COMPENSATION

COMPENSATION

FIFTH EDITION

George T. Milkovich
Cornell University

Jerry M. Newman
State University of New York–Buffalo

With the assistance of Carolyn Milkovich

IRWIN

Chicago • Bogotá • Boston • Buenos Aires • Caracas
London • Madrid • Mexico City • Sydney • Toronto

© Richard D. Irwin, a Times Mirror Higher Education Group, Inc. company, 1984, 1987, 1990, 1993, and 1996

Irwin Book Team

Sponsoring editor: *John E. Biernat*
Developmental editor: *Jennifer R. McBride*
Project editor: *Gladys True*
Production supervisor: *Bette K. Ittersagen*
Assistant manager, graphics: *Charlene R. Breeden*
Designer: *Larry J. Cope*
Cover designer: *Jessica Phillip, Neo Graphics, Inc.*
Art studio: *Benoit and Associates*
Compositor: *Bi Comp, Inc.*
Typeface: *10/12 Times Roman*
Printer: *R. R. Donnelley & Sons Company*

Times Mirror
Higher Education Group

Library of Congress Cataloging-in-Publication Data

Milkovich, George T.
　　Compensation / George T. Milkovich, Carolyn Milkovich and Jerry
　M. Newman. -- 5th ed.
　　　　p.　cm.
　　Includes bibliographical references and indexes.
　　ISBN 0-256-14145-2
　　1. Compensation management.　I. Milkovich, Carolyn.　II. Newman,
　Jerry M.　III. Title.
　HF5549.5.C67M54　1996
　658.3′2—dc20　　　　　　　　　　　　　　　　95–16253

Printed in the United States of America

1 2 3 4 5 6 7 8 9 0 DO 2 1 0 9 8 7 6 5

Preface

When Green Giant discovered that the quality of the pea pack in one of its canned-vegetable plants was down—too many insect parts—it designed a bonus plan for employees whose job was to remove insects from the vegetables. The plan designers got what they paid for: more insects, ostensibly removed from the vegetables. Except employees were bringing insects from home and adding them to the vegetables just prior to their removal.

Sears Automotive wanted to boost its auto repair business and so designed a plan that gave mechanics a larger cut of the fee for doing muffler replacements. Sears got what it paid for, too: Muffler replacements soared as mechanics recommended replacements for everyone, necessary or not. A $15 million lawsuit alleging fraud was settled out of court.

Motorola cellular telephone trashed its old-fashioned pay system that employees said "guaranteed a raise every six months if you were still breathing" and replaced it with one that required learning new skills and working in teams. Very contemporary. Sounded good. It wasn't. Employees resented team members leaving for six weeks of schooling at full pay while remaining team members whose political connections weren't quite so good were left to do the work. Motorola was forced to trash its new-fashioned system, too.

We live in interesting times. Economic and social pressures are forcing managers to reexamine how people get paid and what difference it makes. Traditional approaches to compensation are being questioned and rejected. But what is being achieved by all this experimentation and change? We have lots of fads and fashions, but is it all folderol? Where are the results?

In this book, we strive to cull the beliefs from facts, wishful thinking from demonstrable results, and pay pundits' opinions from scholarly research. Yet when all is said and done, managing compensation is an art. Like any art, not everything that can be learned can be taught.

ABOUT THIS BOOK

This book is based on four strategic choices involved in the compensation management process. We introduce these choices in the compensation model in Chapter 1 and use the model as an integrating framework throughout the book. We examine each of these strategic decisions and discuss the major compensation issues. Discussion occurs in the context of current theory and research and state-of-the-art practice. We draw upon practices that a wide variety of employers actually use. The practices illustrate new developments as well as established approaches to compensation decisions.

Finally, this book provides an opportunity for you to develop decision-making skills through real-life "Your Turn" exercises that apply the concepts and techniques discussed in each chapter. A workbook with a more extensive case and computer applications is also available directly from the authors (telephone or fax 607-257-3859). Completing these exercises will help you develop skills readily transferable to future jobs and assignments.

But caveat emptor! One manager recently told us that she searched for this book in her local Walden Bookstore. The store personnel finally found the listing in their information system—under fiction!

WHAT'S NEW

All chapters of this edition have been completely revised. New chapters on performance-based pay dig into all forms of variable pay such as profit sharing, gain-sharing, and team-based approaches. Person-based plans are contrasted with job-based plans, including recent developments in skill and competency approaches. The increased use of market pricing, broadbanding, and total compensation is also discussed. Employee benefits, always changing and always important, are treated in two new chapters. The strategic approach is integrated throughout the book, and it is contrasted with emerging views such as resource-based models. We have always used international examples in every section; this edition includes a new chapter on international compensation.

Research and surveys about compensation are burgeoning. We have included the best and most relevant of it, along with a new reader's guide on how to be an informed consumer of this material.

ACKNOWLEDGMENTS

In addition to our Walden shopper, many people have contributed to our understanding of compensation and to the preparation of this textbook. We owe a special, continuing debt of gratitude to our students. In the classroom, they motivate and challenge us, and as returning seasoned managers, they try mightily to keep our work relevant.

We appreciate the contributions of those compensation managers who shared their ideas and reactions with us for this and earlier editions of the book. Although we cannot hope to recognize all of them, a few went beyond the call of duty:

Jeanie Adkins *Mercer Meidinger Hansen*

Bob Anderson *Computer Task Group*

Richard Blough *Electro-Wire Products*

John Bronson *PepsiCo*

John Butler *Nabisco*

Lisa Colten *American Express*

Dennis Donovan *General Electric*

Andrew Doyle *Toshiba, Japan*

Larry Drake *Graphic Controls*

Stan Durda *3M*

Joel Goldberg *RJR-Nabisco*

Steve Gross *Hay*

Michael Guthman *Hewitt*

Doris Hauser *Office of Personnel Management*

Steve Kane *Baxter*

Dae-Ki Kim *Yukong Limited, Korea*

Tae-Jin Kim *Yukong Limited, Korea*

Rich Koerner *Cliffstar*

Michael Byungnam Lee *Lucky Goldstar, Korea*

John Markowski *consultant*

David Ness *Medtronics*

Bob Ochsner *Hay*

Sandra O'Neal *Towers Perrin*

Ray Olsen *TRW*

Larry Phillips *Citicorp*

Walt Read *consultant*

Jan Reicis *Graphic Controls*

Robert Rusek *AT&T*

Fumie Urashima *Johnson & Johnson, Japan*

Our universities, Cornell and Buffalo, provide forums for the interchange of ideas among students, experienced managers, and academic colleagues. We value this interchange. Other academic colleagues also provided helpful comments on this and earlier editions of the book.

Robert Amann *St. Thomas University*

C. Anderson *Clarion University*

David L. Aronson   *University of South Dakota*
Ronald Ash   *University of Kansas*
Donald L. Ashbaugh   *University of Northern Iowa*
Thomas Atchison   *University of Washington, Tacoma*
David Balkin   *University of Colorado, Boulder*
Melissa Barringer   *University of Massachusetts*
Kathryn M. Bartol   *University of Maryland*
Doug Benton   *University of Colorado, Fort Collins*
Chris Berger   *Purdue University*
Meg Birdseye   *Augusta College*
George Bohlander   *Arizona State University*
Anthony Bonaro   *Park College*
James T. Brakefield   *Western Illinois University*
Matthew Bloom   *Cornell University*
Renae Broderick   *Cornell University*
Constance R. Campbell   *Georgia Southern University*
Robert Cardy   *Arizona State University*
Charles E. Carlson   *University of Wisconsin at Milwaukee*
Shawn M. Carraher   *University of Wisconsin at Milwaukee*
Elizabeth Cooper   *University of Rhode Island*
Eric Cousineau   *York University*
John W. Crim   *Columbus College*
Michael Crino   *Clemson University*
Ulku Dicle   *Rhode Island College*
Larry Donnelly   *Xavier University*
Donald Drost   *California State, San Bernardino*
Bruce Eberhardt   *University of North Dakota*
Robert A. Figler   *University of Akron*
John Fossum   *University of Minnesota*
Cynthia Fukami   *University of Denver*
Richard Gaffney   *Cedar Crest College*
Barry Gerhart   *Cornell University*
Jai Ghorpade   *San Diego State University*
Luis Gomez-Mejia   *Arizona State University*
Deborah Good   *University of Pittsburgh*
Brian Graham-Moore   *The University of Texas at Austin*
Nancy J. Gussett   *Baldwin-Wallace College*
E. Hammer   *University of Tennessee at Chattanooga*
John Hannon   *Purdue University*
Charmine Hártel   *University of Tulsa*

Linda Hartenian   *University of Wisconsin at Oshkosh*

John W. Henry   *Georgia Southern University*

James Hodgetts   *Memphis State University*

Gregory Hundley   *University of Oregon*

Tom Hyclak   *Lehigh University*

W. Roy Johnson   *Iowa State University*

Jiri Kamenicek   *Charles University, Czech Republic*

Jeffrey Kane   *University of North Carolina at Greensboro*

Erik Kansen   *The University of Utah*

Paul N. Keaton   *University of Wisconsin at LaCrosse*

Sookon Kim   *Kyunghee University, Korea*

S. L. Knowlton   *Central Michigan University*

Thomas A. Kolenko   *Kennesaw State College*

Gerald J. Koppes   *Loras College*

Daniel Koys   *DePaul University*

Linda Krefting   *Texas Tech University*

Frank Krzystofiak   *State University of New York at Buffalo*

Stewart D. Langdon   *Spring Hill College*

Terry L. Leap   *Clemson University*

Jay Liebowitz   *Duquesne University*

Thomas Mahoney   *Vanderbilt University*

Robert Mathis   *University of Nebraska at Omaha*

Donald R. McCarty   *University of Pittsburgh at Johnstown*

Sarah Milkovich   *Phillips Exeter Academy*

Ed Montemeyer   *Michigan State University*

Michael Moore   *Michigan State University*

Oliver Mulford   *Mankato State University*

Tom Noble   *University of Tennessee at Martin*

Craig Olson   *University of Wisconsin at Madison*

Leo B. Osterhaus   *St. Edwards University*

Charles Parsons   *Georgia Tech*

Robert J. Paul   *Kansas State University*

Steven Lance Popejoy   *Central Missouri State University*

Janez Prasnikar   *University of Ljubljana, Slovenia*

Bonnie Rabin   *Ithaca College*

Sara Rasch   *Winona State University*

Bob Reber   *Western Kentucky University*

Robin Remick   *Cornell University*

Monika Renard   *West Virginia University*

Robert K. Robinson   *The University of Mississippi*

Yoko Sano *Keio University, Japan*
Sho Sato *Cornell University*
Edward Schneiderman *Monroe College*
Jerry Schoenfeld *James Madison University*
Donald Schwab *University of Wisconsin*
Susan Schwochau *University of Iowa*
Michael Sturman *Cornell University*
Glenn Thiel *Robert Morris College*
Peg Thomas *Ohio State University*
Steve Thomas *Southwest Missouri State University*
Craig A. Tunwall *Ithaca College*
Linda Tibbetts *University of Dayton*
Richard Ward *Bowling Green State University*
James L. Wahlers *Georgia College*
Theresa Welbourne *Cornell University*
Larry L. Wilson *Texas A&M University*
Nada Zupan *University of Ljubljana, Slovenia*

Brief Contents

Contents

PART II

**External Competitiveness:
Determining the Pay Level**

PART VI

Managing the System

15 Budgets and Administration 549

16 Compensation of Special Groups 581

Strategic Issues and the Pay Model

A friend of ours writes that she is in the touring company of the musical *Cats*. In the company are two performers called *swings* who sit backstage during each performance. Each swing must learn five different lead roles in the show. During the performance, the swing sits next to a rack with five different costumes and makeup for each of the five roles. Our friend, who has a lead in the show, once hurt her shoulder during a dance number. She signaled to someone offstage, and by the time she finished her number, the swing was dressed, in makeup, and out on stage for the next scene.

Our friend is paid $1,500 per week for playing one of the cats in the show. She is expected to do a certain number of performances and a certain number of rehearsals per week. She gets paid for the job she does. The swing gets paid $2,000 per week, whether she performs 20 shows that week or none. She is paid for knowing the five roles, whether she plays them or not.

Think of all the other employees, in addition to the performers, required to put on a performance of *Cats*. Electricians, trombonists, choreographers, dressers, janitors, nurses, vocal coaches, accountants, stagehands, payroll supervisors, ushers, lighting technicians, ticket sellers—the list goes on. Consider the array of wages paid to these employees. Why does the swing get paid more than other performers? Why does the performer get paid more (or less) than the trombonist? Why does the *Cats* trombonist get paid more (or less) than the trombonist in a regional orchestra? How are these decisions made, and who is involved in making them? Whether it's our own or someone else's, compensation questions engage our attention.

Managers of compensation are immersed in one of society's greatest challenges: the efficient and equitable distribution of the returns for work. As already noted, compensation decisions are many and varied. They include how much to pay people who perform both similar and different types of work; whether to use pay to recognize variations in employees' experience and/or performance; and how to allocate pay among cash and benefits and services. Such basic decisions must be made by every employer, no matter how large or small.

Increasingly, employers believe that how employees are paid can be a source of competitive advantage. Further, these decisions must be consistent both with society's changing values about what constitutes fair pay and with government regulations.[1] Consequently, decisions about compensating people for the work they perform are increasingly critical.

This book is about the management of compensation. Its purpose is to give you the background required to make pay decisions.

COMPENSATION IN CONTEMPORARY SOCIETY

Perceptions of compensation vary. Society may see it as a measure of equity and justice. For example, a comparison of U.S. 1994 median weekly earnings of fully

---

[1] G. T. Milkovich and R. F. Broderick, "Developing a Compensation Strategy," in *Compensation Handbook*, 3rd ed., ed. M. L. Rock and L. A. Berger (New York: McGraw-Hill, 1991); L. R. Gomez-Mejia and D. B. Balkin, *Compensation, Organization Strategy, and Firm Performance* (Cincinnati: Southwestern, 1992).

employed women ($395) with that of men ($515) highlights apparent inequities in pay decisions, which many consider an indication of discrimination against women.[2] The good news is that the gender pay gap in the United States narrowed from 64 percent in 1980 to 76 percent in 1994. The bad news is that part of this improvement is due to a decline in male earnings as a result of a shift in the U.S. economy away from well-paid manufacturing jobs mainly held by men.[3]

Others may see high pay as a cause of loss of U.S. jobs to less developed economies. The fact that production workers in Mexico earn, on average, 16 percent of their U.S. counterparts' hourly pay ($15.39) is, to many, a prime example of the flight of high-paying, lower-skilled production jobs from the United States to less developed economies.[4] However, as Exhibit 1.1 reveals, U.S. average labor costs for manufacturing jobs are now less than those paid in Japan and Europe. And *consumers* who seek the highest quality at the lowest costs do not believe that higher labor costs are to their benefit. *Voters* may see compensation, pensions, and health care for public employees as the cause of increased taxes. Public *policymakers* and legislators may view changes in average pay as guides for adjusting eligibility for social services (medical assistance, food stamps, and the like).

To *stockholders*, executive pay is of special interest. Particularly befuddling was the pay of Robert Stempel, who made nearly $2.2 million in 1990, the same year his company, General Motors, lost $4.5 billion and announced the elimination of 74,000 jobs. However, General Motors' Board of Directors replaced him with John E. Smith, who earned $6.1 million in 1994, while GM reported $4.9 billion in profits. Contrary to popular belief, CEO pay does go down—occasionally. Merck's past CEO, Roy Vageles, saw his pay fall 11 percent as profits also fell 11 percent. Mattel's profits slumped 26 percent in 1993 and its CEO's pay dropped 41 percent.[5] And the CEO of Procter & Gamble reduced his own bonuses by $100,000 in the wake of company losses in 1994.

In contrast to the perspective of society and stockholders, *employees* may see compensation as a return for services rendered or as a reward for a job well done. Compensation to some reflects the value of their personal skills and abilities, or the return for the education and training they have acquired. Benefits such as medical insurance, pensions, or wellness programs help protect employees and their dependents. The pay individuals receive for the work they perform is usually the major source of personal income and financial security, and hence a vital determinant of an individual's economic and social well-being.

---

[2] F. D. Blau and L. M. Kahn, "Race and Gender Pay Differentials," (Working paper, no. 4120, National Bureau of Economic Research, June 1992); June O'Neill, Michael Brien, and James Cunningham, "Effects of Comparable Worth Policy: Evidence from Washington State," *AEA Papers and Proceedings* 79, no. 2 (May 1989), pp. 305–9.

[3] "Gender Pay Gap Eased over Last Decade," *The Wall Street Journal*, May 4, 1994, p. B1.

[4] *International Comparisons of Hourly Compensation Costs for Production Workers in Manufacturing, 1994.* Report 766 (Washington, DC: U.S. Department of Labor, Bureau of Labor Statistics, 1995).

[5] Stephen F. O'Byrne, "What Pay for Performance Looks Like: The Case of Michael Eisner," *Journal of Applied Corporate Finance*, 1994, pp. 135–36; "That Eye-Popping Executive Pay: Is Anyone Worth This Much?" *Business Week*, April 25, 1994, pp. 48–52.

EXHIBIT 1.1   Japan is No. 1 (In Labor Costs)

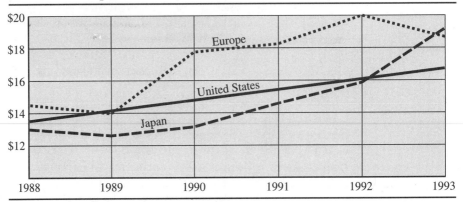

Rather than a return or a reward, some employees in Central Europe and Russia believe their pay is an entitlement: their just due, regardless of their own performance or that of their employer's. They are not yet able to shrug off the past for the freedoms and uncertainties of the market-based economies. Political leaders in these countries often regulate wage increases to ensure political stability of the workforce.[6] As we shall see in the international chapter (18), the perceptions as well as definitions of compensation vary among countries.

Managers also have a stake in compensation; they view it from two perspectives. First, it is a *major expense*. Competitive pressures, both internationally and domestically, force managers to consider the affordability of their compensation decisions. Studies show that in many enterprises labor costs account for more than 50 percent of total costs. Among some industries, such as service or public employment, this figure is even higher. Recent studies report that labor costs as a percent of total costs vary even among individual firms within one industry. This has led many to conclude that compensation decisions can be a source of competitive advantage.[7]

In addition to viewing compensation as an expense, a manager also views it as a possible *influence on employee work attitudes and behaviors* and their organization performance. The way employees are paid may affect the quality of their work; their focus on customer needs; their willingness to be flexible and learn new skills, to suggest innovations and improvements; and even their interests in unions or legal action against their employer. This potential to influence employees' work attitudes and behaviors, and subsequently the productivity and

---

[6] "The Wages of Inequality," *Financial Times*, July 5, 1994, p. 19.

[7] Luis Gomez-Mejia and David Balkin, *Compensation, Organization Strategy, and Firm Performance* (Cincinnati: Southwestern, 1992); Luis Gomez-Mejia and Theresa Vukovich Wellbourne, "Compensation Strategy: An Overview and Future Steps," *Human Resource Planning* 11 (1988), pp. 173–89.

effectiveness of the organization, is another reason why many believe that pay decisions can become a source of competitive advantage.[8]

These contrasting perspectives of compensation—**societal, employee,** and **managerial,** each with different stakes in compensation decisions—can account for the relevance of the topic. But these perspectives can also cause confusion unless everyone is talking about the same thing. So let's define what we mean by compensation.

FORMS OF PAY

Compensation, or pay (the words are used interchangeably in this book), is defined in the following terms:

◈

Compensation refers to all forms of financial returns and tangible services and benefits employees receive as part of an employment relationship.

Exhibit 1.2 shows the variety of forms of compensation. Pay may be received directly in the form of cash (e.g., wages, merit increases, incentives, cost of living adjustments) or indirectly through benefits and services (e.g., pensions, health insurance, paid time off). Programs that distribute compensation to employees can be designed in an unlimited number of ways, and a single employer typically will use more than one program. These pay delivery programs typically fall into four forms: base wage, merit pay, incentives, and employee services and benefits.

Base Wage.   Base wage is the basic cash compensation that an employer pays for the work performed. Base wage tends to reflect the value of the work itself and generally ignores differences in contribution attributable to individual employees. For example, the base wage for a word processor's work may be $12 an hour, but some individual operators may receive more because of their experience and/or performance. Some pay systems set base wage as a function of the skill or education an employee possesses; examples include engineers, scientists, and craft workers. Periodic adjustments to base wages may be made on the basis of changes in the overall cost of living or inflation, changes in what other employers are paying for the same jobs, or changes in experience/performance/skill of employees.

A distinction is often made between salary and wage, with *salary* referring to pay for those workers who are exempt from regulations of the Fair Labor

---

[8] George Milkovich and Renae Broderick, "Developing Compensation Strategies," in *Handbook of Wage and Salary Administration*, 3rd ed., ed. M. Rock (New York: McGraw-Hill, 1990); Barry Gerhart and George Milkovich, "Employee Compensation," in *Handbook of Industrial and Organizational Psychology*, vol. 3, ed. M. D. Dunnette and L. Hough (Palo Alto, CA.: Consulting Psychologists Press, 1992).

EXHIBIT 1.2   Forms of Compensation

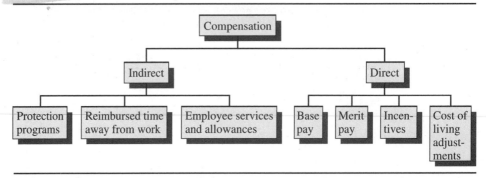

Standards Act, and hence do not receive overtime pay.[9] Managers and professionals usually fit this category. We refer to such employees as *exempts*. Their pay would be calculated at an annual or monthly rate rather than hourly, because hours worked do not need to be recorded. In contrast, workers who are covered by overtime and reporting provisions of the Fair Labor Standards Act—*nonexempts*—usually have their pay calculated at an hourly rate referred to as a *wage*. Some employers, such as Hewlett-Packard and IBM, label all base pay as salary in an attempt to support a management philosophy that all employees are working as a team, rather than being divided into salaried and wage earners.[10] GM's Mr. Smith earned a salary of $1.5 million in 1994, up 9 percent from a year earlier.

Merit. Merit pay rewards past work behaviors and accomplishments. Given as increments to the base pay, merit programs are commonly designed to pay different amounts (often at different times) depending on the level of performance. Thus, outstanding performers may receive a 10 to 12 percent merit increase nine months after their last increase, whereas a satisfactory performer may receive, say, a 6 to 8 percent increase after 12 or 15 months. According to surveys, 90 percent of U.S. firms use pay for performance.[11]

Incentives. Incentives also tie pay directly to performance. Sometimes referred to as nontraditional compensation, incentives may be long or short term, and

---

[9] U.S. Department of Labor Employment Standards Administration, Wage and Hour Division.

[10] *Employee Buy-In to Total Quality*, Report 974 (New York: The Conference Board, 1991); *Hewlett-Packard Personnel Policies and Guidelines*.

[11] Robert Heneman, *Merit Pay: Linking Pay Increases to Performance Ratings* (Reading, MA.: Addison-Wesley, 1992); Robert Bretz, Jr., George Milkovich, and Walter Read, "The Current State of Performance Appraisal Research and Practice: Concerns, Directions, and Implications," *Journal of Management*, 1992; *Performance Appraisal Practice in Leading Companies* (Wyatt, 1991); Buck Consultants, *Compensation Budget Survey 1994,* 500 Plaza Drive, Secaucus, NJ 07096.

can be tied to the performance of an individual employee, a team of employees, a total business unit, or often some combination of individual, team, and unit. Usually very specific performance standards are used in short-term incentive programs. For example, at Union Carbide's Chemicals and Plastics Division, for every quarter that an 8 percent return on capital target is met or exceeded, bonus days of pay are awarded. A 9.6 percent return on capital means two extra days of pay for every participating employee for that quarter. Twenty percent return on capital means 8.5 extra days of pay. Performance results may be defined as cost savings, volume produced, quality standards met, revenues, return on investments, or increased profits; the possibilities are endless.

Long-term incentives are intended to focus employee efforts on longer range (multiyear) results. Top managers or professionals are often offered long-term incentives (e.g., stock ownership, bonuses) to focus on long-term organizational objectives such as return on investment, market share, return on net assets, and the like.[12] Some firms such as Merck grant shares of stock to selected "Key Contributors" who make outstanding contributions to the firm's success. And employee stock ownership (ESOP) plans in which all employees own shares of their employer are believed by some to motivate performance.[13] GM's Mr. Smith received in 1994 both an annual bonus of $1.9 million (to be paid out in cash and restricted stock) and a long-term incentive award of $2.3 million (paid primarily in stock and distributed in installments, with the last payment due when he retires).

Incentives and merit pay differ. Although both may influence performance, incentives do so by offering pay as an inducement. Merit, on the other hand, is a reward that recognizes outstanding past performance. The distinction is a matter of timing. Incentive systems are offered prior to the actual performance. Sales commissions are an example; an auto sales agent knows the commission on a Cadillac versus that on a Chevy prior to making the sale. Gainsharing is another example. Corning employees at their Blacksburg, Virginia, facility know the amount of the bonus they will receive if their plant exceeds its financial goals. Merit pay, on the other hand, typically is not communicated beforehand,

---

[12] *Executive Compensation: Principles and Guidelines for Roundtable Member Companies* (New York: Business Roundtable, 1992); M. C. Jensen and K. J. Murphy, "CEO Incentives: It's Not How Much You Pay, But How," *Harvard Business Review*, May–June 1990, pp. 138–53; Graef Crystal, *In Search of Excess* (New York: W. W. Norton, 1991); "Overview of CEO and Director Compensation," *Compensation Briefs,* October 1994 (Washington, DC: Peat Marwick); J. D. Bloedorn and P. T. Chingos, "Executive Pay and Company Performance," *ACA Journal*, Autumn 1994, pp. 70–79.

[13] Some believe greater stock ownership motivates performance; others argue that the link between individual job behaviors and the vagaries of the stock market are tenuous at best. J. L. Pierce and C. A. Furo, "Employee Ownership: Implications for Management," *Organizational Dynamics*, Winter 1990, pp. 32–43; J. L. Pierce, S. A. Rubenfeld, and S. Morgan, "Employee Ownership: A Conceptual Model of Process and Effects," *Academy of Management Review* 16, no. 1, 1991, pp. 121–44.

and the amount of money to fund merit increases is usually not known very far in advance.

Merit and incentives are clearly related. Insofar as employees begin to anticipate their merit pay, it acts as an incentive to induce performance. Thus, anticipated rewards become incentives. Merit is typically based on individual performance; incentives may be based on the performance of an individual, team, or unit. However, merit pay increasingly depends on how well an employee can operate in a team.

Perhaps the most important distinction is that merit pay usually adds into and permanently increases base pay, whereas incentives are one-time payments and do not have a permanent effect on labor costs. When performance declines, incentive pay automatically declines, too.

Services and Benefits. Employee benefits range from time away from work (vacations, jury duty), services (drug counseling, financial planning, cafeteria support), and protection (medical care, life insurance, and pensions). Because the cost of providing these services and benefits has been rising (for example, employers pay nearly half the nation's health care bills, and health care expenditures have been increasing at annual rates in excess of 15 percent), they are an increasingly important form of pay.[14] In a recent Gallup poll, people claimed they would require $5,000 more in extra pay to choose a job without pension, health care, and life insurance. Many employers now manage benefits as closely as they manage direct compensation.

Services and benefits vary widely from country to country. For example, in response to shortages and high costs, Yukong Petroleum and the Hyundai shipyards and auto company in Korea include housing (dormitories and apartments) and transportation allowances in their pay package. Many Japanese companies—Toshiba and Toyota are examples—provide similar allowances, plus they offer a family allowance based on family size (though this latter practice is declining).

These four pay forms make up the total compensation package paid to employees. The compensation manager is responsible for designing and managing all elements of pay/total compensation.

Alternative rewards are excluded from this definition, yet they affect employee behaviors. Recognition ceremonies, celebration of achievements, personal satisfaction from continually learning and successfully facing new challenges, working with great coworkers, and the like, undoubtedly are an important part of the total returns people receive from their work. Such factors may be thought of as part of an organization's "total reward system" and are often coordinated with compensation.[15] So while this book is about compensation, let's not forget

---

[14] See the entire special issue on employee benefits, in *Human Resource Management Review*, 4, no. 2, ed. Margaret Williams (1994).

[15] N. K. Sethia and M. A. Glinow, "Arriving at Four Cultures by Managing the Reward System," in *Gaining Control of the Corporate Culture*, ed. K. M. Saxton and R. Serpa (San Francisco: Jossey-Bass, 1991).

that compensation is only one of many factors affecting people's decisions. Even an offer of better wages, an expense account, and a company car couldn't compete with the alternative rewards songwriter Roger Miller's hero found in his job in this popular song from the 1960s:

> Got a letter just this morning, it was postmarked Omaha
> It was typed and neatly written offering me a better job,
> Better job and higher wages, expenses paid, and a car.
> But I'm on TV here locally, and I can't quit, I'm a star.
>
> I come on TV a grinnin', wearin' pistols and a hat,
> It's a kiddie show and I'm the hero of the younger set.
> I'm the number one attraction in every supermarket parking lot.
> I'm the King of Kansas City. No thanks, Omaha, thanks a lot.
>
> (refrain)
> Kansas City Star, that's what I are . . .[16]

Returns in an Implicit Exchange

Taken literally, *compensation* means to counterbalance, to offset, to make up for. So compensation makes up for the effort an employee exerts on the employer's behalf. In this sense, pay is a "return" for services. But sometimes pay systems are referred to as *reward systems*. To some, the distinction between rewards and returns is not very important. A reward is given for good performance. A return is given in exchange for something of value. But it's unlikely that employees see their pay as a reward. Rather, they are more likely to describe it as a return received *in exchange* for efforts and ideas given to an employer.

Psychological Contract.   Exchange is the key. Some suggest that an implicit psychological contract is formed in the employment relationship.[17] Employees and employers, parties to this exchange, form beliefs about their mutual obligations and returns. Compensation becomes part of that transaction. In some cases, employees form unions to negotiate more explicit terms of exchange. Unanticipated changes in compensation often breech this implicit understanding. Introducing incentives in place of annual pay increases or requiring employees to pay more of their health care costs are examples.

   Social contracts in the workplace introduce a critical third party to the employment exchange: the government. Implicit social contracts recognize that public policies (e.g., minimum wages, tax laws, social security, health care provisions, union-management regulations, etc.) play a significant role in the exchange

---

[16] Lyrics to "Kansas City Star" written by Roger Miller.

[17] Research about implicit psychological contracts is beginning to appear. The entire Fall 1994 issue of *Human Resource Management* is devoted to psychological contracts. See particularly, D. Rousseau and M. Greller, "HR Practices: Administrative Contract Makers," pp. 385–401; and M. Lucero and R. Allen, "Employee Benefits: A Growing Source of Psychological Contract Violation," pp. 425–46. Also Kathryn Troy, "If Not Loyalty, What About Commitment?" *HR Briefing: The New Employee-Employer Contract*, Winter 1994–95, p. 3.

between individuals and employers. In much of the world, governments play a dominant role in the workplace. Globally, a wide variety of social contracts exist, reflecting the shared understanding with citizens and employees and employers about the employment exchange.

Debates over social contracts are brewing round the world, some heated, some just simmering. For example, the proposed Social Charter for the European Union sets minimum standards and allowances for all member states, including minimum wages, unemployment allowances, national health provisions, overtime provisions, and the like.[18] It also stipulates the types of employee participation (worker councils, board membership) in organization decision making. It is important to realize that compensation forms part of the implicit exchange. Compensation is a psychological relationship between employers and employees, plus it is part of a social contract in which government regulations play a critical role.

Expected Costs and Stream of Earnings

Up to this point compensation has been static, something paid or received at a moment in time. But compensation decisions have a temporal quality. Think about the manager who makes you a job offer—say $30,000. Assume you stay with the firm 5 years and receive an annual increase of 7 percent in each of those 5 years. You will be earning $39,324 in 5 years. The expected cost commitment of the decision to hire you turns out to be $224,279 ($30,000 base compounded by 7 percent for 5 years, plus benefits equal to 30 percent of base). So the decision to hire you implies a commitment of at least a quarter of a million dollars from your employer. Few students, even accounting/finance wonks, seem to evaluate competing job offers in terms of present value of a stream of future earnings. A present value perspective shifts the choice from comparing today's initial offers to include consideration of future bonuses, merit increases, and promotions. Andersen Consulting, for example, convinces some students every year that their relatively low starting offers will be overcome over time by larger future pay increases. In effect, Andersen is selling the present value of the stream of earnings at Andersen. But few students apply those same financial skills to calculate the future increases required to offset the lower initial offers.

The point is that compensation can be both simple and complex. It is pay. It can be treated as a stream of future earnings, costs, or investment. It can include nonfinancial and psychological returns as in a total reward system. And it can take several forms: cash, benefits, and services. We turn now to a pay

---

[18] U.S. Department of Labor/U.S. Department of Commerce, *Commission on the Future of Worker-Management Relations Final Report* (Washington, DC: U.S. Government Printing Office, January 1995); Commission of the European Community, *Social Charter Europe in 1994*, Directorate of General Employment, Social Affairs, Brussels, Belgium; M. Hansenne, "Promoting Social Justice in the New Global Economy," *Monthly Labor Review*, September 1994, pp. 3–8; K. Swinnertan and G. K. Schoepfle, "Labor Standards in the Context of a Global Economy," *Monthly Labor Review*, September 1994, pp. 52–58.

model that will serve as both a framework for examining current pay systems and a guide for much of this book.

A PAY MODEL

The pay model shown in Exhibit 1.3 contains three basic components: (1) the strategic policies that form the foundation of the compensation system, (2) the techniques that make up much of the mechanics or technology of compensation management, and (3) the compensation objectives. Each of these components and the relationships among them are discussed in turn.

Compensation Objectives

Pay systems are designed and managed to achieve certain objectives. The basic objectives, shown at the right side of the model, include efficiency, equity, and compliance with laws and regulations. These objectives in the model are broadly conceived. The *efficiency* objective is typically stated more specifically: (1) im-

Exhibit 1.3   The Pay Model

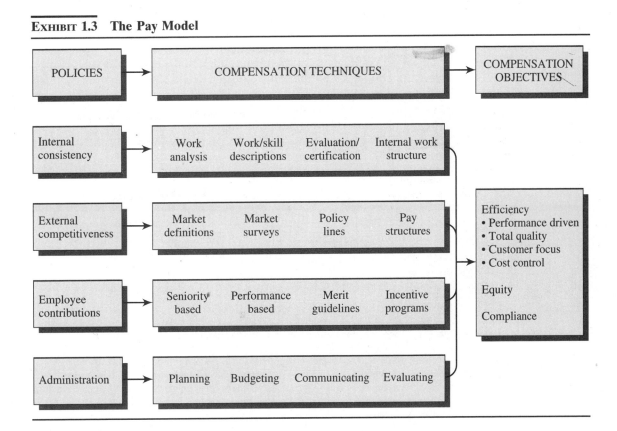

EXHIBIT 1.4   Comparisons of Pay System Objectives

Pay Objectives at Astra-Merck and Hewlett-Packard

Astra-Merck	Hewlett-Packard
• Share commitment and responsibility; foster teamwork	• Help H-P continue to attract creative and enthusiastic people who contribute to its success
• Balance immediate and strategic interests	• Pay among the leaders
• Celebrate performance	• Reflect sustained relative contribution of unit, division, and H-P
• Promote fairness	• Be open and understandable
• Achieve simplicity	• Ensure fair treatment
• Be market competitive; pay at the 75th percentile of competitors	• Be innovative, competitive, and equitable

proving performance, achieving total quality, focusing on customer needs and (2) controlling labor costs. Hewlett-Packard and Astra-Merck's compensation objectives are contrasted in Exhibit 1.4. Note the emphasis on performance and business success reflected in their objectives.

Equity is also a fundamental theme in pay systems. Statements such as "fair treatment for all employees" or "a fair day's pay for a fair day's work" reflect a concern for equity. Thus, the equity objective attempts to ensure fair pay treatment for all participants in the employment relationships. The equity objective focuses on designing pay systems that recognize both employee *contributions* (e.g., offering higher pay for greater performance or greater experience or training) and employee *needs* (e.g., providing a "living wage," as well as fair procedures).

Procedural equity, often overlooked by both managers and researchers, is concerned with the processes used to make decisions about pay.[19] It suggests that the way a pay decision is made may be as important to employees as the results of the decision. As an objective for a pay system, procedural equity helps ensure that employees, managers, and other relevant parties have a voice in the design of pay plans and an opportunity to voice any dissatisfaction with the pay received.

---

[19] Daniel J. Koys, "Process Equity in Employee Compensation: Report to Survey Participants," Presentation at 1992 American Compensation Association Meetings, Anaheim, CA; Jerald Greenberg, "Looking Fair vs. Being Fair: Managing Impressions of Organizations Justice," in *Research in Organizational Behavior*, vol. 12, ed. B. M. Staw and L. L. Cummings (Greenwich, CT : JAI Press, 1990); R. Folger and M. Konovsky, "Effects of Procedural and Distributive Justice on Reactions to Pay Raise Decisions," *Academy of Management Journal* 32, no. 1, pp. 115–30; T. M. Welbourne, D. Balkin, and L. R. Gomez-Mejia, "Gainsharing and Mutual Monitoring: A Combined Agency–Procedural Justice Interpretation," Working paper 93–12, Center for Advanced Human Resource Studies, Ithaca, NY.

Compliance as a pay objective involves conforming to various federal and state compensation laws and regulations. As these laws and regulations change, pay systems often need to be adjusted to ensure continued compliance.

There are probably as many statements of pay objectives as there are employers. In fact, highly diversified firms such as TRW and General Electric, which compete in multiple lines of businesses, may have different pay objectives for different business units. Astra-Merck's and Hewlett-Packard's pay objectives in Exhibit 1.4 emphasize high-quality and innovative performance (productivity), competitiveness (costs—pay among leaders), ability to attract and retain quality people (productivity), and equity (employee communications, openness, and simplicity).

Objectives serve several purposes. First, they guide the design of the pay system. Consider the employer whose objective is to reward outstanding performance. That objective will determine the pay policy (e.g., pay for performance) as well as the elements of pay plans (e.g., merit and/or incentives). Another employer wishes to develop a flexible, continuously learning work force. This employer believes that flexibility is increased through job design, training, and team-building techniques. A pay system that is consistent with this employer's objectives may have a policy of paying salaries that at least equal those of competitors and that recognize increased skills or knowledge. The point is that different objectives guide the design of different pay systems.

Besides affecting the design of the plan, objectives serve as the standards for judging the success of the pay system. If the objective is to attract and retain a highly competent staff, yet skilled employees are leaving to take higher paying jobs at other employers, the system may not be performing effectively. Although there may be many nonpay reasons for turnover and some turnover is probably desirable, objectives provide standards for evaluating the effectiveness of a pay system.

Four Basic Policy Decisions

The pay model in Exhibit 1.3 rests on four basic policies that every employer must consider in managing compensation. The policy decisions shown on the left side of the pay model include (1) internal consistency, (2) external competitiveness, (3) employee contributions, and (4) administration of the pay system. These policies form the building blocks, the foundation on which pay systems are built. These policies also serve as guidelines within which pay is managed to accomplish the system's objectives. Taken together, they make up the *compensation strategy* of the organization.

Internal Consistency.   Internal consistency, often called *internal equity,* refers to comparisons among jobs or skill levels *inside* a single organization. The focus is on comparing jobs and skills in terms of their relative contributions to the organization's objectives. How, for example, does the work of the word processor compare with the work of the computer operator, the programmer, and the software engineer, who together contribute to the organization's objectives? Does one contribute to satisfying customers and shareholders more than the others? Does one require more skill or experience than another? Internal consistency becomes a factor in determining the pay rates both for employees doing equal work and for those doing dissimilar work. In fact, determining what is an appropriate difference in pay for people performing different work is one of the key challenges facing managers.

Determining appropriate pay focuses on two dimensions:

1. The relative similarities and differences in the work or the skills/competencies required.
2. The relative contribution of the work or skills/competencies to the organization's objectives.

The content of one set of tasks and behaviors (a job) is either equal to or different from another set of tasks and behaviors. A job's relative worth is based on its differing work content and its differing contribution to achieving the objectives of the organization. For example, the contribution of a systems analyst who works directly with customers to design a new inventory or production control system is typically considered to be greater than that of the programmer of the system. Similarly, one set of skills is either equal to or different from another set, and the relative value of each depends on how it helps the organization achieve its objectives. Managers have several policy options; they can opt for many (or few) levels of work; they can select larger (or smaller) differences in pay rates among jobs; and they can place greater (or less) emphasis on what other employers are paying. In Exhibit 1.4, Astra-Merck is addressing internal consistency when it mentions teamwork and fairness. Hewlett-Packard also seeks to "ensure fair treatment."

Internal consistency policies affect all three compensation objectives. Equity and compliance with legislation are directly affected, while efficiency is affected more indirectly. As we shall see in Part I of the text, pay relationships within the organization affect employee decisions to stay with the organization, to become more flexible by investing in additional training, or to seek greater responsibility. By motivating employees to choose increased training and greater responsibility in dealing with customers, pay relationships indirectly affect the efficiency of the work force and hence the effectiveness of the total organization.

External Competitiveness.   External competitiveness refers to how an employer positions its pay relative to what competitors are paying. How much do we wish to pay accountants in comparison to what other employers would pay them? Employers have several policy options. Recall that Astra-Merck's policy is to pay at the 75th percentile of competitors, while Hewlett-Packard's policy is to pay among the leaders. Some employers may set their pay levels higher than their competition, hoping to attract the best applicants. Of course, this assumes that someone is able to identify and hire the "best" from the pool of applicants. Another might set its base pay lower than its competitors but offer bigger bonuses for better results. Yet another employer may offer lower base pay but greater opportunity to work overtime or better benefits. Or pay and benefits may be lower, but job security may be higher.

The policy regarding external competitiveness has a twofold effect on objectives: (1) to ensure that the pay rates are sufficient to attract and retain employees—if employees do not perceive their pay as equitable in comparison to what other organizations are offering for similar work, they may be more likely to leave—and (2) to control labor costs so that the organization's prices of products or services can remain competitive. So external competitiveness directly affects both the efficiency and equity objectives. And it must do so in a way that complies with relevant legislation.

Employee Contributions.   The policy on employee contributions refers to the relative emphasis placed on performance. Should all such employees receive the same pay? Or should one programmer be paid differently from another if one has better performance and/or greater seniority? Or should all employees share in the organization's financial successes (and failures) via profit sharing? Perhaps more productive teams of employees should be paid more than less productive teams? The degree of emphasis to be placed on performance and/or seniority is an important policy since it may have a direct effect on employees' attitudes and work behaviors and hence on efficiency and equity. Employers with strong pay for performance policies are more likely to place greater emphasis on incentive and merit schemes as part of their pay systems. Astra-Merck seeks to "celebrate performance." Hewlett-Packard emphasizes performance at the unit, division, and companywide level.

Administration.   Policy regarding administration of the pay system is the last building block in our model. While it is possible to design a system that incorporates internal consistency, external competitiveness, and employee contributions, the system will not achieve its objectives unless it is managed properly. The greatest system design in the world is useless without competent management. Managers must plan the elements of pay that should be included in the pay system (e.g., base pay, short-term and long-term incentives), evaluate how the pay system is operating, communicate with employees, and judge whether the system is achieving its objectives. Are we able to attract skilled workers? Can we keep them? Do our employees feel our system is fair? Do they understand the factors used to set their pay? Do they agree that these factors are important? Do employees have channels for raising questions and voicing complaints about their pay? How do the better performing firms, with better financial returns and a larger share of the market, pay their employees? Are the systems used by these firms different from those used by less successful firms? How do our labor costs compare to our competitors'? Such information is necessary to tune or redesign the system, to adjust to changes, and to highlight potential areas for further investigation. Hewlett-Packard's objectives include a plan designed to be "open and understandable." Astra-Merck hopes to "achieve simplicity."

EXHIBIT 1.5   An Illustration: Alternative Compensation Strategies

Policy Choices	Cost Leader	Innovator
Internal Consistency: Emphasis on		
• Assessing job content/person's skills or competencies	High	Low
• Evaluating relative contribution of work to organization's success	High	Moderate
External Competitiveness: Emphasis on		
• Positioning against competitors' pay	High	High
• Variable (performance-based) over fixed cost (seniority or across-the-board increases)	Low	High
Employee Contributions: Emphasis on		
• Merit- or incentive-based pay over cost-of-living or seniority adjustments	Moderate	High
Administration: Emphasis on		
• Control over flexibility	High	Low

Adapted from Montemayor, "Aligning Pay Systems with Market Strategies," *ACA Journal,* Winter 1994, pp. 44–53.

Four Policies →The Pay Strategy

The balance or pattern among the four basic policies becomes an employer's compensation strategy. Two alternative strategies, Cost Leader and Innovator, are illustrated in Exhibit 1.5. A cost leader strives to achieve desired quality at the lowest price for its products/services.[20] The pay strategy supports driving costs out by emphasizing efficiency, quality control, and customer satisfaction. By contrast, innovators strive to constantly introduce new products by shortening cycle times from product idea to manufacturing and marketing and by focusing on customer satisfaction with innovative products/services. There are similarities and differences in their compensation strategies.

Note that the innovator places less emphasis on assessing and evaluating jobs or skills (internal consistency is less important), greater emphasis on performance-based pay (employee contributions), and is more concerned about ensuring flexibility (versus control) in the administration of the pay system. Both emphasize external competitiveness, yet the cost leader does this via pay increases based on seniority (security to experienced workers). This may seem odd. Why wouldn't the cost leader opt for more performance-based increases than seniority-based? Clearly, more than one route to success exists. Perhaps the logic is that highly experienced employees possess the know-how to get the work done more efficiently, while maintaining quality. Experience and knowledge matter, and seniority-based increases retain that experience.

---

[20] Ediberto F. Montemayor, "Aligning Pay Systems with Market Strategy," *ACA Journal*, Winter 1994, pp. 44–53.

On the other hand, a competing cost leader could emphasize performance-based pay increases (defining performance as cost reduction). Which strategy is better? Research is only now beginning to study the relationship between the overall compensation strategy and organization performance. At this point, it is only necessary to recognize that (1) the compensation strategy is the overall pattern of policy decisions that affect organization success; and (2) different compensation strategies exist. All four policy choices that make up the pay strategy—internal consistency, external competitiveness, employee contributions, and administration—are critical in the management of pay systems. We will discuss strategic perspectives in more detail later in this chapter after a brief look at the techniques used to translate these strategies into practice.[21]

Pay Techniques

The remaining portion of the pay model in Exhibit 1.3 shows the pay techniques. The exhibit provides only an overview since techniques are the topic of much of the rest of the book. Techniques tie the four basic policies to the pay objectives. Internal consistency is typically established through a sequence of techniques starting with analysis of the work done. Analysis involves collecting information about work, which is then evaluated. Based on these evaluations, a structure of the work performed is built.

This structure depicts relationships among jobs and skills or competencies inside an organization. It is based on the relative importance of the work in achieving the organization's objectives. The goal is to establish a structure that supports the organization's objectives and is internally equitable. The equity of the pay system will affect employee attitudes and behaviors as well as the organization's regulatory compliance.

External competitiveness is established by setting the organization's pay level in comparison with what the competition pays for similar work. But who precisely is the "competition"? The pay level is determined by defining the relevant labor markets in which the employer competes, conducting surveys to find out what other employers pay, and using that information in conjunction with the organization's policy decisions to generate a pay structure. The pay structure influences how efficiently the organization is able to attract and retain a competent work force and to control its labor costs.

The relative emphasis on employee contributions is established through performance- and/or seniority-based increases, incentive plans, and salary increase guidelines. If an organization decides to pay employees on the basis of performance, it must have some way to evaluate employee performance and

---

[21] G. T. Milkovich and R. F. Broderick, "Developing a Compensation Strategy," in *Compensation Handbook*, 3rd ed., ed. M. L. Rock and L. A. Berger (New York: McGraw-Hill, 1991); L. R. Gomez-Mejia and D. B. Balkin, *Compensation, Organization Strategy, and Firm Performance* (Cincinnati: Southwestern, 1992); R. Schuster and P. K. Zingheim, *The New Pay: Linking Employee Strategy and Organization Performance* (New York: Lexington Books, 1992).

must adjust pay on the basis of that evaluation. Many organizations use some form of incentive plan to share their success with employees. In addition to managing costs, these practices are all intended to affect employee attitudes and behaviors, in particular the decisions to join the organization, to stay, and to perform effectively. They are also designed to control costs.

Uncounted variations in pay techniques exist; many are examined in this book. Surveys have studied differences in compensation policies and techniques among firms.[22] It is clear from these surveys that the variations in compensation approaches arise from differences in the environments in which the organizations operate, the organizations themselves, and in the objectives they are trying to achieve with pay. Such variations may also be derived from the various strategies organizations adopt to accomplish their objectives.

STRATEGIC PERSPECTIVES

So far our discussion has highlighted the major views of compensation and the basic components of the pay model. Upcoming chapters will discuss the particulars of various techniques. But examining and dissecting techniques can be so seductive that they become the ends in themselves. All too often, pay systems seem to have been designed in response to some historical but long-forgotten situation. Questions such as "So what does this technique do for (to) us?" How does it help achieve our objectives?" or "Why bother with this technique?" are not asked. Throughout this book, we hope you will be asking yourself "so what" questions. And when your future employer asks why your proposal makes sense, you will shape your answer to explain "so what."

So before proceeding to the particulars of pay systems, we pause to consider some major strategic issues related to pay. The issues to which we will pay special attention include matching compensation to the organization's strategic and environmental conditions, its culture and values, the needs of its employees, and its union/management relationship.

Reflect the Organization's Strategies

All pay systems have a purpose. Answer the question, "What do we want to get for our money?" and you'll begin to specify the objectives of the pay system. Some objectives are clearly identified, as in our pay model; others must be inferred from the actions of employers. A currently popular prescription found in almost every textbook and consultant's report is for managers to tailor their pay systems to support the organization's strategic conditions.[23]

---

[22] Most of the leading consulting firms also survey pay practices of firms, for example, Towers Perrin, *Benchmarking Employee Compensation Practices*, 1994; Hewitt Associates, *Benchmarking Best Practices*, 1994; Hay Associates, *Annual Employee Compensation Survey of Practice*, 1994.

[23] Robert C. Ochsner, "Strategic Compensation," *Compensation and Benefits Management,* Fall 1991, pp. 79–80; George T. Milkovich, "A Strategic Perspective on Compensation Strategy,"

The notion is seductive; the reasons offered seem persuasive. They are based on contingency notions. That is, differences in a firm's strategies should be supported by corresponding differences in human resource policies, including compensation policies. The underlying premise is that the greater the alignment, or fit, between the organization conditions and the compensation system, the more effective the organization. Further, different pay system designs should be aligned with changes in strategic conditions. An example is Pepsi-Cola's decision to compete globally with its arch-rival Coca-Cola. PepsiCo has focused on domestic U.S. markets, even though it operates in many other countries. As Exhibit 1.6 reveals, only about 15 percent of PepsiCo's earnings flow from its international operations, compared to about 80 percent at Coke. The exhibit also reveals that Pepsi and Coke pursue very different business strategies. Coke is essentially a global beverage marketing company. Pepsi is in three lines of business: beverages (Pepsi-Cola), food (Frito-Lay), and restaurants (Pizza Hut, Taco Bell, and KFC). Further, Pepsi owns most of its businesses, the bottlers, and the restaurants. Coke, on the other hand, makes greater use of independent bottlers to bottle and distribute its beverages.

The decision by PepsiCo to compete internationally is strategic. It reflects a fundamental change in direction. Organization resources—financial, capital, and human—will need to be deployed in a manner consistent with the new direction.

As Exhibit 1.7 depicts, compensation systems can be designed to support the business strategies adopted by organizations and to adapt to the competitive and regulatory pressure faced in the environment. The ultimate purpose is to gain competitive advantage—to achieve the organization's objectives.

Support the Business Strategy.   In the example above, PepsiCo corporate strategy shifted from primarily a domestic focus to doing business globally. This shift to international has strategic implications for human resources above and beyond compensation. Top managers in all the PepsiCo business units, for example, face decisions about operating in different regions of the world. Decisions about running bottling plants in China and Brazil include negotiating with government agencies and national unions, hiring and developing local nationals to manage these business units, and learning how to operate effectively in different cultures. While the beverage unit PepsiCola faced these decisions in the past, Pizza Hut, KFC, Taco Bell, and Frito-Lay employees have less international expertise. In

in *Research in Human Resource Management*, ed. K. Rowland and G. Ferris (Greenwich, Conn.: JAI Press, 1988); George T. Milkovich and Renae Broderick, "Developing Compensation Strategies," in *Handbook of Wage and Salary Administration*, 3rd ed., ed. M. Rock (New York: McGraw-Hill, 1990); L. R. Gomez-Mejia and D. B. Balkin, *Compensation, Organization Strategy, and Firm Performance* (Cincinnati: Southwestern, 1992); V. Fuehrer, "Total Reward Strategy," *Compensation and Benefits Review*, January–February 1994, pp. 44–53; V. Pucik, N. Tichy, and C. Barnett, eds., *Globalizing Management: Creating and Leading the Competitive Organization* (Wiley, 1992).

EXHIBIT 1.6   The Pepsi Challenge

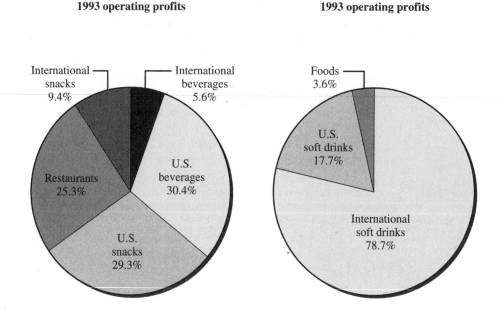

| PepsiCo
1993 operating profits | Coca-Cola
1993 operating profits |

The Pepsi Challenge: to get its paltry profits from international beverages anywhere near Coke's.

Source: Annual Reports.

sum, the overall strategy for managing human resources involves decisions about staffing, organization design, development, employee relations, and compensation. The critical strategic compensation decisions facing managers can be considered in terms of the four basic policies in our pay model.

Consistency.   How should different levels of work be paid within each country? In some countries, notably Japan and Korea, employees' wages are based on their education and seniority, not on the job they perform. Most European and Asian countries use smaller pay differences than North and Latin America. How large should the differences in pay be? And most importantly, what difference will these decisions make? How do these decisions help Pepsi achieve competitive advantage?

Competitiveness.   How should facilities in each country pay in comparison to local wage rates? Many countries negotiate nationwide collective agreements with unions that set the floor for wages. Pepsi could opt to use "adders" on top of the agreed-upon rates to attempt to attract key talent. Should PepsiCola have nationwide rates the way AT&T pays its operators and technicians, or General

Exhibit 1.7   Strategic Perspective: An Illustration

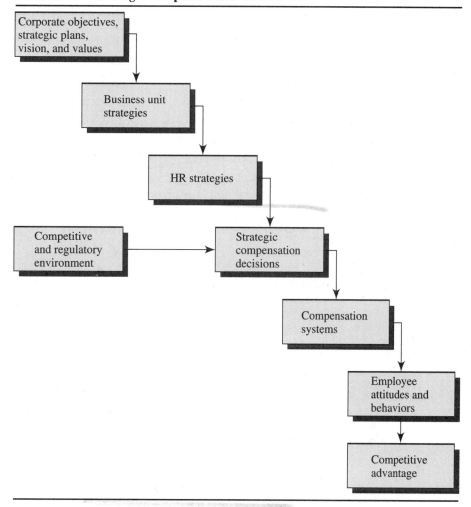

Motors pays its assemblers? Or should rates be based on local comparable jobs? Again, so what? Do these decisions really matter in terms of PepsiCo's objectives?

Employee Contributions.   Should pay increases for PepsiCo employees worldwide be based on individual or team performance, on experience and seniority, on changes in the cost of living, on each business unit's performance (Frito-Lay, Pizza Hut, etc.) or on PepsiCo's performance? With 300,000 employees worldwide, Pepsi has become a behemoth. Pepsi wants each employee to "act like an owner, not a hired hand." Uh-huh! To attempt to sustain this "owner" idea, PepsiCo gave all 300,000 employees, from truck drivers to Pizza Hut bakers, stock options. At current prices, the yearly options are equivalent to 10 percent of the base pay. But considering the different tax laws in different countries, will employees in other countries place any value on these stock options?

Administration.   What should the policy be toward the employee unions? How involved should employees be in the design of these pay systems? What role will each manager play in the design and management of pay systems? Will it be centralized at corporate headquarters in Purchase, New York, or regionally by business unit, or decentralized to each plant?

Exhibit 1.7 shows how the results of these four basic policy choices translate into the compensation system. Our point is that the *techniques that make up the compensation system translate strategic policy into practice.*

"Fit" Environmental and Regulatory Pressures

In Exhibit 1.7, the compensation environment also affects the compensation choices. Environment refers to a wide range of pressures, including competitive pressures from product and labor markets, legal and regulatory requirements, changing work force demographics, values and expectations, and the like. In the case of PepsiCo, its business is very people intensive. Consequently, PepsiCo managers expect that an increasingly diverse work force may desire increasing diverse forms of pay (child care, educational reimbursements, employee assistance programs).[24]

Work force diversity takes on a whole new meaning in a global business. Regional norms about minorities' and women's work roles and pay differ and may be at odds with PepsiCo corporate policies. Different regions of the world may require different approaches to pay. And Pepsi managers probably do not expect to sit by passively while Congress considers whether to impose taxes on benefits paid to employees. Similarly, the European Union's social contract becomes a matter of interest for the PepsiCo leadership. Pepsi intends to shape the environment as well as be shaped by it.

Reflect the Organization's Culture and Values

Not only are pay programs related to strategic conditions and environment, they are also related to the organization's culture and values. The notions of culture and values are complex. But the values underlying an employer's treatment of its employees can be reflected in its pay system. Some employers articulate their philosophies, such as those for AT&T and Honeywell, which are shown in Exhibit 1.8. These philosophies give us a sense of how these two firms treat employees and serve as guides for their pay systems. Note that Honeywell's principles (number 4) reflect its decentralized approach in which each business unit is responsible for its own pay system.

---

[24] Joseph Coates, *Future Work: Seven Critical Forces Reshaping Work and the Work Force in North America* (Washington, DC: J. F. Coates, 1991).

EXHIBIT 1.8 Comparison of AT&T and Honeywell Philosophies

AT&T Values

Help the Customer Succeed	Continuous Improvement	People	Integrity	Profit
To support customers' success, each of us will • Interact with customers as a partner • Know our customers' business • Anticipate what is required for our customers' success • Identify and know our value to our customer • Develop creative/innovative ways to serve our customer • Be responsive and flexible in providing quality products and services to our customers • Provide value-added solutions • Provide unconditional customer satisfaction	In the uncompromising pursuit of quality, we will make decisions based on data and will continuously • Measure and improve customer satisfaction • Improve the "value add" we provide our customers • Analyze and simplify our business process • Promote change as an opportunity to improve • Promote continuous learning • Evaluate our operations and perform only that which has value for the customer • Recognize no limits to improvement	Each of us is important in determining the success of AT&T. Therefore, each of us • Is empowered and expected to act • Will treat each other with respect and dignity • Is expected to grow and achieve • Shares responsibility for the success of our customers and company	Integrity and a high standard of ethics are fundamental in our business, community, and interpersonal relationships; therefore, each of us will • Make and keep commitments • Operate at the highest ethical standards • Act in a forthright and honest manner • Conform to the spirit and letter of the laws that govern our worldwide operations	Sustained profitability is the ultimate measure of how well we serve our customers and is necessary to • Be a reliable partner and foster beneficial relationships with our 　Customers 　Investors 　Communities 　Vendors • Execute long-term plans • Provide opportunity for personal growth and reward

Honeywell's Philosophy and Principles

Philosophy

• Honeywell is one company, made up of different businesses. These businesses are united by a common set of values and by common technologies. Yet they differ in respect to their products and services, size, customers, locations, and competitors.

• The company's pay philosophy allows each individual business to design pay systems responding to that business's own requirements. It also means that each system must contain certain assurances of Honeywell employment. These assurances are expressed in four basic pay principles.

• In support of these objectives, four basic principles also apply to all Honeywell pay systems.

Principles

Fully Competitive	Fair Internally	Communicated	Business Responsibility
Pay must be fully competitive in the market, as defined by each business	Each individual's pay must be fair in relationship to the pay that other employees receive within the same Honeywell business	The communication must explain general pay principles, the specific pay system applicable, and the process used to determine individual pay levels under the system	Each Honeywell business has the basic responsibility for establishing and maintaining its own pay system

Pay is just one of many systems that make up an organization; its design is also partially influenced by how it fits with the other structures and systems in the organization.[25] A highly centralized and confidential pay system, controlled by a few people in a corporate unit, will not, according to this view, operate effectively in a highly decentralized and open organization.[26] Unfortunately, little research has been done directly on the relationship between pay systems and the culture and values of an organization. This may be because culture and values are ambiguous terms.

The importance of congruency between pay programs and other HR management processes can be illustrated with examples of recruiting, hiring, and promoting. The pay linked with a job offer or a promotion must be sufficient to induce acceptance. Some employers do not maintain significant pay differences among various skill levels and levels of responsibility. Lack of adequate differences in pay diminishes the incentive for employees to take the training required to become more skilled or to accept the promotion to supervisor. The situation is reversed for many engineering and research jobs, where the pay for managerial positions induces people to leave engineering and research positions.

Public Not-For-Profit Sector.   Strategic decisions are also evident in governmental and public not-for-profit organizations. Examples include a university's desire for a winning football team, or a regional symphony orchestra's attempt to gain national recognition. Pay programs can also be tailored to facilitate the strategic directions of these organizations. The orchestra can offer a renowned conductor a share of the revenues gained from recording sales, or the university may increase funding for the coaching staff through a cut of the gate for that particular sport.

For managers of compensation, the key point to remember is that pay coexists with other systems in the organization. It must fit. An effective pay system cannot be designed without taking into account the nature of the organization, its business strategies, and other management systems.

Employee Needs—Flexible Compensation Systems

Within some legally imposed limits, compensation can be delivered to employees in various forms already identified. The allocation of compensation among these pay forms to emphasize performance, seniority, entitlements, or the long versus short term can be tailored to the pay objectives of the organization. It can also be tailored to the needs of the individual employees.

The simple fact that employees differ is too easily and too often overlooked in designing pay systems. Individual employees join the organization, make investment decisions, design new products, assemble components, and judge the quality of results. Individual employees receive the pay. A major limitation

---

[25] Balkin and Gomez-Mejia, "Matching Compensation and Organization Strategies."

[26] L. R. Gomez-Mejia, "Structure and Process of Diversification, Compensation Strategy, and Firm Performance," *Strategic Management Journal*, October 1992.

of contemporary pay systems is the degree to which individual attitudes and preferences are ignored.[27] Older, highly paid workers may wish to defer taxes by putting their pay into retirement funds, while younger employees may have high cash needs to buy a house, support a family, or finance an education. Dual career couples who are overinsured medically may prefer to use more of their combined pay for child care, automobile insurance, financial counseling, or other benefits. Employees who have young children or dependent parents may desire dependent care coverage.[28]

Perhaps it is time to consider letting employees specify their own pay form (a choice that currently would meet with Internal Revenue Service disapproval and be a challenge to administer). Pay systems can be designed to permit employee choices. Flexible benefit plans are examples, and increasing numbers of employers are adopting them.[29] Allowing greater flexibility into the cash compensation is a step that is waiting to be taken. Again, the key question you should be asking is, Does it matter? Will flexible compensation help achieve organization objectives?

Unions.   Pay systems also need to be adapted to the nature of the union-management relationship.[30] Strategies for dealing with unions vary widely. The federal government formed a joint labor-management committee to examine how to strengthen the relationship between pay and performance for federal workers. At the other extreme, Caterpillar started hiring new, nonunion employees five months into a strike by the United Auto Workers. Between these extremes, hundreds of union contracts are negotiated each year with little fanfare or rancor.

Even though unions now represent only 15 percent of the civilian labor force in the United States, union influence on the design and administration of pay systems is significant. Union preferences for different forms of pay (e.g., cost of living adjustments, improved health care) and their concern with job security

---

[27] R. D. Bretz, R. A. Ash, and G. F. Dreher, "Do People Make the Place? An Examination of the Attraction-Selection-Attrition Hypothesis," *Personnel Psychology* 42 (1989), pp. 561–81; K. Davis, W. F. Giles, and H. S. Field, *Benefits Preferences of Recent College Graduates*, Report 88–2 (Brookfield, WI: International Foundation of Employee Benefits Plans, 1988).

[28] Melissa Barringer, George Milkovich, and Olivia Mitchell, "Predicting Employee Health Insurance Selections in a Flexible Benefit Environment" (Working paper 91–21, Center for Advanced Human Resource Studies, Cornell University).

[29] See *Human Resource Management Review* 4, no. 2, 1994, ed. Margaret Williams, Special Issue: Employee Benefits.

[30] Raymond E. Miles, "Adapting to Technology and Competition: A New Industrial Relations System for the 21st Century," *California Management Review*, Winter 1989, pp. 9–28; Charles Heckscher, *The New Unionism* (New York: Basic Books, 1988); E. Applebaum and Rosemary Batt, *The New American Workplace* (Ithaca, NY: ILR Press, 1994); T. A. Kochan and P. Osterman, *The Mutual Gains Enterprise: Forging a Winning Partnership among Labor, Management, and Government* (Cambridge: Harvard Business School Press, 1994); Paul H. Farber and Alan Krueger, "Union Membership in the United States: The Decline Continues" (Working paper 4216, National Bureau of Economic Research, 1994).

affect pay system design. Historically, the allocation between wages and benefits was greatly affected by unions. Unionized workers still have a greater percentage of their total compensation allocated to benefits than do nonunion workers.

In addition to affecting forms of pay, unions also play a role in administering pay. Most negotiated contracts specify pay intervals, minimum rates, and the basis for movement through a wage range. Some employers adopt the maintenance of union-free status as an objective of its pay system. Such policies might include a high pay level, internally consistent pay treatment to avoid feelings of inequitable treatment, emphasis on performance, and a fair and open administration of the compensation system. These policies often translate into rates that are at or above those for the market, merit pay, or an all-salaried work force, and great emphasis on communicating pay and benefit programs and on attitude surveys to monitor employee reactions.

Global Competition

Competitive pressures, particularly from international competitors, also affect pay decisions. In 1985, hourly pay for production workers in West Germany was 74 percent of that of the U.S. worker, and a Korean worker received only 10 percent of the U.S. average wage. Responding to these pressures, U.S. employees accepted wage concessions, wage cuts, smaller pay increases, one-time lump sum increases that did not add into base pay, and health care deductibles. By 1993 U.S. hourly compensation was exceeded by Germany (41 percent higher), France (25 percent higher), and Japan (eight percent higher). Caution should be exercised in interpreting these data, however, because government-provided benefits (health care in Canada and large layoff awards in Germany) are not included. International wage comparisons vary considerably. Fluctuations in currency exchange rates also play a substantial role. Chapter 18 is devoted to international employee compensation.

Comparing pay between countries is often not the whole story, as Exhibit 1.9 illustrates. In comparison to Germany, the United States has relatively lower labor costs ($16.17 versus $25.95), longer work week (40 versus 37.6 hours), shorter vacation days (23 versus 42 days per year), and a longer work year (1,847 versus 1,499 days). These data provide some of the reasons BMW built a new facility in South Carolina rather than Dusseldorf, Germany.

Differences in the actual pay systems among international competitors also cause U.S. managers to reconsider their pay systems.[31] Exhibit 1.10 describes Toshiba's pay system for its managers. Several items in the exhibit stand out. First, note that bonuses make up about 37 percent of a Toshiba manager's pay. Because they are paid out twice a year rather than in a biweekly paycheck, the use of bonuses offers a cash flow advantage to Toshiba. In addition, bonuses are

---

[31] Jerry Bowles and Joshua Hammond, *Beyond Quality* (New York: G. P. Putnam, 1991); Hitoshi Kume, "The Quality Cultural Exchange," *Quality Progress*, October 1990, pp. 33–35; Charles Morris, *The Coming Global Boom: How to Benefit Now from Tomorrow's Dynamic World Economy* (New York: Bantam Books, 1990).

EXHIBIT 1.9   International Comparisons of Pay and Hours Worked

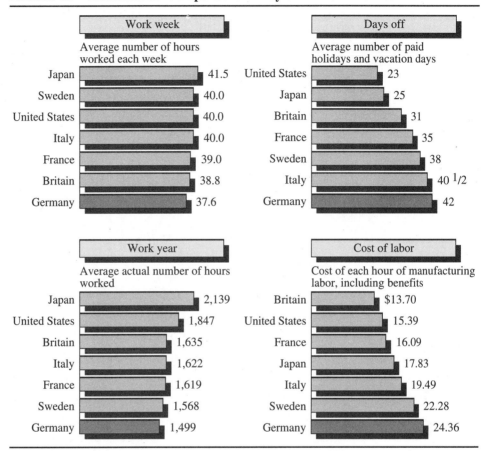

Work week	
Average number of hours worked each week	
Japan	41.5
Sweden	40.0
United States	40.0
Italy	40.0
France	39.0
Britain	38.8
Germany	37.6

Days off	
Average number of paid holidays and vacation days	
United States	23
Japan	25
Britain	31
France	35
Sweden	38
Italy	40 1/2
Germany	42

Work year	
Average actual number of hours worked	
Japan	2,139
United States	1,847
Britain	1,635
Italy	1,622
France	1,619
Sweden	1,568
Germany	1,499

Cost of labor	
Cost of each hour of manufacturing labor, including benefits	
Britain	$13.70
United States	15.39
France	16.09
Japan	17.83
Italy	19.49
Sweden	22.28
Germany	24.36

EXHIBIT 1.10   Toshiba's Managerial Compensation Plan

Pay Elements	Based on	Annual Amount	(%)
1. Core salary	• Performance • Ability • Length of service	¥4,440,000	
			62.8%
2. Position and rank	• Performance	2,280,000	
	Subtotal	**6,720,000**	
3. Bonus* (Example)		3,980,000	37.2
Total		**¥10,700,000**	100%

* Paid twice a year (June and December).

EXHIBIT 1.11 International Perspectives on Competitive Advantage

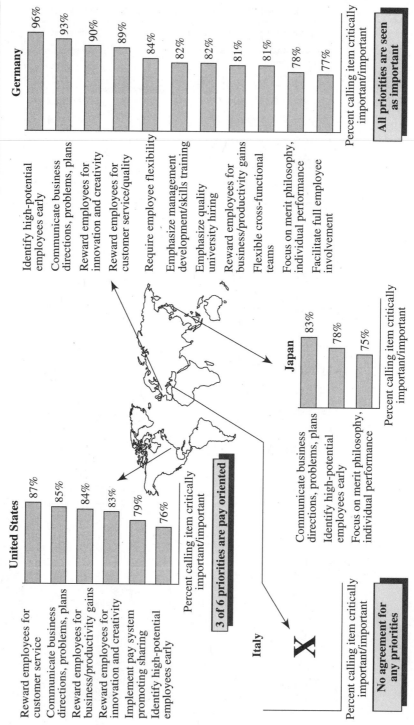

United States

Reward employees for customer service — 87%
Communicate business directions, problems, plans — 85%
Reward employees for business/productivity gains — 84%
Reward employees for innovation and creativity — 83%
Implement pay system promoting sharing — 79%
Identify high-potential employees early — 76%

Percent calling item critically important/important

3 of 6 priorities are pay oriented

Italy

X

Percent calling item critically important/important

No agreement for any priorities

Germany

Identify high-potential employees early — 96%
Communicate business directions, problems, plans — 93%
Reward employees for innovation and creativity — 90%
Reward employees for customer service/quality — 89%
Require employee flexibility — 84%
Emphasize management development/skills training — 82%
Emphasize quality university hiring — 82%
Reward employees for business/productivity gains — 81%
Flexible cross-functional teams — 81%
Focus on merit philosophy, individual performance — 78%
Facilitate full employee involvement — 77%

Percent calling item critically important/important

All priorities are seen as important

Japan

Communicate business directions, problems, plans — 83%
Identify high-potential employees early — 78%
Focus on merit philosophy, individual performance — 75%

Percent calling item critically important/important

NOTE: Priorities identified by 75 percent or more of surveyed managers.

not added into the employee's base pay, so they do not become fixed costs. While a common misperception is that Japanese pay systems are based solely on seniority, notice that Toshiba's managers' pay depends on educational level, experience (i.e., seniority), and performance.[32] The point is that no longer do U.S. managers simply face domestic competitors; they must become knowledgeable in how their global competitors design pay, too.

More than 1,200 experts from 12 different countries were asked how organizations should use human resources to achieve competitive advantage in the 21st century.[33] Some of the results are summarized in Exhibit 1.11. The percentages refer to the amount of agreement among experts. In the United States, 87 percent of the experts agreed that "rewarding employees for customer service" was the top priority for achieving competitive advantage. Of the Germans, 96 percent judged that "identifying high potential employees early" was the highest priority; 85 percent of the Japanese agreed that "communicating business directions, problems, and plans" is a key action; and the Italian experts couldn't agree among themselves about what is important.

Also note that in the United States, four of the six actions the experts agreed upon were pay related (reward employees for customer service, reward employees for business/productivity gains, reward employees for innovation and creativity, implement pay systems promoting sharing). Clearly, U.S. experts see pay as having strategic value in achieving competitive advantage. Japanese experts agreed that only three actions were critical for competitive advantage, and one was pay related: focus on merit pay philosophy and individual performance. Germans agreed on the largest number of actions, 11, and 4 of these were pay related.

Although consensus exists among international experts that pay systems are critical for achieving competitive advantage, significant cross-cultural differences exist over the types of pay programs that are significant. The Japanese, for example, are moving toward individual merit pay, whereas U.S. experts seem to favor more team- and group-based approaches.

BASIC ISSUE: DOES "FIT" PAY OFF?

The basic underlying premise of any strategic perspective is that if managers align pay decisions with the organization strategy and values, are responsive to employees and union relations, and are globally competitive, then the organization is more likely to achieve competitive advantage.

---

[32] Often bonus payments are distributed around major holidays, much as the end-of-year bonus in western companies. Yoko Sano, *HRM Practices in the Japanese Companies*, 1993.

[33] Based on data from an IBM/TPF&C study, 1992. Half the experts were corporate executives, one-fourth were consultants, and one-fourth academics.

| Socio-economic/ political environment | → | Organization strategy | → | HR/compensation policies | → | Competitive advantage |

Up to this point we have stressed that the business strategy leads to the compensation plan. The challenge is to design the "fit" among the environment, business strategy, and pay plan. The better the fit, the greater the competitive advantage.

Now let's turn this perspective on its head.

Resource-Based Perspective: Best Practices →Competitive Advantage

There are those who believe that (1) a set of best pay practices exists, and (2) these practices *should* be applied *independent* of the situation.[34] They challenge the "match-the-business-strategy" view. Does better fit between business strategy and compensation plans really yield better performance? Or is there a set of best practices that yields better performance with almost any business strategy? The latter perspective can be depicted as

| Socio-economic/ political environment | → | HR/compensation policies | → | Organization strategy | → | Competitive advantage |

The underlying premise here is that adopting the best pay practices will allow the employer to gain preferential access to superior human resource talent and competencies (i.e., valued assets). These superior human resources will in turn influence the strategy the organization adopts and be the source of its competitive advantage. This resource-based approach takes literally the oft-heard refrain from corporate public relations: Human resources are our most important asset.

This may appear to be a chicken–egg discussion: Which comes first, the HR/ compensation policies or the business strategy? Yet the answer is critical in the design of a pay plan.

If best practices do exist, what are they? It depends on who you ask. Exhibit 1.12 summarizes two different views. Under the "new pay," employee pay is based primarily on market rates; pay increases depend on performance (not cost

---

[34] P. Cappelli and H. Singh, "Integrating Strategic HR and Strategic Management," Chapter 5, in *Research Frontiers in IR and HR, Industrial and Labor Relations Review*, 1993; P. Wright and G. C. McMahan, "Theoretical Perspectives for Strategic Human Resource Management," *Journal of Management* 18, no. 2 (1992), pp. 295–320; T. Kochan and P. Osterman, *The Mutual Gains Enterprise* (Cambridge: Harvard Business School Press, 1994); J. R. Schuster and P. K. Zingheim, *The New Pay* (New York: Lexington Books, 1992); J. Pfeffer, *Competitive Advantage through People* (Cambridge: Harvard Business School Press, 1994).

EXHIBIT 1.12   **Best Practices Options**

*The New Pay**	*High Commitment†*
• External market-sensitive-based pay; not internal consistency	• High wages: You get what you pay for
• Variable performance-based pay; not annual increases	• Guarantee employment security
• Risk-sharing partnership; not entitlement	• Apply incentives; share gains, not risks
• Flexible opportunities to contribute; not jobs	• Employee ownership
• Lateral promotions; not career path	• Participation and empowerment
• Employability; not job security	• Teams, not individuals, are base units
• Teams; not individual contributors	• Smaller pay differences
	• Promotion from within
	• Selective recruiting
	• Enterprisewide information sharing
	• Training, cross-training, and skill development are crucial
	• Symbolic egalitarianism adds value
	• Long-term perspective matters
	• Measurement matters

* Source: J. R. Schuster, *The New Pay;* E. Lawler, *New Pay.*
† Source: Pfeffer, *Competitive Advantage through People.*

of living or seniority increases), and the employment relationship is uncertain, less secure. The logic is that the implicit contract is a partnership in which successes (and risks) are shared.

The competing view, "high commitment," prescribes high base pay, sharing performance successes only (not risks), guaranteed employment security, promotions from within, and the like. These practices are believed to attract and retain a highly committed work force, which will become the source of competitive advantage. Some political leaders in advanced industrial countries argue that public policies should support high-wage, higher-skilled jobs via laws and tax incentives. Such an approach would encourage less labor-intensive technologies (e.g., Hewlett-Packard, Exxon, Merck) over more labor-intensive operations such as the Wal-Marts and McDonald's.

It would be nice to be able to say whether the "organizational strategy" or the "best practice" perspective has research as well as practical support. Unfortunately, little research that directly examines these competing views has been done. Nevertheless, the evidence to date supports the view that one size does not fit all: that pay policies and plans need to be tailored to match different situations. Early research on the relationship between the fit of business strategies and pay systems and company financial performance suggests that those with better fit perform better.[35] Another study reported that the pay systems adopted under integrated manufacturing strategies (e.g., just in time, statistical quality control, and advanced technologies) were based on how the work was designed in each plant. For example, monthly salaries (versus hourly wages), job-based pay (versus skill based), and individual and group incentives (versus just gain-sharing) were used with jobs that required flexibility and uncertainty in task assignments.[36]

Additional evidence comes from executive pay research, which reveals that firms with higher accounting profits paid their executives more.[37] And top executive pay has also been linked to stockholder returns. Similarly, there is evidence that gain-sharing plans for manufacturing employees are related to improved employee work behaviors (e.g., reduced absenteeism, increased suggestions for productivity improvements, and lower unit costs). And the use of bonuses and stock options for managers, engineers, and other professional employees is also related to firm performance. But caution and more evidence are required in interpreting these results. It may be, for example, that organizations that are successful (higher profits, sales, or appreciating stock values) are better able to afford higher wages and offer incentives and stock options. Rather than the pay system affecting employee behaviors and organization performance, perhaps the reverse occurs: Employees' behaviors and organization performance cause changes in the pay system.

Test for Competitive Advantage—Difficult to Imitate

Designing a pay strategy to achieve competitive advantage is easy to say but difficult to do. One test of competitiveness is whether the strategy is difficult for competitors to imitate. If the pay policies and plans are relatively simple for any competitor to adopt, then how can they possibly provide an advantage? While not much is known about which pay strategies really offer advantages over competitors, an example illustrates the point. Southwest Airlines pilots agreed to a 10-year contract that provides for no wage increases for the first 5 years. In the second five years, the 2,000 pilots agreed to receive stock options plus 3 percent annual wage increases. This strategy will (1) link the financial interests of pilots with those of Southwest stockholders (both benefit if stock prices increase) and (2) help secure Southwest's place as the low-cost provider among

---

[35] E. Montemayer, "Aligning Pay Systems with Market Strategies," *ACA Journal,* Winter 1994, pp. 44–53; L. Gomez-Mejia & D. Balkin, *Compensation, Organization Strategy, and Firm Performance* (Cincinnati: Southwestern, 1992).

[36] Scott A. Snell and James W. Dean, Jr., "Strategic Compensation for Integrated Manufacturing: The Moderating Effects of Jobs and Organizational Inertia," *Academy of Management Journal*, October 1994, pp. 1109–40.

[37] Barry Gerhart and George Milkovich, "Employee Compensation"; A. S. Blinder, ed., *Paying for Productivity* (Washington, DC: Brookings Institute, 1990).

major U.S. airlines. It may also mean that attracting new pilots will become more difficult. Yet it clearly meets the test of being difficult to imitate!

At this point, you may be reminded of the definition of an academic—someone who takes something that works in practice (pay systems) and tries to make it work in theory. But the corollary is that if we can find out why some pay systems work in practice, then we can apply them in other settings, too.

BOOK PLAN

Compensation is such a broad and compelling topic that several books could be devoted to it. The focus of this book will be on the design and management of compensation systems. To aid in understanding how and why pay systems work, a pay model has been presented. This model, which emphasizes the key strategic policies, techniques, and objectives of pay systems, also provides the structure for much of the book.

Strategic policy decisions form the crucial foundation of any pay system. The pay model identifies four basic policy decisions; the first three sections of the book examine each in detail. The first, internal consistency (Part I, Chapters 2 through 5), examines pay relationships within a single organization. What are the pay relationships among jobs and skills or competencies within the organization? What are the relative contributions of each toward achieving the organization's goals? The linkage of pay decisions with the strategic and operating objectives of the organization, the need to establish internal equity, and the importance of ensuring the work relatedness of pay decisions are examined. Job analysis, job evaluation, and skill/competency-based plans are the main techniques for achieving internally consistent pay. Developments and innovations in these techniques, some of them flowing from research efforts and some from organizations' responses to challenges they face, are discussed.

Part II (Chapters 6 and 7) examines external competitiveness—the competitive pay relationships among organizations—and analyzes the influence of market conditions. Pay policies reflect these conditions and are tailored to strategic objectives. Techniques include conducting pay surveys; updating survey data; establishing pay policy lines; and determining pay rates, ranges, and structures.

Once the compensation rates and structures are established, other issues emerge. How much should we pay each individual employee? How much and how often should a person's pay be increased and on what basis? Should employees be paid based on experience, seniority, or performance? Should pay increases be contingent on the unit's or the employee's performance? These are examples of employee contributions, the third building block in the model (Part III, Chapters 8 through 10). Approaches that deliver pay to individual employees are designed with employee knowledge, skills, abilities, needs, preferences, performance, and seniority, as well as the presence or absence of unions, in mind. Recent theoretical and research developments related to motivational effects of pay, goal setting, and performance evaluation are examined in light of the pay decisions that must be made by employers.

Part IV covers employee services and benefits (Chapters 11 and 12). While only two chapters are devoted to employee benefits, this does not imply that the design and management of benefits are unimportant. The opposite is true. Benefits have become so critical that a separate book is required. All we do here is discuss the major benefit forms, the challenges involved in designing and administering the benefit program, and how to tie benefits to the organization's strategic directions.

The government's role in compensation is examined in Part V, Chapters 13 and 14. The government affects compensation through its purchase of goods and services and its employment of a sizable segment of the work force. Additionally, pay practices must comply with legislation and court interpretations.

Managing the compensation system (Part VI, Chapters 15 through 18) includes planning, budgeting, evaluating, communicating, and providing for the special needs of certain groups (e.g., sales representatives, executives, unions). Organizations are becoming more global, with operations in many regions of the world. Even those with only domestic operations are influenced by global competitive forces. In the belief that competence in managing employee compensation includes understanding global pay systems, we have added a new chapter (18) in this edition, "International Compensation."

Even though the book is divided into sections that are reflected in the pay model, that does not mean that pay policies and decisions are necessarily so discrete. All the basic policy decisions are interrelated, and together they form a major system that influences organization performance and employee behaviors. Throughout the book our intention is to examine alternative approaches. We believe that rarely is there a single correct approach; rather, alternative approaches exist or can be designed. The one most likely to be effective depends on the circumstances. We hope that this book will help you become better informed about these options and how to design new ones. Whether as an employee, a manager, or an interested member of society, you should be able to assess effectiveness and equity of pay systems.

CAVEAT EMPTOR—THE IMPORTANCE OF BEING AN INFORMED CONSUMER

Our understanding of compensation management grows as research evidence accumulates. Nevertheless, evidence needs to be evaluated to determine its quality, relevance, and information value. Managers need to be informed consumers. Just as developing a portfolio of high-quality stocks or the successful acquisition of another firm requires judgment, so does understanding the state of knowledge about employee compensation. Whether it is managing your stock portfolio or managing compensation, belief is a poor substitute for informed judgment.

So your challenge is to become an informed consumer. How-to-do-it advice abounds, best-practices prescriptions are plentiful, and academic journals are packed with pay-related theory and research. So we end the chapter with a brief consumer's guide that includes three questions.

1. Does the Research Measure Anything Useful?

How useful are the variables used in the study? How well are they measured? For example, many studies purport to measure organization performance. However, the way performance is actually defined and measured varies. Performance may be accounting measures such as return on assets or cash flow, financial measures such as earnings per share or total shareholder return, operational measures such as scrap rates or defect indicators, or qualitative measures such as customer satisfaction. It may even be the opinions of compensation managers as in, How effective is your gain-sharing plan? (Answer choices are highly effective, effective, some, disappointing, not very effective.) So the informed consumer must say, Help me understand. Does this research measure anything important?

2. Does the Study Separate Correlation from Causation?

Correlation does not mean causation. Many studies investigate the relationship between the use of performance-based pay and performance. Just because the observed use of gain-sharing plans is related to improved performance does not mean it caused the improvement. Other factors may be involved. Perhaps new technology, reengineering, improved marketing, or the general expansion of the local economy underlie the results.

Once we are confident that both performance and pay are accurately defined and measured, we must be sure that they are actually related. Most often this is addressed through the use of statistical analyses. The correlation coefficient is a common measure of association and indicates how changes in one variable are related to changes in another. Many research studies use a statistical analysis known as regression analysis. One output from a regression analysis is the R^2. The R^2 is much like a correlation in that it tells us what percentage of the variation is accounted for by the variables we are using to predict or explain. For example, one study includes a regression analysis of the change in CEO pay due to change in company performance. The resulting R^2s of between 0.8 percent and 4.5 percent indicate that only a very small amount of change in CEO pay is *related to* changes in company performance. Note that *relation* is not necessarily *causation*. For example, just because a manufacturing plant initiates a new incentive plan and the facility's performance improves, we cannot conclude that the incentive plan caused the improved performance. The two changes are associated or related, but causation is a tough link to make.

Too often, case studies or benchmarking surveys are presented as studies that reveal cause and effect. They are not. Case studies are descriptive accounts whose value and limitations must be recognized. Just because the best-performing companies are using a practice does not mean the practice is causing the performance. IBM for a long time pursued a full-employment policy. Clearly, that policy did not cause the value of IBM stock to increase or improve IBM's profitability. However, compensation research often attempts to answer questions of causality. Does the use of performance-based pay *lead to* greater customer satisfaction, improved quality, and better company performance? Causality is one of the most difficult questions to answer and continues to be an important and sometimes perplexing problem for researchers.

3. Are There Alternative Explanations?

Consider a hypothetical study that attempts to assess the impact of a performance-based pay initiative. The researchers measure performance by assessing quality, productivity, customer satisfaction, employee satisfaction, and the facility's performance to plan. The final step is to see if future periods' performance improves over this period's. If it does, can we safely assume that it was the incentive pay that caused performance? Or is it equally likely that the improved performance has alternative explanations such as the passage of NAFTA or the declining value of the dollar or perhaps a change in executive leadership in the facility? In this case, causality evidence seems weak. If the researchers had measured the performance indicators several years prior to and after installing the plan, then the evidence of causality is only a bit stronger. Further, if the researchers repeated this process in other facilities and the results are similar, then the preponderance of evidence is stronger. Clearly, the organization is doing something right, and incentive pay may be part of it.

The best way to establish causation is to account for these competing explanations, either statistically or through control groups. The point is that alternative explanations often exist. And if they do, they need to be accounted for to establish causality. Our experience suggests that it is very difficult to disentangle the effects of pay plans to clearly establish causality. However, it is possible to look at the overall pattern of evidence to make judgments about the effects of pay.

Summary

The model presented in this chapter provides a structure for understanding compensation systems. The three main components of the model include the objectives of the pay system, the policy decisions that provide the system's foundation, and the techniques that link policies and objectives. The following sections of the book examine in turn each of the four policy decisions—internal consistency, external competitiveness, employee contributions, and administration—as well as the techniques, new directions, and related research.

Two questions should constantly be in the minds of managers and readers of this text. First, Why do it this way? There is rarely one correct way to design a system or pay an individual. Organizations, people, and circumstances are too varied. But a well-trained manager can select or design a suitable approach.

Second, So what? What does this technique do for us? How does it help achieve our organization goals? If good answers are not apparent, there is no point to the technique. Adapting the pay system to meet the needs of the employees and to help achieve the goals of the organization is what this book is all about.

The basic premise of this book is that compensation systems do have a profound impact. Yet too often, traditional pay systems seem to have been designed in response to some historical but long-forgotten problem. The practices continue, but the logic underlying them is not always clear or even relevant.

Review Questions

1. How do differing perspectives affect our perceptions of compensation?
2. Do you view pay as a reward or a return? Why?
3. How does the pay model help organize one's thinking about compensation?
 4. What can a pay system do for an organization? For an employee?
5. Under what circumstances would one of the three basic pay policies be emphasized relative to the other two? Try to think of a separate example for each basic pay policy.
6. Answer the three questions in Caveat Emptor for any study or business article that tells you how to pay people.

YOUR TURN:

PSYCHOLOGICAL AND SOCIAL CONTRACTS: IMPLICATIONS FOR EMPLOYEE COMPENSATION

Here are some vignettes providing examples of changes to implicit contracts.* How do you judge them: acceptable or unfair? Explain why.

A. A small photocopy shop has one employee who has worked in the shop for six months and earns about $9.00 per hour. Business continues to be favorable, but a factory in the area has closed and unemployment has increased. Other small shops have hired reliable workers at $7.00 per hour to perform jobs similar to those done by the photocopy shop employee. The owner of the photocopy shop reduces the employee's wage to $7.00 per hour.

_____ Acceptable _____ Unfair

Discuss rationales from both parties' perspectives.

B. Change the vignette: The current employee leaves and the owner decides to pay a replacement $7.00 per hour.

_____ Acceptable _____ Unfair

Discuss in light of your answer to A.

* Vignettes from D. Kahneman, J. Knetsch, and R. Thaler, "Fairness as a Constraint on Profit Seeking: Entitlements in the Market," *American Economic Review*, September 1986, p. 730.

C. A house painter employs two assistants and pays them $9.00 per hour. The painter decides to quit house painting and go into the business of landscape services, where the going wage is lower. He reduces the workers' wages to $7.00 per hour for the landscaping work.

_____ Acceptable _____ Unfair

Again, please discuss this case by extending your answer to questions A and B. What factors do you consider? Which are explicit? Which are implicit or understood?

What are the implications of your answers for the design and management of any compensation system? Does the notion of a social contract change or add to your ideas? How?

Exhibit I.1   The Pay Model

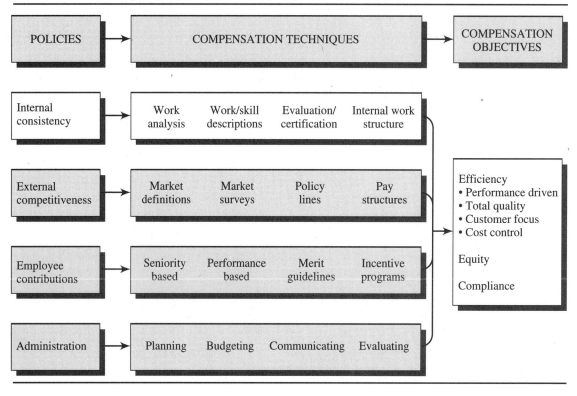

Internal Consistency: Determining the Structure

PART I

Exxon employs a chief executive officer, chemical engineers, plant managers, nurses, market analysts, laboratory technicians, financial planners, hydraulic mechanics, accountants, guards, oil tanker captains, sailors, and word processors. How is pay determined for all these different types of work? Is the financial planner worth more than the accountant, or the mechanic more than the word processor? How much more? What procedures are used to set pay rates and who does it? Should the potential consequences of errors in the job, such as the disastrous Alaskan oil spill blamed on the captain of the *Exxon Valdez*, be considered in setting pay? How important are the characteristics of the employees—their competencies, knowledge, skills, or experience? How important are the characteristics of the work, the conditions under which it is done, or the value of what is produced? What about the employer's financial condition, or employee and union preferences?

Beyond understanding how pay is determined for different types of work, there are other critical questions in compensation management. Does how we pay employees make a difference? Why do we pay the financial planner more than the accountant or the mechanic more than a word processor? Does the compensation system support Exxon's business strategy? Does its compensation system help Exxon attract and retain the talent it needs? Do the procedures used to set pay support the way the work is organized and performed, such as the use of semiautonomous work teams in Exxon's Baytown, Texas, refineries? Or are the procedures bureaucratic burdens that hinder focusing on customers, employee flexibility, and teamwork? Does it matter whether employees are paid based on the jobs they perform versus the skills or competencies they possess?

So two basic questions lie at the core of compensation management: (1) How is pay determined for the wide variety of work performed in organizations?

(2) How does pay affect employees' attitudes and work behaviors and subsequently the success of the organization?

These questions are examined within the framework introduced in Chapter 1 and shown again in Exhibit I.1. This part of the book examines the framework's first strategic policy issue, internal consistency. The focus of these chapters is within the organization. In Chapter 2, the policy of internal consistency—what affects it and what is affected by it—is considered. Chapter 3 discusses various approaches to assess the similarities and differences in work content. Chapters 4 and 5 scrutinize job-based, skill-based, and competency-based approaches for determining internal pay structures.

CHAPTER

Defining Consistency

For the kingdom of heaven is like a householder who went out early in the morning to hire laborers for his vineyard. And having agreed with the laborers for a denarius a day, he sent them into his vineyard. And about the third hour, he went out and saw others standing . . . idle; and he said to them, "Go you also into the vineyard, and I will give you whatever is just." And again he went out about the vineyard, and about the ninth hour, and did as before. . . . But about the eleventh hour he went out and found others . . . and he said to them, "Go you also into the vineyard." When evening came, the owner said to his steward, "Call the laborers, and pay them their wages, beginning from the last even to the first." When the first in their turn came . . . they also received each his denarius. . . . They began to murmur against the householder, saying, "These last have worked a single hour, and thou hast put them on a level with us, who have borne the burden of the day's heat." But answering them, he said, "Friend, I do thee no injustice; take what is thine and go."[1]

Matthew's parable raises age-old questions about internal consistency and pay structures within a single organization.[2] Clearly, the laborers in the vineyard felt that those "who have borne the burden of the day's heat" should be paid more, perhaps because they had contributed more to the householder's economic benefit. According to the laborers, "fair pay" should be based on two criteria: the value of contributions and the time worked. Perhaps the householder was using a third criterion: an individual's needs without regard to differences in the work performed.[3]

Matthew doesn't tell us how the work in the vineyard was organized. Perhaps the laborers had organized into teams, with some members pruning the vines and others pulling weeds or tying the vines. Pay structures in contemporary compensation plans are typically designed by assessing how the work is organized and performed, its relative value, and the skills and knowledge required to perform it. This is done through procedures acceptable to the parties involved, for if the procedures used or the resulting pay structure is unacceptable to managers or employees, they'll probably murmur, too. Is tying more valuable than pruning? Today, murmuring may translate into turnover, unwillingness to try new technology, and maybe even a lack of concern about the quality of the grapes in the vineyard or the customer satisfaction with it.

This chapter examines the strategic policy of internal consistency in pay structures and its consequences for employees' behaviors and the organization's success.

---

[1] Matthew 20: 1–16.

[2] For an excellent history of the different standards for pay, see N. Arnold Tolles, *Origins of Modern Wage Theories* (Englewood Cliffs, NJ: Prentice Hall, 1964).

[3] Several Japanese firms still base a small portion of a worker's pay on the number of dependents. In the early 1900s, workers who were "family men" received a pay supplement in some U.S. firms as well.

INTERNAL CONSISTENCY AND THE PAY MODEL

Two basic concepts—internal consistency and pay structures—need to be clarified.

Internal consistency, often called internal equity, establishes equal pay for work of equal worth and pay differentials for work of unequal worth. But internal consistency involves more than internal equity. It emphasizes the fit between the way work is designed and the pay structure. Pay structures must be consistent with the work itself. They must support the work flow, relationships, and pressures existing within an organization. Consequently, internal consistency includes concerns for fairness of the procedures used to establish the pay structure, as well as concerns for the way the organization is designed and the flow of work. The specific procedures and pay structures must also be designed to (1) elicit employee behaviors and actions that help achieve organizational objectives, (2) gain acceptance from employees and managers, and (3) comply with laws and regulations.

Internal consistency refers to the relationship between the pay structure and the design of the organization and the work. It focuses attention on the importance of designing a pay structure that supports the relationships and pressures internal to the organization: the organization's structure, the flow of work, and the similarities and differences in work and employees performing it.

Pay structure refers to the array of pay rates for different work or skills within a single organization. It focuses attention on the levels, differentials, and criteria used to determine those pay rates.

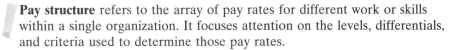

STRATEGY AND PAY STRUCTURES

The basic premise underlying the strategic approach is that fit matters. Pay structures tailored to be consistent with the organization, to support the way the work gets done, and to fit the organization's business strategy will be more likely to lead to success. Misaligned structures may motivate employee behavior that is inconsistent with the organization's strategy. So a low-cost, customer-focused strategy similar to Wal-Mart's is more likely to succeed with a pay structure that generates low labor costs. In contrast, Hewlett-Packard's strategy requires constant product innovation and short product design-to-market cycle time. Hence, its pay structure needs to reinforce innovation and cross-functional flexibility and encourage design, marketing, manufacturing, and customer service personnel to work closely together. Internal consistency focuses on aligning pay structures with employee behaviors that fit the business objectives and ensuring that employees believe their pay is fair.

Another view is emerging, which suggests that, like well-tailored clothes, too tight a fit is not appropriate. Perhaps pay structures should be more loosely coupled to the organization. If organizations are becoming more amoebalike—sort of like Odo the Shape Shifter in Star Trek—then pay structures that facilitate such constant change are required. In the United States, two-thirds of the Fortune 1000 companies both downsized and reduced layers in management in the last decade.[4] If this rate of restructuring continues, then perhaps a more loosely aligned structure is required to facilitate rather than hinder such constant change.

Optional approaches to internal consistency include a closely tailored or a loosely coupled pay structure. In either approach, influencing the attitudes and behaviors of employees remains the goal.

PAY STRUCTURES AND THE PAY MODEL

Pay structures can be described on three dimensions: (1) number of levels, (2) pay differentials among levels, and (3) the criteria used to support the structure. Exhibit 2.1 shows a pay structure for engineers and scientists used at a Martin Marietta division. The structure includes six levels that range from entry to fellows.

Levels

The essence of any pay structure is its hierarchical nature: the number of levels and reporting relationships. Pay structures typically reflect the organization structure and the flow of the work. Therefore, some are more hierarchical with multiple levels; others are flat with few levels. For example, General Electric Plastics uses the five broad basic levels described in Exhibit 2.2 to array its work. These levels, labeled *career bands*, range from professional to executive. If you compare Exhibits 2.1 and 2.2, you will see that Martin Marietta defines the work more specifically than GE Plastics does.

Differentials

The pay differences among levels are referred to as *differentials*. Pay structures typically pay more for work that requires more qualifications to perform, is performed under less desirable working conditions, and/or whose input is more valued. The differential between a hamburger flipper ($5.00) and the front counter supervisor at McDonald's ($6.50) can be expressed as an absolute ($6.50 − $5.00 = $1.50) or as a percentage ([$6.50 − 5.00]/5.00 = 30%). Pay differentials of interest in managing compensation include those between adjacent levels in a career path, between supervisors and subordinates, between

---

[4] General Electric Note to Shareholders, from General Electric Annual Report, 1993, pp. 1–4; E. E. Lawler, "From Job-Based to Competency-Based Organizations," *Journal of Organization Behavior* 15 (1994), pp. 3–15; E. E. Lawler, S. A. Mohrman, and G. E. Ledford, *Employee Involvement and Total Quality Management: Practices and Results in Fortune 1000 Companies* (San Francisco: Jossey Bass, 1992).

EXHIBIT 2.1 Engineering Pay Structure at Martin Marietta

Average rate					
$100,000					
90,000					
80,000					
70,000					
60,000					
50,000					
40,000					
30,000					

$36,750
Engineer
Limited use of basic principles and concepts. Develops solutions to limited problems. Closely supervised.

$45,000
Senior Engineer
Full use of standard principles and concepts. Provides solutions to a variety of problems. Under general supervision.

$55,500
Systems Engineer
Wide applications of principles and concepts, plus working knowledge of other related disciplines. Provides solutions to a wide variety of difficult problems. Solutions are imaginative, thorough, and practicable. Work under only very general direction.

$66,000
Lead Engineer
Applies extensive expertise as a generalist or specialist. Develops solutions to complex problems that require the regular use of ingenuity and creativity. Work is performed without appreciable direction. Exercises considerable latitude in determining technical objectives of assignment.

$78,000
Advisor Engineer
Applies advanced principles, theories, and concepts. Contributes to the development of new principles and concepts. Works on unusually complex problems and provides solutions that are highly innovative and ingenious. Works under consultative direction toward predetermined long-range goals. Assignments are often self-initiated.

$100,000
Consultant Engineer
Exhibits an exceptional degree of ingenuity, creativity, and resourcefulness. Applies and/or develops highly advanced technologies, scientific principles, theories, and concepts. Develops information that extends the existing boundaries of knowledge in a given field. Often acts independently to uncover and resolve problems associated with the development and implementation of operational programs.

Entry Level ——————— **Recognized Authority**

Exhibit 2.2   Managerial/Professional Levels at General Electric Plastics (GEP)

Career Band	Band Description	Developmental Objectives	
Executive	Provides vision, leadership, and innovation to major business segments or functions of GEP	Ability to provide strategic direction and judgment that results in the global objectives of GEP being achieved	
Director	Directs a significant functional area or smaller business segment	Management:	Ability to provide direction and a global perspective to the management of a small business segment or significant functional area
		Individual Contributors:	Direct a project with broad business impact, drawing on others for completion of business objectives while holding accountability for end results
Leadership	Individual contributors leading projects or programs with broad scope and impact, or managers leading functional components with broad scope and impact	Management:	Ability to effectively manage diverse activities within a function and the resolution of decisions in the balanced best interests of the business
		Individual Contributors:	Ability to leverage in-depth technical knowledge in the achievement of business objectives
Technical/ managerial	Individual contributors managing projects or programs with defined scope and responsibility, or first tier management of a specialty area	Management:	Develop management skills and business perspective to effectively resolve cross-functional challenges
		Individual Contributors:	Ability to leverage specialized technical knowledge to achieve project or program results
Professional	Supervisors and individual contributors working on tasks, activities, and/or less complex, shorter duration projects	Ability to work independently on well-defined assignments or shorter term projects	

union and nonunion employees, and between executives and regular employees.[5] The differentials in Exhibit 2.1 vary from 18 to 28 percent, with the largest differential between the top two levels in the structure.

Criteria

Structures may be supported by three criteria: (1) the job or *work performed*, (2) the *skills or competencies* required, or (3) the performance or outcomes of the work. The criterion chosen can influence employee behaviors by describing what is required (i.e., promotion to high level of responsibility, certification of skills/competencies, and/or improved performance) to get higher pay in the structure. The engineering pay structure at Martin Marietta (Exhibit 2.1) uses the work performed as the criterion. General Electric Plastics (Exhibit 2.2) uses the competencies that are required at each level of work. For an example of a performance criterion, recall our discussion of the automobile salesperson in Chapter 1. Selling you a Chevy Nova earns the salesperson $1,000, whereas selling you a BMW earns the salesperson $4,000. The performance creates the structure.

EGALITARIAN VERSUS HIERARCHICAL STRUCTURES

Pay structures can range from egalitarian at one extreme to hierarchical at the other. An egalitarian structure implies a belief that all workers should be treated equally. Some believe that more equal treatment will improve employee satisfaction, aid work team unity, and subsequently affect workers' performance.[6] Egalitarian structures have fewer levels and smaller differentials between adjacent levels and between the highest (CEO) and lowest paid workers.

By contrast, hierarchical structures are consistent with a belief in the motivational effects of recognizing differences in employee skills, responsibilities, and contributions to the organization. Hierarchies are really structures of incentives, in this view. Hierarchical structures have more levels and greater differentials among them. Rather than leading to employee satisfaction, advocates of hierarchies believe that equal treatment will result in the more knowledgeable employees who perform more responsible jobs being unrecognized and unrewarded, which will cause them to leave the organization. Their departure will lower overall performance. So the case can be made for both egalitarian and hierarchical structures.

How egalitarian or hierarchical should pay structures be? The size of the typical differential between CEOs and other employees has generated heated discussion. In the United States, the differentials between CEOs and operatives

---

[5] M. Bloom and G. Milkovich, "Money, Managers, and Metamorphosis," in *Trends in Organizational Behavior,* 3rd ed., ed. D. Rousseau and C. Cooper (New York: John Wiley & Sons, 1996).

[6] E. E. Lawler III, "From Job-Based to Competency-Based Organizations," *Journal of Organization Behavior* 15 (1994), pp. 3–15; Barry Gerhart and George T. Milkovich, "Employee Compensation: Research and Practice," in *Handbook of Industrial and Organizational Psychology* 3, pp. 481–570, ed. M. D. Dunnette and L. Hough (Palo Alto, CA: Consulting Psychologists Press, 1992).

is 35 to 1, the highest among industrialized countries. In Japan, the differential is only 15 to 1. A number of writers have labeled the U.S. differentials excessive and raised concerns over fair treatment of employees.[7] They say the pay gap creates a "trust gap" if executives fatten their own paychecks while cutting jobs and wages for others. For example, Michael Eisner, the chief executive officer of Disney, was paid $750,000 in base salary in 1993.[8] However, his stock options were valued at $298.9 million. Mr. Eisner's pay contrasts to that earned by Disney employees who perform as Mickey or Minnie Mouse. Mickey, Minnie, Pluto, and Goofy are all represented by the Teamsters and earn between $6.50 and $14.00 an hour, compared to $78,081 per hour for Eisner. The effects of such pay differentials are not clear. Some believe they may cause employees to murmur against the executives just as the vineyard laborers once did. Others argue that the large differentials motivate employees to get promoted to earn more.

Yet egalitarian structures can cause problems, too. For example, Ben and Jerry's Homemade, a fast-growing purveyor of premium ice cream, maintains a spread of only 7-to-1 between its highest-paid and lowest-paid employee. (When the company started, the spread was only 5-to-1.) The relatively narrow range reflects the company's philosophy that the prosperity of its production workers and its management should be closely linked. But the narrow spread is often a barrier to recruiting. Ben and Jerry's recently abandoned this policy to hire an accounting manager and a new CEO. Also, the founders Ben and Jerry never publicized the fact that stock options enriched their own total pay to much more than the 7 to 1 ratio.

An egalitarian structure is susceptible to *pay compression*, the narrowing of pay differentials between newly hired and more experienced employees. Compression can lead to a sense of inequity and increased turnover.[9]

So at what point does an egalitarian structure turn into a hiring or "compression problem" and a hierarchical structure into a "trust gap"?[10] Many argue that

---

[7] Arne L. Kalleberg and James R. Lincoln, "The Structure of Earnings Inequality in the United States and Japan," *American Journal of Sociology*, vol. 94, supplement S121–S153; Vladimir Pucik, "Revolution or Evolution: The Transformation of Japanese Personnel Practices" (Working paper, Center for Advanced Human Resource Studies, Cornell University); Takao Kato, "Chief Executive Compensation and Corporate Groups in Japan: New Evidence from Micro Data," *International Journal of Industrial Organization* (in press); Takao Kato and Mark Rockel, "Experiences, Credentials, and Compensation in the Japanese and U.S. Managerial Labor Markets: New Evidence from Micro Data," *Journal of the Japanese and International Economies* 6 (1992), pp. 30–51.

[8] Brian Dumaine, "A Knockout Year," *Fortune*, July 25, 1994, pp. 94–103; Stephen F. O'Byrne, "What Pay for Performance Looks Like: The Case of Michael Eisner," *Journal of Applied Corporate Finance*, October 1994, pp. 135–36; "That Eye-Popping Executive Pay: Is Anyone Worth This Much?" *Business Week*, April 25, 1994, pp. 48–55.

[9] L. R. Gomez-Mejia and D. B. Balkin, "Effectiveness of Individual and Aggregate Compensation Strategies," *Industrial Relations* 28 (1989), pp. 431–45; Luis Gomez-Mejia and David Balkin, *Compensation, Organizational Strategy, and Firm Performance* (Cincinnati: Southwestern, 1992).

[10] Barry Gerhart and George Milkovich, "Employee Compensation: Research and Practice," in *Handbook of Industrial and Organizational Psychology*, 2nd ed., ed. M. D. Dunnette and L. M. Hough, (Palo Alto, CA: Consulting Psychologists Press, 1992).

egalitarian pay supports work teams and cooperative employee relations. They argue that more hierarchical pay structures reflect status, kill employee initiative, and crush creativity.[11] Unions also support egalitarian pay for political and solidarity reasons.[12] Others counter that properly designed hierarchies are more efficient and support initiative and creativity.[13] They say that organizations need to be designed in terms of levels of accountability and skill required. Hierarchies offer incentives to obtain training, to take risks, and to excel. Hierarchies support accountability and responsibility.

Recent research findings offer conflicting views.[14] Behavioralists report finding that the greater the pay differences, the lower the individual's satisfaction, productivity, and willingness to collaborate. These studies were done with college faculty as the subjects. Another set of studies done by economists reports that greater differentials increase individual performance. These studies view pay structures as a *tournament*.[15] In the first example in Exhibit 2.3, 10 team members, each paid $50,000, are competing for one team leader slot. The team leader gets $55,000. In the second example, these 10 members are competing for a $65,000 leader job. The tournament logic is that the greater differential will motivate all members to be the winner, and the bigger the prize, the greater the motivation. So associates on Team 2 will work harder than associates on Team 1.

The research on tournament models is mixed. Raising the total prize money by $100,000 in the Professional Golf Association tournament lowered each player's score, on average, by 1.1 strokes over 72 holes. And the closer the players got to the top prize, the more their scores were lowered. But employment in the real world is probably not a round of golf or teaching college. Employment

[11] E. E. Lawler III, "Pay for Performance: A Strategic Analysis," in *Compensation and Benefits*, ed. L. R. Gomez-Mejia (Washington, DC: BNA, 1989); Sandra O'Neal, "Competencies: The DNA of the Corporation," *Perspectives in Total Compensation* 2, no. 3 (Winter 1994), pp. 6–12; Lawler, "From Job-Based to Competency-Based Organizations."

[12] C. J. Berger, C. A. Olson, and J. W. Boudreau, "The Effect of Unionism on Job Satisfaction: The Role of Work Related Values and Perceived Rewards," *Organizational Behavior and Human Performance* 32 (1983), pp. 284–324; P. Capelli and P. D. Sherer, "Assessing Worker Attitudes under a Two-Tier Wage Plan," *Industrial and Labor Relations Review* 43 (1990), pp. 225–44.

[13] Elliot Jaques, "In Praise of Hierarchies," *Harvard Business Review*, January–February 1990; Ronald G. Ehrenberg and Michael L. Bognanno, "The Incentive Effects of Tournaments Revisited: Evidence from the European PGA Tour," *Industrial Labor Relations Review* 43 (1990), pp. 745–885; Edward Lazear and Sherwin Rosen, "Rank Order Tournaments as an Optimum Labor Contract," *Journal of Political Economy*, October 1989, pp. 41–64; Edward Lazear, "Pay Equality and Industrial Politics," *Journal of Political Economy*, June 1989, pp. 561–80; Charles O'Reilly and Brian S. Main, "Comparisons: A Tale of Two Theories," *Administrative Science Quarterly*, June 1988, pp. 257–74.

[14] Brian E. Becker and Mark A. Huselid, "The Incentive Effects of Tournament Compensation Systems," *Administrative Science Quarterly* 37 (1992), pp. 336–50; Jeffrey Pfeffer and Nancy Langton, "The Effects of Wage Dispersion on Satisfaction, Productivity, and Working Collaboratively: Evidence from College and University Faculty," *Administrative Science Quarterly* (1993), pp. 382–407.

[15] R. G. Ehrenberg and M. L. Bognanno, "The Incentive Effects of Tournaments Revisited: Evidence from the European PGA Tour," *Industrial and Labor Relations Review* 43 (1990), pp. 74–88.

Exhibit 2.3   Structures as Tournaments

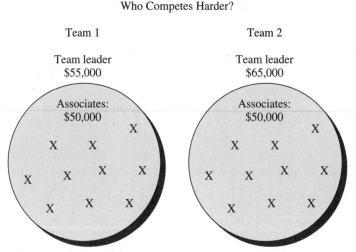

Who Competes Harder?

Tournament theory predicts associates on Team 2 will perform better.

---

involves ongoing and highly interdependent relations with coworkers over time rather than independent competition. Tournaments may accurately model some employment relationships but not others, so their application may be limited. A safe conclusion is that perhaps teachers and athletes are affected differently by pay structures, and economists and behavioralists may disagree.

In practice, the answer to how the structure ought to look probably lies in how the work is organized. It can be organized around teams and cells or around individual performers. The pay structure should support the underlying organization structure. Obviously, this is a simplification. Think of any professional team sport—baseball, football, hockey—versus individual sports such as golf or bowling. Even in team sports, some positions are more valuable than others—a football team's quarterback, a basketball team's point guard and center are leadership roles on the teams. Consequently, these positions are paid more on average based on their relative value to the team's overall performance. So the team/individual distinction is easier to make in theory than in practice.

Distinguishing among Policies

Distinctions among internal consistency (what is the work worth relative to other work in the same organization and does it fit the organization strategy?), external competitiveness (what are competitors paying relative to what we are paying for similar work?), and employee contribution (how much is this employee worth relative to other employees?) are also easier to make in a textbook than in the real world. Internal consistency refers primarily to the relationships among jobs or skills within one employer. The comparison is *not* over pay differences between two individuals or between two firms; the worth of the work/skill itself is determined with little regard to the individual who performs it. For example, word processing may pay $10.50 per hour whether the employee doing the job holds a Ph.D. in journalism or is a vocational school graduate.

Separating internal consistency concerns from employee contribution and individual pay clearly oversimplifies the real world. In some work, particularly that requiring great responsibility and discretion, distinguishing the worth of the job from the individual does not make sense. For example, a Lockheed Director of Special Projects works on the stealth fighter bomber; an Ithaca School District Director of Special Projects works on a pilot program for ninth graders. So although a policy of internal consistency deals primarily with *relationships among jobs/skills/competencies inside a single organization*, equitable pay structures can be based directly on the skills/competencies of employees, as well as the jobs to which they are assigned.[16]

Comparisons of pay structures across organizations reveal significant differences. Some organizations pay the highest jobs 160 times the compensation of the lowest paid job.[17] In other organizations, the differences are considerably less (9 or 10 times). These observed differences raise questions about the design of internal pay structures. What factors influence or determine these structures? What are the consequences of different structures? Each question is considered in turn.

FACTORS INFLUENCING INTERNAL PAY STRUCTURES

The major factors that influence internal structures are shown in Exhibit 2.4. They include societal norms and customs; the economic conditions in which organizations operate; the culture, technology, strategy and objectives of a particular organization; and the particular characteristics of the work and the employees involved. The confluence of these pressures influences the design of pay structures.

Exactly how these factors interact is not well understood. No single theory accounts for all factors. Rather, a number of theories emphasize certain factors over others, and many ignore competing factors. No theory includes all the factors shown in Exhibit 2.4. As we discuss the factors that influence pay structures, we will also look at various theories.

[16] E. E. Lawler III, G. E. Ledford, Jr., and L. Chang, "Who Uses Skill-Based Pay and Why," *Compensation and Benefits Review* 2, no. 5 (1993), pp. 22–26; G. E. Ledford, Jr., "The Effectiveness of Skill-Based Pay," *Perspectives in Total Compensation* 1, no. 1 (1990).

[17] Thomas A. Mahoney, *Compensation and Reward Perspectives* (Burr Ridge, IL: Richard D. Irwin, 1979); Bonnie Rabin, "Measuring Compensation Structures," *Compensation and Benefits Management* 10, no. 4 (1994), pp. 30–40.

EXHIBIT 2.4   Factors Influencing Internally Consistent Pay Structures

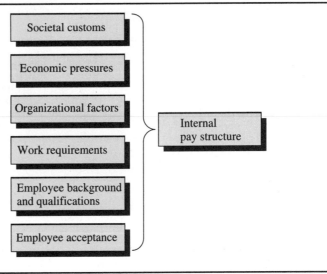

Societal Factors

The historical role of societal conditions can be traced in various theories rationalizing pay differences.[18] These theories draw upon concepts from philosophy, sociology, economics, and psychology. Matthew's parable, for example, reveals an egalitarian philosophy: "the last even to first," regardless of employee qualifications, working conditions, or hours worked.

Just wage doctrine, another approach to pay structures, was a response to 14th century artisans seeking to take advantage of the economic and social chaos that resulted from the death of an estimated one-third of Europe's population due to bubonic plague. Nobles and landholders bid up the prevailing wages of skilled artisans, who were in relatively short supply. The church responded by proclaiming a schedule of "just" wages that reflected that society's class structure. Economic and market forces were explicitly denied as appropriate determinants of pay structures. In this view, *societal norms, customs,* and *tradition* justify pay structures. Present-day manifestations of the just wage doctrine can be seen in debates over minimum wage legislation and comparable worth, which also argue against economic forces as the sole determinant of pay structures.

Toshiba, the major Japanese manufacturer, adheres to a combination of experience and achievement in determining its internal pay structure. Toshiba tries to protect employees from the vagaries of external economic forces but

---

[18] See Tolles, *Origins of Wage Theory*; also see Jerald Greenberg, "Employee Theft as a Reaction to Underpayment or Inequity: The Hidden Cost of Pay Cuts," *Journal of Applied Psychology* 75 (1990), pp. 561–68.

also counsels higher achieving younger employees to respect tradition and "wait; your turn will come." This is a societal custom with increasing appeal to the aging authors of this book. However, competitive economic pressures are forcing Toshiba and other traditional Japanese firms to re-examine their approach.

Economic Factors

The just wage doctrine preserved a privileged position in society for landowners for centuries. Then came the Industrial Revolution. By the end of the 19th century, for the first time, the majority of people were earning wages rather than farming. Adam Smith was an early advocate of letting supply and demand set these wages rather than relying on customs of the past, including just wages.

But as people left the countryside for the new factory jobs, the poverty in the cities contrasted sharply with the rising profits of employers. Theorists who observed this situation assumed that the supply of labor (which closely mirrored the population, since the jobs required little skill, and many could be done by women and children) would continuously expand so that the majority of people would always live at a subsistence level. Wages would always just equal the amount necessary to buy the goods needed to live at a subsistence level. Any deviation from this equilibrium by increasing wages would cause the population to increase, which would soon reestablish the equilibrium, again at the subsistence level. This became known as the *iron law of wages.*

On this foundation, Karl Marx built his theory of *surplus value.*[19] Adam Smith had previously ascribed to labor both exchange and use values. *Exchange value* is the price of labor (the wage) determined in a competitive market: whatever the buyer and seller agree on (i.e., external competitiveness). *Use value*, on the other hand, is determined by the purpose for which the labor is used; the value to the employer of the goods or services labor produces (i.e., internal consistency). Marx said that a capitalistic system will only provide a subsistent wage because it bases wages on exchange value. But labor's use value is higher than its exchange value. The difference between exchange and use value produces a surplus that is being pocketed by the employer, when it should be paid to the worker, according to Marx.

These early theorists concentrated on the *supply* of labor to explain wages. But by the last half on the 19th century, not for the last time, reality disagreed with theory. Wages began to rise. So new theories were offered. Exhibit 2.5 catalogs some of the major contemporary theories related to internal pay structures. The "so what" column highlights each theory's relevance for managing pay structures. We have already discussed some of the theories listed in the exhibit. We will weave the others into our ongoing discussion of factors that influence pay structures.

Marginal productivity theory shifted emphasis to the *demand* for labor. This

---

[19] C. Tucker, ed., *The Marx-Engels Reader*, 2nd ed. (New York: W. W. Norton, 1978).

EXHIBIT 2.5   Theoretical Rationales for Internal Pay Structures

Theory	Description	Application to Compensation
Marginal productivity	Pay should be based upon contributions made to a organizational productivity.	Jobs that have a critical impact on organizational productivity should be paid more than jobs with little or no direct impact.
Human capital	Emphasizes the knowledge, skills, and abilities (KSA) required to perform essential job tasks.	Jobs requiring greater KSA levels should receive higher pay.
Institutional	Companies imitate patterns of behavior (e.g., policies and procedures) exhibited by competitors.	Pay levels should be set relative to those of a company's key competitors.
Internal labor markets	Organizations need very specific skills not available in the external labor market. These skills can only be gained through organization-specific training and experience.	Companies should create job ladders representing successively higher levels of organization-specific skill and experience. Pay increases as one moves up the ladder.
Tournament	Larger differences in pay are more motivating than smaller differences.	Like prize awards in a golf tournament, pay increases should get successively greater as one moves up the job hierarchy. Differential between the top job and second-highest job should be the largest.
Equity	Pay should be based upon contributions made by the employee. Higher effort should be rewarded with higher pay.	Pay should be tied to the performance level of individual employees.

theory says that employers do in fact pay use value.[20] Unless a worker can produce a value equal to the value received in wages, it will not be worthwhile for the employer to hire that worker.

Accordingly, differences in the pay structure reflect differences in use value contributions associated with different work. In this view, work is compensated on the basis of worth to the employing organization, the volume of production or output associated with it, and the net revenue accruing to the organization from sale of the output. Marginalists assert that one job is paid more or less than another because of differences in relative productivity of the job and/or differences in consumer valuation of the output. Hence, differences in productivity provide a rationale for the internal pay structure. These views underlie many contemporary compensation practices.

As we witness the end of the 20th century, economic factors have become global. This globalization of economic competition is having a major impact on pay structures. Entire layers of organizations are disappearing as managers reinvent their organizations in response to global competitive forces. In essence, pay structures are being redesigned to fit the new economic realities. The supply and demand for specific skills also influence pay structures. Pay differences may reflect the availability of critical skills such as software engineering in India or Russia or Europe rather than just in California. The advent of global labor markets, accessed via telecommunications networks, may affect wages and structures within organizations. For example, Hewlett-Packard and Microsoft hire software engineers located in India and Russia for their product development teams centered in California.

Organizational Factors

The *technology* employed is a critical organizational factor influencing the design of pay structures. Technology used in producing goods and services influences organizational structures, functional specialties, work teams, and departments. It influences the work to be performed and the skills required to perform it.

A case in point is the difference in the number of levels in the managerial pay structures at Martin Marietta (6 levels for engineering only) versus GE Plastics (5 levels for all managerial/professional/technical employees). The technology required to produce military hardware differs from that used to manufacture plastics. Aerospace is more labor intensive (more than 50 percent of operating expenses are labor costs) than is plastics (less than 20 percent); hence, different structures emerge.

The organization's *human resource policies* are another influence on pay structures. Most organizations use promotions as an incentive to induce employees to apply for higher-level positions (e.g., machinists to first-line supervisors). In other organizations, offering "titles" are considered a sufficient inducement, and little or no pay differential is offered. If pay differentials are designated as

---

[20] Allan M. Cartter, *Theory of Wages and Employment* (Burr Ridge, IL: Richard D. Irwin, 1959).

a key mechanism to encourage employees to accept greater responsibilities, learn new skills, or leave, then the pay structure must be designed to facilitate that policy.

Institutional theory (Exhibit 2.5) depicts organizations as simply following patterns exhibited by other organizations.[21] By extension, pay structures adopted by each employer would mimic accepted practice rather than be based on differences in productivity or power to procure key resources. Following fads is nothing new, even when it comes to designing pay structures; however, little empirical research supports mimicry as an important factor influencing pay structures. Nevertheless, it is not uncommon for executives to bring back "the answers" discovered at the latest conference. And surveys that benchmark the practices of the best companies facilitate others' copying those practices. Recent examples of such behaviors include the rush to de-layer, to emphasize teams, deemphasize individual contributions, and to shift health care costs to employees, often with little regard to whether any of these practices make sense for the organization or its employees.[22]

The notion of *internal labor markets* (Exhibit 2.5) combines both economic and organizational factors. As depicted in Exhibit 2.6, internal labor markets refer to the rules and procedures that allocate employees among different jobs within a single organization.[23] Individuals tend to be recruited and hired only for specific entry-level jobs and are later allocated (promoted or transferred) to other jobs. Because the employer competes in the external market for people to fill these entry jobs, their pay is tied to the external market. It must be high enough to attract a qualified pool of applicants. In contrast, pay for nonentry jobs (those staffed internally via transfer and promotions) is more heavily influenced by the organization's internal factors such as culture, norms, and/or contribution to the organization's success. In other words, external factors are dominant influences on pay for entry jobs, but the differentials for nonentry jobs tend to reflect the organization's strategic objectives, culture, and traditions.

Internally equitable pay structures must also support progression through jobs and skills, or *career paths*, within an organization.[24] Higher pay is required

---

[21] L. G. Zucker, "Institutional Theories of Organization," *American Review of Sociology* 13 (1987), pp. 443–64; and D. Wazeter, "Determinants and Consequences of Pay Structures" (Ph.D. dissertation, Cornell University, 1991).

[22] Harry Levinson, "Why the Behemoths Fell: Psychological Roots of Corporate Failure," *American Psychologist* 49, no. 5 (1994), pp. 428–36.

[23] Mark Granovetter, "Labor Mobility, Internal Markets, and Job Matching: A Comparison of the Sociological and the Economic Approaches," *Research in Social Stratification and Mobility* 5 (1986), pp. 222–27; Peter Doeringer and Michael J. Piore, *Internal Labor Markets and Manpower Analysis* (Lexington, MA: Heath-Lexington Books, 1971); and Paul Osterman, ed., *Internal Labor Markets* (Cambridge, MA: MIT Press, 1984).

[24] Lester C. Thurow, *Generating Inequality: Mechanisms of Distribution in the U.S. Economy* (New York: Basic Books, 1975); William D. Bridges and Robert L. Nelson, "Markets in Hierarchies: Organizational and Market Influences on Gender Inequality," *American Journal of Sociology* 95, no. 3 (1989), pp. 616–58; Peter Capelli and Wayne Cascio, "Why Some Jobs Command Wage Premiums: A Test of Career Tournament and Internal Labor Market," *Academy of Management Journal* 34, no. 4 (1991), pp. 840–68.

Exhibit 2.6   Illustration of an Internal Labor Market

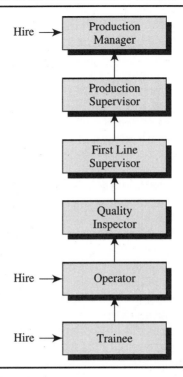

for higher-level jobs to encourage employees to undertake the necessary training and gain the required experience and skills to perform these jobs.

Employee Expectations

It is surprising that so little is known about employee expectations regarding pay differentials. Expectations, like beauty, may be in the eye of the beholder. For example, little research has been reported on whether different employee groups (older versus younger, line versus staff, men versus women, engineers versus personnel specialists, crafts versus office and clerical) hold different ideas about what constitutes fair pay differences among jobs.[25] In one study, business students and compensation administrators were asked to assign pay rates to organization charts.[26] The object of the study was to determine whether different

[25] Jerald Greenberg and Suzy N. Ornstein, "High Status Job Titles as Compensation for Underpayment: A Test of Equity Theory," *Journal of Applied Psychology* 68, no. 2 (1983), pp. 285–97.

[26] Thomas A. Mahoney, "Organizational Hierarchy and Position Worth," *Academy of Management Journal*, December 1979, pp. 726–37.

groups would assign similar pay differentials. Business students and administrators did assign similar differentials; approximately 30 percent was considered appropriate between organization levels.

This finding may be obsolete in light of the current corporate restructuring. Indeed, the very notion of *appropriate differentials* needs attention. Reconsider the career path illustrated in Exhibit 2.7. What will employees expect the appropriate differential to be if the first-line supervisor and production supervisor jobs are de-layered and reengineered? If the operators become associates and are required to become part of self-managing teams, will the 30 percent differential between the production manager (now a process leader) and the operatives (now associates) still be appropriate? What will the impact be on employee behaviors and the organization success? Will those employees facing a 30 percent differential begin to murmur?

Some research suggests that women have lower pay expectations and lower expectations about future pay than do similarly qualified men. For example, studies have reported substantial differences in the pay expectations of male and female MBA students, with women reporting lower career entry and career peak pay expectations than similarly qualified men.[27]

But judgments about equitable differentials are probably a function of many things, including, apparently, the culture. For example, some believe that as more employees are involved in decision making, salaries and benefits will become more equal. That is, the structure becomes more egalitarian; the size of differentials narrows.[28] Our recent work with companies in Central Europe and the Commonwealth of Independent States strongly suggests that employees in past socialist enterprises favor smaller differentials. Perhaps this preference is influenced by the previous norms developed under socialism.

Some assert that societalwide norms of equitable pay exist; that most people would expect approximately the same pay differentials for various levels of work, based on commonly held beliefs.[29] Little evidence supports universally held norms across a highly diverse society. And the number of lawsuits over what constitutes fair pay would seem to indicate that substantial disagreement exists. Nevertheless, even a diverse society may have norms regarding pay differences considered to be excessive. Evidence includes the widespread criticism of the "excessive" difference between executive and regular employee pay in the United States, or Congress granting itself pay increases during economic recessions.

All of these explanations of internal pay structures may have some validity.

---

[27] S. M. Freedman, "The Effects of Subordinate Sex, Pay, Equity, and Strength of Demand on Compensation Decisions," *Sex Roles* 5 (1979), pp. 649–58; B. Major, V. Vanderslie, and D. McFarlein, "Effects of Pay Received: The Conformatory Nature of Initial Expectations," *Journal of Applied Social Psychology* 14, no. 5 (1984), pp. 399–412.

[28] Mary E. Graham and Barry Gerhart, "Starting Salary Differences between Women and Men" (Working paper 93–15, Center for Advanced Human Resource Studies, Ithaca, NY, 1993); Thomas Kochan and Paul Osterman, *The Mutual Gains Enterprise: Forging a Winning Partnership among Labor, Management, and Government* (Cambridge: Harvard University Press, 1994).

[29] Elliot Jaques, *Equitable Payment* (New York: John Wiley, 1961).

<u>**EXHIBIT 2.7**</u>   **Delayered Structure**

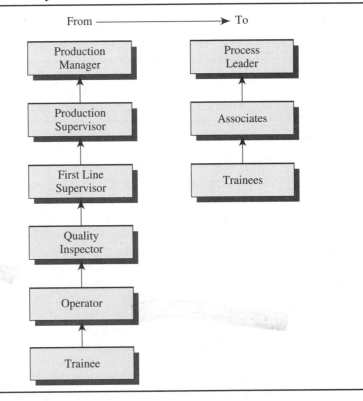

Some pay structures may have been designed to reflect very rational economic reasons, that is, competitive pressures, the technology, and the differences in the work performed. Changes in pay structures may arise in response to economic factors such as skill shortages. Over time, the distorted differential became accepted as equitable and customary; efforts to change it are resisted as destructive of social relationships.[30] Thus, the pay structures established for organizational and economic reasons may be maintained for cultural or other reasons until another economic jolt overcomes the cultural resistance. Then new norms are formed around the new structure.

EMPLOYEE ACCEPTANCE: A KEY TEST

In a classic article on pay structures, Livernash asserts that employees desire fair compensation.[31] He states that employees judge the fairness of their pay through

---

[30] Mahoney, *Compensation and Reward Perspectives.*

[31] E. Robert Livernash, "The Internal Wage Structure," in *New Concepts in Wage Determination,* ed. G. W. Taylor and F. C. Pierson (New York: McGraw-Hill, 1957), pp. 143–72.

comparisons with the compensation paid others for work related in some fashion to their own. He called such interrelated jobs *job clusters*. Accordingly, an important criterion for assessing the internal pay structure is its *acceptability to the employees involved*. Indeed, Livernash's point may echo St. Matthew's laborers who murmured against perceived unfair differentials for work. Effective pay structures depend on employee acceptance. Other factors (societal, economic, and organizational) also influence employee acceptance; but workers' views about what constitutes an equitable wage structure have an important role to play in the determination of wages.[32]

Distributive and Procedural Justice

The fairness of the procedures used to design and administer the pay structure constitutes procedural justice. The actual results—the pay differences, the number of levels, and the criteria used in the structure—pertain to distributive justice: Are the actual pay differences distributed by the structure fair?

The distinction between procedural and distributive justice is important. Suppose you are given a ticket for speeding. *Procedural justice* refers to the process by which a decision is reached: the right to an attorney, the right to an impartial judge, and the right to receive a copy of the arresting officer's statement. *Distributive justice* refers to the fairness of the decision: guilty. Researchers report that employees' perceptions of procedural fairness significantly influence their acceptance of the results; employees and managers are more willing to accept low pay if they believe the way this result was obtained was fair.[33] This research also strongly suggests that pay procedures are more likely to be perceived as fair (1) if they are consistently applied to all employees, (2) if employee participation and/or representation is included, (3) if appeals procedures are available, and (4) if the data used are accurate.

Based on the research on perceptions of procedural and distributive justice, Greenberg argues that employees' impressions can be managed. In effect, he develops a case for marketing to employees and managers the pay structure and the procedures used to design it, just as one would market products or services to consumers. A campaign of public announcements, well-crafted brochures, videos, and articles in the company newsletter should be aimed at managing the belief that the pay structures and procedures are fair. Greenberg is careful to note that he does not condone manipulation—trying to sell an inequitable system.

[32] Gary Burtoless, *A Future of Lousy Jobs: The Changing Structure of U.S. Wages* (Washington, DC: Brookings Institute, 1990); France Levy and Richard J. Murman, "U.S. Earnings Levels and Earnings Inequality: A Review of Recent Trends," *Journal of Economic Literature*, September 1992, pp. 1333–81.

[33] Robert Folger and Mary Konovsky, "Effects of Procedural and Distributive Justice on Reactions to Pay Raise Decisions," *Academy of Management Journal*, March 1989, pp. 115–30; Jerald Greenberg, "Looking Fair vs. Being Fair: Managing Impressions of Organizational Justice," in *Research in Organizational Behavior*, vol. 12, ed. B. M. Staw and L. L. Cummings (Greenwich, CT: JAI Press, 1990).

Rather, the emphasis is on employee perception, which should not be left to chance. If fair procedures and structures have been designed, a necessary step is to ensure that employees believe they are fair.

CONSEQUENCES OF INTERNAL PAY STRUCTURES

But why worry about internal pay structure at all? Why not simply pay employees what it takes to get them to take a job and to stay? Why not simply let external market forces determine wages? The answers can be found in several situations. One is the presence of unique jobs that reflect organizational idiosyncracies. For example, the School of Veterinary Medicine at Cornell University has installed "windows" in the stomachs of several cows to study the animals' digestive processes. Laboratory technicians help install and maintain these windows and perform other equally exotic duties. Without similar jobs with other employers, it is difficult to determine the appropriate wage for such jobs. Other, more common illustrations may be found under titles such as administrative assistant, team leader, or associate. The specific tasks vary with the technologies employed, the manner in which the work is designed, the skills and experiences of the particular incumbent, and so on. The pay for these unique jobs is typically set through comparison of the work with other internal jobs. So the existing internal pay structure provides a basis for arriving at a rate for unique jobs.

Another reason is that some organizations are basing pay structures on the skills or competencies employees possess rather than the jobs they perform. Yet competitive market data are not available to price such skills/competencies as "process leader" (defined as, "possesses the ability to gain and sustain access to key customer decision makers in target markets").

It is also possible that some jobs or skills are valued by a specific organization more or less than the rates reflected for that job in the market. For example, top-notch compensation specialists or accountants may have greater value to a compensation or accounting consulting firm than to heavy manufacturing companies. The consulting firm may pay higher-than-market rates for the greater contribution of the particular job to organization goals. Some genetics and engineering professors are leaving academia to design products for biotech firms—and become eligible for bonuses and stock options that universities cannot match.

The practical question is, Does any of this really matter? Recall the three dimensions of internal pay structures. What difference does the number of levels, the size of pay differentials between levels, and the criteria (job versus skill/competency versus performance) make on the compensation system goals of efficiency, equity, and compliance? Exhibit 2.8 suggests some of the consequences of the internal pay structures.

Efficiency: Competitive Advantage

Why bother with a pay structure? Because it has the potential to lead to better organization performance. If the structure does not motivate employees to help achieve the organization's objectives, then it is a candidate for redesign.

EXHIBIT 2.8   Some Consequences of Pay Structure

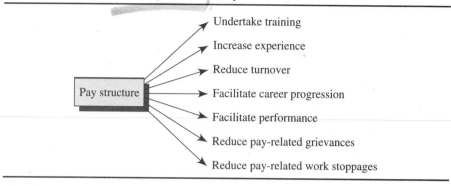

Internal pay structures imply future rewards; they are really structures of incentives. The size of the pay differentials between the entry level in the structure and the highest level may induce employees to undertake the training and obtain the experience required for promotions. *Human capital* theorists (Exhibit 2.5) suggest that pay differentials serve as inducements for employees to invest in themselves by acquiring added knowledge, skills, and experience. Few workers bring fully developed work skills into the labor market. Usually, after obtaining an entry job, skills are acquired either formally or informally through on-the-job training. The incentive to acquire these skills is the pay differential among jobs requiring varying skill levels. According to this view, a computer design engineering job should pay more than a programming job. Without that pay difference, individuals are less likely to go through the education (and forgo earnings while in school) required to become an engineer. Similar logic can be applied to differentials between team leaders and team members, which encourage employees to undertake more responsibilities. Pay differentials within organizations induce employees to remain with the organization, increase their experience and training, and seek greater responsibility.[34]

Equity

Several writers argue that employees' attitudes about the fairness of the pay structure affect their work behaviors. Livernash, for example, asserts that departures from an acceptable wage structure will occasion turnover, grievances, and diminished motivation.[35] Jaques argues that if fair differentials among jobs are not paid, individuals may harbor ill will toward the employer, resist change,

---

[34] Edward Lazear, "Labor Economics and Psychology of Organization," *Journal of Economic Perspectives* 5 (1991), pp. 89–110; David Wazeter, "Determinants and Consequences of Pay Structures."

[35] Livernash, "Internal Wage Structure."

EXHIBIT 2.9   Perceived Equity of a Pay Structure

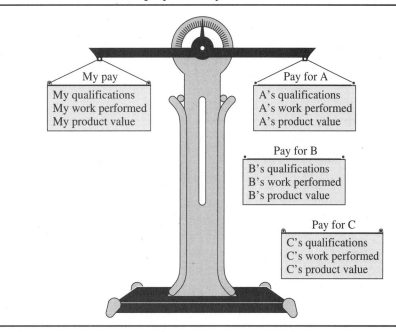

change employment if possible, become depressed, and "lack that zest and enthusiasm which makes for high efficiency and personal satisfaction in work."[36]

Others, including labor unions, have long held the belief that more egalitarian pay structures support team workers, high commitment to the organization, and improved performance. Studies have reported that the greater the wage differences, the more likely employees will vote for unions, and that smaller differences in wages between hourly employees and managers were related to greater product quality.[37]

Since employee judgments about pay structures are so important, we need to understand how employees make these judgments. Exhibit 2.9 shows the main determinants of whether an employee is likely to perceive pay as being equitable. The model, adapted from the distributive justice and equity models, shows that employees' judgments about equity are based on comparisons.[38] A pay structure will be perceived as equitable or inequitable depending on whether the pay for job A compared to its requirements (education, experience), the work performed

[36] Jaques, *Equitable Payment*, p. 123.

[37] William Dickens, Douglas Wholey, and James Robinson, "Correlates of Union Support in NLRB Elections," *Industrial Relations* 26 (1987); pp. 240–52, D. M. Cowherd and David Levine, "Product Quality and Pay Equity between Lower-Level Employees and Top Management," *Administrative Science Quarterly* 37 (1992), pp. 302–20.

[38] E. E. Lawler III, *Pay and Organization Development* (Reading, MA: Addison-Wesley, 1981).

(task, behaviors, working conditions), and the value of contributions (to organization objectives and/or consumers) is congruent with the pay for job B relative to its requirements, work performed, contributions, and so on, through all jobs in the structure. However, very little research addresses the question of what factors influence employees' perceptions of the equity or fairness of pay structures per se.

Most of the research on employee attitudes toward pay has studied pay satisfaction. However, Heneman argues that pay satisfaction needs to be considered in terms similar to the four basic policy areas used in the pay model: satisfaction with the pay structure (internal consistency), the pay level (external competitiveness), individual pay (employee contribution), and the administration of the pay system.[39] Recognizing that employee attitudes may be linked to each of the basic pay-model components permits better analysis of specific aspects of the compensation system and employee satisfaction toward them. Lowering the external competitive position of pay may affect the satisfaction with the pay level, but may leave attitudes toward the pay structure unchanged.

Despite the fact that a great deal of research relating to pay satisfaction and dissatisfaction has been conducted, virtually no research has been directed toward understanding the consequences of *pay differences for different work*. Consequently, there is little to guide us in the design of pay structures that will yield positive employee attitudes.

Compliance

Certainly, all internal pay structures need to comply with government laws and regulations. In the United States, this includes legislation focusing on ensuring nondiscriminatory pay for women and minorities. The Canadian provinces have adopted pay equity legislation that prohibits pay structures that discriminate; the Social Charter of the European Community contains similar legislation. The regulatory influences on compensation management are examined in Chapters 13 and 14. At this point, it is enough to recognize that the design and administration of pay structures need to comply with the regulations of the countries in which the organization operates.

What are the appropriate number of levels, the size of the differentials, and the criteria to advance employees through a structure? We believe the answers lie in understanding the factors discussed in this chapter: the organization's strategic intent, the norms and customs of the culture, the economic circumstances, and, perhaps most importantly, the nature of the work and employees. For example, narrow, egalitarian structures may be related to improving satisfaction and performance when the technology and the nature of the work requires

---

[39] Herbert G. Heneman III, "Pay Satisfaction," in *Research in Personnel and Human Resources Management*, vol. 3, ed. K. M. Rowland and G. R. Ferris (Greenwich, CT: JAI Press, 1985), pp. 115–39.

cooperation and teamwork compared to more independent and autonomous situations. On the other hand, it is not difficult to think of examples in which very large pay differentials exist within highly successful (championship) teams (e.g., Joe Montana and the Kansas City Chiefs; Jerry Seinfeld and the other cast members of his television series; Luciano Pavarotti and the members of the chorus). We believe that aligning the pay structures to fit the organization and the surrounding conditions is more likely to lead to competitive advantage and a sense of fair treatment shared by employees.

Summary

This chapter discusses what is meant by the strategic policy regarding internal consistency and how it affects employees, managers, and employers. *Internal consistency* refers to the pay relationships among jobs/skills/competencies within a single organization. Although the potential consequences of internal pay structures are vital to organizations and individuals, little guidance has emerged from research concerning employee perceptions of internal pay structures.

Pay structures—the array of pay rates for different jobs within an organization—are shaped by societal, economic, organizational, and other factors. Employees judge a structure to be equitable on the basis of comparisons. The ratio of a job's relative pay to its relative requirements, work performed, and value of that performance is compared to the ratio for other jobs in the structure. Congruent ratios are believed to be equitable. Acceptance by employees of the relative pay differentials is the key test of an equitable pay structure.

Keep the goals of the entire compensation system in mind in thinking about internal pay structures. There is widespread belief and considerable research that differences in pay structures influence employees' attitudes and work behaviors and therefore the success of organizations. However, research to date offers little guidance regarding what the appropriate structure is in different situations.

Review Questions

1. Why is internal consistency an important policy issue for the compensation system?
2. Discuss the factors that influence internal pay structures. Based on your own experience, which ones do you think are the most important?
3. How would you go about trying to manage employees' impressions of the pay structure? Is this potentially destructive manipulation?
4. What is the "just wage" doctrine? Can you think of any present-day applications?

5. Contrast job-based versus skill/competency-based structures. Which would you use?

6. What employee behaviors are more egalitarian versus more hierarchical structures likely to affect?

YOUR TURN:

PARCEL PLUS

You are the owner of Parcel Plus, a rapidly growing service that handles all a consumer's mailing needs. Bring in an item, and Parcel Plus will prepare it for shipping and make arrangements with UPS, air freight services, or overnight delivery services. Staff members will advise customers of options and costs.

Because more and more people are working out of their own homes, you have investigated the possibility of expanding service by offering pickup and delivery. Buying your own trucks would also allow handling larger packages that are outside the size and weight limitation set by UPS. Parcel Plus could pick up heavy shipments and take them to nearby larger cities for transfer to one of the nationwide trucking lines. This would help people who do not ship things on a regular basis and do not want to be bothered making the necessary shipping arrangements.

At present Parcel Plus employs 10 people: 8 customer service representatives, an assistant manager, and a manager. The customer service representatives are paid between $5.50 and $6.50 per hour, depending on how long they have been employed. Both the assistant manager and the manager are former customer service representatives, and they are paid $8.50 and $10.00 per hour, respectively. You intend to create a new position, driver/customer service representative, and hire two new employees for this position. The job would consist of truck driving as needed and doing regular customer service representative's duties when not driving. Since the pickup-and-delivery service is new, you aren't sure how much time will be spent driving versus customer ser-

vice work. The proportion spent driving will increase as the demand for this service increases. You feel that $6.50 per hour is a fair wage. But the first person who applied for the job, Carlos Sherman, said $6.50 was too low. "No self-respecting trucker would start at less than $8.50 an hour." You suspect that if you offer $7.50 per hour, he will take the job. Mr. Sherman seems physically strong enough to handle the job, even though he's had no trucking experience. When you shared this opinion with Corrianne Nation, the manager, she became quite upset. "If you hire someone off the street and pay $7.50 an hour, you better be sure no one else hears about it." You thought about this, but when no other job applicants seemed suitable, you decided to renegotiate with Mr. Sherman. You were just about to call him, when two customer service representatives came into your office. They got right to the point. "We think we all deserve a raise."

Discussion Questions

1. How should you handle the customer service representatives? Should you give them an increase? If so, why and how much? If not, why not? Present your case.

2. Should you renegotiate with Mr. Sherman?

3. Is the amount of time on the job spent driving an important factor?

4. What additional information would you like to help you make your decision?

Assessing Work

Chapter Outline

"The End of the Job," trumpets the cover story of *Fortune*, a leading business magazine.[1] The lead story informs us that, "Jobs as a way of organizing work . . . is a social artifact that has outlived its usefulness." If organizations expect to be successful, they need to ". . . get rid of jobs" [and] . . . redesign to get the best out of the de-jobbed worker." If we no longer can expect to hold jobs, then can we at least hold a position? Unfortunately, no. Positions may be "too fixed." Roles? Nope. Too unitary, single-purposed. Skills and competencies then? Guess again: They will become obsolete. Like a fortune teller, *Fortune* tells us that the postjob workers will likely be self-employed contract workers hired to work on projects or teams. Intel and Microsoft are suggested as examples of companies that design work around projects. People will work on six to ten projects, maybe for different employers at one time. Some soothsayers even foresee virtual employers and virtual employees.[2] A skeptic's response to this is, "Okay, how about virtual performance and virtual pay to go along with the virtual organization?" As employees in the old Soviet Union collectives used to say, "If you pretend to pay us, we will pretend to work."

---

[1] William Bridges, "The End of the Job," *Fortune*, September 19, 1994, pp. 62–68.

[2] Marc J. Wallace, Jr., and N. Fredric Crandall, "Winning in the Age of Execution: the Central Role of Work-Force Effectiveness," *ACA Journal*, Winter 1992/1993, pp. 30–47; Robert J. Greene, "Chaos Systems, a Human Resource Management Paradigm for the 1990s?" *ACA Journal*, Winter 1992/1993, pp. 60–67.

Before dismissing *Fortune*'s rhetoric as so much hype to sell magazines, recognize that its underlying premise is relevant to managing compensation. Historically, "a fair day's work for a fair day's pay" provided a simple standard that linked pay to the work performed. But reality is increasingly more complex. *Fortune*'s hype aside, we are in the midst of a revolution in the way work is organized and done. The old concept of work is crumbling. No longer are jobs stable; they are fluid and adapt to changing demands. Organizations are reengineering, restructuring, and de-layering. These are more than buzzwords. Change in the way work is organized is an ongoing fact of life.

Work is increasingly being designed to include an external customer focus.[3] As a result, customers and even suppliers are often included on project teams. Boeing, facing stiff competition from Airbus, used customers and suppliers to help design and produce its new commercial aircraft.[4] Cheaper maintenance, wider aisles, higher ceilings, simpler manufacturing, and adaptable seating arrangements resulted. TRW claims to write more lines of code for computer software than does IBM, yet the bulk of that code is written by teams that include the customers who purchase TRW products. Narrow job definitions seem to be giving way to increased employee flexibility and multiskilling. In the past, General Motors actually organized jobs with titles such as installer, front seats; installer, rear seats; installer, garnish moldings; installer, door panels. A front-seat installer would not install rear seats.[5] Functional hierarchies (finance, personnel, operations, quailty control, purchasing), often labeled functional silos (also called chimneys and ladders—the latent meanings to all the jargon used in compensation is best left to the psychologists), are giving way to cross-functional or cross-specialty organization designs.

So what does this have to do with compensating employees? And more to the point, what does it have to do with establishing an internally consistent pay structure and achieving organization objectives? The answer is that if pay is based on the work is performed, some way is needed to discover the differences and similarities in the work. If pay is to be based on competencies of employees, the same holds true. Some way is needed to discover the differences and similarities in the competencies.

What is required is information that will help ensure that compensation decisions are firmly based on identifiable similarities and differences in the work or the required work-related skills. Achieving some degree of internal consistency is one of the strategic policies, a basic building block, in our compensation model. Recognizing the flow of work and the similarities and differences in the work within an organization are key parts of internal consistency.

---

[3] Peter Leblanc, "Pay for Work: Reviving an Old Idea for the New Customer Focus," *Compensation and Benefits Review*, July/August 1994, pp. 5–10.

[4] Ibid.

[5] Harry Katz, *Shifting Gears: Changing Labor Relations in the U.S. Auto Industry* (Cambridge. MA: MIT Press, 1985).

DIFFERENCES FORM THE INTERNAL PAY STRUCTURE

At Martin Marietta, the differences in the work and skills of an engineer, a word processor, and a phone operator are fairly apparent, even though they all sit in front of a computer and press keys. Differences in pay for each job reflect the relative value of these jobs to Martin Marietta.

But rather than such obviously different jobs, let's consider instead the work in a single occupation: engineering. Recall the engineering pay structure at Martin Marietta discussed in the previous chapter and shown in Exhibit 2.1. How many different levels of work should be included in an engineering pay structure? In the past this division organized it into six levels. However, these levels have changed, partially in response to the massive reordering of spending priorities at the Department of Defense, which is one of Marietta's prime customers, and partially in response to a significant shift in Marietta's marketing and product development strategy. Now Marietta uses only four levels, as shown in Exhibit 3.1. They have merged the position of systems engineer with the lead engineer and the position of entry engineer with the senior engineer. Each distinct level in the structure represents a major difference in the complexities of the account-abilities and knowledge required to perform the work. A major Japanese employer, Toshiba, by comparison, fits all its specialists and managers into a four-level structure, as shown in Exhibit 3.2. A Toshiba employee who moves up one of the ranks shown in the left column of Exhibit 3.2 enjoys a pay increase but no change in job responsibilities. However, colleagues are expected to become more deferential in manner and speech toward the higher-ranked employee.

The point is that information about the actual work performed and the way it is designed is crucial for determining pay structures. This information helps ensure that the compensation decisions are firmly based on identifiable similarities and differences in the work. It is also essential input for designing learning and promotional opportunities that reward employees for increasing their knowledge and undertaking greater responsibilities.

INTERNAL STRUCTURES BASED ON JOBS, SKILLS, OR PERFORMANCE

Pay system design traditionally begins with analyzing the work and building job structures that reflect the relationships among jobs within an organization. The criteria supporting the structure is the job rather than the skills relevant to work. But as Exhibit 3.3 shows, there are alternative criteria. Pay structures can be based on the skills and competencies demonstrated by individuals, performance results of their work, the content of the job they perform, or some combination of all three criteria. Skill/competency-based structures are receiving increasing attention. Surveys report 5 to 15 percent of employers are using these approaches or considering them. However, a recent survey reported that 33 percent of those

EXHIBIT 3.1   Revised Engineering Pay Structure at Martin Marietta

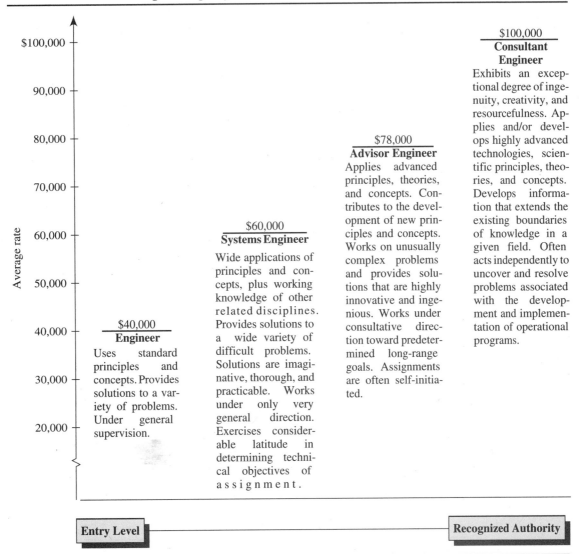

firms using skill-based approaches in 1986 were no longer using them.[6] Job-based structures remain far and away the most common approach. Clearly, the advantages and disadvantages of each approach need to be better understood.

[6] Barbara J. Dewey, "Changing to Skill-Based Pay: Disarming the Transition Landmines," *Compensation and Benefits Review*, January–February 1994, pp. 38–43; Gordon Betcherman and Anil Verma, "Followup to the New Technology Survey," paper presented to the Canadian Industrial Relations Research Association, June 1993.

EXHIBIT 3.2   Ranks and Positions at Toshiba

Ranks	Managerial Positions		Specialist Positions	
Riji	General Manager		Fellow Specialist	
Sanji 1		Senior Manager		Chief Specialist
Sanji 2				
Fuku-sanji			Manager	
Shuji 1				Deputy Manager
Shuji 2				

(diagram: arrows denote promotion across managerial positions — General Manager, Senior Manager, Manager, Deputy Manager — and specialist positions — Fellow Specialist, Chief Specialist, Senior Specialist, Specialist)

Note: Arrow denotes promotion.

Source: *Personnel Management in Toshiba* (Tokyo, Japan: Toshiba Corporation, 1991).

EXHIBIT 3.3   Possible Criteria for Internal Structures

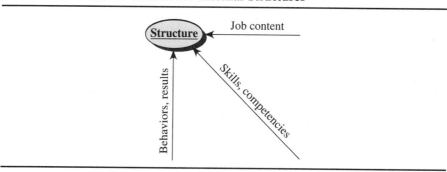

JOB ANALYSIS

If the structure is to be based on jobs, then the first step is to examine the actual jobs. Collecting information about jobs is known as *job analysis* and can be defined as follows:

◈

Job analysis is the systematic process of collecting relevant, work-related information related to the nature of a specific job.

Exhibit 3.4   Determining the Internal Job Structure

Internal relationships within the organization	→	Job analysis	→	Job descriptions	→	Job evaluation	→	Job structure
		Collecting information about the nature of specific jobs		Summary reports that identify, define, and describe the job as it is actually performed		Comparison of jobs within an organization		An ordering of jobs based on their content or relative value

Some Major Issues in Job Analysis
- Analysis for what purpose
- What information to collect
- How to collect information
- Who should be involved
- Usefulness of results

The basic premise underlying job analysis is that jobs are more likely to be described, differentiated, and valued fairly if accurate information about them is available.[7] Exhibit 3.4 shows that job analysis provides the underlying information for preparing job descriptions and evaluating jobs. Job analysis is a prerequisite for job-based pay structures. It is the input for describing and valuing work.

Exhibit 3.4 also identifies the major decisions in designing a job analysis: (1) For what purpose are we collecting job information? (2) What information should be collected? (3) What method should be used? (4) To what extent should the various parties be involved? (5) How useful for compensation purposes are the results?

WHY PERFORM JOB ANALYSIS?

An organization may perform job analysis for a number of reasons. They range from concerns for consistent treatment of employees to more specific uses in compensation and other personnel systems.[8]

---

[7] Particularly valuable sources of information on job analysis definitions and methods are U.S. Department of Labor, Manpower Administration, *Handbook for Analyzing Jobs* (Washington, DC: U.S. Government Printing Office, 1972); Robert J. Harvey, "Job Analysis," in *Handbook of Industrial and Organizational Psychology*, vol. 2, ed. M. D. Dunnette and L. Hough (Palo Alto, CA: Consulting Psychologists Press, 1991), pp. 72–157.

[8] Robert Harvey, "Job Analysis."

Internal Consistency

For most people the pay attached to their job is a matter of stunning importance. Therefore, pay decisions must be shown to be based on work-related logic and administered fairly. If an employer is not consistent in its treatment of its employees or cannot demonstrate the work-related logic of its pay, then it will be hard-pressed to explain its actions to employees or defend them in a lawsuit.[9] Although job analysis is not legally required, the data collected help managers construct a work-related rationale to communicate with employees and defend their decisions when challenged.

Compensation

There are two critical uses for job analysis in compensation: (1) to establish similarities and differences in the content of the jobs and (2) to help establish an internally equitable job structure. If jobs have equal content, then in all likelihood the pay established for them will be equal. If, on the other hand, the job content differs, then those differences, along with the market rates paid by competitors, are part of the rationale for paying jobs differently.

Data collection procedures must gather sufficient detail to distinguish among jobs. Collection methods must be able to withstand challenges from both inside and outside the organization. Job analysis data often become the key supports of an equitable pay structure. If the support is weak, the structure is vulnerable to challenge. Yet balance is required, since analysis in too great detail risks making the process too burdensome and costly.

Additional Uses of Job Analysis Data

Historically, job analysis has been considered the cornerstone of personnel administration. Potential uses for job analysis have been suggested for every major personnel function.[10] Often the type of job analysis data needed varies by function. For example, job analysis is used to identify the skills and experience required to perform the work, thereby clarifying hiring and promotion standards. Training programs may be designed with job analysis data; jobs may be redesigned based on it. In performance evaluation, both employees and supervisors look to the required behaviors and results expected in a job to help assess performance.

---

[9] *Principles for the Validation and Use of Personnel Selection Procedures*, 3rd ed. (College Park, MD: Society for Industrial and Organizational Psychology, Inc., 1987).

[10] R. A. Ash, E. L. Levine, and F. Sistrunk, "The Role of Jobs and Job-Based Methods in Personnel and Human Resource Management," *Research in Personnel and Human Resources Management* 1 (1983), pp. 45–84; Duane Thompson and Toni Thompson, "Court Standards for Job Analysis in Test Validation," *Personnel Psychology* 35 (1982), pp. 865–74; also see Chapter 4, George T. Milkovich and John Boudreau, *Human Resource Management*, 7th ed. (Burr Ridge, IL: Richard D. Irwin, 1994), and Herbert Heneman III, *Selection* (Burr Ridge, IL: Mendota House/Austen Press, 1994).

The key issue for managers of employee compensation is still to ensure that the data collected serve the purpose of making decisions and are acceptable to the employees involved. As the flowchart in Exhibit 3.4 indicates, collecting job information is only an interim step, not an end in itself.

WHAT DATA TO COLLECT?

Recommendations on the types of data to collect can range from the job title (word processor I, spot welder, accountant) to the frequency (daily, twice daily, as needed) with which specific tasks (answer the phone or balance an account) are performed. Generally, a good job analysis collects sufficient information to adequately identify, define, and describe a job.

Identifying a Job.   Data that identify a job include its title, department in which the job is located, the number of people in the organization who hold the job, and whether it is exempt from the Fair Labor Standards Act.

Defining a Job.   The job definition reflects the purpose of the job, why it exists, and how it fits in with other jobs and overall organization objectives. End results that flow from satisfactory performance are typically included, too.

For managerial jobs, statistics on the size of the budget, accountability, and reporting relationships with customers, suppliers, subordinates, and other managers are frequently included. Financial and organizational data such as positions and groups supervised, what functions are the responsibility of this position, and budget and financial responsibilities are included to locate the job in the organization.

Describing a Job.   Exhibit 3.5 lists two main categories of data to describe jobs: those that are job based (content and work characteristics) and those that are employee based (knowledge and prior experience). This list is typical of the kind of information used to describe jobs.[11]

The U.S. Department of Labor's (DOL) work on job analysis over 20 years ago may still be the strongest single influence on job analysis as practiced in the United States. The DOL's *Handbook for Analyzing Jobs* suggests two categories of data: actual work performed (job data) and worker characteristics (employee data). Their functional job analysis (FJA) is still widely used in the public sector. It emphasizes the employee and relates what the employee does to the goals and objectives of the organization. Although few private sector employers use it, all job analysis practices reflect FJA's influence.

Employee characteristics can be further subdivided into two categories: the

---

[11] E. J. McCormick, "Job and Task Analysis," in *Handbook of Industrial and Organizational Psychology*, ed. M. D. Dunnette (Chicago: Rand McNally, 1976), pp. 651–96; E. J. McCormick, *Job Analysis: Methods and Applications* (New York: AMACOM, 1979).

EXHIBIT 3.5   Typical Data Collected for Job Analysis

Data Related to Job

Job content/context factors

Duties	Critical incidents
Functions	Communications network
Tasks	Output (e.g., reports, analyses)
Activities	Working conditions
Performance criteria	Roles (e.g., negotiator, monitor, leader)

Work characteristics

Risk or exposure	Expected/unexpected
Constraints	Pattern or cycle
Choices	Time orientation (short or long)
Conflicting demands	

Data Related to Employee

Employee characteristics

Professional/technical knowledge	Conceptual skills
Prior experience	Managerial skills
Manual skills	Bargaining skills
Verbal skills	Leadership skills
Written skills	Consulting skills
Quantitative skills	Human relations skills
Mechanical skills	

Interpersonal relationships

Internal	External
Boss	Suppliers
Other superiors	Customers
Peers	Regulatory
Subordinates	Consultants
Other juniors	Professional/industry
	Community
	Union/employee group

employee's behavior on the job and the underlying abilities or competencies that make such behavior possible.

The categories of task data, behavior data, and ability data can be confusing because they all look at the same thing—an employee doing a job—and take different approaches to describe what is happening. Perhaps some examples will clarify the differences.

Task Data

Task data involve the elemental units of work, subparts of a job, with emphasis on the purpose of each task. An excerpt from a job analysis questionnaire that collects task data is shown in Exhibit 3.6. The inventory describes communication in terms of actual tasks, for example, "read technical publications" and "consult with coworkers." The other distinguishing characteristic is the emphasis on output, or objective of the task; for example, "read the technical publications to keep current on industry" and "consult with co-workers to exchange ideas and techniques." Task data reveal the actual work performed and its purpose or outcome.

Behavioral Data

This data approach describes jobs in terms of the behaviors that occur. Exhibit 3.7 shows such behavioral observations, again concerned with "communications." This time, the questions focus on verbs that describe the human behavior (e.g., advising, negotiating, persuading). Exhibit 3.7 is from the Position Analysis Questionnaire (PAQ),[12] which groups work information into seven basic factors: information input, mental processes, work output, relationships with other persons, job context, other job characteristics, and general dimensions. Similarities and differences among jobs are described in terms of these seven factors, rather than in terms of specific aspects unique to each job.[13] The communications behavior in Exhibit 3.7 is part of the "relationships with other persons" factor.

Compare the PAQ's approach to communications to the task inventory's approach in Exhibit 3.6. Item 105 of the PAQ: "Nonroutine information exchange (the giving and/or receiving of *job-related* information of a nonroutine or unusual nature)" is probably similar to item 430 on the task inventory: "Consult with co-workers to exchange ideas and techniques." Both are getting at the same aspect of work, by different approaches. But lest you think Exhibit 3.7 offers the beauty of simplicity, note that item 431 lists "consult with members of other technical groups . . . to exchange new ideas and techniques" and item 432 lists "interface with support consultants to clarify . . . design." In fact, the task inventory from which Exhibit 3.7 is excerpted contains 250 items and covers only systems and analyst jobs, whereas the behavioral data in Exhibit 3.7 are from an inventory of 194 items, whose developers claim it can be used to analyze *all* jobs. New task-based questions need to be designed for each new set of jobs, whereas behaviors, at least as defined in the PAQ's seven factors, may be applied across all jobs.

---

[12] Much of the developmental and early applications of the PAQ was done in the 1960s and 1970s. See, for example, McCormick, *Job Analysis*; McCormick, "Job and Task Analysis"; McCormick et al., *A Study of Job Characteristics and Job Dimensions as Based on the Position Analysis Questionnaire* (West Lafayette, IN: Occupational Research Center, Purdue University, 1969). The PAQ is distributed by the University Book Store, 360 West State St., West Lafayette, IN 47906. For more recent discussions, see *PAQ* Newsletters.

[13] R. C. Mecham, E. J. McCormick, and P. R. Jeanneret, *Technical Manual for the Position Analysis Questionnaire (PAQ) System* (Logan, UT: PAQ Services, 1977).

EXHIBIT 3.6   Communications: Task-Based Data

1. Mark the circle in the "Do This" column for tasks that you currently perform.

2. At the end of the task list, write in any unlisted tasks that you currently perform.

3. Rate each task that you perform for relative time spent by marking the appropriate circle in the "Time Spent" column.

   Please use a No. 2 pencil and fill all circles completely.

Time spent in current position

Do This · Very small amount · Much below average · Below average · Slightly below average · About average · Slightly above average · Above average · Much above average · Very large amount

PERFORM COMMUNICATIONS ACTIVITIES	Do This	Time Spent
Obtain technical information		
421. Read technical publications about competitive products.	◯	①②③④⑤⑥⑦⑧⑨
422. Read technical publications to keep current on industry.	◯	①②③④⑤⑥⑦⑧⑨
423. Attend required, recommended, or job-related courses and/or seminars.	◯	①②③④⑤⑥⑦⑧⑨
424. Study existing operating systems/programs to gain/maintain familiarity with them.	◯	①②③④⑤⑥⑦⑧⑨
425. Perform literature searches necessary to the development of products.	◯	①②③④⑤⑥⑦⑧⑨
426. Communicate with system software group to see how their recent changes impact current projects.	◯	①②③④⑤⑥⑦⑧⑨
427. Study and evaluate state-of-the-art techniques to remain competitive and/or lead the field.	◯	①②③④⑤⑥⑦⑧⑨
428. Attend industry standards meetings.	◯	①②③④⑤⑥⑦⑧⑨
Exchange technical information		
429. Interface with coders to verify that the software design is being implemented as specified.	◯	①②③④⑤⑥⑦⑧⑨
430. Consult with co-workers to exchange ideas and techniques.	◯	①②③④⑤⑥⑦⑧⑨
431. Consult with members of other technical groups within the company to exchange new ideas and techniques.	◯	①②③④⑤⑥⑦⑧⑨
432. Interface with support consultants or organizations to clarify software design or courseware content.	◯	①②③④⑤⑥⑦⑧⑨
433. Attend meetings to review project status.	◯	①②③④⑤⑥⑦⑧⑨
434. Attend team meetings to review implementation strategies.	◯	①②③④⑤⑥⑦⑧⑨
435. Discuss department plans and objectives with manager.	◯	①②③④⑤⑥⑦⑧⑨

EXHIBIT 3.7   Communications: Behavioral-Based Data

Section 4   Relationships with Other Persons

This section deals with different aspects of
interaction between people involved in various
kinds of work.

Code Importance to this Job (1)
N   Does not apply
1   Very minor
2   Low
3   Average
4   High
5   Extreme

4.1   Communications

Rate the following in terms of how *important* the activity is to the completion of the job. Some jobs
may involve several or all of the items in this section.

4.1.1   Oral (communicating by speaking)

99 ____   Advising (dealing with individuals in order to counsel and/or guide them with regard to
problems that may be resolved by legal, financial, scientific, technical, clinical, spiritual,
and/or other professional principles)

100 ____   Negotiating (dealing with others in order to reach an agreement or solution, for example,
labor bargaining, diplomatic relations, etc.)

101 ____   Persuading (dealing with others in order to influence them toward some action or point
of view, for example, selling, political campaigning, etc.)

102 ____   Instructing (the teaching of knowledge or skills, in either an informal or a formal manner,
to others, for example, a public school teacher, a machinist teaching an apprentice, etc.)

103 ____   Interviewing (conducting interviews directed toward some specific objective, for example,
interviewing job applicants, census taking, etc.)

104 ____   Routine information exchange: job related (the giving and/or receiving of *job-related*
information of a routine nature, for example, ticket agent, taxicab dispatcher, receptionist,
etc.)

105 ____   Nonroutine information exchange (the giving and/or receiving of *job-related* information
of a nonroutine or unusual nature, for example, professional committee meetings,
engineers discussing new product design, etc.)

106 ____   Public speaking (making speeches or formal presentations before relatively large
audiences, for example, political addresses, radio/TV broadcasting, delivering a sermon,
etc.)

4.1.2   Written (communicating by written/printed material)

107 ____   Writing (for example, writing or dictating letters, reports, etc., writing copy for ads,
writing newspaper articles, etc.; do *not* include transcribing activities described in item 4.3,
but only activities in which the incumbent creates the written material)

Source: E. J. McCormick, P. R. Jeanneret, and R. C. Mecham, *Position Analysis Questionnaire*, copyright © 1969 by Purdue Research
Foundation, West Lafayette, IN 47907. Reprinted with permission.

Abilities Data

Abilities data capture the knowledge and skills a worker must possess to satisfactorily perform the job. One taxonomy that includes (1) pyschomotor abilities, (2) physical proficiency abilities, and (3) cognitive abilities forms the foundation for the ability-based job analysis. AT&T, in conjunction with the Communication Workers of America (CWA) and other unions, developed a set of 16 abilities required in nonmanagerial work at AT&T. Some of these abilities are defined in Exhibit 3.8.[14] "Expression" and "comprehension," the first two factors, probably correspond most closely to the communication aspect we looked at with task and behavior data. Exhibit 3.9 excerpts AT&T's measurement of comprehension abilities required on the job. Note that the behavioral descriptors used to anchor the sales for oral comprehension (e.g., "understand a McDonald's hamburger commercial," "understand instructions for a sport," and "understand a lecture on navigating in space") are not work-specific but are drawn from daily life outside the job. The AT&T–CWA project was not put into practice; yet it is noteworthy because it represents an early effort at developing a competency-based approach to designing pay structures. We will discuss more recent competency approaches later in this chapter.

The "communication" scales shown in Exhibits 3.6, 3.7, and 3.9 illustrate the differences in task, behavior, and ability data. They vary in the way they describe a job. Thus, it is not surprising that varying approaches to job analysis may yield different results. One study examined seven supervisory jobs in a chemical processing plant using all three types of job analysis data.[15] Using the same statistical procedures on all three data sets, they found that different sets yielded different results. In other words, the type of data collected affects the results, and the purpose of the analysis dictates the nature of the data to collect. Other research has identified another factor that affects the results of job analysis: the level of analysis.

Level of Analysis

The nature of the data collected can be considered in terms of a hierarchy, shown in Exhibit 3.10. Some items of the hierarchy are the same as the types of data we just discussed. In the hierarchy, *tasks* represent a grouping of elements or behaviors into a basic accomplishment or duty. For example, elements such as "gathering time cards and using calculators to multiply hours worked by hourly wage" are combined into a task, "calculating the employee wages for time cards." Moving up the hierarchy, tasks are grouped into *positions* that constitute different individuals performing the same group of tasks in a particular organization. In

---

[14] Ken Ross, "Occupational Job Evaluation Study" (Basking Ridge, NJ: AT&T, 1983).

[15] E. T. Cornelius III, T. J. Carron, and M. M. Collins, "Job Analysis Models and Job Classification," *Personnel Psychology* 32 (1979), pp. 693–708.

EXHIBIT 3.8   AT&T–CWA Job Analysis Factors: Abilities-Based

1. *Expression* is speaking and/or writing in words, sentences, or numbers so others will understand. It is measured in terms of the complexity of the information being expressed as well as the comprehension ability of the receiver of the information.

2. *Comprehension* is understanding spoken and/or written words, sentences, or numbers. It is measured in terms of the complexity of the information being received as well as the quality of the information being received.

3. *Fact Finding* is obtaining or selecting pertinent information through observation, research, or questioning. It includes organizing and combining different pieces of information into meaningful order to identify a problem. It does not include the application of this information to solve the problem. An unknown is the key element in fact finding.

4. *Systems Reasoning* is making decisions that involve the selection and application of appropriate business resources or usage of relevant facts to solve identified problems or to achieve a desired result. This is based on knowledge and understanding of products and services, materials, policies, practices, and procedures.

5. *Mathematics* is the selection and application of mathematical methods or procedures to solve problems or to achieve desired results. These systems range from basic arithmetic computations to the most complex statistical techniques or other applications such as occur in physics or engineering problems.

6. *Adaptability* is the need to adapt one's behavior to changing or unusual circumstances to achieve a desired result. This includes changes in personal interactions or work situations.

7. *Persuasion* is influencing the behaviors or actions of others. The changes in others' behaviors or actions may not be observed immediately.

Note: Nine additional factors are omitted from this exhibit.

the illustration in Exhibit 3.10, there are three individuals who hold a Bookkeeper 1 job in firm A. Jobs similar across several firms (bookkeeper, accounting clerk, teller) are in turn considered to belong to an *occupation.* Occupations could be grouped into a *job family* such as a "computing and account recording job family."

What does all this have to do with making pay decisions? The level or unit of analysis chosen may influence the decision of whether the work is similar or dissimilar. At the occupation level, bookkeepers, tellers, and accounting clerks are considered to be similar; yet at the job level, these three are considered dissimilar. An analogy might be looking at two grains of salt under a microscope versus looking at them as part of a serving of french fries. If job data suggest that jobs are similar, then the jobs must be paid equally; if jobs are different, they can be paid differently.

Exhibit 3.9   Communications: Abilities-Based Data

ORAL COMPREHENSION

This is the ability to understand spoken English words and sentences.

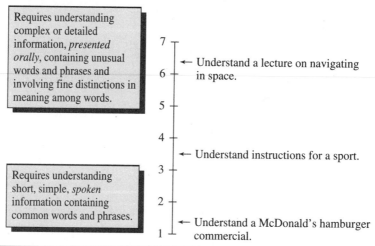

Requires understanding complex or detailed information, *presented orally*, containing unusual words and phrases and involving fine distinctions in meaning among words.

7

6 ← Understand a lecture on navigating in space.

5

4

← Understand instructions for a sport.

3

Requires understanding short, simple, *spoken* information containing common words and phrases.

2

← Understand a McDonald's hamburger commercial.

1

FLEXIBILITY VERSUS COSTS AND BENEFITS OF JOB ANALYSIS

Does job analysis help an organization achieve competitive advantage? Competitive pressures require constant control of costs while increasing the focus on satisfying customers with error-free, high-quality products and services. One response to this pressure is to make work assignments more fluid. Employers who are flexible, adaptable, and responsive can help the organization compete successfully. Does job analysis help do this? In practice, many employers are finding it difficult to justify the time and expense of collecting detailed information.[16] They may collect just position or job-level data and argue that more detailed information is not necessary to determine wages.

Many employers are increasing their flexibility by adopting broad, *generic descriptions* that cover a large number of related tasks akin to the occupation level in Exhibit 3.10. Two employees working in the same broadly defined jobs may be doing enitrely different sets of related tasks. But for pay purposes, they are doing work of equal value. Employees working in very broadly defined jobs

---

[16] Sandra O'Neal, "Competencies: The DNA of the Corporation," *ACA Journal*, Winter 1993/94, pp. 6–13; Randolph William Keuch, "Measuring and Rewarding Performance in the Customer-Driven Organization: A New Measurement Framework," *ACA Journal*, Winter 1993/94, pp. 58–67; Jay R. Schuster and Patricia K. Zingheim, "Building Pay Environments to Facilitate High-Performance Teams," *ACA Journal*, Spring/Summer 1993, pp. 40–51; G. R. Schmidt and J. L. Sulzer, "Defining the Criticality of Job Content: A Survey of Job Analysis Procedures," paper presented at the Annual Conference of the Society for Industrial and Organizational Psychology, Boston, April 1989.

Exhibit 3.10   Levels of Analysis

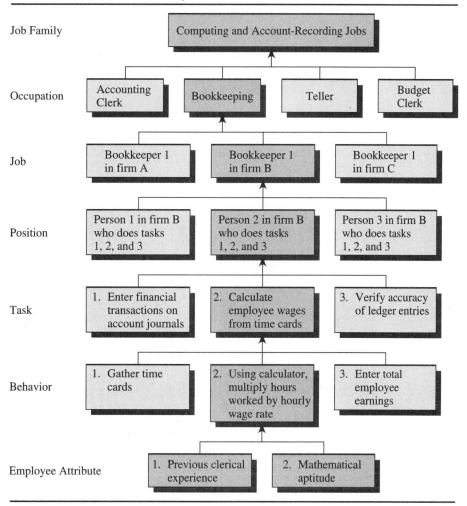

Source: Adapted from K. Pearlman, "Job Families: A Review and Discussion of Their Implications for Personnel Selection," *Psychological Bulletin* 87 (1980), pp. 1–28. Copyright 1980 by the American Psychological Association. Adapted by permission of the author.

can easily be switched to other tasks that fall within the broad range of the same job, without the bureaucratic burden of making job transfer requests and wage adjustments. Thus, employees can more easily be matched to changes in the work flow.

However, such broad, generic descriptions of work leave employers open to challenge regarding potential inequities. At what point is work similar or different for pay purposes? Narrowly defined jobs leave employers (or taxpayers) footing the bill for unneeded employees, as in Philadelphia, where it takes three city employees to change a light bulb. Thanks to that city's union contracts, a building mechanic removes the light panel, an electrician replaces the bulb, and a custodian cleans up any dust and debris. For employees to perform work out of their job descriptions requires extra pay.

Still, a countervailing view deserves consideration. More specific distinctions among jobs represent career paths to employees. Titles may represent promotional opportunities, recognition, and rewards. Reducing the number of levels in a structure may also reduce opportunities for recognition and advancement. Reducing titles or labeling all employees as "associates" signals an egalitarian culture. But it sacrifices a sense of advancement and opportunity.[17] However, a British manager observed, "There are probably more admirals than ships in the British navy. And in some U.S. banks, everyone over 23 seems to be a director." Such title inflation probably deflates the motivating currency of titles and advancement. The challenge in de-layered organizations is to find ways to continue to recognize employee advancement without title inflation or rigid bureaucracies.

So where does this leave us? What data should be collected and what level of analysis should be used? There is no clear-cut answer. It depends on the situation and the resources available. But the more specific and detailed the data, the more likely they are to capture differences in the work and adequately describe the work content. Whether such detailed information is worth the expense involved depends on the circumstances in the organization. Clearly, detailed data may justify pay differences to a skeptical judge presiding over a pay discrimination suit. Yet more broadly defined jobs with generic titles and descriptions offer increased flexibility in work assignments. Properly managed, these more fluid, broader assignments offer employees the promise of enriched and challenging opportunities. Improperly managed, broader assignments have a dark side. Greater discretion lies with managers and improper decisions could result in unequal pay for equal work and unfair opportunities for various individuals. Greater flexibility goes hand in glove with the competence to manage it effectively. Herein lies one of the continuing challenges to managing employee compensation.

HOW CAN THE DATA BE COLLECTED?

After having decided on the purpose, level, and the nature of the data, the next major decision is how to collect it. A wide variety of methods exists; the most common ones are described in Exhibit 3.11. We will combine these methods into two basic types: conventional and quantitative.

Conventional Methods

A common data collection method involves an analyst using a questionnaire to interview job incumbents and supervisors. The questionnaires and interviews

---

[17] Shari Caudron, "HR Revamps Career Itineraries," *Personnel Journal*, April 1994, pp. 64B–64P; Eileen Appelbaum and Rosemary Batt, *The New American Workplace* (Ithaca, NY: ILR Press, 1994).

EXHIBIT 3.11 Data Collection Methods

Method	Descriptions	Characteristics
Questionnaire	Using standardized form, jobholders and/or supervisors describe the work. Data can be gathered either through mailed survey or through individual interview.	Variations include combining questionnaire with individual or group interview. As with all questionnaires, responses may be incomplete or difficult to interpret, a limitation minimized by combining with interviews. Standard format eases mathematical analysis. Interviews, however, may be time consuming, and become more difficult with workers at multiple locations.
Checklist	Jobholders and/or supervisors check items on a task inventory that apply to their particular job. Checklist can be tailor-made or purchased.	Depends on recognition rather than recall. Cheap, easy to administer and analyze. However, care must be taken that all significant aspects of work are included in the list.
Diary	Jobholders record activities as they are performed.	Has the advantage of collecting data as events occur, but it is often difficult to obtain continuous and consistent entries. Obtained data is not in a standardized format.
Observation	Analyst records perceptions formed watching the work being done by one or more jobholders.	The absence of preconceived structures or artificial constraints can lead to richer data. Each job can be studied in any depth desired. However, validity and reliability of data can be a problem, and the relative emphasis of certain work aspects is dependent on the acuteness of the analyst's perceptions. Also, the observation of employee behavior by an analyst influences it.
Activity matrix	Respondents identify time spent in relation to tasks and products or services.	Data collected is amenable to quantitative analysis, and is highly adaptable to other human resource management needs; however, another job analysis procedure must be used initially to develop the matrix.
Critical incidents	Behaviorally oriented incidents describe key job behaviors. Analyst determines degree of each type of behavior present or absent in each job.	Analysis clearly based on concrete behavior. Scales require some expertise to develop.

are structured to achieve a uniform response format. The approach requires considerable involvement of employees and supervisors, which increases their understanding of the process, provides an opportunity to clarify their work relationships and expectations, and increases the likelihood that they will accept the results. Usually, an analyst translates the data collected to a summary job description sheet. Often, both incumbents and supervisors are given an opportunity to modify and approve the job description; this helps ensure its acceptance. In some cases the preparation of these description sheets is left to the supervisors and incumbents, and the analyst role becomes one of trainer/facilitator. Some trainers go so far as to specify "correct" verbs and adjectives to use. Appendix 3–A contains a step-by-step procedure for conducting a conventional job analysis plus a conventional job analysis questionnaire.

Conventional methods place considerable reliance on the analyst's abilities to understand the work performed and to translate it. Certain safeguards, such as multiple approvals (by supervisors and incumbents), may help minimize the difficulties inherent in translating the results of questionnaires and personal discussions into an accurate representation of the job.

In a review of job analysis, McCormick points out that "of the various deficiencies of conventional job analysis procedures, probably the sharpest criticism is that the typical essays of job activities are not adequately descriptive of the jobs in question."[18] Another critic is even more direct: "conventional job analysis . . . [is] floundering in a morass of semantic confusion."[19]

Reducing this semantic confusion is the goal of quantitative job analysis. The critical advantages of quantitative job analysis over conventional approaches are that quantitative analysis lends itself to statistical analysis, is documentable and quantifiable, and *may* be more objective. Additionally, a computerized job analysis holds out the promise of relieving much of the drudgery of collecting and translating job data. To date, that promise remains unrealized.[20]

Quantitative Methods

Inventories are the core of all quantitative job analysis. Inventories are questionnaires in which tasks, behaviors, and abilities are listed. Exhibits 3.6, 3.7, and 3.9 are examples of inventories. Each item is assessed, usually by both job incumbents and supervisors, in terms of time spent, importance to the overall job, and/or learning time. Systematic assessment documents job analysis decisions. The resulting data can then be used for further statistical analysis.

---

[18] McCormick, "Job and Task Analysis."

[19] Quoted in Robert Harvey, "Job Analysis," *Handbook of Industrial and Organizational Psychology*, vol. 2, ed. M. D. Dunnette and L. Hough (Palo Alto, CA: Consulting Psychologists Press, 1991).

[20] For an up-to-date inventory of available software, see Richard Franzreb, ed., *The Personnel Software Census* (Roseville, CA: Advanced Personnel Systems, 1994); *Compensation Software* and *Benefit Software*, both published by the American Compensation Association, Scottsdale, AZ.

Most compensation consulting firms have developed quantitative inventories, which are frequently tailored for a specific organization.[21] The PAQ is the best known and most generally used quantitative job analysis.[22] Exhibit 3.7 is an example of the PAQ.

The Position Information Questionnaire (PIQ) in Appendix 3–B has been developed for 3M by Towers Perrin. PIQ is similar to the products from several other consulting firms (e.g., Wyatt and Hay). PIQ is clearly more structured and systematic than the conventional approach in Appendix 3–A.

Tailoring a Plan

Rather than adopting an existing inventory, some employers opt to tailor one to their specific work and conditions. However, development costs of custom-designed inventories may exceed the value added by the job information collected. Our experience is that employers using quantitative job analysis usually opt to modify predeveloped approaches to fit their situation. The 3M modification of PIQ in Appendix 3–B is an example. However, 3M recently dropped installation of a PIQ in midproject. They determined that the resources and effort required (reportedly up to six professionals over two years) was simply not worth the results obtained.

WHO IS INVOLVED IN JOB ANALYSIS?

Some employers view the job analyst as an entry-level position and adopt the "learn-by-doing" approach: Analyzing work provides a thorough introduction to the company, and after 6 to 12 months, the analyst is ready for a new job assignment. In spite of real-world practice, most textbook writers continue to insist that the analysis should be done by someone who is thoroughly familiar with the organization, its work flow, and its policies and objectives.

Who Collects the Data?

The choice of who collects the data is usually among an analyst, the supervisors, and/or the jobholders.[23] Some firms require the supervisor to perform the analysis, since supervisors are assumed to be knowledgeable, and their involvement may help increase their understanding of exactly what their subordinates do.

---

[21] Information on custom-designed quantitative job analysis plans can be obtained from Towers Perrin, New York, Minneapolis, San Francisco, and other locations; Personnel Decisions Research Institute, Minneapolis; Sibson & Co., Chicago, and other locations; and Wyatt & Company, New York, Detroit, San Francisco, and other locations.

[22] Information on the PAQ is available from PAQ Services, P.O. Box 3337, Logan, UT 84321, (801) 752-5698.

[23] R. Harvey and J. Lozada-Larson, "Influence of Amount of Job Descriptive Information on Job Analysis Rating Accuracy," *Journal of Applied Psychology* 73 (1988), pp. 457–61.

Obvious shortcomings of this arrangement include the possibility of limited knowledge of the actual tasks, skills, and behaviors required on the job. The authors' experience suggests that the employees actually performing the work need to be involved in the process as a way to ensure accuracy and acceptability of resulting pay structures.

Regardless of who collects the data, some training in the process seems to be a requirement. In the absence of more research, publicly available materials from the Department of Labor may be of value in developing training programs.

Who Provides the Data?

The decision on the source of the data (jobholders, supervisors, and/or analyst) hinges on how to ensure consistent, accurate, and acceptable data.[24] Expertise about the work resides with the jobholders and the supervisors; hence, they are the principle sources. For key managerial/professional jobs, supervisors "two levels above" have also been suggested as valuable sources since they may have a more cosmic view of how jobs fit in the overall organization. In other instances, subordinates and employees in other jobs that interface with the job under study are also involved. The number of incumbents per job from which to collect data probably varies with the stability of the job. An ill-defined or changing job will require either the involvement of more respondents or a more careful selection of respondents. Obviously, the more people involved, the more time-consuming and expensive the process.

Finally, the support of top management is absolutely essential. They must be alerted to the cost and time-consuming nature of job analysis. They must also understand the nature of any changes that may result from job analysis. If an organization is not committed to the process and its results, then the effort is probably wasted. The vital importance of employee and operating management involvement has been repeatedly emphasized. This involvement may take several forms, ranging from active participation in describing their own and/or subordinates' work to serving on compensation task forces or committees directly responsible for the design and development of job analysis procedures. Even those employees not directly involved need to be kept informed as to the purposes and progress of all the activity. Employees will guess at the purpose of this work, and it seems only sound compensation practice to help make it an educated guess.

IS JOB ANALYSIS USEFUL?

Job analysis is the Rodney Dangerfield of managing compensation: It gets no respect. It is time-consuming, expensive, and difficult to relate to the bottom

---

[24] Samuel B. Green and Thomas Stutzman, "An Evaluation of Methods to Select Respondents to Structured Job-Analysis Questionnaires," *Personnel Psychology*, Autumn 1986, pp. 543–64; Edwin T. Cornelius III, Angelo S. DeNisi, and Allyn Blencoe, "Expert and Naive Raters Using the PAQ: Does It Matter?" *Personnel Psychology* 37 (June 1984), pp. 453–64.

line. Yet without it, the work relatedness of pay structures is open to challenge and difficult to ensure. Even with it, a high degree of judgement is involved. If it is going to be used, then the comparative usefulness of various methods, particularly their reliability, validity, acceptability, and costs must be considered.

Reliability

Reliability is the consistency of the results obtained. Are the results (whether the work is similar or dissimilar) the same regardless of who is involved (supervisors, incumbents, analysts, consultants) and what methods are used?

Several studies have compared employee-supervisor agreement on work content.[25] They present a mixed picture of the reliability of job analysis. Employees and supervisors often differ in how they view the distribution of time among tasks, the skills required to perform the work, and the difficulties of the tasks performed. In one study, employees did not report 30 percent of the tasks supervisors said were part of their jobs.[26]

Different analysts using the same quantitative methods on the same jobs tend to get the same results. However, even job incumbents may have different perceptions and definitions of the same work. For example, employees who have been on the job a long time may change it by adopting shortcuts and new routines. All these factors may influence the job analysis results.

Conventional job analysis does not usually lend itself to formal reliability analysis because of its unstructured output.[27] This imprecision makes reliability a serious issue for conventional methods. Consistent (reliable) job information does not necessarily mean that it is accurate, comprehensive, or free from bias. To find out whether the results are accurate, we need to consider the validity.

Validity

Research on how to estimate the validity of job analysis is particularly difficult, since there is almost no way to show the extent to which the results are accurate portraits of the work. One reviewer of job analysis research concludes, "Taken together the evidence . . . paints a troubling picture regarding the reliability and

---

[25] Harvey, "Job Analysis;" H. H. Meyer, "Comparison of Foreman and General Foreman Conceptions of the Foreman's Job Responsibility," *Personnel Psychology* 12 (1959), pp. 445–52; A. P. O'Reilly, "Skill Requirements: Supervisor-Subordinate Conflict," *Personnel Psychology* 26 (1973), pp. 75–80; J. T. Hazel, J. M. Madden, and R. E. Christal, "Agreement between Worker-Supervisor Descriptions on the Worker's Job," *Journal of Industrial Psychology* 2 (1964), pp. 71–79.

[26] Robert Harvey, "Incumbent vs. Superior Perception of Jobs," Presentation at SIOP Conference, Miami, 1990.

[27] For an example of the statistical analysis on PAQ results, see R. D. Arvey, S. E. Maxwell, R. L. Gutenberg, and C. Camp, "Detecting Job Differences: A Monte Carlo Study," *Personnel Psychology* 34 (1981), pp. 709–30.

validity of job analysis.[28] The most promising approach may be to examine the convergence of results among multiple sources of job data (analysts, incumbents, supervisors) and multiple methods. A common approach to attempt to increase accuracy of job analysis is to require both the job holder and the manager to "sign off" on the results. Although getting both parties to sign off on the results may reflect their acceptance, it may also reflect their mutual desire to get rid of the analyst and get back to performing the job rather than analyzing it.

Acceptability

Employee acceptability of data collected is important and easily overlooked. No matter how well the rest of the compensation system is administered, if jobholders are dissatisfied with the initial data collected and the process for collecting it, they are not likely to believe in the results.

Conventional job analysis is not always well accepted by the parties involved because of its potential for subjectivity. One writer says, "We all know the classic procedures. One (worker) watched and noted the actions of another . . . at work on (the) job. The actions of both are biased and the resulting information varied with the wind, especially the political wind."[29] But the acceptability of quantitative job analysis is also mixed. Even after four years in development, one application ran into such severe problems that managers refused to use it.[30] The difficulties included:

1. *Employee/manager understanding.* The statistical methods used were difficult to understand, so many managers were unable to communicate the results to employees.

2. *Behaviorally oriented versus "scope" data.* Analyzing work in terms of work behaviors, omitting "scope" data (e.g., size of budgets, total payroll, contribution to organization objectives) caused managers to believe that the questionnaire did not accurately analyze their jobs.

3. *Abstract and ambiguous factors.* The data collected were perceived to be too abstract and ambiguous. Results were considered too subjective and open to personal interpretation.

Practicality

Researchers recognize the necessity of judging the usefulness of job analysis methods according to the purpose of the analysis.[31] Recently 93 experienced job

---

[28] Harvey, "Job Analysis," p. 114.

[29] E. M. Ramras, "Discussion," in *Proceedings of Division of Military Psychology Symposium: Collecting, Analyzing, and Reporting Information Describing Jobs and Occupations,* 77th Annual Convention of the American Psychological Association, Lackland Air Force Base, TX, September 1969, pp. 75–76.

[30] Gomez-Mejia et al., "A Comparison of the Practical Utility of Traditional, Statistical, and Hybrid Job Evaluation Approaches."

[31] Ronald A. Ash and Edward L. Levine, "A Framework for Evaluating Job Analysis Methods," *Personnel* 57, no. 6 (November–December 1980), pp. 53–59; E. L. Levine, R. A. Ash, and

analysts were asked to compare a number of job analysis methods on their utility for 11 different purposes. The researchers concluded that the effectiveness and practicality of each method varied with the purpose. The PAQ was among those rated highest for the purpose of creating job structures. The usefulness of the results obtained is probably the most important criterion on which to judge alternative approaches to job analysis.

There are very few data publicly available on costs of various approaches to job analysis. Our own experience with custom-designed quantitative job analysis plans suggests about 24 to 36 months from design through installation, plus significant time commitments from participating managers who serve on task forces. Considerable time and money are required for any job analysis, with or without computer assistance.

The practical utility of quantitative job analysis, with its relatively complex procedures and analysis, remains in doubt for compensation purposes. Some advocates get so taken with their statistics and computers that they ignore the role that human judgment must continue to play in job analysis. As Dunnette states,

> I wish to emphasize the central role played in all these procedures by human judgment. I know of no methodology, statistical technique or objective measurements that can negate the importance of, nor supplement, rational judgment as an important element in the process of deriving behavior and task information about jobs and of using that information to develop or justify human resources programs.[32]

JOB DESCRIPTIONS

The data collected in job analysis must be put into a form that is usable by employees and managers. Often that form is the job description. A job description identifies, defines, and describes the job as it is being performed. The job description typically contains three sections, which roughly correspond with the purposes of identifying, defining, and describing the job. Recall that these were the categories delineated in deciding what data to collect in job analysis. Exhibits 3.12 and 3.13 are typical job descriptions of a nurse's position, albeit 100 years apart. The job description should indicate the major duties of this jobholder, the specific work performed, how closely supervised this job is, and what controls limit the

---

N. Bennett, "Exploratory Comparative Study of Four Job Analysis Methods," *Journal of Applied Psychology* 65 (1980), pp. 524–35; R. A. Ash, E. L. Levine, and F. Sistrunk, "The Role of Jobs and Job Based Methods in Personnel and Human Resources Management," *Research in Personnel and Human Resources Management* 1 (1983), pp. 45–84; Edward L. Levine, Ronald A. Ash, Hardy Hall, and Frank Sistrunk, "Evaluation of Job Analysis Methods by Experienced Job Analysts," *Academy of Management Journal* 26, no. 2 (1983), pp. 339–48.

[32] M. D. Dunnette, L. M. Hough, and R. L. Rosse, "Task and Job Taxonomies as a Basis for Identifying Labor Supply Sources and Evaluating Employment Qualifications," in *Affirmative Action Planning*, ed. George T. Milkovich and Lee Dyer (New York: Human Resource Planning Society, 1979), pp. 37–51.

Exhibit 3.12   Contemporary Job Description for Registered Nurse

Job Title

   Registered Nurse

Job Summary

Accountable for the complete spectrum of patient care from admission through transfer or discharge through the nursing process of assessment, planning, implementation, and evaluation. Each R.N. has primary authority to fulfill responsibility for the nursing process on the assigned shift and for projecting future needs of the patient/family. Directs and guides patient teaching and activities for ancillary personnel while maintaining standard of professional nursing.

Relationships

Reports to: Head Nurse or Charge Nurse.
Supervises: Responsible for the care delivered by L.P.N.'s, nursing assistants, orderlies, and transcribers.
Works with: Ancillary Care Departments.
External relationships: Physicians, patients, patients' families.

Qualifications

Education: Graduate of an accredited school of nursing.
Work experience: Critical care requires one year of recent medical/surgical experience (special care
                   nursing preferred), medical/surgical experience (new graduates may be considered
                   for noncharge positions).
License or registration requirements: Current R.N. license or permit in the State of Minnesota.
Physical requirements: A. Ability to bend, reach, or assist to transfer up to 50 pounds.
                         B. Ability to stand and/or walk 80 percent of 8-hour shift.
                         C. Visual and hearing acuity to perform job-related functions.

Essential Responsibilities

1. Assesses physical, emotional, and psycho-social dimensions of patients.
   Standard: Provides a written assessment of patient within one hour of admission and at least once
               a shift. Communicates this assessment to other patient care providers in accordance with
               hospital policies.
2. Formulates a written plan of care for patients from admission through discharge.
   Standard: Develops short and long term goals within 24 hours of admission. Reviews and updates
               care plans each shift based on ongoing assessment.
3. Implements plan of care.
   Standard: Demonstrates skill in performing common nursing procedures in accordance with but not
               limited to the established written R.N. skills inventory specific to assigned area. Completes
               patient care activities in an organized and timely fashion, reassessing priorities appropri-
               ately.

Note: Additional responsibilities omitted from exhibit.

EXHIBIT 3.13   Job Description for Nurse 100 Years Ago

In addition to caring for your 50 patients each nurse will follow these regulations:

1. Daily sweep and mop the floors of your ward, dust the patient's furniture and window sills.
2. Maintain an even temperature in your ward by bringing in a scuttle of coal for the day's business.
3. Light is important to observe the patient's condition. Therefore, each day, fill kerosene lamps, clean chimneys, and trim wicks. Wash the windows once a week.
4. The nurse's notes are important in aiding the physician's work. Make your pens carefully, you may whittle nibs to your individual taste.
5. Each nurse on day duty will report every day at 7 A.M. and leave at 8 P.M. except on the Sabbath on which day you will be off from 12:00 noon to 2:00 P.M.
6. Graduate nurses in good standing with the director of nurses will be given an evening off each week for courting purposes, or two evenings a week if you go regularly to church.
7. Each nurse should lay aside from each pay day a goodly sum of her earnings for her benefits during her declining years, so that she will not become a burden. For example, if you earn $30 a month you should set aside $15.
8. Any nurse who smokes, uses liquor in any form, gets her hair done at a beauty shop, or frequents dance halls will give the director good reason to suspect her worth, intentions, and integrity.
9. The nurse who performs her labors and serves her patients and doctors faithfully and without fault for a period of five years will be given an increase by the hospital administration of five cents a day, provided there are no hospital debts that are outstanding.

---

actions of the jobholder. In addition to describing the tasks performd, the training and experience required to perform them may also be included here, or in a separate section called *job specifications*. The description should provide an accurate word picture of the job.

Legal Compliance.   The Americans with Disabilities Act requires that *essential elements of a job* be specified in the job description. These are the elements that cannot be reassigned to other workers. If applicants can perform these essential elements, they are assumed to be able to perform the job. Once essential elements are identified, the employer must consider *reasonable accommodations* that enable an otherwise qualified handicapped person to perform them. Essential elements and reasonable accommodations have to be determined on a case-by-case basis, including legal cases. For those jobs with little discretion, it's relatively easy to list essential tasks, but fewer and fewer such jobs exist. Nevertheless, thorough job analysis and accurate job descriptions are the beginning points for compliance.

Responsibility versus Task-Based Descriptions.   Many employers use results- or responsibility-oriented job descriptions rather than detailed task-oriented ones, particularly for managerial and professional work.[33] Exhibit 3.14 contrasts a programmer/analyst position described in both ways. The responsibility-based description attempts to focus on outcomes, whereas the task-based approach describes the job in greater detail.

Managerial/Professional Jobs

Describing managerial jobs poses special problems. Managers frequently do not perform a prescribed set of duties. Instead of specific tasks with specific outcomes, they have broad accountability for the accomplishment of results that help the organization attain its objectives. For example, a marketing vice president is broadly responsible for moving goods from their site of manufacture to the consumer in a profitable manner. A further difficulty in describing managerial jobs is the expectation that the individuals will change the jobs. Therefore, the format for describing these jobs must be adjusted to adequately describe such work. In addition to sections that identify, defined, and describe the job, the following additions are usually made to managerial job description.

1. *Dimensions.* Provides statistics on the size of the payroll, budget, and number of people supervised. This is an expanded version of the identification section.
2. *Nature and scope.* Identifies how the position fits into the organization, the composition of the supporting staff (e.g., assistant director of personnel, and director of development report to the position) and the key issues to be handled by the person in this job. This is similar to the definition section previously discussed. However, care must be exercised that "scope" data does not just motivate managers to build head count and increase budgets in order to inflate their own jobs at the overall expense of the organization.
3. *Accountabilities.* Delineates the broad end results this position seeks to attain.

Writing the Job Description

Great detail exists on how to write the job descriptions, including specific definitions of verbs. Vague terms (e.g., "many" or "relatively easy") or those with a variety of meanings (e.g., "takes care of," and "handles") are frowned upon. This is not the place for polished prose, or even complete sentences. English

---

[33] R. Bradley Hill, "Get Off the Broadband Wagon," *Journal of Compensation and Benefits,* January–February 1993, pp. 25–29.

EXHIBIT 3.14 Programmer/Analyst Task vs. Responsibility-Based Description

---

Traditional Position Profile: Task Oriented

- Encodes, tests, debugs, and installs operating programs and procedures in coordination with the computer operations and user departments.
- Prepares detailed flow charts and diagrams outlining systems capabilities and processes.
- Develops, tests, installs, and modifies computer software, such as operating systems, compilers, utilities, multiprogramming, and telecommunications systems.

Note: Eight additional tasks omitted from exhibit.

New Position Profile: Responsibility Oriented

- Designs and implements hardware and software modules. Solves problems that have been stated and defined. Makes decisions or recommendations that may require interpretation of policies or regulations or some creativity, but must be made within preestablished technical guidelines or project parameters. Fixes moderately complex bugs.
- Provides technical direction. May lead design activities for a medium-sized project.
- Develops plans with realistic project schedules and resource usage. Modifies plans to adjust for unforeseen situations. Handles complex projects simultaneously.

Note: Four additional responsibilities omitted from exhibit.

Source: Adapted from R. Bradley Hill, "Get Off the Broadband Wagon," *Journal of Compensation and Benefits*, January–February 1993, pp. 25–29.

majors need not apply, since a smooth-flowing writing style may make the crucial information harder to pick out, thus discouraging use of the description.

To ensure equitable comparisons of content across jobs, jobs are typically described in a standardized manner, not only in format but also in choice of words. For example, "supervises" is not the same as "directs," "facilitates," or even "leads."

Although it is necessary to be brief, the description also needs to be accurate. One organization goes so far as to suggest writing a first draft of unlimited length, ensuring inclusion of all necessary detail. The first draft then is reviewed to eliminate all words and sentences that do not contribute to meaning. A length of two to three pages for managerial jobs, fewer for nonmanagerial jobs, is usually considered long enough to be accurate without being unwieldy. The attractiveness of computer-generated job descriptions becomes clear as one begins to write a job description.

We hope the recurring questions you are mumbling at this point are

1. So what does all this detail have to do with compensation?
2. What risks do we run if we skip it?

The answer to the first question lies in ensuring that any potential pay structure is work related, that is, embedded in the work. To design such a structure requires data on the work. The challenge is, How much detail is required? (Once again, all together now, the answer is . . . .) It depends. Internally consistent pay structures need to be designed and managed to achieve the objects discussed in the last chapter: to help set individual employees' pay, encourage continuous learning, increase work force experience, reduce pay-related grievances, and the like. The detail of work information required to do this is a judgment call. The answer to the question of risk if we omit this detailed job analysis and descriptions becomes painfully obvious when inquiring minds want to know, when the employer is challenged to explain or even defend pay decisions to dissatisfied employees or a skeptical judge. Then all eyes shift to the compensation manager.[34] Where is the detail to support the decisions *we* made? How are *you* going to justify *our* decisions about equal pay for equal work and different pay for different work? Clearly, judgments and trade-offs are involved. Perhaps that is why good compensation managers receive those high salaries and offices with windows?

SKILL- AND COMPETENCY-BASED STRUCTURES

The logic seems compelling. As already noted, becoming more competitive requires increasing flexibility, continuous improvement, and learning world-class quality and continuous cost reduction. Some writers say that from a strategic view, pay structures that reinforce flexibility, learning, and improvement fit better with skill- and competency-based plans than those based on job content. Some go as far as to assert that job-based plans are too burdensome, too bureaucratic, too rigid, and too cumbersome to adapt to constant change.[35] First we examine skill- and competency-based plans in some detail; then we will contrast them with job-based plans.

---

[34] Doug Grider and Leslie A. Toombs, "Disproving Valuation Discrimination: A Study of Evaluator Gender Bias," *ACA Journal*, Autumn 1993, pp. 24–33.

[35] Graham L. O'Neill and Deirdre Lander, "Linking Employee Skills to Pay: A Framework for Skill-Based Pay Plans," *ACA Journal*, Winter 1993/94, p. 14–27; Edward E. Lawler III *Strategic Pay: Aligning Organizational Strategies and Pay Systems* (San Francisco: Jossey-Bass, 1990); Kathryn M. Cofsky, "Critical Keys to Competency-Based Pay," *Compensation and Benefits Review*, November–December 1993, pp. 46–52; Theodore Weinberger, "The Strategic Centrality of Jobs: A Measure of Value," *Compensation and Benefits Review*, January–February 1992, pp. 61–68. Nina Gupta, G. Douglas Jenkins, Jr., and William Curington, "Paying for Knowledge: Myths and Realities," *National Productivity Review*, Spring 1986, pp. 107–23; T. P. Schweizer, "Pay-for-Knowledge Systems: An Alternative Approach to Compensation," *Proceedings of the Southwest Academy of Management*, 1986, pp. 159–63.

Skill/Competency Information

Structures based on skill and competencies pay individuals based on what they have demonstrated or acquired rather than on the particular job they are doing. Indeed, a fundamental distinction is that a person is paid for the skills/competencies they can demonstrate, regardless of whether the job they perform requires a particular skill/competency. Exxon pays operators at its refinery in Baytown, Texas, for the multiple skills in which they are certified, whether Exxon assigns them to operations work or to maintenance tasks. Under job-based plans, employees are paid for the job they perform regardless of the skills they possess.

Since many of these plans are relatively new, the terms and definitions are still evolving. Generally, we will follow these definitions:

Skill-based structures link pay to the depth/breadth of the skills, abilities, and knowledge a person acquires that is relevant to the work. Typically applies to operators, technicians, and office work where the work can be specified and defined.

Competency-based structures link pay to the depth/breadth of competencies that are relevant to the work. Typically used in managerial, professional, and technical work where accomplishments are less easy to identify and define.

Skills and competencies differ in their specificity. Consider, for example, the competency described in part in Exhibit 3.15 from Frito-Lay. For its managerial work, Frito-Lay uses four competencies: leveraging technical/business systems, leadership for results, building work force effectiveness, and meeting customer needs. Each of these competencies has three levels: resource, senior resource, and site/area resource. Contrast their approach in Exhibit 3.15 with the skills in Exhibit 3.16, Borg-Warner's skill-based plan that is specifically tied to the actual work of assembling drive chains for automobile transmissions (e.g., stacking, packing, inspecting, measuring) and leadership. Borg-Warner's skills are defined for specific jobs and require shorter times to acquire. Competencies, on the other hand, are tied to careers, and they require a longer time to develop. Since both skills and competencies are acquired over time, both structures support a strategy of continuous learning and improvement.

Specialists and Generalists

Both skill and competency plans can focus on depth (specialists in corporate law, finance, or welding and hydraulic maintenance) or breadth (generalists with knowledge in all phases of operations including marketing, manufacturing, finance, and human resources).

Specialist: In Depth.   Basing pay structures on knowledge possessed by individual employees is not new. The pay structures for your elementary or high school teachers have long been based on their knowledge as measured by education

EXHIBIT 3.15   Competency Levels for Managerial Work at Frito-Lay

	Resource	Senior Resource	Site Resource/Area Resource
Competency			
Leveraging technical/ business systems.	Uses knowledge of one or more systems/ processes to troubleshoot.	Uses broader systems/ process knowledge to solve more complex problem; helps less experienced staff to develop systems/ process knowledge.	Applies expert knowledge of total system to solve broad or new problems; operates as a coach on technical and business issues.
Leading for results.	Makes necessary adjustments to achieve results.	Focuses team on achieving results consistently over time.	Identifies and overcomes system obstacles; influences individuals and results beyond own team.
Building work force effectiveness.	Takes a lead role in delivering on team goals.	Facilitates team effectiveness through teaching and coaching.	Creates alignment across teams; coaches less experienced staff on developing team effectiveness.
Meeting customer needs.	Considers customer needs in making day-to-day decisions.	Identifies and addresses changing customer requirements.	Anticipates and interprets changes in customer requirements to take appropriate action.

EXHIBIT 3.16   Borg-Warner Automotive Assembly Classifications

Pay System		
Job Based	*Skill Based*	
Chain stacker		
Packer		
Cleaner	Skill C	
Ultrasonic inspector		Skill B
Measurer		
Assembler		Skill A
Riveter		
Leadership, Supervisory, and Scheduling Responsibilities		

level. A typical teacher's contract specifies a series of steps, with each step corresponding to a level of education. A bachelor's degree in education is step one and is the minimum required for hiring. To advance a step to higher pay requires additional education. For example, an additional 9 semester hours of coursework earns an increase of $225 in Ithaca, New York. Of course, an additional advancement in pay is also provided for standing in place at the end of the year (called seniority). The result can be that two teachers may receive different pay rates for doing essentially the same job—teaching English to high school juniors. The pay is based on the knowledge of the individual doing the job (measured by number of college credits) rather than job content. The presumption is that teachers with more credits are more effective and more flexible—able to teach seniors, too.

Generalist/Multiskill Based: Breadth.   As with the teachers, employees in a multiskill system earn pay increases by acquiring new knowledge, but the knowledge is specific to a range of related jobs. An example from Borg-Warner (Exhibit 3.16) illustrates the system. Borg-Warner assembles drive chains for automobile transmissions. Originally, seven different jobs were involved in the assembly process, starting with stackers, and moving up through packers, assemblers, and riveters. When Borg-Warner switched to a skill-based pay system, these seven jobs were reorganized into three broad categories: cell operators A, B, and C. Cell operator C is an entry-level position. Once operator Cs can demonstrate mastery of the stacker (through measurer), they are eligible to train for operator B jobs. With each job mastery comes a pay raise. Operator Bs can be rotated among any of the jobs for which they have demonstrated mastery, including C-level jobs. An operator B can do all the jobs required, including stacking, and still receive operator B pay. Operator As can also do all jobs, plus they assume responsibility for scheduling and supervising teams. The advantage to Borg-Warner is workforce flexibility and hence lower staffing levels.

The multiskilled system for operatives at Borg-Warner differs from the competency-based system for engineers, managers, or teachers in that the responsibilities assigned to an employee in a multiskill system can change drastically over a short period of time, whereas teachers, managers, and engineers increase competencies over longer periods. Both systems emphasize increased breadth of knowledge so that employees can perform a variety of assignments. Pay is based on individual skill and competence. Typically, training and certification systems are established to ensure that individuals have adequately mastered and maintain the skills/competency for which they are being paid. These certification and training programs are discussed in greater detail in the next chapter. Here it is important to realize the differences among skill-, competency-, and job-based approaches.

Skill-based structures are currently enjoying a great deal of favorable attention. The idea of basing pay increases on improving employee skills is very appealing. Applications are most common in small- to medium-sized facilities (under 400 employees), especially where a continuous process technology is used.

A recent survey found that on average about 30 percent of the work force in the facility is included in a particular plan.[36] Consulting firms report that competency approaches are among their fastest-growing lines of business.

SKILL/COMPETENCY ANALYSIS

Skill analysis is a systematic process to identify and collect information about skills required to perform work in an organization.

Competency analysis is a systematic process to identify and collect information about the competencies required for the person and the organization to be successful.

The parallels to job analysis should be obvious. If structures are to be based on skills or competencies, some way is needed to determine the different skills or competencies required for the organization to be successful. Data are required to help describe, certify, and value these skills and competencies. Exhibit 3.17 identifies the major skill analysis decisions: (1) What information should be collected? (2) What methods should be used? (3) Who should be involved? (4) How useful are the results for pay purposes?

These are exactly the same decisions managers face in job analysis. However, because skill/competency analysis in compensation is relatively new, little research exists to offer guidance. Currently, the state of practice must be culled from case studies describing applications in a handful of companies.[37]

EXHIBIT 3.17   Determining the Internal Skill-Based Structure

Internal work relationships within the organization → Skill analysis → Skill descriptions → Skill certification → Skill-based structure

Basic Decisions
- What information should be collected?
- What methods should be used?
- Who should be involved?
- How useful are the results for pay purposes?

---

[36] G. Douglas Jenkins, Jr., Gerald E. Ledford, Jr., Nina Gupta, and D. Harold Doty, *Skill-Based Pay* (Scottsdale, AZ: American Compensation Association, 1992).

[37] Gerald E. Ledford, Jr., "Three Case Studies of Skill-Based Pay: An Overview," *Compensation and Benefits Review*, March–April 1991, pp. 11–23. Pages 23–77 of this issue contain case studies of applications at General Mills, Northern Telecom, and Honeywell.

What Information to Collect?

Skill blocks and core competencies are the basic units required to perform the work and to help an organization be successful. There is virtually no systematic guidance about general blocks or cores to look for in the compensation literature. However, reinventing the wheel is not required. Competencies, knowledge, skills, and abilities have long been studied in psychology and education. The military and others have devoted considerable resources to identify work-related knowledge, skills, and abilities (KSAs) for use in selection, placement, and training. Generally, the source of blocks or cores is the staff with the most expertise in the work: employees and managers. Focus groups or teams of employees actually doing the work are asked to answer the question: What are the skills/competencies required to perform the work?

Case studies are also a source of ideas about skill blocks. Each site appears to be somewhat different; a General Mills production plant divides the production process into four basic blocks with different levels within each block. For example, a technical-knowledge block has three levels: (1) limited ability to operate without direction, (2) partial proficiency, and (3) full competency. Northern Telecom uses different blocks for each of three functions: engineering, technician, and support. Dresser Rand uses general skills and applies them across product lines. There are obvious similarities between these skill blocks and the factor "abilities required to perform the work" that we discussed under job analysis.

Skill Blocks.   Skill blocks are the basic units of knowledge employees must master to perform the work. Each block is divided into skill units and elements as illustrated in Exhibit 3.18. In this case, a skill block, bearing-house assembly, includes five skill units and a total 27 skill elements. As you can see in the exhibit, the skill elements can get as detailed as the task statements collected in job analysis.

Competency.   Competencies are the basic units of knowledge and abilities employees need to acquire in a competency-based plan. Astra-Merck, a new joint venture pharmaceutical company, believes its managerial and professional employees need to develop eight competencies that range from the ability to customize products and services to meet unique customer needs to the ability to empower co-workers to act in support of business objectives. Some consulting firms design competencies that are linked to career development. Exhibit 3.19 shows individuals in sales positions who start acquiring competencies as an apprentice and eventually develop into a strategic and mentor role.

Methods to Use/Whom to Involve?

To date, virtually no attention has been focused on alternative methods (e.g., focus groups, interviews, questionnaires) available to collect skill/competency information. Teams of employees and managers groping their way and muddling through seems to be the approach. This has obvious advantages—high participa-

EXHIBIT 3.18   Sample Skill Block

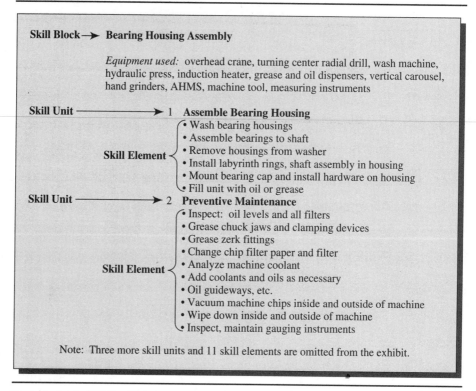

Source: Graham L. O'Neill and Deirdre Lander, "A Framework for Skill-Based Pay Plans," *ACA Journal*, Winter 1993/94, p. 19.

tion and commitment—and equally obvious problems—limited perspective on possible future changes, overreliance on stereotypes, and so on. They are asked the question, "What are the sets of competencies and skills (cores or blocks) required to successfully perform the work, satisfy the customers, and achieve the business objectives?" Our experience has generally shown employee teams to be extremely knowledgeable, highly committed, and fully understanding of the logic underlying the resulting pay structure.

CONTRASTING APPROACHES TO STRUCTURES

Exhibit 3.20 contrasts job-, skill-, and competency-based structures. Pay increases are gained via promotions to more responsible jobs under job-based structures or by acquiring more valued skills/competencies under the other structures. Logically, employees will focus on how to get promoted (experience, performance) or on how to acquire the required skills or competencies (training).

EXHIBIT 3.19   General Competency Profile for Sales Career

Function: Sales
Competency: Industry/Technical Knowledge

Stage I: Apprentice
- Gets to know company, its business units, its policies and procedures
- Learns the business electronics market and how products support customer needs
- Learns differences in competitive product offerings

Stage III: Mentor
- Is looked to as a mentor by others for professional/technical information/guidance
- Applies company's products to customers' conceptual needs (e.g., cost information management, workplace redesign); identifies new applications that extend existing product line

Stage II: Doer
- Applies business electronics design, theory, and concepts to meet various customer needs
- Is familiar with competitive product lines and their strengths and weaknesses
- Presents arguments for using company's products rather than competitor products

Stage IV: Strategic Leader
- Steps outside of existing product line; can see applications and opportunities for major new breakthrough product concepts
- Is sought out by senior management for advice on business issues and product development issues
- Is looked to by others (dealers, end users) as the company's most knowledgeable internal resource regarding marketing and product application

Source: Towers Perrin.

Managers whose employers use job-based plans focus on placing the right people in the right job. A switch to skill/competency-based plans reverses this procedure. Now, managers must assign the right work to the right people, that is, those with the right skills and competencies. As noted earlier, under the skill/competency-based plans, employees are paid for the highest level of skill/competency they have achieved, *regardless of the work they perform.* This is a crucial point about these plans. The top-certified employee at Borg-Warner (see Exhibit 3.16) is certified at A level (which includes B- and C-level skills as well). Even if assigned B- or C-level work, these employees are paid at the higher A rate. This maximizes flexibility in the work force. But it also has risks. If all employees are certified at top rates (which the pay system encourages them to do), an employer may experience higher labor costs than its competitors, which is a price disadvantage in the marketplace. To avoid this, an employer must either control the rate at which employees can certify skill/competency mastery and/or employ fewer people. Absent this offset, the organization's higher labor costs will become a source of competitive disadvantage.

Exhibit 3.20   Comparing Pay Structures Based on Jobs, Skills, and Competencies

	Job-Based	*Skill-Based*	*Competency-Based*
Pay structure	• Based on job performed/market	• Based on skills certified/market	• Based on competency developed/market
Pay increases	• Promotion	• Skill acquisition	• Competency development
Managers' focus	• Link employees to work	• Utilize skills efficiently	• Be sure competencies add value
	• Promotion and placement • Cost control via job pay and budget increase	• Provide training • Control costs via training, certification, and work assignments	• Provide competency-developing opportunities • Control costs via certification and assignments
Employee focus	• Seek promotions to earn more pay	• Seek skills	• Seek competencies
Procedures	• Job analysis • Job evaluation	• Skill analysis • Skill certification	• Competency analysis • Competency certification
Advantages	• Clear expectations • Sense of progress • Pay based on value of work performed	• Continuous learning • Flexibility • Reduced work force	• Continuous learning • Flexibility • Lateral movement
Limitations	• Potential bureaucracy • Potential inflexibility	• Potential bureaucracy • Requires cost controls	• Potential bureaucracy • Requires cost controls

In contrast, a job-based approach controls costs by paying only as much as the work performed is worth, regardless of any greater skills the employee may possess. (Word processors are paid at word-processor rates regardless of whether the person is also qualified to do spreadsheet analysis and fill telephone orders.) So as Exhibit 3.20 suggests, costs are controlled via job rates or via work assignments and budgets.

In addition to potentially higher rates (perhaps offset by fewer employees) and higher training costs, skill/competency plans may have the additional disadvantage of becoming as complex and burdensome as job-based plans. Some recent studies examine the payoffs of skill-based approaches at two facilities. TRW and Ford report that skill-based plans do yield positive productivity improvements while controlling costs. However, no studies have yet been done to assess whether redesigned job-based plans, properly designed and managed, wouldn't be equally effective.[38]

---

[38] Brian Murray and Barry Gerhart, "Early Organization Outcomes from Introduction of Skill-Based Pay," (Working paper 94–26, Center for Advanced Human Resource Studies, Ithaca, NY; Kevin J. Parent and Caroline L. Weber, "Case Study: Does Paying for Knowledge Pay Off," *Compensation and Benefits Review*, September–October 1994, pp. 44–50.

Additionally, questions still remain about a skill/competency system's compliance with the Equal Pay Act. If a member of a protected group has a lower skill-mastery level and lower pay than a white male who is doing the same work, does this violate the equal pay/equal work standard specified in the legislation?[39] Chapters 13 and 14 discuss this and other pay legislation at length.

Summary

Encouraging employee behaviors that help achieve an organization's objectives and foster a sense of fairness among employees are two hallmarks of a useful internal pay structure. One of the first strategic pay decisions is how much to align a pay structure internally compared to aligning it to external market forces. Do not be misled. The issue is not achieving internal consistency versus alignment with external market forces. Rather, the strategic decision focuses on sustaining the optimal balance of internally consistent and externally responsive pay structures that help the organization achieve its mission. Both are required. This section of the book is about one of the first decisions you face in designing pay systems: how much to emphasize pay structures that are internally consistent with the work performed, the organization's structure, and its strategies. Whatever the choice, it needs to support (and be supported by) the organization's overall human resource strategy.

Next, managers must decide whether job and/or individual employee characteristics will be the basic unit of analysis supporting the pay structure. This is followed by deciding what data will be collected, what method(s) will be used to collect it, and who should be involved in the process.

A key test of an effective and equitable pay structure is acceptance of results by managers and employees. The best way to ensure acceptance of job analysis results is to involve employees as well as supervisors in the process. At the minimum, all employees should be informed of purposes and progress of the activity.

If almost everyone agrees about the importance of job analysis for equitable compensation, does that mean everyone does it? Of course not. Unfortunately, job analysis can be tedious and time-consuming. Often the job is given to newly hired compensation analysts, ostensibly to help them learn the organization, but perhaps there's also a hint of "rites of passage" in such assignments.

Alternatives to job-based structures such as skill-based or competency-based systems are being experimented with in many firms. The premise is that basing structures on these other criteria will encourage employees to become more flexible, and fewer workers will be required for the same level of output. Nevertheless, job content remains the conventional criterion for structures.

This completes our discussion of work analysis. The next chapters take the resulting descriptions and evaluate them according to their contributions to the organization goals.

---

[39] G. V. Barrett, "Comparison of Skill-Based Pay with Traditional Job Evaluation Techniques," *Human Resource Management Review* 1, 1991, pp. 97–105.

Review Questions

1. Distinguish between job-based, skill-based, and competency-based structures. Compare their relative advantages and disadvantages.

2. What does job analysis (and skill/competency analysis) have to do with internal consistency?

3. Describe the major decisions involved in job analysis.

4. Distinguish among task, behavioral, and abilities data.

5. What is the critical advantage of quantitative approaches over conventional approaches to job analysis?

6. How would you decide whether to use job-based or skill/competency-based structures?

7. What are the advantages/disadvantages of analyzing a job in great detail versus using a more generic approach?

APPENDIX 3–A

CONVENTIONAL JOB ANALYSIS QUESTIONNAIRE

EXHIBIT 3A.1   General Procedures for Conventional Job Analysis

Step	*Things to Remember or Do*
1. Develop preliminary job information	*a.* Review existing documents in order to develop an initial "big-picture" familiarity with the job: its main mission, its major duties or functions, work flow patterns.
	b. Prepare a preliminary list of duties which will serve as a framework for conducting the interviews.
	c. Make a note of major items which are unclear or ambiguous or that need to be clarified during the data-gathering process.
2. Conduct initial tour of work site	*a.* The initial tour is designed to familiarize the job analyst with the work layout, the tools and equipment that are used, the general conditions of the workplace, and the mechanics associated with the end-to-end performance of major duties.
	b. The initial tour is particularly helpful in those jobs where a first-hand view of a complicated or unfamiliar piece of equipment saves the interviewee the thousand words required to describe the unfamiliar or technical.
	c. For continuity, it is recommended that the first level supervisor-interviewee be designated the guide for the job-site observations.
3. Conduct interviews	*a.* It is recommended that the first interview be conducted with the first-level supervisor who is considered to be in a better position than the jobholders to provide an overview of the job and how the major duties fit together.
	b. For scheduling purposes, it is recommended that no more than two interviews be conducted per day, each interview lasting no more than three hours.
Notes on selection of interviewees	*a.* The interviewees are considered subject matter experts by virtue of the fact that they perform the job (in the case of job incumbents) or are responsible for getting the job done (in the case of first-level supervisors).
	b. The job incumbent to be interviewed should represent the *typical* employee who is knowledgeable about the job (*not* the trainee who is just learning the ropes *nor* the outstanding member of the work unit).
	c. Whenever feasible, the interviewees should be selected with a view towards obtaining an appropriate race/sex mix.

EXHIBIT 3A.1   *(concluded)*

Step	Things to Remember or Do
4. Conduct second tour of work site	*a.* The second tour of the work site is designed to clarify, confirm, and otherwise refine the information developed in the interviews. *b.* As in the initial tour, it is recommended that the same first-level supervisor-interviewee conduct the second walk-through.
5. Consolidate job information	*a.* The consolidation phase of the job study involves piecing together into one coherent and comprehensive job description the data obtained from several sources: supervisor, jobholders, on-site tours, and written materials about the job. *b.* Past experience indicates that one minute of consolidation is required for every minute of interviewing. For planning purposes, at least 5 hours should be set aside for the consolidation phase. *c.* A subject matter expert should be accessible as a resource person to the job analyst during the consolidation phase. The supervisor-interviewee fills this role. *d.* Check your initial preliminary list of duties and questions—all must be answered or confirmed.
6. Verify job description	*a.* The verification phase involves bringing all the interviewees together for the purpose of determining if the consolidated job description is accurate and complete. *b.* The verification process is conducted in a group setting. Types or legibly written copies of the job description (narrative description of the work setting *and* list of task statements) are distributed to the first-level supervisor and the job incumbent interviewees. *c.* Line by line, the job analyst goes through the entire job description and makes notes of any omissions, ambiguities, or needed clarifications. *d.* Collect all materials at the end of the verification meeting.

Job Analysis Report

Date __2-23-95__

Job Analyst __C. Davis__

1. Job Title __Executive Secretary__

2. Department __General Headquarters__

3. No. incumbents ___2___   Interviewed ___2___

4. Relation to other jobs:

    Promotion: From __Secretary-D__   To __Executive Secretary__

    Transfer: From __Administrative Assistant__   To __Executive Secretary__

    Supervision received __From President and/or Chairman of the Board. Works under minimal supervision.__

    Supervision given __Regularly to other clerical personnel.__

5. Summary of Job:

    Personal Secretary to President and/or Chairman of the Board. Performs variety of secretarial and clerical duties including transcribing dictation, filing, routing mail, as well as answering telephone and written inquiries. Exercises discretion in handling confidential and specialized information, screening telephone calls and letters, arranging meetings, and handling inquiries during superior's absence.

6. Equipment used: Typewriter, word processor, dictaphone and telephone.

    Working conditions:

    Hazards (list): N/A   Noise exposure: None
    Work space and quarters: Office environment   Miscellaneous: —

    Job training:

    A. Required experience: (include other jobs)

    Four years of secretarial-stenographic experience or the equivalent.

    B. Outside educational courses:

	Time in semesters/quarters
Vocational courses: Typing, stenography	2 semesters
College courses:	None

C. In-house training courses:

	Time in months
Courses: Basic and Advanced Word Processing	1/2 month

Task Statement Worksheet

Task Statement: Opens and organizes mail addressed to superior.

1. Equipment used—

2. Knowledge required   Must be well versed on superior's responsibilities, how superior's job fits into overall organization.

3. Skills required—

4. Abilities required   Discretion. Organization skills.

5. Time spent and frequency of task performance (hourly, daily, monthly)
   Time varies by assignment. Weekly frequency.

6. Level of difficulty/consequence of error
   Relatively difficult, little effect of error.

Task Statement: Establishes, maintains, and revises files.

1. Equipment used   Typewriter, word processor.

2. Knowledge required   Understanding of organization and responsibilities of superior.

3. Skills required   Typing and word processing, filing.

4. Abilities required   Ability to organize and categorize information.

5. Time spent and frequency of task performance (hourly, daily, monthly)
   One hour spent daily.

6. Level of difficulty/consequence of error   Relatively easy, but moderate to serious consequences if information mishandled.

APPENDIX 3–B

EXAMPLE OF QUANTITATIVE JOB ANALYSIS: THE POSITION INFORMATION QUESTIONNAIRE

Position Information Questionnaire

Introduction

The 3M Position Information Questionnaire (PIQ) is a key part of 3M's job evaluation process. Job evaluation involves a comparison of jobs in relation to other 3M jobs. Job evaluation is a systematic way to help management classify jobs and pay for work appropriately.

The PIQ collects information about the work you do. It takes into account what 3M considers to be most important in the work that you perform. The PIQ asks questions about:

- Skills/Knowledge Applied
- Complexity of Duties
- Impact on Business
- Working Conditions

It will take some time for you to complete the PIQ, but it will be time well-spent. 3M needs the information to properly understand your job and its responsibilities. Your supervisor will give you enough time during normal working hours to complete the PIQ.

Suggestions For Completing The PIQ

Before you begin to write . . .

1. Read through the entire questionnaire.
2. Think about what you do in your work - daily, weekly, and monthly. What are the most important things you do?
3. Make a few notes to yourself, either on a separate sheet of paper or in the margins of the PIQ, outlining the key points you will make on each question.

  Note: If you are unsure about the meaning of a certain question, contact your supervisor, your Human Resources Manager, or call Compensation for assistance.

Then, fill out the questionnaire . . .

1. Begin completing the questions when you feel that you are familiar with the PIQ and have thought through each question.
2. When you have finished filling out the PIQ, put it aside for a day or two. Then reread it to see if you have forgotten anything. Add any additional points you may want to make.

  Important Points to Keep in Mind

  - Since the PIQ is used to describe many jobs, you will probably find questions that do not apply to your job. Do not be concerned about this. What is important is that you find the appropriate places to explain the key parts of your job. If not, there is space for additional comments at the end of the PIQ.

  - The PIQ, and 3M's job evaluation process, considers many aspects of your work. Do not try to explain everything about your job in any one question. You should be able to make each point you feel is important. Again, use the space for additional comments at the end of this document if necessary.

When you have finished the questionnaire . . .

1. Return the completed PIQ to your supervisor who will review it for consistency and completeness. He/she will discuss any possible changes with you.

2. You and your supervisor must sign the last page of the PIQ.

3. Your supervisor will send the completed PIQ to you Human Resources Manager in St. Paul.

Remember . . .

The PIQ is not used to measure your performance on your job. It is not used for performance appraisal. The focus is on the nature of the work that you do, the job's duties and requirements, **not** your performance or personal characteristics.

Obtaining information about what employees do in their work is an important step in defining relationships between jobs and in establishing a competitive pay program. This information helps 3M maintain appropriate relationships between jobs inside 3M, and analyze the competitiveness in pay between 3M jobs and similar jobs outside 3M.

Your input and efforts in completing the PIQ are important. Thank you for participating in this process.

I. Job Overview

Job Summary	What is the main purpose of your job? (Why does it exist and what does the work contribute to 3M?)
	    Examples: To provide secretarial support in our department by performing office and administrative duties.
	                To purchase goods and services that meet specifications at the least cost.
	                To perform systems analysis involved in the development, installation, and maintenance of computer applications.
	
	Hint: It may help to list the duties first before answering this question.

Duties and Respon-sibilities	What are your job's main duties and responsibilities? (These are the major work activities that usually take up a significant amount of your work time and occur regularly as you perform your work.) In the spaces below, list your job's five most important or most frequent duties. Then, in the boxes, estimate the percentage of time you spend on each duty.	Percentage of Time Spent (Total may be less than but not more than 100%)
	1.	
	2.	
	3.	
	4.	
	5.	

II. Skills/Knowledge Applied

Formal Training or Education	What is the level of formal training/education that is needed to start doing your job?
	    Example: High School, 2 Year Vo-Tech in Data Processing, Bachelor of Science in Chemistry.
	In some jobs, a combination of education and job-related experience can substitute for academic degrees.
	    Example: Bachelors Degree in Accounting or completion of 2 years of general business courses plus 3 - 4 years work
	            experience in an accounting field.

	What additional training, certification program, or licensing requirement is needed in order to start doing your job? Example: CPR training, state certification in boiler operation, licensing for pharmacists.

Experience	In addition to the formal training/education or equivalent experience you stated was necessary, how many months or years or previous job-related experience are needed to start doing your job?
	    Note: "None" can be a correct answer. For example, there is typically no previous work experience required for a new
	        college graduate hired as a beginning engineer.
	
	Months: Years: ☐ None

Skills/ Compet-encies	What important skills, competencies, or abilities are needed to do the work that you do? (Please give examples for each skill area you identify.)
	A. Coordinating Skills (such as scheduling activities, organizing/maintaining records)
	Are coordinating skills required? ☐ Yes ☐ No If yes, give examples of specific skills needed
	Example
	B. Administrative Skills (such as monitoring financial data, interpreting policies and procedures)
	Are administrative skills required? ☐ Yes ☐ No If yes, give examples of specific skills needed
	Example
	C. Analytical Skills (such as drawing conclusions from statistical data, examining alternative methods)
	Are analytical skills required? ☐ Yes ☐ No If yes, give examples of specific skills needed
	Example

Note: Additional skills/competencies included on questionnaire:

      D. Engineering Skills

      E. Communication Skills

      F. Influencing Skills

      G. Computer Skills

      H. Creative Skills

      I. Vocational Skills

      J. Basic Leadership Skills

      K. Advanced Leadership Skills

      L. Manual Skills

      M. Mechanical Skills

      N. Short-Term Planning Skills

      O. Long-Term Planning Skills

      P. Mathematical Skills

      Q. Scientific Skills

      R. Software/Word Processing Skills

Skills/ Compet- encies	S. Other Special Skills		
	Are other special skills skills required? ☐ Yes ☐ No If yes, give examples of specific skills needed		
	Example		
	Most Critical Skills	Of all the skills named in the preceding section, which are the most important to the work that you do? In order of importance list the letter codes as used above.	
		Example: 1.C, 2.P, 3.B, 4,R for Analytical, Mathematical, Administrative, and Software/Word Processing Skills	
	1. _____ 2. _____ 3. _____ 4. _____		

III. Complexity of Duties

Structure and Variation of Work	How processes and tasks within your work are determined, and how you do them are important to understanding your work at 3M. Describe the work flow in your job. Think of the major focus of your job or think of the work activities on which you spend the most time.
	1. From whom/where (title, not person) do you receive work?
	2. What processes or tasks do you perform to complete it?
	3. What are typical outputs?
Problem Solving and Analysis	Each job at 3M encounters problem situations, but jobs vary in how solutions are sought and found. Give three examples of problems you must solve in your work on a regular (e.g., daily, weekly, monthly) basis:
	1.
	2.
	3.
	Give an example of a particularly difficult problem that you face in your work.
	Why does it occur?
	How often does it occur?
	What special skills and/or resources are needed to solve this difficult problem?
	Within your work unit, is anyone else able to help solve the problem? Explain.
Creativity and Innovation	In which parts of your job can you be creative and innovative, to introduce new ideas or better ways to do things? Give examples; please be specific. Examples: Finding new uses for an existing product, modifying methods for tracking information, changing procedures to cut 3M shipping costs.

IV. Impact on Business

Independence/ Nature of Work Review	Review of work can occur in different ways; for example, by direct supervision, by computer through built-in checks and balances, or by customers. Who (title, not person) reviews your work?
	What is the reviewer looking for? Examples: Accuracy of work, getting the job done on time, results of specific projects, accomplishment of broad objectives.
	Is all your work reviewed, or does the review focus more on the end result? Explain.
	When you come upon situations that do not fit established policies, procedures or practices, what do you do? Examples: Refer all questions to supervisor, consult with a more experienced co-worker, make a decision and have it approved.

Types of Decisions Made	Give three examples of the types of decisions you regularly make on the job.
	   Examples: Directing a telephone call to the right person, determining the content of a new report, allocating work among those you
	         supervise, approving proposed projects.
	
	1.
	
	2.
	
	3.
	
	If decisions in your job were not made properly, what kinds of errors would be likely to occur?
	   Examples: Inaccurate calculations, misfiling documents, losing data.
	
	What would be the likely results of such errors?
	   Examples: Costly build-up of inventory, significant time loss, delayed production, loss of customer.
	
	What would need to be done to correct the error of errors? Who would be involved?

Restricted Information	What types of 3M restricted information do you see or learn about on your job?
	   Examples: Proprietary processes, trade secrets, costs, human resource-related information.
	
	How often do you see or use this information?
	☐ Regularly ☐ Occasionally ☐ Rarely ☐ Not at all
	In the normal course of doing your job, how often might you have the chance to disclose restricted information?
	☐ Frequently ☐ Occasionally ☐ Once in a while ☐ Not at all Give an example of how disclosure might happen.
	
	What would be the impact if restricted information were disclosed?
	   Examples: Damage to an important division objective, internal dissatisfaction.

Working With Others	This section asks about the level and purpose of your contacts with others while doing your job. In describing the purpose of your contacts, try to use key words such as give, or exchange information, discuss, explain, convince, or persuade.

Internal Contacts

List the titles of other 3M jobs outside your immediate work unit with which you have regular, work-related contact. Describe the purpose and nature of the contacts.

Title	Purpose/Nature
Examples: Division Accountant Purchasing Agent	Discuss pricing strategy Explain invoice price discrepancy

External Contacts

List the titles and, if appropriate, companies/agencies outside 3M with which you have regular, business-related contacts. Describe the purpose of the contacts. List customers as a category, not by individual names.

Title/Company/Agency	Purpose/Nature
Examples: Customers University of Minnesota	Explain product features Discuss research contract

	Multinational/Global Responsibilities
Working With Others (cont.)	Do you have contacts with individuals or companies, including 3M subsidiaries, in countries other than the United States? ☐ Yes ☐ No ➤ If no, go to next section.
	If yes, what is the nature of these contacts? Examples: Telephone conversations, transmitting information, consultations, monitoring plan implementation.
	What percent of time is spent dealing with non-US individuals or companies? ☐ Greater than 50% ☐ 25 - 49% ☐ 10-24% ☐ Less than 10%
	Language Skills
	Do you need to speak, read or write any language other than English to perform your work? ☐ Yes ☐ No ➤ If yes, what are these languages, in order of importance?
	1. 2. 3.
	Explain how these other languages are used on the job. Examples: To explain 3M policies, to take notes in meetings.

Financial Respon-sibility	Some 3M jobs are **accountable** for money management - either income, expenses, assets, or a combination of these. These are typically jobs with leadership, supervisory, or management responsibility.
	Note: To help you decide whether or not you should complete this section, ask yourself this question: "Am I held directly responsible for producing income, controlling expenses, or managing or safeguarding assets?" If your answer is no, enter "4" on each of the lines under the "Impact" column. Otherwise, continue.
	
	How does your job directly affect 3M's revenue, expenses or assets?
	
	Directions:
	1. Estimate the dollar amount(s) for which you are accountable on an annual basis.
	2. Use the impact scale to describe your accountability.
	3. Briefly describe the nature of your financial responsibility in the space provided.
	    Examples: Recommends and monitors spending of advertising budget, approves inventory levels that meet requirements,
	                   minimizes investment in accounts receivable.
	
	Impact Scale
	1 - Overall control or managerial responsibility (Establishes objectives, approves activities)
	2 - Important role in effective management (At liberty to implement approved activities)
	3 - Participative or advisory role in planning/implementation
	4 - No responsibility
	
	Note: A "0" dollar amount followed by a "4" on impact is an acceptable answer.

	Annual Dollars	**Impact**	**Description**
Revenue	$		
Expense	$		
Assets	$		

This action is only for jobs that include responsibility for the work of others. This responsibility can be very limited (example: allocating work), very broad (example: hiring, terminating, merit rating), or indirect (example: leading task forces).

☐ If your job does not have any of these responsibilities, check this box and proceed to the next section. Otherwise, continue.

Please list the number of people for whom you do any of the following: then provide the titles of the jobs supervised.

Note: Do not report intermittent or occasional supervisory duties. Example of what not to list include: process engineers supervising production workers during test runs, filling-in for an absent supervisor or manager, singular (nonrepeating) leadership of a task force or short-term project.

	Type of Work Direction Provided	Number of people	
		Exempt	Nonexempt
Work Direction	Direct supervision of others (conduct performance appraisals, make hiring decisions)		
	Titles of jobs:		
	Work direction of employees who are not direct reports (assign or allocate work, oversee corporate or divisional program)		
	Titles of jobs:		
	Frequent team leadership (task forces, project teams)		
	Titles of jobs:		
	Frequent direct supervision of non-3M employees (contract workers, consultants)		
	Titles of jobs:		
	Other (explain)		
	Titles of jobs:		

V. Working conditions
This section examines each job in terms of physical demands and environmental factors.

Work Position	What percentage of each day do you spend in these work positions? Your responses should total 100%	
	Nonconfined sitting (free to move about at will)	%
	Confined sitting (cannot readily move about)	%
	Standing or walking	%
	Crouching, crawling, climbing, or other nonsitting, nonstanding positions	%
Activity Summary	Approximately what percentage of your work time do you spend on: (Total need not equal 100%. Give examples) **Examples**	
	Section A — Finger/hand manipulation	%
	Section A — Lifting/carrying/pushing/pulling	%
	Approximately what percentage of your work time do you spend on: (Total need not equal 100%. Give examples)	
	Section B — Mental concentration	%
	Section B — Visual concentration	%

Risk Exposure

Describe any risk of injury to which you may be exposed while on the job. State the percentage of the work day you are exposed, assuming normal safety precautions are taken. State the possible consequence if an accident were to occur. Then, check the degree of attention required to minimize risks.

Risk Description & Possible Consequence Example: Chemical spill may require medical care but disability unlikely 5%	%	Precaution Required
.		☐ Ordinary care and attention
		☐ Safety rules, training or protective equipment
		☐ Special skill/high level alertness

Environ-mental Comfort Level	Describe any noises, odors, drafts, dust, temperature extremes, special clothing or other discomforts associated with your job. State the approximate percentage of the work day you are exposed.	
		%
		%

VI. General Comments

General Comments	What percentage of your job duties do you feel was captured in this questionnaire?			
	☐ 0 - 25%	☐ 26 - 50%	☐ 51 - 75%	☐ 76 - 100%
	What aspect of your job was not covered adequately by this questionnaire?			

Important

Review your PIQ to make sure that you have not overlooked any important information.

When you have finished, give the PIQ to your supervisor/manager. He or she will discuss any possible changes with you. Finally, both you and your supervisor must read and sign below.

We have jointly reviewed and discussed the responses to this questionnaire and believe that they are representative of the position being described.

Employee Signature	Date
Supervisor/Manager Signature	Date

Note: Employee signature not required where the supervisor/manager has completed the PIQ for a newly created job.

YOUR TURN

JOB ANALYSIS

1. Use the job analysis questionnaire in Appendix 3–A to describe a specific job you presently hold or have held in the past. This can be a part-time job or volunteer work for which you were not paid. Be sure to put your name on the questionnaire.

2. After you have completed the questionnaire, pick a teammate (or the instructor will assign one) and exchange completed questionnaires with your teammate.

3. Write a job description for your teammate's job. Does the questionnaire give you sufficient information? Is there additional information that would be helpful?

4. Exchange descriptions. Critique the job descriptions written by your teammate. Does it adequately capture all the important job aspects? Does it indicate which aspects are most important?

5. Save the description. We will examine it again in a later case.

CHAPTER

4

Evaluating Work: Job Evaluation, Skill/Competency-Based Plans, and Market Pricing

Chapter Outline

My 14-year-old daughter absolutely refuses to go shopping with me. She's embarrassed by my behavior. (Can you imagine that?) The last time I took her to the mall to help her pick out (and pay for) sneakers, I spent most of my time interrogating the assistant store manager about how he was paid—more precisely, how his pay compared to that of the stock clerks, the manager, and regional managers. My daughter claims I do this everywhere I go. *Compensationitis*, she calls it. And I know it's contagious, because a colleague of mine grills his seatmates on airplanes. He's learned the pay rates for captains who pilot Boeing 747 jets versus those who pilot the 101A Airbus for American Airlines. Reporters often catch compensationitis, too, particularly when writing about salaries that are paid by taxpayers. For example, a recent Associated Press article contrasted the pay and work schedule of piano virtuoso Vladimir Feltsman, a former Soviet dissident, who earns $101,854 a year for teaching 13 music classes a semester at the State University of New York at New Paltz.[1] His pay contrasts with that of graduate assistant Frankie Van Meter, who teaches English at SUNY Albany. She reports spending about 35 hours a week at what is supposed to be a 20-hour-a-week job. Van Meter earns $9,100 a year.

How does any organization, including your school, go about valuing work? The next time you go to the supermarket, check out the different types of work there: store manager, produce manager, front-end manager, deli workers, butchers, stock clerks, checkout people, bakers—the list is long, and the work surprisingly diverse. How does the supermarket value work? Specifically, what techniques does it use, and does the technique really matter? But be careful—compensationitis is contagious, and it can embarrass your friends and relations.

The next two chapters discuss techniques used to value work. The end result is an internally consistent pay structure that will be acceptable to employees and reinforce them for achieving organization objectives through continuous learning, multiskilling, seeking additional responsibilities, promotions, and so on. Ultimately, the pay structure helps the organization achieve its competitive advantage by influencing employee behaviors.

---

[1] David Bauder, "Galaxy of SUNY's Top Stars Under Fire," *Albany Times-Union,* April 30, 1995, pp. A1, A6.

Three basic techniques are examined in this chapter: (1) job evaluation, (2) skill/competency-based plans, and (3) market pricing. This chapter first discusses various perspectives on job evaluation and some of the key decisions, establishing the purposes and choosing among alternative methods. Next, it does the same for skill/competency-based approaches and market pricing. Chapter 5 continues the discussion by focusing on the importance of achieving commitment and involvement of employees, as well as evaluating the usefulness of the various techniques.

JOB-BASED STRUCTURES: JOB EVALUATION

Job evaluation uses information about work to establish a pay structure. Recall the flow chart (Exhibit 3.4) from the last chapter. It pictures everything focusing on information about work. Job analysis collects information. Job descriptions summarize it, and serve as input for evaluating the jobs in order to develop a job structure. The evaluation is based on many factors: content of the work, skills required to perform the work, value of the work to the organization, the culture of the workplace, and external market forces. The potential to blend internal and external market forces represents both a major contribution of job evaluation and a source of controversy. This will become evident as we discuss the variety of definitions and decisions that surround job evaluation.

CONTENT, VALUE, AND MARKET LINKS: DEFINING JOB EVALUATION

Perspectives on job evaluation are as diverse as the blind men's elephant. Job evaluation simultaneously includes (1) distinctions between content and value of the work, (2) linking the content of the work with the external market, and (3) aspects of measurement and administration.

Content and Value

The usual end result of job evaluation is a hierarchy of jobs or groups of jobs in the organization. Perspectives vary on whether these hierarchies are based on the jobs' content, their value, or on some combination of both.

Job content refers to the skills required, the degree of responsibilities assumed, and/or similar factors. The *value* of jobs can refer to the relative value they add to organization goals, to their external market rates, or to some other agreed-upon rates set through collective bargaining or other negotiated process.

A structure based on comparing the relative content of jobs may differ from one based on relative value. This occurs, for example, when the relative value added by the work performed is more (or less) in one organization than in another. The value added by a compensation specialist to a firm whose earnings are generated through sales of manufactured goods or engineering expertise may differ from the value added by that specialist to a consulting firm whose revenues come through the sale of compensation expertise. The skills are similar, yet their relative value to each organization's strategy differs.

Linking Content with the External Market

Some see job evaluation as a mechanism that links job content with the external market rates. In this view, the structure resulting from job evaluation does not completely reflect the job's relative value unless it incorporates external market influences.[2] Consequently, certain aspects of job content (e.g., skills required and customer contacts) take on value based on their relationship to market wages. Because higher skill levels or willingness to work more closely with customers usually commands higher wages in the labor market, then skill level and nature of customer contacts become useful criteria for establishing differences in pay among jobs. If some aspect of job content, such as working conditions, is not related to wages paid in the external labor market, then it is excluded in the job evaluation. Accordingly, since job content obtains value through the external market, it makes little sense to assert that content has an intrinsic value. It is the role of job evaluation to integrate job content with external market forces.

But not everyone agrees. A developer of the Hay job-evaluation plan (perhaps the most widely used plan by large corporations), states that the "measures are independent of the market and encourage rational determination of the basis for pricing job content."[3] They claim that job evaluation establishes the relative values of jobs based on their content, independent of a link to the market. The same issue faces developers of competency-based plans: Do competencies take on value by virtue of their internal fit with the mission of the organization, by their value in the external market, or by some combination?

"Measure for Measure" versus "Much Ado about Nothing"

Some researchers believe that job evaluation takes on the trappings of measurement (objective, numerical, generalizable, documented, and reliable). If it is viewed as a measurement instrument, then job evaluation can be judged according to technical standards. Just as with employment tests, the reliability and validity of job evaluation plans can be compared.

---

[2] Donald P. Schwab, "Job Evaluation and Pay Setting: Concepts and Practices," in *Comparable Worth: Issues and Alternatives*, ed. E. Robert Livernash (Washington, DC: Equal Employment Advisory Council, 1980), pp. 49–77.

[3] Alvin O. Bellak, "Comparable Worth: A Practitioner's View," in *Comparable Worth: Issue for the 80's*, vol. 1 (Washington, DC: U.S. Civil Rights Commission, 1985).

Those involved in actually making pay decisions have a different view. They see job evaluation as a process to help gain acceptance of pay differences among jobs, an administrative procedure through which the parties become involved and committed. It invites give and take—an exchange of views. Employees, union representatives, and managers can haggle over the relative worth of jobs— "the rules of the game." As in sports contests, we are more willing to accept the results if we believe the rules are fair.[4] Consensus building often requires active participation by all those involved.

Livernash summarizes:

> Job evaluation is not a rigid, objective, analytical procedure. Neither is it a meaningless process of rationalization. If a group of people with reasonable knowledge of certain jobs rate (evaluate) them, there will be frequent small differences of opinion, some major differences as well, but also a high degree of general agreement. The application of group judgment through the rating process normally produces an *improved pay structure, but extreme attitudes as to the accuracy of ratings are difficult to defend.*[5]

So users may differ on whether they believe job evaluation is a measurement or merely a procedure. Some say the procedure is eminently just and absolutely fair. Others say it is just fair. The issue will arise again when we discuss comparable worth in Chapter 14, Pay Discrimination. For now, the following definition seems to include many of the nuances attributed to job evaluation.

Job evaluation is a systematic procedure designed to aid in establishing pay differentials among jobs within a single employer.

MAJOR DECISIONS

The major job evaluation decisions are depicted in Exhibit 4.1. They include (1) establish the purpose(s) of job evaluation, (2) decide whether to use single or multiple plans, (3) choose among alternative approaches, (4) obtain the involvement of relevant stakeholders, and (5) evaluate its usefulness. The first three of these decisions are discussed in this chapter; the remaining two are covered in the next.

---

[4] Robert Folger and Mary Konovsky, "Effects of Procedural and Distributive Justice on Reactions to Pay Raise Decisions," *Academy of Management Journal*, March 1989, pp. 115–30; Jerald Greenburg, "A Taxonomy of Organizational Justice Theories," *Academy of Management Review* 12 (1987), pp. 9–22.

[5] E. Robert Livernash, "Internal Wage Structure," in *New Concepts in Wage Determination*, ed. George W. Taylor and Frank C. Pierson (New York: McGraw-Hill, 1957).

EXHIBIT 4.1   Determining an Internally Consistent Job Structure

Internal consistency:
Work relationships
within the   →   Job analysis   →   Job description   →   Job evaluation   →   Job structure
organization

Some Major Decisions in Job Evaluation
- Establish purpose of evaluation.
- Decide whether to use single or multiple plans.
- Choose among alternative approaches.
- Obtain involvement of relevant stakeholders.
- Evaluate plan's usefulness.

Establish the Purpose

Why bother with job evaluation? Because it aids in establishing a pay structure that is internally equitable to employees and consistent with the goals of the organization.

More specific purposes of job evaluation often include the following:

- Signal to employees what is valued in their work and what supports the organization's strategy and its success.
- Help integrate pay with a job's relative contributions to the organization.
- Establish a workable, agreed-upon pay structure.
- Assist employees to adapt to organization changes by improving their understanding of what is valued.
- Simplify and rationalize the pay relationships among jobs and reduce the role that chance, favoritism, and bias may play.
- Aid in setting pay for new, unique, or changing jobs.
- Reduce disputes and grievances over pay differences among jobs.
- Support other human resource programs such as career planning and training.

However, no one has studied the effects of formal job evaluation on any of these objectives.[6] Since they guide the design and administration of job evaluation,

---

[6] Sandra M. Emerson, "Job Evaluation: A Barrier to Excellence?" *Compensation and Benefits Review*, January–February 1991, pp. 38–51; Richard Bunning, "Models for Skill-Based Pay Plans," *HR Magazine*, February 1992, pp. 62–64.

objectives need to be specified. But initially established objectives too often get lost in complex procedures and bureaucracy that sprout around job evaluation.

Lawler derides job evaluation, saying it "emphasizes control and focuses on carefully prescribed and described activities. It supports a top down, control oriented, bureaucracy."[7] These criticisms have validity when job evaluation is used for its own sake rather than as an aid to achieve behavioral objectives. Similar criticisms have been leveled at skill/competency-based approaches, especially by managers who have extended experience with them. Recently, a vice president at General Mills lamented that the skill-based approach at one of its facilities was more bureaucratic and technically complex than the job evaluation plan it replaced.[8] So an organization is best served by establishing its objectives for the job evaluation process and using them as a constant yardstick to evaluate the usefulness of these techniques.

Single versus Multiple Plans

Rarely will an employer evaluate all jobs in the organization at one time. More typically, related groups of jobs, for example, production, engineering, or marketing, will receive attention. Many employers design different evaluation plans for different types of work. They do so because they believe that the work content is too diverse to be adequately evaluated by one plan. For example, production jobs may vary in terms of working conditions, manipulative skills, and knowledge of statistical quality control required. But engineering and marketing jobs do not vary on these factors, nor are those factors particularly important in engineering or marketing work. Rather, other factors such as technical knowledge and skills and the contacts with customers may be relevant.

The decision about single versus multiple plans is also important in the comparable-worth controversy. The issue is whether the jobs usually found within a single firm can be adequately evaluated by a single plan.[9] Advocates argue that an operational definition of comparable worth hinges on the application of a single evaluation system across all job families, both to rank order and to set salaries.[10] Yet to define universal factors in such a way that they accurately evaluate all jobs within a single employer and at the same time remain acceptable

---

[7] E. E. Lawler, "What's Wrong with Point-Factor Job Evaluation," *Compensation and Benefits Review*, March–April 1986, pp. 20–28.

[8] G. V. Barrett and D. Doverspike, "Another Defense of Point-Factor Job Evaluation," *Personnel*, March 1989, pp. 33–36.

[9] Donald J. Treiman and Heidi J. Hartmann, eds., *Women, Work and Wages: Equal Pay for Jobs of Equal Value* (Washington, DC: National Academy Press, 1981); D. Treiman, ed., *Job Evaluation: An Analytic Review*, Interim Report to the Equal Employment Opportunity Commission (Washington, DC: National Academy Press, 1981).

[10] Helen Remick, *Comparable Worth and Wage Discrimination* (Philadelphia: Temple University Press, 1984). See also Karin Allport, "Equal Pay for Equal Work? Of Course," *Across the Board* 17, no. 10 (October 1980).

to all parties imposes a burden on a single plan.[11] This issue is examined again in Chapter 14, Pay Discrimination.

Rather than using either universal factors or entirely unique factors for each type of work, some employers, notably Hewlett-Packard, use a core set of common factors and another set of factors unique to particular occupational or functional areas (finance, manufacturing, software and systems, sales). Their experience suggests that unique factors tailored to different job families are more likely to be acceptable to employees and managers and easier to verify as work related than are generalized universal factors.

Choose among Methods

*getting all involved
μ GT – SUPV – WORKER*

Three fundamental job evaluation methods are in use: ranking, classification, factor comparison, and point method. Uncounted variations of these methods exist. The point method is by far the most commonly used method. The following sections examine each of the methods and provide examples of some adaptations. All of the methods assume that an accurate job analysis has been translated into useful job descriptions.

RANKING

Ranking simply orders the job descriptions from highest to lowest based on a definition of relative value or contribution to the organization's success. Our experience suggests that it is common in small- to medium-sized firms. Ranking is the simplest, fastest, easiest to understand and explain to employees, and the least expensive method, at least initially. However, you shall see that if used improperly, it can create problems by posing difficult and potentially expensive solutions.

Two ways of ranking are usually considered: alternation ranking and paired comparison. *Alternation ranking* orders job descriptions alternately at each extreme. Exhibit 4.2 illustrates the method. Agreement is reached among evaluators on which jobs are the most and least valuable, then the next most and least valued, and so on, until all the jobs have been ordered. In the exhibit, evaluators agreed that the job of master welder was the most valued of the six jobs listed in the exhibit and that receiving clerk was the least valued. Then they selected most and least valued from the four remaining jobs on the list.

The *paired comparison* method compares all possible pairs of jobs using a matrix as shown in Exhibit 4.3. Starting at the top left cell and moving to the

---

[11] Legislation in Ontario, Canada, requires single plans for each bargaining unit with an employer. Thus, a single employer could have three plans if the Teamsters Union represented one occupation, and the Sheetmetal Workers Union another. An additional plan is required for employees who are not in a bargaining unit. *Pay Equity Implementation Series* (Toronto, Ontario, Canada: The Pay Equity Commission, 1994).

EXHIBIT 4.2   Alternation Ranking

Jobs		Rank
Number	Title	Most Valued
1	Shear operator	Master welder
2	Electrician	Electrician
3	Punch press operator	
4	Master welder	
5	Grinder	
6	Receiving clerk	Receiving clerk
		Least Valued

EXHIBIT 4.3   Paired Comparison Ranking

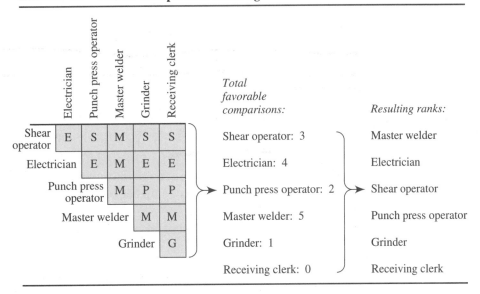

right, each pair of jobs is compared. The higher-ranked job is entered in the cell. For example, of the shear operator and the electrician, the electrician is ranked higher. The electrician is entered in the cell. Of the shear operator and the punch press operator, the shear opertor is ranked higher. When all comparisons have been completed, the job most frequently judged "more valuable" becomes the highest ranked job, and so on. Alternation ranking and paired comparison methods may be more reliable (produce similar results consistently) than simple ranking.

Ranking Has Drawbacks.   The criteria or factors on which the jobs are ranked are usually so poorly defined, if they are specified at all, that the evaluations can become subjective opinions that are difficult, if not impossible, to explain and justify in work-related terms. Further, evaluator(s) using this method must be knowledgeable about every single job under study. The numbers alone turn what should be a simple task into a formidable one—50 jobs require 1,225 comparisons; and as organizations change, it is difficult to remain knowledgeable about all jobs. Some organizations try to overcome this difficulty by ranking jobs within single departments and merging the results. However, even though the ranking appears simple, fast, and inexpensive, in the long run, the results are difficult to defend, and costly solutions may be required to overcome the problems created. However, in simplified structures with broad, generic jobs (e.g., Martin Marietta's four levels of engineers), ranking is appealing.

CLASSIFICATION

Picture a large bookcase with many shelves. Each shelf is labeled with a paragraph describing the kinds of books on that shelf and, perhaps, one or two representative titles. This same approach describes the classification system of job evaluation. Job descriptions are slotted into a series of classes that cover the range of jobs. Class descriptions are the labels that serve as the standard for comparing job descriptions. Each class is described in such a way that it captures sufficient work detail, yet is general enough to cause little difficulty in slotting each job onto its appropriate "shelf" or class.

The classes may be described further by naming benchmark jobs that fall into each class. A benchmark job has the following characteristics:

- Its contents are well known, and relatively stable over time.
- The job is common across a number of different employers. It is not unique to a particular employer.
- It represents the entire range of jobs being evaluated.
- It is accepted in the external labor market for setting wages.

Writing class descriptions can be troublesome when jobs from several occupations or job families are covered by a single plan. Although greater specificity of class definition improves the reliability of evaluation, it also limits the variety of jobs that can easily be classified. For example, class definitions written with sales jobs in mind may make it difficult to slot office or administrative jobs and vice versa. You can see the difficulty by examining the class definitions from the federal government's 18-class evaluation system (see Exhibit 4.4). The point of using benchmark jobs is to anchor the comparisons for each job class. Anchoring the classes in this way has the advantage of illustrating the typical job in a class.

In practice, the job descriptions not only are compared to the standard class descriptions and benchmark jobs but also to each other, to ensure that jobs

EXHIBIT 4.4 Examples of General Schedule Descriptions for the Federal Government's Job Classification Method

Grade-General Schedule 1 includes all classes of positions the duties of which are to be performed, under immediate supervision, with little or no latitude for the exercise of independent judgment, (1) the simplest routine work in office, business, or fiscal operations, or (2) elementary work of a subordinate technical character in a professional, scientific, or technical field.

Grade-General Schedule 5 includes all classes of positions the duties of which are (1) to perform, under general supervision, difficult and responsible work in office, business, or fiscal administration, or comparable subordinate technical work in a professional, scientific, or technical field, requiring in either case (A) considerable training and supervisory or other experience, (B) broad working knowledge of a special subject matter or of office, laboratory, engineering, scientific, or other procedure and practice, and (C) the exercise of independent judgment in a limited field; (2) to perform, under immediate supervision, and with little opportunity for the exercise of independent judgment, simple and elementary work requiring professional, scientific, or technical training equivalent to that represented by graduation from a college or university of recognized standing but requiring little or no experience; or (3) to perform other work of equal importance, difficulty, and responsibility, and requiring comparable qualifications.

Grade-General Schedule 9 includes all classes of positions the duties of which are (1) to perform, under general supervision, very difficult and responsible work along special technical, supervisory, or administrative experience which has (A) demonstrated capacity for sound independent work, (B) thorough and fundamental knowledge of a special and complex subject matter, or of the profession, art, or science involved, and (C) considerable latitude for the exercise of independent judgment; (2) with considerable latitude for the exercise of independent judgment, to perform moderately difficult and responsible work, requiring (A) professional, scientific, or technical training equivalent to that represented by graduation from a college or university of recognized standing, and (B) considerable additional professional, scientific, or technical training or experience which has demonstrated capacity for sound independent work; or (3) to perform other work of equal importance, difficulty, and responsibility, and requiring comparable qualifications.

Grade-General Schedule 13 includes all classes of positions the duties of which are (1) to perform, under administrative direction, with wide latitude for the exercise of independent judgment work of unusual difficulty and responsibility along special technical, supervisory, or administrative lines, requiring extended specialized, supervisory, or administrative training and experience which has demonstrated leadership and marked attainments; (2) to serve as assistant head of a major organization involving work of comparable level within a bureau; (3) to perform, under administrative direction, with wide latitude for the exercise of independent judgment, work of unusual difficulty and responsibility requiring extended professional, scientific, or technical training and experience which has demonstrated leadership and marked attainments in professional, scientific, or technical research, practice, or administration; or (4) to perform other work of equal importance, difficulty, and responsibility, and requiring comparable qualifications.

within each class are more similar to each other than to adjacent classes. The final result is a series of classes with a number of jobs in each. The jobs within each class are considered to be equal (similar) work and will be paid equally. Jobs in different classes should be dissimilar and may have different pay rates.

The Federal Government's General Schedule

Classification systems are widely used in the public sector. Although classification is more complex than ranking, it still is relatively inexpensive to develop and simple to install and understand. Probably the best known example is the Office of Personnel Management's General Schedule (GS), with 18 classes (which the government calls "grades"), distinguished by level of difficulty.[12] Most jobs are in 15 grades; the top 3 have been combined into a "supergrade" that covers senior executives. Employees in these top three grades are eligible for bonuses and special stipends based on performance. Collapsing the top three classes into one supergrade provides flexibility by making it easier to move people at this level among different agencies in order to best utilize these particular employees' skills and meet different agency needs.

The Federal Classification Act of 1923 provided the early impetus for job classification in the federal government. Classification and job descriptions provided the basis for internal consistency and a uniform job terminology, which allowed centralized financial control. The argument at the time was that centralization made better, more efficient government a possibility. (Not a reality, only a possibility.)

Subsequent legislation further refined and expanded the use of the classification method. Currently, the Factor Evaluation System (FES) uses nine factors to classify approximately 1 million nonsupervisory general schedule positions. These factors are listed in Exhibit 4.5. With the plan, jobs as diverse as conservationist in the Agriculture Department, border patrol officer in Immigration, and account auditor in the Internal Revenue Service are placed in the same GS level. Each factor also receives point values that reflect the factor's importance in a job. The sum total of the factor ratings equals the job's total worth. The general class descriptions are written to capture the varying emphasis on these factors. The Factor Evaluation System gives managers three potential comparisons to guide their evaluation of a job: the general class description, the factor comparisons, and the benchmark jobs that anchor each class.

The Factor Evaluation System is not the only job evaluation system within the federal government.[13] The government's approach seems to be similar to

---

[12] We have avoided referring to *job grades* because of possible confusion with *pay grades*, discussed in Chapter 7. However, the federal government refers to the results of its classification as *grades*, rather than *classes*.

[13] Paul A. Katz, "Specific Job Evaluation Systems: White Collar Jobs in the Federal Civil Service," in *Handbook of Wage and Salary Administration*, ed. Milton Rock (New York: McGraw-Hill, 1984), pp. 14/1–14/10; Steven W. Hays and T. Zane Reeves, *Personnel Management in the Public Sector* (Boston: Allyn and Bacon, 1984); *Modernizing Federal Classification: An Opportunity for Excellence* (Washington, DC: National Academy of Public Administration, 1991).

EXHIBIT 4.5   Factor Evaluation System: Nine Factors with Subfactors

Knowledge required by the position
1. Nature or kind of knowledge and skills needed.
2. How the knowledge and skills are used in doing the work.

Supervisory controls
1. How the work is assigned.
2. The employee's responsibility for carrying out the work.
3. How the work is reviewed.

Guidelines
1. The nature of guidelines for performing the work.
2. The judgment needed to apply the guidelines or develop new guides.

Complexity
1. The nature of the assignment.
2. The difficulty in identifying what needs to be done.
3. The difficulty and originality involved in performing the work.

Scope and effect
1. The purpose of the work.
2. The impact of the work product or service.

Personal contacts

Purpose of contacts

Physical demands

Work environment

that of private industry: pick, choose, and adapt, according to specific needs. It is unclear how the jobs listed in Exhibit 4.6 are classified.

Many states and other governmental units use variations of the classification system, too.[14] In addition, classification is applied to a wide variety of private sector jobs. High-technology and defense-related businesses have frequently developed four to six job classes for engineers. However, the differences among classes in this setting are often more related to experience or "years-since-degree" than to differences in work done by engineers.

POINT METHOD

Point methods have three common characteristics: (1) compensable factors, with (2) factor degrees numerically scaled, and (3) weights reflecting the relative importance of each factor.[15] Appendix 4–B provides factor definitions and weights for a plan used for manufacturing jobs. In point methods, each job's relative value, and hence its location in the pay structure, is determined by the total points assigned to it. A job's total point value is the sum of the numerical values for each degree of compensable factor that the job possesses.

---

[14] See, for example, H. G. Doggett, *Advancing Managerial Excellence: A Report on Improving the Performance Management and Recognition System* (Washington, DC: Office of Personnel Management, 1994).

[15] Factor comparison, another method of job evaluation, bears some similarities to the point method in that comprehensible factors are clearly defined and the external market is linked to the job evaluation results. However, factor comparison is used by less than 10 percent of employers who use job evaluation. The method's complexity makes it difficult to explain to employees and managers, which limits its usefulness. For a detailed description of the method, see previous editions of this textbook.

EXHIBIT 4.6   How Your Tax Dollars Go to Protecting Smokey and Keeping Supreme Court Justices in Stitches

---

Ten Most Unusual Federal Jobs

- Smokey Bear's manager
- The Army civilian marksmanship chief
- The fish watcher
- The Supreme Court seamstress
- The gold stacker
- The (legal) cocaine importer
- The condom tester
- The currency reconstructor
- The Air Force art curator
- The White House gift appraiser

Source: David Wessel, *The Wall Street Journal*, October 9, 1989, p. A14.

Point plans are the most commonly used approach to establish pay structures in the United States. They represent a significant change from ranking and classification methods in that they make explicit the criteria for evaluating jobs: compensable factors. Compensable factors are defined on the basis of the strategic direction of the business and how the work contributes to that strategy. Compensable factors are then scaled to reflect the degree to which they are present in each job and weighted to reflect their overall importance to the organization. Points are then attached to each factor weight. The total points for each job determines its position in the job structure.

The following steps are involved in the design of a point plan.

- Conduct job analysis.
- Determine compensable factors.
- Scale the factors.
- Weight the factors according to importance.
- Communicate the plan and train users; prepare manual.
- Apply to nonbenchmark jobs.

The end product of this design process is an evaluation plan that helps develop and explain the pay structure.

Conduct Job Analysis

Just as with ranking and classification, point plans begin with job analysis. Typically a representative sample of jobs, that is, all benchmark jobs, is drawn for analysis. The content of these jobs serves as the basis for defining, scaling, and weighting the compensable factors.

Determine Compensable Factors

Compensable factors play a pivotal role in the point plan. These factors reflect how work adds value to the organization. They flow from the work itself and the strategic direction of the business.

Compensable factors are those characteristics in the work that the organization values, that help it pursue its strategy and achieve its objectives.

To select compensable factors, an organization asks itself, What is it about the work that adds value? One company chose decision making as a compensable factor. As shown in Exhibit 4.7 the definition of decision making is three dimensional: (1) the risk and complexity (hence the availability of guidelines to assist in making the decisions), (2) the impact of the decisions, and (3) the time that must pass before the impact is evident.

In effect, this firm determined that its competitive advantage depends on decisions employees make in their work. And the relative value of the decisions depends on their risk, their complexity, and their impact on the company. Hence, this firm is signaling to all employees that jobs will be valued based on the nature of the decisions required by employees in those jobs. Jobs that require riskier decisions with greater impact have a higher relative worth than jobs that require fewer decisions of relatively little consequence.

To be useful, compensable factors should be

• Based on the work performed.
• Based on the strategy and values of the organization.
• Acceptable to the stakeholders affected by the resulting pay structure.

Based on the Work Itself.   Employees are the experts in the work actually done in any organization. Hence, it is important to seek their answers to what should be valued in the work itself. Some form of documentation (i.e., job descriptions, job analysis, employee and/or supervisory focus groups) must support the choice of factors. Work-related documentation helps gain acceptance by employees and managers, is easier to understand, and can withstand a variety of challenges to the pay structure. For example, managers may argue that the salaries of their employees are too low in comparison to those of other employees, or that the salary offered to a job candidate is too low. Union leaders may face questions from members about why one job is paid differently from another. Allegations of pay discrimination may be raised. Employees, line managers, union leaders, and compensation managers must understand and be able to explain why work is paid differently or the same. Differences in factors that are obviously based on the work itself provide that rationale. Properly selected factors may even diminish the likelihood of the challenges arising.

EXHIBIT 4.7   Example of a Compensable Factor Definition: Decision Making

---

Compensable Factor Definition: Evaluates the extent of required decision making and the beneficial or detrimental effect such decisions would have on the profitability of the organization. Consideration is given to the:
- Risk and complexity of required decision making
- Impact such action would have on the company

What type of guidelines are available for making decisions?

_____ 1. Few decisions are required; work is performed according to standard procedures and/or detailed instructions.

_____ 2. Decisions are made within an established framework of clearly defined procedures. Incumbent is only required to recognize and follow the prescribed course of action.

_____ 3. Guidelines are available in the form of clearly defined procedures and standard practices. Incumbent must exercise some judgment in selecting the appropriate procedure.

_____ 4. Guidelines are available in the form of some standard practices, well-established precedent, and reference materials and company policy. Decisions require a moderate level of judgment and analysis of the appropriate course of action.

_____ 5. Some guidelines are available in the form of broad precedent, related practices and general methods of the field. Decisions require a high level of judgment and/or modification of a standard course of action to address the issue at hand.

_____ 6. Few guidelines are available. The incumbent may consult with technical experts and review relevant professional publications. Decisions require innovation and creativity. The only limitation on course of action is company strategy and policy.

What is the impact of decisions made by the position?

_____ 1. Inappropriate decisions, recommendations or errors would normally cause minor delays and cost increments. Deficiencies will not affect the completion of programs or projects important to the organization.

_____ 2. Inappropriate decisions, recommendations or errors will normally cause moderate delays and additional allocation of funds and resources within the immediate work unit. Deficiencies will not affect the attainment of the organization's objectives.

_____ 3. Inappropriate decisions, recommendations or errors would normally cause considerable delays and reallocation of funds and resources. Deficiencies will affect scheduling and project completion in other work units and, unless adjustments are made, could affect attainment of objectives of a major business segment of the company.

_____ 4. Inappropriate decisions, recommendations or errors would normally affect critical programs or attainment of short-term goals for a major business segment of the company.

_____ 5. Inappropriate decisions, recommendations or errors would affect attainment of objectives for the company and would normally affect long-term growth and public image.

The effectiveness of the majority of the position's decisions can be measured within:

_____ 1. One day. _____ 4. Six months.
_____ 2. One week. _____ 5. One year.
_____ 3. One month. _____ 6. More than a year.

Source: Jill Kanin-Lovers, "The Role of Computers in Job Evaluations: A Case in Point," *Journal of Compensation and Benefits* (New York: Warren Gorham and Lamont, 1985).

Based on the Strategy and Values of the Organization.   The leadership of any organization is the best source of information on where the business should be going and how it is going to get there. Clearly, their input into factors in the work that help create value is crucial. So if the business strategy involves providing innovative, high quality products and services designed in collaboration with customers and suppliers, then jobs with greater responsibilities for product innovation and customer contacts should probably be highly valued, and these factors will be compensable. Or if the business strategy is more Wal-Mart-like, "providing goods and services to delight customers at the lowest cost and greatest convenience possible," then compensable factors might include impact on cost containment, customer relations, and so on. The point is that compensable factors need to reinforce the organization's culture and values as well as its business direction and the nature of the work.

Changes in the organization or its strategic directions may require that the compensable factors also change. For example, both 3M and TRW recently added international responsibilities, as shown in Exhibit 4.8, as a factor in their managerial job-evaluation plans. The factor is defined in terms of the type of responsibility, the percent of time devoted to international issues, and the number of countries covered. In both firms, strategic business plans call for increased emphasis on international operations. Consequently, the compensable factors include international responsibilities as well.

EXHIBIT 4.8   Compensable Factor Definition: Multinational Responsibilities

---

This factor concerns the multinational scope of the job. Multinational responsibilities are defined as line or functional managerial activities in one or several countries.

---

1. **The multinational responsibilities of the job can best be described as:**
   A. Approving major policy and strategic plans.
   B. Formulating, proposing, and monitoring implementation of policy and plans.
   C. Acting as a consultant in project design and implementation phases.
   D. Providing procedural guidance and information on well-defined topics.
   E. Not applicable.

2. **Indicate the percentage of time spent on multinational issues:**
   A. > 50%
   B. 25–49%
   C. 10–24%
   D. < 10%

3. **The number of countries (other than your unit location) for which the position currently has operational or functional responsibility:**
   A. More than 10 countries
   B. 5 to 10 countries
   C. 1 to 4 countries
   D. Not applicable

By the same token, factors may be eliminated if they no longer support the business strategy. The railway company Burlington Northern recently revised its job evaluation plan to omit the factor number of subordinates supervised. Although many plans include a similar factor, Burlington Northern decided that a factor that values increases to staff runs counter to the organization's objective of reducing the work force size. Major shifts in the business strategy or values are not daily occurrences, but when they do occur, the factors need to be reexamined to ensure that they are consistent with the new directions.

Acceptable to the Stakeholders.   Acceptance of the pay structure by managers and employees is critical. This is also true of compensable factors used to slot jobs into the pay structure. To achieve acceptance of the factors, all the relevant parties' viewpoints need to be considered.

An example illustrates the point. A senior manager refused to accept a job evaluation plan unless the factor working conditions was included. The compensation specialist, a recent college graduate, demonstrated through statistical analysis that working conditions did not vary enough among 90 percent of the jobs under study to have a meaningful effect on the resulting pay structure; statistically, working conditions did not affect the results. The manager rejected these data, pointing out that the compensation wonk had never worked in the other 10 percent of the jobs, which were in the plant's foundry. The manager knew that working conditions were important to the foundry employees. To get the plan and pay decisions based on it accepted, the plan was redesigned to include working conditions. In sum, compensable factors need to be work related, business related, and acceptable.

Adapting Factors from Existing Plans.   Although a wide variety of factors are used in standard existing plans, the factors tend to fall into four generic groups: skills required, effort required, responsibility, and working conditions. These four were used more than 50 years ago in the National Electrical Manufacturers Association (NEMA) plan and are also included in the Equal Pay Act (1963) to define equal work.

Many of the early points plans, such as those of National Metal Trades Association (NMTA) and NEMA, and the Steel Plan, were developed for nonexempt manufacturing and/or office jobs. Since then, point plans have also been applied to managerial and professional jobs. The Hay Guide Chart—Profile Method of Position, used by 5,000 employees worldwide (130 of the 500 largest U.S. corporations), is perhaps the most widely used. The classic three Hay factors—know-how, problem solving, and accountability—and an example of the guide charts are included in Appendix 4–A.

However, even the venerable Hay Guide Charts shown in Appendix 4–A are changing. Recently, Hallmark Cards, Inc., reengineered its operations. As a long-time user of the Hay job-evaluation plan, Hallmark leadership judged that the original factors no longer adequately reflected what Hallmark wanted to

EXHIBIT 4.9   Original and Revised Hay Factors

Original factors	Proposed factors
1. Know-how	1. Capacity
Functional expertise	Business systems
Managerial skills	Integrating resources
Human relations	Teaming skills
2. Problem solving	2. Improvement opportunities
Environment	Context
Challenge	Challenge
3. Accountability	3. Scope
Freedom to act	Empowerment
Impact of end results	Impact of end results
Magnitude	Reach

value in the work and its business strategy. Hay and Hallmark teamed to redesign the factors.[16] The results are shown in Exhibit 4.9.

The major changes add team involvement and leadership and deemphasize functional expertise to favor more generalized, cross-functional (process-oriented) expertise. So even the classic Hay Method is adapting to reflect the changed business operations.

Employee Involvement.   Factors are usually developed by a task force consisting of key decision makers (or their representatives) from various area such as finance, operations, engineering, and marketing. Joint union–management development of compensable factors is common. Dresser Rand and the electrical workers' union and Borg-Warner and the machinists' union jointly developed their plans. Not only is increased employee acceptance of a jointly developed plan likely, but employees provide valuable expertise, since they are usually the most knowledgeable about the actual work performed.

J. C. Penney involved more than 5,000 of the 15,000 managers whose jobs would eventually be covered by a job evaluation plan in focus groups. A compensation committee combined the lists of factors suggested by the focus groups, refined the factor definitions, and eliminated overlapping factors. In the end, six compensable factors were approved by top management:

- Decision making impact on the company's objectives.
- Communications.
- Supervision and management.
- Knowledge requirements.

---

[16] Hay Associates does not define its guide chart-profile method as a variation of the point method. Whether it is a point method or factor comparison is less important than recognizing that it is a widely used plan that combines characteristics of both methods.

- Internal customers.
- External customers.

Two additional factors, stress and employee development, were eliminated after further discussions with the executive management. Penney decided that these two factors were difficult to quantify and tended to be a function of the person, not the job (i.e., what I find stressful, you may find energizing). Since the compensable factors were suggested by such a cross section of the managers, there is little question of their acceptability to those same managers when used to determine pay structures.

Several consulting firms adopt a more selective approach to soliciting factors. Early in the design of the point plan, key executives and senior managers are interviewed to collect information on a variety of issues. Bank of America, Digital Equipment, and 3M followed this less elaborate (and less expensive) process using a task force of about 20 employees and managers. Questions can cover what the executives see as inequities in current practices, their views on the firm's value system, and future business directions.

How Many Factors?   A remaining issue to consider is how many factors should be included in the plan. Some factors may have overlapping definitions or may fail to account for anything unique in the criterion chosen. We have already noted that factors must often be included to ensure the plan's acceptance. More than 40 years ago, researchers demonstrated that a few factors will yield practically the same results as many factors. Three to five factors explained most of the variation in the job hierarchy. In one study, a 21-factor plan produced the same job structure that could be generated using only 7 of the factors. Further, the jobs could be correctly slotted into classes using only 3 factors. Yet the company decided to keep the 21-factor plan because it was "accepted and doing the job."

Scale the Factors

Once the factors are chosen, scales reflecting the different degrees within each factor are constructed. Each degree may also be anchored by the typical skills, tasks, and behaviors taken from the benchmark jobs that illustrate each factor degree. Exhibit 4.10 shows NMTA's scaling for the factor of knowledge.

A major problem in determining degrees is to make each degree equidistant from the adjacent degrees (interval scaling). The following criteria for determining degrees have been suggested: (1) limit to the number necessary to distinguish among jobs, (2) use understandable terminology, (3) anchor degree definition with benchmark job titles, and (4) make it apparent how the degree applies to the job.[17] Using too many degrees makes it difficult for evaluators to accurately

---

[17] Charles Fay and Paul Hempel, "Whose Values? A Comparison of Incumbent, Supervisor, Incumbent-Supervisor Consensus and Committee Job Evaluation Ratings" (Working paper, Rutgers University, 1991).

EXHIBIT 4.10   Illustration of Factor Scaling from National Metal Trades Association

1. Knowledge

This factor measures the knowledge or equivalent training required to perform the position duties.

1st Degree

Use of reading and writing, adding and subtracting of whole numbers; following of instructions; use of fixed gauges, direct reading instruments and similar devices; where interpretation is not required.

2nd Degree

Use of addition, subtraction, multiplication and division of numbers including decimals and fractions; simple use of formulas, charts, tables, drawings, specifications, schedules, wiring diagrams; use of adjustable measuring instruments; checking of reports, forms, records and comparable data; where interpretation is required.

3rd Degree

Use of mathematics together with the use of complicated drawings, specifications, charts, tables; various types of precision measuring instruments. Equivalent to 1 to 3 years applied trades training in a particular or specialized occupation.

4th Degree

Use of advanced trades mathematics, together with the use of complicated drawings, specifications, charts, tables, handbook formulas; all varieties of precision measuring instruments. Equivalent to complete accredited apprenticeship in a recognized trade, craft or occupation; or equivalent to a 2-year technical college education.

5th Degree

Use of higher mathematics involved in the application of engineering principles and the performance of related practical operations, together with a comprehensive knowledge of the theories and practices of mechanical, electrical, chemical, civil or like engineering field. Equivalent to complete 4 years of technical college or university education.

choose the appropriate degree. This, in turn, reduces the acceptability of the system.

Weight the Factors According to Importance

Once the degrees have been assigned, the factor weights must be determined. Different weights reflect differences in importance attached to each factor by the employer. For example, the National Electrical Manufacturers Association plan weights education at 17.5 percent; another employer's association weights it at 10.6 percent; a consultant's plan recommends 15.0 percent; and a trade association weights the same factor at 10.1 percent.

Exhibit 4.11   Job Evaluation Form

Compensable Factors	Degree	x	Weight	=	Total
Working Conditions:	1 2 3 4 5				
Environment	X		10%		10
Hazards	X		10%		10
Skill:					
Education	X (deg 2)		40%		120
Experience	X (deg 2)		40%		120
Mental	X (deg 3)		40%		160
Manual/Specific	X (deg 1)		40%		80
Effort:					
Physical	X (deg 2)		30%		60
Mental	X (deg 3)		30%		120
Responsibility:					
Effect of Error	X (deg 4)		20%		80
Inventiveness/ Innovation	X (deg 3)		20%		60
					(820)

Job __bookstore manager__

Check one: ☒ Administrative   ☐ Technical

There are two basic methods used to establish factor weights: *committee judgment* and *statistical analysis.*

Judgment.   Members of the compensation committee or, in some rare cases, groups of employees are asked to allocate 100 percent of value among the factors. Some structured decision process such as delphi or other nominal group technique may be used to facilitate consensus. In the illustration in Exhibit 4.11, the point plan has four factors (skills required, effort required, responsibility, and working conditions) with five degrees of each factor.

Additionally, the factors are weighted. The "skills required" item carries a greater weight (40 percent of the total points) for this employer than does working conditions (10 percent of the total points). Thus, a job's 240 total points may result from two degrees of skills required ($2 \times 40 = 80$), three each of effort required ($3 \times 30 = 90$) and responsibility ($3 \times 20 = 60$), and one of working conditions ($1 \times 10 = 10$); ($80 + 90 + 60 + 10 = 240$). Weighting reflects the relative value of a factor to an employer. In this illustration, the weighting of factors represents the judgment of the compensation committee.

Statistically. Statistical approaches were developed more than 40 years ago.[18] The weights are statistically derived in such a way as to correlate as closely as possible to pay rates that are agreed upon by the parties involved. Typically, those rates are the agreed-upon pay structure for benchmark jobs. By statistically analyzing an agreed-upon pay structure for benchmark jobs on the factor degrees assigned to each job, a set of weights is derived that will produce total job evaluation scores that will closely match the agreed-upon pay structure.

Most major consulting firms use this approach to establish both factor weights and scales. Although each firm's model and computer software are proprietary, as best we can judge, the basic approaches are similar statistically. Basically, they derive factor weights and scales that best fit a criterion pay structure.

The Key—Criterion Pay Structure. The choice of the criterion is a critical decision since the factor weights and degrees are modeled to reproduce it. Several options are available: (1) current wage rates paid by the firm for benchmark jobs. This criterion is used when the firm simply wants a job evaluation plan that will reproduce the current structure or (2) competitive rates paid in the labor market for benchmark jobs. The premise in this case is that the firm wants to set its pay structure to match the structure found in the labor market at a particular time.

Some people object to using market rates since they may not be linked to the firm's business strategy. Still others object because they believe wage rates for jobs held predominantly by women are artificially depressed due to historical gender discrimination.[19] Therefore, duplicating the existing pay structure, whether within the firm or in the market, perpetuates this discrimination. Other possible criteria include (3) the rates for jobs held predominantly by men (on the grounds that they are the best estimates of bias-free rates) and (4) wage rates that have been negotiated with employees through collective bargaining.

The statistical approach is often labeled as *policy capturing* to contrast it with the committee judgment approach. Both approaches are policy capturing; only the policy or criterion captured may vary and the method used to capture that policy may vary (statistical versus judgmental).

Often the initial results of either the committee judgment or statistical approach for deriving factor weights and degrees may not be completely satisfactory. The job evaluation results and the agreed-upon pay structure may not agree.

---

[18] Paul M. Edwards, "Statistical Methods in Job Evaluation," *Advanced Management*, December 1948, pp. 158–63; J. L. Otis and R. H. Leukart, *Job Evaluation: A Basis for Sound Wage Administration* (Englewood Cliffs, NJ: Prentice Hall, 1954); Kermit Davis, Jr., and William Sauser, Jr., "Effects of Alternative Weighting Methods in a Policy-Capturing Approach to Job Evaluation: A Review and Empirical Investigation," *Personal Psychology* 44 (1991), pp. 85–127.

[19] Donald J. Treiman, "Effect of Choice of Factors and Factor Weights in Job Evaluation," in *Comparable Worth and Wage Discrimination*, ed. H. Remick (Philadelphia: Temple University Press, 1984), pp. 79–89.

Several procedures are commonly used to overcome this disagreement. First, the sample of benchmark jobs is often changed by adding or deleting jobs. Second, the factor degree assigned to each benchmark job may be adjusted. Third, the pay structure serving as a criterion may be adjusted. Or the weighting scheme may be adjusted. Thus, a task force beginning with exactly the same factors and degrees could end up with very different job-evaluation plans, depending on the specific benchmark jobs, the pay structure chosen as the criterion, and the method used to weight the factors.

Combining Factor Scales and Weights.   To translate weights and factor scales into actual job points, the maximum number of points to be used in the system is first divided among the factors according to their weights. The points for each factor are then attached to that factor's scale. For example, if the knowledge factor scaled in Exhibit 4.9 is weighted 20 percent in a 500-point system, then a total of 100 points is assigned to this factor, and each of the five degrees of knowledge is worth 20 points; for example, fourth degree $= 4 \times 20 = 80$ points.

BALANCING CONTROL AND CHAOS

Many job-evaluation plans afford flexibility to adapt to changing conditions. Sufficient ambiguity usually exists in the compensable factor descriptions to permit interpretation as the situation requires. This inherent flexibility accommodates the introduction of new technology or the restructuring of operations. Flexibility may be very attractive to managers coping with increased competitive pressures and the need to restructure work. However, the lack of business- and work-related evaluations cut two ways: Generic factors and vague descriptions such as "associates" or "technicians" may not provide sufficient business- and work-related information to justify pay decisions. This lack of detail clearly avoids bureaucracy, leaving managers free to manage. But it also reduces control and may increase the likelihood of equal-pay lawsuits or make it harder to placate disgruntled employees who believe the work they do is undervalued. Some balance between chaos and control is required.

Prior to the widespread use of job evaluation, employers in the 1930s and 1940s had irrational pay structures—the legacy of decentralized and uncoordinated wage-setting practices. Pay differences were a major source of unrest among workers. American Steel and Wire, for example, had more than 100,000 pay rates. Employment and wage records were rarely kept before 1900; only the foreman knew with any accuracy how many workers were employed in his department and the rates they received. Foremen were "free to manage," but they used wage information to play favorites by varying the day rate or assigning favored workers to jobs where piece rates were loose. What's the point? History suggests that when flexibility without guidelines exists, chaotic and irrational pay rates too frequently result. Removing inefficient bureaucracy is important, but balanced guidelines are necessary to ensure that employees are treated fairly and that pay decisions support the organization's strategy and help it achieve its objectives.

SKILL/COMPETENCY-BASED STRUCTURES

We have already pointed out that internal pay structures do not need to be based on jobs; rather, they can be based on skill or competency. With these methods, employees' pay is based on the required competency or skills they possess rather than the jobs they perform or whether they actually use the competency or skills in their work.[20]

MAJOR DECISIONS

Even with the renewed interest in how to design and manage skill/competency-based structures, there is as yet no well-established, agreed-upon approach. However, we can identify the major decisions involved in designing a skill/competency-based plan. They are depicted in Exhibit 4.12 and include the following:

1. Establish the purpose for the plan.
2. Determine the skill blocks/competencies and levels.
3. Establish certification methods.
4. Obtain involvement and commitment of stakeholders.
5. Evaluate the plan's usefulness.

EXHIBIT 4.12   Determining the Skill/Competency-Based Structure

Internal consistency: work relationships within the organization	→	Skill/Competency analysis	→	Skill/Competency certification	→	Skill/Competency-based structure

Some major decisions in skill/competency assessment and certification
- Establish the purpose of the plan.
- Determine the skill blocks/competencies and level.
- Establish certification methods.
- Obtain involvement and commitment of stakeholders.
- Evaluate the plan's usefulness.

---

[20] G. Douglas Jenkins, Jr., Gerald E. Ledford, Jr., Nina Gupta, and D. Harold Doty, *Skill-Based Pay* (Scotsdale, AZ: American Compensation Association, 1992).

As with job evaluation, the first three of these decisions are discussed in this chapter, and the remaining two are covered in the next. Examples of Borg-Warner's and FMC's skill-based plan are found in Appendix 4–B and Exhibit 4.14.

Establish the Purpose

Under these plans, employees are paid for either the skills or competencies they are capable of using rather than the jobs they are performing. The key objectives for these plans include the following:

- Signal to employees that continuous learning is valued and is a key to the organization's success.
- Provide employees with incentives to acquire additional skills and competencies.
- Remove job barriers to encourage flexibility: "It's not in my job description."
- Establish a workable, agreed-upon pay structure.
- Explain/reduce disputes in terms of skill differences.
- Help ensure that the pay structure supports other human resource programs such as training and career planning.[21]

Note that those objectives are practically identical to those listed for job evaluation on page 128. The major difference is that a structure based on skills/competencies signals to employees that advancement coupled with pay increases depends on continuously learning relevant information, whereas job-based structures tell workers that performing jobs that add greater value to the organization is the way to advance and increase pay.

Other potential differences such as flexibility through multiskilling and cross-functional career moves really depend on the design of each approach. It should be clear that it is possible to design a job-based plan with generic descriptions and broad classifications that encourage flexibility, too. Contrasts among job evaluation and skill and competency-based plans are further illustrated in Exhibit 4.13. The basic question, What is valued in the work? is answered through compensable factors in job evaluation and through skill blocks and competencies in the person-based approaches. These factors, blocks and competencies, are defined and made more specific through the development of degrees, weights, and levels. Finally, just as the link between job-evaluation points and pay depends on the criteria pay structure selected (e.g., the rates paid to benchmark jobs or some negotiated rates), the dollars attached to each skill or competency depend on conversion to market rates and certification.

---

[21] E. E. Lawler III, "From Job-Based to Competency-Based Organizations," *Journal of Organization Behavior* 15, pp. 3–15, 1994.

EXHIBIT 4.13   Contrasting Approaches

	Job evaluation	Skill-based	Competency-based
What is valued	Compensable factors	Skill blocks	Competencies
Quantify the value	Factor degree weights	Skill levels	Competency levels
Mechanisms to translate into pay	Assign points that reflect criterion pay structure	Certification and market pricing	Certification and market pricing

Determine Skill Blocks and Levels

Skill blocks, as noted in Chapter 3, are the different types of skills required to perform the work. Just as with compensable factors used in job evaluation, skill blocks should be (1) derived from the work to be performed, (2) focused on developing a highly flexible work force, and (3) understood and acceptable to the stakeholders involved.[22]

Skill levels are simply the degrees within a particular skill block. For example, the General Mills plan has three levels within each block. The levels reflect the proficiency of the employee. In the technical skill block, the three levels include (1) limited abilities to apply principles, (2) partially proficient, and (3) fully competent. Borg-Warner's skill-based evaluation plan (see Appendix 4–B) uses levels of each skill block, similar to degrees of a compensable factor in a job evaluation plan.

A skill-based plan for technicians at FMC is shown in Exhibit 4.14. The plan has three skill blocks: foundation, core electives, and optional electives. The levels within the core elective block are calibrated by points assigned to each specific skill. The technician pay structure has five rates ranging from an entry rate of $10.50 per hour to a Technician IV rate of $14.50 per hour. The three skill blocks are described as follows:

- *Foundation.* This block includes a quality seminar, videos on materials handling and hazardous materials, a three-day safety workshop, and a half-day orientation. All foundation competencies are mandatory and must be certified to reach the Technician I rate ($11).

---

[22] Gerald E. Ledford, Jr., "Three Case Studies on Skill-Based Pay: An Overview," *Compensation and Benefits Review*, March–April 1991, pp. 11–23; Richard Bunning, "Models for Skill-Based Pay Plans," *HR Magazine*, February 1992, pp. 62–64.

EXHIBIT 4.14 Technician Skill-Based Structure

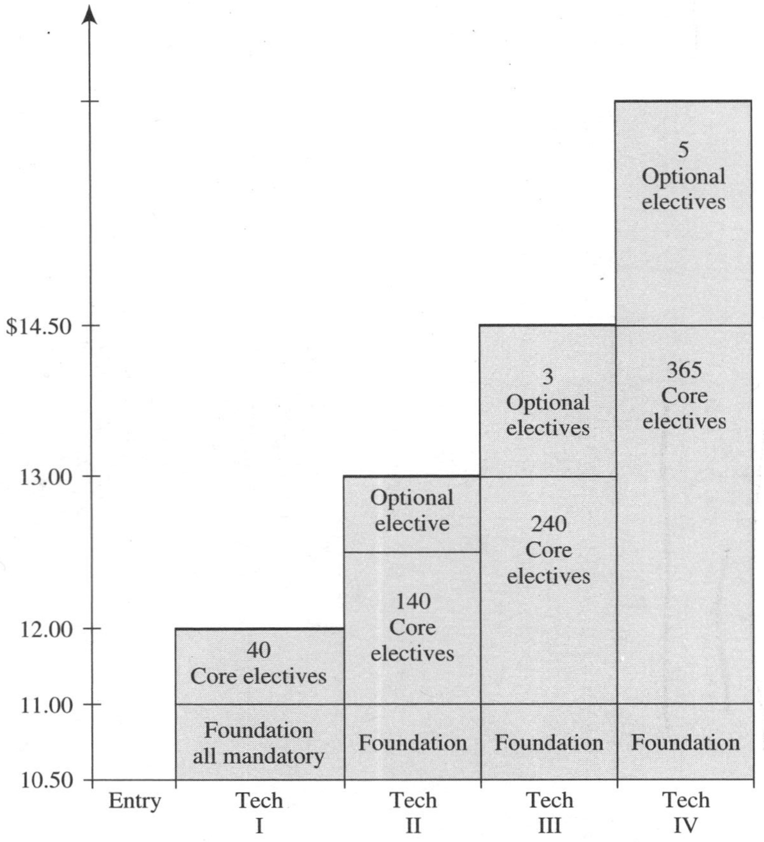

Foundation

Quality course
Shop floor control
Materials handling
Hazardous materials video
Safety workshop
Orientation workshop

Core Electives

Skills	Points	Skills	Points
Longeron Fabrication	10	Leak Check/Patch Weld	5
Panel Fabrication	15	Final Acceptance Test	10
Shell Fabrication	15	Welding Inspection	15
End Casting Welding	20	Flame Spraying	15
Finishing—Paint	20	Assembly Inspection	5
Finishing—Ablative/Autoclave	20	Safe % Arm Assembly	15
Finishing—Surface Prep	10	MK 13 Machining	25
MK 13 Assembly	15	MK 14 Machining	25
MK 14 Assembly	15	Tool Set Up	10
Finishing Inspection	5	NC1 Inspection	30
Machining Inspection	20	Degrease	10
Pad Welding	15	Guide Rail Assembly	5
		Receiving Inspection	5

Optional Electives

Maintenance	Career Development
Logistics—JIT	Group Decision Making
Plant First Aid	Public Relations
Geometric Tolerancing	Group Facilitator
Computer-Lotus	Training
Computer-dBASE III	Group Problem Solving
Computer-Word Processing	Administration
Assessment Center	Plant Security
Consensus Building	

- *Core electives.* These are necessary to the facility's operations (e.g., fabrication, welding, painting, finishing, assembly, inspection). Each skill is assigned a point value.

To reach Technician II ($12 per hour), 40 core elective points (of 370) must be certified, in addition to the foundation competencies. To reach Technician III, an additional 100 points of core electives must be certified, plus three optional electives.

- *Optional electives.* These are additional specialized competencies ranging from computer applications to team leadership and consensus building.

A fully qualified Technician IV (e.g., certified as mastering foundations, 365 points of core electives, and five optional electives) is able to perform all work in a cell at the facility. Technician IV earns $14.50 per hour and can be assigned to any task, Technician III earns $13 per hour and can handle more tasks than Technician II, and so on.

The FMC approach should look familiar to any college student: required courses, required credits chosen among specific categories, electives, and optional electives. There is a minor difference, of course—FMC employees get paid for passing these skills, whereas college students pay their schools to take courses!

Determine Competencies and Levels

At this point in development, competencies usually refer to managerial and professional work, whereas skills are used to value technical and blue-collar work. Competencies tend to be more general than skill blocks. Nevertheless, like compensable factors, they are derived from the executive leadership's beliefs about the organization and its strategic intent. In essence, competencies are the basic attributes of employees that create value for the organization. Indeed, one consultant calls competencies "the DNA of organizations."[23]

Determining competencies is relatively new; however, the procedures seem to parallel those used to define compensable factors. Some additional examples are shown in Exhibits 4.15 and 4.16. Note that these competencies, *understanding and meeting customer needs* (Exhibit 4.15) and *establishing and developing teams* (Exhibit 4.16), capture the same notion as the compensable factors used in the revised Hallmark/Hay plan.

Advocates of competency-based approaches seem to reject these parallels, believing instead that somehow the competencies lie within the person, not the work itself. Perhaps this is a basic point, or perhaps some of these nuances are salient only to compensation wonks. The key is whether either approach helps accomplish the organization's objectives and offers a sense of fair treatment to

---

[23] Sandra O'Neal, "Competencies: The DNA of the Corporation," *Perspectives in Total Compensation*, Winter 1994, pp. 6–12.

EXHIBIT 4.15   **Example of a Customer-Service Competency and Related Behavioral Anchors**

Understanding and Meeting Customer Needs

"Understanding and meeting customer needs" is the demonstrated desire to work with, serve or do something helpful for customers. This includes initiative and tenacity in understanding the needs of others, including internal customers, external customers, suppliers and vendors.

Behavioral Anchors (from Low to High Level)

1. **Follows Up On Customer Issues.**   Follows through on customer inquiries, requests or complaints. Keeps customers up-to-date about progress of projects or services but does not explore customers' issues or problems.

2. **Seeks To Understand Customer Issues.**   Maintains clear communication with customers regarding mutual expectations. Monitors customer satisfaction. Listens and responds to customers' concerns. Is sensitive to resource concerns of customers.

3. **Takes Full Personal Responsibility for Resolving Issues.**   Personally sees that customer problems or concerns are addressed satisfactorily. Demonstrates leadership in resolving conflicts with customers. Is fully available to customers, especially during critical periods.

4. **Adds Value Beyond Customer Issues.**   Works to add value to the customer and to make things better than the customer may expect.

5. **Assesses Underlying Customer Needs.**   Seeks information about the real, underlying needs of customers beyond those expressed initially and matches these needs to available or customized services. Looks for long-term benefits to the customer.

6. **Becomes a Trusted Advisor.**   Gets personally involved in customer activities and decisions. Develops an independent opinion on customers' current and long-term needs, problems, opportunities and alternatives for implementation. Acts on this opinion, for example, by recommending appropriate approaches that are new and different from those requested by the customer.

7. **Sacrifices Short-Term Benefits for Long-Term Benefits.**   Takes customer's side against the organization, as necessary, with long-term mutual benefit to customers and the organization.

Source: Sharon A. Tucker and Kathryn M. Cofsky, "Competency-Based Pay on a Banding Platform: A Compensation Combination for Driving Performance and Managing Change" *ACA Journal*, Spring 1994, pp. 30–45.

EXHIBIT 4.16A Competency: Establish and Maintain a Team-Based, Empowered Organization

			Competencies		
Proficiency Levels	Creates a Culture of Empowerment that Promotes Teamwork	Supports Policies and Systems that Promote Teams	Works Effectively in Teams as Leader or Member	Facilitates Team Effectiveness Within and Across Teams	Provides Meaningful Performance Feedback
• Sets strategy • High-level decision making • Excellent knowledge of industry • Thought leader	Clarifies roles and relationships, rewards teamwork, empowered behavior, and risk taking.	Facilitates team dynamics. Works effectively as a leader. Integrates multiple perspectives across teams. Creates policies that support a team-based environment.	Models leadership behavior. Supports team members and colleagues	Champions team development and cooperation. Coaches/ counsels team members.	Champions systems that facilitate performance feedback. Is accessible to team members.
• Plans and manages • Analyzes and synthesizes • Knows the industry • Demonstrates expertise in field of specialty • Mentor/coach	Provides effective teamwork and empowerment. Holds others accountable for their actions. Secures resources for team. Takes intelligent risks.	Performs major activities in cross-functional teams. Integrates multiple perspectives across teams. Facilitates team dynamics. Creates systems that promote team effectiveness.	Can shift from leader to member as team requirements change. Supports team members.	Facilitates team development/ cooperation and conflict resolution. Gives feedback. Coaches/counsels team members.	Demonstrates effective feedback and communication skills. Is accessible to team members.
• Analyzes • Executes and plans • Continuing to develop knowledge of industry and field	Facilitates effective teamwork. Accepts accountability. Takes intelligent risks.	Works effectively in a team-based structure. Uses tools that promote team effectiveness.	Supports leadership role of others. Acts as team member or leader.	Demonstrates teamwork. Understands/deals with conflict.	Actively solicits feedback. Provides feedback to team members.
• Gathers information • Supports strategy/ plans • Developing knowledge of field and industry	Demonstrates empowerment within agreed upon boundaries. Works effectively in teams.	Works effectively in team-based organizational structure.	Contributes to team. Supports leadership role.	Understands principles of team effectiveness.	Actively solicits feedback from superiors.

Adapted from Astra-Merck.

EXHIBIT 4.16B Competency: Establish and Sustain Strategic Partnerships

Proficiency Levels	Competencies				
	Negotiates Win–Win Agreements With Strategic Partners	*Executes Win–Win Contracts With Strategic Partners*	*Understands the Needs of Strategic Partners*	*Shares Information With Strategic Partners*	*Mobilizes Company Resources in Support of Strategic Partnerships*
• Sets strategy • High-level decision making • Excellent knowledge of industry • Thought leader	Establishes negotiating strategy. Develops long-term relationships and focus. Closes win–win deals.	Communicates win–win attitude. Provides resources needed to ensure results. Seeks solutions to problems arising in contract.	Leverages research to educate teams. Seeks input from partners. Responds to partner's needs by providing services and products they value.	Uses technology to enhance information exchange. Shares relevant information with decision-makers.	Allocates resources. Continually adjusts business plans. Brings right skills & resources together at the right time.
• Plans and manages • Analyzes and synthesizes • Knows the industry • Demonstrates expertise in field of specialty • Mentor/coach	Negotiates and links licenser and customer needs. Strives to develop long-term relationships.	Secures resources to ensure win–win results. Seeks solutions to problems arising during the contract. Conducts day-to-day business.	Uses effective feedback mechanisms. Responds to partners' needs by providing services and products they value.	Uses technology to provide all relevant product information. Shares knowledge and expertise.	Prioritizes use of resources. Brings right skills and resources together at the right time.
• Analyzes • Executes and plans • Continuing to develop knowledge of industry and field	Participates in development of strategy. Researches and analyzes licenser and customer needs.	Conducts day-to-day business.	Collects and analyzes input. Shares input and feedback. Contributes work that adds value.	Provides all relevant information to decision makers. Collects and organizes relevant information.	Supports the allocation of resources.
• Gathers information • Supports strategy/plans • Developing knowledge of field and industry	Researches licenser and customer needs. Supports development of negotiating strategy.	Conducts day-to-day business.	Analyzes and reports on input from partners. Contributes work that adds value.	Supports efforts to collect, organize, and share information.	Uses resources in order to meet partner needs.

Adapted from Astra-Merck.

employees. The answer, to date, lies in beliefs rather than research. Virtually no systematic evidence exists that supports job evaluation over competency- or skill-based approaches.

Descriptions of competency levels can become relatively specific. The definitions and proficiency levels for "Establish and Maintain a Team-Based, Empowered Organization" and "Establish and Sustain Strategic Partnerships" (Exhibits 4.16A and 4.16B) are very closely tailored to the organization business strategy and its values. Employees who exhibit and/or acquire the competency to "create a culture of empowerment" at a proficiency level of "strategic–thought leader" will be among the top leaders in the organization and paid accordingly.

Establish Certification Methods   *Measure or certify*

How should employees be certified that they possess the skill or competency and are able to apply it? Who should be involved in the process? Practice varies widely. Some organizations use successful completion of courses to verify certification. Elementary and secondary school teachers get pay increases for completing additional college courses. Other organizations use peer review, on-the-job demonstrations, and tests for certification. This is similar to the traditional craft approach (i.e., apprentice, journeyman, and master). Still others require successful completion of formal courses, plus time on the job. Northern Telecom uses a preassessment meeting between supervisor and employee to discuss skill accomplishments and goals and training needs. Subsequently, a certification committee made up of employees and supervisors examines employees to determine whether they can be certified in the skills. Honeywell's plan calls for evaluating employees during the six months after they have learned the skills. Again, leaders and peers are used in the certification process.[24]

The certification of competencies is hardly discussed by advocates. In light of the detailed bureaucracy that has grown up around job evaluation, we confidently predict a growth of procedures here, too.[25] The whole approach to certification may be fraught with potential legal vulnerabilities if employees who fail to be certified challenge the process. At this point, very little attention has been devoted to assessor training or validating the certification process. On the face of it, just as employment tests used for hiring and promotion decisions are vulnerable to regulatory pressures, so too are certification procedures used to determine pay increases. Clearly, there is a need to ensure that procedures are work related and free of bias.

[handwritten margin note: Be sure to love involvement]

---

[24] G. Douglas Jenkins, Jr., Gerald E. Ledford, Jr., Nina Gupta, and D. Harold Doty, *Skill-Based Pay* (Scottsdale, AZ: American Compensation Association, 1992).

[25] E. E. Lawler III, G. E. Ledford, Jr., and L. Chang, "Who Uses Skill-Based Pay and Why," *Compensation and Benefits Review* 2, no. 5 (1993), pp. 22–26. G. E. Ledford, Jr. "The Effectiveness of Skill-Based Pay," *Perspectives in Total Compensation* 1, no. 1 (1990).

MARKET PRICING

The third technique for valuing work differs markedly from job evaluation and skill/competency-based approaches. Market pricing involves setting pay structures almost exclusively by relying on rates paid in the external market.

Employers following such an approach typically match a large percentage of their jobs with market data and collect as much market data as possible. Opting for market pricing may reflect an emphasis on external competitiveness and a deemphasis on internal consistency. Organizations adopting "bands," discussed in Chapter 7, increasingly use market pricing for the specific jobs within each band.[26] Organizations that fill large proportions of their job vacancies with new hires from the outside may also become market pricers. The potential problems with market pricing stem from giving up internal consistency among jobs to the vagaries of the external market and therefore to competitors' decisions. In effect, market pricing lets competitors determine an employer's internal pay structure.

Market pricers often use the ranking method to determine the pay for jobs unique to their firms. Often called *rank to market,* it involves first determining the competitive rates for positions for which external market data are available and then blending the remaining (nonbenchmark) jobs into the pay hierarchy. At Pfizer, for example, job analysis results in written job descriptions. This is immediately followed by labor market analysis and market pricing for as many jobs as possible. Exhibit 4.17 shows Pfizer's pay comparisons with comparable jobs at surveyed companies. After that, the internal job relationships are reviewed to be sure they are *reasonable in light of organization needs*. The final step is pricing those jobs not included in the survey. These remaining jobs are compared to the survey positions in terms of their total value to Pfizer. This internal evaluation seeks to ensure consistency with promotion opportunities and to properly reflect internal job values across functions.

Market Pricing Each Job.   Market pricing appears to be increasingly popular. It goes beyond market-pricing benchmark jobs and then slotting nonbenchmarks. Some employers are attempting to establish most if not all of their internal pay structure based on external market rates. Hence, over 20 percent of jobs pay rates that are based on the external market. In effect, these organizations are using the structures established in external markets as their internal pay structures, breaking down the boundaries between the internal organization and external market forces. One company we know even attempts to specify the forms of pay for each job according to its competitors in the market. For example, if the average rate paid by competitors for a controller job is $120,000, then the company pays $120,000. If 70 percent of the $120,000 is base pay, 25 percent is

---

[26] Frederic W. Cook, "Compensation Surveys Are Biased," *Compensation and Benefits Review*, September–October 1994, pp. 19–22.

EXHIBIT 4.17   Market Pricing at Pfizer

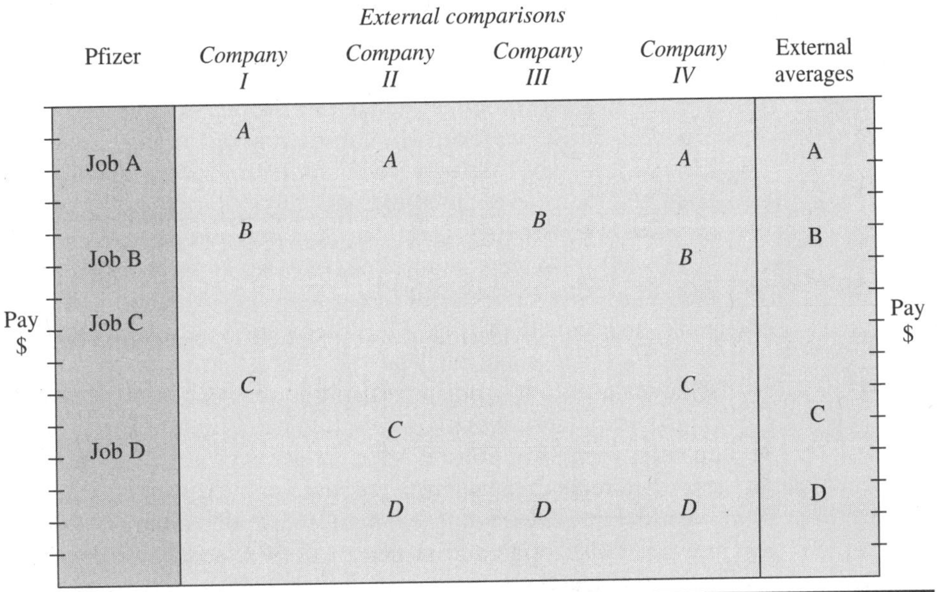

External comparisons

	Pfizer	*Company I*	*Company II*	*Company III*	*Company IV*	External averages

annual bonus, and 5 percent is stock options, then the company matches it. Another $120,000 job, say director of market analysis, may have 60 percent base, 30 percent bonus, and 10 percent stock options among market competitors.

Letting Competitors Determine Pay Structure.   Note what is going on here. The approach to achieving internal consistency really is to match the competition. Market pricing carried to this extreme deemphasizes internal consistency completely. Gone is any attempt to align internal pay structures with the business strategy and the work performed. Rather, the internal pay structure is aligned with competitors' decisions that are reflected in the market.

This approach raises several issues. Among them: Just how valid is market data?[27] How specific and finely calibrated is market data? Does it really lend itself to such decisions? Why should competitors' pay decisions be the sole or even primary determinant of your company's pay structure? If it is, then how your company pays is no longer a source of competitive advantage because it only matches competitors. We will return to these and other external market issues in Chapters 6 and 7.

---

[27] S. Rynes and G. Milkovich, "Wage Surveys: Dispelling Some Myths about the 'Market Wage,'" *Personnel Psychology*, Spring 1986, pp. 71–90; Frederic W. Cook, "Compensation Surveys Are Biased," *Compensation and Benefits Review*, September–October 1994, pp. 19–22.

Summary

The differences in the rates paid for different jobs and skills affect the ability of managers to achieve their business objectives. Differences in pay matter. They matter to employees, because their willingness to take on more responsibility and training, to focus on adding value for customers and improving quality of products, and to be flexible enough to adopt to change all depend at least in part on how pay is structured for different levels of work. Differences in the rates paid for different jobs and skills also influence how fairly employees believe they are being treated. Unfair treatment is ultimately counterproductive.

So far we have examined three basic approaches for determining how to design pay differences for different work: job evaluation, skill/competency-based plans, and market pricing. All three need to be understood as procedures used to help design an internal pay structure that is based on the work, will help achieve the business objectives, and is acceptable to the key stakeholders.

Job evaluation has evolved into many different forms and methods. Consequently, wide variations exist in its use and how it is perceived. This chapter discussed some of the many perceptions of the role of job evaluation and reviewed the criticisms leveled at it. No matter how job valuation is designed, its ultimate use is to help design and manage a work-related, business-focused, and agreed-upon pay structure.

We also examined the emerging state of practice regarding skill/competency-based plans. Both clearly signal that continuous learning is valued. Finally, the market pricing approach was also examined.

At this point, we have examined three alternative approaches to valuing work. In the next chapter, we look at ensuring the involvement of the relevant parties, administering these plans, and evaluating their usefulness.

Review Questions

1. Distinguish among job evaluation, skill/competency-based plans, and market pricing.
2. What do these three approaches have to do with a policy of internal consistency?
3. How does the concern over flexibility, control, and chaos relate to these three approaches?
4. What are the pros and cons of using multiple plans within an organization?
5. Consider your college or school. What are the competencies required for your college to achieve its objectives? To gain competitive advantage over other schools? How would you go about identifying such competencies?
6. You are the manager of 10 employees. Everyone becomes very suspicious and upset upon receiving a memo from the personnel department saying jobs are going to be evaluated. How will you reassure the employees?

APPENDIX 4–A

HAY GUIDE CHART—PROFILE METHOD OF POSITION

KNOW-HOW
DEFINITIONS

DEFINITION: Know-How is the sum total to every kind of skill, however acquired, required for acceptable job performance. This sum total which comprises the overall "savvy" has 3 dimensions – the requirements for:

1 Practical procedures, specialized techniques, and scientific disciplines.

2 Know-How of integrating and harmonizing the diversified functions involved in managerial situations occurring in operating, supporting, and administrative fields. This Know-How may be exercised consultatively (about management) as well as executively and involves in some combination the areas of organizing, planning, executing, controlling and evaluating.

3 Active, practicing, face-to-face skills in the area of human relationships (as defined at right).

MEASURING KNOW-HOW: Know-How has both scope (variety) and depth (thoroughness). Thus, a job may require some knowledge about a lot of things, or a lot of knowledge about a few things. The total Know-How is the combination of scope and depth. This concept makes practical the comparison and weighing of the total Know-How content of different jobs in terms of: "How much knowledge about how many things."

3 HUMAN RELATIONS SKILLS

1. BASIC: Ordinary courtesy and effectiveness in dealing with others.

2. IMPORTANT: Understanding, influencing, and/or serving people are important, but not critical considerations.

3. CRITICAL: Alternative or combined skills in understanding, selecting, developing and motivating people are important in the highest degree.

KNOW-HOW 1

		I. MINIMAL			II. RELATED			III. DIVERSE			IV. BROAD		
		1.	2.	3.	1.	2.	3.	1.	2.	3.	1.	2.	3.
	A. PRIMARY	50	57	66	66	76	87	87	100	115	115	132	152
		57	66	76	76	87	100	100	115	132	132	152	175
		66	76	87	87	100	115	115	132	152	152	175	200
	B. ELEMENTARY VOCATIONAL	66	76	87	87	100	115	115	132	152	152	175	200
		76	87	100	100	115	132	132	152	175	175	200	230
		87	100	115	115	132	152	152	175	200	200	230	264
	C. VOCATIONAL	87	100	115	115	132	152	152	175	200	200	230	264
		100	115	132	132	152	175	175	200	230	230	264	304
		115	132	152	152	175	200	200	230	264	264	304	350
	D. ADVANCED VOCATIONAL	115	132	152	152	175	200	200	230	264	264	304	350
		132	152	(152)	175	200	230	230	264	304	304	350	400
		152	175	200	200	230	264	264	304	350	350	400	460
	E. BASIC TECHNICAL-SPECIALIZED	152	175	200	200	230	264	264	304	350	350	400	460
		175	200	230	230	264	304	304	350	400	400	460	528
		200	230	264	264	304	350	350	400	460	460	528	608
	F. SEASONED TECHNICAL-SPECIALIZED	200	230	264	264	304	350	350	400	460	460	528	608
		230	264	304	304	350	400	400	460	528	528	608	700
		264	304	350	350	400	460	460	528	608	608	700	800
	G. TECHNICAL-SPECIALIZED MASTERY	264	304	350	350	400	460	460	528	608	608	700	800
		(304)	350	400	400	460	528	528	608	(700)	700	800	920
		350	400	460	460	528	608	608	700	800	800	920	1056
	H. PROFESSIONAL MASTERY	350	400	460	460	528	608	608	700	800	800	920	1056
		400	460	528	528	608	700	700	800	920	920	1056	1216
		460	528	608	608	700	800	800	920	1056	1056	1216	1400

Left vertical labels: PRACTICAL PROCEDURES · SPECIALIZED TECHNIQUES · SCIENTIFIC DISCIPLINES · MANAGERIAL KNOW-HOW

KH	PS	AC	TOTAL
152			

SUPERVISOR KEY PUNCH

KH	PS	AC	TOTAL
304			

ACTUARIAL SPECIALIST RESEARCH ASSOCIATE

KH	PS	AC	TOTAL
700			

AREA MANAGER

PROBLEM SOLVING
DEFINITIONS

DEFINITION: Problem Solving is the original, "self-starting" thinking required by the job for analyzing evaluating, creating, reasoning, arriving at and making conclusions. To the extent that thinking is circumscribed by standards, covered by precedents, or referred to others, Problem Solving is diminished, and the emphasis correspondingly is on Know-How.

MEASURING PROBLEM SOLVING: Problem Solving measures the intensity of the mental process which employs Know-How to (1) identify, (2) define, and (3) resolves a problem. "You think with what you know." This is true of even the most creative work. The raw material of any thinking is knowledge of facts, principles and means; ideas are put together from something already there. Therefore, Problem Solving is treated as a percentage utilization of Know-How.

Problem Solving has two dimensions:

1 The thinking environment in which the problems are solved.

2 The thinking challenge presented by the problem to be solved.

PROBLEM SOLVING

	THINKING CHALLENGE				
1 → **2**→	1. REPETITIVE	2. PATTERNED	3. INTERPOLATIVE	4. ADAPTIVE	5. UNCHARTED
A. STRICT ROUTINE	10% 12%	14% 16%	19% 22%	25% 29%	33% 38%
B. ROUTINE	12% 14%	16% 19%	22% 25%	29% 33%	38% 43%
C. SEMI-ROUTINE	14% 16%	19% 22%	25% 29%	33% 38%	43% 50%
D. STANDARDIZED	16% 19%	22% 25%	29% (33%)	38% 43%	50% 57%
E. CLEARLY DEFINED	19% 22%	25% 29%	33% 38%	43% 50%	57% 66%
F. BROADLY DEFINED	22% 25%	29% 33%	38% 43%	50% 57%	(66%) 76%
G. GENERALLY DEFINED	25% 29%	33% 38%	43% 50%	(57%) 66%	76% 87%
H. ABSTRACTLY DEFINED	29% 33%	38% 43%	50% 57%	66% 76%	87% 100%

KH	PS	AC	TOTAL
152	**50**		

SUPERVISOR KEY PUNCH

KH	PS	AC	TOTAL
304	**200**		

**ACTUARIAL SPECIALIST
RESEARCH ASSOCIATE**

KH	PS	AC	TOTAL
700	**400**		

AREA MANAGER

ACCOUNTABILITY
DEFINITIONS

DEFINITION: Accountability is the answerability for action and for the consequences thereof. It is the measured effect of the job on end results. It has three dimensions in the following order of importance.

1 **FREEDOM TO ACT** – the degree of personal or procedural control and guidance as defined in the left-hand column of the chart.

2 **JOB IMPACT ON END RESULTS** – as defined at right.

3 **MAGNITUDE** – indicated by the general dollar size of the area(s) most clearly or primarily affected by the job.

2 **IMPACT Of JOB ON END RESULTS**

Indirect:

REMOTE: Informational, recording, or incidental services for use by others in relation to some important end result.

CONTRIBUTORY: Interpretive, advisory, or facilitating services for use by others in taking action.

Direct:

SHARED Participating with others (except own subordinates and supervisors), within or outside the organizational unit, in taking action.

PRIMARY: Controlling impact on end results, where shared accountability or others is subordinate.

ACCOUNTABILITY 1	(1) VERY SMALL OR INDETERMINATE				(2) SMALL				(3) MEDIUM				(4) L	
	R	C	S	P	R	C	S	P	R	C	S	P	R	C
A. PRESCRIBED	10	14	19	25	14	19	25	33	19	25	33	43	25	33
	12	16	22	29	16	22	29	38	22	29	38	50	29	38
	14	19	25	33	19	25	33	43	25	33	43	57	33	43
B. CONTROLLED	16	22	29	38	22	29	38	50	29	38	50	66	38	50
	19	25	33	43	25	33	43	57	33	43	57	76	43	57
	22	29	38	50	29	38	50	66	38	50	66	87	50	66
C. STANDARDIZED	25	33	43	57	33	43	57	76	43	57	76	100	57	76
	29	38	50	(66)	38	50	66	87	50	66	87	115	66	87
	33	43	57	76	43	57	76	100	57	76	100	132	76	100
D. GENERALLY REGULATED	38	50	66	87	50	66	87	115	66	87	115	152	87	115
	43	57	76	100	57	76	100	132	76	100	132	175	100	132
	50	66	87	115	66	87	115	152	87	(115)	152	200	115	152
E. DIRECTED	57	76	100	132	76	100	132	175	100	132	175	230	132	175
	66	87	115	152	87	115	152	200	115	152	200	264	152	200
	76	100	132	175	100	132	175	230	132	175	230	304	175	230
F. ORIENTED DIRECTION	87	115	152	200	115	152	200	264	152	200	264	350	200	264
	100	132	175	230	132	175	230	304	175	230	304	400	230	304
	115	152	200	264	152	200	264	350	200	264	350	460	264	350
G. BROAD GUIDANCE	132	175	230	304	175	230	304	400	230	304	400	528	304	400
	152	200	264	350	200	264	350	460	264	350	460	(608)	350	460
	175	230	304	400	230	304	400	528	304	400	528	700	400	528
H. STRATEGIC GUIDANCE	200	264	350	460	264	350	460	608	350	460	608	800	460	608
	230	304	400	528	304	400	528	700	400	528	700	920	528	700
	264	350	460	608	350	460	608	800	460	608	800	1056	608	800
I. GENERALLY UNGUIDED	304	400	528	700	400	528	700	920	528	700	920	1216	700	920
	350	460	608	800	460	608	800	1056	608	800	1056	1400	800	1056
	400	528	700	920	528	700	920	1216	700	920	1216	1390	920	1216

KH	PS	AC	TOTAL
152	50	**66**	268

SUPERVISOR KEY PUNCH

KH	PS	AC	TOTAL
304	200	**115**	619

ACTUARIAL SPECIALIST RESEARCH ASSOCIATE

KH	PS	AC	TOTAL
700	400	**608**	1708

AREA MANAGER

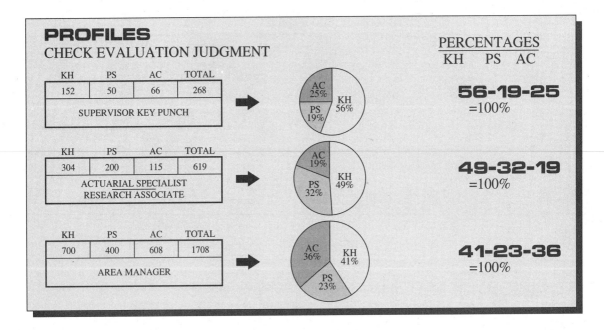

APPENDIX 4–B

FACTOR WEIGHTS AND DEFINITIONS IN BORG-WARNER'S SKILL-BASED PLAN

Factor 1: Basic Knowledge

1st Degree (22 points).   Ability to read, write, add and subtract basic mathematics, interpret and complete simple instructions.

2nd Degree (47 points).   Knowledge of higher mathematical calculations such as basic decimal and fractional equations, ability to read and follow semicomplicated written instructions and to use basic measuring equipment.

3rd Degree (72 points).   Knowledge of a variety of manufacturing skills, specific training, work experience equivalent to trade school or high school, ability to read semicomplicated measuring equipment, graphics, technical or written reports.

4th Degree (111 points).   Extensive specific skills training in a specialized field; equivalent to one–two years of college or vocational (technical) training or master trade certificate.

Factor 2: Electrical/Electronic Skills

Application of the principles of electricity, electronic logic, and integrated transmission technologies, such as lasers. This includes understanding circuits, their component parts, and how they work together.

1st Degree (7 points).   Operational knowledge of electrical/electronic equipment without understanding the electrical/electronic principles on which the equipment operates.

2nd Degree (15 points).   Operational knowledge of electrical/electronic equipment with understanding the electrical/electronic principles on which the equipment operates.

3rd Degree (23 points).   Application of principles of electronic circuitry and appropriate wiring procedures.

4th Degree (37 points).   Application of principles of miniaturized electronic circuits and digital and analog transmission concepts.

Factor 3: Mechanical Skills

The application of mechanical knowledge of how/why mechanical equipment works. It includes the operation, repair, or maintenance of machinery/mechanical systems.

1st Degree (5 points).   This includes the use of basic mechanical ability to operate/adjust single or multiple pieces of mechanical or electromechanical equipment. It includes, but is not limited to, such elements as clearing jams and setting feed speeds and/or pressure changes.

2nd Degree (12 points).   This includes all elements of 1st Degree basic mechanical ability, with the exceptions that the incumbent is required to have the skills to perform preventive maintenance, disassemble/reassemble specific components, change tools, and the like.

3rd Degree (25 points).   Perform servicing and procedural repair activities on mechanical systems/machinery as the primary function.

4th Degree (31 points).   Apply advanced principles of mechanical skills to repair, rebuild, service to a close tolerance level of fit.

5th Degree (37 points).   Perform sophisticated diagnostic and repair activities on complex mechanical or electromechanical machinery/systems.

Factor 4: Graphics

Reading, interpreting, and/or preparing graphic representations of information, such as maps, plans, drawings, blueprints, diagrams, schematics, and timing/flowcharts.

1st Degree (5 points).   Understand basic blueprints and/or prepare rough sketches.

2nd Degree (12 points).   Understand more complex blueprints and/or prepare simple graphic information.

3rd Degree (25 points).   Understand complex, technical graphic representations of information and/or prepare technical graphics.

4th Degree (31 points).   Prepare and/or interpret complex, technical graphic representations of a wide range of information.

5th Degree (37 points).   Develop, prepare, and/or interpret highly complex, sophisticated graphic representations.

Factor 5: Mathematical Skills

The selection and application of mathematical methods or procedures to solve problems or to achieve desired results.

1st Degree (8 points).   Simple arithmetic computations involving addition, subtraction, multiplication, or division.

2nd Degree (15 points).   Computations involving decimals, percentages, fractions, and/or basic statistics.

3rd Degree (23 points).   Computations involving algebra (e.g., solving for an unknown) or geometry (e.g., areas, volumes).

4th Degree (38 points).   Computations involving the use of trigonometry (properties of triangles and circles including sine, cosine, and tangent functions), logarithms and exponents, and advanced statistics.

Factor 6: Communication/Interpersonal Skills

This factor measures the scope and nature of relationships with others.

1st Degree (28 points).   Little or no contact with others. Relationships involving providing and/or receiving information or documents.

2nd Degree (56 points).   Some contact with others. Relationships often require explanation or interpretation of information.

3rd Degree (84 points).   Substantial contact with others. Relationships usually involve discussions with stakeholders or recommendations on issues regarding policies, programs, and so on. Impact is considerable and may be limited to individual departments/programs.

4th Degree (140 points).   Extensive contact with others. Relationships usually include decisions in a broad sense and will affect several areas within the manufacturing unit.

Factor 7: Safety Skills

This factor measures the requirements for adherence to prescribed safety and personal security practices in the performance of required tasks. These safety and personal security practices are generally required to minimize exposure to hazard or risk in the work environment.

1st Degree (10 points).   Perform work in accordance with a few simple safety procedures to minimize potential for injury.

2nd Degree (40 points).   Perform work in accordance with several specific safety procedures to minimize potential for injury.

3rd Degree (80 points).   Perform work in accordance with a wide range of safety procedures to minimize some potential for injury.

4th Degree (100 points).   Perform work in a highly variable environment where safety principles and procedures need to be tailored to deal with unforeseen hazards to minimize high potential for serious injury.

Factor 8: Decision Making/Supervision Required

This factor measures the degree of decision making required without being checked by others, and the degree to which immediate supervisor is required to outline the procedures to be followed and/or the results to be attained on the job.

1st Degree (36 points).   Limited decision making by the incumbent. Progress of work is checked by others most of the time, and/or 60–90 percent of activities are defined by someone other than the incumbent.

2nd Degree (89 points).   Routine decision making based on specific criteria. Progress of work is often checked by others, and/or 40–60 percent of activities are defined by someone other than the incumbent.

3rd Degree (112 points).   Significant decision making based on established guidelines and experience. Progress of work is checked by others some of the time, and/or 25–40 percent of activities are defined by someone other than the incumbent.

4th Degree (180 points).   Extensive decision making based on broad policies, procedures, and guidelines. Progress of work is seldom checked by others, and/or less than 25 percent of activities are defined by someone other than the incumbent.

YOUR TURN:

JOB EVALUATION FOR THE STATE

Your state is enjoying economic growth. Tax revenues are up, but so is the workload for government employees. Recently there have been increasing complaints about pay. Some employees believe that their salary is out of line in comparison to the amount received by other employees. As a first step, the state personnel director hired you to perform job analysis and write job descriptions. The results are shown below. Now a job structure is needed.

1. Divide into teams of four to six students each. Each team should evaluate the eight jobs and prepare a job structure based on its evaluation. Assign titles to each job, and list your structure by title and job letter.

2. Each team should describe the process the group went through to arrive at that job structure. Job evaluation techniques and compensable factors used should be described, and the reasons for selecting them should be stated.

3. Each team should give each job a title and put its job structure on the board. Comparisons can then be made among job structures of the various teams. Does the job evaluation method used appear to affect the results? Do compensable factors chosen affect the results? Does the process affect the results?

4. Evaluate the job descriptions. What parts of them were most useful? How could they be improved?

Job A

Kind of Work.   Directs a large and complex fiscal management program in a large state department, agency, or institution. Provides technical and supervisory financial support to carry out policies and programs established by the department head. Serves as the chief liaison to activity managers to ensure

coordination of their activities in planning with the accounting division. Maintains a close working relationship with the finance agency controller to ensure compliance with budgetary and financial planning requirements of the Department of Finance. Considerable latitude is granted employee in this class for developing, implementing, and administering financial methods and procedures. Typically reports to a high-level department manager with work reviewed through periodic conferences and reports.

Essential Responsibilities

- Directs all accounting functions of the department, agency, or institution so that adequate financial records and fiscal controls are maintained.

- Provides supervisory and high professional skills for the financial operations of the department consistent with the appropriate state and federal laws and regulations so that state and federal funds are utilized in the most efficient and effective manner.

- Provides coordination with other state and federal agencies relating to financial matters so that the department head and agency controller are informed as to matters pertaining to policies, procedures, and programs that may have an effect on the financial operation of the department.

- Develops authorized department budgets and financial plans, goals, and objectives for review and approval by the agency controller and the department head so that maximum use will be made of financial resources.

- Consults with and advises the department head, managers, supervisors, and the agency controller on financial policies and procedures, organizational changes, and interpretation of financial data and reports to ensure efficient and effective fiscal management.

Job B

Kind of Work.   Keeps financial records where the accounts are relatively complex or assists higher-level accountants and accounting technicians when the accounts are complex and extensive.

Receives direction from higher-level accounting personnel in the form of a review of work for accuracy and completeness. In some cases, may provide lead work direction to account clerks or clerical personnel engaged in the bookkeeping operation. Prepares relatively simple reports, makes preliminary analyses of financial conditions for use by other employees, and implements minor procedural and transactional changes in the fiscal operation. Emphasis is on bookkeeping procedures and the smooth transition of fiscal operations.

Essential Responsibilities

- Maintains the financial records of a moderate-sized department according to established procedures and makes adjustments to the records as directed.

- Prepares special analytical data for use by others in preparing budget requests or other reports.

- Approves and processes travel, account, invoice, and claim documents for payment.

- Codes and records all receipts and disbursement of funds.

- Reviews encumbrance or liquidation documents for accuracy and conformity with procedures and expedites financial transactions.

- Accesses or inputs information to the statewide accounting system.

- Investigates errors or problems in the processing of fiscal transactions and recommends changes in procedures.

- Issues purchase orders.

- Provides lead work direction to other bookkeeping and clerical employees.

- Performs related work as required.

Job C

Kind of Work.   Serves as section chief or top assistant to an accounting director or other high-level fiscal management officer in a moderate or large-sized state department. Directs the activities of an accounting or fiscal management section consisting of several subsections or assists the supervisor with the supervision of a very large and complex accounting operation. Works closely with the chief fiscal officer in formulating fiscal policies and independently establishes new accounts in payroll procedures to accomplish the department's program. Considerable independence of action is granted the employee, with work reviewed through reports and conferences.

Essential Responsibilities

- Prepares and administers the department budget, confers with operating officials on projected needs, and devises methods of adjusting budgets so that agency programs may be carried on efficiently and effectively.

- Provides technical accounting assistance and guidance to operational accounting units within a large- or medium-sized agency so that operating procedures and staff skills will be upgraded on a continuing basis with resultant improvement in quality and reduction in cost.

- Produces special accounting plans, reports, and analyses involving complex accounting methods and principles as a basis for decision making by the chief fiscal officer and the department head.

- Constructs and maintains the department's accounting structure and cost accounting capabilities so the department can conform to legislative intent, meet state and federal regulatory requirements, and provide the department with reporting capabilities.

- Assists in the coordination and ongoing analysis and control of fiscal matters relevant to satellite institutions under departmental supervision.

Job D

Kind of Work. Performs professional accounting work as the fiscal officer of a small department, institution, or major division, or as an assistant to a higher-level accountant in a large fiscal operation. Work involves providing a wide range of accounting services to professional and managerial employees. Assists in the development and maintenance of broad fiscal programs. Regularly performs complex fiscal analysis, prepares fiscal reports for management, and recommends alternative solutions to accounting problems. May supervise account clerks, accounting technicians, or clerical employees engaged in the fiscal operation. Receives supervision from a higher-level accountant, business manager, or other administrative employee.

Essential Responsibilities

- Helps administrative employees develop budgets to ensure that sufficient funds are available for operating needs.

- Monitors cash flow to ensure minimum adequate operating balance.

- Produces reports so that management has proper fiscal information.

- Submits reports to federal and state agencies to ensure that financial reporting requirements are met.

- Analyzes and interprets fiscal reports so that information is available in useful form.

- Instructs technicians and clerks in proper procedures to ensure smooth operation of accounting functions.

- Investigates fiscal accounting problems so that adequate solutions may be developed.

- Recommends and implements new procedures to ensure the efficient operation of the accounting section.

- Interprets state laws and department policies to ensure the legality of fiscal transactions.

Job E

Kind of Work. Performs semiprofessional accounting work within an established accounting system. Responsible for maintaining accounting records on a major set of accounts, preauditing transactions in a major activity, or handling cash receipts in a major facility, and for classifying transactions, substantiating source documents, balancing accounts, and preparing reports as prescribed. Responsible for recognizing errors or problems in the fiscal transactions of an agency and recommending alternative solutions for consideration by other staff. Must regularly exercise initiative and independent judgment and may provide lead-work direction to account clerks or clerical employees engaged in the fiscal operation. Receives supervision from other accounting personnel.

Essential Responsibilities

- Controls expenditures so they do not exceed budget totals and prepares allotment requests in the agency's budgetary accounts.

- Processes encumbrance changes of expenditures authorization and adjusts budget as necessary and desired.

- Reconciles department accounting records with the statewide accounting system and records documents so that funds may be appropriated, allotted, encumbered, and transferred.

- Authorizes reimbursement for goods and services received by a major department.

- Develops and maintains a system of accounts receivable, including issuance of guidelines for participants and preparation of state and federal reports.

- Provides daily accounting on loans receivable or financial aids for a major college.

- Audits cost vendor statements for conformity within departmental guidelines.

- Supervises cash accounting unit and prepares reports on receipts and deposits.

- Performs related work as required.

Job F

Kind of Work.   Keeps financial records when the accounts are relatively simple, or assists others in assigned work of greater difficulty where accounting operations are more complex and extensive. The work involves a combination of clerical and book-keeping responsibilities requiring specialized train-ing or experience. Receives direction from higher-level accounting personnel in the form of detailed instructions and close review for accuracy and con-formance with law, rules, or policy. Once oriented to the work, employee may exercise independent judgment in assigned duties.

Essential Responsibilities

- Maintains complete bookkeeping records independently when scope, volume, or complexity is limited or maintains a difficult part of an extensive bookkeeping operation.

- Codes and records all receipts and disbursement of funds.

- Prepares travel, account, invoice, and claim documents for payment.

- Reviews encumbrance or liquidation documents for accuracy and conformity with procedures and expedites financial transactions.

- Prepares financial information of reports and audits, invoices, and expenditure reports.

- Keeps general, control, or subsidiary books of accounts such as cash book appropriation and disbursement ledgers and encumbrance records.

- Accesses or inputs information to the statewide accounting system as directed.

- Performs related tasks as required.

Job G

Kind of Work.   Performs varied and difficult semi-professional accounting work within an established accounting system. Maintains a complex set of ac-counts and works with higher management outside the accounting unit in planning and controlling ex-penditures. Works with higher-level employees in providing technical fiscal advice and service to func-tional activities. Receives supervision from higher-level management or accounting personnel. May pro-vide lead work to lower-level accounting, bookkeep-ing, or clerical personnel.

Essential Responsibilities

- Assists the chief accounting officer in the preparation of all budgets to ensure continuity in financial operations.

- Prepares and assembles the biennial budget and coordinates all accounting functions for a small department according to overall plan of department head and needs expressed by activity managers.

- Maintains cost coding and allocation system for a major department to serve as a basis for reimbursement.

- Provides accounting and budgetary controls for federal, state, and private grants including reconciling bank statements and preparing reports on the status of the budget and accounts.

- Evaluates the spending progress of budget activities, ensures that budgetary limits are not exceeded, and recommends or effects changes in spending plans.

- Provides technical services to divisions of an agency in the supervision of deposits, accounts payable, procurement, and other business management areas.

- Performs related work as required.

Job H

Kind of Work.   Maintains a large and complex system of accounts. Serves as a section chief in the finance division of a very large department, maintains large state-federal or state-county accounts, and oversees a major statewide accounting function in the Department of Finance. Responsible for coordinating and supervising the various phases of the accounting function. Responsibility extends to the development of procedure and policies for the work involved. Supervises a staff of accounting personnel.

Essential Responsibilities

- Provides regular budget review so that program managers have adequate funds to be effective.
- Conducts financial analysis for economical and equitable distribution or redistribution of agency resource.
- Prepares long- and short-range program recommendations for fiscal action so that agency policies are consistent.
- Plans and directs the computerization of systems applied to fiscal services to ensure efficient operation.
- Develops and defines accounting office procedures to ensure the efficient delivery of fiscal services.
- Reviews and analyzes cost accounting computer output to ensure proper documentation of projected cost as required by federal policy and procedures.
- Prepares and supervises the preparation of federal budgets and grant requests, financial plans, and expenditure reports so that they accurately reflect needs and intent of the agency.
- Develops accounting and documentation procedures for county welfare departments so that state and federal auditing and reporting requirements are met.
- Establishes and maintains a financial reporting system for all federal and other nonstate funding sources so that all fiscal reporting requirements are adhered to on a timely and accurate basis.
- Assists grantee agencies in proper reporting procedures under federal grant programs so that requirements for reimbursement may be made on a timely basis.
- Determines the statewide indirect costs so that all state agencies are allocated their proportionate share of indirect costs.
- Supervises the review and processing of all encumbrance documents submitted to the Department of Finance so that necessary accounting information is recorded accurately and promptly in the accounting system.

YOUR TURN:

SKILL-BASED PAY AT BORG-WARNER

Borg-Warner (BW), a 600-person facility, manufactures the world's highest-quality timing and drive chains. These chains, similar in concept to the chain on a bicycle, are used in car and light truck transmissions. General Motors, Ford, and BMW use BW as the primary supplier of drive chains for their vehicles. Honda and Toyota also order BW chains, although these Japanese manufacturers also produce their own chains. For the last 10 years, BW's chains have had a worldwide reputation for quality, but their consumers pay a premium price for BW's product.

Recently, the quality differential between chains manufactured by foreign competitors, primarily the Japanese and South Koreans, and BW has narrowed. And foreign-produced chains are lower priced. Although BW remains the "supplier of choice" for its major customers, its management is concerned about its ability to remain competitive.

The Advanced Engineering Unit developed a series of changes for the current manufacturing process. These changes have the potential to vary the quality of chains depending on the customers' specifications. For example, some high performance cars such as GM's Corvette and BMW's 500 and 700 series all demand tight tolerances. In contrast, the tolerances for chains in other product lines such as light trucks and standard cars are looser. Beyond these changes in the current manufacturing process, Advanced Engineering has developed a computer–integrated manufacturing (CIM) technology. The CIM project will introduce even greater changes to the current manufacturing process.

Modifying the BW manufacturing process is inevitable in light of foreign competition and advances in technology. The general manager at the BW facility is ready and eager to move on the first set of changes and has increased the research budget allocated to Advanced Engineering's CIM project.

The general manager also assembled a task force, including an industrial engineer, a member of the advanced engineering group, a production supervisor, and you. Your mission is to develop an implementation process for the first series of changes to position BW for the future. The task force assembled the following information.

Background

- It is clear that flexibility is going to have to be a permanent feature of life at BW.
- The human resource philosophy and practices at BW currently emphasize the importance and dignity of the individual employee, team work, and employee participation. This philosophy is reflected in BW's practices. For example, BW's top managers meet with all employees in groups of 50–60 each to report the facility's financial condition, its future business prospects, and answer any questions employees may wish to raise. These group meetings with the "brass," held on company time, are well attended and lively.

Current Compensation

Employee compensation includes profit sharing (based on the facility's profit performance and paid annually), benefits that match those of U.S. competitors, plus a competitive base pay. Two critical jobs also have individual incentive schemes. Base pay is determined by conventional job analysis and evaluation plans that define each job's duties and tasks and evaluate them using four factors: skill, effort, responsibility, and working conditions. Thus, the base pay employees receive is based on the *job* they hold. Based on attitude surveys and other feedback, employees seem very satisfied with the job evaluation results and the pay relationships among different jobs.

Incentive Pay

Only two jobs, chain assembler and riveter, have incentives. The incentive is a standard piece rate plan

EXHIBIT 1   Current Work Flow and Structure

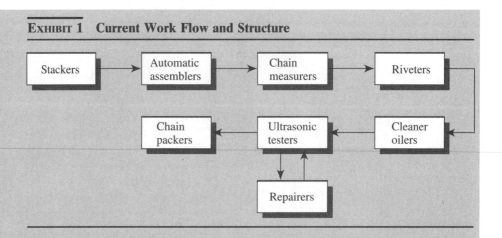

with the standard based on the industrial engineering department's time studies. Employees report that these standards are fair; they have remarked, however, that the existing plans emphasize quantity produced rather than quality. Chain quality is controlled through two jobs, ultrasonic tester and inspector/repairer.

Work Flow and Structure

The facility's current work flow and job structure are described in Exhibit 1. Note that bringing the chain parts from inventory to the assembly line is performed by employees in the stacker job. Automatic assemblers operate machines that assemble the chains, chain measurers operate equipment that measures and cuts chains to appropriate lengths, and riveters hook up and perform the final assembly of the chain. Next, the chains are prepared by the chain cleaner and oiler to undergo quality control inspection by the ultrasonic tester. A defective chain goes to the repairer job and, once reassembled, it is rerouted to the ultrasonic tester. Finally, chains that meet BW's quality standards are prepared for shipment by the chain packer.

Current and Proposed Structure

The task force is considering converting the *job-based structure* to one based on employees' *knowledge or skill* required to perform the work. Exhibit

2 compares the current job structure and pay rates to the proposed skill-based structure. Note that BW currently requires seven jobs (10 employees) for each assembly group. With the proposed technological changes in the manufacturing process, each "manufacturing cell" will require three basic skills levels; A, B and C. Skill C basically incorporates the skills and knowledge required to perform five current jobs (stacker, cleaner/oiler, ultrasonic tester, repairer, and chain stacker). Skill B includes those skills currently involved in assembler and riveter, in addition to all the skill C jobs. Finally, skill A will include *all* the skills and knowledge required in all seven jobs plus some supervisory and team leadership skills. Employees who attain the level of skill A will be able to perform any tasks in the team, and they will assume some of the leadership, coordination, and scheduling tasks formerly performed by first-level supervision.

The ideal mix of skills required for each new cell is not clear, but the task force anticipates that five to seven employees will be required to produce the same volume of chains as the current manufacturing groups. At the minimum, one employee must have obtained each level of skill and a minimum of five employees would be required for a cell to operate.

Discussion Questions

1. What are the major advantages and limitations of internal pay structure based on skills? What

EXHIBIT 2   Current Job-Based Pay Structure and Proposed Skill-Based Structure

	Current—Job Based		
Hourly Pay Rate	*Employees*	*Job Classification*	*Proposed Skill Based*
6.50	1	Chain Stacker	
6.60	2	Chain Packer	
6.60	1	Cleaner/Oiler	Skill C
6.75	1	Ultrasonic Tester	Skill B
6.80	1	Chain Repairer	
11.65*	2	Chain Assemblers/Measurers	
10.50*	2	Riveters	
			Skill A

* Average hourly rate earned under current piece rate incentive plan.

are *the key differences between the two approaches* (job evaluation and job-based structures compared to skill-based structures)?

2. What rates of pay for each skill level do you recommend? What is the rationale for your proposal? Will you keep the individual incentive schemes for skill B?

3. How would you go about introducing the skill-based approach to employees? What are some key issues involved in the actual implementation of such an approach? Based on the information provided, discuss whether you would recommend the proposed skill-based plan. What are the costs of each approach? Has the task force considered all the implications of a skill-based approach (e.g., training programs and skill evaluation procedures required)? What, if anything, will be done with any surplus employees? Finally, what two or three pieces of additional information should the task force gather and how would you recommend it use the information to aid its decision making?

CHAPTER

Evaluating Work: Administration

Chapter Outline

American Telephone & Telegraph Co. (AT&T) for years had little competition. Its local operating companies petitioned state commissions for rate changes that more often than not were granted. Prices for phone services were calculated on some sense of "adequate return on investment," and profits generated by improved technology in long distance lines were used to hold down charges for local service. But antitrust lawsuits led to the breakup of AT&T. Faced for the first time with aggressive competitors, AT&T transformed itself. AT&T is no longer only the phone company. It has transformed itself into a network of communications and information/technology units in strategic alliances with other companies, many of them competitors, around the world. AT&T has become a network of integrated business units that market different products/services in different regions of the world. In 1994 the company had 20-plus decentralized units with approximately 300,000 employees; about 55,000 of them worked outside the United States.[1]

Gone is AT&T's protective, predictable, nurturing employment relationship and culture. "Ma Bell" has become an amoebalike creature continually reshaping itself. Its business strategy now emphasizes adding economic value for its customers, its shareholders, and its employees. As a result of this new strategy, the compensation system has also changed. AT&T continuously redesigns its managerial pay structures to support flexibility and mobility across functions and business units. Each business unit designs its employee compensation system to ensure its competitive advantage while supporting AT&T's overall strategy.

To support this diversity, each business unit has the flexibility to determine whether job evaluation, skill/competency-based plans, and/or market pricing best aligns it with the prevailing business/socio/political environment. The management job evaluation plan (MJE/Hay) at AT&T was redesigned to include compensable factors that more accurately value the new global competitive environment. AT&T management asked, What is it we want to pay for? and got a set of answers that differed from the answers under its regulated environment. The new plan includes team-oriented, customer-centered, and internationally oriented factors. Two AT&T units, Universal Cards and Paradyne, have experimented with skill/competency-based approaches. Recently acquired NCR, now renamed Global Information Solutions, continues to use a modified version of the original Hay plan. However, the glue that binds this network of business units and strategic alliances is adherence to AT&T's policy of adding value for its customers, shareholders, and employees.

As you might imagine, the transformation has not been easy. CBS News reported the suspension of AT&T employees (who were scheduled for layoffs anyway) for wearing to work T-shirts with the motto: "Road Kill on the Information Superhighway." So much for adding value.

While all this discussion of amoebalike change and flexible compensation systems is heady stuff for compensation wonks, some of us occasionally yearn for the "old days." This yearning surfaces whenever I call a business whose

---

[1] AT&T Annual Report 1994. Personal communication with Jorg Kasparek, Robert Rusek, and Tappas Sen of AT&T.

phone is answered by mellow software that orders me, "If you wish to place an order, press 1. If you wish to inquire about an order, press 2. If you wish to etc., etc., etc.," and greets me at the end with a dial tone. While we do not telephone Dave Barry with any regularity, rumor has it that his even mellower telephone software says, "If you wish to press one, press one. If you wish to press two, press two."

For AT&T employees, the shift to more competitive environments means designing internal pay structures that support acquiring the skills and competencies that add value. The AT&T experience illustrates the underlying premise of this book: Compensation decisions, properly made, can be a source of competitive advantage. Improperly made, they will place an organization at a disadvantage.

We began our discussion of evaluating work in the previous chapter. We examined three basic approaches: job evaluation, skill-based plans, and market pricing. Also recall what the last three chapters are all about: designing and managing the internal pay structures that help the organization treat employees fairly. The major decisions already discussed include (1) determining the purpose of evaluating work, (2) deciding whether to use single or multiple plans, and (3) choosing among alternative approaches. This chapter discusses the remaining decisions: (4) ensuring the involvement of key stakeholders and (5) evaluating the usefulness of the plans and resulting structure.

WHO SHOULD BE INVOLVED?

Who should be involved in evaluating work? The choice is usually among compensation managers, operating managers, and/or employees. Regardless of the approach, if the process is to aid managers and if ensuring high involvement and commitment from employees is important, those managers and employees with a stake in the resulting structures need to be involved.

Committees, Task Forces, and Teams

A common approach to understanding pay decisions and gaining their acceptance is the use of committees, task forces, and teams. Membership in these groups seems to vary among firms. All of them typically include representatives from key operating functions, and many include nonmanagerial employees. In some cases, the group's role is only advisory; in others, it designs the evaluation approach and approves all major changes. Some go so far as to prescribe roles for members similar to those shown in Exhibit 5.1.

The Design Process Matters

Case studies emphasize the importance of identifying key stakeholders to champion the approach internally.[2] Often the champions or advocates tend to be line

---

[2] Gerald E. Ledford, Jr., "Three Case Studies on Skill-Based Pay: An Overview," *Compensation and Benefits Review*, March–April 1991, pp. 11–23.

EXHIBIT 5.1   Roles of Evaluation Group Members

Leader	Members	Facilitator	Expert
• Understand evaluation plan	• Understand evaluation plan	• Understand evaluation plan	• Clarify job analysis data
• Listen	• Listen	• Listen	• Provide additional information
• Keep the group moving	• Discuss facts and assumptions	• Ask questions to facilitate objectives	• Serve as an adviser
• Encourage participation	• Analyze information objectively	• Make suggestions on group process	• Can be a temporary "voting" member
• Prevent individuals from dominating	• Ask questions	• Help group reach a consensus	
• Express own opinion	• Formulate and express opinions	• Can be a full committee member	
• Encourage consensus	• Encourage and reach consensus	• Maintain documentation	
	• Commit to participation and timetable		

Source: Jill Kanin-Lovers, "Using Committees to Evaluate Jobs," *Journal of Compensation and Benefits* (New York: Warren Gorham and Lamont, 1986).

managers. The design teams focus on achieving employee and manager ownership of the results. This practice is less common in the design of job evaluation and market pricing plans and may help explain the growing interest in skill/competency plans.

Procedural equity, discussed in Chapter 2, is highly related to employee involvement and acceptance. Research strongly suggests that attending to the equity of the design process and the approach chosen (job evaluation, skill/competency-based plan, and market pricing) rather than focusing solely on the results (the internal pay structure) is likely to achieve employee and management commitment, trust, and acceptance of the results.[3] And achieving procedural equity is related to the design process and who participates.

---

[3] One of the key findings of a National Academy of Science report that examined virtually all research on pay was that the process used to design pay plans is vital to achieving high commitment. George Milkovich and Alexandra Wigdor, eds., *Pay and Performance* (Washington, DC: National Academy Press, 1991). Also, see Edward E. Lawler III and J. Richard Hackman, "Impact of Employee Participation in the Development of Pay Incentive Plans: A Field Experiment," *Journal of Applied Psychology* 53, no. 6 (December 1969), pp. 467–71; Carl F. Frost, John W. Wakely, and Robert A. Ruh, *The Scanlon Plan for Organization Development: Identity, Participation, and Equity* (East Lansing: Michigan State Press, 1974); K. C. Sheflen, E. E. Lawler III, and J. R. Hackman, "Long-Term Impact of Employee Participation in the Development of Pay Incentive Plans: A Field Experiment Revisited," *Journal of Applied Psychology* 55 (1971), pp.

Case descriptions report improved employee attitudes toward their pay at both the General Mills and Honeywell sites following the use of high employee involvement in the design of skill/competency-based plans.[4] But recall the caveats on case descriptions that we discussed in Chapter 1. These results need to be treated with a tad of caution. The reported improvement in attitudes may have been due to high involvement or the skill/competency-based plan or to any number of other factors not controlled, including the attention and interest paid to employees, or the possibility that employees believe they will get higher pay under the new plans. Research does show that higher pay is related to higher satisfaction with pay—no great surprise.[5]

The absence of participation may make it easier for employees and managers to imagine ways the structure might have been rearranged to their personal liking. Crepanzano and Folger observed ". . . if people do not participate in decisions, there is little to prevent them from assuming that things would have been better, 'if I'd have been in charge.'"[6] Additional research is needed to ascertain whether the payoffs from increased participation offset potential costs (time involved to reach consensus, potential problems caused by disrupting current perceptions, etc). For example, the involvement of both subunit and corporate managers raises the potential for conflict due to their differing perspectives. Managers at AT&T's Universal Card wish to gain greater flexibility in order to funnel more pay to key individuals. AT&T corporate types, aware of the difficulties resulting from emphasizing Universal's short-term needs rather than the overall AT&T strategy, may disagree. Note the difference in focus. The Universal Card manager has operating objectives to achieve, does not want to lose key individuals, and views compensation as a mechanism to help accomplish these goals. AT&T corporate, on the other hand, adopts a corporatewide perspective and focuses on ensuring that the decisions are consistent with AT&T's overall strategic intent.

Unions' Stake

To what extent should unions be involved? Management probably will find it advantageous to include union representation as a source of ideas and to help

182–86; E. A. Locke and D. M. Schweiger, "Participation in Decision Making: One More Look," *Research in Organization Behavior* (Greenwich, CT: JAI Press, 1979); J. F. Carey, "Participative Job Evaluation," *Compensation Review*, Fourth Quarter 1977, pp. 29–38; G. J. Jenkins, Jr. and E. E. Lawler III, "Impact of Employee Participation in Pay Plan Development," *Organizational Behavior and Human Performance* 28 (1981), pp. 111–28.

[4] Ledford, "Three Case Studies."

[5] Herbert Heneman III, "Pay Satisfaction," in *Research in Personnel and Human Resources Management*, vol. 3, ed. K. M. Rowland and G. R. Ferris (Greenwich, CT: JAI Press, 1985), pp. 115–39; Barry Gerhart and George Milkovich, "Employee Compensation," in *Handbook of Industrial and Organizational Psychology*, vol. 3, ed. M. D. Dunnette and L. Hough (Palo Alto, CA): Consulting Psychologists Press, 1992).

[6] R. Crepanzano and R. Folger, "Referent Cognitions and Task Decision Autonomy: Beyond Equity Theory," *Journal of Applied Psychology*, September 1989, pp. 17–23.

promote acceptance of the results. For example, union–management task forces participated in the design of new evaluation systems for both a Borg-Warner facility and the federal government.[7] Their roles involved mutual problem solving. But other union leaders believe that philosophical differences prevent their active participation.[8] They take the position that collective bargaining yields more equitable results than do job evaluation or skill-based plans. In other cases, union and management representatives evaluated jobs jointly and submit disagreements to an arbitrator. So the extent of union participation varies. No single perspective exists on the value of active participation in the process, just as no single management perspective exists.

Union involvement with the current wave of skill-based plans is relatively new. Our experience with the employees' unions at Dresser Rand and Colgate-Palmolive suggests that in a reasonably trusting relationship, union officials make invaluable contributions to the design and administration of an evaluation plan.

ADMINISTERING THE PLAN

Our previous chapter led us through the technical decisions involved in evaluating work. The output of the technical phase is typically a manual to assist in applying the plan. The manual becomes the "yardstick" for the plan. It contains information on the plan and a description of the method. Compensable factors are defined and enough information is provided to allow the user to recognize varying degrees of each factor. Skill blocks and levels, competencies, and certification procedures are detailed in the manual. Information needs to be detailed enough to permit accurate and rapid application of whatever approach is used.

Appeals/Review Procedures

No plan anticipates all situations. It is inevitable that some jobs will be incorrectly evaluated, or at least employees and managers may suspect incorrect evaluation. Or some individuals may believe that a skill level should have been certified. Consequently, the manual needs to contain review procedures to handle such cases and to help ensure procedural equity.[9] Often the compensation manager

---

[7] *Modernizing Federal Classification: An Opportunity for Excellence* (Washington DC: National Academy of Public Administration, 1991).

[8] Mike Burns, *Understanding Job Evaluation* (London: Institute of Personnel Management, 1978).

[9] R. Folger and M. A. Konovsky, "Effects of Procedural and Distributive Justice on Reactions to Pay Raise Decisions," *Academy of Management Journal*, March 1989, pp. 115–30; J. Greenberg, "Reactions to Procedural Injustice in Payment Distributions: Do the Ends Justify the Means?" *Journal of Applied Psychology* 72 (1987), pp. 55–61; R. Folger and J. Greenberg, "Procedural Justice: An Interpretative Analysis of Personnel Systems," in *Human Resources Management*, vol. 3, ed. K. M. Rowland and G. R. Ferris (Greenwich, CT: JAI Press, 1985), pp. 141–83.

EXHIBIT 5.2 **Job Evaluation Process**

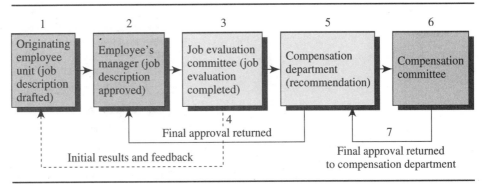

handles reviews, but increasingly, peer or team reviews are being used.[10] Very occasionally, these reviews take on the trappings of formal grievance procedures (e.g., documented complaints and responses and levels of approval). The problems may also be handled by managers and the employee relations generalists through informal discussions with employees.[11]

Training

Once the manual is complete, those who will be applying the methodology require training in its proper use. These employees may also need background information on the entire pay system and how it relates to the overall human resource strategies and the organization's business strategy.

Control: Approval and Certification

When the evaluations are completed, approval by higher levels of management is usually required. The particular approval process differs among organizations; Exhibits 5.2 and 5.3 are examples. The approval process serves as a control. It helps ensure that any changes that result from evaluating work are consistent with the organization's operations and directions.

Where control resides is important. In Exhibit 5.2, control could be shifted to the manager and include only the shaded boxes 1, 2, and 6, deleting steps 3, 4, and 5 (and even 6) from the process. Reengineering advocates thrive on this sort of redesign—quicker decisions and less bureaucracy. However, the real issue is to ensure that the decisions support objectives. Perhaps shifting compensation managers into the advisory role (and out of the "control" role) makes sense.

---

[10] Sharon A. Tucker and Kathryn Cofsky, "Competency Based Pay on a Banding Platform," *ACA News*, Spring 1994, 3, no. 1, pp. 30–40.

[11] T. B. Carver and A. A. Vondra, "Alternative Dispute Resolution: Why It Doesn't Work and Why It Does," *Harvard Business Review*, May–June 1994, pp. 120–29.

EXHIBIT 5.3   Skill Assessment Process

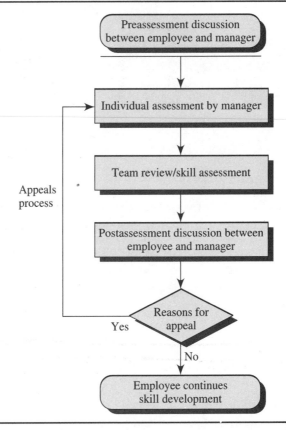

Source: Peter Leblanc, "Skill Based Pay Case #2: Northern Telecom," *Compensation and Benefits Review*, March–April 1991, p. 50.

Managing Expectations: Communication

Employee and managerial understanding and acceptance of the process requires communication. Either through brochures, videos, information sessions, or other communication devices, the goals of the system, the stakeholders' roles in it, and the final results need to be explained to all employees. Employees have a right to know what a system does for (to?) them.

Final Result: Internal Structure

The final result of the administration phase is a hierarchy of work. This hierarchy translates the employer's internal consistency policy into practice. Exhibit 5.4 shows four hypothetical job structures within a single evaluation. These structures were obtained via different approaches to evaluating work. The jobs are arrayed

EXHIBIT 5.4 Resulting Internal Structures—Job, Skill, and Competency Based

Managerial Group	Technical Group	Manufacturing Group	Administrative Group
		Assembler I Inspector I	
Vice Presidents	Head/Chief Scientist	Packer	Administrative Assistant
Division General Managers	Senior Associate Scientist	Materials Handler Inspector II	Principal Administrative Secretary
Managers	Associate Scientist	Assembler II	Administrative Secretary
Project Leaders	Scientist	Drill Press Operator Rough Grinder	Word Processor
Supervisors	Technician	Machinist I Coremaker	Clerk/Messenger
↑ Job Evaluation	↑ Competency-Based	↑ Skill-Based	↑ Job Evaluation

in hierarchies within four basic functions: managerial, technical, manufacturing, and administrative. The managerial and administrative structures were obtained via a point job evaluation plan, and technical and manufacturing work via two different skill-based plans; the manufacturing plan was negotiated with the union. The point of the exhibit is to illustrate the results of evaluating work: structures that are consistent with the policy of internal consistency. Organizations commonly have multiple structures derived through multiple approaches. Consistency in such cases may be interpreted as consistency within each functional group or unit. Although some employees in one structure may wish to compare the procedures used in another structure with their own, the underlying premise in Exhibit 5.4 and in practice is that internal consistency is most influenced by fair and equitable treatment of employees doing similar work in the same skill group.

Once the structure or structures are established, managers must ensure that they remain internally consistent and equitable. This requires seeing that jobs and skills that employees believe are incorrectly evaluated are recertified and reevaluated (e.g., appeals/review procedures) and that new jobs or those that experience significant changes get reevaluated.

Competencies as compensable factors can become obsolete as strategies shift. Under skill-based plans employees often are required to be recertified, since the work they perform may not require them to use all the skills for which they were certified. Airplane pilots, for example, must go through an emergency-landing simulation every 12 months, since the airlines' objective is to ensure that such crucial skills are not actually demonstrated on the job with any frequency. Similarly, the introduction of new skill requirements and the obsolescence of previous skills require recertification. At its Ome facility in Tokyo, Toshiba requires all team members to recertify their skills every 24 months. Those who fail have the opportunity to retrain and attempt to recertify before their pay rate is reduced. However, the pressure to keep up-to-date and avoid obsolescence is intense. The same sense of urgency to avoid obsolescence does not pervade competency-based schemes since competencies are more general and less specific to a particular job or project.

EVALUATE USEFULNESS

The usefulness of any management system is a function of how well it accomplishes its objectives. Job evaluation, skill/competency-based plans, and market pricing approaches need to be judged on their usefulness. In Chapter 2 we noted that pay structures influence a wide variety of employee behaviors, such as reducing the need for additional training, increasing willingness to take on new assignments, and decreasing turnover and absenteeism. Fortunately, research is beginning to assess the structures in terms of their ability to affect employee behaviors.

Job-Evaluation Research: The Counterculture.   Research on job evaluation has focused on the procedures, not on whether job evaluation pays off or affects employee behaviors. In general, the research treats job evaluation as a measurement device and considers its reliability, its validity, the costs involved in its design and implementation, and its compliance with laws and regulations. Let us review some of the work that has been reported.

Reliability: Do Different Evaluators in Different Circumstances Obtain Different Results?

Reliability refers to the consistency of results obtained under different conditions. For example, to what extent do different evaluators come to similar conclusions? Few employers or consulting firms report the results of their studies. However, several research studies by academics present a mixed picture; some report relatively high consistency whereas others report lower agreement on the values assigned to each specific compensable factor.[12] Some evidence also reports that

---

[12] Several studies on the reliability of job evaluation plans have been reported. Four reviews provide useful overviews: R. D. Arvey, "Sex Bias in Job Evaluation Procedures," *Personnel Psychology*, Summer 1986, pp. 315–35; D. P. Schwab, "Job Evaluation and Pay Setting: Concepts and Practices," in *Comparable Worth: Issues and Alternatives*, ed. E. R. Livernash (Washington, DC: Equal Employment Advisory Council, 1980), pp. 49–78; R. J. Snelgar, "The Comparability

evaluators' background and training may affect reliability.[13] An evaluator's affiliation with union or management appears to have little effect.

Using evaluators who are familiar with the jobs appears to enhance reliability.[14] This result lends support to the practice of involving employees in the evaluation process. One study reports that results obtained through a group consensus process were similar to those obtained by independent evaluators or an average of individual evaluators' results.[15] Yet group consensus is widely used in practice. Each evaluator makes a preliminary independent evaluation. Then, meeting as a job evaluation committee, evaluators discuss their results until consensus emerges.

Although all this research is interesting, it fails to address a key issue: to what extent does the degree of reliability of job evaluation influence pay decisions, employees' attitudes, and work behaviors? Only two studies have directly addressed this issue. Madigan examined three different job evaluation plans: a guide chart method similar to the Hay Guide Charts presented in Appendix 4–A, the Position Analysis Questionnaire discussed in Chapter 3, and a custom-designed point plan using six factors (knowledge, experience, interpersonal skill, and supervisory, decision-making, and fiscal responsibilities). Although he found high consistency among raters, when he examined the impact of the results from different plans on actual pay decisions, he found significant differences. For example, when different evaluators used the custom-designed point plan, their pay recommendations for the jobs agreed in only 51 percent of jobs. The differences in results translated into a range of ±160 evaluation points, which meant significant pay differences for affected employees. Madigan points out that by traditional academic standards, the reliability of these three methods are acceptable. However, managers and affected employees probably wouldn't agree. (Nor would academics if it were their pay.) Madigan observes, "The assessment of potential error . . . in job evaluation must go beyond reliability estimates to include the estimates of impact of pay decisions."[16]

---

of Job Evaluation Methods," *Personnel Psychology* 36 (1983), pp. 371–80; and R. M. Madigan, "Comparable Worth Judgments: A Measurement Properties Analysis," *Journal of Applied Psychology* 70 (1985), pp. 137–47.

[13] T. Naughton, "Effects of Female-Linked Job Titles on Job Evaluation Ratings," *Journal of Management* 14, no. 4 (1988), pp. 567–78; Vandra Huber, "Comparison of Supervisor-Incumbent and Female-Male Multidimensional Job Evaluation Ratings," *Journal of Applied Psychology* 76, no. 1 (1991), pp. 115–21. C. H. Lawshe, Jr., and P. C. Farbo, "Studies in Job Evaluation: 8. The Reliability of an Abbreviated Job Evaluation System," *Journal of Applied Psychology* 33 (1949), pp. 158–66.

[14] J. M. Madden, "The Effect of Varying the Degree of Rater Familiarity in Job Evaluation," *Personnel Administrator* 25 (1962), pp. 42–45; R. E. Cristal and J. M. Madden, *Effect of Degree of Familiarity in Job Evaluation* (Lackland Air Force Base, TX: Personnel Laboratory, Wright Air Development Division, 1960).

[15] D. P. Schwab and H. G. Heneman III, "Assessment of a Consensus-Based Multiple Information Source Job Evaluation System," *Journal of Applied Psychology* 71 (1986), pp. 354–56.

[16] Madigan, "Comparable Worth Judgments."

EXHIBIT 5.5   Illustration of Plan's Hit Rate as a Method to Judge the Validity of Job Evaluation Results

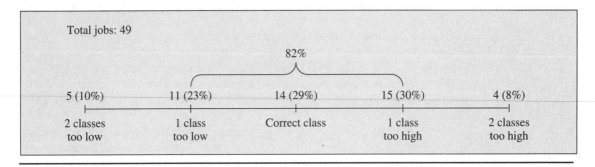

Validity: Do Results Depend on the Method?

The choice among evaluation approaches depends on the circumstances and objectives. Does it make any difference? Do the results differ?

Validity refers to the degree to which an evaluation method yields the desired results. The desired results can be measured several ways: (1) the hit rate (percentage of correct decisions it makes), (2) convergence (agreement with results obtained from other evaluation plans), and (3) employee acceptance (employee and manager attitudes about the evaluation process and the results).[17]

Hit Rates: Agreement with Predetermined Benchmark Structures.

The hit rate approach focuses on the ability of the job evaluation plan to replicate a predetermined, agreed-upon job structure. The agreed-upon structure, as we discussed in the last chapter, can be based on several criteria. The jobs' market rates, or a structure negotiated with a union or a management committee, or rates for jobs held predominantly by men, or some combination of these are all examples. Exhibit 5.5 shows the hit rates for a hypothetical job evaluation plan. The agreed-upon structure has 49 benchmark jobs in it. This structure was derived through negotiation among managers serving on the job evaluation committee. The job evaluation plan placed only 14 (29 percent) of the jobs into their current (agreed-upon) pay classes and came within ± one pay class on 82 percent of the jobs in the agreed-upon structure. In one study the reported hit rates for six different plans ranged from 49 to 73 percent of the jobs classified within ±1 class of their

---

[17] Validity can also be reflected in the R^2 and standard error of estimate generated via regressing benchmark job's wages on compensable factors. R^2 alone is insufficient because it reflects only the strength of the relationship. The error terms are also important, since they reflect the precision with which job grades and pay decisions can be made. Hit rates, in a general sense, capture the R^2 and standard error information. For an early discussion of validation and job evaluation, see William M. Fox, "Purpose and Validity in Job Evaluation," *Personnel Journal* 41 (1962), pp. 432–37.

current, agreed-upon classes.[18] Hit rates in another study ranged from 27 to 73 percent, depending on the scoring method used.[19]

Is a job evaluation plan valid (i.e., useful) if it can correctly place only one-third of the jobs? As with so many questions in compensation, the answer is "It depends." It depends on the alternative approaches available, on the costs involved in designing and implementing these plans, and on the magnitude of errors involved in missing a "direct hit." If, for example, being within ±1 pay class translates into several hundred dollars in pay, then employees probably aren't going to express much confidence in the "validity" of this plan. If, on the other hand, the pay difference between ±1 class is not great *or* the plan's results are treated only as an estimate to be adjusted by the job evaluation committee, then its validity (usefulness) is more likely.

Convergence of Results.   Evaluation plans can also be judged by the degree to which different plans yield similar results. The premise is that convergence of the results from independent methods increases the chances that the results, and hence the methods, are valid. Different results, on the other hand, point to lack of validity. We again turn to Madigan's report on the results of three job evaluation plans (guide chart, PAQ, and point plan).[20] He concludes that the three methods generate different and inconsistent job structures. An employee could have received up to $427 per month more (or less), depending on the job evaluation method used.

Another study applied three variations on a point plan to 15 jobs from three different job families: blue collar, clerical, and professional/technical. Although all three plans gave similar results, none of them matched the employer's rankings in any of the job groups. The authors conclude that the methods were reliable, but not necessarily valid or correct, because all three of them ranked a police officer higher than a detective.[21] Fans of the television series "Homicide" have no doubt that Detective Frank Pembleton outranks the "uniforms."

These results are provocative. They are consistent with the proposition that job evaluation, as traditionally practiced and described in this and other textbooks, is not a measurement procedure.[22] This is so because it fails to consistently

---

[18] L. R. Gomez-Mejia, R. C. Page, and W. W. Tornow, "A Comparison of the Practical Utility of Traditional, Statistical, and Hybrid Job Evaluation Approaches," *Academy of Management Journal* 25 (1982), pp. 790–809.

[19] R. M. Madigan and D. J. Hoover, "Effects of Alternative Job Evaluation Methods on Decisions Involving Pay Equity," *Academy of Management Journal*, March 1986, pp. 84–100.

[20] Madigan, "Comparable Worth Judgments"; D. Doverspike and G. Barrett, "An Internal Bias Analysis of a Job Evaluation Instrument," *Journal of Applied Psychology* 69 (1984), pp. 648–62.

[21] Judith Collins, "Job Evaluation" (Working paper, University of Arkansas–Little Rock, 1992).

[22] Kermit Davis, Jr., and William Sauser, Jr., "Effects of Alternative Weighting Methods in a Policy-Capturing Approach to Job Evaluation: A Review and Empirical Investigation," *Personnel Psychology* 44 (1991), pp. 85–127.

exhibit properties of reliability and validity. However, it is important to maintain a proper perspective in interpreting these results. Few compensation managers consider job evaluation a measurement tool in the strict sense of that term. More often, it is viewed as a procedure to help rationalize an agreed-upon pay structure in terms of job and business-related factors. As such, it becomes a process of give and take, not an immutable yardstick. This perspective leads us to a third criteria to judge the validity of a job evaluation plan: its acceptance by the parties involved.

Acceptability.   Several devices are used to assess and improve acceptability. An obvious one is the inclusion of a *formal appeals process,* discussed earlier. Employees who believe their jobs are evaluated incorrectly should be able to request reanalysis and/or skills reevaluation. Most firms respond to such requests from managers, but few extend the process to all employees, unless those employees are represented by unions who have negotiated a grievance process. No matter what the outcome from the appeal, the results need to be explained in detail to anyone who requests reevaluation.

A second method of assessing acceptability is to include questions about it in *employee attitude surveys.*[23] Questions can assess perceptions of how useful evaluation is as a management tool. Another method is to *audit* how the plan is being used on a series of measures of use. Exhibit 5.6 lists examples of indexes used by various employers. These indexes range from the percentage of employees who understand the reasons for evaluation to the percentage of jobs with current descriptions, to the rate of requests for revaluation. Acceptability is a somewhat vague test of the job evaluation—acceptable to whom is an open issue. Clearly, managers and employees are important constituents because acceptance makes it a useful device. But as we will discuss in the chapter on pay discrimination (Chapter 14), others outside the firm also have a stake in job evaluation and pay structure.

Costs

Two types of costs associated with evaluation can be identified: (1) design and administration costs and (2) labor costs that result from pay structure changes occasioned by evaluation. The labor cost effects will be unique for each application. Little recent data have been published on design and administration costs, though a rule of thumb of 1 to 3 percent of covered payroll as the cost for traditional job evaluation has been offered. Costs can range from a few thousand dollars for a small organization to more than $500,000 in consultant fees alone for major projects in large firms. This does not include the costs of the compensation professionals, managers, and employees involved. Little cost data for skill-based

---

[23] Sanford Jacoby, "Employee Attitude Surveys in Historical Perspective," *Industrial Relations* 27, no. 1 (Winter 1988), pp. 74–93.

EXHIBIT 5.6 Illustrations of Audit Indexes

A. Overall indicators.
 1. Ratio of number of current descriptions to numbers of employees.
 2. Number of job descriptions evaluated last year and previous year.
 3. Number of jobs evaluated per unit.
   (*a*) Newly created jobs.
   (*b*) Reevaluation of existing jobs.
B. Timeliness of job descriptions and evaluations.
 1. Percent of total jobs with current descriptions.
 2. Percentage of evaluation requests returned within 7 working days, within 14 working days.
 3. Percentage of reevaluation requests returned with changed (unchanged) evaluations.
C. Workability and acceptability of job evaluation.
 1. Percentage of employees (managers) surveyed who know the purposes of job evaluation.
 2. The number of employees who appeal their job's evaluation rating.
 3. The number of employees who receive explanations of the results of their reevaluation requests.

---

or competency-based plans have been published, although consulting firms report tremendous interest in both approaches.

Gender Effects in Evaluation

Much attention has been directed at job evaluation as both a potential source of bias against women and a mechanism to reduce bias.[24] Although Chapter 14 presents an extended discussion of pay discrimination, it has been widely speculated that job evaluation is susceptible to gender bias. To date, three ways that job evaluation can be biased against women have been studied.[25] Unfortunately, no studies of gender effects in skill-based or competency-based plans exist.

Jobholder's Gender. Direct bias occurs if jobs held predominantly by women are undervalued relative to jobs held predominantly by men, simply because of the jobholder's gender. Evidence does not support the proposition that the

---

[24] D. J. Treiman and H. I. Hartmann, eds., *Women, Work and Wages: Equal Pay for Jobs of Equal Value* (Washington, DC: National Academy of Sciences, 1981); H. Remick, *Comparable Worth and Wage Discrimination* (Philadelphia: Temple University Press, 1984); R. G. Blumrosen, "Wage Discrimination, Job Segregation, and Title VII of the Civil Rights Act of 1964," *University of Michigan Journal of Law Reform* 12, no. 3 (1979), pp. 397–502.

[25] This discussion is adapted from D. Schwab and R. Grams, "Sex-Related Errors in Job Evaluation: A 'Real-World' Test," *Journal of Applied Psychology* 70, no. 3 (1985), pp. 533–59; Arvey, "Sex Bias in Job Evaluation Procedures."

gender of the jobholder influences the evaluation of the job. One study found no effects when it varied the gender of jobholders using photographs and recorded voices.[26] Another study reported a slight bias in favor of female-linked *job titles* (e.g., orderly vs. nurse's aide). The evaluators received extensive training in potential gender bias; hence, they may have "bent over backwards" to avoid it.[27] Simply telling evaluators that varying proportions of men and women performed the jobs made no difference.[28]

However, specific compensable factors may be biased for or against gender-segregated jobs.[29] A study found that those compensable factors related to job content (contact with others and error in judgment) did reflect bias, but others pertaining to employee requirements (education and experience required) did not.[30] Two job descriptions were evaluated. The female-linked title, executive secretary, was reportedly undervalued on the job content factors. The psychological literature identifies a common tendency to make stereotypical assumptions, usually to the detriment of women and minorities. Perhaps by calling out the job-related criteria for making judgments, job evaluation is able to avoid this bias.[31]

Wages Criteria Bias. The second potential source of bias affects job evaluation indirectly, through the current wages paid for jobs. In this case, job evaluation results may be biased if the jobs held predominantly by women are incorrectly underpaid. Treiman and Hartmann argue that women's jobs are unfairly underpaid simply because women hold them.[32] If this is the case and if job evaluation is based on the current wages paid, then the job evaluation results simply mirror any bias in the current pay rates. Considering that many job evaluation plans are purposely structured to mirror the existing pay structure, it should not be

---

[26] Richard D. Arvey, Emily M. Passino, and John W. Lounsbury, "Job Analysis Results As Influenced by Sex of Incumbent and Sex of Analyst," *Journal of Applied Psychology* 62, no. 4 (1977), pp. 411–16; Carol T. Schreiber, "Job Evaluation and the Minority Issue," Paper presented at Industrial Relations Counselors Symposium, Atlanta, September 1978, pp. 14–15; J. Goodman and J. Morgan, "Job Evaluation without Sex Discrimination," *Personnel Management* 11, no. 10 (October 1979), pp. 158–67; Catherine M. Meek, "Auditing Your Job Evaluation Plan—A Case Study," *EEO Today*, Spring 1979, pp. 21–27.

[27] Michael K. Mount and Rebecca A. Ellis, "Investigation of Bias in Job Evaluation Ratings of Comparable Worth Study Participants," *Personnel Psychology*, Spring 1987, pp. 85–96.

[28] R. Grams and D. Schwab, "An Investigation of Systematic Gender-Related Error in Job Evaluation," *Academy of Management Journal* 28, no. 2 (1985), pp. 279–90.

[29] Gerald V. Barrett and Dennis Doverspike, "Another Defense of Point-Factor Job Evaluation," *Personnel*, March 1989, pp. 33–36.

[30] Arvey, "Sex Bias in Job Evaluation Procedures."

[31] L. A. Krefting, P. K. Berger, and M. J. Wallace, Jr., "The Contribution of Sex Distribution, Job Content, and Occupational Classification to Job Sextyping," *Journal of Vocational Behavior* 13 (1978), pp. 181–91; L. A. Krefting, P. K. Berger, and M. J. Wallace, Jr., "Sextyping by Personnel Practitioners," Paper presented at Academy of Management national meetings, San Francisco, 1978.

[32] Treiman and Hartmann, *Women, Work and Wages.*

surprising that the current wages for jobs influence the results of job evaluation. In one study, 400 experienced compensation administrators were sent information on current pay, market, and job evaluation results. They were asked to use this information to make pay decisions for a set of nine jobs. Half of the administrators received information on jobs traditionally held by men (e.g., security guards) and half received information on jobs traditionally held by women (e.g., secretary II). The results revealed that (1) market data had a substantially larger effect on pay decisions than did job evaluations or current pay data and (2) the jobs' gender had no effect.[33]

This study is a unique look at several factors that may affect pay structures. If market rates and current pay already reflect gender bias, then these biased pay rates could work indirectly through the job evaluation process to deflate the evaluation of jobs held primarily by women.[34] Clearly, the criteria used in the design of evaluation plans are crucial and need to be business and work related.

Evaluator's Gender.   The third possible source of gender bias in evaluation is the gender of the individual evaluators. Some argue that male evaluators may be less favorably disposed toward jobs held predominantly by women. However, there is no evidence that the job evaluator's gender affects the results. Several recommendations seek to ensure that job evaluation plans are bias free. The recommendations include the following:

1. Define the compensable factors and scales to include the content of jobs held predominantly by women. For example, working conditions should include the noise and stress of office machines and the repetitive movements associated with the use of word processors.
2. Ensure that factor weights are not consistently biased against jobs held predominantly by women. Are factors usually associated with these jobs always given less weight?
3. Apply the plan in as bias-free a manner as feasible. Ensure that the job descriptions are bias free, exclude incumbent names from the job evaluation process, and train women as evaluators.

Some writers see job evaluation as a friend of those who wish to combat pay discrimination.[35] Without a properly designed and applied system, "employers will face an almost insurmountable task in persuading the government that

---

[33] S. Rynes, C. Weber, and G. Milkovich, "The Effects of Market Survey Rates, Job Evaluation, and Job Gender on Job Pay," *Journal of Applied Psychology* 74 (1989), pp. 114–23; also see Doverspike and Barrett, "An Internal Bias Analysis."

[34] Grams and Schwab, "Investigation of Systematic Gender-Related Error in Job Evaluation."

[35] Paula England, *Comparable Worth: Theories and Evidence* (New York: Aldine De Gruyter, 1992).

ill-defined or whimsical methods of determining differences in job content and pay are a business necessity."[36] On the other hand, some lawyers recommend that employers avoid job evaluation on the grounds that the results will lead to lawsuits. This issue will be discussed again in the chapter on pay discrimination.

At the risk of pointing out the obvious, all issues concerning job evaluation also apply to skill-based and competency-based plans. For example, the acceptability of the results of skill-based plans can be studied from the perspective of measurement (reliability and validity) and administration (costs and returns). The various points in skill certification at which errors and biases may enter into judgment (e.g., different views of skill-block definitions, potential favoritism toward team members, defining and assessing skill obsolescence) and whether skill block points and evaluators make a difference all need to be studied. A cynic might observe that one reason skill-based plans seem to be increasing in popularity is that they have yet to take on all the administrative and regulatory baggage to which job evaluation has been subjected.

SKILL-BASED RESEARCH

Most of the literature on skill- and competency-based plans are descriptions of specific applications. These are valuable because they share ideas on "how to do it," but they do not answer, "Okay, now I know how to do it. But does it really matter?" A few studies have asked compensation specialists how they liked the plans (sort of like asking a fox what it thinks of the chicken coop it designed). Recall our earlier caution about research reports in Chapter 1.

Two recent studies have gone beyond case descriptions. One study compared two Ford parts plants located in Ontario, Canada.[37] One plant used a skill-based plan; the other did not. They were studied over a 10-month period. The weekly wages in the skill-based facility were based on job level and seniority. Under the skill-based plan weekly wages increased 5 percent when an employee successfully completed one of four skill blocks (health and safety, theory of plastics processing, operating molding equipment, and statistical process control). The other plant paid the hourly wage plus annual seniority-based increases. The non-skill-based facility reported higher productivity rates (10 percent) than the skill-based facility. However, the skill-based plant reported better product quality (10 percent), lower absenteeism (6 percent), and lower accident rates (2 percent). The researchers suggest that newer equipment at the non-skill-based plant may contribute to the productivity gap.

---

[36] Marsh W. Bates and Richard G. Vail, "Job Evaluation and Equal Employment Opportunity: A Tool for Compliance—A Weapon for Defense," *Employee Relations Law Journal* 1, no. 4 (1984), pp. 535–46.

[37] K. Parent and C. Weber, "Case Study: Does Paying for Knowledge Pay Off?" *Compensation and Benefits Review*, September–October 1994, pp. 44–50.

The second study, conducted at two TRW auto parts assembly plants over 37 months, reported different results.[38] The skill-based facility reported greater productivity (48 percent), lower labor costs per unit (16 percent), and greater work force flexibility. However, injury frequency seemed to increase with the introduction of the skill-based plan. The researchers suggest that the higher injury rate may be due to inexperience (e.g., people new to the job) and will decline over time.

The lower labor cost per unit under the skill-based plan may also be explained by the percentage of employees who had attained the top pay rate (topping out). As more employees certify for the top-paid skill block (top out), we would expect unit costs to increase unless fewer people are employed or more product is produced. The results of these two studies, although different, confirm the theory that alternative pay initiatives can affect employee behaviors and costs.

Short-Term Payoffs, Long-Term Not

A potential Achilles heel of skill-based approaches is that over time, more and more of the work force will certify for the top rate. At some point the entire work force will top out. Prior to this time, labor costs per unit will be lower, but the competitive advantage declines over time as more and more employees top out. So perhaps skill-based approaches are short-term initiatives to achieve flexibility through multiskilling. At some point, having all chefs and no dishwashers (and having to pay chef wages to those who are assigned to scrub pots and pans) is uncompetitive. And probably dissatisfying to certified chefs with dishpan hands.

This notion of *short-term payoff, long-term not,* may account for Motorola's experience.[39] Motorola implemented a skill-based plan in one of its cellular phone plants. The objective sounds familiar: to develop a more flexible, multiskilled work force. Yet within three years, Motorola shifted back to a more conventional job-based approach with broad job descriptions. Motorola cited difficulties in achieving sufficient return on investment in the skill-based approach. Similar experiences are reflected in a Canadian survey in which about one-third of those who reported using a skill-based system were no longer using it after five years.[40] Motorola cited the following dilemma: if at the end of three years, everyone topped out at $10 per hour (by accumulating the necessary skill blocks), what happens next year? Does everybody automatically receive a pay increase? What about the year after that? In a firm with labor intensive products, the increased labor costs under skill-based plans may be a source of competitive

[38] B. Murray and B. Gerhart, "Early Organization Outcomes from Introduction of Skill-Based Pay," (CAHRS Working paper 94–26, Center for Advanced Human Resource Studies, Ithaca, NY).

[39] K. Davidson, "Motorola Transitions from Skill-Based," *ACA News*, July 1993, p. 3.

[40] Gordon Betcherman and Anil Verma, "Followup to the New Technology Survey," Paper presented to the Canadian Industrial Relations Research Association, June 1993.

disadvantage. In contrast, under a job-based plan, employees are paid according to the value of the job they perform.

Some of the issues to consider before adopting a skill-based plan include the following:

1. Is the facility labor or capital intensive? The financial risks in labor intensive operations may be greater under skill-based approaches.

2. Is the work force individual or team based? Interestingly, Motorola reported that skill-based pay is easier to administer in a setting that adheres to an individual achievement philosophy. Under a team environment, an individual may have to postpone training and the accompanying pay increase in order to meet the needs of the team better.

3. Is the work stable or dynamic? Under rapidly changing technologies, skills may become obsolete rapidly, making constant revision of skill-based plans and recertification an administrative burden.

4. Is a jack-of-all-trades really the master of none? Some research in operations management suggests that the greatest impact on results occurs after just a small amount of increased flexibility.[41] Greater increments in flexibility achieve fewer improvements. More skills may not necessarily improve productivity. So there may be an optimal number of skills for any individual to possess. Beyond that number, productivity returns are less than the pay increases.

Summary

This section of the book started by examining pay structures within an organization. The importance placed on internal consistency in the pay structures was the basic policy issue addressed. We pointed out that the basic premise underlying a policy that emphasizes internal consistency is that internal pay structures need to be tailored to be consistent with the organization's business strategy and values, the design of the work flow, and a concern of fair treatment of employees. Internal equity, the work relationships within a single organization, is an important part of a policy of internal consistency. Equitable structures, acceptable to the stakeholders involved, affect satisfaction with pay, the willingness to seek and accept promotions to more responsible jobs, the effort to undertake additional training, and the propensity to remain with the employer; they also reduce the incidence of pay-related grievances.

The techniques for establishing internally consistent structures typically include job evaluation, skill/competency-based plans, and market pricing. Although

---

[41] P. Park and P. Bobrowski, "Job Relevance and Labor Flexibility in A Dual Resume Job Shop," *Journal of Operations Management*, 8 no. 3 (1989), pp. 230–49.

viewed by some as bureaucratic burdens, these techniques can aid in achieving the objectives of the pay system when they are properly designed and administered. Without them, our pay objectives of improving competitiveness and equity are more difficult to achieve.

We have now finished the first part of the book. In it, you were introduced to strategic perspectives on compensation, the key policy issues in compensation management, and the model that provides a framework for the book. Managing compensation requires adapting the pay system to support the organization strategies, its culture and values, and the needs of individual employees. We examined the first basic policy issue: internal consistency of the pay structure. We discussed the techniques used to establish consistency as well as its effects on compensation objectives. The next section of the book focuses on the second major policy issue in our pay model: external competitiveness.

Review Questions

1. What are the pros and cons of having employees involved in compensation decisions?

2. Think back to the earlier chapters on job and skill/competency analysis and evaluation, including job evaluation and skill/competency. What forms can employee involvement take?

3. Why does the process used in the design of the internal pay structure matter? Distinguish between the process used to design and administer the structure and the techniques or mechanics used.

4. If you were managing employee compensation, how would you recommend that your company evaluate the usefulness of its job evaluation or skill-based plans?

5. Based on the research on job evaluation, what are the sources of possible gender bias in skill/competency-based plans?

6. How can a manager ensure that job evaluation or skill/competency-based plans support a customer-centered strategy?

YOUR TURN:

DISCRIMINATORY JOB FACTORS

The chart below is taken from a United Kingdom Equal Opportunities Commission report. It deals with gender bias in job factors and describes some factors that, in the opinion of commission members, strongly favor males or females, weakly favor males or females, or are neutral.

1. Use this chart to analyze the job descriptions in Chapter 3, Exhibits 3.12, 3.13 (nurses) and 3.14 (programmer). For each description, list any factors that appear to
   a. Strongly favor males
   b. Weakly favor males
   c. Be neutral

d. Weakly favor females
e. Strongly favor females
What is your overall assessment of the possibility of gender bias in these descriptions?

2. In the same way, analyze the job description you and your teammate prepared following Chapter 3. Is there a gender bias?

3. Analyze the competencies described in Exhibit 3.15 for bias. Do you think competencies allow more or less possibility for bias than job evaluation?

EXHIBIT 1 Gender-Biased and Gender-Neutral Job Factors Cited by United Kingdom Equal Opportunities Commission

	Favors Male Jobs		Neutral	Favors Female Jobs	
	Strongly	*Weakly*		*Weakly*	*Strongly*
Factors with a time dimension	Length of service Experience	Age Qualifications Education Knowledge Breadth of know-how	Training period Level of skill Depth of know-how		
Factors with a seniority dimension	Responsibility for cash or assets Discretion Responsibility Effect of decisions Supervision of subordinates Accountability Decision making Planning	Confidential data/ information			
Factors with a relationship dimension			Safety of others Cooperation Supervising Creating new business Communication Coordination Personal appearance Expression	Contacts: internal/ external Human relations responsibility Public relations responsibility Accuracy	Caring

(continued)

EXHIBIT 1 (concluded)

| | Favors Male Jobs | | | Favors Female Jobs | |
	Strongly	Weakly	Neutral	Weakly	Strongly
Factors with a physical activity dimension	Heavy lifting Physical hazards Spatial ability Unpleasant working conditions	Technical expertise Responsibility for equipment Physical skills Physical effort Responsibility for standards Operational knowledge Knowledge of machinery, tools, and materials	Safety of others Stamina Responsibility for materials Versatility Procedural know-how Fatigue	Monotony Visual concentration Scanning and location of details	Dexterity Typing keyboard skills
Factors with a mental activity dimension		Numerical calculation Knowledge Numerical ability Mathematical reasoning Problem solving	Initiative Originality Ingenuity Judgment Mental effort Complexity of job Planning Verbal comprehension Verbal expression	Concentration Memory Information ordering	
Factors with a sensory activity dimension		Differentiating sounds	Differentiating tastes Differentiating smells Visual concentration Aesthetic appreciation Tactic sensitivity Artistic/Musical creativity		

Exhibit II.1   The Pay Model

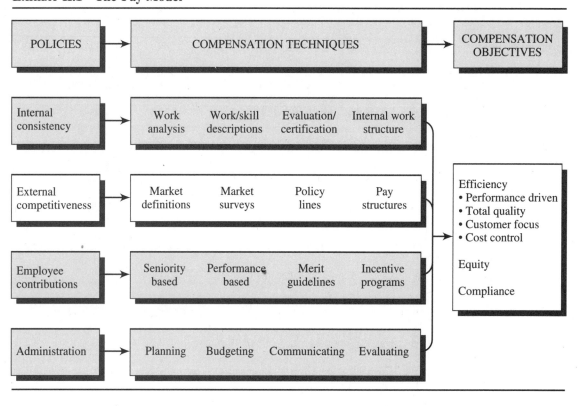

External Competitiveness: Determining the Pay Level

"Thank God it's Friday" is such a popular refrain in American pop culture that a restaurant chain expropriated it. "Get your money every Friday" is a refrain in the Three Penny Opera. Every Friday, Gerald M. Levin, CEO of Time Warner, picks up $407,000 (that's $21,164,000 annually). Natmata Katongole, a customer service representative for Time Warner, picks up $711.54 ($37,000 annually). Gerry's deal is even sweeter than David Letterman's $14 million deal with CBS, which pays him $269,230.76 every Friday. From there it's a dramatic drop to Barbara Walters' $10 million ($192,307.69 every Friday) or Sam Donaldson's $2 million (only $38,461.54 every Friday). Meanwhile, over at the Wyndham Hotel, Manuel Castillo, the front-desk clerk, walks out every Friday with $641.13 ($33,339 annually); Rudy Eason, the chambermaid there, gets only $496.96 ($25,842 annually).

Astonishing differences in salaries are shown in Exhibit II.2. How in the world are these salaries determined? For some people, these examples confirm what they have always suspected: that pay is determined without apparent reason or justice. These are figures employers have arrived at when they position their pay relative to other organizations who compete in the same labor and product markets. David Letterman is able to command such a high salary because (1) other employers were also interested in his services and (2) they all believe that Mr. Letterman can create a stream of earnings for them that will be greater than his pay.

The objective of Part II is to discuss how employers position their pay relative to other employers who compete in the same labor and product/service markets. Exhibit II.1 shows that the external competitiveness policy fits into the total pay model. It represents the second of the four major strategic decisions in the model.

External competitiveness varies in its importance among companies and among countries. In the United States, for example, many of the new approaches

Exhibit II.2 Who Makes How Much?

Tom Brokaw	NBC anchor	$ 2,000,000
Ronald Carey	president, Teamsters Union	45,000
Carolina Slim	street musician, blues guitarist	15,000
John Caruso	sanitation worker, NYC Dept. of Sanitation	32,000
Phil Caruso	president, Patrolmen's Benevolent Association	49,000
Manuel Castillo	front-desk clerk, Wyndham Hotel	33,339
Elaine L. Chao	president and CEO, United Way of America	195,000
Dr. Chou	acupuncturist	40,000
Bill Clark	NYC detective 1st grade	74,000
Chris Cozzone	executive editor, *Prison Life* magazine	44,700
Macaulay Culkin	actor	16,000,000
Christopher Czekaj	team leader, AT&T international multilingual center	37,000
Luiz Desales	shoe-shine man, Daily News—building lobby	15,000
Bo Bieti	private investigator and security consultant	150,000
Laura Drager	criminal court judge	90,450
Mary Drayer	teacher, Lexington School for the Deaf	25,124
Glenn Drewes	studio, freelance, and Broadway horn player	80,000
Karen Durbin	editor, *The Village Voice*	125,000
Rudy Eason	chambermaid, Wyndham Hotel	25,842
Robert J. Eaton	chairman and CEO, Chrysler Corp.	9,260,000
Andrew Friedman	criminal lawyer	65,000
Louis C. Gerstner, Jr.	chairman and CEO, IBM	2,625,000
Dr. Spencer Gibbs	president, NYC Council of Churches	0
Allen Ginsberg	distinguished professor, CUNY	96,228
Rudolph Giuliani	mayor, New York City	130,000
Cora Glasser	personal-injury/bankruptcy lawyer	90,000
Nelson Gonzales	Harvard Club dishwasher	20,000
Jose M. Hernandez	Harvard Club laundry worker	10,000
Geri Jordan	U.S. letter carrier, Brownsville, Brooklyn	31,000
Namata Katongole	customer service representative, Time Warner Cable	37,000
Jules Kenny	True Value pharmacist	60,000
"Kimberley"	exotic dancer	49,500
Brian Leetch	Rangers defenseman	1,805,000
Spiros Mastoras	hot dog and pretzel vendor	17,000
Michael Metry	Olympia Trails bus driver	31,000
Jennifer Jo Moyer	prekindergarten teacher, Grace Church School	31,000
Daniel Patrick Moynihan	U.S. senator	133,600
Michael Rubin	air-traffic-control specialist, La Guardia Airport	70,000
Daniel Ryniec	gardener, Brooklyn Botanic Gardens	37,400
Mario Silva	Harvard Club waiter	29,000
George Soros	Soros Fund Management	1,100,000,000
Robert Sturner	interior designer	125,000
J. F. Welch, Jr.	chairman and CEO, General Electric Co.	4,391,046
Mary Jo White	U.S. attorney, Southern District	113,500

Source: *New York Magazine,* "Who Makes How Much," September, 19, 1994.

to designing organizations and organizing work deemphasize the traditional focus on internal relationships and place greater reliance on external market comparisons to arrive at pay rates. But in Japan very little hiring is done in the external market for other than entry-level positions. Consequently, pay rates in the external market for many jobs may be less relevant. However, Japanese employers still emphasize pay level, headcount (i.e., labor costs), and productivity comparisons with their competitors. Toyota is acutely aware of how much auto assemblers in Germany, Korea, Italy, and South Carolina earn.

External competitiveness translates into practice when the company establishes a pay level. Three pure policy alternatives exist: to lead competitors' pay, to match it, or to lag below it. But as we shall see in Chapter 6, variations exist. Chapter 6 discusses the major factors affecting external competitiveness policies, consequences of these policies, and theories and research related to them. Chapter 7 has two parts. First, it discusses the decisions and techniques that translate an employer's competitiveness policy into pay level. Second, it discusses how to integrate market data with the structures we designed in Part I.

CHAPTER

Defining Competitiveness

January is always a good month for travel agents in Ithaca, New York. In addition to the permanent population eager to flee Ithaca's leaden skies (our computer has a screen-saver color titled *Ithaca;* it consists of 256 shades of gray), graduating students from Ithaca's two colleges are traveling to job interviews with employers across the country—at company expense, and at full fare. No Saturday night stayovers required. During this recruiting season, students compare notes and find that even for people receiving the same degree in the same field from the same college, the offers vary. At first, students attribute these differences to themselves: differences in grades, courses taken, work experience, interviewing skills, and so on. But as students accept offers and reject others, an interesting phenomenon occurs. Many companies whose offers were rejected now extend the identical offer to other students.

If an individual's qualifications do not explain differences in offers, what does? Location has an effect: firms in San Francisco and New York City make higher offers. The work also has an effect: jobs in employment pay a little less than jobs in compensation and employee relations. (Now aren't you glad you didn't drop this course?) And the industry to which the different firms belong has an effect: Pharmaceuticals, brokerage houses, and petroleum firms tend to offer more than consumer products, insurance, banking, and heavy manufacturing firms.[1] What determines these differences in pay levels? What effects do they have? This chapter addresses these questions.

Readers have told us this chapter can be heavy going. The reasons are the sheer volume of relevant theories and research. Another reason is that the reality of the decisions doesn't always match the theories. The key to this chapter is to always ask, So what? How will this information help me?

COMPETITIVENESS AND THE PAY MODEL

The key to competitiveness is its relative nature: comparisons with other employers. Although pay level is a primary component, competitiveness also includes the mix of pay forms (i.e., use of bonuses, benefits), career opportunities, training, challenging assignments, or financial stability of the organization. Pay competitiveness is expressed by setting pay rates that are above, below, or equal to rates paid by competitors. Within an organization, the average of the array of rates set for various jobs is that organization's pay level.

External competitiveness refers to the pay relationships among organizations—the organization's pay relative to its competitors.

Pay level refers to the average of the array of rates paid by an employer.

An organization's competitiveness policy translates into practice in the employer's pay-level decisions.

Pay level focuses attention on two objectives: (1) control labor costs and (2) attract and retain employees.[2]

---

[1] Richard H. Thaler, "Interindustry Wage Differentials," *The Winner's Curse* (NY: Free Press, 1992); William T. Dickens and Lawrence F. Katz, "Inter-Industry Wage Differences and Industry Characteristics," in *Unemployment and the Structure of Labor Markets,* ed. K. Lang and J. Leonard (Oxford, England: Basil Blackwell, 1987); William T. Dickens and Lawrence F. Katz, "Inter-Industry Wage Differences and Theories of Wage Determination" (Working paper 2271, National Bureau of Economic Research, Cambridge, MA, 1987); Alan B. Krueger and Lawrence H. Summers, "Reflections on the Inter-Industry Wage Structure," in *Unemployment and the Structure of Labor Markets,* ed. K. Lang and J. Leonard (Oxford, England: Basil Blackwell, 1987); Alan B. Krueger and Lawrence H. Summers, "Efficiency Wages and the Inter-Industry Wage Structure," *Econometrica,* March 1988, pp. 259–93; Summer Slichter, "Notes on the Structure of Wages," *Review of Economics and Statistics* 32 (1950), pp. 80–91.

[2] S. L. Rynes and A. E. Barber, "Applicant Attraction Strategies: An Organizational Perspective," *Academy of Management Review,* 1990; Margaret L. Williams and George Dreher, "Compensation System Attributes and Applicant Pool Characteristics," *Academy of Management Journal,* August 1992; H. J. Holzer, "Wages, Employer Costs, and Employee Performance in the Firm," *Industrial and Labor Relations Review* 43 (1990), pp. 147S–164S; S. L. Rynes, "Compensation Strategies for Recruiting," *Topics in Total Compensation* 2 (1987), pp. 185–96.

Control Labor Costs

Pay level decisions significantly impact most organizations' total expenses. Other things being equal, the higher the pay level, the higher the labor costs (Exhibit 6.1). Furthermore, the higher the pay level relative to what competitors pay, the greater the relative costs to produce similar products or provide similar services. For example, pilots at major U.S. airlines are nicknamed "flying vice presidents" because of their high salaries and their interest in how the company is managed. Exhibit 6.2 shows that pilot's pay varies by employer. After five years of experience, pilots at US Air ($85,000), Delta ($79,000), and Southwest and United ($78,000) earn the most. But after 10 years Northwest pilots lead the pack ($125,000) and can earn more—over 67 percent more—than Southwest pilots, who max out at about $120,000. The same work is paid differently by different employers. Why would Northwest pay more than America West? What could justify a pay level above whatever minimum amount is required to attract and retain pilots?

Attract and Retain Employees

In fact, all else is rarely equal. Northwest may believe its higher pay for pilots is offset by savings resulting from more productive employees. Northwest pilots may be more experienced, which may reassure white-knuckle passengers. Or maybe they are more flexible and can deal more satisfactorily with the nonroutine (!) events in the air. Or they may be less likely to quit, which can cut down on recruiting and training costs. Or Northwest pilots may just have more negotiating power with Northwest management. These other factors may justify a decision to set a high pay level. In reality, employers set a variety of pay levels. That is why there is no single "going rate" in the labor market for a specific job.

EXHIBIT 6.1   Pay Level Decision Impacts Labor Cost

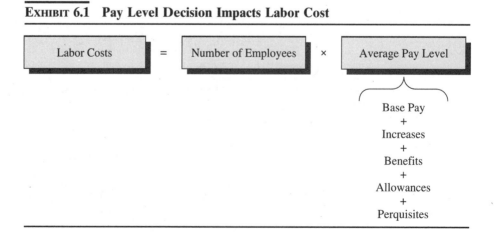

EXHIBIT 6.2   Structure Differences: Do They Matter?

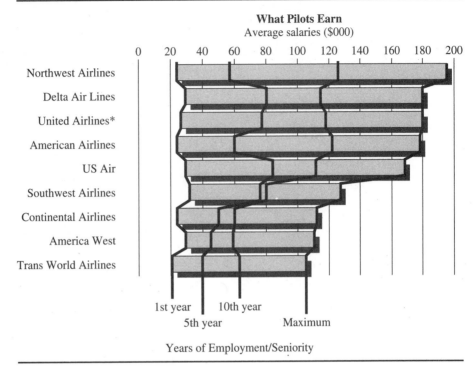

What Pilots Earn
Average salaries ($000)

Years of Employment/Seniority

* Adjusted to reflect concessions the pilots made in exchange for an equity stake.
Source: Air Inc., Atlanta.

No Single "Going Rate"

Just as graduating students discover each year, the rates paid for similar jobs and skills vary among employers.[3] An array of rates exists. Notice that in Exhibit 6.3, the wages paid to the secretary of the chief executive officer (CEO) vary with the size of the company (top secretaries that report to CEOs in companies with revenues of $5 billion or more can expect to earn approximately 5 to 10 percent more than average); with the region of the country (salaries are highest in the metropolitan New York area, lowest in the South Central region); and with the industry (the top secretaries in financial services average $60,300, but only $46,700 in natural resources and exploration). Although some of this variation may be attributable to such factors as experience and seniority of the secretary (their average tenure in this survey is 18 years with the company and 7

---

[3] *College Placement Council Salary Survey* is published quarterly by the College Placement Council, Bethlehem, PA. It reports starting salary offers to college graduates as collected by college placement offices. Data are reported by curriculum, by functional area, and by degree. It is one of several sources employers may use to establish the offers they extend to new graduates.

Exhibit 6.3   **Secretary to the Chief Executive Officer**

	Avg. Base Salary	Avg. Bonus	Avg. Total Cash		Avg. Base Salary	Avg. Bonus	Avg. Total Cash
By Revenues (billions)				**By Industry**			
$10 and over	$64,900	$5,700	$66,900	Chemical and			
$5–$10	57,700	6,400	60,900	pharmaceuticals	$52,500	—	$53,000
$2–$5	50,700	2,800	51,500	Consumer products	57,600	$7,500	59,800
Less than $2	48,500	4,900	50,600	Technology and			
				equipment	57,300	6,300	59,000
By Region				Natural resources			
Metro New York	62,100	7,200	63,800	and exploration	46,700	—	47,300
North Central	48,800	3,600	50,200	Financial services	60,300	4,400	63,800
Northeast*	48,900	2,200	49,900	Utilities	57,700	5,500	60,400
South Central	47,700	8,500	52,000	Other service			
Southeast	58,800	4,300	61,200	organizations	52,100	5,000	54,400
West Coast	56,800	5,700	59,100				

* Excluding Metro New York.

Source: Executive Resource Group.

years with the job), much of it also reflects different pay levels among survey respondents.

Pay level also varies among job families within a single company. For example, a survey of 21 aerospace firms found that the top-paying firm paid more than 21 percent above the average pay and the bottom one paid more than 13 percent below the overall average pay (Exhibit 6.4).[4] Even more interesting are the profiles of different competitive positions for different job families. Company A paid 10.5 percent below the market overall, but its pay level for sales and market positions was almost 40 percent above the market for those positions. Its CEO was paid 30 percent below the market. Obviously, company A's pay strategy placed great importance on sales and marketing. Company B displayed a completely different pattern. While it was 2.6 percent above the market overall, its CEO's pay was 7 percent above the market and the pay of its sales and marketing people was 3 percent above the market. The internal pay structure at company B closely mirrored the pay relationships found in the external market; company A's pay structure did not. The data suggest that B is a market pricer and A emphasizes internal consistency.

Although it is risky to infer a specific competitive policy from these data, it is clear that different employers in the same industry adopt different policies

---

[4] Ken Foster, "An Anatomy of Company Pay Practices," *Personnel*, September 1985, pp. 67–71.

EXHIBIT 6.4   The Relationship of Company Pay Scales to Market Average

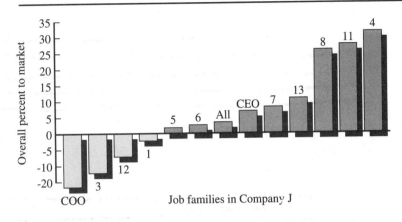

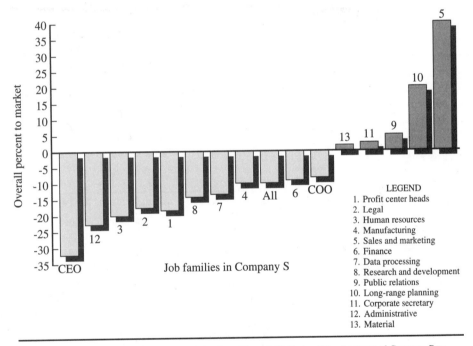

LEGEND
1. Profit center heads
2. Legal
3. Human resources
4. Manufacturing
5. Sales and marketing
6. Finance
7. Data processing
8. Research and development
9. Public relations
10. Long-range planning
11. Corporate secretary
12. Administrative
13. Material

Source: Reprinted by permission of the publisher from Kenneth E. Foster, "An Anatomy of Company Pay Practices," *Personnel*, September 1985, pp. 69–70. © 1985 by the American Management Association.

and practices regarding external competition and pay levels.[5] The next section discusses the theories and research related to understanding these differences.

---

[5] Barry Gerhart and George Milkovich, "Employee Compensation: Research and Practice," in *Handbook of Industrial and Organizational Psychology*, 2nd ed., ed. M. D. Dunnette and L. M. Hough (Palo Alto, CA: Consulting Psychologists Press, 1992).

FACTORS INFLUENCING EXTERNAL COMPETITIVENESS

The factors that affect the pay level and consequently external competitiveness are grouped in Exhibit 6.5. They include the pressures exerted by (1) competition in labor markets for workers with sought-after skills and abilities; (2) competition in product and service markets, which affects the financial condition of the firm; and (3) characteristics unique to each organization and its work force, such as its business strategies and the productivity and experience of its work force. These factors act in concert to influence pay-level decisions.

LABOR MARKET FACTORS

Economists describe two basic types of markets: the quoted price and the bourse. Stores that label each item's price or ads that list a job opening's starting wage are examples of *quoted price markets*. Buying at a flea market or haggling over the terms and conditions in professional athletes' contracts are examples of *bourses*. Graduating students usually find themselves in a quoted labor market, though some haggling over terms may occur.[6] Both types of market involve an exchange between buyers (the employers) and sellers (the workers). If the inducements offered by the employer and the skills offered by the worker are mutually acceptable, a contract is executed. The contract may be formal, such as those made with unions, professional athletes, and executive officers, or informal, with an implied understanding or a brief letter. The result of the workings of the labor market is the allocation of employees to opportunities at specified pay rates.

EXHIBIT 6.5   Factors Influencing Pay Level

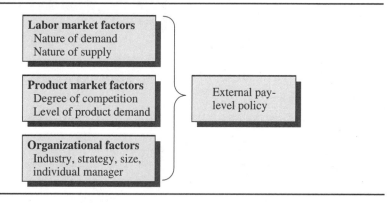

---

[6] Barry Gerhart and Sara Rynes, "Determinants and Consequences of Salary Negotiations by Male and Female MBA Graduates," *Journal of Applied Psychology* 76, no. 2 (1991), pp. 256–62; Kathryn Bartol and David Martin, "When Politics Pays: Factors Influencing Managerial Compensation Decisions," *Personnel Psychology* 43 (1990), pp. 599–614.

How Markets Work

Neoclassic labor market theory begins with four basic assumptions.

1. Employers always seek to maximize profits.
2. Human resources are homogenous and therefore interchangeable; a business school graduate is a business school graduate is a business school graduate.
3. The pay rates reflect all costs associated with employment (e.g., holidays, benefits, and training).
4. The markets faced by employers are competitive, so there is no advantage for a single employer to pay above or below the market rate.

Although these assumptions oversimplify reality, they provide a framework for understanding labor markets. As we shall see later, as we change our assumptions, our theories change, too.

Compensation managers often refer to the "market." "Our pay levels are based upon the market," "We pay competitively with the market," or "We are market leaders." Understanding how markets work requires analysis of the demand and supply of labor. The demand side focuses on the *employer:* how many employees they seek and what they are able and willing to pay. The supply side looks at the *workers:* their qualifications and the pay they are willing to accept in exchange for their services.

Exhibit 6.6 shows a simple illustration of demand for and supply of business school graduates. The vertical axis represents pay rates from $20,000 to $70,000 a year. The horizontal axis is the number of business school graduates in the market, ranging from 100 to 1,000. In Exhibit 6.6, the line labeled demand is the sum of all employers' hiring requirements for business graduates at various pay levels. If the pay for business graduates is $70,000, only 100 of them will be hired. (Few firms will be able to afford them.) If the pay is $20,000, then companies can afford to hire 1,000 business graduates. However, as we look at the line labeled supply, we see that there aren't 1,000 business graduates willing to be hired at $20,000. In fact, only 100 are. As pay rates rise, more graduates become interested in working, so the labor supply line slopes upward. The lines for labor demand and labor supply cross. The point where the lines intersect determines the market rate. In this illustration, the interaction among all employers and all business graduates determines the $45,000 market rate. Because any single employer can hire all the business graduates it wants at $45,000 and all business graduates are of equal quality (assumption #2), there is no reason for any wage other than $45,000 to be paid.

Labor Demand

So if $45,000 is the market-determined rate for business graduates, how many business graduates will a specific employer hire? The answer requires an analysis

Exhibit 6.6   Supply and Demand for M.B.A.s in the Short Run

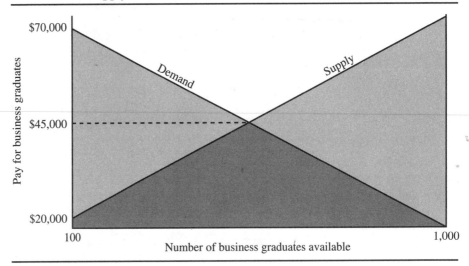

of labor demand. In the near term, when an employer cannot change any other factor of production (i.e., technology, capital, or natural resources), its level of production can change only if the level of human resources (HR) employed, its labor demand, is changed. Under such conditions, a single employer's demand for labor coincides with the marginal product of labor.

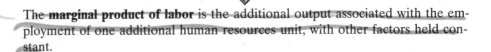

The **marginal product of labor** is the additional output associated with the employment of one additional human resources unit, with other factors held constant.

The **marginal revenue of labor** is the additional revenue generated when the firm employs one additional unit of human resources, with other factors held constant.

Marginal Product

Assume that two business graduates form a consulting firm that provides services to 10 clients. They hire a third person and add five more clients. The marginal product (the change in output associated with the additional unit of labor) of employing the third business graduate is 5. But the marginal product of a fourth hire may not be the same as the marginal product of the third. In fact, adding a fourth business graduate generates only four new clients. This diminishing marginal productivity results from the fact that each additional graduate has a progressively smaller share of the other factors of production with which to work. In the short term, other factors of production (e.g., office space, computer service) are fixed. As more business graduates are brought into the firm without changing other production factors, the marginal productivity must eventually decline.

Marginal Revenue

Now let's look at marginal revenue. Marginal revenue is the money generated by the sale of the marginal product; the additional output associated with the employment of one additional HR unit. In the case of the consulting firm, it's the revenues generated by each additional business graduate. If the graduate's marginal revenue exceeds its costs of $45,000, profits are increased by the additional hiring. Conversely, if marginal revenue is less than $45,000, the employer would lose money on the last hire. Recall that our first labor market theory assumption is that employers seek to maximize profits. Therefore, the employer will continue to employ additional graduates until the marginal revenue generated by that last hire is equal to the expenses associated with employing that worker. Because other potential costs will not change in the short run, the level of demand that maximizes profits is that level at which the marginal revenue of the last hire is equal to the wage rate for that hire.

Exhibit 6.7 shows the connection between the labor market model and conditions facing a single employer. On the left is the same supply and demand model from Exhibit 6.6 showing that pay level ($45,000) is determined by the interaction of all employers' demand for business graduates. The right side of the exhibit shows supply and demand at the level of the individual employer. At the market-determined rate ($45,000), the individual employer can hire as many business graduates as desired. Therefore, supply is now a horizontal line representing an unlimited supply of graduates. The demand line still slopes downward, so that the two lines intersect at 20; that is, for this employer, the

EXHIBIT 6.7   Supply and Demand at the Market and Individual Employer Level

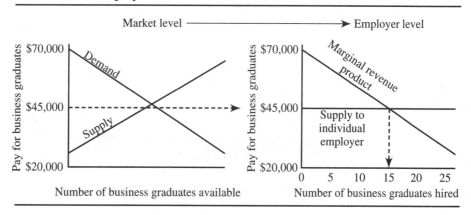

marginal revenue of the 20th graduate is $45,000. The marginal revenue of the 19th graduate may be $47,000, and the marginal revenue of the 21st graduate may be $43,000. The point at which the incremental income that hiring the graduate brings to the firm—the marginal revenue product—just equals the wage rate is 20. Until this level of employment is reached, additional graduates contribute more to revenues than they do to costs, so it is worthwhile for the individual employer to continue to hire.[7]

So the manager of compensation who uses the marginal product model must do only two things: (1) determine the pay level set by market forces and (2) determine the marginal revenue generated by each potential new employee. These two pieces of information will decide how many people to hire. Simple? Of course not.

Although this model of labor supply and demand provides a valuable analytical framework, it has a number of limitations when applied to managing compensation. The first is that the model's assumptions oversimplify the real world. For example, the assumed degree of competition among buyers and sellers does not exist, nor are factors of production homogeneous, nor are all firms profit maximizers (some maximize market share, long-term profits, and so on). The second objection is that managers have no idea what the marginal revenue and marginal products are. Difficulties in trying to operationalize these concepts of marginal revenue and marginal product include the following:

1. Placing a value on the goods or services each individual employee produces.
2. Determining individual values on products and services that are produced through joint efforts of different workers with a variety of talents. Think about this the next time you are in the local supermarket, the symphony hall, or even your college. It will be immediately obvious that labor is heterogeneous, not homogeneous.
3. Factoring out the contributions of other resources (capital and raw materials) in the production process.

Since measuring marginal product and revenue directly is difficult, managers often use other factors that they believe reflect value. In the last two chapters, we discussed compensable factors, skill blocks, and competencies. When the compensable factors define what organizations value in work, job evaluation based on these factors assesses the job's contribution to organization goals. Thus, job evaluation results may be in some sense a proxy for marginal revenue product. However, compensable factors are usually defined as input (skills required, problem solving required, responsibilities), rather than as the value of the output of a job. The same logic applies to skills and competencies.

Marginal productivity concepts may be relevant to establish the maximum

[handwritten margin note: limitations]

---

[7] Paul Milgrom and John Roberts, *Economics, Organization and Management* (Englewood Cliffs, NJ: Prentice Hall, 1992).

pay rates for jobs or to link pay increases to performance. For example, the highest pay rates or performance payments should not exceed the marginal revenue product, or how much can be received for what the employee produces. But managers rarely make such a direct link between an individual's pay and the value of what is produced. Managers may have a "feel" for the link between maximum pay and what the organization can afford, but links to marginal revenue product are theoretical only. As to linking performance to pay, any gains from such a link must be traded off against the cost of measuring, or even estimating, performance.[8] If output from a job is easily measurable, then calculating marginal revenue and linking it to pay may be possible. But for most work, the requirements of having easily measured output and placing a value on it simply cannot be met.

Labor Supply

The labor supply level in Exhibit 6.6 represents different numbers of employees available at different pay rates. Like demand, the exact shape of the line representing the supply of labor depends on the assumptions. In perfectly competitive markets, an individual employer faces a horizontal supply; that is, the market determines the price, and the individual employer can hire all the employees it wants, at that price. (See the right side of Exhibit 6.7.) This model assumes that many workers are seeking jobs, that they possess accurate information about all job openings, and that no barriers to mobility (discrimination, licensing provisions, or union membership requirements) among jobs exist.

As in the analysis of labor demand, these assumptions greatly simplify the real world. As the assumptions of the model change, so does the supply. The upward-sloping line or curve we have looked at so far implies that as pay increases, more people are willing to take a job. But if unemployment rates are low, individual offers of higher pay may not increase supply. If the higher offer is matched quickly by competitors, the employer may face a higher pay level but no increase in supply. For example, when Giant Foods raised its hourly pay 50 cents above the minimum wage in the Chicago area, Wendy's and Burger King quickly followed suit. The result was that the supermarket was paying more for the employees it already had but was still shorthanded.

An employer who dominates the local labor market, such as Corning Glass in Corning, New York, may also find that raising wages doesn't necessarily attract more applications simply because the supply has dried up. People who are conveniently located to Corning and interested in work are already there. Any increase in employment requires that additional applicants must be induced to enter the labor supply, perhaps from schools, retirement, or more distant areas. A dominant employer has relatively wide latitude in determining pay levels,

---

[8] Charles Brown, "Firms' Choice of Method of Pay," *Industrial and Labor Relations Review* 40 (1990), pp. S165–S182.

since few local labor market competitors exist. However, once the local labor supply is exhausted, small increases in the pay levels may not attract more applicants. The supply curve, although sloping upward, may take on the shape of a "step" function and may require large pay increases to attract additional people. Although many firms find lowering the job requirements and hiring less-skilled workers a better choice than raising wages, any pay savings may be offset by increased training expenses.

MODIFICATIONS TO THE DEMAND SIDE

The story is told of the economics professor and the student who were strolling through campus. "Look," the student cried, "there's a $100 bill on the path!"

"No, you are mistaken," the wiser head replied. "That cannot be. If there were actually a $100 bill, someone would have picked it up."

The point of the story is that economic theories must frequently be revised to account for reality. We started this chapter by observing that different employers offer different pay rates for similar jobs to similar people. This reality differs from what the economic model assumes and predicts. So economists and psychologists modify the model to make it better conform to what actually happens when we change our focus from *all* the employers in an economy to a *particular* employer. A particularly troublesome issue for economists is why an employer would pay more than what theory states is the market-determined rate. Let us look at some modifications to explain this phenomenon. Three modifications to the classic economic model address the pay-level decisions of individual employers: compensating differentials, efficiency wage, and signaling. (See Exhibit 6.8.) Generally, these modifications seek to explain why employers pay rates that may be above or below "market."

Compensating Differentials

More than 200 years ago, Adam Smith argued that individuals consider the "whole of the advantages and disadvantages of different employments" and make decisions based on the alternative with the greatest "net advantage."[9] If a job has negative characteristics, that is, if the following apply, then employers must offer higher wages to compensate for these negative features.

1. More time and expense are necessary to acquire the skill and experience required to perform the work.
2. Job security is tenuous.
3. Working conditions are disagreeable.
4. Chances of succeeding on the job are lower.

---

[9] Thomas A. Mahoney, *Compensation and Reward Perspectives* (Burr Ridge, IL: Richard D. Irwin 1979), p. 123.

Exhibit 6.8   Labor Demand Theories and Implications

Theory	Prediction	So What?
Compensating differentials	Work with negative characteristics requires higher pay to attract workers.	Compensable factors must capture these negative characteristics.
Efficiency wage	Above-market wages will improve efficiency by inducing employees to work better.	Staffing programs must have the capability of selecting the best employees; work must be structured to take advantage of employees' greater efforts.
Signaling	Pay policies signal the kinds of behavior the employer seeks.	Pay policy must accurately reflect the employer's strategy and objectives.

Such *compensating differentials* explain the presence of various pay rates in the market. Although the notion is appealing, it is hard to document, due to the difficulties in measuring and controlling all the factors that go into a net advantage calculation.

Efficiency Wage Theory

Efficiency wage theory challenges the basic assumption of the employer as a powerless payer of market-determined wages. Instead, this theory posits that sometimes an employer can reduce unit labor costs by paying above-market wages. The high wages may induce employees to be more efficient. Five mechanisms are commonly advanced as channels for this increased efficiency.

1. Attracting higher-quality applicants.
2. Lowering turnover.
3. Increasing worker effort, out of "gratitude" toward the employer.
4. Reducing worker "shirking" (what economists say when they mean "screwing around") due to the increased cost of being fired.
5. Reducing the need to supervise employees.

Notice that the first four mechanisms assume that the same number of employees will be hired, even at higher rates. The additional costs are offset by increased productivity. Only the last mechanism, reduced supervision, opens the possibility of increasing efficiency by hiring fewer employees. So basically, efficiency increases by hiring better employees or motivating average employees to work harder. The underlying assumption is that pay level determines effort—again, an appealing notion that is difficult to document. Few employees believe that they are overpaid.

There is some research on efficiency wage theory.[10] One study looked at shirking behavior by examining the relationship between rates of employee discipline and higher wages in several plants of the same firm. Shirking was measured as the number of disciplinary layoffs. (A union contract forbade dismissals without work-related cause.) Higher wages were associated with lower levels of shirking. Shirking was also lower where labor market conditions raised the costs of shirking, that is, high unemployment made it more difficult for fired workers to find alternative employment. So while the higher wages cut shirking, the authors were unable to say whether it was cut enough to offset the higher wage bill.[11]

Another study tested the relationship between wages paid by employers for recent high school graduates and job tenure. The assumption was that the higher wages would reduce turnover, which would increase tenure, or time on the job. While the study correlated higher wages with longer job tenure, it wasn't clear whether the higher wages did in fact lead to greater profits.[12] In other words, did the money saved on hiring and training offset the higher wages? More basically, was any money saved on hiring and training?

Other research shows that high-wage employers also expend greater efforts on recruiting. This dichotomy is explained by the greater selectivity in hiring that is made possible by the large number of applicants attracted by the high wages. If better applicants are hired, then greater productivity may offset the higher labor costs per employee. However, few companies evaluate their recruiting programs well enough to show that higher wages do in fact allow them to choose superior applicants.[13] Although high pay attracts more qualified applicants, it also attracts people with poor qualifications and motivation. So an above-market wage does not always guarantee a more productive work force. Superior selection and recruiting programs are also required.

Does an above-market wage allow an organization to operate with fewer supervisors? Some research evidence says yes. For example, a study of hospitals found that those that paid high wages to staff nurses employed fewer nurse supervisors.[14] However, the researchers did not speculate on whether the higher wages attracted *better* nurses or caused *average* nurses to work harder. Also, we don't know whether the higher wages allowed the hospital to reduce overall nursing costs.

---

[10] Carl M. Campbell III, "Do Firms Pay Efficiency Wages? Evidence with Data at the Firm Level," *Journal of Labor Economics* 11, no. 3 (1993), pp. 442–69.

[11] Peter Cappelli and Keith Chauvin, "An Interplant Test of the Efficiency Wage Hypothesis," *Quarterly Journal of Economics*, August 1991, pp. 769–87.

[12] Holzer, "Wages, Employer Costs, and Employee Performance."

[13] S. L. Rynes and J. W. Boudreau, "College Recruiting in Large Organizations: Practice, Evaluation, and Research Implications," *Personnel Psychology* 39 (1986), pp. 729–57.

[14] Erica Groshen, "Why Do Wages Vary Among Employees?" *Economic Review* 24 (1988), pp. 19–38; E. Groshen and A. B. Krueger, "The Structure of Supervision and Pay in Hospitals," *Industrial and Labor Relations Review*, February 1990, pp. 134S–46S.

A variation on the notion that an above-market wage induces workers to increase efforts (rationale 3) is the *fair-wage model*.[15] This model says firms will pay above-market wages whenever employees' perceived fair wage exceeds competitive wage. The model predicts that employees of high-profit industries will perceive that fairness requires the firm to pay more and so the firm will do so. The model does explain why secretaries and janitors in high-wage industries (e.g., petroleum) are paid more than secretaries and janitors doing the same tasks in other industries (e.g., education). Unfortunately, many secretaries and janitors in low-wage industries also perceive that fairness requires their employers to pay more, but they don't. And some professors who write compensation textbooks perceive that fairness requires their publishers to pay more, but they don't.

Signaling

Another variation on the demand model seeks to explain the variability in employees' pay levels, including paying wages that may be *below* the market.[16] *Signaling theory* says that employers may deliberately design pay policies as part of a strategy that signals to both prospective and current employees what kinds of behaviors are sought. A policy of paying below the market for base pay yet offering generous bonuses or training opportunities sends a different signal, and presumably attracts different applicants, than a policy of paying market wage without bonus tied to performance. For example, an employer who combines low base with high bonuses may be signaling that employees are expected to be risk takers. The proportion of people within the organization who are eligible for bonuses signals the extent to which the reward system is geared to all employees (versus managers only). One theorist suggests that in the absence of complete and accurate information about the job, applicants make inferences about nonmonetary job attributes (colleagues, job assignments, etc.) based on what they know about an employer's relative pay level. If this is so, then pay level signals a whole raft of information, both intended and unintended, accurate and inaccurate.

---

[15] R. W. Rice, S. M. Phillips, and D. B. McFarlin, "Multiple Discrepancies and Pay Satisfaction," *Journal of Applied Psychology* 75 (1990), pp. 386–93; R. Thaler, "Interindustry Wage Differentials"; Lawrence F. Katz and Lawrence H. Summers, "Industry Rents and Industrial Policy," Brookings Papers on Economic Activity (forthcoming); Assar Lindbeck and Dennis Snower, "Cooperation, Harassment, and Involuntary Unemployment: An Insider-Outsider Approach," *American Economic Review*, March 1988, pp. 167–88; George Akerlof, Andrew Rose, and Janet Yellen, "Job Switching and Job Satisfaction in the U.S. Labor Market," Brookings Papers on Economic Activity (forthcoming); R. Thaler, *The Winner's Curse* (New York: Free Press, 1992).

[16] Allison Barber, "Pay as a Signal in Job Choice" (Graduate School of Business Administration, Michigan State University); and J. M. Barron, J. Bishop, and W. C. Dunkelberg, "Employer Search: The Interviewing and Hiring of New Employees," *The Review of Economics and Statistics* 67 (1985), pp. 43–52.

As noted, a number of studies have shown that pay level is a significant factor in attracting applicants. Not surprisingly, employers are reluctant to set relatively low pay levels for openings filled from the external market or filled by applicants who are well positioned to exchange information: college students. A study of college students approaching graduation found that a variety of pay characteristics beyond pay level affects their job decisions.[17] Students were more likely to pursue jobs that offer higher pay levels, but they also showed a preference for individual-based (rather than team-based) pay, fixed (rather than variable) pay, job-based (rather than skill-based) pay, and flexible benefits (choices available). This study also rated job seekers on various personal dimensions, materialism, confidence in their abilities, and risk aversion, and then related these dimensions to pay preferences. Materialists placed greater emphasis on pay level than did non-materialists. (One wonders what the psychologists expected to find?) Pay level was also less important to individuals who emphasized continuous personal improvement and to those who were risk averse. The point is that applicants appear to self-select among job opportunities based on the perceived match between their personal dispositions and the signals they receive from the characteristics of the employer's pay system. Pay level is only one pay characteristic that sends a signal.

Signaling works on the supply side of the model, too, as suppliers of labor signal to potential employers. Individuals who are better trained, have higher grades in relevant courses, and/or have related work experience signal to prospective employers that they are likely to be better performers. Presumably they signal with the same degree of accuracy as employers. So both investments in human capital (degrees, grades, experience) and pay decisions about level (lead, match, lag) and mix (higher bonuses, benefit choices) act as signals and presumably help employees and organizations exchange information.

MODIFICATIONS TO THE SUPPLY SIDE

Turning to the supply side of the model, which focuses on employees rather than employers, the question becomes: What affects worker behavior? We'll discuss three theories shown in Exhibit 6.9: reservation wage, human capital, and job competition.

Reservation Wage

Economists are renowned for their linguistic creativity and their great sense of humor. So it is not surprising that many of them describe pay as "noncompensatory."[18] What they mean is that job seekers have a *reservation wage* below which

---

[17] Daniel M. Cable and Timothy A. Judge, "Pay Preferences and Job Search Decisions: A Person-Organization Fit Perspective," *Personnel Psychology*, Summer 1994, pp. 317–48.

[18] C. Brown, "Firms' Choice of Method of Pay," *Industrial and Labor Relations Review*, February 1990, pp. S165–S182.

Exhibit 6.9   Labor Supply Theories and Implications

Theory	*Prediction*	*So What?*
Reservation wage	Job seekers will not accept jobs whose pay is below a certain wage, no matter how attractive other job aspects.	Pay level will affect ability to recruit.
Human capital	The value of an individual's skills and abilities is a function of the time and expense required to acquire them.	Higher pay is required to induce people to train for more difficult jobs.
Job competition	Workers compete through qualifications for jobs with established wages.	As hiring difficulties increase, employers should expect to spend more to train new hires.

they will not accept a job offer, no matter how attractive the other job attributes. If pay does not meet their minimum standard, no other job attributes can make up (i.e., compensate) for this inadequacy. Other theorists go a step further and say that some job seekers—satisfiers—take the first job offer they get in which the pay meets their reservation wage. A reservation wage may be above or below the market wage. The theory is seeking to explain differences in workers' responses to offers.

Human Capital

The theory of *human capital*, perhaps the most influential economic theory for explaining pay differences, is based on the premise that higher earnings flow to those who improve their productive capabilities by investing in themselves (e.g., education, training, experience).[19] The theory assumes that people are in fact paid at the value of their marginal product. Improving productive abilities by investing in training or even in one's physical health will increase one's marginal product. The value of an individual's skills and abilities is a function of the time, expense, and resources expended to acquire them. Consequently, jobs that require long and expensive training (engineering, physicians) should receive higher pay levels than jobs that require less investment (clerical work, elementary school teaching). The time and expenses associated with acquiring the skills restrict entry into occupations. Increasing the pay level for these occupations will induce people to overcome the restrictions. So as pay level increases, the number of people willing to overcome barriers increases, which creates an upward-sloping supply.

---

[19] Gary S. Becker, *Human Capital* (Chicago: University of Chicago Press, 1975); Barry Gerhart, "Gender Differences in Current and Starting Salaries: The Role of Performance, College Major, and Job Title," *Industrial and Labor Relations Review* 43 (1990), pp. 418–33.

Research does support the relationship between years of education and experience and earnings, although some evidence suggests that carrying this to a ridiculous extreme (i.e., getting a Ph.D.) is not as sound an investment as getting a bachelor's and/or master's degree.

Job Competition

Job competition theory is somewhat similar to human capital theory in that both imply that a decreased labor supply is associated with higher costs for the employer. The human capital theory says these higher costs are the result of higher pay levels. The job competition model says the higher costs take the form of additional training expenses that the employer must bear.[20]

The job competition model asserts that workers do not compete for pay in labor markets. Rather, pay for jobs is "quoted" or established, and workers compete through their qualifications for the job opportunities. A pool of applicants develops for every opportunity. Individuals in the pool are ranked by prospective employers according to the skills, abilities, and experience required for the job. As the employer dips further and further into the applicant pool, individuals require more training and are less productive, even though they receive the same wage. Accordingly, the total costs (pay plus training) associated with each additional unit of labor in the pool increases as the market demand increases.

A number of additional factors affect the supply of labor available to an employer. Geographic barriers to mobility among jobs, union requirements, lack of information about job openings, the degree of risk involved, and the degree of unemployment also influence labor market conditions.

PRODUCT MARKET FACTORS AND ABILITY TO PAY

Any organization must, over time, generate enough revenue to cover expenses, including compensation. It follows that an employer's pay level is constrained by its ability to compete in the product/service market. So product market conditions to a large extent determine what the organization can afford to pay.

The degree of competition and product demand are the two key product market factors. Both affect the ability of the organization to change the prices it charges for its products and services. If prices cannot be changed without decreasing sales and thereby losing income, then the ability of the employer to set a higher pay level is constrained.

Product Demand

Although the labor market conditions put a floor on the pay level required to attract sufficient employees, the product market puts a lid on the maximum pay level that an employer can set. If the employer pays above the maximum, it must

---

[20] Barron et al., "Employer Search."

either pass on the higher pay level through price increases or hold prices fixed and allocate a greater share of total revenues to cover labor costs.

For many years, U.S. automakers solved this affordability dilemma by routinely passing on increased pay in the form of higher car prices. Although competition among the "Big Three" automakers existed, they all passed on the pay increases. But a gasoline shortage (induced by oil-producing nations) changed the nature of product demand almost overnight. Suddenly, everyone wanted less expensive cars that got good gas mileage. U.S. automakers couldn't profitably produce such cars, but Japanese automakers could. At the same time, the total demand for cars actually declined, because the oil shortage slowed oil-dependent economies throughout the world. Both of these factors constrained the U.S. auto firms' ability to change the pay level. In response, some auto workers took pay cuts, accepted smaller wage increases, and agreed to job redesign intended to improve productivity. Publicly available data suggest that General Motors' direct labor costs still account for about 25 percent of total costs, compared to the 15 to 20 percent experienced by Toyota and Honda in their U.S. plants. The wage rates are equal, but because of design differences in both products and plants, the Japanese transplants require fewer direct labor hours per car.

Degree of Competition

Employers in highly competitive markets such as manufacturers of generic drugs are less able to raise prices without loss of revenues. At the other extreme, single sellers of a product, such as Merck with its patented drugs that reduce cholesterol, are able to set whatever price they choose for that drug. However, setting too high a price invites government scrutiny, as Merck sadly discovered. It also invites increased competition. Extremely high profit margins will encourage other drug companies to fund research and development of competing drugs that can also be patented.

Other factors besides the product market conditions affect pay level. Some of these have already been discussed. The productivity of labor, the technology employed, the level of production relative to plant capacity available, and the extent of nonhuman resource expenses all affect ability to pay. These factors vary more *across* than *within* industries. The technologies employed and consumer preferences may vary among auto manufacturers, but the differences are relatively small when compared to the technologies and product demand of auto manufacturers versus the oil or banking industry. These across-industry differences permit firms to adopt different pay levels.

A Dose of Reality: What Managers Say

A recent study of compensation managers provides insight into how all of these economic factors translate into actual pay decisions.[21] A number of scenarios

---

[21] David I. Levine, "Fairness, Markets, and Ability to Pay: Evidence from Compensation Executives," *American Economic Review*, December 1993, pp. 1241–59.

were presented in which unemployment, profitability, and labor market conditions varied. The managers were asked to make wage adjustment recommendations for several positions. *Level of unemployment* made almost no difference. One manager was incredulous at the suggestion: "You mean take advantage of the fact that there are a lot of people out of work?" (She must not have taken Economics 101.) Differing levels of *profitability* were deemed a factor for higher management to consider in setting the overall pay budget rather than a factor for these compensation managers to consider. While numerous indicators of *ability to pay* were mentioned, what it boiled down to was, Whatever the chief financial officer says we can afford! They were sympathetic to a company forced to pay less due to its own financial circumstances, but if a company had the resources, the compensation managers saw it as shortsighted to pay less, even though market conditions would have permitted lower pay. This mind-set probably helps explain *wage's downward stickiness.* Pay goes up more easily than it falls. In direct contradiction to efficiency wage theory, these managers believed that high turnover and difficulty in attracting applicants is a result of poor management rather than a compensation issue. The managers did not recommend increasing wages to solve these problems. Instead, they offered the opinion that, "supervisors try to solve with money their difficulties with managing people."[22]

ORGANIZATION FACTORS

Although product and labor market conditions create a range of possibilities within which managers may set the pay level, other organizational factors such as the type of industry, its strategy, and even its size may influence pay level decisions.[23]

Industry

The industry in which an organization chooses to compete dictates the particular technologies it employs. Labor intensive industries, such as education and services, tend to be lower paying than are industries whose technologies are less labor intensive, such as petroleum and pharmaceuticals. The importance of qualifications and experience tailored to particular technologies is often overlooked in theoretical analysis of labor markets. But machinists and millwrights who build diesel locomotives for General Electric in Erie, Pennsylvania, have very different qualifications from those machinists and millwrights who build airplanes for Boeing in Seattle, Washington.

Some of these industry differentials result from custom. Almost 40 years ago, Dunlop noted that Boston coal truck drivers were paid wage rates about

---

[22] Ibid., p. 1250.

[23] Erica L. Groshen, "Sources of Intra-Industry Wage Dispersion: How Much Do Employers Matter?" *Quarterly Journal of Economics*, August 1991, pp. 869–84.

EXHIBIT 6.10   International Correlations with U.S. Wages for Manufacturing Jobs (Logs)*

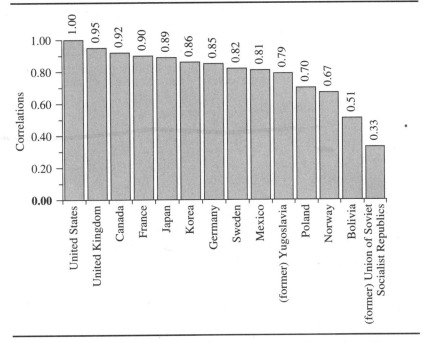

* Log scales measure ratios rather than actual dollar differences, and therefore are less subject to distortion caused by magnitude of flat dollar differences.

Source: Alan B. Krueger and Lawrence H. Summers, "Reflections on the Inter-Industry Wage Structure," in *Unemployment and the Structure of Labor Markets,* ed. Kevin Lang and Jonathan S. Leonard (Oxford: Basil Blackwell, 1987).

25 percent less than Boston oil truck drivers.[24] Furthermore, these industry effects are remarkably stable over time. A more recent study compared executive pay data from the 1930s with similar 1970s data for U.S. and British firms.[25] After adjusting all data to 1981 dollars, the industries that paid high in the 1930s also paid high in the 1970s. So the relatively high-paying industries such as autos and pharmaceuticals of 70 years ago continue to be relatively high paying today; low-wage industries such as education (ouch!) and insurance continue to be lower paying.

In fact, industry wage patterns are consistent internationally, too, especially among developed, market-based countries. As Exhibit 6.10 shows, correlations between industry wages in the United States and those in Canada, France, Japan,

---

[24] John Dunlop, "The Task of Contemporary Wage Theory," in *New Concepts in Wage Determination*, ed. George W. Taylor and Frank C. Pierson (New York: McGraw-Hill, 1957).

[25] Peter Kostiuk, "Firm Size and Executive Compensation," *Journal of Human Resources*, XXV–I, pp. 91–105.

Germany, Korea, Sweden, and the United Kingdom all exceed 0.80. A high correlation indicates a relatively similar pattern of industry wage differences (i.e., high-wage industries in the United States, such as automobile manufacturing and petroleum, are also high-wage industries in other developed, capitalist countries; low-wage industries in the United States, such as educational services and shoe manufacturing, are also low-wage industries in other countries). But we must also remember the data shown earlier in this chapter. Not only do pay levels for the same job differ by industry, but they also differ among employers within the same industry and the same geographic location.

Employer Size

There is consistent evidence that large organizations tend to pay more than small ones. For example, earlier you read about CEO secretaries' pay: those in larger organizations received 5 to 10 percent above the average.[26] Another example: a study of manufacturing firms found that firms with 100 to 500 workers paid 6 percent higher wages than did smaller firms; firms of more than 500 workers paid 12 percent more than did the smallest firms. The study controlled for differences in worker characteristics.[27] A comparison of executive pay data from the 1930s and 1970s found that today's correlation between organization size and pay level existed in the 1930s, too.

This relationship between organization size and pay is consistent with economic theory that says the marginal value of having more able people increases with organization size because their talents can influence more people and decisions. The underlying assumption is that the market operates efficiently, that is, the more qualified people are allocated to the more influential positions from where they can have a larger economic impact. Think of the advertising revenue that David Letterman can bring to CBS versus the potential revenue to station WBNS if his late-night show was only seen in Athens, Ohio. WBNS could not generate enough revenue to be able to afford to pay him $14 million; CBS can.

Organization Strategy

An organization's business strategy also affects its pay-level decision. Some employers adopt a *low-cost/low-wage strategy;* they compete by producing mass market goods as cheaply as possible. Others adopt a *mutual commitment strategy* that combines high wages with an emphasis on quality, innovation, and customer service.[28] They believe that high wages are essential to reinforce cooperation and

---

[26] Executive Secretarial Survey 1993 (Wilton, CT: Executive Resource Group, 1994); Tamar Lewin, "As the Boss Goes, So Goes the Secretary: Is it Bias?" *New York Times,* March 17, 1994, pp. A1, B9.

[27] Wesley Mellow, "Employer Size and Wages," *Review of Economics and Statistics* 64, no. 3 (August 1982), pp. 495–501.

[28] Thomas Kochan and Paul Osterman, *The Mutual Gains Enterprise: Forging A Winning Partnership Among Labor, Management and Government* (Cambridge: Harvard University Press, 1994); Lee Dyer, "Human Resources as a Source of Competitive Advantage" (Working paper, Cornell University Center for Advanced Human Resource Studies, Ithaca, NY, 1994); Peter Cap-

participation and will lead the way to a better living standard for all employees. In fact, according to some, the failure to adopt this mutual commitment strategy is what's wrong with the country today.[29] (Who says academics can't be passionate?) Lagging productivity and noncompetitive product quality are undermining our entire national economy. But the situation can be fixed by paying higher wages. This view is consistent with the resource-based strategic perspective discussed in Chapter 1, in which resources and assets, including human resources, drive the organization's strategy rather than a perspective in which business strategy drives resource allocation. A high pay level relative to competitors is a critical component of this approach.

Some research has looked at the pay levels used with different organization strategies. For example, Gomez-Mejia and Balkin propose that "Defenders" (organizations that seek to maintain their market share and profitability) will pay above the market in the short run but below market in the long run. "Prospectors" (those seeking to grow market share and innovate with new products) will pay below market in the short run and above market in the long run. They conclude that organizations that choose pay strategies that "fit" their business strategies actually do perform better.[30]

Individual Manager

Most economic models make heroic assumptions about how individual employees react to different pay levels. Rational behavior, or optimizing expected value, is the basic assumption of individual behavior. But human behavior is often nonrational. Behavioral decision models offer insights into how managers may actually make pay-level decisions. Two features of these models, *representativeness* and *anchoring,* often lead to nonrational decisions.

Representativeness refers to how a particular event represents the entire population. For example, let's say that a manager's top-performing employee recently took a higher-paying job in another city. The manager assumes the problem is that the competitor's pay level is higher. But what if the employee left to follow a job-changing spouse? The manager relies on one recent and very salient event, even though the cause of that event may have been unique and therefore not indicative of a pay problem in that firm.

---

pelli and Harbir Singh, "Integrating Strategic Human Resources and Strategic Management," in *Research Frontiers in IR and HR,* ed. D. Lewin, O. Mitchell, and P. Sherer (Madison, WI: Industrial Relations Research Association, 1992); Jeffrey Pfeffer, *Competitive Advantage Through People* (Boston: Harvard University Press, 1994).

[29] Thomas Kochan and Lee Dyer, "Managing Transformational Change: The Role of HR Professionals" (Working paper, Cornell University Center for Advanced Human Resource Studies, Ithaca, NY, 1993).

[30] Luis Gomez-Mejia and David Balkin, *Compensation, Organizational Strategy, and Firm Performance* (Cincinnati: Southwestern, 1992). See also Henry L. Tosi and Steve Werner, "Managerial Discretion and the Design of Compensation Strategy" (Working paper, University of Florida, Gainesville, 1995).

Anchoring refers to decision makers who focus on the first objective data provided and make only small adjustments from this position. For example, the manager who lost the employee to a competitor's higher pay will assume that the competitor's rate is the going rate in the market and will be loathe to deviate from it. The rate serves as an anchor regardless of how accurately the employee reported it or how or whether the job to which that wage is attached is even the same.

Both representativeness and anchoring in behavioral decision models attempt to capture how managers actually make decisions rather than presuming a rational model.

RELEVANT MARKETS

Up to this point, we've examined labor market, product market, and organization factors that influence the pay level. Next, we focus on relevant markets. Although the notion of a single homogeneous labor market may be an interesting analytical device, it does not mirror reality. Rather, each organization operates in many labor markets, each with unique demand and supply. Managers must define the markets that are relevant for pay purposes and establish the appropriate pay level in these markets. The three factors usually used to determine the relevant labor markets are the occupation (qualifications required), geography (willingness to relocate and/or commute), and the other employers that directly compete in the same product market.

Occupations

The skills and qualifications required in an occupation are important because they tend to limit mobility among occupations. Qualifications include licensing and certification requirements as well as training and education. Accountants, for example, would have difficulty becoming dentists. However, unless they bill themselves as certified public accountants, dentists would break no laws if they started selling accounting services.

Geography

Qualifications interact with geography to further define the scope of the relevant labor markets. Degreed professionals (accountants, engineers, dentists) are typically recruited nationally. Technicians, craftspeople, and operatives are usually recruited regionally, and office workers, locally. However, the geographic scope of a market is not fixed. It changes in response to workers' willingness to relocate or commute certain distances. This propensity to be mobile in turn may be affected by personal and economic circumstances as well as the employer's pay level. Configurations of local markets are even shaped by the availability of convenient public transportation. Furthermore, the geographic limits may not

EXHIBIT 6.11   Pay Variance by Location

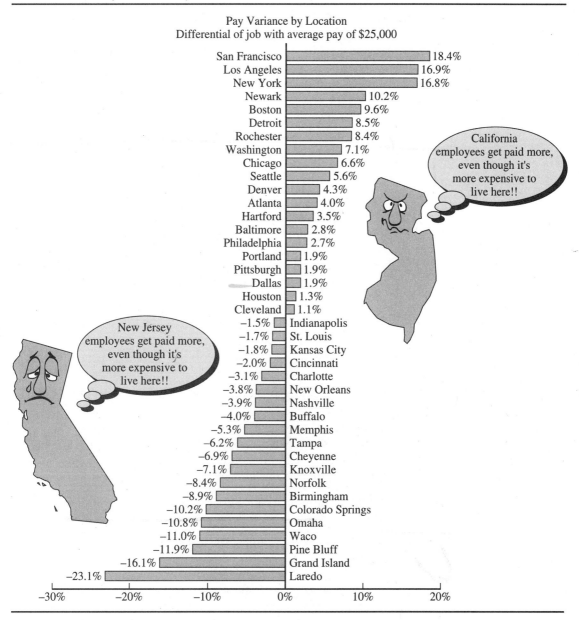

Pay Variance by Location
Differential of job with average pay of $25,000

Source: Data from Mercer & Co.

be the same for all in a broad skill group. All accountants do not operate in a national market; some firms recruit them regionally, others locally. As Exhibit 6.11 shows, pay differentials vary among localities. A job that averages $26,000 nationally can range from $19,225 in Laredo to $29,600 in San Francisco.

Product Market Competitors

In addition to the occupation and geography, the industry in which the employer competes also affects the relevant labor markets by relating the qualifications required to particular technologies. Product market comparisons also focus on comparative labor costs.

How do employers choose their relevant market? Surprisingly little research has been done on this issue. But if the markets are incorrectly defined, the estimates of other employer's pay rates may be incorrect and the pay level inappropriately established. One study divided the process of collecting pay rates into two decisions.[31]

1. Which companies to request data from.
2. Whose data to use and how to weight it.

The first decision is based on known characteristics of the companies: industry, union status, location, size, and hiring practices. But whose data are actually used depends on the quality of the data received. (See Chapter 7 for more specifics.)

Whose data are weighted most heavily in defining the relevant market, the product market competitors' or the labor market competitors'? The data of product market competitors are likely to receive greater weight when the following factors apply:

1. Labor costs are a large share of total costs.
2. Product demand is responsive to price changes; that is, people won't pay $2.50 for a bottle of Leinenkugel; they'll have a Budweiser instead.
3. Supply of labor is not responsive to changes in pay. Recall the earlier Corning example.
4. Employee skills are specific to the product market and will remain so. (Recall the Boeing millwrights versus the Detroit Diesel millwrights. However, if Boeing begins to emphasize small twin-engine planes, the product market comparisons may become less important.)

On the other hand, labor market comparisons will be more important if the following are true:

1. The organization is having difficulty attracting and retaining employees.
2. Recruiting costs are higher.[32]

Economic and behavioral theories offer some help in understanding the variations in pay levels we observe among employers. Relevant markets blend the factors in the labor and product market and the organization. But so what?

---

[31] Chockalingham Viswesvaran and Murray Barrick, "Decision Making Effects on Compensation Surveys: Implications for Market Wages" (Working paper, University of Iowa, 1991).

[32] Gerhart and Milkovich, "Employee Compensation."

EXHIBIT 6.12   The Relative Importance of Factors Used to Set Wage Objectives in Corporations in 1978 and 1983

Rank	1978	1983
1	Industry patterns	Productivity or labor trends in this company
2	Local labor market conditions and wage rates	Expected profits of this company
3	Expected profits of this company	Local labor market conditions and wage rates
4	Productivity or labor cost trends in this company	Industry patterns
5	Consumer price index increases	Consumer price index increases
6	Influence of this settlement on other wage settlements or nonunion wage levels, or both	Internal (company) wage patterns (historical)
7	Potential losses from a strike	Influence of this settlement on other settlements or nonunion wage levels, or both
8	Internal (company) wage patterns (historical)	Internal (company) benefit patterns (historical)
9	Internal (company) benefit patterns (historical)	Potential losses from a strike
10	Major union settlements in other industries	National labor market conditions and wage rates
11	National labor market conditions and wage rates	Major union settlements in other industries

Note: The sample comprised 197 major U.S. corporations, which, in both 1978 and 1983, ranked factors used in setting company wage objectives, with 1 being the most important factor and 11, the least important.

Source: Audrey Freedman, *The New Look in Wage Policy and Employee Relations* (New York: The Conference Board, 1985).

How, in fact, do managers set pay-level policy, and what difference does it make? In the remainder of this chapter, we will discuss those two issues.

COMPETITIVE PAY POLICY OPTIONS

There are three conventional pay-level policies: to lead, to meet, or to follow competition. How do managers choose a policy? Sixty-three firms responding to a survey in 1948 said that the most important factors in setting pay-level policies were rates paid by other employers in the area or industry and union pressures. The least important factors were the firm's financial position and company profits. A Conference Board survey of 280 firms in 1978 and 1983 reports a shift in the importance of factors.[33] As shown in Exhibit 6.12, industry

---

[33] *The New Look in Wage Policy and Employee Relations* (New York: The Conference Board, 1983).

EXHIBIT 6.13   Probable Relationships Between External Pay Policies and Objectives

Policy	Compensation Objectives				
	Ability to Attract	Ability to Retain	Contain Labor Costs	Reduce Pay Dissatis-faction	Increase Productivity
Pay above market (lead)	+	+	?	+	?
Pay with market (match)	=	=	=	=	?
Pay below market (lag)	–	?	+	–	?
Hybrid policy	?	?	+	?	+
Employer of choice	+	+	+	–	?

patterns remained the most important factor in 1978, just as they had 30 years earlier. But industry patterns dropped to fourth place in 1983, whereas a firm's specific financial situation and its productivity or labor costs and expected profits (ability to pay) were listed as the most important. Union-related factors, rated extremely important in the 1948 study, were among the least important in the more recent Conference Board studies. Consequently, although the factors considered in setting pay level may be stable, their relative importance may vary over time. A study of the factors used in the 1990s is needed.

What difference does the competitive pay policy make? The basic premise is that the competitiveness of pay will affect the organization's ability to achieve its compensation objectives, which in turn will affect the organization's performance. The probable effects of alternative policies are shown in Exhibit 6.13.

Pay with Competition (Match)

Given the choice to match, lead, or lag, the most common policy is to match rates paid by competitors.[34] Managers historically justify the "matching" policy for three reasons: (1) failure to match competitors' rates would cause employee dissatisfaction, (2) lower rates would limit the organization's ability to recruit, and (3) management was somehow obligated to pay prevailing rates. Nonunionized companies frequently try to lead or at least match competition to discourage unionism.[35] However, a firm's actual pay policy may differ from its stated policy, depending on which surveys and statistics are used, whether or not all forms of compensation are considered (base pay, incentives, benefits, etc.) and how well

---

[34] C. Weber and S. Rynes, "Effects of Compensation Strategy on Job Pay Decisions," *Academy of Management Journal*, March 1992, pp. 86–109.

[35] P. D. Lineneman, M. L. Wachter, and W. H. Carter, "Evaluating the Evidence on Union Employment and Wages," *Industrial and Labor Relations Review* 44 (1990), pp. 34–53.

jobs are matched across competitors.[36] A pay with competition policy tries to ensure that an organization's wage costs are approximately equal to those of its product competitors and that its ability to attract people to apply for employment will be approximately equal to its labor market competitors. This policy avoids placing an employer at a disadvantage in pricing products or in maintaining a qualified work force. But it may not provide an employer with a competitive advantage in its labor markets. Most classical economic models, those relying on competitive markets and marginal productivity concepts, would predict that employers would meet competitive wages.

Lead Policy

A lead policy maximizes the ability to attract and retain quality employees and minimizes employee dissatisfaction with pay. Or a lead policy may offset less attractive features of the work. Military combat pay is a classic example. The relatively high pay offered by brokerage firms that offsets the lack of employment security is another. These illustrate Adam Smith's notion of net advantage.

We have already observed that sometimes an entire industry can pass high pay rates on to consumers if pay is a relatively low proportion of total operating expenses or if the industry is highly regulated. But what about specific firms within a high-pay industry? For example, if Chevron or Exxon adopts a pay leadership position in their industry, do any advantages actually accrue to them? If all firms in the industry have similar technologies and operating expenses, then the lead policy must provide some competitive advantage to Chevron or Exxon that outweighs the higher costs.

Does a lead policy really permit the employer to select the best of the applicant pool? Assuming that the employer is able to select the most qualified from this pool, does this higher quality talent translate into greater productivity, lower unit labor costs, improved product quality, and increased innovation? One study estimated that approximately 50 percent of higher wage costs were offset by benefits in recruiting and training.[37] Although the number of assumptions required for this analysis limits confidence in the precision in the estimate, a number of researchers have linked high wages to ease of attraction, reduced vacancy rates and training time, and better-quality employees. A study of government employees found that as wages increase, both the quality and quantity of applicants also increased.[38] Research also suggests that increasing pay levels

[36] J. J. Chrisman, C. W. Hofer, and W. R. Boutton, "Toward a System of Classifying Business Strategies," *Academy of Management Review* 13 (1988), pp. 413–28.

[37] Ibid.

[38] A. B. Krueger, "Efficiency Wages,"; M. B. Tannen, "Is the Army College Fund Meeting Its Objectives?" *Industrial and Labor Relations Review* 41 (1987), pp. 50–62; Hyder Lakhani, "Effects of Pay and Retention Bonuses on Quit Rates in the U.S. Army," *Industrial and Labor Relations Review* 41 (1988), pp. 430–38.

reduces turnover and absenteeism. One study found no evidence that pay level affected an organization's return on assets (ROA).[39] However, this study found that the use of variable forms of pay (bonuses and long-term incentives) was linked to a higher ROA.

The problem with much pay level research is that it focuses on base pay and ignores bonuses, incentives, and other nonbase payments; yet base pay represents only a portion of compensation. Indeed, many managers seem increasingly convinced that they get more bang for the buck by allocating dollars away from base pay and into variable forms that more effectively shape employee behavior.[40]

There are possible down sides to a lead policy. If an employer leads only when hiring new employees but does not adjust wages of current employees, these more experienced employees may murmur against the employer just as those vineyard laborers did in Matthew's parable referred to in Chapter 3. For example, we know an associate professor at Texas A&M's business school who makes less than a new assistant professor. The associate professor is considering becoming one of those highly paid new hires at a new location.

Because relatively higher pay makes recruiting easier, it may mask other job attributes that contribute to high turnover later on (e.g., lack of challenging assignments or hostile colleagues).[41] Recall the compensation managers' consensus that high turnover was likely to be a managerial problem rather than a compensation problem.[42]

Lag Policy

Setting a lag pay policy to follow competitive rates may hinder a firm's ability to attract potential employees. However, if pay level is lagged in return for the promise of higher future returns (e.g., stock ownership in a high-tech startup firm), such a promise may increase employee commitment and foster teamwork, which, according to some, will increase productivity. Andersen Consulting, a software and systems firm, tells college recruits that its starting offers are lower than its competitors but that successful performers will make more than competitors within two to four years. Clearly, Andersen runs a risk of not being able to attract highly qualified talent. But the promise of the bigger carrot seems to attract enough good students, especially in a down economy. Thus, a lag policy's effect on hiring and motivating employees is not clear. Additionally, it is possible to lag competition on pay but to lead on other aspects of rewards (e.g., challenging work, desirable location, outstanding colleagues).

---

[39] B. Gerhart and G. Milkovich, "Organizational Differences in Managerial Compensation and Financial Performance," *Academy of Management Journal* 33 (1990), pp. 663–91. Variable pay is discussed in Chapters 8 through 10. *Variable* indicates that the pay increase (bonus) is not added to base pay; hence, it is not part of fixed costs but is variable, since the amount may vary next year.

[40] The Conference Board, *Variable Pay: New Performance Rewards*, Research Bulletin 246 (New York, 1990).

[41] Rynes, "Compensation Strategies."

[42] Levine, "Fairness, Markets, and Ability to Pay."

Although lower pay levels probably contribute to turnover, pay may be only one of many factors influencing an employee to quit. For example, alternative jobs available and length of service undoubtedly play a role. It is unclear how dissatisfied employees must be with pay before they will actually leave. Our experience suggests that individuals seem to vary in their tolerance for relatively lower pay, given other returns and rewards.

Match, lead, and lag are the conventional policy options. Some employers adopt nonconventional policies; they may mix policies for different employee groups, or may place their policy in a broader HR context in an effort to become the employer of choice.

Hybrid Policies

In practice, many employers have more than one policy. They may vary the policy for different occupational families, that is, above market for critical skill groups but below or at market for others. Or they may vary the policy for different pay elements. A Denver insurance company describes its policy: "It is our goal to position ourselves competitively above market value in total compensation, slight-to-somewhat-below in base salary, and well-above average in incentive compensation."[43]

Under this variable pay policy, higher earnings through profit sharing or incentive pay are offered if the firm's performance is strong. Union Carbide's Chemicals and Plastic Division offers employees the opportunity to earn a bonus of up to 40 days' pay if the division's operating profits exceed certain targets ($280 million in 1990). However, Carbide repositioned its base pay to 5 percent below its usual "match" in the market position. So, in effect, Carbide lags the market by 5 percent but pays a bonus that yields a slight lead position when the company has a good year. This competitive position has several potential effects. The variable pay policy is intended to focus employee attention on the firm's financial performance and motivate productivity improvements. Its effects on turnover and ability to attract probably depend on individual employees. Some employees may want to share the gains and risks inherent in a business. Others may prefer greater certainty in their pay increases. The effect on costs is a little more certain. The 5 percent lag reduces labor costs. The variable pay controls labor costs as a percentage of corporate income.

Employer of Choice

An *employer of choice* policy is more complex than the other options. Basically, it embeds a firm's external competitive position into its entire set of HR policies. The competitive policy may be to offer challenging work, employment security, and pay that in some sense fits these other policies. For example, IBM leads its competitors with its extensive training opportunities, employee assistance

---

[43] Stephenie Overman, "In Search of Best Practices," *HR Magazine*, December 1993, pp. 48–50.

programs, and the like. But it meets or even follows with its cash compensation. A competitor such as Apple Computer may lead with pay but lag on the extensive nonfinancial aspects of employment. IBM's competitiveness policy views pay as part of the total pattern of HR policies.

Which Policy Achieves Competitive Advantage?

Adopting a competitive pay policy is akin to establishing a niche in the market. Unfortunately, there is little evidence of the consequences of these different options. It is not known whether the effects of pay level on the financial performance of a firm, its productivity, or its ability to attract and retain employees is sufficient to offset the effects on payroll costs. Nor is it known how much of a pay level variation makes a difference; will 5 percent, 10 percent, or 15 percent be a noticeable difference? Although lagging competitive pay could have a noticeable reduction in short-term labor costs, it is not known whether this savings is accompanied by a reduction in the quality and performance of the work force. Similarly, we simply do not know the effects of the variable pay or employer of choice options. It may be that an employer's pay level will not gain any competitive advantage; however, the wrong pay level may put the organization at a serious disadvantage.

Research on the effect of alternative pay-level policies is difficult because companies' stated policies often do not correspond to reality. For example, HR managers at 124 companies were asked to define their firm's target pay level. All 124 of them reported that their companies paid above the median![44] But there is no place other than Garrison Keillor's Lake Wobegon where the laws of statistics allow everyone to be above the median. One study proposes a utility model to assess the financial impact of alternative pay-level policies.[45] The model looks at the financial trade-offs between wage costs and work force quality. For example, if we know that pay level significantly affects applicant acceptance of job offers, how much do acceptance rates have to increase in order to financially justify a higher pay level, that is, lead to productivity increases with the financial impact equal to the cost of the higher pay? Conversely, how much of a decrease in acceptance rates is tolerable before the break-even point with reduced labor costs is reached?

The researchers began with the assumption that the organization's current policy is to match the market. Their model predicted that the payoff is highest when moving from a match position to a lag position, next highest when retaining a match position, and lowest when moving from a match position to a lead position. Their point is not to determine which policy is best; rather, they provide a way to make estimates that, while imprecise, help improve decision making.

---

[44] Gerhart and Milkovich, "Employee Compensation."

[45] Brian Klaas and John A. McClendon, "To Lead, Lag, or Match: Estimating the Financial Impact of Pay Level Policies" (Working paper, University of South Carolina, Columbia, 1994).

So where does this leave the compensation manager? In the absence of convincing evidence, the least-risk approach may be to set the pay level to match competition, though as we said, some employers set different policies for different skills. They may adopt a lead policy for skills that are critical to the organization's success, a match policy for less critical skills, and a lag policy for jobs that are easily filled in the local labor market. TRW, a large, highly decentralized firm, allows its different business units to establish a variety of pay level policies. Some of these differences reflect different industries in which the units operate (financial services, automotive- and defense-related units). Other differences reflect varying labor market conditions (high unemployment in Redondo Beach, California, for their military products versus lower unemployment in Mesa, Arizona, for the air bag facility) and business strategies (cost-plus defense contracts versus the highly competitive auto parts supplier market). Other diversified firms also encourage each of their business divisions to set pay-level policies independently. More employers are considering a hybrid policy that includes base pay set at or below competitive market rates plus performance-based bonuses that vary with the unit's profitability. An obvious concern with such decentralization is to achieve some degree of control and uniformity, at least at the corporate level.

CONSEQUENCES OF PAY LEVEL DECISIONS

Earlier we noted that the degree of competitiveness of the pay level has two major consequences: (1) its effect on operating expenses and (2) its effect on employee attitudes and work behaviors. These consequences, shown in Exhibit 6.14, have been discussed throughout this chapter. All we will do here is to note again that the competitive policy and the pay level are key decisions that affect the performance of the organization. The pay level directly affects the compensation objectives of efficiency, equity, and compliance.

EXHIBIT 6.14   Some Consequences of Pay Levels

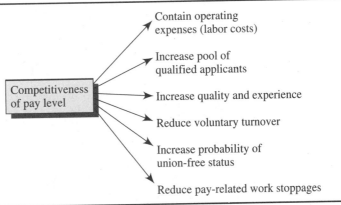

Efficiency

Wages paid represent an expense, so any decision that affects their level is important. A variety of theories make assumptions about the effects of relative pay levels on an organization's effectiveness. Some believe that lead policies diminish shirking, permit hiring better-qualified applicants, and so on. Yet other models (e.g., free markets and marginal productivity) support a policy of matching competitors. The utility model just discussed supported a lag policy. Virtually no research evidence guides managers in which policy yields the most efficient results or is the source of competitive advantage under different circumstances.

Pay level indirectly affects revenues through the quality of the work force induced to join and the productivity and experience levels of those who stay. Reduction in turnover of high performers, increased experience levels, increased probability of remaining union free, and reduction of pay-related grievances and work stoppages are examples of the work behaviors presumed to be affected by pay level decisions.

Equity

Employees' sense of fair treatment regarding pay is clearly affected by the level of their pay. As noted in Chapter 2, satisfaction with pay is directly related to the pay level: more is better.[46] But as with most things, the relationship between pay and equity is more complex. Employees' sense of pay equity also is related to how others are paid and how they expected to be paid. A friend of ours at Stanford told us that if all but one of the faculty in the Stanford Business School got $1 million and that one person received $1 million plus $1, the others would all be murmuring against the dean and asking for an explanation of why one person got the extra dollar.

Compliance

It's not enough to say that an employer must pay at or above the legal minimum wage. Provisions of prevailing wage laws and equal rights legislation must also be met. In fact, we will return to the subject of market wages again when we discuss pay discrimination in Chapter 14. From a practical perspective, the manager of the pay system must consider all these factors. From a research perspective, disentangling the relationship among pay level decisions and employee behaviors and organization performance is difficult. The links between pay levels and many of the behaviors listed in Exhibit 6.14 remain to be studied.

No matter the external pay policy, it needs to be translated into practice. The starting point is measuring the market through use of a salary survey. For this, we turn to the next chapter.

---

[46] H. G. Heneman III, "Pay Satisfaction," *Research in Personnel and Human Resource Management* 3 (1985), pp. 115–39.

Summary

The pay model used throughout this book emphasizes four strategic policy issues: consistency, competitiveness, contributions, and administration. Policies regarding these four issues need to be designed to achieve specific pay objectives. This section is concerned with external competitiveness, or pay comparisons among organizations. Does Apple Computer pay its accountants the same wage that Virginia Electric and Power pays its accountants? Probably not. Different companies pay different rates; the average of the overall array of rates in an organization constitutes the pay level. Each integrated job structure or career path within the organization may have its own pay level and competitive position in the market. To achieve the objectives stipulated for the pay system, the pay level must be properly positioned relative to competitors. The next chapter considers the decisions involved and the variety of techniques available to implement decisions.

Before we proceed, let us reemphasize that the major reason we are interested in the external competitiveness policy and the pay level is that they have profound consequences on the organization's objectives. Theories and practical experience support this belief. As we have also noted, very little research exists to guide us in making pay-level decisions. We have clearly established that differences among organizations' competitive policies and pay levels exist. We have examined the factors that determine these differences. What remains to be better demonstrated are the potential effects that different policies will have.

Review Questions

1. Distinguish policies on external competitiveness from policies on internal consistency. Why is external competitiveness so important?
2. What factors influence an organization's external competitiveness?
3. What does marginal revenue product have to do with pay?
4. What pay level does the efficiency wage theory predict? Does the theory accurately predict organization behavior? Why or why not?
5. How do behavioral decision models modify the conventional economic perspective on pay levels?
6. What are the consequences of a lead and/or lag policy?
7. What are the advantages and limitations of a hybrid policy?

YOUR TURN:

UPSTART AIRLINES

Pilots are critical resources. They directly affect the success of any airline. Suppose you faced a clean slate: A group of investors is about to invest in a new startup, a regional (midwest) airline based at the new Denver airport, but serving the entire midwest, including Laramie, Cody, Jackson Hole, and Rock Springs, Wyoming.

These investors hired you to help them determine pilots' pay. Go back to Exhibit 6.2. Based solely on the information in that exhibit, what would you advise?

1. What policy regarding external competition would you advise? List the options and the pros and cons of each policy option. Offer the rationale for your recommendation.

2. Consider the theories and research presented in this chapter. Which ones did you use to support your recommendation?

3. List three pieces of additional information you would like to have to refine your recommendation. Explain how this information would help you.

Designing the Pay Structure

Chapter Outline

> The desired position in compensation is to be above the market—equal to or better than.
>
> Our pay philosophy is to be, on the average, better than average.
>
> The policy for pay and benefits is to be in the top 10 percent.
>
> The company pays a slight premium in its nonunion plans over the wages paid in the general geographic area for similar work at union plants.
>
> The pay policy, an unwritten one, is to be competitive with the area. We use our own surveys. We check midpoints, and while the policy is to pay slightly above, in practice we pay at the midpoint. The salaried employees are below midpoint and the hourly people are at the midpoint.
>
> Our goal is to be in the 65th percentile nationally.[1]

All these statements refer to different organizations' pay competitiveness policy. Competitive position refers to the comparison of the compensation offered by one employer relative to that paid by its competitors. In the last chapter, we discussed the factors that influenced these policies. The level and types of compensation that competitors offer—base salary, incentive bonuses, benefits—are critical. Labor market factors that influence policy include the supply of qualified workers and the demand for these workers from other firms. Organizational factors such as the employer's financial condition, technology, size, strategy, productivity, and the influence of unions and employee factors such as demographics may also affect a firm's competitive pay policies. In this chapter, we examine how managers use these factors to design pay levels and structures.

---

[1] Fred K. Foulkes, *Personnel Policies in Large Nonunion Companies* (Englewood Cliffs, NJ: Prentice Hall, 1980).

EXHIBIT 7.1   Determining Externally Competitive Pay Levels and Structures

External competitiveness: Pay relationships among organizations	→	Policy determination	→	Market definition	→	Conduct pay surveys	→	Draw policy lines	→	Competitive pay levels and structures

Some Major Decisions in Pay Level Determination
- Determine pay level policy.
- Define purpose of survey.
- Design and conduct survey.
- Interpret and apply results.
- Design ranges, flat rates, incentives.

MAJOR DECISIONS

The major techniques and decisions involved in setting externally competitive pay and designing the corresponding pay structures are shown in Exhibit 7.1. They include (1) establishing the employer's external pay policy; (2) determining the issues to be addressed in a survey; (3) designing and conducting surveys; (4) interpreting and applying survey results; (5) designing ranges, flat rates, and/or incentives; and (6) adjusting the structure to balance internal and external considerations and employee contributions. The first decision, establishing the external pay policy, was discussed in the previous chapter. The remaining decisions are discussed in the rest of this chapter. As you read through the chapter, you will become aware that each new decision may cause an employer to revise previous decisions. The process may be better described as circular than linear. For example, the use of incentives (decision 5) may cause the employer to revise its external policy or decide that a specialized survey is needed to determine what types of incentives other employers are using. Or a firm may discover that it is losing employees to competitors who offer child care. As information changes, policy decisions may change.

WHY CONDUCT A SURVEY?

Surveys provide the data for setting the pay policy relative to competition and translating that policy into pay levels and structures.

A **survey** is the systemic process of collecting and making judgments about the compensation paid by other employers.

Most firms conduct or participate in several different pay surveys. Some writers claim that large employers participate in up to 100 surveys in a single year, although they base their compensation decisions on data from only a few surveys.[2]

An employer conducts or participates in a survey for a number of reasons: (1) to adjust the pay level in response to changing external pay rates, (2) to establish or price the pay structure, (3) to analyze personnel problems that may be pay related, or (4) to attempt to estimate the labor costs of product market competitors.

Adjust Pay Level

Most organizations make adjustments to employees' pay on a regular basis. Such adjustments can be based on cost of living, performance, seniority, or simply the overall upward movement of pay rates among competitors. Periodic changes in overall rates must be known to maintain or adjust a firm's pay level in relationship to its competitors in the relevant market.

Adjust Pay Structure

Many employers use market surveys to validate their own job evaluation results. For example, job evaluation may place data processing jobs at the same level in the job structure as some secretarial jobs. But if the market shows vastly different pay rates for the two types of work, most employers will recheck their evaluation process to see whether the jobs have been properly evaluated. Some may even establish a separate structure for the data processing work. Thus, the job structure that results from job evaluation may not match the pay structure found in the external market. Reconciling these two pay structures is a major issue. Informed judgment based on the organization's specific circumstances and objectives is required.

Recall in our market pricing discussion in Chapter 4 that many fast-changing organizations are keeping their job evaluations but moving to more generic jobs that focus on the person more than the job. Determining pay for such jobs requires greater reliance on the market, as any former equivalence between job evaluation points and dollars no longer holds.

Pay-Related Personnel Projects

Information from a specialized survey may shed light on a pay-related problem. Many special studies appraise the starting salary offers or current pay practices for targeted groups, for example, patent attorneys, retail sales managers, or chemical engineers. Survey data may help justify pay differences between men and women in discrimination lawsuits. Employers have successfully argued that the difference in pay between nurses and craft workers is due to pay differences

---

[2] Milton Rock and Lance Berger, eds., *The Compensation Handbook,* 3rd ed. (New York: McGraw-Hill, 1991).

found in the external market for these skills. This argument rests on the defensibility of the market data collected through wage surveys. Consequently, managers need to ensure that their surveys will withstand legal challenges.[3]

Estimate Competitors' Labor Costs

Some firms, particularly those in highly competitive businesses, such as microcomputer, auto, or specialty steel production, use salary survey data in their financial analysis of competitors' product pricing and manufacturing practices. Industrywide labor cost estimates are reported in the Employment Cost Index (ECI), one of four types of salary surveys published regularly by the Department of Labor. The ECI measures quarterly changes in employer costs for employee compensation. It allows a firm to compare its average costs to an all-industry or specific-industry average. However, this comparison has limited value because industry averages may not reflect relevant competitors. Also, the ECI gives a lot of weight to unionized firms.[4]

Survey results serve as crucial input for decisions that ultimately affect a firm's compensation objectives of efficiency, equity, and compliance. An employer's labor costs and the competitiveness of its products can be affected by conclusions drawn from survey data. Because their results are so significant to the organization, businesses should design and manage their surveys carefully. A first step to ensure careful management is to identify the key issues the employer seeks to resolve in the survey.

DEFINING THE RELEVANT MARKET

In Chapter 6, we pointed out that employers compete in many labor markets. The relevant market depends on the purpose of the survey. To make decisions about pay levels and structures or to estimate competitors' labor costs, the relevant labor market includes those employers with whom an organization competes for employees. Although a statistician may design a survey to sample a broad population, salary surveys are typically designed to capture a narrower population of employers (i.e., the competition). As we observed in Chapter 6, competitors forming the relevant markets are typically defined by the following:

1. Employers who compete for the same occupations or skills required.
2. Employers who compete for employees within the same geographic area.
3. Employers who compete with the same products.

---

[3] Sara L. Rynes and G. T. Milkovich, "Wage Surveys: Dispelling Some Myths about the 'Market Wage,'" *Personnel Psychology,* Spring 1986, pp. 71–90; Frederic Cook, "Compensation Surveys Are Biased," *Compensation and Benefits Review,* September–October 1994, pp. 19–22.

[4] Thomas Stone and Sarosh Kuruvilla, "The Wage Comparison Process in a Local Labor Market" (Working paper, University of Iowa, 1988).

Perhaps a fourth criterion will eventually be added: employers who use the same basis for their structure (e.g., job versus skill/competency based). As less traditional approaches become more common (skill/competency-based structures, use of contingent and temporary employees, broadbanding, etc.), separate surveys, or at least the flexibility to analyze data from competitors using skill/competencies, will be required. Presently, managers using other structures face special problems getting comparable market data at the same time that they are relying more on that external market data.[5] So the definition of relevant labor market will vary, depending on the purpose of the survey and the particular jobs and skills being examined.

Exhibit 7.2 shows how qualifications interact with geography to define the scope of relevant labor markets. As the importance of the qualifications and the complexity of qualifications increase, the geographic limits also increase. Competition tends to be national for managerial and professional skills, but local or regional for clerical and production skills. However, these generalizations do not always hold true. In areas with high concentrations of scientists, engineers, and managers (e.g., Boston, Dallas, or Palo Alto), the primary market comparison may be regional, with national data used only secondarily. Exhibit 7.3 translates these generalities into policy for a pharmaceutical manufacturer. For top managerial jobs, national surveys of companies with sales between $1 billion and $4 billion are used. For research jobs, only data from pharmaceutical industry firms are used. For clerical jobs, local data from a wide range of industries and organization sizes are used.

In major metropolitan areas, the relevant market may be further restricted by commuting times and patterns. But the amount of time people are willing to commute varies by locale as well as by personal and economic circumstances. Tokyo's 90-minute train rides and Los Angeles' 90-minute traffic jams are legendary. Further, managers can influence the willingness of people to commute with actions other than setting higher pay levels. For example, a firm may lobby the local transit authority for convenient bus routes and schedules or may sponsor company-owned vans and car-pooling programs. One New York City department store buses 160 workers from Brooklyn to its suburban stores during busy holiday seasons so that the stores will have an adequate supply of sales personnel.

From the perspective of cost control and ability to pay, including competitors in the product/service market is crucial.[6] The pay rates of product/service competitors will affect both costs of operations and financial condition (e.g., ability to pay). However, this becomes a problem when the major competitors are based in countries with far lower pay rates, such as China or Mexico. In fact, the

---

[5] Consulting firms are in the process of redesigning products to address these needs. For example, Executive Alliance's Semiconductor, Computer, and High Performance Systems Total Compensation Survey (Marlboro, MA) permits customizing reports on a number of options. Towers Perrin and Wyatt are testing methodologies for conducting surveys based on competencies.

[6] Barry Gerhart and George Milkovich, "Employee Compensation," in *Handbook of Industrial and Organizational Psychology,* 2nd ed., ed. M. D. Dunnette and L. M. Hough (Palo Alto, CA: Consulting Psychologists Press, 1992).

EXHIBIT 7.2 Relevant Labor Markets by Geographic and Employee Groups

Geographic Scope	Production	Office and Clerical	Technicians	Scientists and Engineers	Managerial Professional	Executive
Local: Within relatively small areas such as cities or Metropolitan Statistical Areas (e.g., Dallas metropolitan area)	Most likely	Most likely	Most likely			
Regional: Within a particular area of the state or several states (e.g., oil-producing region of southwestern United States)	Only if in short supply or critical	Only if in short supply or critical	Most likely	Likely	Most likely	
National: Across the country				Most likely	Most likely	Most likely
International: Across several countries				Only for critical skills or those in very short supply	Only for critical skills or those in very short supply	Sometimes

EXHIBIT 7.3   Labor Market Competitors

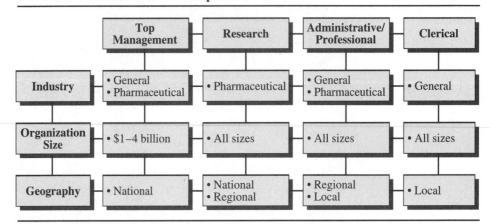

Source: Jane A. Bjorndal and Linda K. Ison, *Mastering Market Data* (Scottsdale, AZ: American Compensation Association, 1991).

increasingly international character of business has spawned interest in global survey data, particularly for managerial and professional talent.[7]

But even if an employer possesses good international survey data, utilizing that data still requires careful judgment. For example, Sun Microsystems pays its Russian engineers in Moscow between $260 and $320 a month. While these salaries are absurdly low by Western standards, they are 25 to 30 times the salaries paid to other engineers outside the Sun-funded unit at the same institute. Sun probably can afford to pay more, even in light of all the other expenses and bureaucratic headaches associated with such an undertaking. But does it make sense to inflate salaries for some to a U.S. level, when colleagues at other institutes or support staff at the same institute do not receive comparable salaries?

Sun isn't the only U.S. company wrestling with this issue in the former Soviet republics. AT&T's Bell Laboratories supports 120 fiber-optics researchers in Moscow. Corning has a contract with 115 scientists in Saint Petersburg to study optics and silicate chemistry. Borg-Warner has brought Russian scientists to the U.S. to work on projects. Sun's Russian engineers claim they are satisfied with their salaries. "If somebody offers us more, then we'll feel underpaid," their leader comments.[8]

Some writers argue that if the skills are tied to a particular industry, as underwriters, actuaries, and claims representatives are to insurance, it makes

---

[7] *Expatriate Compensation Survey* (Organization Resource Counselors) and *International Benefit Guidelines* and *Compensation Benefits Survey* (William M. Mercer) are just some of the surveys conducted annually. Most major consulting firms offer international survey.

[8] Deborah Stead and Robert D. Hof, "Math Genius with Lab. Will Work for Food," *Business Week,* June 14, 1993, pp. 84, 86; Sheila M. Puffer and Stanislav V. Shekshnia, "Compensating Local Employees in Post-Communist Russia: In Search of Talent or Just Looking for a Bargain?" *Compensation and Benefits Review,* September–October 1994, pp. 35–43.

sense to define the market on an industry basis.[9] If accounting, sales, or clerical skills are not limited to one particular industry, industry considerations are less important. But this position ignores financial objectives of the employer. Pricing labor competitively with others who offer similar products and services is necessary to achieve the organization's financial objectives. Within these product/service market constraints, occupational and geographic factors come into play. Additionally, a firm's size (number of employees, total revenues, and assets) reflects its market dominance. Omitting a dominant firm would not accurately capture the market.

Equal Employment Opportunity Considerations

A final consideration in determining the relevant market relates to equal employment opportunity (EEO). As noted earlier, market data are frequently used in pay discrimination litigation to explain pay differentials.[10] If market data are to serve as criteria to explain and justify pay practices, the definition of the relevant markets and the survey methodology must be defensible. This means that procedures and decisions must be

1. *Documented.* An organization's policies regarding external wage comparisons are specified, and actions taken in conducting surveys are consistent with these policies.
2. *Business related.* Firms competing with similar products/services are included.
3. *Work related.* Employers of similar skills within similar geographic areas are included. Caution should be exercised here since some employers, by virtue of the nature of their product market or pressure from their unions, may be able and/or willing to pay more. For example, Price Waterhouse may be willing to pay its accountants in Chicago more than Marshall Field's department store pays its Chicago accountants, since accountants are more critical to generating revenues to Price Waterhouse than they are to Marshall Field's.

How Many Employers?

There are no firm rules on how many employers to include in a survey.[11] Large firms with a lead policy may exchange data with only a few (6 to 10) top-

---

[9] Felicia Nathan, "Analyzing Employers' Costs for Wages, Salaries, and Benefits," *Monthly Labor Review,* October 1987, pp. 3–11.

[10] *Kouba and EEOC* v. *Allstate Insurance Company,* 1982, 691 F.2d 873; *Briggs* v. *City of Madison,* W.D. Wisc. 1982, 436 F. Supp. 435. Also see *In the Matter of Boston Survey Group,* Mass. Superior Court, Docket No. 56341, August 2, 1982; Rynes and Milkovich, "Wage Surveys: Dispelling Some Myths."

[11] Chockalingam Viswesvaran and Murray Barrick, "Decision-Making Effects on Compensation Surveys: Implications for Market Wages," *Journal of Applied Psychology* 77, no. 5 (1992), pp. 588–97.

paying competitors. A small organization in an area dominated by two or three employers may decide to survey only smaller competitors. National surveys conducted by consulting firms may include more than 100 employers. Clients of these consultants often stipulate special analyses that report pay rates by selected industry groups, geographic region, and/or pay levels (e.g., top 10 percent).

Who Should Be Involved?

In most organizations, the responsibility for managing the survey lies with the compensation manager. But since the pricing of HR has a powerful effect on profitability, operating managers and employees need to be involved, too. A recurrent theme in this text has been the need to get user acceptance through involvement in procedure design. Including managers and employees on task forces or surveying employees to discover what firms they use for pay comparisons makes sense.

Outside consulting firms are often used as third-party protection from possible "price-fixing" lawsuits. Suits have been filed alleging that the exchange of survey data violates Section 1 of the Sherman Act, which outlaws conspiracies in restraint of trade. Courts interpret the Sherman Act to find survey participants guilty of price fixing if the overall effect of the information exchange is to *interfere with competitive prices* and *artificially hold down wages*. One case involved the Boston Survey Group, a 34-member association, that exchanged data on wages for a variety of clerical jobs. Each participating firm's information was clearly identified by company name, and the results were reported by industry group. A consent decree agreed to by the Boston Survey Group and the Massachusetts State Attorney General's office stipulates the following:

- The data will no longer be identified by company names.
- Only aggregated information will be reported; salaries of individual employees will not be published.
- No data will be published on a per industry basis.
- Data will not be reported if fewer than 10 people are in a job.
- Members may choose to allow their employees to see the aggregated survey results for their own jobs.

The Utah Society for Healthcare Human Resource Administration, the Utah Hospital Association, and eight hospitals agreed to even stricter requirements in 1994.[12] They had been charged with keeping entry-level wages for registered nurses in the Salt Lake City area artificially low by exchanging wage and budget information, including intentions to increase starting pay offers. As a result of the legal agreement, no health care facility in Utah can design, develop, or

---

[12] Michael B. Shea, "Decrees Offer Survey Guidelines," *ACA News*, June 1994, p. 15; *District of Utah U.S. District Court* v. *Utah Society For Healthcare Human Resources Administration, et al.,* Federal Register 59, no. 58, March 25, 1994, 14203.

conduct a wage survey. They can respond in writing (only) to a written request for information for wage survey purposes from a third party, but only after the third party provides written assurance that the survey will be conducted with particular safeguards.

As with the Boston Survey Group, data must be sufficiently aggregated to prevent identification of source, and only historic data can be provided. Additionally, if a majority of the health care facilities that participate in the survey operate or are headquartered in Utah, the survey may not identify the facilities that participated in the survey, may not disseminate entry-level rates for a particular position, and only may disseminate the average pay rate for that position. The inability to participate in the design and development of the survey, however, probably means that these facilities' only decision is whether to buy what the consultants have to offer. The difficulty is a lack of a clear test to distinguish legitimate attempts to understand market conditions from unlawful agreements that may reduce competition

Hiring a third party instead of managing the survey internally buys legal protection at the cost of control over the decisions that determine the quality and usefulness of the data. A consent decree prohibiting exchange of industry data eliminates the ability to make industry or product market comparisons. This might not be important in clerical jobs, but industry groups are important when making comparisons for wages for other skills/competencies and jobs. For example, a Hewlett-Packard marketer's job is probably more similar to that of an AT&T Information Systems marketer than it is to a Union Carbide marketer. If the competencies in question are generalized and thus transferrable, then industry data can safely be ignored. However, industry data are crucial from a competitive market labor cost perspective. Further, if the skills are highly specialized (e.g., semiconductors designer), then they may be industry specific and therefore not available across industries.

Make or Buy?

The decision to retain outside expertise or to design the survey in-house requires trade-offs. The availability of staff time and talent and the desire to control the quality of analysis and results are often given as reasons to tailor one's own survey. On the other hand, consulting firms offer a wide choice of ongoing surveys covering almost every job family and industry group imaginable.

Consultant surveys are getting better and better. While we would like to attribute the improvement to the fact that our textbook has improved the sophistication of compensation education in the United States (our book was first published in 1985, and at least some of those early readers ought to be in power positions by now), it is more likely that the improvement is the result of technological improvements that make data manipulation easier.

Purchasing Criteria.   Opinions about the value of consultant surveys are rampant; research is not. Do Hay, Mercer, Towers Perrin, Executive Compensation

Services, Executive Alliance, or MCS's 777 surveys of managerial pay yield significantly different results? Can these various surveys successfully withstand pay discrimination litigation? Many firms select one survey as their primary source and use others to cross-check or "validate" the results.

For staffing decisions, professional consultants who design employment tests report the test's performance against a set of measurements (reliability, validity, etc.). For pay decisions, analogous standards have not yet evolved. Issues of sample design and statistical inference are seldom considered. Some employers routinely combine the results of several surveys and weight each survey in this

EXHIBIT 7.4   Example of BLS Survey Data

Occupation and Industry Division	Number of Employees	Average Weekly Hours	Weekly Earnings ($)		
			Mean	Median	Middle Range
Secretarial and Keyboarding Operators					
Secretaries I	924	39.6	$432	$420	$384–485
Private industry	554	39.6	444	439	384–493
Service producing	538	39.7	445	439	384–493
Transportation/utilities	54	39.4	475	481	415–531
State and local government	370	39.7	413	393	364–450
Secretaries II	3115	39.5	491	480	432–539
Private industry	1821	39.2	495	490	439–538
Goods producing	173	39.4	534	520	485–576
Manufacturing	105	39.0	548	524	461–623
Service producing	1648	39.2	491	485	436–534
Transportation/utilities	76	39.6	534	534	461–555
State and local government	1294	39.9	485	460	421–543
Secretaries III	3442	39.3	563	557	509–614
Private industry	2887	39.2	564	559	515–614
Goods producing	215	39.5	574	578	509–626
Manufacturing	142	39.3	583	578	523–614
Service producing	2672	39.2	563	557	515–611
Transportation/utilities	362	40.0	591	599	545–624
State and local government	555	39.8	563	550	451–653
Secretaries IV	1756	39.3	638	634	577–684
Private industry	1585	39.3	636	633	577–678
Goods producing	176	38.9	645	626	592–683
Manufacturing	154	38.8	655	634	597–689
Service producing	1409	39.3	635	634	577–678
Transportation/utilities	252	39.1	663	654	624–676
State and local government	171	39.9	661	636	569–758

Note: Weekly earnings of office workers in establishments employing 500 workers or more in Washington, D.C., January 1994.

composite according to the quality of the data reported.[13] Yet little systematic study of differences in market definition, participating firms, types of data collected, analysis performed, and/or results is available.[14]

Publicly Available Data. The Bureau of Labor Statistics (BLS) is a major source of publicly available pay data. It publishes industry wage studies, the National Survey of Professional, Administrative, Technical, and Clerical Pay (PATC), the Employee Benefits Survey, occupational compensation surveys (formerly called local area wage surveys), and the ECI, the measure of changes in employee compensation costs discussed earlier. In addition, most states and even some counties provide pay data to the public.

Exhibit 7.4 illustrates the nature of the BLS data. The data are inexpensive and readily available. Public sector employers seem to use BLS data more often than do private sector employers. Some private firms track the rate of change in BLS data and the ECI as a cross-check on other surveys and to examine geographic differentials for various nonexempt jobs (e.g., secretary I in Washington, D.C., versus secretary I in Durham, North Carolina). However, most private firms find the data are not specific enough to be used alone.

WHICH JOBS TO INCLUDE?

A general guideline is to keep things as simple as possible. Select as few employers and jobs as necessary to accomplish the purpose. The more complex the survey, the less likely employers are inclined to participate. There are several approaches to selecting jobs for inclusion.

Benchmark Jobs Approach. Benchmark jobs share the following characteristics:

- The contents are well known, relatively stable, and agreed upon by the employees involved.
- The supply and demand for these jobs are relatively stable and not subject to recent shifts.
- They represent the entire job structure under study.
- A sizable proportion of the work force is employed in these jobs.

Typically, only benchmark jobs are included in surveys. Descriptions of the benchmark jobs are included in the survey so that participants can match the survey job within the correct job in their organization.

Some employers also use the percentage of incumbents who are women and

---

[13] L. S. Hartenian and N. B. Johnson, "Establishing the Reliability and Validity of Wage Surveys," *Public Personnel Management* 20, no. 3 (1991), pp. 367–83.

[14] Jane A. Bjorndal and Linda K. Ison, *Mastering Market Data* (Scottsdale, AZ: American Compensation Association, 1991).

men as a defining characteristic of a benchmark job to try to ensure that the benchmarks are free of possible employment discrimination.

Generally, the approach is to ensure that benchmark jobs represent all key functions and levels. The employer in Exhibit 7.5 organizes work into four structures. Selecting benchmark jobs from various levels within each structure ensures coverage of the entire work domain.

Global Approach.   Rarely do several organizations have identical jobs. This is particularly true in organizations that emphasize semiautonomous teams or continuously adapt jobs to meet changing conditions. The global approach may be better suited to survey pay levels in these situations.

With a global approach, the rates paid to every individual employee in an entire skill group or function (e.g., all chemical engineers or all computer scientists) are used. Exhibit 7.6 shows external market data for engineers with bachelor's degrees. Exhibit 7.7 translates those data into percentiles. A survey user can determine the rates paid to engineers (Exhibit 7.6) as well as the rate's relationship to years since degree (YSD) (Exhibit 7.7). Because of this relationship to YSD, the curves in Exhibit 7.7 are often referred to as *maturity curves*. A global approach simply substitutes a particular skill (represented by a B.S. in engineering in the example) and experience or maturity (YSD) for detailed descriptions of work performed.

Low-High Approach.   If an organization is using skill/competency-based structures or generic job descriptions, it may not be able to match jobs with competitors who use a traditional job-based approach. Job-based market data must be converted to fit the skill or competency structure. The simplest approach is to identify

Exhibit 7.5   Benchmarks

Managerial Group	Technical Group	Manufacturing Group	Administrative Group
		Assembler I Inspector I	
Vice Presidents	Head/Chief Scientist	Packer	Administrative Assistant
Division General Managers	Senior Associate Scientist	Materials Handler Inspector II	Principal Administrative Secretary
Managers	Associate Scientist	Assembler II	Administrative Secretary
Project Leaders	Scientist	Drill Press Operator Rough Grinder	Word Processor
Supervisors	Technician	Machinist I Coremaker	Clerk/Messenger

EXHIBIT 7.6 Frequency Distribution—All Engineers, All Companies

YEARS SINCE BS

MONTHLY SALARY	0	1	2	3	4	5	6	7	8	9	10	11	12	13	14	15	16	17	18	19	20	21	22	23	24	25	26	27	28	29	30	31	32	33	34	35	36	37	TOTAL
6950 + OVER																																				1			10
6825 - 6949																														1							1	1	9
5700 - 6824																														1	2			1		1	1	2	12
6575 - 6699																																				1		2	14
6450 - 6574																	1			1		1		1				2		2		2	1				2	9	31
6325 - 6449															1			1			2	2	3	1		2		1	1	1		3	2	3		1	2	5	24
6200 - 6324					2									1			2		1	2			1		3	2	2	2	4	2		4	2	2	2	2	4	4	42
6075 - 6199													1										6	5		3		2		1	3	3	2	1	2	3	2	5	43
5950 - 6074											1			1	1	2	2	1	3	2	4	3	4	4	5	4	2	2	2	3	4	2	4	5	2	1	4	8	44
5825 - 5949															1	1	2	2	2	4	4	4	4	5	2	7	4	4	4	4	4	5	2	2	2	4	2	6	63
5700 - 5824															2			1	6	3	3	2	10	4	10	4	6	4	4	4	4	5	4	5	5	1	6	6	70
5575 - 5699							1								1	2	3	4	1	3	6	4	5	4	8	2	6	4	5	4	4	2	4	2	3	4	6	11	95
5450 - 5574												1			2	5	6	6	6	7	6	10	5	6	10	7	6	6	6	4	4	2	1	6	4	3	3	10	102
5325 - 5449														2	1	5	3	4	9	4	6	5	2	5	8	9	7	3	5	2	4	4	7	6	5	7	7	15	116
5200 - 5324													1		2	5	8	6	5	7	8	10	5	5	6	9	6	7	6	9	5	8	7	7	4	4	5	16	151
5075 - 5199								1				1		2	8	11	8	7	11	13	11	7	12	13	11	8	8	3	11	4	6	5	7	7	4	4	2	17	173
4950 - 5074								4	4	2	1	4	1	8	7	10	8	6	9	12	10	10	10	7	8	6	8	4	6	4	6	4	7	3	4	4	2	18	178
4825 - 4949								1	11	5	8	8	2	10	10	11	13	10	6	13	11	9	12	13	9	8	8	5	3	6	10	4	7	7	5	4	1	27	180
4700 - 4824						1		10	14	12	9	15	6	7	9	10	14	10	13	9	7	8	10	14	16	9	4	4	4	4	8	4	3	3	7	3	4	10	192
4575 - 4699						4	5	10	16	16	12	15	13	4	16	16	13	12	4	6	9	4	13	5	10	9	7	5	6	12	5	1	6	7	5	7	6	20	210
4450 - 4574			2		4	5	6	8	13	10	16	12	8	10	9	11	19	11	9	9	6	5	8	9	16	5	7	6	4	8	4	4	3	4	2	2	4	24	232
4325 - 4449			3	4	9	8	13	18	13	10	16	15	6	10	11	21	14	11	12	13	11	6	18	13	11	5	8	8	6	8	5	10	3	9	4	4	4	24	216
4200 - 4324			5	6	12	8	11	21	20	15	8	12	9	10	19	21	15	9	14	7	6	11	7	15	7	5	2	7	6	12	4	7	10	3	4	9	3	24	290
4075 - 4199	1		6	9	12	8	14	22	7	10	14	10	8	17	17	21	15	13	11	7	9	6	8	15	11	5	4	7	6	9	6	7	3	9	4	9	4	9	281
3950 - 4074			14	6	8	11	14	19	18	8	8	13	5	9	9	13	8	9	4	9	10	8	7	13	7	5	2	7	6	4	6	6	10	3	4	3	3	12	262
3825 - 3949		8	17	24	20	15	11	13	14	10	9	15	13	15	16	10	14	13	10	11	10	8	6	13	8	4	4	6	3	2	10	6	2	3	1	3	2	3	255
3700 - 3824		11	27	19	25	15	18	7	12	15	16	15	16	14	9	16	14	9	4	6	10	4	8	6	6	7	4	5	4	2	8	6	3	4		1	3	2	234
3575 - 3699		27	22	20	14	7	12	13	13	10	12	12	8	16	9	14	13	12	5	5	7	3	5	3	4	7	7	4	6	3	5	4	6		4	1	1	3	205
3450 - 3574		35	17	14	4	7	8	21	19	10	16	8	8	9	16	9	8	10	4	6	6	3	3	3	5	4	2	6	3	3	4	4	3	3	4	3	1	1	193
3325 - 3449		28	10	4	4	8	6	8	13	10	2	11	8	10	9	14	6	5	2	6	6	4	3	2	7	4	4	5	6	2	4	4	2		4	1		3	176
3200 - 3324	1	2	8	9	4	8	13	21	20	15	13	12	9	11	5	1	6	4	4	5	3	6	3	3	3	2		2	2	2	5		3	3		2			174
2950 - 3074		1	5	5	9	8	11	7	7	10	14	10	6	6	8	3	6	2	4	5	6	2	3	5	5	3	3	2	2	1	3		4		3				155
2825 - 2949	4	4	6	6	12	11	14	22	18	10	8	5	5	6	6	3	8	2	2	5	5	3	4	5	3	2	2	2	2	1	3		4	1		1			174
2700 - 2824		11	17	24	20	15	18	13	10	15	4	3	3	3	1	2	1	2	2	5		3	6							1	3	3	1					1	169
2575 - 2699		11	27	22	25	7	12	7	8	7	3	3	3	5	1	2	3	1									2												158
2450 - 2574	29	42	35	17	14	7	8	4	3		1	1		1				2																					172
2325 - 2449	16	37	28	10	4	10	5	2																															116
2200 - 2324	13	11	8	6	6	1	2	2																															48
UNDER 2200	13	10	6																																				29
TOTAL	62	120	142	117	105	87	116	167	165	131	139	166	145	154	193	221	187	170	174	164	179	148	183	170	168	137	128	119	131	124	111	109	103	89	74	91	82	354	5425
MEDIAN	2458	2555	2553	2703	2728	2804	2976	3195	3295	3429	3455	3658	3688	3908	4005	4089	4186	4188	4304	4422	4429	4432	4512	4503	4524	4595	4630	4551	4762	4439	4656	4585	4682	4762	4950	4637	5012	4748	4035
MEAN	2433	2447	2564	2711	2752	2854	3008	3199	3332	3434	3501	3665	3698	3924	4041	4189	4209	4239	4421	4466	4476	4438	4637	4502	4583	4638	4665	4629	4741	4669	4821	4657	4738	4851	4828	4772	4899	4860	4090
STD.DEV.	110	170	243	275	289	344	388	428	479	491	513	583	527	673	678	699	729	798	791	856	932	861	951	807	839	859	819	826	897	979	1097	929	965	1010	1011	943	887	963	1051

Source: Organization Resources Counselors, Inc., New York.

EXHIBIT 7.7   **Percentile Curves: Years since First Degree versus Monthly Salary—All Engineers, All Companies**

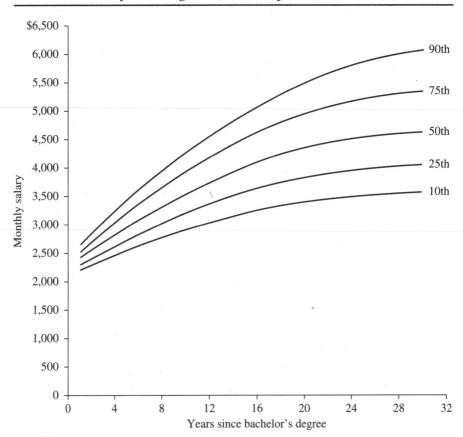

Source: Organization Resources Counselors, Inc., New York.

the lowest- and highest-paid benchmark jobs for the relevant skills in the relevant market and to use the wages for these jobs as anchors for the skill-based structures. Work at various levels within the structure can then be slotted between the anchors. For example, Exhibit 7.8 shows the skill-based system at Borg-Warner. Since the structure begins with unskilled labor, market rates for entry-level unskilled labor would anchor the low end of the structure. Market rates for team leaders should anchor the high end. On a graph with wage rates on the y-axis and the structure on the x-axis, a line can be drawn connecting the rates for the anchors. Wage rates for the rest of the structure can then be slotted on this line. For example, if the entry market rate is $8 per hour and the rate for team leaders is $28 per hour, then the rate for operator Bs can be somewhere between $8 and $28 per hour.

The usefulness of this approach depends on how well the extreme benchmark jobs match the organization's work, and whether they really do tap the entire

EXHIBIT 7.8   Pricing a Skill-Based Structure

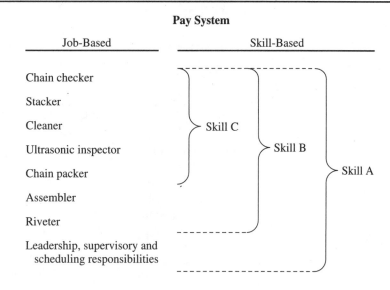

Pay System

Job-Based	Skill-Based

Chain checker

Stacker

Cleaner   Skill C

Ultrasonic inspector   Skill B

Chain packer   Skill A

Assembler

Riveter

Leadership, supervisory and
    scheduling responsibilities

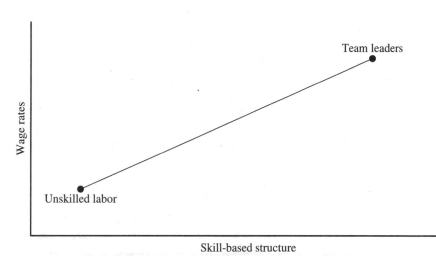

range of skills. Hanging a pay system on two pieces of market data raises the stakes on the accuracy of those data.

Using Skill/Competencies

The dilemma facing those using skill/competency-based approaches is that the market surveys are typically job based. Thus, matching specific combinations of skills/competencies among competitors in the market requires considerable judgment. Some consultants (e.g., Towers Perrin) are piloting skill/competency-based surveys. Until these products become available, most firms are simply "roughing them in." They are converting competencies to (dare we say it?) jobs, and then going to the market to find matches; for example, the combination of competencies for the financial manager role is matched to financial managers in surveys. If skill/competency-based approaches become more commonly used, then consultants will undoubtedly respond with new survey products to meet those needs.

Benchmark Conversion Approach.   This approach to matching survey jobs requires an employer to apply its plan to value the benchmark jobs provided in the survey and to compare those results with internal results. If an organization uses job evaluation, then its job evaluation system is applied to the benchmark jobs, and job evaluation points are assigned to these jobs. If an organization uses skill/competency-based pay, then skill points can be assigned to the survey jobs. The magnitude of difference in skill points or job evaluation points provides a guideline for making similar adjustments in the market data collected for the survey job.

So, the real issue is to ensure that the jobs or skill/competency groups included in the survey provide data that will be useful. Depending on the purpose of the survey, either the benchmark approach, the global approach, the low-high approach, or the benchmark-conversion approach can help.

WHAT INFORMATION TO COLLECT?

Three basic types of data typically are requested: (1) information about the nature of the organization, (2) information about the total compensation system, and (3) specific pay data on each incumbent in the jobs under study. Exhibit 7.9 lists the basic data elements and the logic for including them.

No survey includes all the data that will be discussed. Rather, the data collected depend on the purpose of the survey and the jobs and skills included. Managers must rely on their expertise and experience to decide what data to collect and be sensitive to any guidelines that emerge from consent decrees and legal judgments.

Organization Data.   This information assesses the similarities and differences among survey users. Financial information, size, and organization structure are

EXHIBIT 7.9   Data Elements to Consider for Surveys and Their Rationale

Basic Elements	Examples	Rationale
Nature of Organization		
Identification	Company, name, address, contact person	Further contacts
Financial condition	Assets, sales, profits (after taxes)	Indicates nature of the product/service markets, the ability to pay, size, and financial viability
Size	Profit centers, product lines	Importance of specific job groups to business success
	Total number of employees	Impact on labor market
Structure	Organizational charts	Indicates how business is organized and how important managerial jobs are
Nature of Total Compensation System		
Cash forms used	Base pay, pay increase schedules, long- and short-term incentives, bonuses, cost of living adjustments, overtime and shift differentials	Indicate the mix of compensation offered; used to establish a comparable base
Noncash forms used	Composition of benefits and services, particularly the degree of coverage and contributions to medical and health insurance and pensions	
Incumbent and Job		
Date	Date effective	Need to update rates to current date
Job	Match generic job description	Indicates degree of similarity with survey's key jobs
	Number of employees supervised and reporting levels	Describes scope of responsibilities
Individual	Years since degree, education, date of hire	Indicates training and tenure of incumbents
Pay	Actual rates paid to each individual, total earnings, last increase, bonuses, incentives	

usually included. Surveys of executives and upper-level positions include more detailed financial and reporting relationships data. The logic for including these additional data is that compensation for these jobs is more directly related to the organization's financial performance. More often than not, the financial data are simply used to group firms by size expressed in terms of sales or revenues.

Total Pay System Data.   All the basic forms of pay need to be covered in a survey to assess the similarities and differences in the entire pay packages and to accurately assess competitors' practices.[15] For example, more and more employers offer various forms of team awards and incentives along with the base pay. Some employers roll these awards into the base pay, others do not. Inconsistent reporting (or not reporting) of these awards will distort the data. For example, company I in Exhibit 7.10 may target itself to be at the third quartile among a selected comparison group for cash compensation and benefits. Company I's cash compensation of $250 per week is at the third quartile of comparisons on cash compensation, and Company I's $72 per week for benefits is also at the third quartile of companies for benefits. (See the Appendix for information on quartiles.) But because they surveyed cash compensation and benefits separately, a new profile emerges when the separate surveys are combined. Company I's total pay of $322 is the highest in the group—17 percent higher than its targeted position of third quartile, $275 per week.

It is particularly difficult to include *all* the pay forms in detail. For example, including medical coverage deductibles, flexible benefit options, and vacation policies quickly make a survey too cumbersome to be useful. Methods to handle

EXHIBIT 7.10   The Total May Be Greater than the Sum of the Parts

Remuneration Comparison for a Specific Job										
Company cash compensation	A $100	B $110	C $120	D $130	E $150	F $155	G $170	H $210	I $250	J $255	K $260
Company benefits	J 25	K 30	H 35	A 40	B 45	G 50	D 60	C 65	I 72	E 75	F 77
Company total	A $140	B $155	C $185	D $190	G $220	E $225	F $232	H $245	J $275	K $290	I $322

---

[15] Joseph R. Rich and Carol Caretta Phalen, "A Framework for the Design of Total Compensation Surveys," *ACA Journal,* Winter 1992–93, pp. 18–29; Alan M. Johnson, "Designing Total Compensation Programs," in *The Compensation Handbook,* ed. Milton L. Rock and Lance A. Berger (New York: McGraw-Hill, 1991); Jack Dolmat-Connell, "A New Pardigm for Compensation and Benefits Competitiveness," *Compensation and Benefits Review,* September–October 1994, pp. 51–64.

this problem range from a brief description of a benchmark benefit package to including only the most expensive and variable benefits or asking for an estimate of total benefit expenses as a percentage of total labor costs.

Exhibit 7.11 shows an example of a total compensation summary table. In this example, the participant firm places greater emphasis on cash compensation and less on long-term incentives and benefits than do the competitor firms.

The greatest limitation on total compensation surveys may be understanding how to use all the information. Perhaps as our experience grows, standards will emerge, and the packaging and interpretation of the data will be simplified. For now, total compensation surveys may be thought of as a database project. A well-designed total compensation database will allow each participating firm to determine the models, financial assumptions, and demographic profiles that best reflect its view of the world. In the best total compensation projects, each firm sees the survey as a custom project.

Incumbent Data.   The most important data in the survey are the *actual* rates paid to each incumbent. Total earnings, hours worked, date and amount of last increase, and bonus and incentive payments are included. However, the usefulness of each element needs to be balanced against the cost of trying to collect it.

Enough data must be available to appraise the match between the benchmark jobs in the survey and jobs within each company. The degree of match between the survey's benchmark jobs and each company's jobs is assessed by various means. Hay Associates, for example, has installed the same job evaluation plan in many companies that participate in their surveys. Consequently, jobs in different organizations can be compared on their total job evaluation points and the distribution of points among the compensable factors. Other surveys simply ask participants to judge the degree of match, using a scale similar to the following one.

Please check (   ) degree to which your job matches the benchmark job described in the survey:
My company's job is

Of moderately less value	( )
Of slightly less value	( )
Of equal value	( )
Of slightly more value	( )
Of moderately more value	( )

Still other survey designers periodically send teams of employees familiar with the benchmark jobs to visit each participating organization to discuss the matches. Many public agency and trade association surveys simply rely on each participant to match the benchmark jobs as closely as possible. The BLS has perhaps the most rigorous job-matching process. It includes site visits and detailed job analysis.

International Data.   International competition requires international pay comparisons. Most large consulting firms conduct international surveys. Exhibit 7.12

EXHIBIT 7.11   Example of a Total Compensation Summary Table

Position: Compensation Manager   **Time Frame:** Current
Perspective: Economic Benefit   **Aggregation:** By Position

	Participant Firm			Competitor Firms		
	Valuation	% of Total	% of Base	Valuation	% of Total	% of Base
1. Base salary (including paid time off)	$82.7	87.2%	100%	$74.1	75.3%	100%
2. Eligibility rate, short-term incentives	10%	—	—	20%	—	—
3. Actual participation, short-term incentives	10%	—	—	15%	—	—
4. Target short-term incentives for participants	$7.1	7.5	8.6	$7.0	7.1	9.4
5. Target short-term incentives for all employees	$0.7	0.7	0.9	$1.1	1.1	1.5
6. Eligibility rate, profit-sharing	0%	—	—	24%	—	—
7. Participation rate, profit-sharing	0%	—	—	24%	—	—
8. Target profit-sharing for recipients	$0	0	0	$3.7	3.8	5.0
9. Target profit-sharing for all employees	$0	0	0	$0.9	0.9	1.2
10. Total cash compensation (1 + 5 + 9)	$83.4	88.0	101	$76.1	77.4	103
11. Eligibility rate, long-term incentives	12%	—	—	82%	—	—
12. Participation rate, long-term incentives	12%	—	—	64%	—	—
13. Average long-term incentives for recipients, Black-Scholes valuation	$4.4	4.6	5.3	$8.2	8.3	11.1
14. Average long-term incentives for all employees, Black-Scholes valuation	$0.5	0.5	0.5	$5.2	5.3	7.0
15. Total direct compensation (1 + 5 + 9 + 14)	$83.9	88.5	102	$81.3	82.7	110
16. Health and welfare benefits value	$5.6	5.9	6.8	$6.4	6.5	8.6
17. Retirement/capital accumulation value	$3.2	3.4	3.9	$8.5	8.6	11.5
18. Perquisite value	$2.1	2.2	2.5	$2.1	2.1	2.8
19. Total benefit and perquisite value	$10.9	11.5	12.1	$17.0	17.3	22.9
20. Total compensation (1 + 5 + 9 + 14 + 19)	$94.8	100%	114%	$98.3	100%	132%

Note: Dollar figures in thousands. Totals may not sum because of rounding.
Source: Joseph R. Rich and Carol Caretta Phalen, "A Framework for the Design of Total Compensation Surveys," *ACA Journal*, Winter 1992–93, pp. 18–29.

EXHIBIT 7.12   Example of International Survey Data Reported by Compensation Consulting Firm

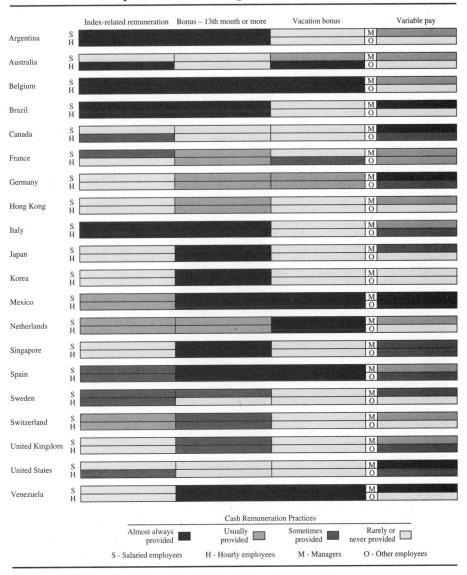

is an example of Towers Perrin's report on cash remuneration practices in 20 countries. International surveys raise additional issues of comparability because legal regulations and tax policies, as well as customs, vary among countries. For example, because of tax reasons, Korean executives rarely receive incentive pay. Some South American countries mandate cost of living adjustments, which makes the timing of the survey data collection crucial. Exhibit 7.13 gives an idea of the

EXHIBIT 7.13   International Benefit Data

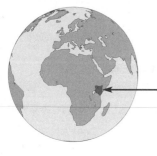

Kenya

Three factors combine to provide a more fertile climate for employee benefit plans
  development than exists in most nonindustrialized African countries—a capitalist
  economy, relative political stability since independence in 1963 (in spite of the
  attempted coup in 1982), and the British origins of most of the country's institutions.

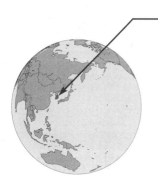

South Korea

The spectacular and consistent levels of economic growth which were seen in Korea
  during the 1970s and 1980s have eased, with a disappointing growth rate of around
  7 percent. Many argue that this reduction in growth is a result of the transition from
  a less developed cheap labor economy to a more mature environment.

Indeed, the era of cheap hard-working labor is drawing to a close as workers demand
  a suitable reward from this growth. Union pressure for wage increases, shorter
  working hours, and better working conditions has intensified with established
  foreign companies being the target for some extreme and occasionally violent
  industrial action. Minimum wages increased by some 15 percent in 1989 with
  average wages increasing by up to 20 percent.

South Korea continues to develop its welfare system. Following the implementation
  of the National Pension Scheme in 1988, 1989 saw the extension of the National
  Medical System to everyone. The next issue on the agenda is the possible
  introduction of unemployment insurance in the 1990s.

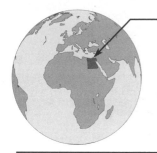

Egypt

The Egyptian government is pursuing its commitment to act to rectify the country's
  economic problems. Inflation was reduced below the 30 percent plus of recent
  years and the level of unemployment has remained stable. Investment laws were
  revised with the intention of stimulating the private sector. Of particular interest to
  foreign investors is the introduction of a Debt Equality Conversion Scheme. Steps
  were taken to liberalize foreign exchange controls and regulations. A favorable
  exchange rate against hard currencies helped the buoyant tourism sector and the
  continued development of manufacturing is expected to benefit the industrial sector.

Source: *1990 International Benefit Guidelines* (William M. Mercer Consultants).

type of background information on benefits in more than 60 countries that Mercer
provides its clients. Companies with worldwide locations use local surveys for
jobs filled locally and international surveys for top executive and managerial jobs.

Opposing Direction: Person-Based Plans and EEO.   Skill/competency-based
plans are often labeled person based to contrast them with job based. According
to this view skills and competencies are possessed or acquired by individuals. If,

then, individual attributes are paid according to how the market values them, then surveys of these individual factors will be necessary. However, early signs emerging from consent-decree guidelines suggest that the courts now require businesses to move away from individual-oriented data because individual data risks fostering discrimination, illegal price fixing, and restraint of trade. The potential opposing forces—increased use of person-based structures versus emerging court guidelines to cease collecting person-level data in the market—will need to be resolved.

Accuracy of Data. Despite the acceptance of courts of market data as legal justification for salary differentials, the whole area of collection, analysis, and interpretation has not been subject to the same scrutiny as hiring practices and testing. Whether it should have been is another question. Certainly, a sound, business-related rationale for every step in the process is important. But fine distinctions using data that are extremely general may be faulty. Some survey data profile a general guide to assess the adequacy of the whole pay structure, but not necessarily pay of specific jobs. Other surveys are designed to price specific jobs, and still others to assess only the rate of change in the rates paid. The purpose of the survey needs to be kept in mind when judging the accuracy of the data.

How to Collect the Data?

Two basic methods are used to collect pay data: interviews (in person or by phone) and mailed questionnaires. The purpose of the survey and the extensiveness of the data required usually determine the method. Special studies or double-checking results are often performed through phone interviews. Mailed questionnaires are probably most common. The BLS, the most experienced wage surveyor of all, uses extensive field interviews. Some organizations use field visits every second or third year to hold down costs and time requirements.

Many aspects of pay surveys have been ignored by researchers. Little can be said about the effects of different formats in the accuracy of the data obtained. Little is known about ensuring comparability of job matches or benefit packages. We don't know how representative surveys are of some markets. The same lack of research plagues the analysis of survey results.

INTERPRET AND APPLY SURVEY RESULTS

To discover how survey data are actually analyzed, Belcher interviewed 34 compensation professionals over a decade ago. He reports:

> Every organization uses its own methods of distilling information from the survey; uses different surveys for different purposes; and uses different methods for company surveys. I could find no commonality in these methods of analysis by industry, by firm size, or by union presence. For example, some did nothing

except read the entire survey, some emphasized industry data, others geographic competitors (commuting distances), some made comparisons with less than five competitors, some emphasized only large firms, others throw out the data from large firms.[16]

His conclusion still holds today. Diversity rules in analyzing survey data. We hope diversity reflects the flexibility of managers who adjust their analysis to deal with a variety of circumstances. We worry that diversity reflects expediency and a lack of business- and work-related logic; such approaches will not be able to withstand close critical scrutiny.

Verify Data

A common first step is to check the accuracy of the job matches. Job descriptions will be included with the survey data. However, even descriptions that match perfectly do not indicate how various companies value the same jobs, or their pay policies in reference to that job.

Exhibit 7.14 is a survey report provided by Organization Resources Counselors, Inc., for participants in its Salary Information Retrieval System. This particular survey report was prepared for company P44, a pharmaceutical firm, and reports wages for a business applications programmer/analyst position. We will use this report to illustrate a survey analysis. Examining the number of employees in each company shows that two clusters of wages seem to exist at $39,894 (297 employees) and at $46,000 to $47,000 (231 employees). Such clustering might raise questions with an analyst. Fortunately, the survey report provides assistance. A modifier key with which to assess the goodness of fit of job description is in the upper-left corner of the exhibit. One company, E17, employs by far the largest number of people whose salaries we are analyzing: 297 in MCS 2—Business, earning an average of $39,894. But this same company, E17, also reports data on 125 people in job MCS 3—Business who earn an average of $46,359. Clearly, company E17 distinguishes between these two jobs and pays them differently. Should both be included here in the same report? Should all the data from company E17 be discarded? Most surveys report only one job match per company, but most surveys also provide little information to assess the strength of that match. The three lines at the bottom of the exhibit disaggregate the salary data according to the goodness of the match.

Leveling.   If the job description is similar but not identical, and the survey data are not disaggregated by closeness of match, the data may be weighted according to the match. This technique is called *survey leveling*. Based on a scale such as the one shown on page 263, if the job in the survey has more responsibility, some analysts adjust the survey data (e.g., multiply it by 0.8) to bring its pay

---

[16] Letter from D. W. Belcher to G. T. Milkovich, in reference to D. W. Belcher, N. Bruce Ferris, and John O'Neill, "How Wage Surveys Are Being Used," *Compensation and Benefits Review,* September–October 1985, pp. 34–51.

EXHIBIT 7.14   Survey Report Prepared by Compensation Consulting Firm

Job: PROGRAMMING/ANALYST-BUSINESS APPLICATIONS

Modifiers: A = **Stronger match**   **Prepared for company P44**
                    B = **Exact match**
                    C = **Weaker match**

Co. #	Modifiers	Job Title	No. of Inc.	Avg.	Low	High	Range Min.	Mid Pt.	Range Max.
D67	B	Prog/Analyst Sr	2	$36,283	$36,108	$36,400	$28,246	$35,351	$42,456
E08	C	Sr Data Analyst	5	36,574	31,682	39,719	28,654	39,719	50,785
P23	B	Prog Analyst Sr	13	39,079	35,817	43,854	28,654	41,787	54,920
D32	B	Mgmt Syst Analyst	2	39,079	37,914	40,185	35,235	44,262	53,289
E09	B	Prog/Analyst Bus	8	39,634	35,280	43,008	32,659	42,403	52,147
E17	B	MCS 2—Business	297	39,894	32,206	51,076	32,905	44,204	55,502
G02	B	Princ Business Prog	1	40,588	40,588	40,588	35,548	44,083	52,617
P19	B	Prog/Analyst Sr	12	41,292	36,108	49,096	35,235	46,679	58,123
E31	B	Prog Analyst Sr	3	41,731	36,960	44,284	32,363	42,107	50,507
E11	C	Prog Analyst Sr	3	42,040	38,707	46,502	32,363	41,442	50,520
P21	B	Prog/Analyst III	1	42,537	42,537	42,537	34,648	44,352	54,055
E08	B	ADP Analyst	4	43,621	39,020	48,339	30,401	44,087	57,774
E35	B	Sr Sys Analyst Gen	22	43,908	30,240	53,978	37,632	47,040	56,448
→ P44	**B**	**Sys Dev Spec III**	**3**	**43,962**	**41,879**	**47,376**	**31,073**	**44,392**	**57,711**
A12	B	Info Syst Prog	9	44,844	40,069	48,863	37,448	48,717	59,987
K15	B	Comp Analyst Sr	7	45,019	34,944	49,397	34,827	44,437	53,988
E20	B	Prog/Analyst Sr	1	45,194	45,194	45,194	40,185	51,804	63,423
E15	C	Prog Analyst II	4	45,267	43,680	49,504	35,002	43,739	52,474
C26	B	Sr Syst Analyst	13	45,651	40,669	53,697	34,832	45,248	55,664
E03	B	Prog/Analyst Sr	6	45,709	42,067	49,392	35,750	44,688	53,625
E17	A	MCS 3—Business	125	46,359	36,865	57,075	35,992	47,611	59,230
E11	B	Syst Analyst Sr	3	46,502	45,696	47,712	36,395	46,643	56,891
B10	B	Prog Analyst III	103	46,784	38,707	57,388	38,707	48,384	58,060
F07	A	Sr Prog/Analyst	24	47,026	33,358	59,068	38,545	50,117	61,676
P12	B	Sr Prog/Analyst	1	47,980	47,980	47,980	36,288	46,480	56,672
E09	A	Prog Analyst	10	48,249	44,634	55,009	37,094	48,451	59,808
S37	B	M/S Analyst	2	48,339	47,349	49,271	34,361	45,718	57,075
E34	B	Analyst Bus Syst	1	50,086	50,086	50,086	35,351	47,552	59,754
Q54	A	Prog Analyst Sr	1	50,435	50,435	50,435	40,127	50,552	60,977
E31	A	Prog Analyst Staff	4	53,128	49,929	59,404	40,992	53,316	63,947
Q18	A	Info Syst Analyst	4	53,424	52,241	54,888	36,624	50,164	63,705
E15	B	Prog Analyst I	1	54,104	54,104	54,104	37,564	46,941	56,318
P05	B	Sr MIS Spec	1	56,551	56,551	56,551	38,321	51,076	61,268
		26 companies							
		Total incumbents	696						
		Company P44 average	**3**	**43,962**	**41,879**	**47,376**	**31,073**	**44,392**	**57,711**
		Market weighted average	693	43,199			34,920	45,919	56,898
		Market simple average		43,216	41,491	49,205	35,280	45,911	56,365
		3 companies matching modifier C	12	40,839	38,023	45,241	32,006	41,633	51,260
		23 companies matching modifier B	513	42,035	41,139	47,955	34,937	45,394	55,677
		6 companies matching modifier A	168	46,920	44,577	55,980	38,229	50,036	61,557

Source: Adapted from Organization Resources Counselors, Inc., New York.

closer in comparability to the employer's job. Conversely, the survey data could be adjusted upward. For example, if you believed that your programmers had slightly more responsibility than the survey job description indicated, you might multiply the $43,199 average salary in the survey by 110 percent and use the result, $47,519, instead. Leveling is another example of the use of judgment in the survey analysis process. It clearly leaves the objectivity of the decisions open to challenge.

Typical Analysis

Becoming familiar with the actual data in a survey is a necessary first step to assessing its accuracy and usefulness. In order to do so, we need to review some simple statistics. We will use the data in Exhibit 7.14 to illustrate some possible analyses.

Frequency Distribution.   Arranging the data from lowest to highest and then tallying the entries allows construction of a frequency distribution. Frequency distributions include an entry for every single measurement. The frequency table in Exhibit 7.15 displays the salary data in intervals of $2,500. The data are then readily converted to a histogram also shown in the exhibit. The histogram helps visualize the information in the survey and may highlight nonconformities. For example, the one salary above $55,000 may be considered an outlier—an extreme that falls outside the majority of the data points. Whether or not to include outliers is a judgment call.

Histograms can vary in their shape. Unusual shapes require further analysis to assess the usefulness of the data. They may reflect problems with job matches, widely dispersed pay rates, or employers with widely divergent pay policies. If the data look reasonable at this point, one wag has suggested that it is probably the result of two large, offsetting errors.

Central Tendency.   The vast amount of information contained in a survey must be reduced to a single number that represents the market wage for programming analysts. The arithmetic average, or mean, is the most widely used, calculated by adding all the numbers in the group and then dividing by the number of numbers. The "simple average" for this survey is $45,216 (e.g., $32,283 + $36,574, + $39,097, etc.) and dividing by 32, the number of positions. (*Note:* Data from the company for which the report was prepared are *not* included in any of these calculations.) This calculation of mean, or arithmetic average, gives equal weight to every *company* in the survey. The programmer wage paid by company G02, which has only one individual in that position, counts as much as the wage paid by E17, which has 297 programmers. An alternative is a *weighted mean,* or weighted average, which gives equal weight to *each individual employee's* wage. Each company's mean wage is weighted by the number of people in that company who occupy that job. A weighted mean gives a more accurate picture of actual labor market conditions, since it better recognizes the size of the supply and demand.

EXHIBIT 7.15   Statistical Analysis of Survey Data

<table>
<tr><th colspan="2">Frequency Table</th><th colspan="2">Quartiles and Percentiles</th></tr>
<tr><td></td><td>*Number of Companies*
Whose Average Wage</td><td>**$36,283**</td><td>◄—— **Minimum**</td></tr>
<tr><td></td><td></td><td>36,574</td><td></td></tr>
<tr><td>*Wage Interval*</td><td>*Falls in This Interval*</td><td>39,079</td><td></td></tr>
<tr><td>$35,001–$37,500</td><td>2</td><td>**39,079**</td><td>◄—— **10th Percentile**</td></tr>
<tr><td>37,501– 40,000</td><td>4</td><td>39,634</td><td></td></tr>
<tr><td>40,001– 42,500</td><td>4</td><td>39,894</td><td></td></tr>
<tr><td>42,501– 45,000</td><td>4</td><td>40,588</td><td></td></tr>
<tr><td>45,001– 47,500</td><td>9</td><td>41,292</td><td></td></tr>
<tr><td>47,501– 50,000</td><td>3</td><td>**41,731**</td><td>◄—— **Quartile 1**</td></tr>
<tr><td>50,001– 52,500</td><td>2</td><td>42,040</td><td></td></tr>
<tr><td>52,501– 55,000</td><td>3</td><td>42,537</td><td></td></tr>
<tr><td>55,001– 57,500</td><td>1</td><td>43,621</td><td></td></tr>
<tr><td></td><td></td><td>43,908</td><td></td></tr>
<tr><td></td><td></td><td>44,844</td><td></td></tr>
<tr><td></td><td></td><td>45,019</td><td></td></tr>
<tr><td></td><td></td><td>45,194</td><td></td></tr>
<tr><td></td><td></td><td>**$45,267**</td><td>◄—— **Quartile 2,**</td></tr>
<tr><td></td><td></td><td>45,651</td><td>**50th Percentile**</td></tr>
<tr><td></td><td></td><td>45,709</td><td></td></tr>
<tr><td></td><td></td><td>46,359</td><td></td></tr>
<tr><td></td><td></td><td>46,502</td><td></td></tr>
<tr><td></td><td></td><td>46,784</td><td></td></tr>
<tr><td></td><td></td><td>47,026</td><td></td></tr>
<tr><td></td><td></td><td>47,980</td><td></td></tr>
<tr><td></td><td></td><td>**48,249**</td><td>◄—— **Quartile 3**</td></tr>
<tr><td></td><td></td><td>48,339</td><td></td></tr>
<tr><td></td><td></td><td>50,086</td><td></td></tr>
<tr><td></td><td></td><td>50,435</td><td></td></tr>
<tr><td></td><td></td><td>53,128</td><td></td></tr>
<tr><td></td><td></td><td>**53,424**</td><td>◄—— **90th Percentile**</td></tr>
<tr><td></td><td></td><td>54,104</td><td></td></tr>
<tr><td></td><td></td><td>**56,551**</td><td>◄—— **Maximum**</td></tr>
</table>

Histogram

An alternative measure of central tendency is the *median,* or the middle number of numbers arranged in either increasing or decreasing order. If the sample contains an even number of entries, the median is the arithmetic average of the two middle numbers after ranking.

Although mean is by far the most common measure of central tendency, outliers (extreme values) can distort it. Therefore, some analysts calculate more than one central tendency measure to compare to the scatter plot and/or frequency distribution before deciding which one best represents "market wage."

What difference does all this make? Central tendency measures summarize all the survey responses into a single wage for each job. Although the frequency distribution shows all the wages, central tendency gives just one. Therefore, the analyst must choose the wage measure that gives the most accurate description of the survey data.

Dispersion.   The distribution of rates around a measure of central tendency is called *dispersion. Standard deviation* is probably the most common statistical measure of dispersion, although its use in salary surveys is less common. Standard deviation refers to how far from the mean each of the items in a frequency distribution is located. In the frequency distribution based on data in Exhibit 7.14, the standard deviation from the mean is $5,029, which means that 68 percent of the salaries lie within $\pm$ 1 standard deviation or between $43,403 and $47,029. Information about dispersion gives the analyst a better idea of the relationship between the central tendency measure and the frequency distribution.

Quartiles and Percentiles.   Quartiles and percentiles are the most common measure of dispersion used in salary survey analysis. Recall from the introduction to this chapter that one organization's policy was to "be in the top 10 percent," and another's was "to be in the 65th percentile nationally." A 65th percentile means that 65 percent of all companies' pay rates are at or below that point, and 35 percent are above. To calculate quartiles, the measures are ordered from lowest to highest. The survey report already has done this. Recall that the median separates the measures into two equal groups. If the measures are separated into four groups, each group contains 25 percent of the measures, and the numbers that separate the groups are called *quartiles.* There are three quartiles (first, second, and third) for any set of scores. The second quartile always corresponds to the median. To say that a measure is in the fourth quartile means that it falls anywhere above the point of separation between the third and fourth quartile. Exhibit 7.15 shows the survey data with quartiles and percentiles marked.

Percentiles separate scores into 100 equal groups, and the points of separation mark the percentiles. Exhibit 7.7 shows the 10th, 25th, 50th, 75th, and 90th percentile curves for engineers' salaries. Ten percent of all engineers in the survey receive salaries below the 10th percentile; 90 percent receive salaries above that line. Quartiles correspond to the 25th (Q1), 50th (Q2), and 75th (Q3) percentiles.

The survey report in Exhibit 7.14 also includes range information and indicates whether the programming analysts receive any bonus or incentive compensation. All these issues will be explained in later chapters.

Where Do We Go from Here?

We have discussed some of the ways to analyze survey data. We looked at ways to calculate central tendency and to visualize the data to assess how "good" they are and how well the central tendency measure reflects the survey data. However, a survey rarely focuses on a single job. Rather, data are gathered for any number of different jobs. These jobs may be related (e.g., computer programmers, computer programming analysts, and computer operators), or they may cover a broader range of work. If the purpose of the survey is to set pay rates for a number of jobs with respect to the market, a way is needed to combine data from all the surveyed jobs. A market pay line does this by summarizing rates of the various jobs found in the market. But before further reviewing more mechanics, it is useful to step back a moment and reconsider what we are trying to accomplish with surveys. The objective is to design pay structures that employees believe are fair and equitable and that will help accomplish management's objectives.

COMBINE INTERNAL STRUCTURE AND EXTERNAL WAGE RATES

Two components of the pay model are emerging, and their relationship to each other is depicted in Exhibit 7.16.

- An *internally consistent structure* has been developed and is shown on the horizontal axis in Exhibit 7.16. For this illustration, our structure consists of jobs A through P, with P being the most complex job in this structure. Jobs B, D, F, G, H, J, M, and P are benchmark jobs that have been matched in a survey. Job M is the programmer analyst surveyed in Exhibit 7.14.
- External wage rates paid by relevant competitors for those benchmark jobs, as measured by the survey, are shown on the vertical (y) axis. The purpose of the survey is to assist the organization to address external competitiveness, much as job analysis addressed internal consistency.

These two components—internal consistency and external competitiveness—come together in the pay structure. The pay structure has two aspects. One is the actual pay policy line, which reflects market rates adjusted to the job structure and pay level policy decisions of the organization. The second is pay ranges, which build flexibility into the structure.

Calculating the Pay Policy Line

Getting from where we are now—wage rates for a number of benchmark jobs—to an actual pay policy line requires three steps.

   1. Construct a market pay line. Recall the frequency distribution for the programmer job M (Exhibit 7.15). If frequency distributions are calculated for all the benchmark jobs B, D, F, H, M, and P, then it is a simple step to transfer all the distributions onto a single graph in Exhibit 7.17, where the employer's job structure (job evaluation points) is the x-axis and wage rates are on the y-axis. The frequency distributions are at right angles to the x- and y-axes, similar to a topographic map. (*Note:* For clarity, only four distributions are shown on the exhibit.) Summarizing the data from all these distributions into a market

EXHIBIT 7.16   Combining Internal Structure with External Wage Rates

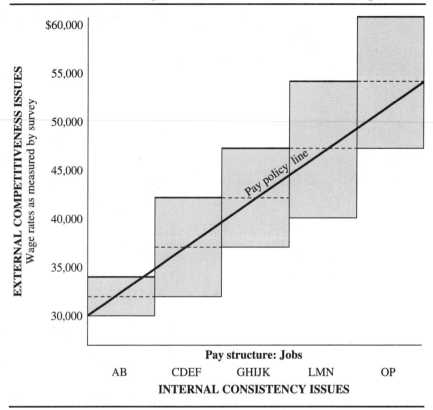

pay line may be as simple as drawing a line that connects the means, percentiles, or other measures of central tendency of the distributions, as in Exhibit 7.17. A straight line or a curve is most useful, even though midpoints for some jobs may not fall on this line. Exactly where this line is drawn will reflect the employer's pay policy. Lines may be drawn to represent various percentiles in the distributions of job rates (e.g., a 60 percent line would indicate that 60 percent of market rates fall below this line). A market line may be drawn freehand on the basis of simple inspection of the data, or statistical techniques, such as regression analysis, may be used. Regression fits a line that minimizes the variance of observations around it. Appendix 7–A provides additional information on regression. The result is a statistically more accurate market pay line that summarizes the distribution of going rates in the market.

Comparing going rates to the employer's rates will show the competitiveness of the current pay rates. Comparisons may be made across job families or by individual jobs. Exhibit 7.18 shows a comparison based on "market index," or the actual salary divided by the market rate. The market index for personnel

EXHIBIT 7.17   Constructing a Market Pay Line

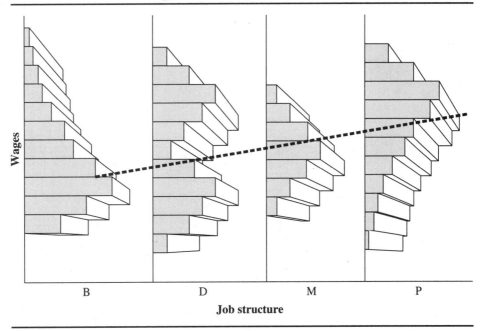

Job structure

representatives is the average salary of the four personnel representatives divided by the market rate for personnel representatives, which yields 86 percent. This low ratio may be the result of deliberate policy choices by the employer (e.g., lag the market for HR positions), the nature of the job, (e.g., personnel reps quickly get promoted into other jobs), or the survey data (e.g., personnel reps in the survey had greater responsibilities). It's up to the analyst to decide whether the variance from the market is explainable and acceptable.

A market index can also be computed for an entire department. To do so, each salary would be weighted by the number of employees (e.g., [4 × $19,600] + [2 × $25,700] + [1 × $33,000] . . . divided by 9) to calculate the average actual salary for the department. This average salary would then be divided by the market average (e.g., $22,700 + $28,000 + $33,500 . . . divided by 5) to get the overall market index for the human resource management department.

2. Update the survey data. The comparison with the market pay line gives the analyst information on the competitiveness of the current pay. The next step is to update or "age" the market data for comparisons at a future time period.

Because they reflect decisions of employers, employees, unions, and government agencies, wages paid by competitors are constantly changing. And competitors adjust their wages at different times. Universities typically adjust to match the academic year. Unionized employers adjust to correspond to dates negotiated in labor agreements. Many employers adjust each employee's pay on the anniver-

EXHIBIT 7.18   Using the Market Index to Determine Competitiveness of Current Pay

Grade	Job Title	Number of Employees	Average Actual Salary	Market Rate Composite	Market Index
1	Personnel representative	4	$19,600	$22,700	86%
3	Senior compensation analyst	2	25,700	28,000	92
4	Security supervisor*	1	33,000	33,500	99
5	Manager, Training*	1	41,000	39,500	104
6	Director, Human Resources*	1	45,000	44,000	102
			Overall market index (Human Resources):		94%
1	Accounting assistant	10	20,000	21,000	95%
2	Accountant	6	24,000	24,500	98
3	Accounting supervisor*	3	31,500	30,000	105
5	Internal auditor	1	38,000	38,000	100
6	Controller*	1	48,000	45,000	107
			Overall market index (Finance):		99%
1	LPN	25	22,000	20,000	110%
2	Registered nurse	100	29,500	27,000	109
3	Nursing instructor	10	34,500	30,500	113
3	Nurse supervisor*	5	38,000	35,000	109
6	Director, Emergency Room*	1	47,500	38,500	123
			Overall market index (Nursing):		110%
1	Programmer	6	21,000	26,500	79%
2	Data entry supervisor*	4	23,500	25,500	92
4	Systems analyst	2	30,000	32,000	94
5	Manager, Computer Operations*	1	38,000	36,500	104
6	Direct, MIS*	1	47,500	46,000	103
			Overall market index (MIS):		90%

* Overall market index for management: 104%.
Overall market index for nonmanagement: 108%.
Source: Jane Bjorndal and Linda Ison, *Mastering Market Data* (Scottsdale, AZ: American Compensation Association, 1991).

sary of the employee's date of hire. Even though these changes do not occur smoothly and uniformly throughout the year, as a practical matter it is common practice to assume that they do. Therefore, a survey that requires three to six months to collect, code, and analyze data is probably outdated before it is available. Consequently, the data are usually updated to forecast the competitive rates for the future date when the pay decisions will be implemented.

The amount to update (often called *aging* or *trending*) is based on several factors, including historical trends in the market economic forecasts, prospects for the economy in which the employer operates, consumer price index, and the manager's judgment, among others.

EXHIBIT 7.19   Choices for Updating Survey Data Reflect Pay Policy

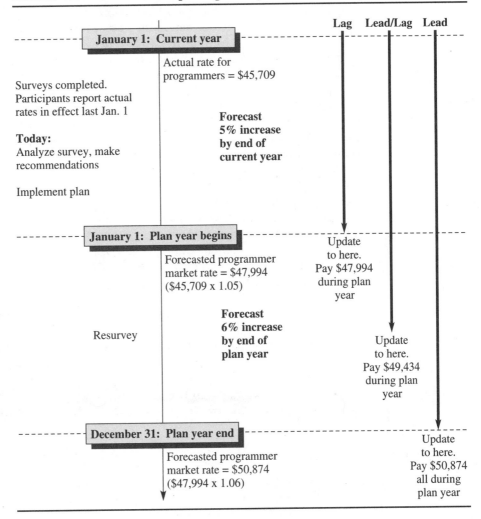

Exhibit 7.19 uses the survey data for the programmer's wage to illustrate updating. In the example, the pay rates collected in the survey were in effect at January 1 of the *current year*. Because this company's stated policy is to "match at the 60th percentile," the figure at A ($45,709) is the 60th percentile of the frequency distribution of the market rates for the programmer's job. The compensation manager will use these data for pay decisions that will go into effect on January 1 of the *plan year*. Assume that pay rates have been increasing by approximately 5 percent annually. If we assume that the future will be like the past, then the market data are multiplied by 105 percent, to account for the rise in pay that is expected to occur by the end of the *current year*. The programmer's $45,709 this past January 1 is updated to $47,994 by the end of the *current year*.

To estimate what the market rates will be by the *end* of the *plan* year, a judgment is made about the rate of increase expected during the plan year and survey results are updated again on the basis of this judgment.

3. Translate pay level policy into practice. The arrows on the right-hand side of Exhibit 7.19 show the practical results of updating. Because an individual company typically adjusts its pay level only once per period, its pay will be at the same point at both the beginning and end of the plan year. But whether an organization updates to the end of the current year (programmer rate = $47,994), the end of the plan year (programmer rate = $50,874), or someplace in between depends on its pay-level policy and how it puts that policy into practice. If the company chooses a market rate comparison consistent with its pay-level policy (60th percentile), updates survey data to the end of the current year/start of the plan year (programmer rate = $47,994), and keeps this rate in effect throughout the plan year, the company will actually be lagging the market, since it matches its desired market pay level only at the beginning of the plan year. The market rates continue to rise throughout the year; the company's rates do not.

To lead competition, an employer can age market data to the *end* of the plan year (programmer = $50,874), then pay at this rate throughout the plan year. Aging the market data to a point halfway through the plan year (middle arrow in Exhibit 7.19), is called *lead/lag*. The original survey rates are updated to the end of the current year plus half the projected amount for the plan year $(1.05 \times 1.03 = 1.0815$; programmer = $49,434).

We have oversimplified this discussion by omitting other possible mechanics. For example, some companies lead by matching the competitor's 75th percentile; others match only a few top-paying competitors or lead for some job families and lag for others. The point is that pay-level policy and actual practice may not coincide, depending on how the policy is translated into practice.

DESIGN PAY RANGES

So far we have constructed a line that reflects market pay rates and projected those rates into the future in a way that reflects the organization's pay level policy. All this is part of designing a pay structure that will reflect the organization's policies on internal consistency and external competitiveness. The next step is to design pay ranges.

Why Bother with Ranges?

The wide variation of market rates paid for similar jobs and skills reflects two *external* pressures:

1. Quality variations (skills, abilities, experience) among individuals in the external market (e.g., company A has stricter hiring requirements for its buyer position than does company B, even though job descriptions are identical).

2. The recognition of differences in the productivity-related value to employers to these quality variations (e.g., buyers for Neiman-Marcus are accountable for different results than are buyers for Wal-Mart).

In addition to these external differences in rates, an organization's internal pay policy may call for differences in rates paid to employees on the same job. A pay range exists whenever two or more rates are paid to employees in the same job. Hence, internal pay ranges reflect the following *internal* pressures:

1. The intention to recognize individual performance variations with pay (e.g., buyer A makes better, more timely decisions for Neiman-Marcus than does buyer B, even though they both hold the same job and have the same responsibilities).
2. Employees' expectations that their pay will increase over time.

From an internal consistency perspective, the range reflects the approximate differences in performance or experience the employer wishes to pay for a given level of work. From an external competitiveness perspective, the range also acts as a control device. A range maximum sets the lid on what the employer is willing to pay for that work; the range minimum sets the floor.

Not all employers use ranges. Skill-based plans establish single *flat rates* for each skill level regardless of performance or seniority. And many collective bargaining contracts establish single flat rates for each job (i.e., all Senior Machinists II receive $14.50 per hour regardless of performance or seniority). This flat rate is often set to correspond to some midpoint on a survey of that job.

Constructing Ranges

Three steps are involved in designing ranges.

1. *Develop Grades.* A *grade* is a grouping of different jobs that are considered substantially equal for pay purposes. Grades enhance an organization's ability to move people among jobs within a grade with no change in pay. In Exhibit 7.20 the horizontal axis is the job structure with the jobs now slotted into grades.

The question of which jobs are substantially equal and therefore slotted into one grade requires the analyst to reconsider the original job evaluation results. Each grade will have its own pay range, and all the jobs within the grade have that same range. Jobs in different grades (e.g., jobs C, D, E, and F in grade 2) should be dissimilar to those in other grades (grade 1 jobs A and B) and will have a different range.

Although grades permit flexibility, they are difficult to design. The objective is for all jobs that are similar for pay purposes to be placed within the same grade. If jobs with relatively close job evaluation point totals fall on either side of grade boundaries (e.g., in Exhibit 7.20, jobs E, F, and G have point totals within 30 points of each other, but E and F are in one grade, and G is in another), the magnitude of difference in salary treatment may be out of proportion to the

---

EXHIBIT 7.20   Developing Pay Grades

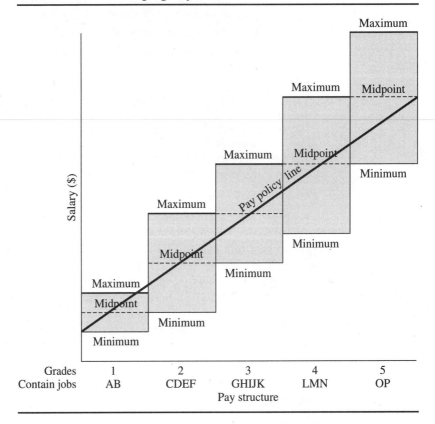

magnitude of difference in job content. Resolving such dilemmas requires an understanding of the specific jobs, career paths, and the flow of work in the organization and supports the interest in broadbanding. Designing the grade structure that fits each organization involves trial and error until one seems to fit the best without too many problems.

2. Establish Ranges (midpoint, minimum, and maximum).   The midpoints for each range are usually set to correspond to the competitive pay level established earlier. The point where the pay policy line crosses each grade becomes the midpoint of the pay range for that grade. The midpoint of the range is often called the *control point*. It specifies the pay objective for a fully trained employee who is satisfactorily performing a job within that grade. It also reflects the competitive position in the relevant market.

The desired range spread is based on some judgment about how the ranges support career paths, promotions, and other organization systems.[17] Range spreads seem to vary between 10 to 120 percent. Top-level management positions commonly have range spreads of 60 to 120 percent; entry to midlevel professional and managerial positions, between 35 to 60 percent; office and production work, 10 to 25 percent. The underlying logic is that wider range spreads in the managerial jobs are designed to reflect the greater opportunity for individual discretion and performance variations in the work.

Another, perhaps better basis on which to determine the desired range spread is what makes good sense for the particular employer. Surveys usually provide data on both the actual maximum and minimum rates paid, as well as the ranges established by policy. Some compensation managers use the actual rates paid, particularly the 75th and 25th percentiles in the survey data, as their maximums and minimums. Others examine alternatives to ensure that the proposed spread includes at least 75 percent of the rates in the survey data. Still others establish the minimum and maximum separately. The amount between the minimum and the midpoint can be a function of the amount of time it takes a new employee to become fully competent. Jobs quickly learned may have minimums much closer to the midpoints. The maximum becomes the amount above the midpoint that the company is willing to pay for sustained performance on the job. In the end, range spread is based on judgment that weighs all these factors.

Once the midpoint (based on the pay policy line) and the range spread (based on judgment) are specified, minimums and maximums are calculated

Minimum = Midpoint ÷ [100% + (1/2 range spread)]
Maximum = Minimum + (Range spread × Minimum)

For example, with a range spread of 30 percent, and a midpoint of $10,000

Minimum = $10,000 ÷ (1 + 0.15) = $8,695
Maximum = $8,695 + (0.30 × $8,695) = 8695 + 2609 = $11,304

Note that these formulas assume symmetrical ranges (i.e., equal distance above and below the midpoint).

An issue related to ranges is the size of pay differentials between supervisors and the employees they supervise. A supervisory job would typically be at least one pay range removed from the jobs it supervises. Although a 15 percent pay differential has been offered as a rule of thumb, large range overlap, combined with possible overtime or incentive pay available in some jobs but not in supervisory jobs, could make it difficult to maintain such a differential. On the other

---

[17] John D. England and David A. Pierson, "Salary Ranges and Merit Matrices: The Time Targeting Approach," *Compensation and Benefits Review,* January 1992, pp. 36–46; Peter V. LeBlanc, "Banding—The New Pay Structure for the Transformed Organization," *ACA Perspectives,* March 1992, pp. 1–6.

hand, some argue that differentials are counterproductive if they force good technical talent (i.e., engineers) to become managers solely because managers command higher incomes. The issue is one of overlap.

3. *Overlap.* If A and B are two adjacent pay grades, with B the higher of the two, the degree of overlap is defined as

$$100 \times \frac{\text{Maximum rate grade A} - \text{Minimum rate grade B}}{\text{Maximum rate grade A} - \text{Minimum rate grade A}}$$

What difference does overlap make? Consider the two extremes shown in Exhibit 7.21. The high degree of overlap and low midpoint differentials in Figure A indicate small differences in the value of jobs in the adjoining grades. Such a structure results in promotions (title changes) without much change in pay. On the other hand, in Figure B, few grades and ranges result in wider range midpoint differentials and less overlap between adjacent ranges, and permit the manager to reinforce a promotion (movement into a new range) with a larger pay increase. At some point, the differential must be large enough to induce employees to seek and/or accept the promotion or to undertake the necessary training required. However, there is little research to indicate how much a differential is necessary to influence employees to take on additional responsibilities or invest in training.

Broadbanding

Figure C collapses the number of salary grades within the structure into only a few broad grades (or bands) with much wider ranges. This technique, known as *broadbanding*, consolidates as many as four or five traditional grades into a single band with one minimum and one maximum. Because the band encompasses so many jobs of differing values, a range midpoint is usually not used.[18]

Supporters of broadbands say they offer two advantages over traditional grade-and-range approaches. First, by acting as *"fat" grades,* they provide flexibility to define job responsibilities more broadly. Thus, they support redesigned, downsized, or boundaryless organizations that have eliminated layers of managerial jobs. They are consistent with a competency- or skill-based structure. Second, they foster cross-functional growth and development in these new organizations. Employees can move laterally across functions within a band in order to gain depth of experience. The emphasis on lateral movement and deemphasis on pay adjustments tied to such movement helps manage the reality of baby boomers confronting flattened organization structures.

Organizations that use broadbanding as fat grades are likely to follow more traditional salary administration practices by using midpoints, zones, or other

---

[18] Carol A. Braddick, Michael B. Jones, and Paul M. Shafer, "A Look at Broadbanding in Practice," *Journal of Compensation and Benefits,* July–August 1992, pp. 17–34; Howard Risher and Robert J. Butler, "Salary Banding: An Alternative Salary-Management Concept," *ACA Journal,* Winter 1993–94, pp. 48–57.

EXHIBIT 7.21   Range Overlap

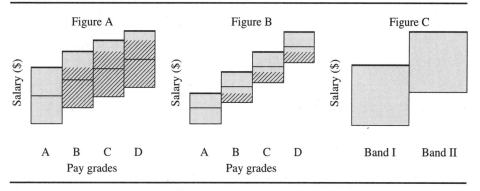

control points within bands to keep the system more structurally intact, according to a recent survey.[19] These organizations tend to create bands that are only about twice as wide as the original salary grades. In contrast, organizations that use broadbanding to enhance career mobility and promote significant cultural change tend to reduce the number of pay levels more dramatically, and they install bands that are three to eight times wider than the previous salary grades. Further, they are less likely to use control points within bands.

Astra-Merck uses five bands for its entire structure with titles ranging from contributor to executive. General Electric Retailer Financial Services' five bands, shown in Appendix 7–B, replace 24 levels. The appendix lists the objectives, competencies, and training expected at each band. However, a survey by Hewitt revealed that fully half of all companies that have implemented bands cover less than 10 percent of their employee population in the banding system.

Bands may be easier to administer, though not all agree. Advocates point to the simplicity of the system. Less time will be spent judging fine distinctions among jobs and building barriers (i.e., that's not in my job description). But others disagree, saying that the time spent judging jobs will now be spent judging individuals, a prospect managers already try to avoid. How will an organization avoid appearance of salary treatment based on personality and politics rather than objective criteria?[20]

Pricing a Band.   Rather than a saving, broadbanding has the potential to be more expensive because the band deemphasizes minimums, midpoints, and maximums as control points for managing salary treatment. These may be replaced with "zones" or shadow grades within the band. Without zones or shadows,

[19] Kenan S. Abosch and Janice S. Hand, *Broadbanding Models* (Scottsdale, AZ: American Compensation Association, 1994).

[20] Hill, "Get Off the Broadband Wagon," *Journal of Compensation and Benefits,* January–February 1993, pp. 25–29.

Exhibit 7.22   From Grades to Bands

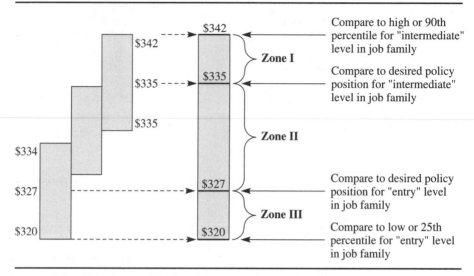

Source: Adapted from Peter V. LeBlanc, "Banding—The New Pay Structure for the Transformed Organization," *Perspectives in Total Compensation,* March 1992, pp. 1–6.

employees may float to the maximum pay, which for many jobs in the band is much higher than market value.

Exhibit 7.22 combines three grades into one band. The lowest minimum and highest maximum become the minimum and maximum for the band. Two additional points are located within the band that correspond to previous grade midpoints. The four band points create three zones, and each job in the band is expected to be paid within a zone. In order to price the band, the four points that create the zones can be matched in the external market.

The key point is that under bands, guidelines for decision making are no longer embedded in the system. Under a grade/range approach, the maximums, midpoints, and minimums provide guides to the appropriate pay for certain levels of work, with levels determined by job evaluation points.

Exhibit 7.23 shows the transition for nonexecutive exempt salaried employees at General Electric. The 14 position levels became four bands with an average width of about 130 percent. Relaxing maximums, midpoints, and minimums offers managers less guidance (read: more flexibility).

Flexibility, Control, and History.   Flexibility is one side of the coin; chaos and favoritism is the other. Banding presumes that managers will manage employee pay to accomplish the organization's objectives (and not their own) and treat employees fairly. Historically, this is not the first time greater flexibility has been shifted to managers and leaders. Indeed, the rationale underlying the use of ranges and grades was to reduce the foremen inconsistencies and favoritism that were destructive to employee relations in the 1920s and 1930s. The challenge

EXHIBIT 7.23   From Levels to Bands at General Electric

GE TRADITIONAL STRUCTURE FOR NONEXECUTIVE SALARIED EMPLOYEES					
Position Level	Minimum $	First Quartile $	Midpoint $	Third Quartile $	Maximum $
14	58,450	67,750	73,050	80,350	87,650
13	51,700	58,175	64,650	71,125	77,600
12	45,950	51,700	57,450	63,200	68,950
11	41,900	47,125	52,350	57,575	62,800
10	38,300	43,075	47,850	52,625	57,400
9	35,100	39,475	43,850	48,225	52,600
8	32,250	36,275	40,300	44,325	48,350
7	29,700	33,425	37,150	40,875	44,600
6	27,250	30,650	34,050	37,450	40,850
5	25,100	28,225	31,350	34,475	37,600
4	23,000	25,875	28,750	31,625	34,500
3	21,000	23,625	26,250	28,875	31,500
2	19,350	21,775	24,200	26,625	29,050
1	18,100	20,350	22,600	24,850	27,100

GE CAREER BANDS FOR NONEXECUTIVE SALARIED EMPLOYEES			
Band Title	Minimum	Maximum	Width
Senior Professional	$48,000	$103,000	115%
Lead Professional	$33,000	$74,000	124%
Professional	$20,000	$52,000	160%
Associate Professional	$15,000	$35,000	133%

Source: Kenan S. Abosch, Dan Gilbert, and Susan M. Dempsey, "Contrasting Perspectives—Broadbanding: Approaches of Two Organizations," *ACA Journal,* Spring 1994, pp. 46–53.

today is to take advantage of flexibility without increasing labor costs or leaving the organization vulnerable to charges of favoritism or inconsistency.

Compression

Compression results when wages for those jobs filled from outside the organization are increasing faster than the wages for jobs filled from within the organization.[21] As pay differentials among jobs become very small, the traditional pay structure becomes compressed. An example is an employer with a large number of jobs at or near the minimum wage. Whenever Congress legislates an increase in the minimum wage, or labor market conditions necessitate raising entry-level wages, the employer must decide whether to shift the entire wage structure upward to maintain differentials, or to narrow it. Either decision can be costly, in dollars and/or employee dissatisfaction.

Compression is also an issue in professional work (engineers, lawyers, professors) when new graduates command salaries almost equal to those of professionals with three to five years of experience. A study of business school professors found that a decision to boost faculty quality by paying premium salaries for the best new assistant professors available backfired, because rates for the rest of the faculty were not also increased.[22] Dissatisfaction among older faculty led to the rapid loss of the best professors, who were able to find other jobs. With only the less-marketable professors remaining, the overall faculty quality declined. (The older the authors of this text get, the more importance we attach to studies that recommend raising salaries for older professors.)

Certain compensation practices can inadvertently narrow the differentials among jobs to cause compression. For example, wide range overlap between adjacent job grades may mean that a job perceived to be harder to do actually pays very little more than a job that is clearly easier. Another example is across-the-board pay increases, with the same dollar amount going to all employees. The technique has an egalitarian appeal, but it also reduces differentials. Employers can minimize compression problems to some extent by utilizing internal employees to fill vacancies as much as possible, thereby reducing exposure to the external market. Part VI, Managing the System, discusses ways to monitor the pay structure to identify possible compression problems. Compensation practices never cease to amaze us. What is compression to some may be egalitarian (smaller pay differences among jobs) to others.

---

[21] Thomas J. Bergmann, Marilyn A. Bergmann, Desiree Roff, and Vida Scarpello, "Salary Compression: Causes and Solutions," *Compensation and Benefits Management,* Fall 1991, pp. 7–16; W. C. Lawther, "Ways to Monitor (and Solve) the Pay Compression Problem," *Personnel,* March 1989, pp. 84–87.

[22] Luis R. Gomez-Mejia and David B. Balkin, "Causes and Consequences of Pay Compression: The Case of Business Schools" (Working paper, University of Florida, Gainesville, November 1984); David Balkin, "Compensation Strategy for Firms in Emerging and Rapidly Growing Industries," *Human Resource Planner* 11, no. 3 (1988), pp. 207–14.

So when does compression become egalitarian? The cynic in us says when it's not our pay that is being compressed.

BALANCING INTERNAL AND EXTERNAL PRESSURES: ADJUSTING THE PAY STRUCTURE

Establishing the pay ranges for work reflects a balance between competitive pressures and pressures for internal consistency and fairness. Up until now, we have tended to make a distinction between the job structure and the pay structure. A *job structure* orders jobs on the basis of total job evaluation points or the skill required to perform them. The *pay structure*, on the other hand, is anchored by the organization's pay policy line, which is set using the market rates paid for benchmark jobs.

Reconciling Differences

The problem with using two methods (market surveys versus job evaluation or skill/competency-based plans) to create a structure is that they are likely to result in two different structures. The order in which jobs are ranked on internal and external factors may not completely agree. Differences between market structures and rates and job evaluation rankings warrant a review of the basic decisions in evaluating and pricing that particular job. This may entail a review of the job analysis, the job description, and the evaluation of the job, or the market data for the job in question. Often this reanalysis solves the problem. Sometimes, however, discrepancies persist; sometimes survey data are discarded; sometimes benchmark job matches are changed.

One study of how differences are actually reconciled found that managers weigh external market data more heavily than internal job evaluation data. In light of all the judgments that go into internal evaluation, market data are often considered to be more objective. Yet market data are also based on judgments.

Sometimes differences arise because a shortage of a particular skill has driven up the market rate. But reclassifying a market-sensitive job (one in which a supply-and-demand imbalance exists) into a higher salary grade, where it will remain long after the imbalance has been corrected, creates additional problems. Creating a special range that is clearly designated as *market responsive* may be a better approach. However, caution is advised. Decisions made on the basis of expediency may undermine the integrity of the pay system.

In sum, the process of balancing internal and external pressures is a matter of judgment, made with an eye to the objectives established for the pay system. Deemphasizing internal pay relationships may lead to feelings of inequitable treatment among employees. These in turn may reduce employees' willingness to share new ideas on how to improve the work or improve the product's quality. Inequitable internal pay relationships may also lead employees to seek other jobs, file grievances, form unions, go out on strike, or refuse to take on increased job responsibilities. Neglecting external pay relationships, however, will affect both the ability to attract job applicants and the ability to hire those applicants who match the organization's needs. External pay relationships also impact labor costs and hence the ability to compete in the product/service market.

Summary

This chapter has detailed the basic decisions and techniques involved in setting pay levels and designing pay ranges. Most organizations survey other employers' pay rates to determine competitive rates paid in the market. An employer using the survey results considers how it wishes to position its pay in the market: to lead, to match, or to follow competition. This policy decision may be different for different business units and even for different job groups within a single organization. Pay policy is translated into practice by setting pay policy lines that reflect the employer's competitive policy and serve as reference points around which pay ranges are established.

The use of ranges is a recognition of both external and internal pressures. No single "going rate" for a job exists in the market; an array of rates exists. This array results from variations in the quality of employees for that job and differences in employer policies and practices. It also reflects the fact that employers differ in the value they attach to the jobs and qualifications. Internally, the use of ranges is consistent with variations in the discretion present in jobs. Some employees will perform better than others; some employees are more experienced than others. Pay ranges permit employers to value and recognize these differences with pay.

Managers are increasingly interested in broadbanding, which offers flexibility to fit the continuously changing work assignments in de-layered organization structures. Broadbanding offers freedom to adapt to changes without requiring approvals, but risks self-serving and potentially inequitable decisions on the part of the manager. Recently, the trend is toward approaches with greater flexibility to adapt to changing conditions.

Let us step back for a moment to review what has been discussed and preview what is coming. We have examined two components of the pay model. A concern for internal consistency meant that analysis and perhaps descriptions and evaluation were important for achieving a competitive advantage. A concern for external competitiveness required policy determination, survey design and analysis, setting the pay policy line, and designing pay ranges. The next part of the book is concerned with employee contributions—paying the individuals who perform the work. This is perhaps the most important part of the book. All that has gone before is a prelude, setting up the pay levels and pay structures within which individual employees are to be paid.

Review Questions

1. Which competitive pay level policy would you recommend to an employer? Why? Does it depend on circumstances faced by the employer? Which ones?

2. How would you design a survey for setting pay for welders? How would you design a survey for setting pay for financial managers? Do the issues differ? Will the techniques used and the data collected differ? Why or why not?

3. What factors determine the relevant market for a survey? Why is the definition of the relevant market so important?

4. In what situations would you recommend your employer use benchmark jobs in a survey? When would you recommend a skill-based or job valuation approach?

5. What do surveys have to do with pay discrimination?

6. Why are pay ranges used? Contrast pay ranges and grades with bands. Why would you use either? Does their use assist or hinder the achievement of internal consistency? External competitiveness?

7. You are the compensation manager for Lomeli Pharmaceuticals, and you directed the survey reported in Exhibit 7.14. Analyze the results. Specify which measure(s) gives the best representation of the market wage for programming analysts. Make the case that Lomeli's pay for its systems development specialist is too high. Make the case that it's too low.

APPENDIX 7–A

STATISTICS TO CALCULATE A MARKET LINE USING REGRESSION ANALYSIS

Using the mathematical formula for a straight line,

$$y = a + bx$$

where

y = dollars
x = job evaluation points
a = the y value (in dollars) at which
$x = 0$ (i.e., the straight line crosses the y-axis)
b = the slope of the line

If $b = 0$, the line is parallel to the x-axis and all jobs are paid the same, regardless of job evaluation points. Using the dollars from the market survey data and the job evaluation points from the internal job structure, solving this equation enables the analyst to construct a line based on the relationship between the internal job structure and market rates. An upward sloping line means that more job evaluation points are associated with higher dollars. The market line can be written as

Pay for job A = a + (b × Job evaluation points for job A)
Pay for job B = a + (b × Job evaluation points for job B), etc.

The issue is to estimate the values of a and b in an efficient manner, so that errors of prediction are minimized. This is what "least squares" regression analysis does.

For many jobs, particularly high-level managerial and executive jobs, job evaluation is not used. Instead, salaries are related to some measure of company size (sales, volume, operating revenues) as a measure of responsibility through the use of logarithms. In such situations, x and y are converted to logarithms (in base 10), and the equation for a straight line becomes

$$\log y = a + b(\log x)$$

where

x = sales or revenues (in millions of dollars)
y = current compensation (in thousands of dollars)

Example

Given sales and compensation levels for a sample of jobs, assume that

a = 1.7390
b = 0.3000

Using the equation $\log y$ = 1.7390 + 0.3000 (log x), one can calculate the current market rate for the chief executive in a company with sales of $500 million.

1. First, set x = 500, that is 500,000,000 with six zeros dropped.
2. Log x = 2.6990.
3. Multiply log x by 0.3000, which is the coefficient of the variable log x in the given equation. This results in a value of 0.8997.
4. Add to 0.8097 the constant in the equation, 1.7390. The result, 2.5487, is the value of log y.
5. The chief executive's total current compensation is the antilog of log y, which is 354.

Read in thousands of dollars, it is $354,000.

Equation: $\log y$ = 1.7390 + 0.3000 (log x)
x = $500,000,000 = 500
$\log x$ = 2.6990
$\log y$ = 1.7390 + 0.3000 (2.6990)
$\log y$ = 1.7390 + 0.8097
$\log y$ = 2.5487
antilog y = 354
y = $354,000

APPENDIX 7–B
BROADBANDING AT GENERAL ELECTRIC RETAILER FINANCIAL SERVICES

	Band I
Objectives	• Develop the self-management, interpersonal communication, and technical skills that are needed to effectively manage your work load and successfully perform as a team member. • Develop a working knowledge of other functional areas and their impact as well as an overall understanding of our clients.
Key competencies	• Plan, organize, and follow through on assignments. • Effectively develop co-worker, customer, and client relationships. • Function effectively as a team member. • Add value through innovative ideas.
Recommended training and education	• Service excellence/quality 100. • Customer service/telephone courtesy. • Technical and procedural training and legal requirements. • Number skills/ergonomics. • RFS systems training. • Cultural diversity awareness training. • Interpersonal and communication skills. • Team awareness and skill building.
	Band II
Objectives	• Develop the leadership, communication, and technical skills that are needed to lead teams and manage projects. • Develop a comprehensive knowledge of clients and a full understanding of RFS.
Key competencies	• Provide the interpersonal and technical leadership skills (such as coaching, relationship-building, and training) to facilitate the completion of work assignments. • Manage multiple and complex situations with co-workers, customers, and clients. • Develop strategies and combined resources to meet defined objectives.
Recommended training and education	• Effective written communication. • Time management. • Facilitator training. • Effective meeting skills. • Interviewing skills. • Problem solving/decision making. • Teambuilding/conflict resolution skills.

Band III

Objectives	• Develop the leadership and business skills to effectively lead people or projects with multi-functional perspectives. • Develop the ability to strategize, initiate plans, and implement projects to meet long-term and short-term objectives.
Key competencies	• Coach, motivate, and lead. • Build and guide high-performance work teams. • Influence others to gain a commitment to your plan or strategy. • Integrate a team's work with that of related functions. • Build relationships with internal and external customers and clients.
Recommended training and education	• Corporate entry leadership conference. • Leadership, interview, and presentation skills. • Facilitator/problem-solving training. • New manager development course. • Interpersonal, negotiating, and managing change skills. • Union awareness. • Cultural diversity awareness/management.

Band IV

Objectives	• Develop the ability to provide a strategic direction and perspective that will have a broad business impact. • Develop the ability to effectively manage and lead diverse activities that incorporate multi-functional perspectives in the balanced best interests of the business.
Key competencies	• Establish, communicate, and gain commitment to a vision and to a system of shared values. • Create organizational structures and systems consistent with your vision. • Conceive and implement changes in system, process, structure, staffing, and culture to better serve the customer and client. • Develop talent by identifying and selecting future leaders. • Create and manage internal and external partnerships. • Develop sound business judgment based on an intuitive process and the exploration of diverse information sources. • Manage innovation and risk taking. • Understand the complete business equation.
Recommended training and education	• Manager development course. • Advanced leadership skills. • Creative thinking. • Advanced functional and technical courses. • Cross-functional and cross-business assignments.

Band V

Objectives	• Develop the ability to direct a major segment or a multi-functional area within a major business.
	• Develop the ability to incorporate a global perspective while proactively establishing a vision.
Key competencies	• Make decisions that reflect global and cross-business considerations.
	• Translate strategic goals and objectives into specific programs which set the culture for the organization.
	• Lead a team in the development of a vision and its business-wide communication and acceptance.
	• Manage community relations.
Recommended training and education	• Business management course.
	• Executive development course.
	• Advanced management marketing seminar.
	• Advanced functional and technical courses.
	• Cross-functional, cross-business, and cross-cultural developmental assignments.

Your Turn:

Are Compensation Surveys Upward Biased?

In an article published in the September–October 1994 issue of *Compensation and Benefits Review,* the consultant Frederic W. Cook lambastes current survey practices. He says that the way surveys are constructed, interpreted, and used artificially inflates wages above the "real" market. He lists 12 reasons, 7 of which are included here. Consider each of his charges and discuss whether you agree or disagree. Then suggest ways to respond to Cook's challenges or minimize the problem he identifies in each of his reasons.

1. User Bias.   Companies that sponsor surveys often do so with an implicit objective: to show the company as paying either competitively or somewhat below the market, so as to justify positive corrective action.

2. Sample Bias.   Companies like to compare themselves against well-regarded, high-paying, and high-performing companies. Those firms that participate in surveys drawing data from a large number of other organizations often have the ability (through computer models) to create a subset of participants with whom they wish to compare. This typically results in a higher competitive pay line than the general survey, thereby showing the user company in a less competitive light in terms of pay rates.

3. Survey Selectivity.   Most companies have access to several surveys covering the same population. Compensation managers tend to disregard, challenge, or downplay those surveys that do not show the company in the desired competitive position.

4. Scope Bias.   The relative "size" of an organization can be measured in any number of ways: revenues, equity, assets, net income, etc. Sponsoring organizations tend to select size variables that let them compare themselves favorably to the survey companies. It is technically feasible for *all* companies to show themselves as paying below the market.

5. Compensation Selectivity.   A total compensation package is composed of many elements, whereas most surveys tend to focus on a few. If a company surveys only those areas where it is light (cash compensation, for example), it should not interpret or use those findings in isolation.

6. Benchmark Bias.   In matching positions against those in the survey, companies tend to match against those that have higher responsibilities and hence higher compensation.

7. Statistical Bias.   By manipulating the variables and assumptions in ways favorable to the company, the interpreter may be able to make an above-market practice appear less generous.

EXHIBIT III.1   The Pay Model

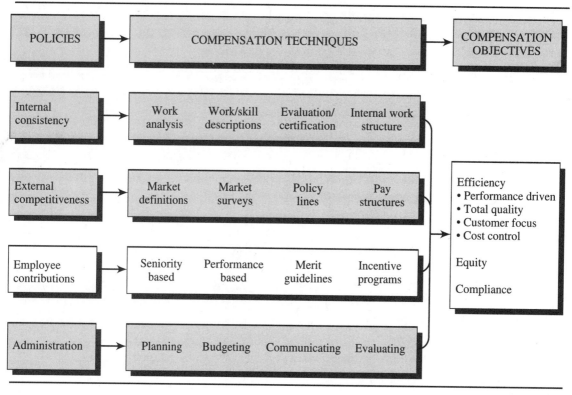

Employee Contributions: Determining Individual Pay

PART III

Thus far we have concentrated on two components of the pay model (Exhibit III.1). Internal consistency and the practices to ensure it—job analysis and job evaluation—provide guidance relating jobs to each other in terms of the content of the work and the relative contributions of the jobs to the organization's objectives. External competitiveness, or comparisons with the external labor market, raises issues of proper survey definitions, setting policy lines, and arriving at competitive pay levels and equitable pay structures. This part of the book deals with a third critical dimension of the pay system design and administration—paying individual employees performing the job.

How much should one employee be paid relative to another when they both hold the same jobs in the same organization? If this question is not answered satisfactorily, all prior efforts to evaluate and price jobs may have been in vain. For example, the compensation manager determines that all systems analysts should be paid between $28,000 and $36,000. But where in that range is each individual paid? Should a good performer be paid more than a poor performer? If the answer is yes, how should performance be measured and what should be the differential reward? Similarly, should the systems analyst with more years' experience (i.e., higher seniority) be paid more than a coworker with less time on the job? Again, if the answer is yes, what is the trade-off between seniority and performance in assigning pay raises? As Exhibit III.1 suggests, all of these questions involve the concept of employee contribution. For the next three chapters we will be discussing different facets of employee contribution.

Chapter 8 considers how pay affects performance. Is there evidence that companies should invest in pay-for-performance plans? In other words, does paying for performance result in higher performance? The answer may seem obvious, but there are many ways to complicate this elegant notion.

Chapter 9 looks at actual pay-for-performance plans. The compensation arena is full of programs that promise to link pay and performance. We identify these plans and discuss their relative advantages and disadvantages.

Chapter 10 acknowledges that performance can't always be measured objectively. What do we do to ensure that subjective appraisal procedures are as free from error as possible? Much progress has been made here, and we provide a tour of the different strategies to measure performance.

CHAPTER

**8**

Pay for Performance: The Evidence

Chapter Outline

The first seven chapters focused primarily on determining the worth of jobs, independent of who performed those jobs. Job analysis, job evaluation, and job pricing all have a common theme. They are techniques to identify the value a firm places on its jobs. Now we introduce people into the equation and declare that different people performing the same job may have different value to the organization. Jim is a better programmer than Sam. Sally knows more programming languages than John.

Entering people into the compensation equation greatly complicates the compensation process. People don't behave like robots. We can't simply tighten a bolt here, oil a joint there, and walk away secure in the knowledge that behaviors will support organizational objectives. Remember, in Chapter 1 we talked about how compensation objectives complement overall human resources objectives, and how this synergy helps an organization achieve its overall strategic objectives. But this begs the question, How does an organization achieve its overall strategic objectives? In this section of the book we argue that compensation decisions and practices should be designed to increase the likelihood that employees will behave in ways that help the organization achieve its strategic objectives. This chapter is organized around employee behaviors. First, we identify the four kinds of behaviors organizations are interested in. Then, we note what theories say about our ability to motivate these behaviors. And finally, we talk about our success, and sometimes lack thereof, in designing compensation systems to elicit these behaviors.

WHAT BEHAVIORS DO EMPLOYERS CARE ABOUT?

Employers care about four general types of behavior.

How do we get good employment prospects to *join* our company?

How do we *retain* these good employees once they join?

How do we get employees to *develop skills* for current and future jobs?

How do we get employees to *perform well* on their current job?

First, how do we get good people to join our company? If our company is the Milwaukee Bucks, for example, we were very concerned in 1994 about ways to structure a pay package that would get NBA star Glenn Robinson to join our team. Even when the decision doesn't involve $50 or $100 million, though, the long run success of any company depends on getting good people to accept employment. And the compensation challenge is to figure out what components of our compensation package are likely to influence this decision to join.

The obvious complement to the decision to join is the decision to stay. How do we retain employees? It doesn't do much good to attract exceptional employees to our company if we lose them a short time later. Once our compensation practices get a good employee in the door, we need to figure ways to ensure its not a revolving door.

We also need to recognize, though, that what we need employees to do today may change, literally, over night. A fast changing world requires employees who can adjust quickly. How do we get employees, traditionally resistant to change, to willingly develop skills today that may not be vital on the current job, but that we expect to be critical to the company's strategic plan? Another compensation challenge!

Finally, we want employees to do well on their current jobs. This means both performing, and performing well, tasks that support our strategic objectives. What motivates employees to succeed? The compensation challenge is to design rewards that enhance job performance.

WHAT DOES IT TAKE TO GET EMPLOYEES TO BEHAVE IN DESIRED WAYS? WHAT MOTIVATION THEORIES SAY

Another way of asking the same question is, What motivates employees? If you know the answer, you're way ahead of the so-called experts! In the simplest sense motivation involves three elements: (1) discovering what is important to a person and (2) offering it in exchange for some (3) desired behavior. In Exhibit 8.1. we briefly summarize some of the important motivation theories. Pay particular attention to the last column where we talk about the implications for employee behavior.

Some of the theories in Exhibit 8.1 focus on content, that is, identifying what is important to people. Maslow and Herzberg, for example, both fall in this category. People have certain needs that influence behavior, for example, physiological, security, and self-esteem. Although neither theory is clear on how these needs influence behavior, presumably if we offer rewards that satisfy one or more needs, employees will behave in desired ways.

A second set of theories, best exemplified by expectancy theory, equity theory, and agency theory, focus less on need states and more on the second element: the nature of the exchange. Expectancy theory argues that people behave as if they cognitively evaluate what behaviors are possible (e.g., the probability that they can complete the task) in relation to the value of rewards offered in exchange. According to this theory, we choose behaviors that yield the most satisfactory exchange. Equity theory also focuses on what goes on inside an employee's head. Not surprisingly, equity theory argues people are highly concerned about equity, or fairness of the exchange process. Employees look at the exchange as a ratio between what is expected and what is received. Some theorists say we judge transactions as fair when others around us don't have a more (or less) favorable balance between the give and get of an exchange.[1] Even greater focus on the exchange process occurs in the last of this second set of theories, agency theory.[2] Here employees are depicted as agents who enter an exchange with principals—the owners or their designated managers. It is assumed that both sides to the exchange seek the most favorable exchange possible and

(handwritten margin note: Content Herzberg Maslow)

---

[1] J. S. Adams, "Toward an Understanding of Inequity," *Journal of Abnormal and Social Psychology* 67 (1963), pp. 442–36; J. S. Adams, "Injustice in Social Exchange," in *Advances in Experimental Social Psychology*, vol. 2, ed. L. Berkowitz (New York: Academic Press, 1965); R. Cosier and D. Dalton, "Equity Theory and Time: A Reformulation," *Academy of Management Review* 8 (1983), pp. 311–19.

[2] B. Oviatt, "Agency and Transaction Cost Perspectives on the Manager-Shareholder Relationship: Incentives for Congruent Interests," *Academy of Management Review* 13 (1988), pp. 214–25.

EXHIBIT 8.1 What Motivation Theories Say

Theory	Essential Features	Predictions About Performance-Based Pay	So What?
Maslow's Need Hierarchy	People are motivated by inner needs. Needs form a hierarchy from most basic (food and shelter) to higher order (e.g., self-esteem, love, self-actualization). Needs are never fully met; they operate cyclically. Higher-order needs become motivators after lower-order needs have been met. When needs are not met, they become frustrations.	1. Base pay must be set high enough to provide individuals with the economic means to meet their basic living needs. 2. An at-risk program will not be motivating since it restricts employees' ability to meet lower-order needs. 3. Success-sharing plans may be motivating to the extent they help employees pursue higher-order needs.	1. Performance-based pay may be demotivating if it impinges upon employees' capacity to meet daily living needs. 2. Incentive pay is motivating to the extent it is attached to achievement, recognition, or approval.
Herzberg's Two-Factor Theory	Employees are motivated by two types of motivators: hygiene factors and satisfiers. The absence of hygiene or maintenance factors prevents behaviors, but their presence cannot motivate performance. These are related to basic living needs, security, and fair treatment. Satisfiers, such as recognition, promotion, and achievement motivate performance.	1. Base pay must be set high enough to provide individuals with the economic means to meet hygiene needs, but it cannot motivate performance. 2. Performance is obtained through rewards; payments in excess of what is required to meet basic needs. 3. Performance-based pay is motivating to the extent it meets employees' needs for recognition, pleasure attainment, achievement, and the like. 4. Other factors such as interpersonal atmosphere, responsibility, type of work, and working conditions influence the efficacy of performance-based pay.	1. Pay level must meet minimum requirements before performance-based pay can operate as motivator. 2. Security plans will induce minimum, but not extra, performance. Success-sharing plans will be motivating. At-risk plans will be demotivating. 3. Other conditions in the working relationship influence the effectiveness of performance-based pay.
Expectancy	Motivation is the product of three perceptions: expectancy, instrumentality, and valence. Instrumentality is an employee's assessment of his or her ability to perform required job tasks. Expectancy is employee's beliefs that requisite job performance will be rewarded by the organization. Valence is the value employees attach to the rewards an organization offers for satisfactory job performance.	1. Job tasks and responsibilities should be clearly defined. 2. The pay–performance link is critical. 3. Performance-based pay returns must be large enough to be seen as rewards. 4. People choose the behavior that leads to the greatest reward.	1. Larger incentive payments are better than smaller ones. 2. Line-of-sight is critical; employees must believe they can influence performance targets. 3. Self-assessment of one's ability is important; organizations should be aware of training and resource needs required to perform at target levels.

Theory			
Equity	Employees are motivated when perceived outputs (e.g., pay) are equal to perceived inputs (e.g., effort, work behaviors). A disequilibrium in the output-to-input balance causes discomfort. If employees perceive that others are paid more for the same effort, they will react negatively (e.g., shirk) to correct the output-to-input balance.	1. The pay-performance link is critical; increases in performance must be matched by commensurate increases in pay. 2. Performance inputs and expected outputs must be clearly defined and identified. 3. Employees evaluate the adequacy of their pay via comparisons with other employees.	1. Performance measures must be clearly defined and employee must be able to affect them through work behaviors. 2. If payouts do not match expectations, employees will react negatively. 3. Fairness and consistency of performance-based pay across employees in an organization is important. 4. Since employees evaluate their pay–effort balance in comparison to other employees, relative pay matters.
Reinforcement	Rewards reinforce (i.e., motivate and sustain) performance. Rewards must follow directly after behaviors to be reinforcing. Behaviors that are not rewarded will be discontinued.	1. Performance-based payments must follow closely behind performance. 2. Rewards must be tightly coupled to desired performance objectives. 3. Withholding payouts is one way to discourage unwanted behaviors.	1. Timing of payouts is very important.
Goal Setting	Challenging performance goals influence greater intensity and duration in employee performance. Goals serve as feedback standards to which employees can compare their performance. Individuals are motivated to the extent that goal achievement is combined with receiving valued rewards.	1. Performance-based pay must be contingent upon achievement of important performance goals. 2. Performance goals should be challenging and specific. 3. The amount of the incentive reward should match the difficulty of the goal.	1. Line-of-sight is important; employees must believe they can influence performance targets. 2. Performance targets should be communicated in terms of specific, difficult goals. 3. Feedback about performance is important. 4. Performance-based payouts should be contingent upon goal achievement.
Agency	Pay directs and motivates employee performance. Employees prefer static wages (e.g., a salary) to performance-based pay. If performance can be accurately monitored, payments should be based upon satisfactory completion of work duties. If performance cannot be monitored, pay should be aligned with achieving organizational objectives.	1. Performance-based pay must be tightly linked to organizational objectives. 2. Employees dislike risky pay and will demand a wage premium (e.g., higher total pay) in exchange for accepting performance-based pay. 3. Performance-based pay can be used to direct and induce employee performance.	1. Performance-based pay is the optimal compensation choice for more complex jobs where monitoring work is difficult. 2. Performance targets should be tied to organizational goals. 3. Performance-based pay requires higher total pay opportunity.

will act opportunistically if given a chance (e.g., might try to "get by" with doing as little as possible to satisfy the contract). Compensation is a major element in this theory, because it is used to keep employees in line: employers identify important behaviors and important outcomes and pay employees for attaining desired levels of each. Such incentive systems penalize employees who try to shirk their duties; they receive proportionately lower rewards.

Finally, at least one of the theories summarized in Exhibit 8.1 focuses on the third element of motivation: desired behavior. A review of this literature indicates that the vast majority of studies on goal setting find that goal setting has a positive impact on performance. Workers assigned "hard" goals consistently do better than workers told to "do your best."[3]

WHAT DOES IT TAKE TO GET EMPLOYEES TO BEHAVE IN DESIRED WAYS? WHAT COMPENSATION PEOPLE SAY

In the past, compensation people didn't ask this question very often. Employees learned what behaviors were important as part of the socialization process or as part of the performance management process.[4] If it was part of the culture to work long hours, you quickly learned this. If your performance appraisal at the end of the year stressed certain types of behaviors, or if your boss said certain things were important to her, then the signals were pretty clear: Do these things! Compensation might have rewarded people for meeting these expectations, but usually the compensation package wasn't designed to be one of the signals about expected performance. Now compensation people talk about pay in terms of a neon light pointing out expected behaviors. Progressive companies ask the questions, What do we want our compensation package to do? How, for example, do we get our product engineers to take more risks? Compensation is then designed to support this risk-taking behavior. In the next section we begin to talk about the different types of reward components, acknowledging that pay isn't the only reward that influences behavior. The remainder of the chapter looks at pay components and what we know about their effectiveness in motivating desired behaviors.

TOTAL REWARD SYSTEM

Compensation is but one of the many rewards that influence employee behavior. Sometimes this important point is missed by compensation experts. Going back

---

[3] E. A. Locke, K. N. Shaw, L. M. Saari, and G. P. Latham, "Goal Setting and Task Performance: 1969–1980," *Psychological Bulletin* 90 (1981), pp. 125–52.

[4] M. R. Louis, B. Z. Posner, and G. N. Powell, "The Availability and Helpfulness of Socialization Practices," *Personnel Psychology* 36 (1983), pp. 857–66; E. H. Schein, "Organizational Socialization and the Profession of Management," *Industrial Management Review* 9 (1968), pp. 1–16.

EXHIBIT 8.2   Components of a Total Reward System

1. Compensation	Wages, commissions and bonuses
2. Benefits	Vacations, health insurance
3. Social interaction	Friendly work place
4. Security	Stable, consistent position and rewards
5. Status/recognition	Respect, prominence due to work
6. Work variety	Opportunity to experience different things
7. Work load	Right amount of work (not too much, not too little)
8. Work importance	Is work valued by society?
9. Authority/control/autonomy	Ability to influence others; control own destiny
10. Advancement	Chance to get ahead
11. Feedback	Receive information helping to improve performance
12. Work conditions	Hazard free
13. Development opportunity	Formal and informal training to learn new knowledge/skills/abilities

at least to Henry Ford, we tend to look at money as the great equalizer. Job boring? No room for advancement? Throw money at the problem. Before we commit the same blunder and talk about monetary solutions to problems, please note that at least 13 general categories of rewards exist in organizations (see Exhibit 8.2).

Now consider two examples that show how compensation decisions have to be integrated with total reward system decisions. If we don't think about the presence or absence of rewards other than money in an organization, we may find the compensation process produces unintended consequences. Consider a team-based work environment where the culture of the organization strongly supports empowerment of workers. Empowerment is a form of reward. In Exhibit 8.2 we call out the dimensions of empowerment (see #9) as *authority* to make decisions, some *control* over factors that influence outcomes, and the *autonomy* to carry out decisions without over-regulation by upper management. For some people empowerment is a very positive inducement and makes coming to work each day a pleasure. Others may view empowerment as just added responsibility, legitimizing demands for more pay! In the first case adding extra compensation may not be necessary. Some have even argued it can lessen motivation![5] In the second case, extra compensation may be a necessity. Is it any wonder that

---

[5] E. L. Deci and R. M. Ryan, *Intrinsic Motivation and Self-Determination in Human Behavior* (New York: Plenum Press, 1985). Note, however, the evidence is not very strong.

companies are having trouble finding *one* right answer to the team compensation question?

Our second example illustrates the relationship between the different forms of monetary rewards and another of the general rewards listed in Exhibit 8.2: security. Normally, we think of security in terms of job security. Drastic reductions in middle management layers during the downsizing decade of the 1980s increased employee concerns about job security and probably elevated the importance of this reward to employees today. For example, there is evidence that compensation at risk leaves employees both less satisfied with their pay level and with the process used to determine pay.[6] Security as an issue is creeping into the domain of compensation. It used to be fairly well established that employees would earn more this year than they did last year. And employees counted on such *security* to plan their purchases and other economic decisions. The trend today is toward less stable and secure compensation packages. The decreased security comes in two forms. First, the 1980s were some tough cost-cutting years, and wage rollbacks were a part of this trend. Between rollbacks and inflation, average wages (adjusted for inflation) declined during the 1980s.[7] Second, the very design of compensation systems today contributes to instability and insecurity. Exhibit 8.3 outlines the different wage components.

Notice that Exhibit 8.3 generally orders compensation components from least risky to most risky for employees. We define risk in terms of *stability of income*, the ability to accurately predict income level from year to year. *Base pay* is, at least as far as there are any guarantees, the guaranteed portion of income. As long as employees remain employed, there are very few years since the Depression when base wages did not rise, or at least stay the same.[8] After base pay, the next seven components are distinguished by increasing levels of uncertainty for employees. In fact, risk sharing plans actually include a provision for cuts in base pay that are only recaptured in years when the organization meets performance objectives.

All of this discussion of risk is only an exercise in intellectual gymnastics unless we add one further observation. Over the last several decades, companies have been moving toward compensation programs higher on the risk continuum. New forms of pay are less entitlement-oriented and more linked to the uncertainties of individual, group, and corporate performance.[9] Employees are increasingly being expected to bear a share of the risks that businesses have borne wholly in the past. It's not entirely clear what impact this shifting of risk will have in the long run, but some authors are already voicing concerns that efforts to build

---

[6] K. Brown and V. Huber, "Lowering Floors and Raising Ceilings: A Longitudinal Assessment of the Effects of an Earnings-at-Risk Plan on Pay Satisfaction," *Personnel Psychology* 45 (1992), pp. 279–311.

[7] G. Koretz, "Was the Last Decade Really So Cruel? Yes . . ." *Business Week,* January 17, 1994, p. 20.

[8] Please note, though, most of the declines experienced in base pay have occurred since 1980.

[9] J. R. Schuster and P. K. Zingheim, *The New Pay: Linking Employee and Organizational Performance* (New York: Lexington Books, 1992).

employee loyalty and commitment may be an early casualty of these new pay systems.[10] Some research suggests that employees may need a risk premium (higher pay) to willingly stay and perform in a company with a pay-at-risk structure.[11] To explore what impact these new forms of pay have, the remainder of this chapter summarizes what we know about the ability of different compensation components to motivate the four general behaviors we noted earlier.

DOES COMPENSATION MOTIVATE BEHAVIOR? GENERAL COMMENTS

Although there are exceptions, in general, linking pay to behaviors of employees, that is, performance-based pay, results in better individual and organizational performance.[12] One report by director's of compensation in 663 companies reported an increase in organizational earnings of $2.34 for every $1 spent on performance-based pay.[13] Similarly, Heneman reports that 40 of 42 studies looking at merit pay claim increased performance occurs when pay is tied to performance.[14] The strength of this relationship holds even in more scientifically controlled studies. One study of 841 union and nonunion companies found gain-sharing and profit sharing plans increased individual and team performance 18 to 20 percent.[15] How, though, does this translate into corporate performance? A review of 26 separate studies gives high marks to profit sharing plans: organizations with such plans had 3.5 to 5 percent higher annual performance.[16] Gerhart and Milkovich took the performance-based pay question one step further finding that, across 200 companies there was a 1.5 percent increase in ROA for every 10 percent increase in the size of a bonus.[17] Further, they found that the variable

---

[10] E. J. Conlon and J. M. Parks, "Effects of Monitoring and Tradition on Compensation Arrangements: An Experiment with Principal-Agent Dyads," *Academy of Management Journal* 33 (1990), pp. 603–22; A. Kohn, *Punished by Rewards: The Trouble With Gold Stars, Incentive Plans, A's, Praise and Other Bribes* (Boston: Houghton-Mifflin, 1993).

[11] Conlon and Parks, "Effects of Monitoring and Tradition."

[12] W. N. Cooke, "Employee Participation Programs, Group Based Incentives, and Company Performance," *Industrial and Labor Relations Review* 47 (1994), pp. 594–610; G. W. Florkowski, "The Organizational Impact of Profit Sharing," *Academy of Management Review* 12 (1987), pp. 622–36; R. Heneman, *Merit Pay: Linking Pay Increases to Performance Ratings* (Reading, MA: Addison-Wesley, 1992); J. L. McAdams and E. J. Hawk, *Organizational Performance and Rewards* (Phoenix, AZ: American Compensation Association, 1994); G. T. Milkovich, "Does Performance-Based Pay Really Work? Conclusions Based on the Scientific Research" (Unpublished document for 3M, 1994); G. Milkovich and C. Milkovich, "Strengthening the Pay Performance Relationship: The Research," *Compensation & Benefits Review* (1992), pp. 53–62.

[13] McAdams and Hawk, *Organizational Performance and Rewards.*

[14] Heneman, *Merit Pay.*

[15] Cooke, "Employee Participation Programs."

[16] D. L. Kruse, *Profit Sharing: Does it Make a Difference?* (Kalamazoo, MI: Upjohn Institue, 1993).

[17] B. Gerhart and G. Milkovich, "Organizational Differences in Managerial Compensation and Financial Performance," *Academy of Management Journal* 33 (1990), pp. 663–90.

EXHIBIT 8.3

Wage Component	Definition	Level of Risk to Employee
Base Pay	The guaranteed portion of an employee's wage package.	As long as employment continues, this is the secure portion of wages.
Across-the-Board Increase	Wage increase granted to all employees, regardless of individual performance. Size related to some subjective assessment of employer about ability to pay. Adds on to base pay in subsequent years.	Some risk to employee since at discretion of employer. But not tied to performance, so risk lower in that respect.
Cost of Living Increase	Same as across-the-board increase, except magnitude based on change in cost of living (e.g., as measured by CPI).	Same as across-the-board increases.
Merit Pay	Wage increase granted to employee as function of some assessment of performance. Adds on to base pay in subsequent years.	Employees face two types of risk. Size of total merit pool at discretion of employer and individual portion of pool depends on performance.
Lump Sum Bonus	As with merit pay, granted for individual performance. Does not add into base pay, though. Distributed as a one time bonus.	Employees face three types of risk. Both types mentioned under merit pay, plus requires annually "re-earning" the added pay.
Individual Incentive Plans	Sometimes this variable pay is an add-on to a fixed base pay. The incentive component ties increments in compensation directly to extra individual production (e.g., commission systems, piece rate). While measures of performance are typically subjective with merit pay and lump sump bonuses, this form of variable pay differs because measures of performance are objective (e.g., sales volume).	Most risky compensation component if sole element of pay, but often combined with a base pay. No or low fixed base pay means each year employee depends on performance to determine pay level.

Success Sharing Plans	A generic category of pay add-on (variable pay) that is tied to some measure of group performance, not individual performance. Not added into base pay. Distinguished from risk sharing plans below because employees share in any success, performance above standard, but are not penalized for performance below standard.	All success sharing plans have some risks as above pay components plus the risk associated with group performance measures. Now the individual worker also depends upon the performance of others, that is, those included in the group.
• Gain Sharing	Differs from profit sharing in that goal to exceed is not financial performance of organization, but some cost index (e.g., labor cost is most common; might also include scrap costs, utility costs).	Less risk to individual than profit sharing because performance measure is more controllable.
• Profit Sharing	Add-on pay linked to group performance (team, division, total company) relative to exceeding some financial goal.	Profit measures are influenced by factors beyond employee control (e.g., economic climate, accounting write-offs). Less control means more risk.
Risk Sharing Plans	Generic category of pay add on (variable pay) that differs from success sharing in that employee shares not only in the successes, but is also penalized during poor performance years. Penalty is in form of lower total compensation in poor corporate performance years. Reward, though, is typically higher than for success sharing programs in high performance years.	Greater risk than success sharing plans. Typically, employees absorb a "temporary" cut in base pay. If performance targets are met, this cut is neutralized by one component of variable pay. Risk to employee is increased, though, because even base pay is no longer totally predictable.

portion of pay had a stronger impact on individual and corporate performance than did the level of base pay.

DOES COMPENSATION MOTIVATE BEHAVIOR? SPECIFIC COMMENTS

This section looks at the role of compensation in motivating the four types of behavior outlined earlier.

Do People Join a Firm Because of Pay?

Not surprisingly, level of pay and pay system characteristics influence a job candidate's decision to join a firm.[18] Pay is one of the more visible rewards in the whole recruitment process. Employment offers spell out level of compensation and may even include discussions about various components of pay such as bonuses and profit sharing participation. Less common are clauses that say: You'll get plenty of work variety or Don't worry about empowerment or The workload isn't too heavy. These other rewards are subjective and tend to require actual time on the job before we can decide if they are positive or negative features of the job. Not so for pay. Being perceived as more objective, it's more easily communicated in the employment offer.

Recent research suggests job candidates look for organizations with reward systems that fit their personalities.[19] Below we outline some of the ways that "fit" is important.

Person Characteristics	*Preferred Reward Characteristics*
• Materialistic	Relatively more concerned about pay level.[20]
• Low self-esteem	Low self-esteem individuals want large, decentralized organization with little pay for performance.[21]
• Risk takers	Pay plans based on performance.[22]
• Individualists (I control my own destiny.)	Pay plans based on individual performance, not group performance.[23]

---

[18] E. E. Lawler, *Pay and Organizational Effectiveness: A Psychological View* (New York: McGraw-Hill, 1971); E. E. Lawler and G. D. Jenkins, "Strategic Reward Systems," in *Handbook of Industrial and Organizational Psychology*, ed. M. D. Dunnette and L. M. Hough (Palo Alto, CA: Consulting Psychologists Press, 1992), pp. 1009–55; W. Mobley, *Employee Turnover: Causes, Consequences and Control* (Reading, MA: Addison-Wesley, 1982).

[19] D. M. Cable and T. A. Judge, "Pay Preferences and Job Search Decisions: A Person-Organization Fit Perspective," *Personnel Psychology* 47 (1994), pp. 317–48.

[20] Ibid.

[21] D. B. Turban and T. L. Keon, "Organizational Attractiveness: An Interactionist Perspective," *Journal of Applied Psychology* 78 (1993), pp. 184–93.

[22] Cable and Judge, "Pay Preferences"; Kohn, *Punished by Rewards*.

[23] Cable and Judge, "Pay Preferences."

None of these relationships are particularly surprising. People are attracted to organizations that fit their personalities. It's not a big jump, then, to suggest organizations should design their reward systems to attract people with desired personalities and values. For example, if we need risk takers maybe we should design reward systems that have elements of risk built into them.

Do People Stay in a Firm (or Leave) Because of Pay?

Some experts argue money is a form of punishment, cheapening the sense of accomplishment we get from a job well done.[24] If so, we might expect the new types of pay systems to lead to more retention problems. Actually, the evidence on pay and retention is mixed. Much of the equity theory research in the 1970s documented that workers who feel unfairly treated in pay (lower than people to whom they compare themselves) sometimes react by leaving the firm for greener pastures.[25] If we consider absenteeism as a mild form of the retention problem, then pay can make a difference. Companies that tie pay and bonuses to absenteeism (i.e., bonuses achieved when absenteeism is below some target level) report lower absenteeism.[26] Similarly, some pay systems also are linked to lower turnover. Skill-based pay packages implemented in 27 companies yielded drops in turnover averaging 75 percent.[27] Of concern, though, is more recent information that suggests some types of performance-based pay may promote turnover.

Consider the following scenario. You work on a group project in school and, as usual, some members don't pull their own weight. Who is likely to want to quit the group? Exactly! The good performers. One recent study supports this gut level intuition. When employees receive individual incentives (i.e., pay tied to their own personal performance) turnover is lower. Group incentive plans, though, are a different matter. Turnover is higher, perhaps because "free riders" bother employees the same way they bother students.[28] Compounding the problem, it seems that turnover is, indeed, more likely among the star performers than others in the group. When AT&T shifted from individual to team-based incentives a number of years ago, star performers either reduced their output or quit. Out of 208 above average performers, only one continued to report performance increases under the group incentive plan. The rest felt cheated

---

[24] Kohn, *Punished by Rewards*.

[25] M. R. Carrell and J. E. Dettrich, "Employee Perceptions of Fair Treatment," *Personnel Journal* 55 (1976), pp. 523–24.

[26] D. L. Scholtzhauer and J. G. Rosse, "A Five-Year Study of Incentive Absence Control Program," *Personnel Psychology* 38 (1985), pp. 575–85.

[27] "Skill Based Pay Boosts Worker Productivity and Morale," *The Wall Street Journal*, June 23, 1992, p. A1.

[28] H. Y. Park, J. Ofori-Dankwa, and D. R. Bishop, "Organizational and Environmental Determinants of Functional and Dysfunctional Turnover: Practice and Research Implications," *Human Relations* 47 (1994), pp. 353–66.

because the incentives for higher individual performance were now spread across all group members.[29]

Clearly, pay can be a factor in decisions to stay or leave. Too little pay triggers feelings of unfair treatment. Result? Turnover. Even the way we pay, though, has an impact on turnover. More evidence is beginning to suggest that some employees are uncomfortable with pay systems that put any substantial future earnings at risk or pay systems that link less to personal effort and more to group effort. We need to make sure, as one critic has noted, that we don't let our design of new reward systems rupture our relationships with employees.[30]

Do Employees More Readily Agree to Develop Job Skills Because of Pay?

We don't know the answer to this question. Skill-based pay (Chapter 4) is intended, at least partially, to pay employees for learning new skills, skills that hopefully will help employees perform better on current jobs and adjust more rapidly to demands on future jobs. Whether this promise is fulfilled is unclear. We do have a few empirical case studies indicating skill-based pay does deliver on these promises, but better we await-controlled experimental evidence.[31]

Do Employees Perform Better on Their Jobs Because of Pay?

Before answering this question, maybe we should ask if employees think any link at all should be made between pay and performance. The answer is yes! Substantial evidence exists that management and workers alike believe pay should be tied to performance.

Dyer and colleagues asked 180 managers from 72 different companies to rate nine possible factors in terms of the importance they should receive in determining size of salary increases.[32] Workers believed the most important factor for salary increases should be job performance. Other research supports these findings.[33] Both college students and a second group of managers ranked job performance as the most important variable in allocating pay raises. Once we move away from the managerial ranks, though, other groups express a different view of the pay–performance link. The role that performance levels should

---

[29] A. Weiss, "Incentives and Worker Behavior: Some Evidence" in *Incentives, Cooperation and Risk Sharing*, ed. H. R. Nalbantian (Totowa, NJ: Rowan & Littlefield, 1987), pp. 137–50.

[30] Kohn, *Punished by Rewards*.

[31] Ledford, G. E., Jr., and Bergel, G., "Skill-Based Pay Case Number 1: General Mills," *Compensation & Benefits Review* 23, no. 1, pp. 24–38; Ledford, G. E., Jr., Tyler, W. R., and Dixey, W. B., "Skill-Based Pay Case Number 3: Honeywell Ammunition Assembly Plant," *Compensation & Benefits Review* 23, no. 1 (1990), pp. 57–77.

[32] L. Dyer, D. P. Schwab, and R. D. Theriault, "Managerial Perceptions Regarding Salary Increase Criteria," *Personnel Psychology* 29 (1976), pp. 233–42.

[33] Fossum and M. Fitch, "The Effects of Individual and Contextual Attributes on the Sizes of Recommended Salary Increases," *Personnel Psychology* 38 (1985), pp. 587–603.

assume in determining pay increases is less clear-cut for blue-collar workers.[34] Unionized workers, for example, prefer seniority rather than performance as a basis for pay increases.[35] Part of this preference may stem from a distrust of subjective performance measurement systems. Unions ask, Can management be counted on to be fair? In contrast, seniority is an objective index for calculating increases. Some evidence also suggests that women might prefer allocation methods not based on performance.[36]

Now we can ask the question, Can pay be used to increase performance? If we are talking about individuals, the answer is probably yes. Numerous studies indicate that tying pay to individual performance has a positive impact on employee performance.[37] Unfortunately, many of these studies are flawed. In one particularly thorough review of merit pay and performance, Heneman concluded that there are very few good scientific studies to help answer the question, Can

---

EXHIBIT 8.4   Examples of Group Incentive Plans

Company	Pay Component
Corning	Competitive base pay. Group bonus based on meeting certain quality measures, customer satisfaction measures, and production targets.
Nucor	Plant manager's base pay 25 percent below market. Five percent of excess over target goes to bonus. Amount of bonus often equals base pay.
Pepsico	Competitive base pay. All employees get stock options equal to 10 percent of base pay. Employees share in corporate triumphs and failures as stock price rises or falls.

---

[34] L. V. Jones and T. E. Jeffrey, "A Quantitative Analysis of Expressed Preferences for Compensation Plans," *Journal of Applied Psychology* 48 (1963), pp. 201–10; Opinion Research Corporation, *Wage Incentives* (Princeton, NJ: Opinion Research Corporation, 1946); Opinion Research Corporation, *Productivity from the Worker's Standpoint* (Princeton, NJ: Opinion Research Corporation, 1949).

[35] D. Koys, T. Keaveny, and R. Allen, "Employment Demographics and Attitudes That Predict Preferences for Alternative Pay Increase Policies," *Journal of Business and Psychology* 4 (1989), pp. 27–47.

[36] B. Major, "Gender, Justice, and the Psychology of Entitlement," *Review of Personality and Social Psychology* 7 (1988), pp. 124–48.

[37] G. Green, "Instrumentality Theory of Work Motivation," *Journal of Applied Psychology* 53 (1965), pp. 1–25; R. D. Pritchard, D. W. Leonard, C. W. Von Bergen, Jr., and R. J. Kirk, "The Effects of Varying Schedules of Reinforcement on Human Task Performance," *Organizational Behavior and Human Performance* 16 (1976), pp. 205–30; D. P. Schwab and L. Dyer, "The Motivational Impact of a Compensation System on Employee Performance," *Organizational Behavior and Human Performance* 9 (1973), pp. 215–25; D. Schwab, "Impact of Alternative Compensation Systems on Pay Valence and Instrumentality Perceptions," *Journal of Applied Psychology* 58 (1973), pp. 308–12.

we increase performance of individuals by tying it to pay?[38] Heneman argues, and we agree, that companies need to do a better job of managing merit pay if they want to improve the chances that employees will respond with better performance. Later in this chapter we talk about pay management.

When we turn to the impact of pay on group performance, the evidence is somewhat clearer. Pay matters! Companies like Corning, Nucor Steel, and Pepsico all strongly support variable pay based on group (all employees in the organization or some subset) performance. Exhibit 8.4 describes elements of the variable pay plan for these companies.

Most well-controlled studies where companies base part of pay on some measure of corporate or division performance report increases in performance of about 4 to 6 percent per year.[39] Typical of these studies is a utility company that placed one division on an experimental group incentive plan and left the other division (the control group) with no pay changes.[40] The goal in the experimental division was to lower unit cost of electricity. The utility set performance goals for such things as operating expenses, maintenance expenses, and absenteeism. If these goals were exceeded, employees would receive a bonus that grew as the goals were exceeded by a larger amount. After implementing this variable pay plan (or group incentive plan), performance improved significantly (relative to a division with no variable pay implemented) on 11 of 12 objective performance measures. As an example, unit production costs fell 6 percent.

Compensation experts estimate that every dollar spent on any performance-based pay plan yields $2.34 more in organizational earnings.[41] Put differently, there is further documented evidence that every 10 percent increase in the ratio of bonus pay to base pay yields a 1.5 percent increase in ROA to the firm.[42]

Before we rush out and develop a variable pay component to the compensation package, though, we should recognize that such plans can, and do, fail. Sometimes the failure arises, ironically, because the incentive works too well,

[38] R. Bretz and G. Milkovich, "Performance Appraisal in Large Organizations: Practice and Research Implications," (Working paper 87-17, NYSSILLR); E. L. Deci, "The Effects of Contingent and Noncontingent Rewards and Controls on Intrinsic Motivation," *Organizational Behavior and Human Decision Processes* 8 (1972), pp. 217–29; Heneman, *Merit Pay*; F. S. Landy, J. L. Barnes, and K. R. Murphy, "Correlates of Perceived Fairness and Accuracy of Performance Evaluations," *Journal of Applied Psychology* 63 (1978), pp. 751–54; J. B. Prince and E. E. Lawler, "Does Salary Discussion Hurt the Developmental Performance Appraisal?" *Organizational Behavior and Human Decision Processes* 37 (1986), pp. 357–75; P. M. Wright, "Testing the Mediating Role of Goals in the Incentive-Performance Relationship," *Journal of Applied Psychology* 74 (1989), pp. 699–705.

[39] Cooke, "Employee Participation Programs"; Kruse, *Profit Sharing*; G. T. Milkovich, "Does Performance-Based Pay Really Work?"; M. M. Petty, B. Singleton, and D. W. Connell, "An Experimental Evaluation of an Organizational Incentive Plan in the Electric Utility Industry," *Journal of Applied Psychology* 77 (1992), pp. 427–36; J. R. Schuster, "The Scanlon Plan: A Longitudinal Analysis," *Journal of Applied Behavioral Science* 20 (1984), pp. 23–28.

[40] Petty et al., "An Experimental Evaluation."

[41] McAdams and Hawk, *Organizational Performance and Rewards.*

[42] Gerhart and Milkovich, "Organizational Differences."

EXHIBIT 8.5   Sears Makes a Mistake

Strategic Goal	Supporting Compensation Component as Translated for Tire and Auto Centers	Unintended Consequence
Cut costs by $600 million; provide facelift to stores; cut prices; make every employee focus on profits.	Set high quotas for generating dollars from repairs. Reward with commissions.	The California Consumer Affairs Division went undercover posing as customers. On 34 of 38 undercover runs, Sears charged an average of $235 for unnecessary repairs.

leading employees to exhibit rewarded behaviors to the exclusion of other desired behaviors. Exhibit 8.5 documents one such embarrassing incident that haunted Sears for much of the early 90s.[43]

Apparently this example is no fluke. Other companies have found poorly implemented incentive pay plans can hurt rather than help. Green Giant, for example, used to pay a bonus based on insect parts screened in its pea-packing process. The goal, of course, was to cut the number of insect parts making their way into the final product (anyone planning on vegetables for dinner tonight?). Employees found a way to make this incentive system work for them. By bringing insect parts from home and inserting and then "finding" them, incentive dollars rose. Clearly, the program didn't work as intended. Experts contend this is evidence the process wasn't managed well. If true, what do we need to know about designing a pay-for-performance plan?

DESIGNING A PAY-FOR-PERFORMANCE PLAN

According to the pay model developed in Chapter 1, we need to be concerned about efficiency, equity, and compliance in designing a pay system.

Efficiency

Efficiency involves three general areas of concern.

Strategy.   Does the pay-for-performance plan support corporate objectives? Is, for example, the plan cost effective, or are we making payouts that bear no relation to improved performance on the bottom line? Similarly, does the plan help us improve quality of service? Some pay-for-performance plans are so focused on quantity of performance that they ignore quality. Defect rates rise;

---

[43] K. Kelly and E. Schine, "How Did Sears Blow This Gasket?" *Business Week*, June 29, 1992, p. 38.

customers must search for someone to handle a merchandise return. Unintended consequences arise from poorly designed plans.

The plan also should link well with HR strategy and objectives. If, for example, other elements of our total HR plan are geared to select, reinforce, and nurture risk-taking behavior, we don't want a compensation component that rewards the status quo.

Structure.   Is the structure of the organization sufficiently decentralized to allow different operating units to create flexible variations on a general pay-for-performance plan? Different operating units may have different competencies, different competitive advantages. We don't want a rigid pay-for-performance system that detracts from these advantages, all in the name of consistency across divisions.

Standards.   Operationally, the key to designing a pay-for-performance system rests in setting up sound output standards. Specifically, we need to be concerned about:

Objectives:	Are they specific yet flexible? Can employees see that their behavior influences their ability to achieve objectives (called the "line-of-sight" issue)?
Measures:	Do employees know what measures (individual appraisals, peer reviews of team performance, corporate financial measures, etc.) will be used to assess whether their performance merits a payout?
Eligibility:	How far down the organization will the plan run? Companies like Pepsico believe all employees should be included. Others think only top management can see how their decisions affect the bottom line.
Funding:	Will the program be funded out of extra revenue generated above and beyond some preset standard? If so, what happens in a bad year? Many employees become disillusioned when they feel they have worked harder, only to find that economic conditions or poor management decisions conspire to cut or eliminate bonuses.

Equity or Fairness

Our second design objective is to ensure that the system is fair to employees. One type of fairness concerns the amount of compensation that is distributed to employees. Not surprisingly, this type of fairness is labeled *distributive justice.*[44]

---

[44] John Thibaut and Laurens Walker, *Procedural Justice: A Psychological View* (Hillsdale, NJ: John Wiley & Sons, 1975).

Does an employee view the amount of compensation received as fair? As we discussed earlier in the section on equity theory, perceptions of fairness depend on the amount of compensation actually received relative to inputs (e.g., productivity).

Notice several of the components of this equity equation are frustratingly removed from the control of the typical supervisor or manager working with employees. A manager has little influence over the size of an employee's pay check. This is influenced more by external market conditions, pay policy decisions of the organization, and the occupational choice made by the employee. Even decisions about how much of a pay increase to give are typically constrained by budget limitations.

Managers do have somewhat more control, though, over a second type of equity. Employees are also concerned about the fairness of *procedures* used to determine the amount of rewards they receive. Employees expect *procedural justice*. Evidence suggests that organizations that use fair procedures and supervisors who are viewed as fair in the means they use to allocate rewards are perceived as more trustworthy and command higher levels of commitment.[45] Some research even suggests that employee satisfaction with pay may depend more on the procedures used to determine pay than on the actual level distributed![46]

A key element in fairness is communications. Employees want to know in advance what is expected of them. They want the opportunity to provide input into these standards or expectations, too. And, if performance is judged lacking relative to these standards, they want a mechanism for appeals. In a union environment, this is the grievance procedure. Something similar needs to be set up in a nonunion environment.[47]

Compliance

Finally, our pay-for-performance system should comply with existing laws. We want a reward system that maintains, and enhances, the reputation of our firm. Think about the companies that visit a college campus. Students naturally gravitate to some of them—their interview schedule fills very quickly indeed! Why? Because of reputation. We tend to undervalue the reward value of a good reputation. To guard this reputation we need to make sure to comply with the laws outlined in Chapters 13 and 14.

---

[45] Robert Folger and Mary Konovsky, "Effects of Procedural and Distributive Justice on Reactions to Pay Raise Decisions."

[46] S. Alexander and M. Ruderman. "The Role of Procedural and Distributive Justice in Organizational Behavior." *Social Justice Research* 1 (1987), pp. 177–98.

[47] G. S. Leventhal, J. Karuza, and W. R. Fry, "Beyond Fairness: A Theory of Allocation Preferences," in *Justice and Social Interaction*, ed. G. Mikula (New York: Springer Verlag, 1980), pp. 167–218.

Summary

Pay-for-performance plans can make a difference in organizational effectiveness. As this chapter indicates, though, success depends on careful design and administration. A poorly designed plan can have unintended consequences: employees doing things that earn incentives but that do not promote organizational success! A poorly administered plan can erode employee trust; and without trust in management's intentions, no pay-for-performance plan can long endure.

Review Questions

1. We try to use money to motivate performance. Defend the position that pay motivates job performance.
2. How can values of people in an organization (and culture) and performance dimensions used in the performance appraisal process conflict with goals of a pay-for-performance system?
3. If you wanted workers to perceive their compensation package as secure, which components would you include and which would you avoid?
4. How does procedural justice differ from distributive justice? Defend the position that supervisors have considerable control over procedural justice in their departments but little control over distributive justice.
5. How might the design of a pay system actually lead to increased turnover?

YOUR TURN:

CLINTON PHARMACEUTICAL

Clinton Pharmaceutical is a medium-sized pharmaceutical company located in Sherwood, New Jersey. Most of Clinton's profits over the past 20 years have been generated by high volume production of drugs that veterinarians use to care for domesticated animals. Since there is only a small markup in this market, Clinton must make its profit from high volume. The somewhat loose quality control laws for drugs distributed to veterinarians has enabled Clinton to achieve unit production levels that are high for the pharmaceutical industry.

Unfortunately, in the past two years productivity has significantly deteriorated at Clinton. (Productivity for the past five years is shown in Exhibit 1.) In addition, turnover and absenteeism are up (Exhibits 2 and 3).

John Lancer, president of Clinton Pharmaceutical, is deeply concerned. The key to Clinton's success has always been its high productivity and resulting low unit production costs. For some reason profits have been down 18 percent during the past two years (1988 = −13 percent; 1989 = −23 percent). Mr. Lancer has an annual stockholders' meeting in two weeks, and he is determined to go in with some answers. Maybe the managers can't correct the decline in time for the meeting, but heads will roll if he doesn't get some answers. All department heads soon receive detailed letters outlining the profit picture and requesting explanations.

Ralph Simpson is the director of Human Resources Management. John Lancer informed him three weeks ago that a marked drop in profits had occurred over the past year. Mr. Simpson offers the data in Exhibit 4 as a possible explanation for the profit decline.

EXHIBIT 1   Clinton Pharmaceutical Productivity Trends, 1991–1995*

1991	1992	1993	1994	1995
127,000	123,000	122,786	104,281	100,222

* Gross revenue generated per employee in constant dollars.

EXHIBIT 2   Turnover Percentages, All Occupations, 1991–1995

1991	1992	1993	1994	1995
14%	12.5	19.0	20.2	21.1

EXHIBIT 3   Absenteeism, Average Days per Employee, 1991–1995

1991	1992	1993	1994	1995
*	*	9.6	9.7	10.2

* Records not available.

Discussion Questions

1. Do Exhibits 1, 2, and 3 suggest any problems that might explain or be related to the profit declines?

2. Given the discussion of motivation theory in this chapter, do the data in Exhibit 4 suggest that productivity declines may be due to motivation problems? What other human resource management explanations are plausible?

EXHIBIT 4   Attitude Survey toward Compensation: Level and Administration

$N = 1,427$ (87 percent response rate)
Questions 1–15

Column A Scaling	*Column B Scaling*	*Column C Scaling*
1 = Very important to me	1 = Very satisfied	1 = Very dependent
2 = Important to me	2 = Satisfied	2 = Dependent
3 = Neither important nor unimportant	3 = Neutral	3 = Unsure
4 = Unimportant to me	4 = Dissatisfied	4 = Rarely dependent
5 = Very unimportant to me	5 = Very dissatisfied	5 = Never dependent

Indicate how important the following rewards available to Clinton employees are to you in column A.
Indicate how satisfied you are with the level Clinton delivers in column B.
How dependent are these rewards on your performance (column C)?

	A	B	C
1. A good salary	2	2	4
2. An annual raise equal to or greater than the cost of living	1	2	5
3. A profit sharing plan	5	3	3
4. Paid sick days	5	3	5
5. Vacation	3	1	5
6. Life insurance	4	1	5
7. Pension	4	1	5
8. Medical plan	3	1	5
9. Opportunity for advancement	2	5	5
10. Job security	1	2	2
11. Good supervisors	2	2	5
12. Opportunity to develop new skills	2	5	5
13. Good coworkers	3	3	5
14. Steady hours	3	2	2
15. Feedback about performance	1	5	3

CHAPTER

Pay-for-Performance Plans

WHAT IS A PAY-FOR-PERFORMANCE PLAN?

What is in a name? The answer is . . . confusion, at least if we are talking about *pay-for-performance* plans. Listen long enough and you will hear about incentive plans, variable pay plans, compensation at risk, earnings at risk, success sharing, etc. Sometimes these names are used interchangeably. They shouldn't be. The major thing all these names have in common is a shift in thinking about compensation. We used to think of pay as primarily an entitlement; if you went to work

321

and did well enough to avoid being fired, you were entitled to your base plus an annual increment. Pay-for-performance plans signal a movement away from entitlement—sometimes a verrryyy slow movement—toward pay that varies with some measure of individual or organizational performance. Of the pay components we discussed in Chapter 8, only base pay and across-the-board increases don't fit the pay-for-performance category. Curiously, though, many of the surveys on pay for performance tend to omit the grandfather of all these plans, merit pay. Maybe the problem is that merit pay is out of favor right now. One survey of 250 companies reports 30 percent are thinking about eliminating merit pay and another 10 percent already have![1] Another survey reports fully one-quarter of a sampled 1,750 organizations may substitute lump sum awards for merit pay.[2] Despite this unrest, merit pay is still a pay-for-performance plan and, as Exhibit 9.1 suggests, still widely used in industry.

In general, pay-for-performance plans are increasingly used to compensate employees at all levels (Exhibit 9.2). Notice that pay-for-performance plans are increasing or staying the same in popularity for all employee groups. Pay-for-performance plans started to grow in popularity in the early 1980s with upper management. This trend now seems to be spreading to lower level employees. These programs are becoming more popular for two reasons. First, increasing

---

EXHIBIT 9.1   Frequency of Adoption for Different Pay-for-Performance Plans

	Type of Pay Plan			
	Merit Pay	*Bonus Plan*	*Skill-Based Pay*	*Any Pay-for-Performance Plan*
Employee Group				
Executives		89*		87‡
Exempt	90†	57*	9†	72‡
Nonexempt		27*		
• Clerical/administrative	87†		10†	60‡
• Production/craft	47†		25†	49‡

* Compflash, "Merit Raises Remain Popular among Fortune 1000," *Compflash*, December 1994, p. 1.

† J. L. McAdams and E. J. Hawk, *Organizational Performance and Rewards* (Phoenix: American Compensation Association, 1994).

‡ Wyatt Data Services, *1994/95 Office Personnel Report* (Ft. Lee, NJ: Wyatt Data Services, 1994).

---

[1] Compflash, "Survey of Merit Pay," *Compflash* (Saranac Lake, NY: American Management Association, January 1994), p. 8.

[2] Compflash, "Towers Perrin Survey of Merit Pay," *Compflash* (Saranac Lake, NY: American Management Association, January 1994), p. 1.

EXHIBIT 9.2   A Growing Trend in Pay-for-Performance Plans[3]

Employee Group	1990 (%)	1992 (%)
Salaried nonexempt	45.2	60
Exempt nonmanagement	61.8	72
Hourly nonexempt	38.5	48.6
Top management	86.9	84
Other management	85.2	86.9

domestic and international competition forces companies to be even more cost conscious than in prior eras. Most of these reward systems attempt to control costs by better linking rewards to performance increases. One study of 4,500 organizations found that the single factor that best explained why organizations adopted alternative reward systems was increases in domestic and foreign competition.[4] As we indicated in Chapter 8, pay-for-performance plans can increase performance and make organizations more competitive on the botton line.

Second, pay-for-performance plans recognize that the rate of technological change seems to be increasing, with new products and new methods of production introduced at what sometimes appears to be a bewildering pace. Organizations that fail to capitalize on new technologies and to recognize new product opportunities face an uncertain future. Their competitors threaten to steal market share and/or erode profits. If this happens, workers face possible layoffs and terminations. To avoid this scenario, compensation experts are focusing on ways to design reward systems so that workers will be able and willing to move quickly into new jobs and new ways of performing old jobs. The ability and incentive to do this comes partially from reward systems that more closely link worker interests with the objectives of the company.

SPECIFIC PAY-FOR-PERFORMANCE PLANS

Merit Pay

A merit pay system links increases in base pay (called *merit increases*) to how highly employees are rated on a subjective performance evaluation. Chapter 10 covers performance evaluation, but as a simple illustration consider the following typical merit pay setup.

---

[3] Compflash, "A Growing Trend: Variable Pay for Lower Level Employees," *Compflash* (Saranac Lake, NY: American Management Association, December 1992), p. 1.

[4] Carla O'Dell, *Major Findings from People, Performance and Pay* (Houston, TX: American Productivity Center, 1986).

Performance rating →	Well above average 1	Above average 2	Average 3	Below average 4	Well below average 5
Merit pay increase →	6%	5%	4%	3%	0%

At the end of a performance year the employee is evaluated, usually by the direct supervisor. The performance rating, 1 to 5 in the above example, determines the size of the increase added to base pay. This last point is important. In effect, what you do this year in terms of performance is rewarded *every year* you remain with your employer. By building merit increases into base pay, the dollar amount, just like the energizer bunny, keeps on going! With compounding, this can amount to tens of thousands of dollars over an employee's work career.[5]

Increasingly, merit pay is under attack. Not only is it expensive, but many argue it doesn't achieve the desired goal: improving employee and corporate performance.[6] In a thorough review of merit pay literature, Heneman concludes that merit pay does have a small, but significant, impact on performance.[7] If we want merit pay to do even better, it needs to be managed better.[8] This requires a complete overhaul of the way we allocate raises: improving the accuracy of performance ratings, allocating enough merit money to truly reward performance, and making sure the size of the merit increase differentiates across performance levels. To illustrate this latter point, consider poor George who works hard all year, earns a 6 percent increase as our guidelines above indicate, and compares himself with Jerry, average performer, who coasts to a 4 percent increase. First Uncle Sam takes out taxes on that extra 2 percent. What's left is spread out over 52 pay checks. It's only a slight exaggeration to suggest the extra money won't pay for a good cup of coffee! Unless we make the reward difference larger for every increment in performance, next time George is going to ask, Why bother?

Lump Sum Bonuses

A popular addition to (and increasingly, substitute for) merit pay is lump sum bonuses. Based on employee or company performance, employees receive an end-of-year bonus that does not build in to base pay. Because employees must

[5] Jerry M. Newman and Daniel J. Fisher, "Strategic Impact Merit Pay," *Compensation and Benefits Review* (Saranac Lake, NY: American Management Association, July–August 1992), pp. 38–45.

[6] Glenn Bassett, "Merit Pay Increases Are a Mistake," *Compensation and Benefits Review* (Saranac Lake, NY: American Management Association, March–April 1994), pp. 20–25.

[7] Robert Heneman, *Merit Pay: Linking Pay Increases to Performance Ratings* (Reading, MA: Addison-Wesley, 1993).

[8] Ibid.

EXHIBIT 9.3   Relative Cost Comparisons

	Pay Package with Merit Pay	Pay Package with Lump Sum Bonus
Base pay	$50,000	$50,000
Year 1 increase	5% ($2,500)	5% ($2,500)
New base pay	$52,500	$50,000
Extra cost total	$ 2,500	$ 2,500
Year 2 increase	5% ($2,625 = .05 * $52,500)	5% ($2,500 = .05 * $50,000)
New base pay	$55,125 ($52,500 + $2,625)	$50,000
Extra cost (y_1, y_2)	7,625 (2,500 + 5,125)	5,000 (2,500 + 2,500)
After 5 years		
New base pay	$63,814	$50,000
Total 5 yr. extra	$40,095	$12,500

earn this increase every year, it is viewed as less of an entitlement than merit pay. As Exhibit 9.3 indicates, lump sum bonuses also can be considerably less expensive than merit pay over the long run. Notice how quickly base pay rises under a merit pay plan. After just five years, base pay is almost $14,000 higher than under a lump sum bonus plan. It should be no surprise that cost conscious firms report switching to lump sum pay. Twenty-five percent of the companies in one large survey report seriously considering such a change away from merit pay.[9]

Individual Spot Awards

Technically, *spot awards* should fall under pay-for-performance plans. About 30 percent of all companies use spot awards.[10] Usually these payouts are awarded for exceptional performance, often on special projects or for performance that so exceeds expectations as to be deserving of an add-on bonus. The mechanics are simple. After the fact, someone in the organization alerts top management to the exceptional performance. If the company is large, there may be a formal mechanism for this recognition and perhaps some guidelines on the size of the spot award (so named because it is supposed to be awarded on the spot). Smaller companies may be more casual about recognition and more subjective about deciding the size of the award.

Individual Incentive Plans: Types

These plans differ from three already mentioned because they offer a promise of pay for some objective, preestablished level of performance. For example,

---

[9] Compflash, "Towers Perrin Survey of Merit Pay," January 1994.

[10] Compflash, "A Growing Trend: Variable Pay for Lower Level Employees," December 1992.

salepeople know up front what level of sales they need to achieve for different levels of commissions.

All incentive plans have one common feature: an established standard against which worker performance is compared to determine the magnitude of the incentive pay. For individual incentive systems, this standard is compared against individual worker performance. From this basic foundation, a number of seemingly complex and divergent plans have evolved. Before discussing the more prevalent of these plans, however, it is important to note that each varies along two dimensions and can be classified into one of four cells illustrated in Exhibit 9.4.

The first dimension on which incentive systems vary is in the *method of rate determination.* Plans either set up a rate based on units of production per time period or in time period per unit of production. On the surface, this distinction may appear trivial but, in fact, the deviations arise because tasks have different cycles of operation.[11] Short-cycle tasks, those that are completed in a relatively short period of time, typically have as a standard a designated number of units to be produced in a given time period. For long-cycle tasks, this would not be appropriate. It is entirely possible that only one task or some portion of it may be completed in a day. Consequently, for longer cycle tasks, the standard is typically set in terms of time required to complete one unit of production.

EXHIBIT 9.4   Individual Incentive Plans

		Method of Rate Determination	
		Units of production per time period	*Time period per unit of production*
Relationship between production level and pay	*Pay constant function of production level*	*(1)* Straight piecework plan.	*(2)* Standard hour plan.
	Pay varies as function of production level	*(3)* Taylor differential piece rate system. Merrick multiple piece rate system.	*(4)* Halsey 50–50 method. Rowan plan. Gantt plan.

[11] Thomas Patten, *Pay: Employee Compensation and Incentive Plans* (New York: Macmillan, 1977); Schwinger, *Wage Incentive Systems.*

Individual incentives are based on whether or not workers complete the task in the designated time period.

The second dimension on which individual incentive systems vary is the specified relationship between production level and wages. The first alternative is to tie wages to output on a one-to-one basis, so that wages are some constant function of production. In contrast, some plans vary wages as a function of production level. For example, one common alternative is to provide higher dollar rates for production above the standard than for production below the standard.

Each of the plans discussed in this section has as a foundation a standard level of performance determined by some form of time study or job analysis completed by an industrial engineer or trained personnel administrator. (Exhibit 9.5 provides an illustration of a time study.) The variations in these plans occur in either the way the standard is set or the way wages are tied to output. As in Exhibit 9.4, there are four general categories of plans.

EXHIBIT 9.5   Example of a Time Study

Task: Drilling operation.

Elements:
1. Move part from box to jig.
2. Position part in jig.
3. Drill hole in part.
4. Remove jig and drop part in chute.

		Elements			
Notes and Remarks	Observation Number	(1)	(2)	(3)	(4)
	1	.17	.22	.26	.29
	2	.17	.22	.27	.34
	3	.16	.21	.28	.39
	4	.18	.21	.29	.29
	5	.19	.20	.30	.36
	6	.25	.21	.31	.31
	7	.17	.23	.29	.33
Observed time		.17 (mode)	.21 (mode)	.29 (median)	.33 (mean)
Effort rating	(130%)	1.30	1.30	1.30	1.30
Corrected time		.2210	.2730	.3370	.4290
Total corrected time					1.2600

Allowances:

Fatigue	5%		
Personal needs	5%		
Contingencies	10%		
Total	20%	(of total corrected time of 1.2600)	.2520
Total alloted time for task			1.5120

Source: From Stephen J. Carroll and Craig E. Schneier, *Performance Appraisal and Review Systems* (Glenview, IL: Scott, Foresman, 1982). Copyright © 1982 by Scott, Foresman and Company. Reprinted by permission.

EXHIBIT 9.6   Illustration of a Straight Piece Rate Plan

Piece rate standard (e.g., determined from time study): 10 units/hour
Guaranteed minimum wage (if standard is not met): $5/hour
Incentive rate (for each unit over 10 units): $.50/unit

Examples of Worker Output	*Wage*
10 units or less	$5.00/hour (as guaranteed)
20 units	20 × $.50 = $10/hour
30 units	30 × $.50 = $15/hour

---

1. *Cell 1.* The most frequently implemented incentive system is a straight piecework system (Exhibit 9.6). Rate determination is based on units of production per time period, and wages vary directly as a function of production level. A standard is developed reflecting the units of output a worker is expected to complete in, say, an hour. Workers are paid for each unit of output. Consequently, workers who consistently exceed the established standard receive higher than average wages.

The major advantages of this type of system is that it is easily understood by workers and, perhaps consequently, more readily accepted than some of the other incentive systems. The major disadvantages center on the difficulty in setting a standard. For example, the industrial engineer charged with establishing a standard for the drilling operation in Exhibit 9.5 may be expected to observe numerous drillers performing the task. The time study expert would then derive a standard indicating the number of holes it should be possible to drill in a given time period by workers performing at a normal rate. The accuracy of the industrial engineer's measurements, the workers chosen to observe, and the definition of a normal rate of speed all influence the final standard.[12] An inappropriate standard can result in labor dissension (too high a standard) or excessive labor costs (too low a standard). Either outcome is likely to result in deteriorating labor-management relations. Consequently, great care must be taken to ensure that both management and workers have a role in establishing standards. In unionized firms this is often formally ensured through inclusion of standards as a negotiable issue in the contract language.

2. *Cell 2.* Two relatively common plans set standards based on time per unit and tie incentives directly to level of output: (1) standard hour plans and (2) Bedeaux plans. A *standard hour plan* is a generic term for plans setting incentive rate based on completion of a task in some expected time period. A common example can be found in any neighborhood gasoline station or automobile repair shop. Let us assume that you need a new transmission. The estimate you receive

---

[12] Stephen Carroll and Craig Schneier, *Performance Appraisal and Review Systems* (Glenview, IL: Scott, Foresman, 1982).

for labor costs is based on the mechanic's hourly rate of pay, multiplied by a time estimate for job completion derived from a book listing average time estimates for a wide variety of jobs. If the mechanic receives $30 per hour and a transmission is listed as requiring four hours to remove and replace, the labor costs would be $120. All this is determined in advance of any actual work. Of course, if the mechanic is highly experienced and fast, the job may be completed in considerably less time than indicated in the book. However, the job is still charged as if it took the quoted time to complete. This is the basic mechanism of a standard hour incentive plan. If a task can be completed in less than the designated time, a worker is still paid at a rate based on the standard time allotted for that job times an hourly rate. Standard hour plans are more practical than a straight piecework plan for long-cycle operations and jobs that are nonrepetitive and require numerous skills for completion.[13]

A *Bedeaux plan* provides a variation on straight piecework and standard hour plans. Instead of timing an entire task, a Bedeaux plan requires division of a task into simple actions and determination of the time required by an average skilled worker to complete each action. After the more fine time analysis of tasks, the Bedeaux system functions similarly to a standard hour plan. Workers receive a wage incentive for completing a task in less than standard time. This incentive is a direct function of the time saved in completing the task.

3. *Cell 3.* The two plans included in cell 3 provide for variable incentives as a function of units of production per time period. Both the Taylor plan and the Merrick plan provide different piece rates, depending on the level of production relative to the standard. To illustrate this, consider the contrasts of these plans with a straight piece rate plan. A straight piece rate plan varies wages directly with output. If workers reach standard production, they receive the standard wage. Eighty percent of standard production results in 80 percent of standard wage. Plotting a graph with percentage of standard production on one axis and percentage gain in base hourly rate on the other, the slope for a straight piece rate system would be 1.00. Both the Taylor and Merrick plans would have variable slopes, depending on production levels of workers. For example, the Taylor plan establishes two piecework rates. One rate goes into effect when a worker exceeds the published standard for a given time period. This rate is set higher than the regular wage incentive level. A second rate is established for production below standard, and this rate is lower than the regular wage.

The Merrick system operates in the same way, except that three piecework rates are set: (1) high—for production exceeding 100 percent of standard; (2) medium—for production between 83 and 100 percent of standard; and (3) low—for production less than 83 percent of standard.[14] Exhibit 9.7 compares these two plans.

---

[13] Patten, *Pay: Employee Compensation and Incentive Plans;* Schwinger, *Wage Incentive Systems.*

[14] Schwinger, *Wage Incentive Systems.*

Exhibit 9.7   Illustrations of the Taylor and Merrick Plans

Piece rate standard: 10 units per hour
Standard wage: $5.00/hour
Piecework rate:

Output	Taylor Rate per Unit	Taylor Wage	Merrick Rate per Unit	Merrick Wage
7 units/hour	$.50/unit	$3.50	$.50/unit	$3.50
8 units/hour	$.50/unit	$4.00	$.50/unit	$4.00
9 units/hour	$.50/unit	$4.50	$.60/unit	$5.40
10 units/hour	$.50/unit	$5.00	$.60/unit	$6.00
11 units/hour	$.70/unit	$7.70	$.70/unit	$7.70
12 + units	Calculations at same rate as for 11 units.			

Both systems are designed to reward highly the efficient worker and penalize the inefficient worker. Quite obviously, there are infinite variations on the number and type of piecework rates that could be established. Although these two plans are designed to encourage the highly efficient, they are not as penalty-laden for less efficient workers as their now defunct predecessors.

4. *Cell 4.* The three plans included in cell 4 provide for variable incentives linked to a standard expressed as time period per unit of production. The three plans include the Halsey 50–50 method, the Rowan plan, and the Gantt plan.

The *Halsey 50–50 method* derives its name from the shared split between worker and employer of any savings in direct cost. An allowed time for a task is determined via time study. The savings resulting from completion of a task in less than the standard time are allocated 50–50 (most frequent division) between the worker and the company.

The *Rowan plan* is similar to the Halsey plan in that an employer and employee both share in savings resulting from work completed in less than standard time. The major distinction in this plan, however, is that a worker's bonus increases as time required to complete the task decreases. For example, if the standard time to complete a task is 10 hours and it is completed in 7 hours, the worker receives a 30 percent bonus. Completion of the same task in 6 hours would result in a 40 percent bonus above the hourly wage for each of the 6 hours.

The *Gantt plan* differs from both the Halsey and Rowan plans in that standard time for a task is purposely set at a level requiring high effort to complete. Any worker who fails to complete the task in standard time is guaranteed a preestablished wage. However, for any task completed in standard time or less, earnings are pegged at 120 percent of the time saved. Consequently, workers' earnings increase faster than production whenever standard time is met or exceeded.

Individual Incentive Plans: Advantages and Disadvantages

We already mentioned that incentive plans can lead to unexpected, and undesired, behaviors. Certainly Sears, our example from Chapter 8, did not want mechanics to sell unnecessary repairs. But the incentive program encouraged that type of behavior. This is a common problem with incentive plans: Employees and managers end up in conflict because the incentive system often focuses only on one small part of what it takes for the company to be successful.[15] Employees, being rational, do more of what the incentive system pays them to do. Exhibit 9.8 outlines some of the other problems, as well as advantages, with individual incentive plans.

EXHIBIT 9.8   Advantages and Disadvantages of Individualized Incentive Plans

Advantages

1. Substantial contribution to raise productivity, to lower production costs, and to increase earnings of workers.
2. Less direct supervision is required to maintain reasonable levels of output than under payment by time.
3. In most cases, systems of payment by results, if accompanied by improved organizational and work measurement, enable labor costs to be estimated more accurately than under payment by time. This helps costing and budgetary control.

Disadvantages

1. Greater conflict may emerge between employees seeking to maximize output and managers concerned about deteriorating quality levels.
2. Attempts to introduce new technology may be resisted by employees concerned about the impact on production standards.
3. Reduced willingness of employees to suggest new production methods for fear of subsequent increases in production standards.
4. Increased complaints that equipment is poorly maintained, hindering employee efforts to earn larger incentives.
5. Increased turnover among new employees discouraged by the unwillingness of experienced workers to cooperate in on-the-job training.
6. Elevated levels of mistrust between workers and management.

Source: T. Wilson, "Is It Time to Eliminate the Piece Rate Incentive System?" *Compensation and Benefits Review* 24, no. 2 (1992), pp. 43–49; Pinhas Schwinger, *Wage Incentive Systems* (New York: Halsted, 1975).

---

[15] Thomas Wilson, "Is It Time to Eliminate the Piece Rate Incentive System?" *Compensation and Benefits Review*, March–April 1992, pp. 43–49.

EXHIBIT 9.9   Lincoln Electric's Compensation System

Description of culture:	High level of trust. Long history of employment stability even under severe economic downturns. Employees with three-plus years' seniority are guaranteed (on one-year renewable basis) at least 75 percent full-time work for that year. In exchange, employees agree to flexible assignment across jobs.
Base wages:	Market rate determined. Time-study department sets piece rate so average worker can earn market rate.
Bonus (short term):	Board of directors sets year-end bonus pool as function of company performance. Employee share in pool is function of semi-annual performance review (see below).
Incentive (long term):	Employees share in long-term company successes/ failures in form of employee stock ownership plan (ESOP). Employees now own 28 percent of outstanding stock shares.
Performance review:	Employees rated on four factors: (1) dependability, (2) quality, (3) output, and (4) ideas and cooperation in comparison to others in department.

Individual Incentive Plans: Examples

Even though individual incentive systems are less popular than they used to be, there are still notable successes. Of course, most sales positions have some part of pay based on commissions, a form of individual incentives. Perhaps the longest running success with individual incentives, going back to 1914, belongs to a company called Lincoln Electric. As we describe the compensation package for factory jobs at Lincoln Electric, notice how the different pieces fit together (Exhibit 9.9). This isn't a case of an incentive plan operating in a vacuum. All the parts complement each other. Lincoln Electric's success is so striking that it is the subject of many case analyses.[16]

Group Incentive Plans: Types

Corporate America is thinking teams![17] When we move away from individual incentive systems and start focusing on people working together, we shift to

---

[16] Kenneth Chilton, "Lincoln Electric's Incentive System: A Reservoir of Trust," *Compensation and Benefits Review*, November–December 1994, pp. 29–34.

[17] Jon Katzenbach and Douglas Smith, *The Wisdom of Teams* (New York: Harper Collins, 1993).

EXHIBIT 9.10   The Choice between Individual and Group Plans

Characteristic	Choose an Individual Plan when . . .	Choose a Group Plan when . . .
Performance measurement	Good measures of individual performance exist. Task accomplishment not dependent on performance of others.	Output is group collaborative effort. Individual contributions to output cannot be assessed.
Organizational adaptability	Individual performance standards are stable. Production methods and labor mix relatively constant.	Performance standards for individuals change to meet environmental pressures on relatively constant organizational objectives. Production methods and labor mix must adapt to meet changing pressures.
Organizational commitment	Commitment strongest to individual's profession or superior. Supervisor viewed as unbiased and performance standards readily apparent.	High commitment to organization built upon sound communication of organizational objectives and performance standards.
Union status	Nonunion. Unions promote equal treatment. Competition between individuals inhibits "fraternal" spirit.	Union or nonunion. Unions less opposed to plans that foster cohesiveness of bargaining unit and which distribute rewards evenly across group.

group incentive plans. The group might be a work team. It might be a department. Or we might focus on a division or the whole company. The basic concept is still the same. A standard is established against which worker performance is compared to determine magnitude of the incentive pay. We measure group performance against some standard or level of expected performance. The standard might be an expected level of operating income for a division; or for a smaller group with no traceable income accountability, the standard might be a customer satisfaction rating on questionnaires mailed to new purchasers. The point is, we are now concerned about the performance of the group. This presents both problems and opportunities. As Exhibit 9.10 illustrates, we need to decide if a group incentive plan is a better choice than an individual plan.

Team Incentives.   Of course, it's not essential that work teams are paid with incentives. One survey of 36 companies with a team-based work environment found the following breakdown:[18]

---

[18] Sam Johnson, "Work Teams: What's Ahead in Work Design and Rewards Management," *Compensation and Benefits Review*, March–April 1993, pp. 35–41. (Numbers do not add to 35 because some companies use multiple components.)

Form of Pay	Number of Companies
Fixed hourly rate	14
Skill-based pay	12
Group incentives	11

One of the problems with team compensation is that teams come in many varieties. There are permanent full-time teams (work group organized as a team). There are part-time teams that cut across functional departments (e.g., experts from different departments pulled together to improve customer relations). There are even full-time team teams that are temporary (e.g., cross-functional teams pulled together to help ease the transition into a partnership or joint venture). With so many varieties, it's hard to argue for one consistent type of compensation plan. Companies that do use team incentives typically set team performance standards based on productivity improvements (38 percent), customer satisfaction measures (37 percent), financial performance (34 percent), or quality of goods and services (28 percent).[19] For example, Colgate-Palmolive uses a combination of merit pay, skill-based pay, and a group incentive based on operating criteria (quality, safety, and productivity).[20] Similarly, Hannaford Brothers Company offers regular compensation plus gain-sharing and a team-share bonus based on financial results.[21] Despite all the experimentation, companies report they generally are not satisfied with the way their team compensation systems work.[22] So, the experiments continue.

Gain-Sharing Plans.   As the name suggests, employees share in the gains in these types of group incentive plans. With profit-sharing plans the sharing involves some form of profits. Realistically, though, most employees feel as if there is little they can do to affect profits—that top management decisions influence profits more! Rather, gain-sharing looks at cost components of the income ledger and identifies savings over which employees have more impact (e.g., reduced scappage, lower labor costs, reduced utility costs).

The following issues must be considered before selecting any gain-sharing or profit-sharing plans.[23]

---

[19] Compflash, "Team-Based Pay: Approaches Vary, but Produce no Magic Formulas," *Compflash* (Saranac Lake, NY: American Management Association, April 1994), p. 4.

[20] Richard Wellins, William Byham, and George Dixon, *Inside Teams* (San Francisco: Jossey Bass, 1994).

[21] Ibid.

[22] Compflash,"Team-Based Pay," April 1994.

[23] Max Bazerman and Brian Graham-Moore, "PG Formulas: Developing a Reward Structure to Achieve Organizational Goals," in *Productivity Gainsharing*, ed. Brian Graham-Moore and Timothy Ross (Englewood Cliffs, NJ: Prentice Hall, 1983).

1. *Strength of reinforcement.*   What role should base pay assume relative to incentive pay? Incentive pay tends to encourage only those behaviors that are rewarded. For example, try returning an unwanted birthday present to a store that pays its sales force solely for new sales! Tasks that carry no rewards are only reluctantly performed (if at all!).

2. *Productivity standards.*   What standard will be used to calculate whether employees will receive an incentive payout? Almost all group incentive plans use a historical standard. A historical standard involves choice of a prior year's performance to use for comparison with the current year. Which baseline year should be used, though? If too good (or too bad) a comparison year is used, the standard will be too hard (or too easy) to achieve, with obvious motivational and cost effects. One possible compromise is to use a moving average of several years (e.g., the average for the past five years, with the five-year block changing by one year on an annual basis).

3. *Sharing the gains.*   Part of the plan must address the relative split between management and workers of any savings generated. This also includes discussion of whether an emergency reserve (gains withheld from distribution in case of future emergencies) will be established in advance of any sharing of profits.

4. *Scope of the formula.*   Formulas can vary in the scope of inclusions for both the labor inputs in the numerator and productivity outcomes in the denominator.[24] Recent innovations in gain-sharing plans broaden the types of productivity standards considered appropriate. Arguing that organizations are complex and require more complex measures, performance measures have expanded beyond traditional financial measures. For example, with the push for greater quality management, we could measure retention of customers or some other measure of customer satisfaction. Similarly, other measures include delivery performance, safety, absenteeism, turnaround time, and number of suggestions submitted. Three specific examples are:[25]

What Is Rewarded	Goal	Bonus per Month
Productivity	38,500 pounds per month	$20
Product damage	15 per 10,000 cases	10
Customer complaints	14 per million pounds	15

Great care must be exercised with these alternative measures, though, to ensure that the behaviors reinforced actually affect the desired bottom-line goal. Getting workers to expend more effort, for example, might not always be the desired behavior. Increased effort may bring unacceptable levels of accidents. Or it may

---

[24] Newman, "Selecting Incentive Plans to Complement Organizational Strategy."

[25] John G. Belcher, "Gainsharing and Variable Pay. The State of the Art," *Compensation and Benefits Review*, May–June 1994, pp. 50–60.

be preferable to encourage cooperative planning behaviors that result in smarter, rather than harder, work.

5. *Perceived fairness of the formula.* Not all incentive systems cover all employees in a firm.[26] In fact, it is common to limit eligibility to individuals in key positions whose income exceeds certain minimum standards.[27] When multiple plans with different goals and covering different employee groups are implemented, coordination to ensure equity becomes increasingly important.

6. *Ease of administration.* Sophisticated plans with complicated calculations for profits or costs can become too complex for existing company information systems. Increased complexities also require more effective communications and higher levels of trust among participants.

7. *Production variability.* One of the major sources of problems in group incentive plans is failure to set targets properly.[28] For example, consider the company that sets a target of 6 percent return on investment. When this level is reached, it triggers an incentive for eligible employees. Yet, in a product market where the average for that year is 15 percent return on investment, it is apparent that no incentive is appropriate for our underachiever.[29] Such problems are particularly insidious during economic swings and for organizations that face volatile economic climates. Care must be taken to ensure that the link between performance and rewards is sustained. This means that environmental influences on performance, not controllable by plan participants, should be factored out when identifying incentive levels. One alternative would be to set standards that are relative to industry performance. To the extent data are available, a company could trigger gain-sharing when performance exceeds some industry norm. The obvious advantage of this strategy is that economic and other external factors hit all firms in the industry equally hard. If our company performs better, relatively, it means we are doing something as employees to help achieve success.

Exhibit 9.11 illustrates some of the important ingredients in setting up a gain-sharing plan.[30]

Exhibit 9.12 illustrates three different formulas that can be used as the basis for gain-sharing plans. The numerator, or input factor, is always some labor cost variable, expressed in either dollars or actual hours worked. Similarly, the denominator is some output measure such as net sales or value added. Each of the plans determines employees' incentive based on the difference between the

---

[26] John Belcher, "Design Options for Gain Sharing" (Unpublished paper, American Productivity Center, 1987).

[27] Ellig, "Incentive Plans: Short Term Design Issues."

[28] Rich and Larson, "Why Some Long Term Incentives Fail."

[29] Patten, "Why Incentive Plans Fail."

[30] Jay Schuster and Patricia Zingheim, "Designing Incentives for Top Financial Performance," *Compensation and Benefits Review* 18, no. 3 (1986), pp. 39–48; Dong-One Kim, "Determinants of Effectiveness in Gainsharing Programs: Findings and Implications," Proceedings of the 46th Annual Meeting IRRA, January 1994, pp. 279–88.

EXHIBIT 9.11 Determinants of a Successful Gain-Sharing Plan

Factor	What the Best Companies Do	What the Rest Do
Eligibility	To be eligible a person must impact on some measurable factor of importance to the company	Based on job level
Compensation	At risk is larger percentage of total pay with 200–300% of base pay typical	At-risk pay is no more than 100% of base pay
Mix: basis of reward formula	Performance	More attuned to what competitors give than any measure of performance
Time period	Plan length geared to time necessary to achieve objectives	Calendar or fiscal year yardstick
Distribution of rewards	20% receive no award 20% receive minimum 20% receive more than minimum but less than maximum 40% receive fully competitive cash incentive	Many more receive maximum award

Source: Adapted from J. Schuster and P. Zingheim, "Designing Incentives for Top Financial Performance," *Compensation and Benefits Review* 18, no. 3 (1986), pp. 39–48.

EXHIBIT 9.12 Three Gain-Sharing Formulas

	Scanlon Plan (single ratio volume)	Rucker Plan	Improshare
Numerator of ratio (input factor) Denominator of ratio (outcome factor)	Payroll costs Net sales (plus or minus inventories)	Labor cost Value added	Actual hours worked Total standard value hours

Source: Adapted from M. Bazerman and B. Graham-Moore, "PG. Formulas: Developing a Reward Structure to Achieve Organizational Goals," in *Productivity Gainsharing*, ed. B. Graham-Moore and T. Ross (Englewood Cliffs, NJ: Prentice Hall, 1983).

current value of the ratio and the ratio in some agreed-upon base year. The more favorable the current ratio relative to the historical standard, the larger the incentive award.[31] The three primary types of gain-sharing plans, differentiated by their focus on either cost savings (the numerator of the equation) or some measure of profits (the denominator of the equation), are noted in Exhibit 9.12.

Scanlon Plan.   Scanlon plans are designed to lower labor costs without lowering the level of a firm's activity. Incentives are derived as a function of the ratio between labor costs and sales value of production (SVOP).[32] The SVOP includes sales revenue and the value of goods in inventory. To illustrate how these two figures are used to derive incentives under a Scanlon plan, consider Exhibit 9.13.

In practice, the $50,000 bonus in Exhibit 9.13 is not all distributed to the work force. Rather, 25 percent goes to the company, 50 percent is distributed as bonus, and the remainder is withheld and placed in an emergency fund to reimburse the company for any future months in which a "negative bonus" is earned (i.e., when the actual wage bill is greater than the allowable wage bill). The excess remaining in the emergency pool is distributed to workers at the end of the year. Appendix 9–A illustrates a variant of the Scanlon plan adopted at Dresser Rand's Painted Post facility.

Rucker Plan.   The Rucker plan involves a somewhat more complex formula for determining worker incentive bonuses than does a Scanlon plan. Essentially,

---

Exhibit 9.13   Examples of a Scanlon Plan

1989 Data (base year) for Alcon, Ltd.		
SVOP	=	$10,000,000
Total wage bill	=	4,000,000
$\dfrac{\text{Total wage bill}}{\text{SVOP}}$	=	$4,000,000 \div 10,000,000 = .40 = 40\%$

Operating Month, August 1987		
SVOP	=	$950,000
Allowable wage bill	=	.40 ($950,000) = $380,000
Actual wage bill (August)	=	330,000
Savings	=	50,000

$50,000 available for distribution as a bonus.

---

[31] A. J. Geare, "Productivity from Scanlon Type Plans," *Academy of Management Review* 1, no. 3 (1976), pp. 99–108.
[32] Ibid.

a ratio is calculated to express the value of production required for each dollar of total wage. Consider the following illustration.[33]

1. Assume that accounting records show that the company put $.60 worth of electricity, materials, supplies, and so on into production to produce $1 worth of product. The value added is $.40 for each $1 of sales value. Assume also that records show that 45 percent of the value added was attributable to labor; a productivity ratio (PR) can be allocated from the formula:

2. PR $\times$ 0.45 = 1. Solving yields PR = 2.22.

3. If the wage bill equals $100,000, the *expected* production value is the wage bill ($100,000) $\times$ PR (2.22) = $222,222.22.

4. If *actual* production value equals $280,000, then the savings (actual production value minus expected production value) equals $57,777.78.

5. Since the labor contribution to value added is 45 percent, the bonus to the work force should be 0.45 $\times$ $57,777.78 = $26,000 (rounded).

6. The savings are distributed as an incentive bonus according to a formula identical to the Scanlon plan formula: 75 percent of the bonus is distributed to workers and 25 percent is kept as an emergency fund to cover poor months. Any excess in the emergency fund at the end of the year is then distributed to workers.

Implementation of the Scanlon/Rucker Plans. Two major components are vital to the implementation and success of a Rucker- or Scanlon-type plan: (1) a productivity norm and (2) the development of effective worker committees. Development of a productivity norm requires both effective measurement of base year data and acceptance by workers and management of this standard for calculating bonus incentives. Effective measurement requires an organization to keep extensive records of historical cost relationships and make them available to workers or union representatives to verify cost accounting figures. Acceptance of these figures, assuming that they are accurate, requires that the organization choose a base year that is neither a "boom" nor a "bust" year. The logic is apparent. A boom year would reduce opportunities for workers to collect bonus incentives. A bust year would lead to excessive bonus costs for the firm. The base year chosen also should be fairly recent, allaying worker fears that changes in technology or other factors would make the base year unrepresentative of a given operational year.

The second ingredient of Scanlon/Rucker plans is a series of worker committees (also known as *productivity committees* or *bonus committees*). The primary function of these committees is to evaluate employee and management suggestions for ways to improve productivity and/or cut costs. Operating on a plantwide basis in smaller firms, or a department basis in larger firms, these committees

---

[33] Geare, "Productivity from Scanlon Type Plans."

have been highly successful in eliciting suggestions from employees. It is not uncommon for the suggestion rate to be above that found in companies with standard suggestion incentive plans.[34]

It is the climate that the Scanlon/Rucker plans foster that is perhaps the most vital element of success.[35] Numerous authorities have pointed out that these plans have the best chance for success in companies with competent supervision, cooperative union-management attitudes, strong top management interest and participation in the development of the program, and management openness to criticism and willingness to discuss different operating strategies. It is beyond the scope of this discussion to outline specific strategies adopted by companies to achieve this climate, but the key element is a belief that workers should play a vital role in the decision-making process.

Differences between Individual Incentive Plans and Scanlon/Rucker Plans.
Scanlon and Rucker plans differ from individual incentive plans in their primary focus. Individual incentive plans focus primarily on using wage incentives to motivate higher performance through increased effort. Although this is certainly a goal of the Scanlon/Rucker plans, it is not the major focus of attention. Rather, given that increased output is a function of group effort, more attention is focused on organizational behavior variables. The key is to promote faster, more intelligent, and acceptable decisions through participation. This participation is won by developing a group unity in achieving cost savings, a goal that is not stressed, but often stymied, in individual incentive plans.

Differences between Scanlon and Rucker Plans.
Even though Scanlon and Rucker plans share a common attention to groups and committees through participation as a linking pin, there are two important differences between the two plans. First, Rucker plans tie incentives to a wide variety of savings, not just the labor savings focused on in Scanlon plans.[36] Second, the greater flexibility may help explain why Rucker plans are more amenable to linkages with individual incentive plans.

Improshare.
Improshare (IMproved PROductivity through SHARing) is a relatively new gain-sharing plan that has proven easy to administer and to communicate.[37] First, a standard is developed that identifies the expected hours required to produce an acceptable level of output. This standard comes either from time and motion studies conducted by industrial engineers or from a base period measurement of the performance factor. Any savings arising from production

---

[34] Ibid.

[35] Kim, "Determinants of Effectiveness in Gainsharing Programs," January 1994.

[36] Patten, "Pay: Employee Compensation and Incentive Plans"; Schwinger, *Wage Incentive Plans.*

[37] Graham-Moore and Ross, *Productivity Gainsharing.*

of agreed-upon output in fewer than expected hours are shared by the firm and by the worker.[38]

One survey of 104 companies with an Improshare plan found a mean increase in productivity during the first year of 12.5 percent.[39] By the third year, the productivity gain rose to 22 percent. A significant portion of this productivity gain was traced to reduced defect rates and downtime (e.g., repair time).

Profit Sharing Plans. The second general category of group incentive plans includes *all profit sharing plans*, whether the profit shared is distributed currently or deferred until later (typically at retirement, disability, severance, or death).[40] Although provisions of the Employee Retirement Income Security Act (ERISA) have taken some of the incentive out of implementing incentive plans, recent estimates still suggest that about 37 percent of the private nonfarm work force receives some kind of profit sharing.[41]

Profit sharing, as is evident from the name, focuses on profitability as the standard for group incentives. Both the financial research literature and the human resources management literature currently are debating what is the best measure of profitability.[42] Exhibit 9.14 illustrates measures and their relative merits.

Profit sharing plans typically can be found in one of three combinations. First, current distribution plans provide full payment to participants soon after profits have been determined, usually quarterly or annually. As might be expected, the incentive value of profit distribution declines as the time between performance and payoff increases and as the size of the payoff declines relative to previous years. Second, deferred plans have a portion of current profits credited to employee accounts, with cash payment made at time of retirement, disability, severance, or death.[43] Because of certain tax advantages, this is the fastest-growing type of profit sharing system, with approximately 80 percent of the companies with some form of profit sharing plans using the deferred option.[44] The median range of profits distributed varies from 14 percent to about 33 percent.[45] Third, combination plans incorporate aspects of both current and deferred options. A portion of profits is immediately distributed to employees

---

[38] Newman, "Selecting Incentive Plans to Complement Organizational Strategy."

[39] R. Kaufman, "The Effects of Improshare on Productivity," *Industrial and Labor Relations Review* 45, no. 2 (1992), pp. 311–22.

[40] Robert McCaffery, *Managing the Employee Benefits Process* (New York: AMACOM, 1983).

[41] Bureau of National Affairs, "Incentive Pay Schemes Seen as a Result of Economic Employee Relation Change," *BNA Daily Report*, October 9, 1984, pp. cc–1.

[42] Bruce R. Ellig, "Incentive Plans: Over the Long Term," *Compensation Review* 16, no. 2 (1984), pp. 39–54; and Ellig, "Short Term Design Issues."

[43] Schwinger, *Wage Incentive Systems.*

[44] McCaffery, *Managing the Employee Benefits Process.*

[45] Patten, "Pay: Employee Compensation and Incentive Plans"; Schwinger, *Wage Incentive Systems.*

EXHIBIT 9.14   Common Performance Measures Used in Profit Sharing Plans

Measure	Strength
Rate of Return Indicators • Return on assets • Return on investment	Approximates investors return on equity; links to shareholder value widely understood and data are readily available.
Income Measurements • Operating income • Pretax operating income	Reflects performance of business unit better than net income; excludes extraneous items like extraordinary write-offs.
• Earnings per share	Calls attention to shareholder value; widely reported so comparisons across companies are possible.
Cash Flow Measures	Pinpoints organizations where cash flows are inadequate. Easily distorted, though, by allocations, estimates, and transfer-pricing practices.

Source: Adapted from Francis Walsh, *Measuring Business Unit Performance* (New York: The Conference Board, 1987).

with the remaining amount set aside in designated accounts. About 20 percent of all companies with profit sharing plans have this option.

Profit sharing plans and the other group incentive plans discussed have certain similarities. Both types of plan foster a climate in which cost-cutting suggestions are more acceptable to employees. Furthermore, both types of plan are designed to pay out incentives when the organization is most able to afford them. However, the similarities end here. Although a cash or current distribution profit sharing plan carries some motivational incentive, thus resembling Scanlon/ Rucker plans, deferred payment plans more closely resemble a pension fund. The incentive value of working to increase current profits when rewards are distributed much later is, at best, minimal. To balance this disadvantage, profit sharing plans have two distinct advantages. First, they do not require elaborate cost accounting systems to calculate incentives to be allocated to employees. (See Exhibit 9.14 for common performance measures.) Second, and perhaps more important, profit sharing plans have been implemented in organizations that cover the entire spectrum in size. Admittedly, there is a definite tendency for smaller organizations to opt for a current distribution plan and for larger organizations to choose the deferred option, but until there is more evidence that Scanlon/Rucker plans can be adapted successfully to larger organizations, profit sharing plans seem to represent the major alternative for organizations of any size. Appendix 9–B outlines the profit sharing plan used at 3M as part of its management compensation package.

Earnings-At-Risk Plans. We probably should not designate *earnings-at-risk plans* as a distinct category. In fact, any incentive plan could be an at-risk plan. Think of incentive plans as falling into one of two categories: *success sharing* or *risk sharing*. In success sharing plans, employee base wages are constant and variable pay accrues during *successful years*. If the company does well, you receive some amount of variable pay. If the company does poorly, you simply forego any variable pay; there is no reduction in your base pay, though. In a risk sharing plan, base pay is reduced by some amount relative to the level that would be offered in a success sharing plan. Let's say base pay is set at 80 percent of its previous level. In bad years for the company, your total compensation remains at 80 percent. In good years, though, you are rewarded for having assumed some of the risk. If, for example, the company meets its goals, you might receive your 80 percent base pay, a 20 percent hit to make you "whole," another 20 percent that you might rightfully receive under any success sharing plan, plus (and this is the difference) a 20 percent premium for having assumed some of the business risk. Summarizing, in bad years you get 80 percent, but in goods years you get (at least in this example) 140 percent. Under a success sharing plan the range would have been 100 to 120 percent. Risk sharing means just that: You gamble along with the company. For taking on part of the gamble, things are worse in bad years and better in good years.

Clearly, at-risk plans shift some of the risk of doing business from the company to the employee. The company hedges against the devastating effects of a bad year by mortgaging some of the profits that would have accrued during a good year. Companies like Du Pont and Saturn report considerable success with these, admitedly, fairly new programs. Reports on the employee front are not so positive, though. At-risk plans appear to decrease satisfaction with both pay in general and the process used to set pay.[46]

Employee Stock Ownership Plans. Some companies believe that employees can be linked to the success or failure of a company in yet another way—through employee stock ownership plans.[47] At places like Pepsico and Lincoln Electric, the goal is to increase employee involvement in the organization. It is hoped that involvement will positively influence performance. Toward this end, employees own 28 percent of stock at Lincoln Electric. At Worthington Industries, an oft-praised performer in the steel industry, the typical employee owns stock valued at $45,000.[48] Unfortunately, there is little scientific research to tell us

---

[46] K. Brown and V. Huber, "Lowering Floors and Raising Ceilings: A Longitudinal Assessment of the Effects of an Earnings-at-Risk Plan on Pay Satisfaction," *Personnel Psychology* 45 (1992), pp. 279–311.

[47] T. H. Hammer and R. N. Stern, "Employee Ownership: Implications for the Organizational Distribution of Power," *Academy of Management Journal* 23 (1980), pp. 78–100.

[48] Chilton, "Lincoln Electric's Incentive System"; Howard Rudnitsky, "You Have to Trust the Workforce," *Forbes*, July 19, 1993, pp. 78–81.

Exhibit 9.15   Advantages and Disadvantages of Group Incentive Plans

Advantages

1. Positive impact on organization and individual performance of about 5 percent per year.
2. Easier to develop performance measures than for individual plans.
3. Signals that cooperation, both within and across groups, is a desired behavior.
4. Teamwork meets with enthusiastic support from most employees.
5. May increase participation of employees in decision-making process.

Disadvantages

1. *Line of sight* may be lessened, that is, employees may find it more difficult to see how their individual performance affects their incentive payouts.
2. May lead to increased turnover among top individual performers who are discouraged because they must share with lesser contributors.
3. Increases compensation risk to employees because of lower income stability. May influence some applicants to apply for jobs in firms where base pay is larger compensation component.

---

whether ESOPs affect either performance or employee involvement. Some experts argue, though, that ESOPs can make a difference when coupled with a genuine employee participation plan.[49]

Group Incentive Plans: Advantages and Disadvantages

Clearly, group pay-for-performance plans are gaining popularity while individual plans are stable or declining in interest. Why? A big part of the reason is the changing nature of work processes. Teams as the basic work unit are growing in popularity. The interdependence of jobs and the need for cooperation means compensation must reinforce working together. Efforts to reinforce these group efforts with compensation generally have been successful (Chapter 8). Exhibit 9.15 outlines some of the general positive and negative features of group pay-for-performance plans.[50]

---

[49] J. Tucker, S. L. Nock, and D. J. Toscano, "Employee Ownership and Perceptions of Work," *Work and Occupations* 16 (1989), pp. 26–42.

[50] These observations are drawn from a variety of sources, including: Brown and Huber, "Lowering Floors and Raising Ceilings"; D. Collins, L. Hatcher, and T. Ross, "The Decision to Implement Gainsharing: The Role of Work Climate, Expected Outcomes and Union Status," *Personnel Psychology* 46 (1993), pp. 77–103; Compflash, "Team-Based Pay," April 1994; W. N. Cooke, "Employee Participation Programs, Group Based Incentives and Company Performance," *Industrial and Labor Relations Review* 1, no. 47 (1994), pp. 594–610; G. W. Florowski, "The Organizational Impact of Profit Sharing," *Academy of Management Review* 12, no. 4 (1987), pp. 622–36.

EXHIBIT 9.16 Examples of Group Incentive Plans at Some Major Corporations

GE Information Systems	A team-based incentive with links to individual payouts. Team and individual performance goals are set. If the team hits its goals, the team members earn their incentive only if they also hit their individual goals. The team incentive is 12 to 15 percent of base pay and is paid monthly.
Corning Glass	A gain-sharing program (goal sharing) where 75 percent of the payout is based on unit objectives such as quality measures, customer satisfaction measures, and production targets. The remainder is based on Corning's return on equity.
3M	Operates with an earnings-at-risk plan. Base pay is fixed at 80 percent of market. Employees have a set of objectives to meet for pay to move to 100 percent of market. Additionally, there is a modest profit sharing component.
Saturn	Earnings-at-risk plan where base pay is 93 percent of market. Employees meet individual objectives to capture at-risk component. All team members must meet objectives for any to get at-risk money. A profit sharing component is based on corporate profits.
Du Pont Fibers	Earnings-at-risk plan where employees receive reduced pay increases over five years, resulting in 6 percent lower base pay. If the department meets annual profit goal, employees collect all 6 percent. Variable payout ranges from 0 (department reaches less than 80 percent of goal) to 12 percent (150 percent of goal).

Group Incentive Plans: Examples

Incentive plans, as we noted earlier, can be described by (1) the size of the group that participates in the plan, (2) the standard against which performance is compared, and (3) the payout schedule. Exhibit 9.16 illustrates some of the more interesting components of incentive plans.

Summary

Pay-for-performance plans can work. But as this chapter demonstrates, the design and effective administration of these plans is key to their success. Having a good idea is not enough. The good idea must be followed up by sound practices that use rewards to shape employee behavior.

Review Questions

1. Why are variable pay plans increasing in popularity?

2. When are group incentive plans preferable to individual incentive plans?

3. How is an earnings-at-risk plan different from an ordinary gain-sharing or profit sharing plan?

4. If you wanted to create a work enviroment where employees offered more new product suggestions, what type of plan might you recommend? What are some of the problems you need to be aware of?

APPENDIX 9–A

GAIN-SHARING AT DRESSER RAND

History

Let's start with some background on the history of gain-sharing and the Painted Post Gain-Sharing Plan.

Gain-sharing plans have been on the American industrial scene for almost 50 years. One of the first gain-sharing plans was developed by the late Joseph Scanlon. Scanlon was a one-time prize fighter; cost accountant; later, he went to work in a steel mill where he became a local union president. Scanlon eventually joined the United Steelworkers of America staff as its research director.

In 1938 the steel mill where Scanlon worked was on the verge of bankruptcy. The men were desperately anxious to protect their jobs. Scanlon, who had worked on the management side as an accountant and on the union side as union president, realized that the productivity of the plant was exceedingly low.

Scanlon convinced the president of the company to join him in a visit to the office of Mr. Clinton S. Golden, vice president of the Steelworkers, to talk things over. Mr. Golden encouraged them to go back and devise a plan whereby the union and management could work together to save the company. As a result, the first plan of its type was worked out between the management and the union. A new principle was introduced—the principle of employee participation. Later on, Scanlon became a professor at the Massachusetts Institute of Technology, but he died an untimely death in 1956.

Scanlon's work is being carried on by a small group of mostly university professors who are committed to cooperation and team work in American industry. One of those professors, Dr. Michael Schuster of Syracuse University, was commissioned by Ingersoll-Rand management to conduct a feasibility study to see if gain-sharing was an idea that might help Painted Post.

The results of the feasibility study were positive. A recommendation was made to implement a productivity gain-sharing program at Painted Post. The plan is modeled after plans used in many other companies, but has several unique features which are unique to Painted Post. Painted Post was the first Ingersoll-Rand location to attempt a gain-sharing plan. It was started July 1, 1985. If you would like more details about gain-sharing, stop into the Plant Personnel Office.

Now let's get down to the plan itself. Its basic purpose is to tap the huge reservoir of know-how, skill, and experience that is present in every work force. The plan permits and encourages all employees to participate in the solution to productivity, quality, and cost problems.

In addition, each employee shares in the success of the plan through the bonus program. In short, the plan gives each employee a financial stake in the business.

Key Features of the Painted Post Gain-Sharing Plan

1. A productivity, quality, and cost reduction formula to recognize employees for their efforts. Employees can earn a bonus by:

   - Increasing productivity
   - Improving quality
   - Saving on shop supplies

   This element of the plan gives employees a triple opportunity to be productive and, at the same time, conscious of quality, material, and shop supplies.

2. An expansion of the Employee Involvement Teams (EITs) to provide employees with an opportunity to solve problems that can increase productivity and quality, while reducing the costs of material and shop supplies.

3. A Bonus Committee composed of four union and four management representatives responsible for the overall administration of the program.

4. The program recognizes Painted Post employees for performance efforts that exceed the plant's 1984 levels.

5. Teamwork and employee participation are the key ingredients of the plan. Both require your support and commitment in order for the program to be successful.

The Employee Involvement Teams

The success of the Painted Post Gain-Sharing Plan will largely be determined by the extent to which all employees, hourly and salary, get involved in making Painted Post a successful business once again. The vehicle for doing this is through an expanded and modified process of employee involvement. ALL EMPLOYEES MUST GET INVOLVED IF WE ARE TO MAKE THIS GAIN-SHARING PLAN A SUCCESS.

You know more about your work operations than anyone else. You know best how they can be improved, what shortcuts can be taken, how materials can be saved and scrap minimized, and how work can be performed more efficiently.

The best suggestions are those which recognize the problem and propose a solution.

There will be Employee Involvement Teams (EITs) in each department of the plant, and where possible on the second shift as well. The primary purpose of the EITs should be in the areas of cost reduction, quality, and productivity. The teams will have the option of seeking their own projects. The Steering Committee will also form task forces, task teams, and project teams to work on specific projects, which, in the view of the Steering Committee, might contribute to reducing costs, increasing quality, or reducing production inefficiencies and bottlenecks. Other companies have found that expansion of the EITs will allow us to:

- Use our creative powers in our daily tasks to make suggestions which will improve productivity and quality that will result in better earnings and bonuses.
- Communicate clearly with each other—management to employees and employees to management.
- Join fully and cooperatively in the common effort to increase productivity, quality, and earnings.
- Keep an open-minded attitude to change.

When an EIT team has developed a solution to a problem and the supervisor agrees with the solution, it may be implemented immediately if the cost of the solution is less than $200 and it does not impact on another department. The reason for this is that we want all employees to take greater responsibility for the success of the business.

If, after discussion and analysis, the employees feel the idea is still a good one, and the supervisor or area manager does not, the employees may ask for a review by the EIT Steering Committee. The reason for this is that no one employee, hourly or salaried, can be permitted to stand in the way of a good idea being heard.

The only bad idea is one that is not suggested. You may think your suggestion is not important enough to bring up. **WRONG**. It may prove to be catalyst needed by your fellow employee to trigger another idea.

There will be an Employee Involvement Steering Committee which will coordinate all employee involvement activities. The EIT Steering Committee will have the following functions:

- Oversee the operation of the EIT teams.
- Encourage the teams to take on significant projects.
- Review ideas that have been rejected by supervisors or managers.
- Coordinate review of ideas that cut across more than one department.
- Provide regular communications on the activities of the EITs.
- Act as a mechanism that will create greater trust, confidence, and teamwork.

The Bonus Committee

The Bonus Committee is made up of four union and four company representatives. It is one of the most effective means of communication between employees and management. The committee meets once each quarter to review the bonus computation for the previous quarter and analyze why it was, or was not, favorable. Accurate minutes will be kept by the Bonus Committee.

The Gain-Sharing Bonus

The productivity bonus is paid to recognize employees for their efforts. **The bonus is not a gift.** It will be paid when it has been earned by exceeding 1984 performance levels for labor costs, quality, and shop supplies.

The program utilizes three measurement points when calculating the bonus payout:

Productivity (as measured in labor costs)

Quality (as measured by spoilage, scrap, and reclamations)

Shop supplies

The Painted Post Gain-Sharing Plan permits gains in productivity to be enhanced by savings in scrap and reclamation expenses and shop supplies. Thus, a bonus is determined by the following formula:

$$\text{Gain-sharing} = \text{Productivity} \pm \text{Quality} \pm \text{Shop supplies}$$
$$\text{bonus} \qquad \text{(Labor costs)} \quad \text{(Spoilage, scrap, \& reclamation)}$$

However, if quality falls below the stated target, it will reduce the bonus earned from a productivity gain. Conversely, if productivity falls below the stated target, it will reduce a bonus that could have been earned from a quality improvement.

Thus, employees are required to focus on three very important indicators of plant performance. This measurement system ensures that productivity gains are not achieved at the expense of quality and prudent shop supply usage. At Painted Post, the dual importance of productivity and quality must be recognized by all employees.

The Role of Quality

Maintaining and increasing the quality of Painted Post products is achieved with this measurement formula in two ways.

First, only "good product" is to be recognized in accounting for sales.
Second, "bad product" will be scrapped and will adversely affect spoilage, scrap, and reclamation, as well as labor costs.

Thus, there is a double benefit for employees to produce good quality products and a severe penalty for failure to do so.

Calculation of the Gain-Sharing Bonus

Employees will receive a bonus when they exceed their own levels of performance in 1984. Bonuses from the Painted Post Gain-Sharing Plan are not based upon management or employee opinion of how much work should be done and of what quality. Instead, the bonus is based upon improvements in how the work force actually performed in 1984. Following is an example of how the gain-sharing bonus will be calculated.

PAINTED POST
Gain-Sharing Calculation Example

Net sales	$ 9,000,000
Inventory change sales value	+ 1,000,000
Sales value of production	10,000,000

Labor Bonus Pool

Target labor and fringe (16.23%)	1,623,000
Actual labor and fringe	1,573,000
Labor/fringe savings bonus	50,000
Actual percent of sales value	15.73%

Waste Savings Bonus Pool

Target spoiled and reclaimation (3.34)	$ 334,000
Actual spoiled and reclamation	294,000
Waste savings bonus	40,000
Actual percent of sales value	2.94%

Operating Supplies Bonus Pool

Target operating supplies (4.00%)	$ 400,000
Actual operating supplies	370,000
Operating supplies savings bonus	30,000
Actual percent of sales value	3.70%

Distribution

Total all savings bonus pools	$ 120,000
Less: Current quarter reserve provision	40,000
Apply to prior quarter loss	–0–
Available for distribution	80,000
Employee share (65%)	52,000
Participating payroll	1,000,000
Employee share—percentage of participating payroll	5.20%
Reserve balance	$ 40,000

The reserve is established in order to safeguard the Company against any quarters with lower than normal output. At the end of each plan year, whatever is left in the reserve will be paid out with 65 percent going to the employees and 35 percent to the Company.

On the next several pages we examine the bonus formula in detail. Please read this information carefully. It is very important for every employee to understand how we arrive at a bonus.

PAINTED POST GAIN-SHARING PLAN
XXXX QUARTER 19XX
(Example 1)

Net Sales are the combination of the following:	$ 9,000,000
Gas compressor sales	
Air compressor transfers	
V & R transfers	
Transfers to repair centers	
Transfers to DRCS	
In short, **New Sales** is what Painted Post receives for what it does.	
± Inventory Change Sales Value	±1,000,000
Inventory is work in progress and finished goods that have not been shipped.	
SALES VALUE OF PRODUCTION	$10,000,000
The actual quarterly sales plus or minus the inventory increases or decreases.	
Incidentally, if we can get some price increases, that should increase the sales value of production and help us to earn a bonus.	

PAINTED POST GAIN-SHARING PLAN
XXXX Quarter 19XX
(Example 2)

SALES VALUE OF PRODUCTION	$10,000,000
Target Labor and Fringe (16.23%)	1,623,000
The historical relationship between payroll cost (less pension) and sales for the year 1984. Payroll costs were adjusted to reflect the 1985 contract changes.	
This is the amount of labor we would expect if we had $10,000,000 in sales. It is the target we must beat if we are to earn a bonus.	
Actual Labor and Fringes	1,573,000
The actual monies paid during the quarter for wages and fringes.	
LABOR COSTS SAVINGS	$ 50,000
The difference between what we would have expected in labor costs from what actually occurred.	
Can we do better than the past and earn a bonus?	
Answer: There is nothing the Painted Post work force can't do when it tries.	

PAINTED POST GAIN-SHARING PLAN
XXXX Quarter 19XX
(Example 3)

Target Spoilage and Reclamation (3.34%)	$334,000
The historical relationship between spoilage, scrap, and reclamations and sales for the year 1984.	
This is the cost of spoilage, scrap, and reclamation we would expect if we had $10,000,000 in sales.	
Actual Spoilage and Reclamation	294,000
The actual costs of spoilage, scrap, and reclamations for the quarter.	
QUALITY SAVINGS	$ 40,000
The difference between what we would have expected in quality costs and what actually occurred.	
Can we reduce the costs of quality?	
Answer: Painted Post has one of the most highly skilled work forces anywhere.	
We can improve our quality and probably increase our sales as a result.	

PAINTED POST GAIN-SHARING PLAN
XXXX Quarter 19XX
(Example 4)

Target Operating Supplies (4.00%)	$400,000
The historical relationship between operating supplies and sales for the year 1984.	
This is the cost of shop supplies we would expect if we had $10,000,000 in sales.	
Actual Operating Supplies	370,000
The actual costs of operating supplies for the quarter.	
OPERATING SUPPLIES SAVINGS	$ 30,000
The difference between what we would have expected in operating supply costs and what actually occurred.	
Does anyone know where savings might be found in operating supplies?	
Answer: Everyone knows.	

PAINTED POST GAIN-SHARING PLAN
XXXX Quarter 19XX
(Example 5)

TOTAL ALL SAVINGS BONUS POOLS		$120,000
Labor	+ $ 50,000	
Quality	+ 40,000	
Supplies	+ 30,000	
	$120,000	
Less 1/3 as current Qtr. Reserve Provision		40,000
Apply to prior quarter loss		–0–
Available for Distribution		80,000
Employee share of savings 65%		52,000
Participating Payroll		1,000,000
Employee Share—% of Participating Payroll		5.20%
(Participating payroll is total wages for all hours worked.)		
RESERVE BALANCE		40,000

The Reserve is established to provide some safeguard for the Plan against quarters with lower than normal efficiency where we fail to meet our stated labor costs, spoilage, scrap and reclamation, and shop supplies goals. At the end of the gain-sharing year, the money remaining in the Reserve Account will be distributed.

Questions and Answers

Q: What should an employee do if he or she has a question about the plan or an idea that might increase the bonus?

A: Questions or ideas should be referred to the employee's supervisor, the EIT Steering Committee, the Plant Personnel office, or the Gain-Sharing Committee.

Q: Will being absent or tardy affect my bonus?

A: Employees will only receive a bonus for actual hours worked. The employee who has lost time will not be paid a bonus for that period of absences.

Q: What about other pay-for-time-not-worked benefits?

A: Bonuses will be excluded from all pay-for-time-not-worked benefits, such as vacations, holidays, death in family, jury duty, etc.

Q: What if there is ever a question as to the accuracy of the calculation of the bonus formula?

A: If there is ever a question as to the accuracy of the information, the company has agreed to permit Price Waterhouse to conduct an audit.

Q: How long will the program last?

A: The Gain-Sharing Plan will exist for the life of the present collective bargaining agreement. Since the plan is an annual plan, each year the nature of the plan will be reviewed. The Union and the Company will have the right to meet to review the plan if either becomes dissatisfied with it.

Appendix 9–B

Profit-Sharing at 3M

Prologue

". . . In years of unusual company prosperity, incomes under a properly designed plan may go up, allowing the employee to participate in the company's prosperity; and during lean years, incomes automatically decrease. It seems to me that those in important positions should recognize that it is proper to expect their incomes to vary somewhat in relation to the prosperity of their division, subsidiary, and/or the prosperity of the company as a whole."

> William L. McKnight
> Chairman 1949–1966

3M's management compensation system is designed to reinforce the manager's responsibility to improve profitability. The formula is based on a simple philosophy; the individual manager's income should vary with the business unit's profitability. This booklet explains how "profit-sharing" converts this philosophy into practice.

Salary Surveys

Our management compensation system starts with a review of competitive pay rates in the marketplace. For 3M, the "marketplace" is not the average U.S. corporation, but rather, respected companies that are similar to us in management philosophies and human resource principles. In other words, the "peer" companies with which we compete for talent.

The survey process involves asking our peers for information about base salaries, discretionary bonuses, and any special incentive programs. These components are added together to provide the basis for 3M's salary range structure.

As you'll see, as a manager part of your total cash compensation is paid to you as base salary, and the remainder as profit-sharing. The relationship of your total pay to the market rate determined by survey is illustrated by this diagram.

MARKET	**3M RANGE MIDPOINT**
BONUS/ SPECIALS	PROFIT-SHARING (VARIABLE)
BASE SALARY	BASE SALARY
PEERS	3M

The diagram helps to illustrate a very important concept. Your profit-sharing is not an "over and above" payment, nor is it a bonus. Rather, it is a variable portion of your total cash compensation that will fluctuate with the success of your business unit.

Definitions

Before explaining how a profit-sharing plan is developed, we must discuss two important terms.

As noted earlier, profit-sharing is a variable part of your cash compensation. In order to calculate the variable payment, it is first necessary to assign a fixed number of profit-sharing "shares." These shares are not owned, nor do they have a market value; they are a device to calculate profit-sharing. Then, after the end of each quarter, the number of shares is multiplied by the profit-sharing "rate." The rates vary with profitability; hence, your profit-sharing payment will increase or decrease, depending upon profitability.

The Rate Calculations section of this booklet describes how profit-sharing rates are determined.

Your Initial Plan

When you are first appointed to management, 5 percent to 10 percent of your new total compensation is normally allocated to profit-sharing. Let's go through an example to show how the initial plan is developed. The example assumes you work for an operating division; if you are a staff manager, you will normally receive company shares instead of the division shares referred to in the example.

Let's assume that when you are appointed, your total cash compensation is $45,600 per year, and you receive a promotional increase of approximately 15 percent. The computation works like this.

$45,600	Total compensation
×1.15	15% promotional increase
$52,520	New total compensation
×0.05	5% allocated to profit-sharing
$ 2,600	Amount allocated to profit-sharing

The next step is to determine your number of shares. To do this, your profit-sharing dollar allocation is divided by your division's four-quarter profit-sharing rate (the sum of the most recent four quarter's rates). In our example, the four-quarter rate is $0.17391. Accordingly,

$$\frac{\$2,600 \text{ Dollar Allocation}}{\$0.17391 \text{ Division Rate}} = 14,950 \text{ Division Shares}$$

Your annualized profit-sharing compensation plan would then be:

Base Salary	$49,920 Paid Monthly
Division Profit-Sharing	
14,950 Shares at $0.17391	2,600 Paid Quarterly
	$52,520 Total Compensation

Generally, your initial share assignment is division shares only, since, as a new manager, your most significant contributions will be at the division level. However, as your responsibilities increase, you may be assigned group and company shares. As a staff manager, you will receive company shares which will be increased as responsibilities increase.

Rate Calculations

The 3M profit-sharing system provides for profit-sharing at the division, group, and company level. All three types of profit-sharing rates are described in this section.

All profit-sharing rates are calculated quarterly. Quarterly profit is determined as follows:

$$\begin{array}{l}\text{Year-to-date profit, current quarter}\\[-2pt] \underline{-\ \text{Year-to-date profit, previous quarter}}\\[2pt] =\ \text{Current quarter profit}\end{array}$$

Division Rates.   A division's quarterly profit-sharing rate is determined by dividing the division's current quarter profit by the number of 3M common shares outstanding at the end of the previous quarter. As an example, let's assume your division had a $5,000,000 profit and there were 115 million shares of 3M common stock outstanding.

$$\frac{\$\ 5{,}000{,}000\ \text{Quarterly Profit}}{115{,}000{,}000\ \text{3M Common Stock}} = \frac{\$0.04348\ (\text{Division Profit-}}{\text{Sharing rate per share})}$$

Since the number of outstanding shares of 3M common stock remains relatively constant, the quarterly rate will increase if division profit increases. This creates the opportunity for you to earn more than your planned income; remember, your share allocation was based on the four-quarter rate at the time your shares were assigned. Conversely, if profit declines, the quarterly rate declines and you will be paid less than your planned income.

Group Rates.   Group quarterly profit-sharing rates are calculated using the same formula as division rates. That is, group quarterly profit is divided by the number of 3M common shares outstanding. For example, if your group's quarterly income was $18,750,000 your group rate would be:

$$\frac{\$18{,}750{,}000\ \text{Group Profit}}{115{,}000{,}000\ \text{3M Common Stock}} = \frac{\$0.16304\ (\text{Group Profit-}}{\text{Sharing rate per share})}$$

The assignment of group shares is determined using the most recent four-quarter group rate in the manner described for division share assignments.

Company Rates.   The formula used to calculate company quarterly profit-sharing rates differs from the division/group formula.

The formula is: Current quarter 3M consolidated net income, minus 2.5% of the previous quarter's Stockholders' Equity (Assets minus Liabilities), divided by the previous quarter's number of 3M common shares outstanding. Using representative numbers, the quarterly calculation looks like this:

Reserve for Return on Stockholders' Equity

Total Assets	$6,593,000,000
Less Total Liabilities	2,585,000,000
Stockholders' Equity	$4,008,000,000
	× 2 1/2%
Minimum Reserve	$ 100,200,000

Income Available for Profit-Sharing

Consolidated Net Income	$ 186,450,000
Less Minimum Reserve	100,200,000
Adjusted Net Income	$ 86,250,000

Company Share Rate

$$\frac{\$86,250,000 \text{ Profit-Sharing Income}}{115,000,000 \text{ 3M Common Stock}} = \$0.750 \text{ (Company Profit-Sharing rate per share)}$$

By establishing the minimum reserve, this formula recognizes the fact that the shareholders own the company and are entitled to a reasonable return before profits are shared with management. And, the inclusion of assets and liabilities in the calculation provides an incentive for managers to use assets wisely in their efforts to increase profits.

The assignment of company shares uses the same four-quarter rate method described for division share assignments.

Another Example

Now that you understand rate calculations, let's go through another example that will build on the first.

Your initial plan was designed to pay you a total of $52,520, of which $2,600 was to be profit-sharing. However, since that plan became effective, your division's four-quarter rate increased from $0.17391 to $0.20000. As a result, your plan is now paying at an annual rate of $52,910, as follows:

Base Salary	$49,920 Paid Monthly
Division Profit-Sharing	2,990 Paid Quarterly
14,950 shares @ $0.20000	$52,910 Total

Your manager has decided that:

- You have earned a 6 percent merit increase.
- You should have 10 percent of your total pay in profit-sharing (up from 5 percent).
- You should receive some group and company shares.
- The value of the group/company profit-sharing should be 10 percent of your profit-sharing.

Assuming that the four-quarter group and company rates are $0.65216 and $3.000 respectively, your new plan would look like this.

Base Salary	$50,460 Paid Monthly
Division Profit-Sharing:	
25,200 shares @ $0.2000	5,040 Paid Quarterly
Group Profit-Sharing:	
425 shares @ $0.65216	277 Paid Quarterly
Company Profit-Sharing:	
100 shares @ $3.000	300 Paid Quarterly
	$56,077 Total Planned Pay

It's important to note that your 6 percent increase was calculated at a value determined by the current four-quarter rate, and not from the rate used when your shares were originally assigned. In other words, $56,077 is 106 percent of $52,910.

The addition of group/company shares and a change in the percent allocated to profit-sharing is most often timed to correspond with a merit or promotional increase. Other changes to your plan, called "conversions," are explained in the last section of this booklet.

You've noted that your profit-sharing allocation was not divided equally between division, group, and company profit-sharing. The reasons are explained in the next section.

Profit-Sharing Mix

Our example illustrated an important feature of the 3M profit-sharing system. Because your most important contributions will always be at the division level (as long as you have a division job), division profit-sharing will always be the most important. However, as your responsibility level increases, the value of the group/company portion may increase, to about 40 percent of the total profit-sharing allocation. When group shares are used, the value of group and company profit-sharing will normally be kept approximately equal (up to 20 percent for each). The desired mix is achieved by adjusting the number of shares (without subtracting division shares), generally at the time of an increase.

Profit-Sharing/Base Salary Balance

It is also important to maintain a proper relationship between profit-sharing and base salary. As you advance in management, more dollars are assigned to profit-sharing, increasing your potential for an increase or decrease in earnings as a result of business unit profitability. For example, as a new or first-level manager, no more than 15 percent of your total planned compensation will be assigned to profit-sharing, whereas senior managers may have up to 40 percent of their total planned compensation in profit-sharing. At the time of compensation plan changes, increases are planned so as to retain the desired balance between base salary and profit-sharing in your plan (without reducing base salary).

Participation Limits

Profit-sharing is intended to provide significant increases in total cash compensation during periods of improving profitability; however, profit growth rates vary by division, and sometimes dramatically. As a consequence, managers in divisions experiencing rapid or even explosive growth can significantly outearn their counterparts in divisions with lower profit growth or even declining profits. When profit growth is more related to the business/product cycle of the division than to relative managerial effectiveness, excessive earnings are not justified. To maintain internal equity while still permitting increased earnings through profit-sharing, participation limits have been established.

Participation limits are calculated as a percent of your base salary, and they vary by salary grade. Participation limits are calculated on a year-to-date basis. It is important to emphasize that participation limits do not stop profit-sharing; they only restrain the rate at which you participate in profit growth.

Suppose, using our last example, your division is extremely successful. The division, group, and company four-quarter profit-sharing rates have jumped to $0.75000, $1.00000, and $3.500, respectively. At those rates, the annualized value of your profit-sharing has increased by approximately 350 percent.

Type	Planned	Now Paying
25,200 Division Shares	$5,020	$18,900
425 Group Shares	277	425
100 Company Shares	300	350
	$5,597	$19,675

However, at your salary grade, the participation limit is 35 percent. Here's how it works.

Base Salary	$50,420
	× 35%
100% participation up to	$17,647
50% participation in the next	$17,647
25% participation in the remainder	

So, in our example you would receive:

100% participation	$17,647
50% participation in excess ($2,028)	1,014
Total	$18,661

Normally, after participation limits are reached, the plan will be revised to provide the desired balance between base salary and profit-sharing without a loss in planned total compensation. The resulting new plan effectively captures the level of compensation attained and allows for full participation in future profit growth.

Conversions

Occasionally, events such as the sale or transfer of commodities, the acquisition or divestiture of a subsidiary or business, or the reorganization of a division will affect division profits, resulting in an increase or decrease in the profit-sharing rate that does not reflect operating results. If the event results in a net change of 3 percent in a division's rate or a 6 percent change in a group rate, the Compensation Department will automatically "convert" your plan.

Conversion is simply restating the number of shares you have in your plan, based on the four-quarter profit-sharing rates. For example, the number of division shares you are assigned will decrease if your division rate increased because of added profit, and they will increase if your division lost profit. The intent, of course, is to cancel the influence of the event and allow the profit-sharing rate to reflect normal changes in business operations.

Summary

The 3M Management Profit-Sharing Compensation system has and continues to:

- Focus management attention on profits and the effective use of assets,
- Provide a measure of variable compensation,
- Allow managers to participate in the growth and decline of the profits of their division, group, and the company.

If there are any questions still unanswered, you should contact your manager, your Human Resource Manager, or the Compensation Department.

YOUR TURN:

J. MARTIN GAMES: COSTING OUT AN INDIVIDUAL INCENTIVE SYSTEM

A competitor to GTM Toys has decided to implement an individual incentive plan to improve productivity. As a first step in this process, the company hired an industrial engineer to do time studies for the three assembler positions involved in assembling the Dunk-it Basketball Game. General descriptions of the three positions follow:

Position 1: Remove basketball hoop and miniature backboard from feeder lines and attach hoop to backboard with available screws.

Position 2: Remove net from number 2 feeder line and attach to hoop.

Position 3: Assemble Dunk-it Basketball Game box and enclose foam rubber basketball and assembled hoop.

Time studies indicate that each of the jobs should take an allotted time (with allowance for fatigue and other contingencies) (see Exhibit 1). Current pay and productivity for the three position incumbents is also available (see Exhibit 2).

What is the likely response of the three position incumbents if they are put on a straight piecework schedule as noted in Exhibit 1 and they continue to perform at the level noted in Exhibit 2?

EXHIBIT 1   Time Study

Position	Allotted Time (minutes, seconds)		Established Standard (units/hour)
1	–0–	45	80
2	–0–	36	100
3	–0–	54	66

EXHIBIT 2   Productivity and Wage Data

Position	Incumbent	Wages/Hour	Units/Hour
1	Arnold	$7.50	71
2	Ramirez	$7.50	88
3	Friedman	$7.50	59

Subjective Performance Evaluation and Merit Pay

Chapters 8 and 9 covered the merits of pay-for-performance plans. A key element of these plans is some measure of performance. Sometimes this measure is objective and quantifiable. Certainly, when we are measuring performance for a group incentive plan, objective financial measures may be readily available. As we move down to the level of the individual and the team, these "hard" measures are not as readily available. This chapter discusses in more detail the difficulties of measuring performance, particularly when we use subjective procedures.

THE ROLE OF PERFORMANCE APPRAISAL IN COMPENSATION DECISIONS

By the year 2000 employees may have between 10 to 15 percent of their pay determined by their level of performance. This is up from 5 percent in 1980 and 6.8 percent in 1991.[1] If we also add in other forms of compensation tied to performance (group performance and company performance), another 10 to 15 percent of total compensation depends on some accurate measure of performance.[2] This emphasis on performance and effective use of human resources is further evident in the continuing emphasis on total quality management. One of the major requirements for winning the Baldridge Award, the superbowl of quality recognition, is effective measurement of performance.[3]

At times, measurement of performance can be quantifiable. Indeed, some good estimates suggest between 13 (hourly workers) and 70 percent of the time (managerial employees) employee performance is tied to these quantifiable measures.[4] Just because something is quantifiable, though, doesn't mean it is an objective measure of performance. As any accounting student knows, financial measures are arrived at through a process that involves some subjective decision making. Which year we choose to take write-offs for plant closings, for example, affects the bottom line reported to the public. Such potential for subjectivity has led some experts to warn that so-called objective data can be deficient and not tell the whole story.[5] Despite these concerns, most HR professionals probably would prefer to work with objective data. Sometimes, though, objective performance standards are not feasible. Either job output is not readily quantifiable or the components that are quantifiable do not reflect important job dimensions. A secretarial job could be reduced to words per minute and errors per page of typing. But many secretaries, and their supervisors, would argue this captures only a small portion of the job. Courtesy in greeting clients and in answering phones, initiative in solving problems without running to the boss, dependability under deadlines—all of these intangible qualities can make the difference between a good and a poor secretary. Such subjective goals are less easily measured. The end result, all too often, is a performance appraisal process that is plagued by errors.

---

[1] Amanda Bennett, "Paying Workers to Meet Goals Spreads, but Gauging Performance Proves Tough," *The Wall Street Journal*, June 7, 1990, pp. B1, B8.

[2] Ibid.

[3] Towers Perrin, *1991 Survey of Top HR Goals* (New York: Towers Perrin, 1991).

[4] Susan E. Jackson, Randall S. Schuler, and J. Carlos Rivero, "Organizational Characteristics as Predictors of Personnel Practices," *Personnel Psychology* 42 (1989) pp. 727–86.

[5] Robert L. Cardy and Gregory H. Dobbins, *Performance Appraisal: Alternative Perspectives* (Cincinnati: Southwestern Publishing, 1994).

Perhaps the biggest attack against appraisals in general, and subjective appraisals in particular, comes from top names in the total quality management area. Edward Deming, the grandfather of the quality movement here and in Japan, launched an attack of appraisals because, he contended, the work situation (not the individual) is the major determinant of performance.[6] Variation in performance arises many times because employees don't have necessary information, technology or control to adequately perform their jobs.[7] Further, Deming argued, individual work standards and performance ratings rob employees of pride and self-esteem.

Rather than throwing out the entire performance appraisal process, some experts argue we should apply total quality management principles to improving the performance appraisal process.[8] A first step, of course, is recognition that part of performance is influenced more by the work environment and system than by employee behaviors. For example, sometimes when students say the dog ate my paper (1990s version, the computer ate my disk) . . . it really happened. When we tell teachers, or other raters, that the system sometimes does control performance, raters are more sympathetic (i.e., rate higher).[9]

A second step in this direction, one that involves most of the remainder of this chapter, concerns identifying strategies to understand and measure job performance better. This may help us reduce the number and types of rating errors illustrated in Exhibit 10.1.

COMMON ERRORS IN APPRAISING PERFORMANCE

Suppose you supervised 1,000 employees. How many would you expect to rate at the highest level? How many would be average or below? If you're tempted to argue the distribution should look something like a normal curve, you might get an A in statistics, but fail Reality 101. One survey of 1,816 organizations reported the following distribution of performance ratings (shown in Exhibit 10.2) for its managers.

Now, we might argue that managers got to that organization level because they are better than average performers.[10] So, of course they rate mostly average or better in their jobs. But the truth is, as raters we tend to make mistakes. Our

---

[6] W. E. Deming, *Out of the Crisis* (Cambridge, MA: MIT Press, 1986).

[7] David Waldman, "The Contributions of Total Quality Management to a Theory of Work Performance," *Academy of Management Review* 19 (1994) pp. 510–36.

[8] David Antonioni, "Improve the Performance Management Process before Discontinuing Performance Appraisals," *Compensation and Benefits Review*, May–June 1994, pp. 29–37.

[9] R. L. Cardy, C. L. Sutton, K. P. Carson, and G. H. Dobbins, "Degree of Responsibility: An Empirical Examination of Person and System Effects on Performance Ratings," Paper presented at the national meeting of the Academy of Management, San Francisco, 1990.

[10] Compflash, "Top Performers? Most Managers Rated Average or Better," *Compflash* (Saranac Lake, NY: American Management Association, 1992), p. 3.

EXHIBIT 10.1   Common Errors in the Appraisal Process

Halo error	An appraiser giving favorable ratings to all job duties based on impressive performance in just one job function. For example, a rater who hates tardiness rates a prompt subordinate high across all performance dimensions *exclusively because of this one characteristic.*
Horn error	The opposite of a halo error. Downgrading an employee across all performance dimensions *exclusively because of poor performance on one dimension.*
First impression error	Developing a negative (positive) opinion of an employee early in the review period and allowing that to negatively (positively) influence all later perceptions of performance.
Recency error	The opposite of first impression error. Allowing performance (either good or bad) at the end of the review period to play too large a role in determining an employee's rating for the entire period.
Leniency error	Consistently rating someone higher than is deserved.
Severity error	The opposite of leniency error. Rating someone consistently lower than is deserved.
Central tendency error	Avoiding extremes (both high and low) in ratings across employees.
Clone error	Giving better ratings to individuals who are like the rater in behavior and/or personality.
Spillover error	Continuing to downgrade an employee for performance errors in prior rating periods.

ratings differ from what would occur if we could somehow, in a moment of clarity, divine truth. We make errors in ratings. Recognizing and understanding the errors noted in Exhibit 10.1 are the first steps to communicating and building a more effective appraisal process.

Not surprisingly, the potential for errors causes employees to lose faith in the performance appraisal process. One poll, in fact, found that 30 percent of employees believed their performance appraisals were ineffective. Employees, quite naturally, will be reluctant to have pay systems tied to such error-ridden

EXHIBIT 10.2   Ratings of Managers

Rating	Percent of Managers Receiving This Rating
Above average	46.4%
Average	49.0%
Below average	4.6%

performance ratings. At the very least, charges that the evaluation process is political will abound.[11] To counter such problems, companies and researchers alike have expended considerable time and money to identify ways performance ratings can be improved.

STRATEGIES TO BETTER UNDERSTAND AND MEASURE JOB PERFORMANCE

Early research to understand and measure job performance centered on identifying the best appraisal format. If only the ideal format could be found, so the argument goes, raters would use it to measure job performance better, that is, make more accurate ratings. More recent attention has focused less on the rating format and more on the raters themselves. One branch of this work identifies possible categories of raters (e.g., supervisor, peers, subordinates, self) and asks if the roles each assumes in the firm lead to more or less accurate ratings. The second branch of this research about raters attempts to identify how raters process information about observed job performance and translate it into performance ratings. Such information, including an understanding of the role irrelevant information plays in the evaluation of employees, may yield strategies to reduce the flaws in the total process. Finally, data also suggest that raters can be trained to increase the accuracy of their ratings. The following sections discuss each of these different approaches to better understand and measure performance.

Strategy One: Improve Appraisal Formats

Types of Formats.   Evaluation formats can be divided into two general categories.[12] In one category are all ranking procedures. *Ranking formats* require the rater to compare employees against each other to determine the relative ordering of the group on some performance measure (usually some measure of overall performance). Exhibit 10.3 illustrates three different methods of ranking employees.

The *straight ranking procedure* is just that: Employees are ranked relative to each other. *Alternation ranking* recognizes that raters are better at ranking people at extreme ends of the distribution. Raters are asked to indicate the best employee and then the worst employee. Working at the two extremes permits a rater to get more "practice" prior to making the harder distinctions in the vast middle ground of employees. Finally, the *paired comparisons ranking* method simplifies the ranking process by forcing raters to make ranking judgments about only discrete pairs of people. Each individual is compared separately with all

---

[11] Clinton Longnecker, Henry Sims, and Dennis Gioia, "Behind the Mark: The Politics of Employee Appraisal," *Academy of Management Executive* 1, no. 3 (1987), pp. 183–93.

[12] Daniel Ilgen and Jack Feldman, "Performance Appraisal: A Process Focus," *Research in Organizational Behavior* 5 (1983), pp. 141–97.

EXHIBIT 10.3 Three Ranking Formats

Straight Ranking Method

Rank		Employee's Name
Best	1.	_____
Next Best	2.	_____
Next Best	3.	_____

Alternation Ranking

Rank		Employee's Name
Best performer	1.	_____
Next best	2.	_____
Next best	3.	_____
Etc.	4.	_____
Next worst	3.	_____
Next worst	2.	_____
Worst performer	1.	_____

(Alternate identifying best performer, then worst performer, best of those left then worst of those left, etc.)

Paired Comparison Ranking Method

	John	Pete	Sam	Tom	Number of Times Ranked Higher
Bill	x	x	x	x	4
John		x	x	x	3
Pete			x	x	2
Sam				x	1

x indicates the person in the row who is ranked higher than the person in the column. The highest ranking goes to person with most "ranking wins."

others in the work group. The person who "wins" the most paired comparisons is ranked top in the group, and so on. Unfortunately, as the size of the work group goes above 10 to 15 employees, the number of paired comparisons becomes unmanageable.

The second category of appraisal formats involves ratings, rather than rankings, of employees. In general, rating forms are more popular than ranking systems.[13]

The various *rating formats* share two underlying commonalities. First, in contrast to ranking formats, rating formats require raters to evaluate employees

---

[13] Cardy and Dobbins, *Performance Appraisal: Alternative Perspectives.*

on some absolute standard rather than relative to other employees. Second, each performance standard has attached to it a measurement scale indicating varying levels of performance on that dimension. Appraisers rate employees by checking the point on the scale that best represents the appraisee's performance level. Possible performance variation is described along a continuum from good to bad. The types of descriptors used in anchoring this continuum provide the major difference in rating scales. These descriptors include adjectives, behaviors, and outcomes. When adjectives are used as anchors, the format is called a *standard rating scale.* Exhibit 10.4 shows a typical rating scale with adjectives as anchors (well above average to well below average).

When behaviors are used as anchors, a second type of rating scale results: behaviorally anchored rating scales (BARS). Although there are variants on this scale and small differences in construction and explanation (e.g., behavioral observation scale, behavioral expectation scale), BARS seems to be the most common behavioral format. By anchoring scales with concrete behaviors, firms adopting a BARS format hope to make evaluations less subjective. When raters try to decide on a rating, they have a common definition (in the form of a behavioral example) for each of the performance levels. This directly addresses a major criticism of standard rating scales: Different raters carry with them into the rating situation different definitions of the scale levels (e.g., different raters have different ideas about what "average work" is). Appendix 10–A illustrates a behaviorally anchored rating scale.

Overall performance is calculated as some weighted average (weighted by the importance the organization attaches to each dimension) of the ratings on all dimensions. The appendixes to this chapter give examples of rating scales and the total appraisal form for some well-known organizations. As a brief illustration, though, consider Exhibit 10.5.

The employee evaluated in Exhibit 10.5 is rated slightly above average. An alternative method for obtaining an overall rating is to allow the rater discretion in rating both performance on the individual dimensions and in assigning an overall evaluation. In this case, the weights from the far right column of Exhibit

Exhibit 10.4   Rating Scales Using Absolute Standards

Standard Rating Scale with Adjective Anchors					
Communications skills: Written and oral ability to clearly and convincingly express thoughts, ideas, or facts in individual or group situations					
Circle the number that best describes the level of employee performance	1	2	3	4	5
	Well above average	Above average	Average	Below average	Well below average

EXHIBIT 10.5   An Example of Employee Appraisal

Employee: Kelsey T. Mahoney

Job Title: Supervisor, Shipping and Receiving

Performance Dimension	Dimension Rating					Dimension Weight
	Well Below Average 1	*Below Average* 2	*Average* 3	*Above Average* 4	*Well Above Average* 5	
Leadership ability				X		0.2 (× 4) = 0.8
Job knowledge					X	0.1 (× 5) = 0.5
Work output				X		0.3 (× 4) = 1.2
Attendance			X			0.2 (× 3) = 0.6
Initiative			X			0.2 (× 3) = 0.6

Sum of rating × weight = 3.7

Overall rating = 3.7

10.5 would not be used and the overall evaluation would be based on a subjective and internal assessment by the rater.

In addition to adjectives and behaviors, outcomes also are used as a standard. The most common form is management by objectives (MBO). Management by objectives is both a planning and appraisal tool that has many different variations across firms.[14] As a first step, organization objectives are identified from the strategic plan of the company. Each successively lower level in the organizational hierarchy is charged with identifying work objectives that will support attainment of organizational goals. Exhibit 10.6 illustrates a common MBO objective. Notice that the emphasis is on outcomes achieved by employees. At the beginning of a performance review period, the employee and supervisor discuss performance objectives (column 1).[15] Months later, at the end of the review period, the two again meet to record results formally (of course, multiple informal discussions should have occurred before this time). Results are then compared against objectives, and a performance rating is then determined based on how well objectives were met.

---

[14] Mark L. McConkie, "A Clarification of the Goal Setting and Appraisal Processes in MBO," *Academy of Management Review* 4, no. 1 (1979), pp. 29–40.

[15] Ibid.

EXHIBIT 10.6   Example of MBO Objective for Communications Skill

1. Performance Objective	*2. Results*
By July 1 of this year, Pat will complete a report summarizing employee reactions to the new performance appraisal system. An oral presentation will be prepared and delivered to all nonexempt employees in groups of 15 to 20. All oral presentations will be completed by August 31, and reactions of employees to this presentation will average at least 3.0 on a 5-point scale.	Written report completed by July 1. All but one oral presentation completed by August 31. Last report not completed until September 15 because of unavoidable conflicts in vacation schedules. Average rating of employees (reaction to oral presentation) was 3.4, exceeding minimum expectations.

A review of firms using MBO indicates generally positive improvements in performance for both individuals and the organization. This performance increase is accompanied by managerial attitudes toward MBO that become more positive over time, particularly when the system is revised periodically to reflect feedback of participants. Managers are especially pleased with the way that MBO provides direction to work units, improves the planning process, and increases superior/ subordinate communication. On the negative side, MBO appears to require more paperwork and increases both performance pressure and stress.[16]

Exhibit 10.7 shows some of the common components of an MBO format and the percentage of experts who judge this component vital to a successful evaluation effort.

A final type of appraisal format does not easily fall into any of the categories yet discussed. In an *essay* format, supervisors answer open-ended questions in essay form describing employee performance. Since the descriptors used could range from comparisons with other employees to the use of adjectives describing performance, types of behaviors, and goal accomplishments, the essay format can take on characteristics of all the formats discussed previously.

Evaluating Performance Appraisal Formats.   Appraisal formats are generally evaluated against five criteria: (1) employee development potential (amount of feedback about performance that the form offers), (2) administrative ease, (3) personnel research potential, (4) cost, and (5) validity. Admittedly, different

---

[16] J. S. Hodgson, "Management by Objectives: The Experiences of a Federal Government Department," *Canadian Public Administration* 16, no. 4 (1973), pp. 422–31.

EXHIBIT 10.7   Components of a Successful MBO Program

	Total Number of Responses*	Percentage of Authorities in Agreement
1. Goals and objectives should be specific.	37	97%
2. Goals and objectives should be defined in terms of measurable results.	37	97
3. Individual goals should be linked to overall organization goals.	37	97
4. Objectives should be reviewed "periodically."	31	82
5. The time period for goal accomplishment should be specified.	27	71
6. Wherever possible, the indicator of the results should be quantifiable; otherwise, it should be at least verifiable.	26	68
7. Objectives should be flexible; changed as conditions warrant.	26	68
8. Objectives should include a plan of action for accomplishing the results.	21	55
9. Objectives should be assigned priorities of weights.	19	50

* In this table the total number of responses actually represents the total number of authorities responding; thus, percentages also represent the percentage of authorities in agreement with the statements made.

Source: Mark L. McConkie, "A Clarification of the Goal Setting and Appraisal Process in MBO," *Academy of Management Review* 4, no. 1 (1979), pp. 29–40. © 1979, Academy of Management Review.

organizations attach different weights to these dimensions. For example, a small organization in its formative years is likely to be very cost conscious. A large organization with pressing affirmative action commitments might place relatively high weight on validity and nondiscrimination and show less concern about cost issues. A progressive firm concerned with employee development might demand a format allowing substantial employee feedback. Other organizations might be concerned solely with costs. These criteria are explained below.[17]

Employee Development Criterion.   Does the method communicate the goals and objectives of the organization? Is feedback to employees a natural outgrowth of the evaluation format, so that employee developmental needs are identified and can be attended to readily?

Administrative Ease Criterion.   How easily can evaluation results be used for administrative decisions concerning wage increases, promotions, demotions, terminations, and transfers? Comparisons among individuals for personnel action require some common denominator for comparison. Typically this is a numerical

---

[17] Bruce McAfee and Blake Green, "Selecting a Performance Appraisal Method," *Personnel Administrator* 22, no. 5 (1977), pp. 61–65.

rating of performance. Evaluation forms that do not produce numerical ratings cause administrative headaches.

Personnel Research Criterion.   Does the instrument lend itself well to validating employment tests? Can applicants predicted to perform well be monitored through performance evaluation? Similarly, can the success of various employees and organizational development programs be traced to impacts on employee performance? As with the administrative criterion, though, evaluations typically need to be quantitative to permit the statistical tests so common in personnel research.

Cost Criterion.   Does the evaluation form require a long time to develop initially? Is it time-consuming for supervisors to use in rating their employees? Is it expensive to use? All of these factors increase the format cost.

Validity Criterion.   By far the most research on formats in recent years has focused on reducing error and improving accuracy. Success in this pursuit would mean that decisions based on performance ratings (e.g., promotions, merit increases) could be made with increased confidence. In general, the search for the "perfect format" to eliminate rating errors and improve accuracy has been unsuccessful. The high acclaim, for example, accompanying the introduction of BARS has not been supported by research.[18]

Exhibit 10.8 is a "report card" on the five most common rating formats relative to the criteria just discussed.

Which of these appraisal formats is the "best"? Unfortunately, the answer is a murky "it depends." Keely suggests that the choice of an appraisal format is dependent on the type of tasks being performed.[19] He argues that tasks can be ordered along a continuum from those that are very routine in nature to those for which the appropriate behavior for goal accomplishment is very uncertain. In Keeley's view, different appraisal formats require assumptions about the extent to which correct behavior for task accomplishment can be specified. The choice of an appraisal format requires a matching of formats with tasks that meet the assumptions for that format. At one extreme of the continuum are behavior-based evaluation procedures that define specific performance expectations against which employee performance is evaluated. Keeley argues behaviorally anchored rating scales fall into this category. The behavioral anchors specify

---

[18] H. John Bernardin, "Behavioral Expectation Scales v. Summated Ratings: A Fairer Comparison," *Journal of Applied Psychology* 62 (1977), pp. 422–27; H. John Bernardin, Kim Alvares, and C. J. Cranny, "A Recomparison of Behavioral Expectation Scales to Summated Scales," *Journal of Applied Psychology* 61 (1976), pp. 284–91; C. A. Schriesheim and U. E. Gattiker, "A Study of the Abstract Desirability of Behavior-Based v. Trait-Oriented Performance Rating," *Proceedings of the Academy of Management* 43 (1982), pp. 307–11; F. S. Landy and J. L. Farr, "Performance Rating," *Psychological Bulletin* 87 (1980), pp. 72–107.

[19] Michael Keeley, "A Contingency Framework for Performance Evaluation," *Academy of Management Review* 3 (July 1978), pp. 428–38.

EXHIBIT 10.8 An Evaluation of Performance Appraisal Formats

	Employee Development Criterion	Administration Criterion	Personnel Research Criterion	Economic Criterion	Validity Criterion
Ranking	Poor—ranks typically based on overall performance, with little thought given to feedback on specific performance dimensions.	Poor—comparisons of ranks across work units to determine merit raises are meaningless. Other administrative actions similarly hindered.	Average—validation studies can be completed with rankings of performance.	Good—inexpensive source of performance data. Easy to develop and use in small organizations and in small units.	Average—good reliability but poor on rating errors, especially halo.
Standard rating scales	Average—general problem areas identified. Some information on extent of developmental need is available, but no feedback on necessary behaviors/outcomes.	Average—ratings valuable for merit increase decisions and others. Not easily defended if contested.	Average—validation studies can be completed, but level of measurement contamination unknown.	Good—inexpensive to develop and easy to use.	Average—content validity is suspect. Rating errors and reliability are average.
Behaviorally anchored rating scales	Good—extent of problem and behavioral needs are identified.	Good—BARS good for making administrative decisions. Useful for legal defense because job relevant.	Good—validation studies can be completed and measurement problems on BARS less than many other criterion measures.	Average—expensive to develop but easy to use.	Good—high content validity. Some evidence of interrater reliability and reduced rating errors.
Management by objectives	Excellent—extent of problem and outcome deficiencies are identified.	Poor—MBO not suited to merit income decisions. Level of completion and difficulty of objectives hard to compare across employees.	Poor—nonstandard objectives across employees and no overall measures of performance make validity studies difficult.	Poor—expensive to develop and time-consuming to use.	Excellent—high content validity. Low rating errors.
Essay	Unknown—depends on guidelines or inclusions in essay as developed by organization or supervisors.	Poor—essays not comparable across different employees considered for merit or other administrative actions.	Poor—no quantitative indices to compare performance against employment test scores in validation studies.	Average—easy to develop but time-consuming to use.	Unknown—unstructured format makes studies of essay method difficult.

performance expectations representing different levels of performance possible by an employee. Only for highly routine, mechanistic tasks is it appropriate to specify behavioral expectations. For these routine tasks it is possible to identify the single sequence of appropriate behaviors to accomplish a goal. Consequently, it is possible to identify behavioral anchors for a performance scale that illustrate varying levels of attainment of the proper sequence of activities.

However, when tasks become less routine, it becomes more difficult to specify a single sequence of procedures that must be followed to accomplish a goal. Rather, multiple strategies are both feasible and appropriate to reach a final goal. Under these circumstances, Keeley argues the appraisal format should focus on evaluating the extent to which the final goal can be specified.[20] Thus, for less certain tasks an MBO strategy would be appropriate. As long as the final goal can be specified, performance can be evaluated in relation to that goal without specifying or evaluating the behavior used to reach that goal. The focus is exclusively on the degree of goal accomplishment.

At the other extreme of the continuum are tasks that are highly uncertain in nature. A relatively low consensus exists about the characteristics of successful performance. Moreover, the nature of the task is so uncertain it may be difficult to specify expected goals. For this type of task, Keeley argues that judgment-based evaluation procedures—as exemplified by standard rating scales—may be most appropriate. Raters make subjective estimates about the levels of employee performance on tasks for which neither the appropriate behavior nor the final goal are well specified. The extent of this uncertainty makes this type of appraisal very subjective and may well explain why trait-rating scales are openly criticized for the number of errors that result in inaccurate performance evaluations.

Strategy Two: Select the Right Raters

A second way that firms have tried to improve the accuracy of performance ratings is to focus on who might conduct the ratings and which of these sources is more likely to be accurate.

Supervisors as Raters. Who rates employees? Some estimates indicate more than 80 percent of the input for performance ratings comes from supervisors.[21] There is good reason why supervisors play such a dominant role. Supervisors assign (or jointly determine) what work employees are to perform. This makes a supervisor knowledgeable about the job and the dimensions to be rated. Also, supervisors frequently have considerable prior experience in rating employees, thus giving them some pretty firm ideas about what level of performance is required for any given level of performance rating. Supervisor ratings also tend

---

[20] Ibid.

[21] Jackson, Schuller, and Rivero, "Organizational Characteristics as Predictors of Personnel Practices."

to be more reliable than those from other sources.[22] On the negative side, though, supervisors are particularly prone to halo and leniency errors.[23]

Peers as Raters.   One of the major strengths of using peers as raters is that they work more closely with the ratee and probably have an undistorted perspective of typical performance, particularly in group assignments (as opposed to what a supervisor might observe in a "causal" stroll around the work area). Balanced against this positive are at least two powerful negatives. First, peers may have little or no experience in conducting appraisals, leading to rather mixed evidence about the reliability of this rating source. Second, in a situation where teamwork is promoted, placing the burden of rating ones peers or coworkers can either create group tensions (in the case of low evaluations) or yield ratings second only to self-ratings in level of leniency.[24] Motorola, one of the leaders in the use of teams and in peer ratings, reports that peer ratings helps team members exert pressure on fellow workers to perform better.[25]

Self as Rater.   Some organizations have experimented with self-ratings. Obviously, self-ratings are done by someone who has the most complete knowledge about the ratee's performance! Unfortunately, though, self-ratings are generally more lenient and possibly more unreliable than ratings from other sources.[26] One compromise in the use of self-ratings is to use them for developmental rather than administrative purposes. Increasingly firms are asking employees to rate themselves, as the first step in the actual appraisal process. Forcing employees to think about their performance in advance may lead to more realistic assessments, ones that are also more in tune with a supervisor's own perceptions.

Customers as Raters.   This is the decade of the customer. The drive for quality means more companies are recognizing the importance of customers. One logical outcome of this increased interest is ratings from customers. For example, Burger King surveys its customers, sets up 800 numbers to get feedback, and hires mystery customers to order food and report back on the service and treatment they receive. Increasingly we can expect the boundaries between organizations and the outside world to fade. While much of the customer-rating movement is directed at performance of business units, we can expect some of this to distill down to individual workers.

---

[22] E. Pulakos and W. Borman, *Developing the Basic Criterion Scores for Army-Wide and MOS-Specific Ratings* (Alexandria, VA: U.S. Army Research Institute, 1986).

[23] F. S. Landy and J. L. Farr, "Performance Rating," *Psychological Bulletin* 87 (1980), pp. 72–107.

[24] M. M. Harris and J. Schaubroeck, "A Meta Analysis of Self-Supervisor, Self-Peer and Peer-Supervisor Ratings," *Personnel Psychology* 4 (1988), pp. 43–62.

[25] Personal communication.

[26] Harris and Schaubroeck, "A Meta Analysis of Self-Supervisor, Self-Peer and Peer-Supervisor Ratings."

Strategy Three: Understand Why Raters Make Mistakes

A third way to improve job performance ratings is to understand how raters think. When we observe and evaluate performance, what else influences ratings besides an employee's performance? We know, for example, that feelings, attitudes, and moods influence raters. If your supervisor likes you, independent of how well you perform, you are likely to get better ratings.[27] Your boss's general mood also influences performance ratings. Hope for a rater who is generally cheerful rather than grumpy; it could influence how you are evaluated![28]

Researchers continue to explore how raters process information about the performance of the people they rate. In general, we think the following kinds of processes occur. First, the rater observes behavior of a ratee. Second, the rater encodes this behavior as part of a total picture of the ratee (i.e., one way of saying that the rater forms stereotypes). Third, the rater stores this information in memory, which is subject to both short and long term decay. Simply put, they forget things! Fourth, when it comes time to evaluate a ratee, the rater reviews the performance dimensions and retrieves stored observations/impressions to determine their relevance to the performance dimensions. Finally, the information is reconsidered and integrated with other available information as the rater decides on the final ratings.[29] Quite unintentionally, this process can produce information errors and they can occur at any stage.

Errors in the Rating Process.   Ideally raters should notice only performance-related factors when they observe employee behavior. In fact all of the processing stages should be guided by *performance relevancy*. Unless a behavior (or personality trait) affects performance it should not influence performance ratings! Fortunately, studies show that performance actually does play an important role, perhaps the major role, in determining how a supervisor rates a subordinate.[30]

---

[27] R. L. Cardy and G. H. Dobbins, "Affect and Appraisal Accuracy: Liking as an Integral Dimension in Evaluating Performance," *Journal of Applied Psychology* 71 (1986), pp. 672–78.

[28] G. Alliger and K. J. Williams, "Affective Congruence and the Employment Interview," in *Advances in Information Processing in Organizations,* vol. 4, ed. J. R. Meindl, R. L. Cardy, and S. M. Puffer (Greenwich, CT: JAI Press), pp. 31–44.

[29] Landy and Farr, "Performance Rating"; A. S. Denisi, T. P. Cafferty, and B. M. Meglino, "A Cognitive View of the Performance Appraisal Process: A Model and Research Propositions," *Organizational Behavior and Human Performance* 33 (1984), pp. 360–96; Jack M. Feldman, "Beyond Attribution Theory: Cognitive Processes in Performance Appraisal," *Journal of Applied Psychology* 66, no. 2 (1981), pp. 127–48; W. H. Cooper, "Ubiquitous Halo," *Psychological Bulletin* 90 (1981), pp. 218–44.

[30] Leo Leventhal, Raymon Perry, and Philip Abrami, "Effects of Lecturer Quality and Student Perception of Lecturer Experience on Teacher Ratings and Student Achievement," *Journal of Educational Psychology* 69, no. 4 (1977), pp. 360–74; Angelo Denisi and George Stevens, "Profiles of Performance, Performance Evaluations, and Personnel Decisions," *Academy of Management* 24, no. 3 (1981), pp. 592–602; Wayne Cascio and Enzo Valenzi, "Relations among Criteria of Police Performance," *Journal of Applied Psychology* 63, no. 1 (1978), pp. 22–28; William Bigoness, "Effects of Applicant's Sex, Race, and Performance on Employer Performance Ratings: Some Additional Findings," *Journal of Applied Psychology* 61, no. 1 (1976), pp. 80–84; Dorothy

Employees who are technically proficient and who do not create problems on the job tend to receive higher ratings than others who score lower on these dimensions.[31] On the negative side, though, performance-irrelevant factors appear to influence ratings, and they cause errors in the evaluation process.[32]

Errors in Observation (Attention).   Generally, researchers have varied three types of input information to see what raters pay attention to when they are collecting information for performance appraisals. First, it appears that raters are influenced by general appearance characteristics of the ratees. Males are rated higher than females (other things equal). A female ratee is observed, not as a ratee, but as a female ratee. A rater may form impressions based on stereotypic beliefs about women rather than the reality of the work situation. The gender of the ratee influences performance ratings quite apart from any performance information. Interestingly, it seems that females are only rated less accurately when the rater has a traditional view of women's "proper" role. Raters with nontraditional stereotypes of "women's place" are not prone to such errors.[33] Race also matters in performance ratings. Blacks (whites) are rated higher when the rater is of the same race.[34] In general, if supervisors see ratees as similar to themselves, there is a positive influence on performance ratings, independent of actual performance.[35]

Researchers also look at change in performance over time to see if this influences performance ratings. Both the pattern of performance (performance gets better vs. worse over time) and the variability of performance (consistent vs. erratic) influence performance ratings, even when the overall level of perfor-

---

P. Moore, "Evaluating In-Role and Out-of-Role Performers, *Academy of Management Journal* 27, no. 3 (1984), pp. 603–18; and W. Borman, L. White, E. Pulakos, and S. Oppler, "Models of Supervisory Job Performance Ratings," *Journal of Applied Psychology* 76, no. 6 (1991), pp. 863–72.

[31] Ibid.

[32] H. J. Bernardin and Richard Beatty, *Performance Appraisal: Assessing Human Behavior at Work* (Boston: Kent Publishing, 1984).

[33] G. Dobbins, R. Cardy, and D. Truxillo, "The Effects of Purpose of Appraisal and Individual Differences in Stereotypes of Women on Sex Differences in Performance Ratings: A Laboratory and Field Study," *Journal of Applied Psychology* 73, no. 3, (1988), pp. 551–58.

[34] Edward Shaw, "Differential Impact of Negative Stereotyping in Employee Selection," *Personnel Psychology* 25 (1972), pp. 333–38; Benson Rosen and Thomas Jurdee, "Effects of Applicant's Sex and Difficulty of Job on Evaluations of Candidates for Managerial Positions," *Journal of Applied Psychology* 59 (1975), pp. 511–12; Gail Pheterson, Sara Kiesler, and Philip Goldberg, "Evaluation of the Performance of Women as a Function of their Sex, Achievement, and Personal History," *Journal of Personality and Social Psychology* 19 (1971), pp. 114–18; W. Clay Hamner, Jay Kim, Lloyd Baird, and William Bigoness, "Race and Sex as Determinants of Ratings by Potential Employers in a Simulated Work Sampling Task," *Journal of Applied Psychology* 59, no. 6 (1974), pp. 705–11; Neal Schmitt and Martha Lappin, "Race and Sex as Determinants of the Mean and Variance of Performance Ratings," *Journal of Applied Psychology* 65, no. 4 (1980), pp. 428–35.

[35] D. Turban and A. Jones, "Supervisor-Subordinate Similarity: Types, Effects and Mechanisms," *Journal of Applied Psychology* 2, no. 73 (1988), pp. 228–34.

mance is controlled.[36] Workers who start out high in performance and then get worse are rated lower than workers who remain consistently low.[37] Not surprisingly, workers whose performance improves over time are seen as more motivated, while those who are more variable in their performance are tagged as lower in motivation. All of us have seen examples of workers (and students) who intuitively recognize this type of error and use it to their advantage. The big surge of work at the end of an appraisal period is often designed to "color" a raters perceptions.

Errors in Storage and Recall.   Research suggests that raters store information in the form of traits.[38] More importantly, people also tend to recall information in the form of trait categories. For example, a rater observes a specific behavior, for example, an employee resting during work hours. The rater stores this information not as the specific behavior, but rather in the form of a trait, such as "that worker is lazy." Specific instructions to recall information about the ratee, as for a performance review, elicit the trait—lazy. Further, in the process of recalling information, a rater may remember events that didn't actually occur, simply because they are consistent with the trait category.[39] The entire rating process then, may be heavily influenced by trait categories that the rater adopts, regardless of their accuracy!

Errors in storage and recall also appear to arise from memory decay. At least one study indicates that rating accuracy is a function of the delay between performance and subsequent rating. The longer the delay, the less accurate the ratings.[40] Some research suggests that memory decay can be avoided if raters

---

[36] Denisi and Stevens, "Profiles of Performance, Performance Evaluations, and Personnel Decisions"; William Scott and Clay Hamner, "The Influence of Variations in Performance Profiles on the Performance Evelution Process: An Examination of the Validity of the Criterion," *Organizational Behavior and Human Performance* 14 (1975), pp. 360–70; Edward Jones, Leslie Rock, Kelly Shaver, George Goethals, and Laurence Ward, "Pattern of Performance and Ability Attributions: An Unexpected Primacy Effect," *Journal of Personality and Social Psychology* 10, no. 4 (1968), pp. 317–40.

[37] B. Gaugler and A. Rudolph, "The Influence of Assessee Performance Variation on Assessor's Judgments," *Personnel Psychology* 45 (1992), pp. 77–98.

[38] Landy and Farr, "Performance Rating"; Bernardin and Beatty, *Performance Appraisal: Assessing Human Behavior at Work.*

[39] N. Cantor and W. Mischel, "Traits v. Prototypes: The Effects on Recognition and Memory," *Journal of Personality and Social Psychology* 35 (1977), pp. 38–48; R. J. Spiro, "Remembering Information from Text: The 'State of Schema' Approach," in *Schooling and the Acquisition of Knowledge,* ed. R. C. Anderson, R. J. Spiro, and W. E. Montague (Hillsdale, CA: Erlbaum Assoc., 1977); T. K. Srull and R. S. Wyer, "Category Accessibility and Social Perception: Some Implications for the Study of Person Memory and Interpersonal Judgments," *Journal of Personality and Social Psychology* 38 (1980), pp. 841–56.

[40] Robert Heneman and Kenneth Wexley, "The Effects of Time Delay in Rating and Amount of Information Observed on Performance Rating Accuracy," *Academy of Management Journal* 26, no. 4 (1983), pp. 677–86.

keep a diary, and record information about employee performance as it occurs.[41]

Errors in the Actual Evaluation.   The context of the actual evaluation process also can influence evaluations.[42] Several researchers indicate that the purpose of an evaluation affects the rating process.[43] For example, performance appraisals sometimes serve a political end. Supervisors have been known to deflate performance to send a signal to an employee, You're not wanted here.[44]

If the purpose of evaluation is to divide up a fixed pot of merit increases, ratings also tend to be less accurate. Supervisors who know ratings will be used to determine merit increases are less likely to differentiate among subordinates than when the ratings will be used for other purposes.[45] Being required to provide feedback to subordinates about their ratings also yields less accuracy than a secrecy policy.[46] Presumably anticipation of an unpleasant confrontation with the angry ratee "persuades" the rater to avoid confrontation. How? By giving ratings which are higher than justified.

TRAINING RATERS TO RATE MORE ACCURATELY

Although there is some evidence that training is not effective,[47] or is less important in reducing errors than other factors,[48] most research indicates rater training is an effective method to reduce appraisal errors.[49] Rater-training pro-

---

[41] B. P. Maroney and R. M. Buckely, "Does Research in Performance Appraisal Influence the Practice of Performance Appraisal? Regretfully Not," *Public Personnel Management* 21 (1992), pp. 185–96.

[42] Robert Liden and Terence Mitchell, "The Effects of Group Interdependence on Supervisor Performance Evaluations," *Personnel Psychology* 36, no. 2 (1983), pp. 289–99.

[43] See, for example, Dobbins, Cardy, and Truxillo, "The Effects of Purpose of Appraisal and Individual Differences in Stereotypes of Women on Self Differences in Performance Ratings."

[44] G. R. Ferris and T. A. Judge, "Personnel/Human Resource Management: A Political Influence Perspective," *Journal of Management* 17 (1991), pp. 1–42.

[45] Winstanley, "How Accurate are Performance Appraisals?"; Landy and Farr, "Performance Rating"; Heneman and Wexley, "The Effects of Time Delay in Rating and Amount of Information Observed on Performance Rating Accuracy."

[46] Cummings and Schwab, *Performance in Organizations.*

[47] H. J. Bernardin and E. C. Pence, "Effects of Rater Training: Creating New Response Sets and Decreasing Accuracy," *Journal of Applied Psychology* 6 (1980), pp. 60–66.

[48] Sheldon Zedeck and Wayne Cascio, "Performance Appraisal Decision as a Function of Rater Training and Purpose of the Appraisal," *Journal of Applied Psychology* 67, no. 6 (1982), pp. 752–58.

[49] H. J. Bernardin and M. R. Buckley, "Strategies in Rater Training," *Academy of Management Review* 6, no. 2 (1981), pp. 205–12; D. Smith, "Training Programs for Performance Appraisal: A Review," *Academy of Management Review* 11, no. 1 (1986), pp. 22–40; B. Davis and M. Mount, "Effectiveness of Performance Appraisal Training Using Computer Assisted Instruction and Behavioral Modeling," *Personnel Psychology* 3 (1984), pp. 439–52; H. J. Bernardin, "Effects of Rater Training on Leniency and Halo Errors in Student Ratings of Instructors," *Journal of Applied Psychology* 63, no. 3 (1978), pp. 301–8; J. M. Ivancevich, "Longitudinal Study of the Effects of Rater Training on Psychometric Error in Ratings," *Journal of Applied Psychology* 64, no. 5 (1979), pp. 502–8.

grams can be divided into three distinct categories:[50] (1) *Rater-error training*, in which the goal is to reduce psychometric errors (e.g., leniency, severity, central tendency, halo) by familiarizing raters with their existence; (2) *performance dimension training* exposes supervisors to the performance dimensions to be used in rating; and (3) *performance-standard training* provides raters with a standard of comparison or frame of reference for making appraisals. Several generalizations about ways to improve rater training can be summarized from this research. First, straightforward lecturing to ratees (the kind we professors are notorious for!) about ways to improve the quality of their ratings generally is ineffective. Second, individualized or small group discussion sections are more effective in conveying proper rating procedures. Third, when these sessions are combined with extensive practice and feedback sessions, rating accuracy significantly improves. Fourth, longer training programs (more than 2 hours) generally are more successful than shorter programs. Fifth, performance-dimension training and performance-standard training (as explained above) generally work better than rater-error training, particularly when they are combined. Finally the greatest success has come from efforts to reduce halo errors and improve accuracy. Leniency errors are the most difficult form of error to eliminate. This shouldn't be surprising! Think about the consequences to a supervisor of giving inflated ratings versus accurate or even deflated ratings. The latter two courses are certain to result in more complaints and possibly reduced employee morale. The easy way out is to artificially inflate ratings.[51] Unfortunately, this positive outcome for supervisors may come back to haunt them—with everyone receiving relatively high ratings there is less distinction between truly good and poor performers. Obviously, it is also harder to pay for real performance differences.

PUTTING IT ALL TOGETHER: THE PERFORMANCE EVALUATION PROCESS

A good performance evaluation doesn't begin on the day of the performance interview. We outline here some of the key elements in the total process, from day one, that make for a good outcome in the appraisal process.[52] First, we need a sound basis for establishing the performance appraisal dimensions and scales associated with each dimension. Performance dimensions should be relevant to the strategic plan of the company. If innovation of new products is key to success, we'd better have something in our performance dimensions that assesses individual performance. And these performance dimensions also should reflect what employees are expected to do in their jobs, that is, their job descriptions. If the job descriptions include nothing on quality (admittedly an unlikely event), the appraisal should not measure quality. Second, we need to involve employees in every stage of developing performance dimensions and building scales to

---

[50] Bernardin and Buckley, "Strategies in Rater Training."

[51] Longnecker, Sims, and Gioia, "Behind the Mask: The Politics of Employee Appraisal."

[52] Robert Heneman, *Merit Pay: Linking Pay Increases to Performance Ratings* (Reading, MA: Addison-Wesley, 1992).

EXHIBIT 10.9   Tips on Appraising Employee Performance

Preparation for the Performance Interview
1. Keep a weekly log of individual's performance. Why?
    A. It makes the task of writing up the evaluation simpler. The rater does not have to strain to remember six months or a year ago.
    B. It reduces the chances of some rating errors (e.g., recency, halo).
    C. It gives support/backup to the rating.
2. Preparation for the interview should *not* begin a week or two before it takes place. There should be continual feedback to the employee on his/her performance so that (*a*) problems can be corrected before they get out of hand, (*b*) improvements can be made sooner, and (*c*) encouragement and support are ongoing.
3. Allow sufficient time to write up the evaluation. A well-thought-out evaluation will be more objective and equitable. Sufficient time includes (*a*) the actual time necessary to think out and write up the evaluation, (*b*) time away from the evaluation, and (*c*) time to review and possibly revise.
4. Have employees fill out an appraisal form prior to the interview. This prepares employees for what will take place in the interview and allows them to come prepared with future goal suggestions, areas they wish to pursue, and suggestions concerning their jobs or the company.
5. Set up an agreed-upon, convenient time to hold the interview (at least one week in advance). Be sure to pick a nonthreatening day.
6. Be prepared!
    A. Know what you are going to say. Prepare an outline (which includes the evaluation and future goal suggestions).
    B. Decide on developmental opportunities *before* the interview. Be sure you know of possible resources and contacts.
    C. Review performance interview steps.
7. Arrange the room in such a way as to encourage discussion.
    A. Do not have barriers between yourself and the employee (such as a large desk).
    B. Arrange with secretary that there be no phone calls or interruptions.

Performance Appraisal Interview (Steps)
1. Set the subordinate at ease. Begin by stating the purpose of the discussion. Let the individual know that it will be a two-way process. Neither superior nor subordinate should dominate the discussion.
2. Give a general, overall impression of the evaluation.
3. Discuss each dimension separately. Ask the employee to give his/her impression on own performance first. Then explain your position. If there is a problem on some, try *together* to determine the cause. When exploring causes, urge the subordinate to identify three or four causes. Then, jointly determine the most important ones. Identifying causes is important because it points out action plans which might be taken.
4. Together, develop action plans to correct problem areas. These plans will flow naturally from the consideration of the causes. Be specific about the who, what, and when. Be sure to provide for some kind of follow-up or report back.
5. Close the interview on an optimistic note.

Exhibit 10.9   *(concluded)*

Communication Technique Suggestions
1. Do not control the interview—make it two-way. Do this by asking open-ended questions rather than submitting your own solutions. For example, rather than saying, "Jim, I'd like you to do these reports over again," it would be better to say, "Jim, what sort of things might we do here?" Avoid questions that lead to one-word responses.
2. Stress behaviors and results rather than personal traits. Say, "I've noticed that your weekly report has been one to two days late in the last six weeks," rather than, "You tend to be a tardy, lazy person."
3. Show interest and concern. Instead of saying, "Too bad, but we all go through that," say, "I think I know what you're feeling. I remember a similar experience."
4. Allow the subordinate to finish a sentence or thought. This includes being receptive to the subordinate's own ideas and suggestions. For example, rather than saying, "You may have something there, but let's go back to the real problem," say, "I'm not certain I understand how that relates to this problem. Why don't you fill me in on it a bit more?"

These last four suggestions emphasize problem analysis rather than appraisal. Of course, appraisal of past performance is a part of problem analysis, but these suggestions should lead to a more participative and less defensive subordinate role. These suggestions will also help improve creativity in problem solving. The subordinate will have a clearer understanding of why and how he/she needs to change work behavior. There should be a growth of climate of cooperation, which increases motivation to achieve performance goals.

measure how well they perform on these dimensions. Third, we need to make sure raters are trained in use of the appraisal system and that all employees understand how the system operates and what it will be used for. Fourth, we need to make sure raters are motivated to rate accurately. One way to achieve this is to ensure that managers are rated on how well they utilize and develop human resources. A big part of this is evaluation and feedback to employees. Fifth, raters should maintain a diary of employee performance, both as documentation and to jog the memory.[53] This will help ensure that supervisors are knowledgeable about subordinate performance.[54] Sixth, raters should attempt a performance diagnosis to determine in advance if performance problems arise because of motivation, skill deficiency, or external environmental constraints[55]; this process in turn tells the supervisor whether the problem requires motivation building, training, or efforts to remove external constraints. Seventh, the actual appraisal process should follow the guidelines outlined in Exhibit 10.9. At a minimum this should include:

---

[53] A. DeNisi, T. Robbins, and T. Cafferty, "Organization of Information Used for Performance Appraisals: Role of Diary-Keeping," *Journal of Applied Psychology* 74, no. 1, (1989), pp. 124–29.

[54] F. J. Landy, J. L. Barnes, and K. R. Murphy, "Correlates of Perceived Fairness and Accuracy of Performance Evaluations," *Journal of Applied Psychology* 63 (1978), pp. 751–54.

[55] Snell and Wexley, "Performance Diagnosis: Identifying the Causes of Poor Performance."

1. Genuine participation between superior and subordinate in the appraisal process—not unilateral "discussion."
2. Supervisors and their employees working together as a team to achieve results.
3. Goal setting to focus work efforts and provide a basis for comparison of results to goals.
4. Focused discussions about job performance and ways to improve it.
5. Minimal criticism, with focus on the future and strategies to achieve future goals.
6. Developmental goals designed to help correct perceived performance deficiencies.[56]

EQUAL EMPLOYMENT OPPORTUNITY AND PERFORMANCE EVALUATION

Equal employment opportunity (EEO) and affirmative action have influenced HR decision making for almost 30 years now. While there are certainly critics of these programs, at least one important trend can be traced to the civil rights vigil in the workplace. Specifically, EEO has forced organizations to document employment decisions and to ensure they are firmly tied to performance or expected performance. Nowhere is this more apparent than in the performance appraisal area. Performance appraisals are subject to the same scrutiny as employment tests. Consider the use of performance ratings in making decisions about promotions. In this context, a performance appraisal takes on all the characteristics of a test used to make an initial employment decision. If employees pass the test (i.e., are rated highly in the performance evaluation process), they are predicted to do well (i.e., have promotion potential) at higher level jobs. This interpretation of performance evaluation as a test, subject to validation requirements, was made in *Brito* v. *Zia Company*.[57] In this case, Zia Company used performance ratings based on a rating format to lay off employees. The layoffs resulted in a disproportionate number of minorities being discharged. The court held that:

> Zia, a government contractor, had failed to comply with the testing guidelines issued by the Secretary of Labor, and that Zia had not developed job-related criteria for evaluating employees' work performance to be used in determining employment promotion and discharges which is required to protect minority group applicants and employees from the discriminatory effects of such failure.[58]

---

[56] Landy et al., "Correlates of Perceived Fairness and Accuracy of Performance Evaluations."
[57] Brito v. *Zia Company,* 478 F.2d 1200 (1973).
[58] Ibid.

Since the *Brito* case, there has been growing evidence that the courts have very specific standards and requirements for performance appraisal.[59] The courts stress six issues in setting up a performance appraisal system.[60]

1. Courts are favorably disposed to appraisal systems that give specific written instructions on how to complete the appraisal. Presumably, more extensive training in other facets of evaluation would also be viewed favorably by the courts.

2. Organizations tend to be able to support their cases better when the appraisal system incorporates clear criteria for evaluating performance. Performance dimensions and scale levels that are written, objective, and clear tend to be viewed positively by courts in discrimination suits.[61] In part, this probably arises because behaviorally oriented appraisals have more potential to provide workers feedback about developmental needs.

3. As pointed out by every basic personnel book ever printed and reinforced by this text, the presence of adequately developed job descriptions provides a rational foundation for all forms of personnel decision making. The courts reinforce this by ruling more consistently for defendants (company) when their appraisal systems are based on sound job descriptions.

4. Courts also approve of appraisal systems that require supervisors to provide feedback about appraisal results to the employees affected. Absence of secrecy permits employees to identify weaknesses and to challenge undeserved appraisals.

5. The courts seem to like evaluation systems that incorporate a review of any performance rating by a higher level supervisor(s).

6. Perhaps most importantly, the courts consistently suggest that the key to fair appraisals depends on consistent treatment across raters, regardless of race, color, religion, sex, and national origin.

The focal question then becomes, Are similarly situated individuals treated similarly? This standard is particularly evident in a recent court case involving perfor-

---

[59] G. L. Lubben, D. E. Thompson, and C. R. Klasson, "Performance Appraisal: The Legal Implications of Title VII," *Personnel* 57, no. 3 (1980), pp. 11–21; H. Field and W. Halley, "The Relationship of Performance Appraisal System Characteristics to Verdicts in Selected Employment Discrimination Cases," *Academy of Management Journal* 25, no. 2 (1982), pp. 392–406; *Albermarle Paper Company* v. *Moody,* U.S. Supreme Court, nos. 74–389 and 74–428, 10 FEP Cases 1181 (1975); also *Moody* v. *Albermarle Paper Company,* 474 F.2d 134.

[60] Feild and Hally, "The Relationship of Performance Appraisal System Characteristics to Verdicts in Selected Employment Discrimination Cases"; Gerald Barrett and Mary Kernan, "Performance Appraisal and Terminations: A Review of Court Decisions since *Brito* v. *Zia* with Implications for Personnel Practices," *Personnel Psychology* 40 (1987), pp. 489–503.

[61] D. Martin and K. Bartol, "The Legal Ramifications of Performance Appraisal: An Update," *Employee Relations* 17, no. 2 (1991).

mance appraisal and merit pay.[62] A black male filed suit against General Motors, claiming race discrimination in both the timing and amount of a merit increase. The court found this case without merit. General Motors was able to show that the same set of rules were applied generally across all individuals.

TYING PAY TO SUBJECTIVELY APPRAISED PERFORMANCE

Think, for a moment, about what it really means to give employees merit increases. Bill Peterson makes $40,000 per year. He gets a merit increase of 5 percent, the approximate average increase over the past few years.[63] Bill's take-home increase (adjusted for taxes) is a measly $27 more than he used to make. Before we console Bill, though, consider Jane Krefting, who is a better performer than Bill, and receives an 8 percent merit increase. Should she be thrilled by this pay for performance differential and motivated to continue as a high achiever? Probably not. After taxes, her paycheck (assuming a base salary similar to Bill's) is only $15 dollars per week more than Bill's check.

The central issue involving merit pay is: How do we get employees to view raises as a reward for performance? Chapter 8 illustrated this difficulty in theoretical terms. Now it is addressed from a pragmatic perspective. Very simply, organizations frequently grant increases that are not designed or communicated to be related to performance. Perhaps the central reason for this is the way merit pay is managed. Many companies view raises not as motivational tools to shape behavior but as budgetary line items to control costs.[64] Frequently this results in pay increase guidelines with little motivational impact. The three pay increase guidelines that particularly lead to low motivation will be discussed briefly before outlining a standard that *attempts* to link pay to performance.[65]

Two types of pay increase guidelines with low-motivation potential provide equal increases to all employees regardless of performance. The first, a general increase, typically is found in unionized firms. A contract is negotiated that specifies an across-the-board (equal) increase for each year of the contract. Similar increases occur because of cost-of-living adjustments (COLA), but these would be triggered by changes in the consumer price index (CPI) (Chapter 17).

The third form of guideline comes somewhat closer to tying pay to performance. Longevity (seniority) increases tie pay increases to a preset progression pattern based on seniority. For example, a pay grade might be divided into 10 equal steps, and employees move to higher steps based on seniority. To the

---

[62] *Payne* v. *General Motors*, 53 Fair Employment Practice Cases (BNA) 471 (D, C, Kan. 1990).

[63] G. Milkovich and C. Milkovich, "Strengthening the Pay-for-Performance Relationship," *Compensation and Benefits Review,* in press.

[64] Ibid.

[65] *Compensating Salaried Employees during Inflation: General vs. Merit Increases,* Report no. 796 (New York: The Conference Board, 1981).

EXHIBIT 10.10   Performance-Based Guideline

	1	2	3	4	5
Performance level	Outstanding	Very satisfactory	Satisfactory	Unsatisfactory	Marginally unsatisfactory
Merit increase	6–8%	5–7%	4–6%	2–4%	0%

extent that performance improves with time on the job, this method has the rudiments of paying for performance.

By far the most prevalent form of pay guideline for exempt employees is one intended to link pay and performance.[66] Invariably this guideline takes one of two forms. The simpler version (Exhibit 10.10) specifies pay increases permissible for different levels of performance.

Increases expressed in the form of ranges may be warranted if the goal is to give supervisors some discretion in the amount of increases. A twist on this guideline would vary the time between increases. Better performers might receive increases every 8 months; the poorest performers might have to wait 15 months to two years for their next increase.

A more complex guideline ties pay not only to performance but also to position in the pay range. Exhibit 10.11 illustrates such a system for a food market firm. The percentages in the cells of Exhibit 10.11 are changed yearly to reflect changing economic conditions. Despite these changes, though, two characteristics remain constant. First, as would be expected in a pay-for-performance system, lower performance is tied to lower pay increases. In fact, in many

EXHIBIT 10.11   Performance Rating Salary Increase Matrix

Position in Range \ Performance Rating	Unsatisfactory	Needs Improvement	Competent	Commendable	Superior
Fourth quartile	0%	0%	4%	5%	6%
Third quartile	0	0	5	6	7
Second quartile	0	0	6	7	8
First quartile	0	2	7	8	9
Below minimum of range	0	3	8	9	10

---

[66] Jackson, Schuller, and Rivero, "Organizational Characteristics as Predictors of Personnel Practices."

organizations, the poorest performers receive no merit increases. The second relationship is that pay increases at a decreasing rate (percentage) as employees move through a pay range. For the same level of performance, employees low in the range receive higher percentage increases than employees who have progressed farther through the range. In part this is designed to forestall the time when employees reach the salary maximum and have salaries frozen. In part, though, it is also a cost-control mechanism tied to budgeting procedures, as discussed in Chapter 15.

Performance- and Position-Based Guidelines

Given a salary increase matrix, merit increases are relatively easy to determine. As Exhibit 10.11 indicates, an employee at the top of a pay grade who receives a "competent" rating would receive a 4 percent increase in base salary. A new trainee starting out below the minimum of a pay grade would receive a 10 percent increase for a "superior" performance rating.

Designing Merit Guidelines

Designing merit guidelines involves answering four questions. First, what should the poorest performer be paid as an increase? Notice that this figure is seldom negative! Wage increases are, unfortunately, considered an entitlement. Wage cuts tied to poor performance are very rare. Most organizations, though, are willing to give no increases to very poor performers.

The second question involves average performers. How much should they be paid as an increase? Most organizations try to ensure that average performers are kept whole (wages will still have the same purchasing power) relative to cost of living. This dictates that the midpoint of the merit guidelines equals the percentage change in the local or national CPI. Following this guideline, the 6 percent increase for an average performer in the second quartile of Exhibit 10.11 would reflect the change in CPI for that area. In a year with lower inflation, all the percentages in the matrix probably would be lower.

Third, how much should the top performers be paid? In part, budgetary considerations (Chapter 15) answer this question. But there is also growing evidence that employees do not agree on the size of increases that they consider meaningful (Chapter 8). Continuation of this research may help determine the approximate size of increases needed to "make a difference" in employee performance.

Finally, matrices can differ in the size of the differential between different levels of performance. Exhibit 10.11 basically rewards successive levels of performance with 1 percent increases (at least in the portion of the matrix in which any increase is granted). A larger jump between levels would signal a stronger commitment to recognizing performance with higher pay increases. Most companies balance this, though, against cost considerations. Larger differentials cost more. When money is tight, this option is less attractive. Exhibit 10.12 shows how a merit grid is constructed when cost constraints (merit budget) are known.

EXHIBIT 10.12   Merit Grids

Merit grids combine 3 variables: level of performance, distribution of employees within their job's pay range, and merit increase percentages.

Example:

1. Assume a performance rating scale of A through D: 30 percent of employees get A, 35 percent get B, 20 percent get C, and 15 percent get D. Change to decimals.

A	B	C	D
.30	.35	.20	.15

2. Assume a range distribution as follows: 10 percent of all employees are in the top (fourth) quartile of the pay range for their job, 35 percent are in the third quartile, 30 percent in second quartile, and 25 percent in lowest quartile. Change to decimals.

1	.10
2	.35
3	.30
4	.25

3. Multiply the performance distribution by the range distribution to obtain the percent of employees in each cell. Cell entries = Performance × Range.

	A	B	C	D
1	.30 × .10 = .03	.35 × .10 = .035	.20 × .10 = .02	.15 × .10 = .015
2	.30 × .35 = .105	.35 × .35 = .1225	.20 × .35 = .07	.15 × .35 = .0525
3	.30 × .30 = .09	.35 × .30 = .105	.20 × .30 = .06	.15 × .30 = .045
4	.30 × .25 = .075	.35 × .25 = .1225	.20 × .25 = .05	.15 × .25 = .0375

   Cell entries tell us that 3 percent of employees are in top quartile of pay range AND received an A performance rating, 10.5 percent of employees are in second quartile of pay range AND received an A performance rating, etc.

4. Distribute increase percentage among cells, varying the percentages according to performance and range distribution, for example, 6 percent to those employees in cell A1, 5 percent to those employees in B1.

5. Multiply increase percentages by the employee distribution for each cell. Sum of all cells should equal the total merit increase percentage.

   Example: 6% × cell A1 = .06 × .03 = .0018
                 5% × cell B1 = .05 × .035 = .00175
                      etc.   _____

   Targeted merit increase percentage = Sum

6. Adjust increase percentage among cells if needed in order to stay within budgeted increase.

PROMOTIONAL INCREASES AS A PAY-FOR-PERFORMANCE TOOL

Let's not forget that firms have methods of rewarding good performance other than raises. One of the most effective is a promotion accompanied by a salary increase, generally reported as being in the 8 to 12 percent range. This method of linking pay to performance has at least two characteristics that distinguish it from traditional annual merit pay increases. First, the very size of the increment is approximately double a normal merit increase. A clearer message is sent to employees, both in the form of money and promotion, that good performance is valued and *tangibly rewarded.* Second, promotion increases represent, in a sense, a return to employees for commitment and exemplary performance over a sustained period of time. Promotions are not generally annual events. They complement annual merit rewards by showing employees that there are benefits to both single-year productivity and to continuation of such desirable behavior.

Summary

The process of appraising employee performance can be both time-consuming and stressful. These costs are compounded if the appraisal system is poorly developed or if a supervisor lacks appropriate training to collect and evaluate performance data. Development of a sound appraisal system(s) requires an understanding of organizational objectives balanced against the relative merits of each type of appraisal system. For example, despite its inherent weaknesses, an appraisal system based on ranking of employee performance may be appropriate in small organizations that, for a variety of reasons, choose not to tie pay to performance. In contrast, a sophisticated MBO appraisal system may not be appropriate for such a company.

Training supervisors effectively to appraise performance requires an understanding of organizational objectives. We know relatively little about the ways in which raters process information and evaluate employee performance. However, a thorough understanding of organizational objectives combined with a knowledge of common errors in evaluation can make a significant difference in the quality of appraisals.

Review Questions

1. LeBoy Corporation manufactures specialty equipment for the auto industry (e.g., seat frames). One job involves operation of machines that form heat-treated metal into various seat shapes. The job is fairly low level and routine. Without any further information, which of the five types of appraisal formats (see Exhibit 10.8) do you think would be most appropriate for this job? Justify your answer.

2. Employees in your department have formed semiautonomous work teams (they determine their own production schedule and individual work assignments). Individual performance is assessed using four performance dimensions: quantity of work, quality of work, interpersonal skills, and teamwork. Should the supervisor have a role in the rating process? What role, if any, should other members of the work team have in the assessment process?

 3. What do you think should be included in the design of a performance appraisal process to lessen the probability that your company would be accused of discrimination in performance appraisal?

4. If you wanted to ensure that employees had good feedback about performance problems and strengths, which appraisal format would you recommend using? Why?

5. Assume that you had one employee fall into each of the cells in Exhibit 10.11 (25 employees in the company). How much would base salary increase in dollars if the current average salary in the company is $15,000? (Assume that ratings are randomly distributed by salary level; you can use $15,000 as your base salary for calculation in each of the cells.)

APPENDIX 10–A

SAMPLE APPRAISAL FORM: OUTOKUMPU AMERICAN BRASS

Ω outokumpu american brass

Salaried Personnel Performance Appraisal

Name			OAB Employee #	OAB Service Date
				Appraisal Date
(Last)	(First)	(MI)		
Location	Function			Department
Classification Title			Pay Grade	Time in present position
				_____ Years _____ Months

Performance Rating (check one)		
A copy of this form is to be provided to the employee upon completion of the appraisal process. Submit the original to the Human Resources Department	Exceeds Standards — 1 ❑ 2 ❑ Meets Standards — 3 ❑ 4 ❑ 5 ❑ Does Not Meet Standards — 6 ❑ 7 ❑	Comment (if any)

Completed by: _____   Employee Signature: _____

Reviewed by: _____   (your signature does not imply agreement)

Job Knowledge:	The ability to effectively understand, utilize and demonstrate technical concepts and operating procedures applicable to all aspects of the job. People differ in the breadth of knowledge across jobs, the depth of knowledge within jobs, and the ability to innovatively use this knowledge to complete tasks.

Exceeds Standards	1	Displays broad knowledge and innovative ability on technical concepts and operating procedures for even the most complex tasks. Most people in the department consider this person the expert on a wide variety of department jobs.
	2	Broad knowledge of technical and operating procedures for all aspects of own and closely related jobs. If you needed to know both standard and alternative procedures for performing any aspect of this job you would think of this person as the source.
Meets Standards	3	Broad knowledge of standard technical and operating procedures for all aspects of own job. If you needed to know existing or alternative procedures for any aspect of this job, this person could be expected to provide correct information.
	4	Generally knowledgeable about all standard technical and operating aspects of own job. Might be expected to occasionally double check procedures with others on the most complex of tasks.
	5	Generally understands standard job components but may not be versed in all the more complex aspects. Wouldn't normally expect others to go to this person for technical and/or operating information because of these knowledge gaps. Would expect this person to go to others for information rather than perform inadequately because of knowledge gaps.
Does Not Meet Standards	6	Technical and/or operating information about some standard aspects of job may be faulty, leading to occasional improper performance of job. May show desire to improve but progress has been minimal thus far.
	7	Regularly makes mistakes because of faulty knowledge on many standard and more complex aspects of job. Shows little sign of improvement despite prior counseling.

Rating:	Documentation of Rating (optional except for 6 and 7):

Interpersonal Skills: The ability to show understanding, support, courtesy, tact and cooperation in interactions with coworkers, subordinates, customers, and visitors. People differ in the extent they are recognized and sought out to show this skill, the frequency and nature of lapses in this skill, and the ability to recognize and correct lapses as they occur.

Exceeds Standards	1	The understanding, support and tact shown by these employees make them the choice for: difficult negotiations with others; reaction to sensitive business ideas; ability to resolve conflict between individuals. Is recognized company-wide for consistency in interpersonal skills.
	2	This person is seen by others as genuinely interested in their welfare. Able to make others feel comfortable when asked to conduct discussions of even the most sensitive and stressful subjects. Is recognized department wide for consistency in interpersonal skills.
Meets Standards	3	This person could be expected to show courtesy, tact and understanding in interactions with coworkers, subordinates, customers and visitors even under sensitive circumstances.
	4	This person occasionally might have lapses in courtesy, tact and understanding in sensitive and stressful situations, but lapses would be confined to internal employees and not customers / visitors. Person could be expected to recognize and seek to repair damage to relationship immediately.
	5	This person occasionally might have lapses in courtesy, tact and understanding, but lapses would be confined to internal employees. Would be expected to seek to repair damage to relationship immediately if recognized.
Does Not Meet Standards	6	Lapses in courtesy, tact and understanding are not uncommon and not confined to just internal employees. Could be expected to attempt to repair damage to relationship, when it is recognized or pointed out. Seems genuinely interested in improving.
	7	Lapses in courtesy, tact and understanding are not uncommon and not confined to just internal employees. Could be expected to show little remorse and not feel damage repair is personal responsibility.

Rating:	Documentation of Rating (optional except for 6 and 7):

Organization and Planning: Ability to systematically make plans and set objectives, structure tasks to achieve objectives, establish priorities and make schedules.		

Exceeds Standards	1	Can be relied upon to have a plan for accomplishing tasks, even when working from unclear directions or vague strategic goals. Plan shows clear recognition of problems and constraints. Tasks have reasonable timeframes and accurately reflect company or supervisory priorities.
	2	Once understands overall responsibilities as explained by supervisor, could be expected to develop a clear plan for tasks to be completed without being prompted. Plan usually shows clear recognition of problems and constraints. Tasks have reasonable timeframes and accurately reflect supervisor's priorities.
Meets Standards	3	Supervisor explains overall responsibilities. Without prompting, this employee could be expected to develop an effective plan of attack with only occasional assistance from supervisor in one or more of the following: defining tasks to be performed, establishing priorities and timeframes, identifying constraints.
	4	Supervisor explains overall responsibilities. Occasionally requires prompting to develop plan for completing tasks. Supervisor provides occasional assistance in: defining tasks to be performed, establishing priorities and timeframes, identifying constraints.
	5	Supervisor explains overall responsibilities. Occasionally requires prompting to develop plan for completing tasks. Supervisor occasionally (on complex tasks) must monitor planning and organizing to ensure no gaps in: defining tasks to be performed, establishing priorities and timeframes, identifying constraints.
Does Not Meet Standards	6	Supervisor explains overall responsibilities and must assist employee in outlining tasks to be performed. Planning and organization still show gaps and possible errors. Employee misses deadlines because of poor plan of attack or prioritization of tasks.
	7	Without direct intervention by supervisor this employee could be expected to work without any clear plan for completing tasks; has only vague ideas about priorities, time tables and constraints.

Rating:	Documentation of Rating (optional except for 6 and 7):

Communications Skills:	Written and oral ability to clearly and convincingly express thoughts, ideas or facts in individual or group situations.

Exceeds Standards	1	Through clarity and logic of communications is able to persuade others to adopt policies and practices, even those which may have been unpopular initially. Makes complex ideas understandable for all levels and types of audiences. Would be a top choice for presenting an unpopular subject to a hostile audience.
	2	Clearly and logically presents ideas in a way that makes even complex subjects easy to grasp for a wide variety of audiences. Frequently is able to persuade others to adopt policies and practices, even those which may have been unpopular initially. Not normally among the first people considered to present an unpopular subject to a hostile audience.
Meets Standards	3	Typically presents ideas clearly and logically without assistance from others. Recognizes when content of message is not understood and is able to reexplain ideas in a different manner to clarify. Communications ability may not have the power to convert unsympathetic listeners.
	4	Ideas are clear and logical, but success may come only after pretesting arguments with others and clarifying content of message. Recognizes when content of message is not understood and usually is able to rephrase in a way that clarifies.
	5	With help of others can develop clear and logical communications. Occasionally, may not be clear when ideas are first presented in casual conversations or in written drafts, but on own or with help, recognizes where message is not understood. Struggles to find ways to clarify message and is usually successful.
Does Not Meet Standards	6	Occasionally unclear in formal presentations and in final papers, either because of failure to seek input from others or because of inability to act upon that input. May not be able to recognize when listeners or readers do not understand message. May not be able to clarify message even when gap in understanding is recognized. Gives appearance of trying to improve these skills.
	7	Frequently unclear in communications of both casual and great importance. Shows little ability or interest in understanding where misunderstanding is or in correcting same.

Rating:	Documentation of Rating (optional except for 6 and 7):

Judgment:	Ability to obtain and evaluate information form all relevant sources. Uses information effectively to arrive at conclusions which are appropriate to the situation.

Exceeds Standards	1	Readily perceives existent or potential problems, collects information relevant to solution from affected sources. Makes effective decisions which reflect sensitivity to Financial, Operating and Human Resource constraints of both short- and long-term nature.
	2	Readily perceives existing problems. Usually able to identify potential problems before they occur. With occasional direction from others is able to identify and obtain information from parties who will be affected by decision. Decisions effective for short-term perspective and usually reflect consideration of long-term concerns.
Meets Standards	3	Good at perceiving existing problems. May need help to identify potential problem areas, but responds quickly when identified. Understands importance of getting input from affected parties, and able to identify many of these sources on own. Usually needs help, though, to identify input sources. Decisions are typically quite good from a short-term perspective and at least reflect consideration of long-term issues.
	4	Responsive to claims by others that potential or current problems exist. Frequently is aware of these concerns on own. Seeks and obtains help in identifying appropriate sources for input information. First pass at problem solution may be incomplete, but is diligent in seeking input from others before errors result. Final decisions are typically good from a short-term perspective and at least reflect consideration of long-term issues.
	5	Responsive to claims by others that potential or current problems exist. Not always perceptive on own, though, that problems exist or are developing. First pass at problem solution may be incomplete, but is diligent in seeking input from others before errors result. Final decisions are acceptable but sometimes not optimal, either in short- or long-term perspective.
Does Not Meet Standards	6	Occasionally fails to recognize existing or potential problems and may let them magnify before acting on advice of others. Once acts, though, can be spurred by others to seek information from some, but not always all, relevant sources. Not always diligent in getting input to final decision. Decisions regularly are unacceptable from short- and/or long-term perspective.
	7	Shows little effort to recognize or deal with problems unless forced by others. Decisions lack input of relevant sources and are usually unacceptable.

Rating:	Documentation of Rating (optional except for 6 and 7):

Initiative-Dependability:	Ability to fulfill responsibilities on time and according to expectations of supervisor. Includes recognition and quality completion of necessary tasks beyond the scope of initial instructions.

Exceeds Standards	1	Recognizes tasks which need to be performed to complete overall mission. Undertakes such tasks, even if beyond initial instructions of supervisor, checking for approval where appropriate. Completes these and other assigned tasks on time, even if efforts beyond the norm are required.
	2	Receives task assignments from supervisor and regularly finds ways to exceed requirements. Completes tasks on time and according to directions of supervisor, even if efforts beyond the norm are required
Meets Standards	3	Receives task assignments from supervisor and occasionally finds ways to exceed requirements. Completes tasks on time and according to directions of supervisor, even if efforts beyond the norm are required.
	4	Receives task assignments from supervisor and occasionally finds ways to exceed requirements. Completes top priority tasks on time, and few modifications are needed. Usually completes less important tasks on time and without reminders. This work may have minor flaws which employee might catch and correct immediately, causing deadline to be narrowly missed. Occasionally exerts efforts beyond those normally required.
	5	Rarely would expect this person to complete tasks beyond those assigned by supervisor. Completes top priority tasks accurately and on time, but occasionally may need to be reminded to do so. Less important tasks are completed, but sometimes reminders are needed when deadlines are drawing close. May leave these tasks to the last minute such that, to meet deadline, minor flaws are not corrected. Corrects flaws immediately when noted. Wouldn't be expected to regularly and willingly exert efforts beyond those normally required.
Does Not Meet Standards	6	Does work assigned but occasionally misses important deadlines, and more often misses lesser deadlines, unless closely supervised. Work regularly does not meet supervisor expectations, but employee can be expected to try to make corrections. Only reluctantly exerts efforts beyond those normally required.
	7	Can not be counted on to meet deadlines except under very close supervision. Employee begrudgingly corrects work if demanded, but errors may still exist. Only works beyond normal hours when directly instructed.

Rating:	Documentation of Rating (optional except for 6 and 7):

Teamwork:		Ability to contribute to group performance, to draw out the best from others, to foster activities building group morale, even under high pressure situations.
Exceeds Standards	1	Seeks out or is regularly requested for group assignments. Groups this person works with inevitably have high performance and high morale. Employee makes strong personal contribution and is able to identify strengths of many different types of group members and foster their participation. Wards off personality conflicts by positive attitude and ability to mediate unhealthy conflicts, sometimes even before they arise. Will make special effort to insure credit for group performance is shared by all.
	2	Seen as a positive contributor in group assignments. Works well with all types of people and personalities, occasionally elevating group performance of others. Good ability to resolve unhealthy group conflicts that flare up. Will make special effort to insure strong performers receive credit due them.
Meets Standards	3	Seen as a positive personal contributor in group assignments. Works well with most types of people and personalities. Is never a source of unhealthy group conflict and will encourage the same behavior in others.
	4	When group mission requires skill this person is strong in, employee seen as strong contributor. On other occasions will not hinder performance of others. Works well with most types of people and personalities and will not be the initiator of unhealthy group conflict. Will not participate in such conflict unless provoked on multiple occasions.
	5	Depending on the match of personal skill and group mission, this person will be seen as a positive contributor. Will not be a hindrance to performance of others and avoids unhealthy conflict unless provoked.
Does Not Meet Standards	6	Unlikely to be chosen for assignments requiring teamwork except on occasions where personal expertise is vital to group mission. Not responsive to group goals, but can be enticed to help when personal appeals are made. May not get along with other members and either withdraw or generate unhealthy conflict. Seeks personal recognition for team performance and/or may downplay efforts of others.
	7	Has reputation for noncontribution and for creating conflicts in groups. Cares little about group goals and is very hard to motivate towards goal completion unless personal rewards are guaranteed. May undermine group performance to further personal aims. Known to seek personal recognition and/or downplay efforts of others.

Rating:	Documentation of Rating (optional except for 6 and 7):

Quantity / Quality: Amount of high quality work completed in a variety of situations relative to expectations.

Exceeds Standards	1	Consistently exceeds expectations in both quality and quantity of work for tasks requiring widely different skills.
	2	Output often exceeds standards and is of the highest quality, even across tasks requiring widely different skills.
Meets Standards	3	Consistently exceeds expectations in both quality and quantity of work for tasks in area of known competence. For tasks requiring developed skill, meets expectations for both quantity and quality.
	4	Consistently meets, and occasionally exceeds, expectations in both quality and quantity of work for tasks in area of known competence. For tasks requiring less developed skills, may initially not meet expectations, but will quickly develop to a satisfactory level.
	5	Meets expectations in quality and quantity of work for tasks in area of known competence. On rare occasions when expectations aren't met initially, employee makes effort to correct problem immediately. For tasks requiring less developed skills, may initially not meet expectations but will quickly develop to a satisfactory level.
Does Not Meet Standards	6	Does not consistently meet expectations in quality and quantity of work for tasks in area of known competence. May attempt to correct problem, but still fall below expectations. Shows little interest and capability to achieve acceptable quantity / quality standards in areas of less developed skills.
	7	Frequently marginally misses quality / quantity expectations on a wide variety of tasks or misses by a wide margin on a few tasks, even after prior counseling.

Rating:	Documentation of Rating (optional except for 6 and 7):

Management of Human Resources:	The ability to effectively select, utilize and develop subordinates. Also requires recognition and compliance with accepted and required personnel policies and procedures. (RATING IN THIS AREA REQUIRED ONLY FOR SUPERVISORY POSITIONS)	
Exceeds Standards	1	Widely recognized in the company as very good at selecting good people, placing them in jobs which utilize their skills effectively, and providing developmental experiences which increase their value to the organization. Is conscientious in keeping current and following accepted and required personnel policies and procedures. Insists on same from subordinates.
	2	Employees within the department would characterize this person as one of the top people in selecting, utilizing and developing subordinates. Complaints by subordinates about treatment rarely occur, and are never traceable to improper behavior by this person. Is conscientious in keeping current and following accepted and required personnel policies and procedures. Insists on same from subordinates.
Meets Standards	3	Good at utilizing and developing better employees. Occasionally has employees who don't meet expectations. Likely to consult HR staff and others for strategies to assist these employees. Such strategies are typically successful. Complaints by subordinates about treatment rarely occur, handled appropriately when they do. Conscientious in keeping current and following accepted and required personnel policies and procedures. Subordinates don't always follow these guides as closely.
	4	Has a mixed group of employees in terms of effectiveness. Is concerned about placement and development and will respond to suggestions if offered, but not particularly proactive except for top subordinates. Complaints by subordinates about treatment are handled quickly and effectively. Few lapses of the same type arise later. Will attempt to comply with accepted and required personnel policies and procedures, but both self and subordinates have occasional lapses which are quickly corrected when pointed out.
	5	Mixed group of employees in terms of effectiveness. Concerned about placement and development and will respond to suggestions offered, but not particularly proactive except for top subordinates. Complaints by subordinates about treatment sometimes follow patterns previously observed, but are handled quickly and usually effectively, at least in short run. Attempts to comply with accepted and required personnel policies and procedures, but both self and subordinates have occasional lapses which are quickly corrected when pointed out.
Does Not Meet Standards	6	Seems concerned about selecting and developing good employees, but is a continuing source of complaints. Shows the same pattern of mistakes over time. Corrects problems with help from HR department, but does not seem to have sense of ways to avoid problem in the future. Lapses in compliance with accepted and required personnel policies and procedures are not uncommon for self and subordinates. Responds, at least in short run, to notification about infractions.
	7	Regularly has complaints from employees about treatment. Will respond only when complaint is voiced and pursued outside department. Not unusual to trace violations of accepted personnel policies and procedures back to this department. Shows little talent and/or motivation for changing treatment of employees.
Rating:	Documentation of Rating (optional except for 6 and 7):	

Performance Against Standards:	The ability to achieve objectives as agreed upon by supervisor and employee. (RATING IN THIS AREA OPTIONAL FOR NONEXEMPT EMPLOYEES)

Exceeds Standards	1	Exceeds expectations on all objectives.
	2	Exceeds expectations on all priority objectives and most remaining objectives. Any problems are generally traceable to external constraints not under control of employee.
	3	Meets or exceeds expectations on all objectives. Exceeds expectations on one, but not all, priority objectives.
Meets Standards	4	Meets expectations on all priority objectives. May occasionally fall below standards on one or a few remaining objectives, but this is balanced against performance exceeding expectations on an equal number of other objectives.
	5	On average, performance meets expectations, but there is variability across objectives. Performance which does not meet standards on one objective is balanced against high performance on another objective of approximately equal importance.
Does Not Meet Standards	6	On average, performance does not meet expectations. Either the employee generally meets standards on most objectives with a few (more than one) sub marginal ratings, or, on average, good performance (exceeds standards) does not balance out occasions of poor performance. Does not meet standards on at least one priority objective.
	7	On average, does not meet standards for a majority of objectives. More than one objective not met.

Rating:	Documentation of Rating (optional except for 6 and 7):

1st Priority Objective and Desired Results (One of top three or four priorities in this business unit)	Actual Results and Comments	Rating (Exceeded, met, not met or deferred)

2nd Priority Objective and Desired Results	Actual Results and Comments	Rating (Exceeded, met, not met or deferred)

3rd Priority Objective and Desired Results	Actual Results and Comments	Rating (Exceeded, met, not met or deferred)

4th Priority Objective and Desired Results	Actual Results and Comments	Rating (Exceeded, met, not met or deferred)

Other Objectives and Desired Results Include here tasks performed but not anticipated at start of plan year	Actual Results and Comments	Rating (Exceeded, met, not met or deferred)

What training programs or other activities will be scheduled to increase this person's job related skills?

Employee Comments (Optional): Employee comments must be reviewed and initialed by all supervisors involved in the process.

Reviewers' Initials: 1. _____   2. _____   3. _____   4. _____

APPENDIX 10–B
SAMPLE APPRAISAL FORM: HEWLETT PACKARD

HEWLETT PACKARD	PLEASE PRINT OR TYPE	
	Date of Evaluation	
	Evaluating Manager	
	Reviewing Manager (Next Level)	

**PERFORMANCE EVALUATION AND
DEVELOPMENT PLAN**

Employee No	Name (Last, First, MI)	Date Hired
Entity and Department	Job Title	Time in Position

TO THE EMPLOYEE:

This evaluation is to let you know how you have performed in the judgement of your managers. You and your manager should discuss, assess, and summarize your performance based upon responsibilities, objectives, and performance factors.

You and your manager should clarify expectations, set objectives, and identify actions you can take to maintain or increase your effectiveness.

1. *RESPONSIBILITIES:* Summarize major responsibilities and specific objectives:

2. *RESULTS:* Describe specific accomplishments since last evaluation.

3. *PERFORMANCE FACTORS:* Explain specific strengths and weaknesses.

You may check *"IMPROVEMENT REQUIRED"* in conjunction with *"MEETS OR EXCEEDS AN ACCEPTABLE LEVEL OF PERFORMANCE"* when the trend of the employee's performance is declining or is approaching unacceptable for the performance factor.

TECHNICAL COMPETENCE/JOB KNOWLEDGE Demonstrates the skills needed to perform the job. Understands the work environment, the job requirements, and the customer needs. Completed assignments with minimum direction.	[ ] Meets or exceeds an acceptable level of performance. Improvement Required [ ] [ ] Unacceptable
EXPLAIN:	

QUALITY Demonstrates a commitment to quality and the quality process. Completes assignments in an accurate and thorough manner. Produces work that meets standards.	[ ] Meets or exceeds an acceptable level of performance. Improvement Required [ ] [ ] Unacceptable
EXPLAIN:	

PRODUCTIVITY Organizes work activities to improve results. Uses resources efficiently and effectively.	[ ] Meets or exceeds an acceptable level of performance. Improvement Required [ ] [ ] Unacceptable
EXPLAIN:	

DEPENDABILITY Completes assigned tasks. Meets schedules and other time commitments. (Include comments on attendance if appropriate.)	[ ] Meets or exceeds an acceptable level of performance. Improvement Required [ ] [ ] Unacceptable
EXPLAIN:	

TEAMWORK Establishes and maintains cooperative and productive work relationships with all employees.	[ ] Meets or exceeds an acceptable level of performance. Improvement Required [ ] [ ] Unacceptable
EXPLAIN:	

JUDGEMENT Demonstrates ability to make well-reasoned and timely decisions that favorably affect work performance.	[ ] Meets or exceeds an acceptable level of performance. Improvement Required [ ] [ ] Unacceptable
EXPLAIN:	

CUSTOMER SATISFACTION Responds actively and sensitively to the needs of internal and external customers.	[ ] Meets or exceeds an acceptable level of performance. Improvement Required [ ] [ ] Unacceptable
EXPLAIN:	

INITIATIVE Demonstrates ability to think and act effectively. Originates new ideas or methods to improve the job or to complete assigned tasks.	[ ] Meets or exceeds an acceptable level of performance. Improvement Required [ ] [ ] Unacceptable
EXPLAIN:	

WORK ENVIRONMENT AND SAFETY Maintains a safe and pleasant work environment, follows safety regulations, and actively contributes to work safety.	[ ] Meets or exceeds an acceptable level of performance. Improvement Required [ ] [ ] Unacceptable
EXPLAIN:	

FLEXIBILITY Responds willingly to changes in procedure, technology, responsibility, or assignment. *(Use if appropriate for this employee.)*	[ ] Meets or exceeds an acceptable level of performance. Improvement Required [ ] [ ] Unacceptable
EXPLAIN:	

PLANNING AND ORGANIZATION Coordinates resources, prioritizes activities, and establishes schedules to complete assignments. Ensures that plans are consistent with overall work group objectives. *(Use if appropriate for this employee.)*	[ ] Meets or exceeds an acceptable level of performance. Improvement Required [ ] [ ] Unacceptable
EXPLAIN:	

4. *PERFORMANCE SUMMARY*

Summarize the employee's overall performance considering responsibilities, results, performance factors and processes used. This summary may reflect how the employee performed against objectives without comparing this performance to others doing similar work.

SUMMARIZE

5. *RELATIVE RANKING*

DATE OF LAST RANKING

Rank indicated below reflects the sustained relative performance and contribution of this employee as compared to other HP employees doing similar work and as compared against management expectations. The annual pay plan will be based on this relative ranking and the employee's ability to sustain this level of performance over the time period of the salary plan.

[ ] PERFORMANCE RANK BAND 5   [ ] UNACCEPTABLE
[ ] PERFORMANCE RANK BAND 4   [ ] NEW TO JOB
[ ] PERFORMANCE RANK BAND 3
[ ] PERFORMANCE RANK BAND 2
[ ] PERFORMANCE RANK BAND 1/ACTION NEEDED

6. *EMPLOYEE COMMENTS:* You are encouraged to add comments to this review. If you need additional space, attach a separate sheet to this form.

SIGNATURES

My signature indicates that my manager and I have discussed this evaluation.

EMPLOYEE	DATE	EVALUATING MANAGER	DATE

This evaluation will not become part of the employee's file until the reviewing manager has signed it.

REVIEWING MANAGER	DATE		

7. DEVELOPMENT PLAN/OBJECTIVES FOR THE COMING YEAR

Establish a development plan and objectives with your employee for the coming year. This plan will include specific actions the employee can take to maintain or increase effectiveness. The objectives are results the employee intends to achieve and are the basis for the next performance evaluation. This section must accompany the performance evaluation in the employee's personnel file.

NAMES AND SIGNATURES

Employee No.	Name (Print or type)		Evaluating Manager (Print or type)	
Employee Signature		Date	Evaluating Manager Signature	Date

YOUR TURN:

POLICY IMPLICATIONS OF MERIT PAY GUIDES

GEMCAR is a manufacturer of decals and hood ornaments for all varieties of American cars. During the past four years, profits have plummeted 43 percent. This decline is attributed to rising costs of production and is widely believed to have triggered the resignation of GEMCAR's longtime president, C. Milton Carol. The newly hired CEO is Winston McBeade, a former vice president of finance and of human resources management at Longtemp Enterprises, a producer of novelty watches. As his first policy statement in office, Mr. McBeade declared a war on high production costs. As his first official act, Mr. McBeade proposed implementing a new merit pay guide (see Exhibits 1 and 2 for former and revised pay guides). What can you deduce about Mr. McBeade's "philosophy" of cost control from both the prior and newly revised merit guides? What implications does this new philosophy have for improving the link between pay and performance and, hence, productivity?

EXHIBIT 1   Merit Pay Guide for Last Year

		Performance				
		Well Below Average	Below Average	Average	Above Average	Well Above Average
	Above Grade Maximum (red circle)	0 — 0	2 — 0	3 — 10	4 — 5	5 — 15
	Q4	0 — 0	3 — 0	4 — 5	5 — 10	6 — 15
Position in Salary Range	Q3	0 — 0	4 — 0	5 — 10	6 — 25	7 — 10
	Q2	2 —	5 — 2	6 — 9	7 — 9	8 — 10
	Q1	2 — 0	6 — 3	7 — 6	8 — 5	9 — 9

Notes: 1. Cost of living rose 5 percent last year.
2. The number at the lower right corner of each cell represents the number of employees falling into that cell during the previous year.

EXHIBIT 2   Revised Pay Guide

		Performance				
		Well Below Average	*Below Average*	*Average*	*Above Average*	*Well Above Average*
	Above grade maximum (red circle)	0	0	0	0	0
	Q4	0	0	2	4	6
Position in Salary Range	Q3	0	0	3	5	7
	Q2	0	0	4	6	8
	Q1	0	0	5	7	9

Note: Cost of living is expected to rise 5 percent this year.

Exhibit IV.1   The Pay Model

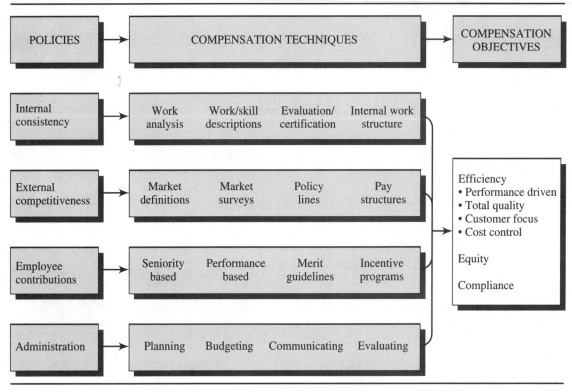

Employee Benefits

Employee benefits is one of the hottest areas in compensation today. The reason is quite simple: We know markedly less about this high-cost area than almost any other subject in compensation. An exaggeration, you say! Think about what we know that is fact, not faith, in the benefits area. Does the pay model (Exhibit IV.1) tell us *how* the administration of employee benefits facilitates organization performance? The answer is unclear. We do know that benefit costs affect the bottom line (admittedly an important measure of organization performance). But what about other design and administrative efforts? Do they complement organization strategy and performance? We don't know. Or do employee benefits affect an organization's ability to attract, retain, and motivate employees? Conventional wisdom says employee benefits can affect retention, but there is little research to support this conclusion. A similar lack of research surrounds each potential payoff of a sound benefits program.

Employee benefits cost over $1 trillion today! Is it any wonder, then, that companies are increasingly paying more attention to this reward component. It represents a labor cost with no apparent returns.

Compounding this problem is the ever present entitlement problem. Employees perceive benefits as a right, independent of individual or company performance. Efforts to reduce benefit levels or eliminate parts of the package altogether always meet with employee resistance and dissatisfaction.

Operating on the assumption that the probable truth about employee benefits is somewhere between these two perspectives, this part of the book takes the position that organizations must control costs of benefits wherever possible and learn to maximize the returns from benefit expenditures. As a first step in this direction, Chapter 11 identifies the issues that organizations face in developing and maintaining a benefits program. A model of the benefits determination process outlines a structure for thinking about employee benefits. Chapter 12 provides a summary of the state of employee benefits today. We hope this will provide the groundwork for innovative and effective benefits packages in the future.

CHAPTER

The Benefits Determination Process

Chapter Outline

What can you do with $1 trillion? Help balance the budget? Buy several copies of this book? Cover the cost of employee benefits in the United States today? It's hard to believe that employee benefits cost this much; it works out to $14,807 per worker in 1993, more than double the 1983 cost of $7,000 per worker.[1] These figures are particularly revealing when we take a peek at what passed as benefits in the not-too-distant past.

- A carriage shop published a set of rules for employees in 1880 that stated, in part:

  Working hours shall be from 7 A.M. to 9 P.M. every day except the Sabbath. . . . After an employee has been with the firm for five years he shall receive an added payment of five cents per day, provided the firm has prospered in a manner to make it possible. . . . It is the bounden duty of each employee to put away at least 10 percent of his monthly wages for his declining years so he will not become a burden upon his betters.

- In 1915 employees in the iron and steel industry worked a standard 60 to 64 hours per week. By 1930 that schedule had been reduced to 54 hours.

- It was not until 1929 that the Blue Cross concept of prepaid medical costs was introduced.

- Prior to 1935 only one state (Wisconsin) had a program of unemployment compensation benefits for workers who lost their jobs through no fault of their own.

- Before World War II very few companies paid hourly employees for holidays. In most companies employees were told not to report for work on holidays and to enjoy the time off, but their paychecks were smaller the following week.

In comparison to these "benefits" from the past, today's reality seems staggering. Exhibit 11.1 illustrates the rapid rise in employee benefit costs, jumping from about 25 percent of payroll costs in 1959 to just over 41 percent today.[2] These average figures vary considerably by industry. Department stores are on the low end, paying benefits averaging only 30 percent of payroll.[3] The chemical industry is on the high end, with benefits averaging 45 percent of payroll.[4] By any standard, though, benefits represent a huge cost for the private sector. As a tangible example of the cost to industry, General Motors estimates that it pays more for employee medical benefits alone than it does for all the steel necessary to produce its yearly output of automobiles![5]

Over one 20-year period (1955–1975), employee benefit costs rose at a rate almost four times those of employee wages or the CPI.[6] A similar comparison

---

[1] U.S. Chamber of Commerce, *Employee Benefits, 1993* (Washington, DC: U.S. Chamber of Commerce, 1994).

[2] Ibid.

[3] Ibid.

[4] Ibid.

[5] Hallie Kintner and Ernest B. Smith, "General Motors Provides Health Care Benefits to Millions," *American Demographics,* May 1987, pp. 44–45.

[6] John Hanna, "Can the Challenge of Escalating Benefits Costs Be Met?" *Personnel Administration* 27, no. 9 (1977), pp. 50–57.

Exhibit 11.1   Changes in Benefit Costs: 1959, 1969, 1990, 1993

	1959	*1969*	*1990*	*1993*
Percentage of payroll (total)	24.7	31.1	38.4	41.3
Legally required benefits	3.5	5.3	8.8	8.7
Pension, insurance, and other agreed upon payments	8.5	10.4	15.9	18.3
Rest periods and lunch breaks	2.2	3.1	2.4	2.3
Payment for time not worked (holidays, vacations, etc.)	8.4	10.1	10.5	10.4
Miscellaneous	2.1	2.2	0.8	1.6

Note: Costs are reported as a percentage of payroll.
Source: Adapted from U.S. Chamber of Commerce Annual Benefits Surveys.

for the period 1964–1987 shows that the rate of growth has slowed (benefit costs rose only twice as fast as wage costs), but organizations still express extreme concern for controlling the cost of benefits.[7] Experts agree that this concern is legitimate, and the problem is expected to worsen. The aging of the work force alone could add billions to the cost of pensions and medical care. The ratio of retired people to workers is currently 20 per 100. By 2050 this number will jump to 38 per 100![8] Before exploring ways to rationally plan and administer benefits programs in a cost-effective manner, we outline the reasons for this growth in employee benefits in the next section.

WHY THE GROWTH IN EMPLOYEE BENEFITS?

Wage and Price Controls

During both World War II and the Korean War, the federal government instituted strict wage and price controls. The compliance agency charged with enforcing these controls was relatively lenient in permitting reasonable increases in benefits. With strict limitations on the size of wage increases, both unions and employers sought new and improved benefits to satisfy worker demands.

Unions

The climate fostered by wage and price controls created a perfect opportunity for unions to flex the muscles they had recently acquired under the Wagner Act of 1935. Several National Labor Relations Board rulings during the 1940s

---

[7] U.S. Chamber of Commerce, *Employee Benefits, 1993.*
[8] E. Davis and M. K. Krouze, "A Maturing Benefit: Eldercard after a Decade," *Employee Benefits Journal* 19, no. 3 (1994), pp. 16–19.

conferred legitimacy upon negotiations over employee benefits. Absent the leverage to raise wages very much, unions fought for the introduction of new benefits and the improvement of existing benefits. Success on this front during the war years led to further postwar demands. Largely through the efforts of unions, most notably the auto and steelworkers, several benefits common today were given their initial impetus: pattern pension plans, supplementary unemployment compensation, extended vacation plans, and guaranteed annual wage plans.[9]

Employer Impetus

It would be a mistake to assume that the war years provided the only incentive fostering a receptive benefits climate. In fact, many of the benefits in existence today were provided at employer initiative. Much of this employer receptivity can be traced to pragmatic concerns about employee satisfaction and productivity. Rest breaks often were implemented in the belief that fatigue increased accidents and lowered productivity. Savings and profit sharing plans (e.g., Procter & Gamble's profit sharing plan initiated in 1885) were implemented to improve performance and provide increased security for worker retirement years. Indeed, many employer-initiated benefits were designed to create a climate in which employees perceived that management was genuinely concerned for their welfare.

Cost-Effectiveness of Benefits

Another important impetus for the growth of employee benefits is their cost effectiveness in three situations. The first cost advantage is that most employee benefits are not taxable. Provision of a benefit rather than an equivalent increase in wages avoids payment of federal and state personal income tax. Remember, though, that recurrent tax reform proposals continue to threaten the favorable tax status granted to many benefits. Already there has been one minor casualty, with the Deficit Reduction Act (Defra) of 1984 limiting the types of benefits that can be included in cafeteria or flexible benefit plans (e.g., no parking fees paid, limits on vacation homes). Obviously, taxation of any or all of these benefits would reduce or eliminate their advantage over allocating the corresponding amount to direct wages.

A second cost-effectiveness component of benefits arises because many group-based benefits (e.g., life, health, and legal insurance) can be obtained at a lower rate than could be obtained by employees acting on their own. Group insurance also has relatively easy qualification standards, giving security to a set of employees who might not otherwise qualify (e.g., an employee with a heart condition who becomes eligible for group life insurance at a nonprohibitive rate after being denied individual insurance).

---

[9] Robert W. McCaffery, *Managing the Employee Benefits Program* (New York: American Management Association, 1983).

Third, a well-conceived benefits plan that meets employee needs may yield advantages far beyond the dollar cost. In an economic sense, if the utility of the cash value of a benefit is less than the utility of the benefit itself, the organization is better off providing the benefit.

Government Impetus

Obviously, the government has played an important role in the growth of employee benefits. Three employee benefits are mandated by either the state or federal government: worker's compensation (state), unemployment insurance (federal), and Social Security (federal). In addition, most other employee benefits are affected by such laws as the Employee Retirement Income Security Act (ERISA—affects pension administration) and various sections of the Internal Revenue Code.

THE VALUE OF EMPLOYEE BENEFITS

Exhibit 11.2 shows the relative importance that employees attached to different types of benefits across three different studies.[10]

Exhibit 11.2   Ranking of Employee Benefits

	Study		
	1	*2*	*3*
Medical	1	1	3
Pension	2	3	8
Paid vacation and holidays	3	2	—
Sickness	4	—	5
Dental	5	—	6
Profit sharing	6	—	2
Long-term disability	7	—	7
Life insurance	8	—	4

Note: Dashes indicate that the item was not rated.

---

[10] This table was compiled from three different sources. Some of the reward components rated in some of the studies were not traditional employee benefits and have been deleted from the rankings here. The three studies were "The Future Look of Employee Benefits," *The Wall Street Journal* September 8, 1988, p. 23 (Source: Hewitt Associates); Kermit Davis, William Giles, and Hubert Feild, *How Young Professionals Rank Employee Benefits: Two Studies* (Brookfield, WI: International Foundation of Employee Benefit Plans, 1988); Kenneth Shapiro and Jesse Sherman, "Employee Attitude Benefit Plan Designs," *Personnel Journal*, July 1987, pp. 49–58.

In general, the three studies reported in Exhibit 11.2 show fairly consistent results. For example, medical payments regularly are listed as one of the most important benefits employees receive. These rankings take on added significance when we note that health care costs are the most rapidly growing and the most difficult to control of all the benefit options offered by employers.[11] Since 1980 medical care costs have risen 169 percent, totaling $2,851 per employee for insurance premiums in 1993.[12]

These costs would not seem nearly so outrageous if we had evidence that employees place high value on the benefits they receive. Unfortunately, there is evidence that employees frequently are not even aware of, or undervalue, the benefits provided by their organization. For example, in one study employees were asked to recall the benefits they received. The typical employee could recall less than 15 percent of them! In another study, MBA students were asked to rank order the importance attached to various factors influencing job selection.[13] Presumably, the large percentage of labor costs allocated to payment of employee benefits would be partially justified if benefits turned out to be an important factor in attracting good MBA candidates. Of the six factors ranked, employee benefits received the lowest ranking. Opportunity for advancement (1), salary (2), and geographic location (3) all ranked considerably higher than benefits as factors influencing job selection. Compounding this problem, these students also were asked to estimate the percentage of payroll spent on employee benefits. Slightly less than one half (46 percent) of the students thought that benefits represented 15 percent or less of payroll. Nine of 10 students (89 percent) thought benefits accounted for less than 30 percent of payroll. Only 1 in 10 students had a reasonably accurate or inflated perception of the magnitude of employee benefits.[14]

The ignorance about the value of employee benefits inferred from those studies is further accompanied by complacency. Benefits are taken for granted. Employees view them as a right with little comprehension of, or concern for, employer costs.[15]

One possible salvation from this money pit comes from reports that employees are not necessarily looking for more benefits, but rather greater choice in

---

[11] Mary Fruen and Henry DiPrete, "Health Care in the Future" (Boston, MA: John Hancock, 1986); HRM Update, "Health Plan Increases" (New York: The Conference Board, May 1988); Kintner and Smith, "General Motors Provides Health Care Benefits to Millions"; Health Research Institute, "1985 Health Care Cost Containment Survey"; North West National Life Insurance Co., "Ten Ways to Cut Employee Benefit Costs" (1988).

[12] U.S. Chamber of Commerce, *Employee Benefits, 1993.*

[13] Richard Huseman, John Hatfield, and Richard Robinson, "The MBA and Fringe Benefits," *Personnel Administration* 23, no. 7 (1978), pp. 57–60.

[14] Ibid.

[15] Foegen, "Are Escalating Employee Benefits Self-Defeating?" *Pension World* 14, no. 9 (September 1978).

the benefits they receive.[16] In fact, up to 70 percent of employees in one study indicated they would be willing to pay more out of pocket for benefits if they were granted greater choice in the design of their own benefits package. This leads us to the issues of benefits planning, design, and administration. All three offer an opportunity to improve benefits effectiveness.

KEY ISSUES IN BENEFITS PLANNING, DESIGN, AND ADMINISTRATION

Benefits Planning and Design Issues

First, and foremost, the benefits planning process must address this vital question: What is the relative role of benefits in a total compensation package?[17] For example, if a major compensation objective is to attract good employees, we need to ask: What is the best way to achieve this? The answer is not always, nor even frequently, Let's add another benefit. Consider a company that needs to fill some entry-level jobs that pay minimum wage. One temptation might be to set up a day care center to attract more mothers with preschool children. Certainly this is a popular response today, judging from all the press that day care needs are receiving. A more prudent compensation policy would ask the question: Is day care the most effective way to achieve my compensation objective? Sure, day care may be popular with working mothers. But can the necessary workers be attracted to the company using some other compensation tool that better meets company goals?

As a second example, how do we deal with undesirable turnover? We might be tempted to design a benefits package that improves progressively with seniority, thus providing a reward for continuing service. This would only be the preferred option, though, if other compensation tools (e.g., increasing wages, introducing incentive compensation) are less effective.

In addition to integrating benefits with other compensation components, the planning process also should include strategies to ensure external competitiveness and adequacy of benefits. Competitiveness requires an understanding of what other firms in your product and labor markets offer as benefits. Firms conduct benefits surveys much as they conduct salary surveys. Either our firm must have a package comparable to that of survey participants, or there should be a sound justification of why deviation makes sense for the firm.

In contrast, ensuring that benefits are adequate is a somewhat more difficult task. Adequacy is defined by the financial liability of employees with and without a particular benefit (e.g., employee medical expenses with and without medical

---

[16] Employee Benefit Research Institute, *America in Transition: Benefits for the Future* (Washington, DC: EBRI, 1987).

[17] Jerry Rosenbloom and G. Victor Hallman, *Employee Benefit Planning* (Englewood Cliffs, NJ: Prentice Hall, 1991).

expense benefits). There is no magic formula for defining benefits adequacy.[18]
In part, the answer must be tempered by the relationship between benefits
adequacy and the third plan objective: cost of effectiveness. More organizations
need to consider whether employee benefits are cost justified. All sorts of ethical
questions arise when we start asking this question. How far should we go with
elder care? Can we justify a $250,000 operation that will likely buy only a few
months more of life? Companies face these impossible questions when they build
a benefits administration system.

Benefits Administration Issues

Three major administration issues arise in setting up a benefits package: (1) Who
should be protected or benefited? (2) How much choice should employees have
among an array of benefits? (3) How should benefits be financed?[19]

Every organization has a variety of employees with different employment
statuses. Should these individuals be treated equally with respect to benefits
coverage? Exhibit 11.3 illustrates that companies do indeed differentiate treatment based on employment status. For example, part-timers receive, proportionately, far fewer benefits than do full-time employees.

As a second example, should retired automobile executives be permitted to
continue purchasing cars at a discount price, a benefit that could be reserved
solely for current employees? In fact, a whole series of questions needs to
be answered:

1. What probationary periods (for eligibility of benefits) should be used
   for various types of benefits? Does the employer want to cover
   employees and their dependents more or less immediately upon
   employment or provide such coverage for employees who have
   established more or less "permanent" employment with the employer?
   Is there a rationale for different probationary periods with different
   benefits?
2. Which dependents of active employees should be covered?
3. Should retirees (as well as their spouses and perhaps other
   dependents) be covered, and for which benefits?
4. Should survivors of deceased active employees (and/or retirees) be
   covered? And if so, for which benefits? Are benefits for surviving
   spouses appropriate?
5. What coverage, if any, should be extended to employees who are
   suffering from disabilities?

---

[18] M. Meyer, *Profile of Employee Benefits,* Report no. 813 (New York: The Conference Board,
1981), p. 2.

[19] Rosenbloom and Hallman, *Employee Benefit Planning,* pp. 427–31.

EXHIBIT 11.3   Benefits Comparison: Part-Timers versus Full-Timers

	Percent of Firms Giving Benefits to			
	Part Timers		Full Timers	
Benefit	1990	1993	1990	1993
All benefits	17.0%	28%	100%	100%
Health	22.0	22	99	97
Retirement	31.6	37	85	83
Vacation	33.2	37	98	98

Source: U.S. Chamber of Commerce, *Employee Benefits, 1993* (Washington, DC: U.S. Chamber of Commerce, 1994).

6. What coverage, if any, should be extended to employees during layoff, leaves of absence, strikes, and so forth?

7. Should coverage be limited to full-time employees?[20]

The answers to these questions depend on the policy decisions regarding adequacy, competition, and cost effectiveness discussed in the last section.

The second administrative issue concerns choice (flexibility) in plan coverage. In the standard benefits package, employees typically have not been offered a choice among employee benefits. Rather, a package is designed with the "average" employee in mind and any deviations in needs simply go unsatisfied. The other extreme is represented by "cafeteria-style," or flexible benefit plans. Under this concept, employees are permitted great flexibility in choosing benefits options of greatest value to them. Picture an individual allotted *x* number of dollars walking down a cafeteria line and choosing menu items (benefits) according to their attractiveness and cost. The flexibility in this type of plan is apparent. Exhibit 11.4 illustrates a typical choice among packages offered to employees under a flexible benefits system.

Even companies that are not considering a flexible benefits program are offering greater flexibility and choice. Such plans might provide, for example, (1) optional levels of group term life insurance, (2) the availability of death or disability benefits under pension or profit sharing plans, (3) choices of covering dependents under group medical expense coverage, (4) a variety of participation, cash distribution, and investment options under profit sharing, thrift, and capital accumulation plans.[21]

Exhibit 11.5 summarizes some of the major advantages and disadvantages of flexible benefits. Judging from the recent acceleration in the use of flexible

---

[20] Ibid.

[21] Kenneth Shapiro, "Flexibility in Benefit Plans," *Hay Compensation Conference Proceedings* (Philadelphia: Hay Management Consultants, 1983).

Exhibit 11.4   Example of Possible Options in a Flexible Benefits Package

	Package			
	A	*B*	*C*	*D*
Health	No	No	No	Yes
Dental	No	No	No	Yes
Vision	No	Yes	Yes	Yes
Life insurance	1 × AE*	2 × AE	2 × AE	3 × AE
Dependent care	Yes	No	No	No
401-K savings	No	No	No	No
Cash back	Yes	No	No	No

* AE = Average earnings.

Exhibit 11.5   Advantages and Disadvantages of Flexible Benefit Programs

Advantages
1. Employees choose packages that best satisfy their unique needs.
2. Flexible benefits help meet the *changing* needs of a *changing* work force.
3. Increased involvement of employees and families improves understanding of benefits.
4. Flexible plans make introduction of new benefits less costly. The new option is added merely as one among a wide variety of elements from which to choose.
5. Cost containment—the organization sets the dollar maximum. Employee chooses within that constraint.

Disadvantages
1. Employees make bad choices and find themselves not covered for predictable emergencies.
2. Administrative burdens and expenses increase.
3. Adverse selection—employees pick only benefits they will use. The subsequent high benefit utilization increases its cost.
4. Subject to nondiscrimination requirements in Section 125 of the Internal Revenue Code.

benefits, it seems that employers consider the advantages noted in Exhibit 11.5 to far outweigh the disadvantages.[22] Between 1980 and 1988, the number of major employers offering flexible benefit plans grew from 8 to 800.[23] Recent evidence indicates the growth trend continues.[24] Two recent studies also support adoption of flexible benefits plans. Benefits satisfaction, job satisfaction, and organizational commitment may rise with movement to flexible benefits.[25]

A key consideration in the continued popularity of flexible benefit plans may well be the increased scrutiny of the Internal Revenue Service. Section 125 of the Internal Revenue Code outlines a series of requirements that a company must meet in setting up a flexible benefits package.[26] The most important of these restrictions is a nondiscrimination clause, that is, a plan may not give significantly higher benefits to highly compensated executives relative to average employees. In fact, the average benefits for nonhighly compensated employees must equal or exceed 75 percent of the average benefits for highly compensated executives.

The final administrative issue involves the question of financing benefits plans. Alternatives include the following:

1. Noncontributory (employer pays total costs).
2. Contributory (costs shared between employer and employee).
3. Employee financed (employee pays total costs for some benefits—by law the organization must bear the cost for some benefits).

Exhibit 11.6 presents the arguments for each of these three methods of financing. In general, organizations prefer to make benefits options contributory, reasoning that a "free good," no matter how valuable, is less valuable to an employee. Furthermore, employees have no personal interest in controlling the cost of a free good.

COMPONENTS OF A BENEFITS PLAN

Exhibit 11.7 outlines a model of the factors influencing benefits choice, from both the employer and employee perspective. The remainder of this chapter briefly examines each of these factors.

---

[22] B. T. Beam and J. M. McFadden, *Employee Benefits*, 3rd ed. (Chicago: Dearborn Financial Publishing, 1992).

[23] Hewitt Associates, *Fundamentals of Flexible Compensation* (New York: Wiley, 1988).

[24] Hay Group, *Compensation and Benefits Strategies for 1993 and Beyond* (Philadelphia: Hay Management Consultants, 1992).

[25] Barber, A. E., R. B. Dunham and R. Formisano. "The Impact of Flexible Benefit Plans on Employee Benefit Satisfaction." Presented at 50th annual meeting of the Academy of Management, San Francisco, CA, 1990; Brian Heshizer, "The Impact of Flexible Benefit Plans or Job Satisfaction, Organizational Commitment and Turnover Intentions," *Benefits Quarterly* 4 (1994), pp. 84–90.

[26] Richard Johnson, *Flexible Benefits: A How to Guide* (Brookfield, WI: International Foundation of Employee Benefit Plans, 1986).

EXHIBIT 11.6   Advantages of Different Types of Benefit Financing Plans

Arguments for *Noncontributory Financing*

1. *Coverage for all eligible employees:* Under a noncontributory plan, all eligible employees who have completed the probationary period, if any, are covered by the plan. This feature can avoid employee and public relations problems that might arise under a contributory plan. For example, otherwise eligible employees may not elect coverage under a contributory plan and hence, they and/or their dependents may not be covered when a loss or retirement occurs.

2. *Tax efficiency:* In most cases, employer contributions to an employee benefit plan do not result in current gross income to the covered employees for federal income tax purposes, even though these contributions are normally deductible by the employer as a reasonable and necessary business expense.

3. *Group purchasing advantages:* To the extent that all eligible employees are covered, as opposed to less than all under a contributory plan, the employer may be able to secure more favorable group rates or other conditions of coverage than would otherwise be the case.

4. *Union or collective bargaining pressures:* Labor unions generally favor noncontributory plans.

5. *Ease and economy of administration:* Since payroll deducation is not necessary under a noncontributory plan, benefit and accounting records are easier to maintain.

Arguments for *Contributory Financing*

1. *More coverage and/or higher benefits possible:* Given a certain level of employer contribution toward the cost of an employee benefit plan, employee contributions may make possible a more adequate plan, or they may enable a plan to be installed in the first place.

2. *Possible enhanced employee appreciation of the plan:* When employees contribute to a plan, they will have greater appreciation for the benefits that they are helping to finance. They will not take such benefits for granted.

3. *Possible lessening of abuses of benefits:* In a vein similar to the previous argument, employees will be less likely to abuse an employee benefit plan if they know that such abuses may increase their own contribution rates.

Arguments for *Employee-Pay-All Financing*

1. *Separate optional plans offered:* Some employers offer employees the opportunity of purchasing additional, supplementary coverage at group rates, without individual underwriting, which is separate from the benefits of the regular employee benefit plan. This coverage might include, for example, additional accident insurance, or hospital-indemnity coverage to supplement Medicare. This additional coverage is normally on an employee-pay-all basis.

2. *Benefits not otherwise available:* Employee-pay-all financing may be the only basis on which an employer believes it can offer the coverage. In the future, such a plan might be shifted to a contributory or even to a noncontributory basis.

Source: Jerry Rosenbloom and G. Victor Hallman, *Employee Benefit Planning* (Englewood Cliffs, NJ: Prentice Hall, 1991), pp. 427, 429–34. Reprinted by permission of Prentice Hall, Englewood Cliffs, NJ.

427

EXHIBIT 11.7   Factors Influencing Choice of Benefits Package

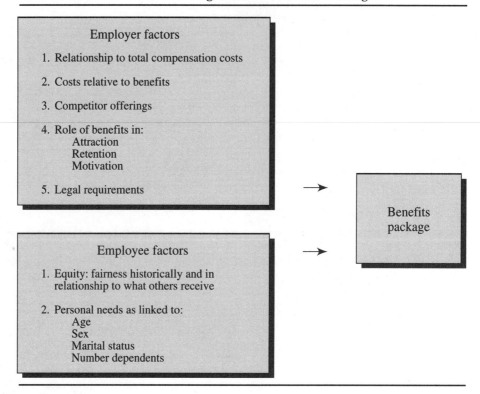

Employer Preferences

As Exhibit 11.7 indicates, a number of factors affect employer preference in determining desirable components of a benefits package.

Relationship to Total Compensation Costs.   A good compensation manager considers employee benefit costs as part of a total package of compensation costs. Frequently, employees think that just because an employee benefit is attractive, the company should provide it. A good compensation manager thinks somewhat differently: Is there a better use for this money? Could we put the money into some other compensation component and achieve better results? Benefit costs are only one part of a total compensation package. Decisions about outlays have to be considered from this perspective.

Costs Relative to Benefits.   A major reason for the proliferating costs of benefits programs is the narrow focus of benefits administrators. Too frequently in the past the costs/benefits of a particular benefit inclusion were viewed in isolation, without reference to total package costs or forecasts of rising costs in future years. To control spiraling benefits costs, administrators should adopt a broader, cost-centered approach. As a first step, this approach would require policy decisions on the level of benefits expenditures acceptable both in the short and long term. Historically, benefits managers negotiated or provided benefits on a "package" basis rather than a cost basis. The current cost of a benefit would be identified and, if the cost seemed reasonable, the benefit would be provided for (or negotiated with) employees. The crucial error in this process was a failure to recognize that rising costs of this benefit were expected to be borne by the employer. The classic example of this phenomenon is health care coverage. An employer considering a community-based medical plan like Blue Cross during the early 1960s no doubt agreed to pay all or most of the costs of one of the Blue Cross options. As costs of this plan skyrocketed during the 1960s and 1970s, the employer was expected to continue coverage at the historical level. In effect, the employer became locked into a level of coverage rather than negotiating a level of cost. In subsequent years, then, the spiraling costs were essentially out of the control of the benefits manager.

This cost-centered approach would require benefits administrators, in cooperation with insurance carriers and armed with published forecasts of anticipated costs for particular benefits, to determine the cost commitments for the existing benefits package. Budget dollars not already earmarked may then be allocated to new benefits that best satisfy organizational goals. Factors affecting this decision include an evaluation of benefits offered by other firms and the competitiveness of the existing package. Legal compliance is also important (Chapter 12). Finally, the actual advantage of a new option must be explored in relation to employee preferences. Those benefits that top the list of employee preferences should be evaluated in relation to current and future costs. Because future cost estimates may be difficult to project, it is imperative that benefits administrators reduce uncertainty. If a benefit forecast suggests that future cost containment may be difficult, the benefit should be offered to employees only on a cost-sharing basis. Management determines what percentage of cost it can afford to bear within budget projections, and the option is offered to employees on a cost-sharing basis, with projected increases in both employer and employee costs communicated openly. In the negotiation process, then, employees or union representatives can evaluate their preference for the option against the forecasted cost burden. In effect, this approach defines the contribution an employer is willing to make in advance.

Competitor Offerings.   Equity issues arise with employee benefits, as well. What is the absolute level of benefits payments relative to important product and labor market competitors? What should be the benefit's position relative to the market? What is the "fit" with the total compensation policy? Many employers adopt a benefit that a competitor has initiated only to find some time later that it is inappropriate given the makeup of the organization. A classic example is the employer who installs an education reimbursement plan in an organization with an aging work force. Data suggest that older employees are less likely to use this benefit and consequently place a relatively low value on it.

One of the best strategies to determine *external equity* is to conduct a benefits survey. Alternatively, many consulting organizations, professional associations, and interest groups collect benefits data that can be purchased. Perhaps the most widely used of these surveys is the annual benefits survey conducted by the U.S. Chamber of Commerce.[27]

Role of Benefits in Attraction, Retention, and Motivation.   Given the rapid growth in benefits and staggering cost implications, it seems only logical that employers would expect to derive commensurate return on this investment. In fact, there is at best only anecdotal evidence that employee benefits are cost justified. This evidence falls into three categories.[28] First, employee benefits are widely claimed to help in the retention of workers. Benefit schedules are specifically designed to favor longer term employees. For example, retirement benefits increase with years of service, and most plans do not provide for full employee eligibility until a specified number of years of service has been reached. Equally, amount of vacation time increases with years of service, and, finally, employee savings plans, profit sharing plans, and stock purchase plans frequently provide for increased participation or benefits as company seniority increases. By tying these benefits to seniority, it is assumed that workers are more reluctant to change jobs.

There is also some research to support this common assumption that benefits increase retention. Two studies uncovered a negative relationship between fringe benefit coverage and job change patterns.[29] Higher benefits reduced mobility. A more detailed follow-up study, though, found that only two specific benefits curtailed employee turnover: pensions and medical coverage.[30] Virtually no other employee benefit had a significant impact on turnover. Some people argue, though, that this reduction in turnover because of benefits may not always be good. One poll found that 3 Americans in 10 have, at one time or another, stayed in a job they wanted to leave simply because they could not give up their health care coverage.[31] This job lock probably is not a desirable situation for employers.

Second, employee benefits are lauded for their presumed impact on employee satisfaction. One survey by the International Survey Research Corporation casts doubt on this claim, though. Today only 50 percent of workers consider their

---

[27] U.S. Chamber of Commerce, *Employee Benefits, 1993.*

[28] Donald P. Crane, *The Management of Human Resources,* 2nd ed. (Belmont, CA: Wadsworth, 1979); Foegen, "Are Escalating Employee Benefits Self-Defeating?" pp. 83–84, 86.

[29] Olivia Mitchell, "Fringe Benefits and Labor Mobility," *Journal of Human Resources* 17, no. 2 (1982), pp. 286–98; Bradley Schiller and Randal Weiss, "The Impact of Private Pensions on Firm Attachment," *Review of Economics and Statistics* 61, no. 3 (1979), pp. 369–80.

[30] Olivia Mitchell, "Fringe Benefits and the Cost of Changing Jobs," *Industrial and Labor Relations Review* 37, no. 1 (1983), pp. 70–78.

[31] New York Times and CBS poll, as reported in the *Human Resource Management News* (Chicago: Remy Publishing, 1991).

benefits adequate. This is down from 83 percent in the early 1980s.[32] The lowest satisfaction marks go to disability, life, and health insurance.[33] Why have satisfaction ratings fallen? One view holds that benefits satisfaction falls as cost-cutting companies attempt to reduce coverage and also shift more of the costs to employees.[34] A second view is more pessimistic, arguing that benefits plans fail to meet either employer or employee needs. In this view, simply pumping more money into benefits is inappropriate. Rather, employers must make fundamental changes in the way they approach the benefits-planning process. Companies must realize that declining satisfaction with benefits is a result of long-term changes in the work force. Ever-increasing numbers of women in the labor force, coupled with increasing numbers of dual career families and higher educational attainments, suggest changing values of employees.[35] Changing values, in turn, necessitate a reevaluation of benefits packages.

Finally, employee benefits also are valued because improved retention and increased satisfaction will, some organizations hope, have bottom line effects on profitability. This is consistent with the old adage: "A happy worker is a productive worker."

Unfortunately, the research supporting these declarations is relatively scant, particularly in relation to the huge costs incurred in the name of employee benefits.

Legal Requirements.   Employers obviously want a benefits package that complies with all aspects of the law. Exhibit 11.8 shows part of the increasingly complex web of legislation in the benefits area. Greater details on the three legally mandated benefits (workers' compensation, Social Security, and unemployment insurance) are provided in Chapter 12.

Absolute and Relative Compensation Costs.   Any evaluation of employee benefits must be placed in the context of total compensation costs. Cost competitiveness means the total package must be competitive—not just specific segments. Consequently, decisions on whether to adopt certain options must be considered in light of the impact on total costs and in relationship to expenditures of competitors (as determined in benefits surveys such as the Chamber of Commerce survey mentioned earlier in this chapter).

Employee Preferences

Employee preferences for various benefit options are determined by individual needs. Those benefits perceived to best satisfy individual needs are most highly desired. In part these needs arise out of feelings of perceived equity or inequity.

---

[32] Conte, "Flexible Benefit Plans Grow More Popular," p. A1.

[33] *The Wall Street Journal,* April 30, 1985, p. 1.

[34] George Dreher, Ronald Ash, and Robert Bretz, "Benefit Coverage and Employee Cost: Critical Factors in Explaining Compensation Satisfaction," *Personnel Psychology* 41 (1988), pp. 237–54.

[35] Ibid.

EXHIBIT 11.8 Impact of Legislation on Selected Benefits

Legislation	Impact on Employee Benefits
Fair Labor Standards Act, 1938	Created time and one-half overtime pay. Benefits linked to pay (e.g., social security) increase correspondingly during those overtime hours.
Employee Retirement Income Security Act, 1974	If an employer decides to provide a pension (it is not mandated!), specific rules must be followed. Plan must vest (employee has right to both personal and company contributions into pension) after five years of employment. Pension Benefit Guaranty Corporation, as set up by this law, provides workers some financial coverage when a company and its pension plan goes bankrupt.
Tax Reform Act, 1982, 1986	Permit individual retirement accounts (IRAs) for eligible employees. Established 401-K programs, a matched contributions saving plan (employer matches part or all of employee contribution) that frequently serves as part of a retirement package.
Health Maintenance Act, 1973	Required employers to offer alternative health coverage (e.g., health maintenance organizations) options to employees.
Discrimination legislation (Age Discrimination in Employment Act, Civil Rights Act, Pregnancy Disbility Act, various state laws)	Benefits must be administered in a manner that does not discriminate against protected groups (or basis of race, color, religion, sex, national origin, age, pregnancy).
Consolidated Omnibus Budget Reconciliation Act (COBRA), 1984	Employees who resign or are laid off through no fault of their own are eligible to continue receiving health coverage under employer's plan at a cost borne by the employee.

Equity. To illustrate the impact of equity, consider the example of government employees working in the same neighborhood as auto workers. Imagine the dissatisfaction with government holidays created when government employees leave for work every morning knowing that their autoworker neighbors are home in bed for the whole week between Christmas and New Year's Day. The perceived unfairness of this difference need not be rational. But it is, nevertheless, a factor that must be considered in determining employee needs. Occasionally this comparison process leads to a bandwagon effect in which new benefits offered by a competitor are adopted without careful consideration, simply because the employer wants to avoid hard feelings. This phenomenon is particularly apparent for employers with strong commitments to maintaining a totally or partially nonunion work force. Benefits obtained by a unionized competitor or a unionized segment of the firm's work force are frequently passed along to nonunion employees. Although the effectiveness of this strategy in thwarting unionization efforts has not been demonstrated, many nonunion firms would prefer to provide the benefit as a safety measure.

Personal Needs of Employees.   A major assumption in empirical efforts to determine employee preferences is that preferences are somehow systematically related to what are termed *demographic differences.* The demographic approach assumes that demographic groups (e.g., young versus old, married versus unmarried) can be identified for which benefits preferences are fairly consistent across members of the group. Furthermore, it assumes that meaningful differences exist between groups in terms of benefit preferences.

There is some evidence that these assumptions are only partially correct. One study extensively reviewed patterns of group preferences for particular benefits.[36] As one might expect, older workers showed stronger preferences than younger workers for pension plans.[37] Also, families with dependents had stronger preferences for health/medical coverage than families with no dependents.[38] The big surprise in all these studies, though, is that many of the other demographic group breakdowns fail to result in differential benefit preferences. Traditionally, it has been assumed that benefit preferences ought to differ among males versus females, blue collar versus white collar, married versus single, young versus old, and families with dependents versus those with none. Few of these expectations have been borne out by these studies. Rather, the studies have tended to be more valuable in showing preference trends that are characteristic of all employees. Among the benefits available, health/medical and stock plans are highly preferred benefits, but such options as early retirement, profit sharing, shorter hours, and counseling services rank among the least preferred options. Beyond these conclusions, most preference studies have shown wide variation in individuals with respect to benefit preferences.

The weakness of this demographic approach has led some organizations to undertake a second and more expensive empirical method of determining employee preference: surveying individuals about needs. One way of accomplishing this requires development of a questionnaire on which employees evaluate various benefits. For example, Exhibit 11.9 illustrates two types of questionnaire formats.

While other strategies for scaling are available (e.g., paired comparison), the most important factor to remember is that a consistent method must be used in

---

[36] William F. Glueck, *Personnel: A Diagnostic Approach* (Plano, TX: Business Publications, 1978).

[37] Ludwig Wagner and Theodore Bakerman, "Wage Earners' Opinions of Insurance Fringe Benefits," *Journal of Insurance,* June 1960, pp. 17–28; Brad Chapman and Robert Otterman, "Employee Preference for Various Compensation and Benefits Options," *Personnel Administrator* 25 (November 1975), pp. 31–36.

[38] Stanley Nealy, "Pay and Benefit Preferences," *Industrial Relations,* October 1963, pp. 17–28.

EXHIBIT 11.9   Questionnaire Formats for Benefits Surveys

A. Ranking Method

Rank order the following benefits from 1 (high) to 4 (low) in terms of their value to you.

_____ Health/medical coverage

_____ Extended holiday schedule

_____ Pension plan

_____ Life insurance

B. Likert-Type Scale

How important are each of the following benefits to you (check one for each benefit).

	(1) Very Important	*(2)* Important	*(3)* Neutral	*(4)* Unimportant	*(5)* Very Unimportant
Health/holiday coverage	_____	_____	_____	_____	_____
Extended holiday schedule	_____	_____	_____	_____	_____
Pension plan	_____	_____	_____	_____	_____
Life insurance	_____	_____	_____	_____	_____

assessing preferences on a questionnaire. Switching between a ranking method and a Likert-type scale may, by itself, affect the results.[39]

A third empirical method of identifying individual employee preferences is commonly known as a *flexible benefit plan* (also called, at various times, a *cafeteria-style plan* or a *supermarket plan*). As previously noted, employees are allotted a fixed amount of money and permitted to spend that amount in the purchase of benefit options. From a theoretical perspective, this approach to benefits packaging is ideal. Employees directly identify the benefits of greatest value to them, and by constraining the dollars employees have to spend, benefits managers are able to control benefits costs.

ADMINISTERING THE BENEFITS PROGRAM

The job description for an employee benefits executive found in Exhibit 11.10 indicates that administrative time is spent on three functions that require further discussion: (1) communicating about the benefits program, (2) claims processing, and (3) cost containment.[40]

---

[39] George T. Milkovich and Michael J. Delaney, "A Note on Cafeteria Pay Plans," *Industrial Relations,* February 1975, pp. 112–16.

[40] McCaffery, *Managing the Employee Benefits Program.*

EXHIBIT 11.10   Job Description for Employee Benefits Executive

Position
The primary responsibility of this position is the administration of established company benefits programs. Develops and recommends new and improved policies and plans with regard to employee benefits. Ensures compliance with ERISA requirements and regulations.

Specific Functions
1. Administers group life insurance, health and accident insurance, retirement programs, and savings plans.
2. Processes documents necessary for the implementation of various benefits programs and maintains such records as are necessary.
3. Recommends and approves procedures for maintenance of benefits programs and issues operating instructions.
4. Participates in the establishment of long-range objectives of company benefits programs.
5. Conducts surveys and analyzes and maintains an organized body of information on benefits programs of other companies.
6. Informs management of trends and developments in the field of company benefits.
7. Gives advice and counsel regarding current developments in benefits programs.
8. Acts as liaison between company and banks, insurance companies, and other agencies.
9. Conducts special studies as requested by management.

In addition, the employee-benefits executive may be responsible for various employee services, such as recreation programs, advisory services, credit unions, and savings bond purchase programs.

Source: Robert McCaffery, *Managing the Employee Benefits Program* (New York: American Management Association, 1983), p. 25.

EMPLOYEE BENEFITS COMMUNICATION

Companies that effectively communicate benefits can expect increased employee satisfaction.[41] The most frequent method for communicating employee benefits is probably the employee benefits handbook.[42] A typical handbook contains a description of all benefits, including levels of coverage and eligibility requirements. To be most effective, this benefits manual should be accompanied by

---

[41] B. R. Rabin, "Benefits Communication: Its Impact on Employee Benefits Satisfaction under Flexible Programs," *Benefits Quarterly* 10, no. 4, pp. 67–83.
[42] Towers, Perrin, Forster, and Crosby, "Corporate Benefit Communication . . . Today and Tomorrow," 1988.

group meetings and videotapes.[43] Although some organizations may supplement this initial benefits discussion with periodic refreshers (e.g., once per year), a more typical approach involves one-on-one discussions between the benefits administrator and an employee seeking information on a particular benefit. There are also a number of excellent newsletters published by firms to update employees on changes in benefits.

In recent years, the dominance of the benefits handbook has been challenged by computer-generated personalized benefits statements. These tailor-made reports break down the package components and list selected cost information about the options. Many experts predict that in the future benefits communications will include interactive computer programs that provide basic benefits counseling.[44]

Despite such innovative plans to communicate employee benefit packages, failure to understand benefits components and their value is still one of the root causes of employee dissatisfaction. We believe an effective communications package must have three elements. First, an organization must spell out its benefit objectives and ensure that any communications achieve these objectives. Exhibit 11.11 outlines typical benefits objectives. Second, the program should make use of the most effective presentation media. Exhibit 11.12 indicates the effectiveness ratings for a variety of communications tools. And, finally, the content of the communications package must be complete, clear, and free of the complex jargon

EXHIBIT 11.11   Typical Benefits Objectives

Objective	Respondents Indicating This Is a Primary Objective (%)
1. Increase employee understanding of plan objectives	82%*
2. Increase employee appreciation of the benefits program	81
3. Increase employee knowledge of the cost of providing benefits	41
4. Obtain employee cooperation in controlling benefit costs	36
5. Encourage employees to take responsibility for their own financial security	16
6. Maintain the company's commitment to open employee communications	16

Note: * Multiple responses permitted.
Source: Towers, Perrin, Forster, and Crosby (1988), "Corporate Benefit Communication . . . Today and Tomorrow."

[43] Ibid.
[44] Ibid.

EXHIBIT 11.12   Effectiveness of Different Communications Tools

Communications Tool	Rating
Memos	3.4
Special brochures	3.8
Employee handbooks	3.3
Small group meetings	4.2
Personalized benefits statements	4.3
Letters to employee's home	3.5
Company-wide publications	3.3
"Live" slide shows	3.8
Large group meetings	3.6
Bulletin boards	3.1
Videotapes	4.0
Employee annual reports	2.4
Slides/audiotapes	3.7
Individual discussions with supervisors	3.4
Benefits newsletters	3.6
Telephone hotlines	3.6
Electronic communications	3.3
Films	3.5

Note: 5 = Highly effective; 1 = Highly ineffective.
Source: Towers, Perrin, Forster, and Crosby (1988), "Corporate Benefit Communication . . . Today and Tomorrow."

that so readily invades benefits discussions. The amount of time/space devoted to each issue should vary closely with both perceived importance of the benefit to employees and with expected difficulty in communicating option alternatives.[45]

CLAIMS PROCESSING

Claims processing begins when an employee asserts that a specific event (e.g., disablement, hospitalization, unemployment) has occurred and demands that the employer fulfill a promise of payment.[46] As such, a claims processor must first determine whether the act has, in fact, occurred. If it has, the second step involves determining whether the employee is eligible for the benefit. If payment is not denied at this stage, the claims processor calculates payment level. It is particu-

---

[45] "How Do You Communicate? It May Not Be Nearly As Well As You Think," *Benefits,* December 1988, pp. 13–15; Kevin Greene, "Effective Employee Benefits Communication," in *New Perspectives on Compensation*, ed. David Balkin and Luis Gomez-Mejia (Englewood Cliffs, NJ: Prentice Hall, 1987).

[46] Bennet Shaver, "The Claims Process," in *Employee Benefit Management,* ed. H. Wayne Snider (New York: Risk and Insurance Management Society, 1980), pp. 141–52.

larly important at this stage to ensure coordination of benefits. If multiple insurance companies are liable for payment (e.g., working spouses covered by different insurers), a good claims processor can save from 10 to 15 percent of claims cost by ensuring that the liability is jointly paid.[47]

Although these steps are time consuming, most of the work is quite routine in nature. The major job challenges come in those approximately 10 percent of all claims when payment is denied. A benefits administrator must then become an adroit counselor explaining the situation to the employee in a manner that conveys the equitable and consistent procedures used.

COST CONTAINMENT

Cost containment is easily the largest issue in benefits planning and administration today. Escalating costs of the 1960s, 1970s, and 1980s, combined with disappointing evidence that benefits have little impact on shaping positive employee behaviors, have molded the cost-cutting drives of the 1990s. Increasingly, employers are auditing their benefits options for cost-containment opportunities. The terminology of cost containment is becoming a part of every employee's vocabulary; Exhibit 11.13 defines some common cost-containment terms.

EXHIBIT 11.13   A Basic Primer of Cost-Containment Terminology

Deductibles—the requirement that the first x amount of dollars in a year be paid by the claimant when an employee makes a claim for insurance coverage.

Coinsurance (copayment)—a proportion of insurance premiums paid by the employee.

Benefit cutbacks—corresponding to wage concessions, negotiations by some employers with employees to eliminate or reduce employer contributions to selected options.

Defined contribution plans—limits of employers' responsibility for employee benefits in terms of dollar contribution maximum.

Defined benefits plans—limits of employers' responsibility for employee benefits in terms of a specific benefit and the options included. As the cost of these options rises in future years, the employer is obligated to provide the benefit as negotiated despite its increased cost.

Dual coverage—in families in which both spouses work, coverage of specific claims from each employee's benefit package. Employers cut costs by specifying payment limitations under such conditions.

Benefit ceiling—a maximum payout for specific claims (e.g., limiting liability for extended hospital stays to $150,000).

---

[47] Thomas Fannin and Theresa Fannin, "Coordination of Benefits: Uncovering Buried Treasure," *Personnel Journal,* May 1983, pp. 386–91.

Summary

Given the rapid escalation in the cost of employee benefits over the past 15 years, organizations would do well to evaluate the effectiveness of their benefits adoption, retention, and termination procedures. Specifically, how does an organization go about selecting appropriate employee benefits? Are the decisions based on sound evaluation of employee preferences balanced against organizational goals of legal compliance and competitiveness? Do the benefits chosen serve to attract, retain, and/or motivate employees? Or are organizations paying billions of dollars of indirect compensation without any tangible benefit? This chapter has outlined a benefits determination process that identifies major issues in selecting and evaluating particular benefit choices. The next chapter catalogs the various benefits available and discusses some of the decisions confronting a benefits administrator.

Review Questions

1. Your CEO is living proof that a little bit of knowledge is dangerous. He just read in *The Wall Street Journal* that employee benefits cost, on average, 38 percent of payroll. To save money, he suggests the company fire its two benefits administrators, do away with all benefits, and give employees a 38 percent pay hike. What arguments would you use to persuade the CEO this is not a good idea?

2. Assume that an organization (company A) develops a benefits program in the following way. First it identifies the major demographic groups in the organization. Then the company offers benefits known to be highly desired by people in those demographic groups in general (i.e., more senior employees prefer larger allocations to pensions). What kinds of problems could arise using this type of strategy to design a benefits program?

3. Explain how a flexible benefits package might save an organization money.

4. Why do many experts negatively characterize employee benefits as an entitlement?

5. Is there ever a time an organization should lag the market in wages but lead in employee benefits? Why or why not?

YOUR TURN:
MONDAILLE HYDRAULICS

Mondaille Hydraulics manufactures pumps for construction equipment and residential homes. In six months contract negotiations are scheduled with the bargaining representative for all blue-collar workers, Local 1099 of the United Auto Workers. The president of your company, Forrest Sutton, is convinced that he must get concessions from the workers if Mondaille is to compete effectively with increasing foreign competition. In particular, Mr. Sutton is displeased with the cost of employee benefits. He doesn't mind conceding a small wage increase (maximum 3 percent), but he wants the total compensation package to cost 3 percent less for union employees during the first year of the new contract. Your current costs are shown in Exhibit 1.

Your labor relations assistant has surveyed other companies obtaining concessions from UAW locals.

You also have data from a consulting firm that indicates employee preferences for different forms of benefits (Exhibit 2). Based on all this information, you have two possible concession packages that the union just might accept, labeled Option 1 and Option 2 (Exhibit 3).

1. Cost out these packages given the data in Exhibits 1 and 2 and the information contained from various insurance carriers and other information sources (Exhibit 4).

2. Which package should you recommend to the president? Why?

3. Which of the strategies do you think need not be negotiated with the union before implementation?

EXHIBIT 1   Current Compensation Costs

Average yearly wage	$24,336.00
Average hourly wage	12.17
Dollar value of yearly benefits, per employee	10,284.00
Total compensation (wages plus benefits)	34,620.00
Daily average number of hours paid	8.0

Benefits (by category)	Dollar/Cost/ Employee/Year
1. Legally required payments (employer's share only)	$ 2,141.00
a. Old-age, survivors, disability, and health insurance (FICA) taxes	1,509.00
b. Unemployment compensation	292.00
c. Workers' compensation (including estimated cost of self-insured)	311.00
d. Railroad retirement tax, railroad unemployment and cash sickness insurance, state sickness benefits insurance, etc.	29.00
2. Pension, insurance, and other agreed-upon payments (employer's share only)	$ 3,129.00
a. Pension plan premiums and pension payments not covered by insurance-type plan (net)	1,460.00
b. Life insurance premiums; death benefits; hospital, surgical, medical, and major medical insurance premiums, etc. (net)	1,427.00
c. Short-term disability	83.00
d. Salary continuation or long-term disability	57.00
e. Dental insurance premiums	51.00
f. Discounts on goods and services purchased from company by employees	27.00
g. Employee meals furnished by company	–0–
h. Miscellaneous payments (compensation payments in excess of legal requirements, separation or termination pay allowances, moving expenses, etc.)	24.00

(continued)

EXHIBIT 1   *(concluded)*

Benefits (by category)	Dollar/Cost/ Employee/Year
3. Paid rest periods, lunch periods, wash-up time, travel time, clothes-change time, get-ready time, etc. (60 minutes)	$ 727.00
4. Payments for time not worked	$ 2,703.00
a. Paid vacations and payments in lieu of vacation (16 days average)	1,558.00
b. Payments for holidays not worked (9 days)	973.00
c. Paid sick leave (10 days maximum)	172.00
d. Payments for state or national guard duty; jury, witness, and voting pay allowances; payments for time lost due to death in family or other personal reasons, etc.	66.00
5. Other items	$ 157.00
a. Profit-sharing payments	–0–
b. Contributions to employee thrift plans	71.00
c. Christmas or other special bonuses, service awards, suggestion awards, etc.	–0–
d. Employee education expenditures (tuition refunds, etc.)	40.00
e. Special wage payments ordered by courts, payments to union stewards, etc.	46.00
Total	$10,284.00

EXHIBIT 2   Benefit Preferences

Benefit Type or Method of Administering	Importance to Workers
Pensions	87
Hospitalization	86
Life insurance	79
Paid vacation	82
Holidays	82
Long-term disability	72
Short-term disability	69
Paid sick leave	70
Paid rest periods, lunch periods, etc.	55
Dental insurance	51
Christmas bonus	31
Profit sharing	21
Education expenditures	15
Contributions to thrift plans	15
Discount on goods	5
Fair treatment in administration	100

Note: 0 = Unimportant; 100 = Extremely important.

EXHIBIT 3   Two Possible Concession Packages

Option 1

Implement COPAY for Benefit	*Amount of* *COPAY*
Pension	$200.00
Hospital, surgical, medical, and major medical premiums	250.00
Dental insurance premiums	15.00

Reduction of Benefit

Eliminate 10-minute paid break (workers leave work 10 minutes earlier)
Eliminate one paid holiday per year
Coordination with legally required benefit; Social Security coordinated with
  Mondaille pension plan

Option 2

Improved claims processing
  Unemployment compensation
  Workers' compensation
  Long-term disability
Require probationary period (one year) before eligible for
  Discounts on goods
  Employee meal paid by company
  Contributions to employee thrift plans
Deductible ($100 per incident)
  Life insurance; death benefits; hospital, etc.
  Dental insurance

COPAY	*Amount of* *COPAY*
Hospital, surgical, medical and major medical premiums	$200.00

EXHIBIT 4   **Analysis of Cost Implications for Different Cost-Cutting Strategies: Mondaille Hydraulics**

Cost-Saving Strategy	Savings as Percent of Benefit-Type Cost
COPAY	Dollar-for-dollar savings equal to amount of COPAY
Deductible ($100 per incident)	
Life insurance premiums, death benefits, hospital, etc.	6%
Dental insurance	30
Require probationary period before eligible (one year)	
Discount on goods and services	10
Employee meals furnished by company	15
Contributions to employee thrift plans	10
Improved claims processing	
Unemployment compensation	8
Workers' compensation	3
Long-term disability	1
Coordination with legally required benefits	
Coordinate Social Security with Mondaille pension plan	15

CHAPTER

Benefits Options

Chapter Outline

Human resources professionals share three widely held views about benefits administration. First, the number of employee benefits and the laws affecting them have been escalating rapidly. Second, a good benefits administrator can save an organization substantial sums of money through proper benefits plan design and effective administration of benefits. Third, proficiency in benefits plan administration requires years of experience. The first two of these statements were endorsed in Chapter 11. The third statement, however, requires qualification. Admittedly, the number of benefit options and choices is overwhelming. Even trained human resource professionals can err in their evaluation of a benefits package. For example, one study asked both college graduates and HR recruiters to rank order 11 different benefits equated for costs to a company.[1] The HR recruiters' role was to estimate the graduates' responses. Surprisingly, at least to the recruiters, the college graduates placed high value on medical/ life insurance, company stock, and pensions. They placed less importance on holidays and scheduling conveniences (e.g., flextime, four-day work week). The recruiters systematically underestimated the value of most of the top benefits and overestimated the value of the leisure and work-schedule benefits. Despite the surprises, though, and despite the huge quantity of benefits information, some basic issues can be identified as relevant to most organizations. These common concerns serve as a foundation for aspiring benefits plan administrators. After categorizing benefits, these issues will be discussed as they relate to each benefit category. Exhibit 12.1 provides the most widely accepted categorization of employee benefits. In its annual report based on a nationwide survey of employee benefits, the U.S. Chamber of Commerce identifies seven categories of benefits.[2] Since this breakdown is familiar to all benefits plan administrators, it will be used to organize this chapter and illustrate important principles affecting administration of each benefit type.

Exhibit 12.2 provides data on employee participation in selected benefits programs from the private sector (both small and large companies) and the public sector.[3] Notice the high rate of participation for benefits such as life/ health insurance and pension plans in all except small firms. These participation rates are exceeded only by those of legally required benefits. In general, private sector employees are more likely to have benefits plans than their public sector peers. The one major exception is pension coverage. Typically, state and local government employees are more likely to have some form of retirement coverage than are their private sector counterparts.

---

[1] Kermit Davis, William Giles, and Hubert Feild, "Compensation and Fringe Benefits: How Recruiters View New College Graduates' Preferences," *Personnel Administrator,* January 1985, pp. 43–50.

[2] U.S. Chamber of Commerce, *Employee Benefits, 1993* (Washington, DC: Chamber of Commerce, 1994).

[3] U.S. Department of Labor, *Employee Benefits in Medium and Large Firms,* 1986, Bulletin 2281 (Washington, DC: U.S. Department of Labor, 1987).

LEGALLY REQUIRED BENEFITS

Statutory or common law *somehow affect* virtually every employee benefit; many of the limitations are imposed by tax laws. In this section the primary focus will be on laws that mandate the inclusion of certain benefits: workers' compensation, social security, unemployment compensation, family/medical leaves, and the Consolidated Omnibus Budget Reconciliation Act (COBRA).

Workers' Compensation

Workers' compensation is an insurance program, paid for by the employer, that is designed to protect employees from expenses incurred for a work-related injury or disease. An injury or disease qualifies for workers' compensation if it results from an accident that arose out of, and while in, the course of employment. There are five categories of workers' compensation benefits:[4]

1. Permanent total disability and temporary total disability.
2. Permanent and temporary partial disability (i.e., loss of use of a body member).
3. Survivor's benefits in cases of fatal injuries.
4. Medical expenses.
5. Rehabilitation.

Temporary total disability is both the most frequent type of claim and one of the two most costly (permanent partial disability is the other).[5]

Workers' compensation can consist of either monetary reimbursement or payment of medical expenses. The amount of compensation is based on fixed schedules of minimum and maximum payments. Disability payments are often tied to the employee's earnings, modified by such economic factors as number of dependents.

The employee receives workers' compensation regardless of fault in an accident. State statute requires detailed recordkeeping of work accidents, illnesses, and deaths.

States require that employers obtain workers' compensation insurance through a private carrier or, in some states, through participation in a state fund. The employer is liable for premium payments; the employee does not pay for this insurance.

Some states provide "second injury funds." These funds relieve an employer's liability when a preemployment injury combines with a work-related injury to produce a disability greater than that caused by the latter alone. For example, if a person with a known heart condition is hired and then breaks an arm in a fall triggered by a heart attack, medical treatment for the heart condition would

---

[4] Ronald G. Ehrenberg, "Workers' Compensation, Wages, and the Risk of Injury," in *New Perspectives in Workers Compensation,* ed. John Burton (Ithaca, NY: ILR Press, 1988).

[5] Ibid.

EXHIBIT 12.1   Categorization of Employee Benefits

1. Legally required payments (employer's share only).
   a. Old-age, survivors, disability, and health insurance (employer FICA taxes), and railroad retirement tax.
   b. Unemployment compensation.
   c. Workers' compensation (including estimated cost of self-insured).
   d. State sickness benefits insurance.
2. Retirement and saving plan payments (employer's share only).
   a. Defined benefit pension plan contributions (e.g., 401-K).
   b. Defined contribution plan payments.
   c. Profit sharing.
   d. Stock bonus and employee stock ownership plans (ESOP).
   e. Pension plan premiums (net) under insurance and annuity contracts (insured and trusted).
   f. Administrative and other cost.
3. Life insurance and death benefits (employer's share only).
4. Medical and medically related benefit payments (employer's share only).
   a. Hospital, surgical, medical, and major medical insurance premiums (net).
   b. Retiree (payments for retired employees) hospital, surgical, medical, and major medical insurance premiums (net).
   c. Short-term disability, sickness, or accident insurance (company plan or insured plan).
   d. Long-term disability or wage continuation (insured, self-administered, or trust).
   e. Dental insurance premiums.
   f. Other (vision care, physical and mental fitness benefits for former employees).
5. Paid rest periods, coffee breaks, lunch periods, wash-up time, travel time, clothes-change time, get-ready time, etc.
6. Payments for time not worked.
   a. Payment for or in lieu of vacations.
   b. Payment for or in lieu of holidays.
   c. Sick leave pay.
   d. Parental leave (maternity and paternity leave payments).
   e. Other.
7. Miscellaneous benefit payments.
   a. Discounts on goods and services purchased from company by employees.
   b. Employee meals furnished by company.
   c. Employee education expenditures.
   d. Child care.
   e. Other.

Source: U.S. Chamber of Commerce, *Employee Benefits, 1993* (Washington, DC: U.S. Chamber of Commerce, 1994).

EXHIBIT 12.2   Percentage Participation in Selected Benefits

Benefit Type	Small Firms (100 or less)		Larger Firms			State and Local Governments	
	1985	1990	1980	1985	1989	1987	1990
Paid holiday	?	84%	99%	98%	97%	81%	74%
Paid vacation	59%	88	100	99	97	72	67
Sickness and accident insurance	34	26	54	52	43	14	21
Long-term disability	?	19	40	48	45	31	27
Health insurance	42	69	97	96	92	94	93
Life insurance	33	64	96	96	94	85	88
Retirement	18	42				93	96
Defined benefit plan	?	20	84	80	63	?	90
Defined contribution plan	?	31	?	41	48	9	9

Source: Selected volumes from Bureau of Labor Statistics: *Employee Benefits in Medium and Large Firms; Employee Benefits in State and Local Government; National Federation of Independent Businesses, Small Business Employee Benefits,* 1985; 1990 data from J. S. Placentini and T. J. Cerino, *EBRI Databook on Employee Benefits, 1992* (Washington, DC: EBRI, 1993).

not be paid from workers' compensation insurance; treatment for the broken arm would be compensated.

Exhibit 12.3 summarizes the most common features of the various state laws.[6]

The cost of workers' compensation, as well as level of protection, varies widely from state to state. In some states employers pay more for workers' compensation than they do for state income tax. In 1990, more than 44 billion dollars were paid out in workers' compensation claims.[7] Between 1950 and 1990 workers' compensation benefits as a percentage of payroll more than tripled, from .36 to 1.2 percent.[8] Some employers argue that these high costs are forcing them to uproot established businesses in states with high costs and relocate in lower-cost states.[9]

Why these rapid cost increases? At least three factors seem to play a role. First, medical costs continue to skyrocket. Medical expenses, as a percent of workers' compensation costs, increased from 30 to 40 percent during the 1980s.

---

[6] U.S. Chamber of Commerce, *Analysis of Workers' Compensation Laws, 1985* (Washington, DC: Chamber of Commerce, 1985).

[7] J. S. Placentini and T. J. Cerino, *EBRI Databook on Employee Benefits* (Washington, DC: EBRI, 1992), p. 17.

[8] Robert Lampman and Robert Hutchens, "The Future of Workers' Compensation," in *New Perspectives in Workers Compensation;* data for 1990 from J.S. Placentini and T. J. Cerino, *EBRI Databook on Employee Benefits, 1992,* p. 29.

[9] Ibid.

EXHIBIT 12.3   Commonalities in State Workers' Compensation Laws

Issue	Most Common State Provision
Type of law	
	• Compulsory (*N* = 47 states).
	• Elective (*N* = 3 states).
Self-insurance	
	• Self-insurance permitted (*N* = 47 states).
Coverage	
	• All industrial employment.
	• Farm labor, domestic servants, and casual employees usually exempted.
	• Compulsory for all or most public sector employees (*N* = 47 states).
Occupational diseases	
	• Coverage for all diseases arising out of and in the course of employment. No compensation for "ordinary diseases of life."

By the end of this century, this number is expected to be 50 percent.[10] Second, some employees use workers' compensation as a surrogate for more stringent unemployment insurance programs. Rising numbers of employees, fearing recession and possible layoffs, fake new illnesses or stall reporting back after existing illnesses. Finally, workers' compensation also faces a serious threat from the mandated inclusion of new illnesses, such as stress-related ailments. By 1990, stress-related ailments constituted over 10 percent of all occupational disease claims.[11]

Unfortunately, these cost problems appear to be spiraling. Several studies indicate that the number of workers' compensation claims moves with the size of benefits specified in the state law.[12] When benefits rise, more people find reasons to file claims. Equally disturbing, though, when the number of claims rise, state legislators have a tendency to vote for more generous benefits.[13]

Spiraling costs have led to several containment strategies by states. Of course, some of the traditional *cost-containment* measures (copayment, deductibles) cannot be used with workers' compensation because it provides for "first-dollar" coverage. Instead, states are using some traditional *managed care* practices such

---

[10] Orin Kramer and Richard Briffault, *Workers Compensation: Strengthening the Social Compact* (New York: Insurance Information Institute, 1991), p.6.

[11] Kramer and Briffault, *Workers Compensation*, p. 21.

[12] Ehrenberg, "Workers' Compensation, Wages, and the Risk of Injury," J. Paul Leigh, "Analysis of Workers' Compensation Using Data on Individuals," *Industrial Relations* 24, no. 2 (1985), pp. 247, 256.

[13] Ibid.

as: (1) preferred-provider organizations for health care delivery, (2) utilization-review procedures, and (3) hospital/medical bill audit.[14]

Some experts argue that the only way to break this cost spiral is to dramatically change existing laws. Some state legislatures appear to be listening. At least 27 states have fee schedules to control physician charges.[15] A handful of states have enacted, or are considering, comprehensive managed care programs.[16]

Further progress in cutting costs may require a more comprehensive education effort for legislators and the public about the intent, functioning, and problems in workers' compensation. Below we provide a brief history of workers' compensation. This is followed by a discussion of program objectives and an evaluation of the plan's success in meeting its objectives.

The first workers' compensation state laws to survive the constitutionality question were passed in 1911. By 1920 all but six states had passed some form of workers' compensation law; all 50 states now have a workers' compensation law. The passage of the early laws is attributable to two related circumstances. First, prior to the passage of the first state law (1907–1908), the accident rate in industry was excessive: "approximately 30,000 workers died from occupational-related accidents."[17]

In addition to this high accident rate, workers had no protection for work-related accidents. The only source of remedy for workers was the courts, and prevailing law heavily favored employer rights over those of employees. As accident rates mounted, however, public support grew for some form of worker compensation.

The result of this rising sentiment, tempered by more than 70 years of experience and modification, is the modern workers' compensation system. According to the National Commission on State Workmen's Compensation Laws, the existing workers' compensation system is designed to achieve five major objectives.[18] The following paragraphs outline these objectives and assess the degree to which they have been achieved.

First, workers' compensation is designed to pay prompt and reasonable compensation to victims of work accidents. Little can be said about the promptness of payments, since few jurisdictions collect or report such data. The reasonableness of compensation, however, is more easily assessed. Most states attempt to provide an injured worker with two-thirds of gross or 80 percent of net lost income.[19] According to one authority, though, this compensation level frequently is not achieved in practice.[20] Numerous states set maximum weekly benefits that

---

[14] Barbara Solomon, "The State of Worker's Compensation," *Compflash* (Saranac Lake, NY: American Management Association, January 1993), p. 6.

[15] Ibid.

[16] Ibid.

[17] Robert J. Paul, "Workers Compensation: An Adequate Employee Benefit?" *Academy of Management Review,* October 1976, p. 113.

[18] Ibid.

[19] Kramer and Briffault, *Workers Compensation,* p. 24.

[20] Ibid.

fall below the target policy. Of even more concern, many jurisdictions only provide benefits that are below the poverty threshold.

Second, workers' compensation attempts to eliminate delays, costs, and waste in personal injury litigation. The existing system is based on the no-fault concept, presumably eliminating the need to undertake costly legal battles to establish guilt or innocence. This goal has been largely achieved, despite some administrative problems.

Third, the law attempts to reduce the number of accident cases. Although data on accident reduction records are not widely available, workers' compensation has two components that act as incentives for developing a safe work environment. First, since most employers are *experience rated* (insurance premiums vary directly with the number of accidents), they have a monetary incentive to reduce accidents.[21] Second, most laws require accurate records on accident data that help design safer work environments. Unfortunately, many employers do not respond to this component of the law. Consequently, the resulting accident data are often sketchy and of little value for accident prevention programs.

Perhaps the most convincing evidence that workers' compensation laws have not met public expectations about accident prevention can be inferred from passage of the Occupational Safety and Health Act (OSHA) of 1970.[22] The provisions of OSHA are designed to improve working conditions in industry, thereby reducing worker accidents and job-related illness. Passage of the act suggests that the reactive approach (i.e., after-the-fact response through compensation) is insufficient incentive to stem job-related accidents.

Fourth, workers' compensation requires businesses to provide prompt and adequate medical treatment. This provision has been a major success for the workers' compensation law. Most jurisdictions provide full medical treatment for injured workers without legal limitation on the time or cost of treatment.

Fifth, the law provides for rehabilitation of workers unable to return to their former jobs. Prior to the early 1970s, this provision was the least effective aspect of existing workers' compensation programs. However, massive reforms of the law during the 1970s resulted in additional rehabilitative benefits for disabled employees enrolled in a retraining program.

Social Security

When Social Security became effective in 1937, only about 60 percent of all workers were eligible.[23] Today, most working Americans and their families are protected by Social Security. Whether a worker retires, becomes disabled, or dies, Social Security benefits are paid to replace part of the lost family earnings.

---

[21] Ibid.

[22] James Ledvinka, *Federal Regulation of Personnel and Human Resource Management* (Belmont, CA: Wadsworth Publishing, 1982).

[23] Employee Benefit Research Institute, *Fundamentals of Employee Benefit Programs* (Washington, DC: EBRI, 1990).

EXHIBIT 12.4 Social Security through the Years

> **Original Provisions of the 1935 Law**
> Federal old-age benefits program.
> Public assistance for the aged, blind, and dependent children
>   who would not otherwise qualify for Social Security.
> Unemployment compensation.
> Federal state program for maternity care, crippled children's
>   services, child-welfare services.
> Public health services.
> Vocational rehabilitation services.
>
> **Changes in the Law since 1935**
> 1939:   Survivor's insurance added to provide monthly life insurance
>   payments to the widow and dependent children of a deceased
>   worker.
> 1950–1954:   Old-age and survivor's insurance was broadened.
> 1956:   Disability insurance benefits provided to workers and
>   dependents of such employees.
> 1965:   Medical insurance protection to the aged and later (1973) the
>   disabled under age 65 (Medicare).
> 1972:   Cost-of-living escalator tied to the consumer price
>   index—guaranteed higher future benefits for all beneficiaries.
> 1974:   Existing state programs of financial assistance to the aged, blind,
>   and disabled were replaced by SSI (supplemental security
>   income) administered by the Social Security Administration.
> 1983:   Effective 1984, all new civilian federal employees are covered.
>   All federal employees covered for purpose of Medicare.

Indeed, ever since its passage the Social Security Act has provided a foundation of basic security for American workers and their families. Exhibit 12.4 identifies initial coverage of the law and subsequent broadening of this coverage over the years.[24]

The money to pay these benefits comes from the Social Security contributions made by employees, their employers, and self-employed people during working years. As contributions are paid in each year, they are immediately used to pay for the benefits to current beneficiaries. Herein lies a major problem with Social Security. The number of retired workers continues to rise (because of earlier retirement and longer life spans), but there is no corresponding increase in the number of contributors. Combine the increasing number of recipients with other

[24] William J. Cohen, "The Evolution and Growth of Social Security," in *Federal Policies and Worker Status Since the Thirties,* ed. J. P. Goldberg, E. Ahern, W. Haber, and R. A. Oswald (Madison, WI: Industrial Relations Research Association, 1976), p. 62; Burton T. Beam, Jr., and John J. McFadden, *Employee Benefits,* 3rd ed. (Dearborn Financial Publishing, 1992).

EXHIBIT 12.5   Tax Rates, Maximum Earnings Base, and Maximum Social Security Tax

	Employer and Employee Each							
	OASDI			HI			Total Contribution	
	Max. Tax Earnings	% OASI	% DI	Max. Tax Earnings	% HI	%	%	$
1980	25,900	4.52	.56	25,900	1.05		6.13	1,587.67
1981	29,700	4.7	.65	29,700	1.3		6.65	1,975.05
1982	32,400	4.575	.825	32,400	1.3		6.7	2,170.80
1983	35,700	4.775	.625	35,700	1.3		6.7	2,391.90
1984	37,800	5.2	.5	37,800	1.3		7.0	2,646.00
1985	39,600	5.2	.5	39,600	1.35		7.05	2,791.80
1986	42,000	5.2	.5	42,000	1.45		7.15	3,003.00
1987	43,800	5.2	.5	43,800	1.45		7.15	3,131.70
1988	45,000	5.53	.53	45,000	1.45		7.51	3,379.50
1989	48,000	5.53	.53	48,000	1.45		7.51	3,604.80
1990	51,300	5.6	.6	51,300	1.45		7.65	3,924.45
1991	53,400	5.6	.6	125,000	1.45		7.65	5,123.30
1992	55,500	5.6	.6	130,200	1.45		7.65	5,328.90
1993	57,600	5.6	.6	135,000	1.45		7.65	5,528.70
1994	60,600	5.6	.6	No max.	1.45		7.65	—
1995	61,200	5.6	.6	No max.	1.45		7.65	—
1996+	To be announced	5.49	.71	To be announced	1.45		7.69	—

Source: *Social Security Bulletin, Annual Statistical Supplement* (1994).

cost stimulants (e.g., liberal cost of living adjustments), and the huge expense is not surprising. To maintain solvency, there have been dramatic increases in both the maximum earnings base and the rate at which that base is taxed. Exhibit 12.5 illustrates the trends in tax rate, maximum earnings base, and maximum tax for Social Security.

The combined impact of these schedules for employers is twofold. Consider, for example, employees who earned $45,000 in 1995. Their Social Security deduction is $3,442 (7.65 percent of $45,000). The first obvious impact on employers is that they must also pay $3,442. In addition, employers should factor this Social Security contribution into any other contribution they make to a private pension plan. A targeted level of pension benefits that neglects Social Security contributions results in retirement incomes that exceed employer intentions.

It is generally agreed that current funding levels will produce a massive surplus throughout the 1990s. Current baby boomers will reach their peak earnings potential and subsidize a much smaller generation born during the 1930s. Forecasts project a $70 billion surplus in 1996 alone! This surplus is expected to turn into a substantial shortfall sometime after the year 2015.[25] By that time baby boomers will be at retirement age, and too few workers will be contributing to the fund to balance the outflow. One proposed solution is to set aside current surpluses rather than using the money to finance part of the general debt. Unfortunately, there is no evidence that Congress has this much self-control.

Benefits under Social Security.   The majority of benefits under Social Security fall into one of four categories: (1) old age or disability benefits paid to the covered worker, (2) benefits for dependents of retired or disabled workers, (3) benefits for surviving family members of a deceased worker, and (4) lump sum death payments. To qualify for these benefits, a worker must work in a covered employment and earn a specified amount of money ($620 in 1994) for each quarter year of coverage.[26] Forty quarters of coverage will insure any worker for life. The amount received under the four benefits categories noted above varies, but in general is tied to the amount contributed during eligibility quarters. The average monthly benefit rose from $571 in 1990 to $625 for disabled workers[27] and $652 for retired workers in 1992.

Unemployment Insurance

The earliest union efforts to cushion the effects of unemployment for their members (c. 1830s) were part of benevolence programs of self-help. Working members made contributions to their unemployed brethren.[28] With passage of the unemployment insurance law (as part of the Social Security Act of 1935), this floor of security for unemployed workers became less dependent upon the philanthropy of fellow workers. Since unemployment insurance laws vary by state, this review will cover some of the major characteristics of different state programs.

Financing.   Employers who pay federal and state unemployment insurance tax are the exclusive financiers of unemployment compensation. Each state determines both the minimum and maximum tax rate, as well as the taxable wage base (which must exceed or equal the first $7,000 of each worker's earnings).[29] All states allow for *experience rating*, that is, charging lower percentages to employers who have terminated fewer employees. The tax rate may fall to 0 percent in some states for employers who have had no recent experience with

---

[25] Robert Myers, "The Role of the Social Security in the Smoke-and-Mirrors Budget Deficit," *Benefits Quarterly* (1994), pp. 17–21.

[26] *Social Security Bulletin* 56, no. 4 (Winter 1993).

[27] *Social Security Bulletin, Annual Statistical Supplement* (1993).

[28] Raymond Munts, "Policy Development in Unemployment Insurance," in *Federal Policies and Worker Status Since the Thirties,* ed. Goldberg, Ahern, Haber, and Oswald.

[29] Saul J. Blaustein, *Unemployment Insurance in the United States* (Kalamazoo, MI: W. E. Upjohn Institute for Employment Research, 1993), pp. 316, 321.

former employees collecting chargeable unemployment insurance, or it may rise to 10 percent for organizations with large numbers of layoffs. The federal unemployment insurance tax, currently .8 percent, is used for administrative costs and to repay government loans to the extended unemployment compensation account.[30]

Eligibility.   To be eligible for benefits, an unemployed worker must: (1) be able, available, and actively seeking work; (2) not have refused suitable employment; (3) not be unemployed because of a labor dispute (except in Rhode Island and New York); (4) not have left a job voluntarily; (5) not have been terminated for gross misconduct; and (6) have been previously employed in a covered industry or occupation, earning a designated minimum amount for a specified period of time.

Coverage.   All workers except a few agricultural and domestic workers are currently covered by unemployment insurance (UI) laws. These covered workers (97 percent of the work force), though, must still meet eligibility requirements to receive benefits.

Duration.   Until 1958 the maximum number of weeks any claimant could collect UI was 26 weeks. However, the 1958 and 1960–1961 recessions yielded large numbers of claimants who exhausted their benefits, leading many states to temporarily revise upward the maximum benefits duration.

In 1991 the Emergency Unemployment Compensation Act was passed to alleviate the hardships of sustained unemployment. As a temporary measure, this act was supposed to expire in 1992, but it has been renewed through 1996. The act gives extended benefits, an extra 13 to 20 weeks, under one of two conditions:

1. When total state unemployment averages 9 percent or more over a six-month period.
2. When a state's insured unemployment rate (insured unemployed plus claimants who have exhausted regular benefits in the last three months) averages 5 percent or more over a 13-week period.

Weekly Benefits Amount.   Those unemployed workers who do meet eligibility requirements are entitled to a weekly benefit amount designed to equal 50 percent of their lost wages. One study indicates, though, that most states don't reach this 50 percent target level.[31] Nor do benefits appear to cover even minimum nondeferable expenditures (e.g., minimum outlay for food and housing).[32] Recognizing this problem, some states have recently raised their benefits levels.

---

[30] Ibid.

[31] Elchanan Cohn and Margaret Capen, "A Note on the Adequacy of UI Benefits," *Industrial Relations* 26, no. 1 (1987), pp. 106–11.

[32] Ibid.

Controlling Unemployment Taxes.   An unemployed worker's unemployment benefits are "charged" against the firm or firms that most recently employed the worker. The more money paid out on behalf of a firm, the higher its unemployment insurance rate. Efforts to control these costs quite logically should begin with a well-designed HR planning system. Realistic estimates of HR needs will reduce hasty hiring and morale-breaking terminations. Additionally, though, a benefits administrator should attempt to audit prelayoff behavior (e.g., tardiness, gross misconduct, absenteeism, illness, leaves of absence) and compliance with UI requirements after termination (e.g., job refusals, insufficient duration of covered work).

Family and Medical Leave Act

The 1993 Family and Medical Leave Act (FMLA) entitles all eligible employees to receive unpaid leave up to 12 weeks per year for specified family or medical reasons. Under FMLA employees may be required to provide 30 days' notice for intended leave, proof of illness when appropriate, and periodic status reports. Common reasons for leave under FMLA include caring for an ill family member or adopting a child.

Consolidated Omnibus Budget Reconciliation Act

In 1985, Congress enacted the Consolidated Omnibus Budget Reconciliation Act (COBRA) to provide current and former employees and their spouses and dependents with a temporary extension of group health insurance when coverage is lost due to qualifying events (e.g., layoffs). All employers with 20 or more employees must comply with COBRA; an employer may charge individuals up to 102 percent of the premium for coverage that can extend up to 36 months, depending on the category of the qualifying event.

RETIREMENT AND SAVINGS PLAN PAYMENTS

The last chapter noted that a strong relationship exists between employee age and preference for a pension plan. Although the need for old age security may become more pronounced as workers age, it is also evident among younger workers.

The security motive and certain tax advantages have fostered the rise of *pension programs*. As Exhibit 12.2 indicates, the vast majority of employers choose to provide this benefit as part of their overall package. Pension programs provide income to an employee at some future time as compensation for work performed now. Two types of pension plans will be discussed here: (1) *defined benefit* and (2) *defined contribution*. As you read these descriptions, keep in mind that defined benefit plans may be a dying breed. Only 34 percent of employers surveyed in 1993 offered a defined benefit plan, while 66 percent provided a defined contribution plan.[33]

Defined Benefit Plans

In a defined benefit plan an employer agrees to provide a specific level of retirement pension that is expressed as either a fixed dollar or percentage-of-earnings amount that may vary (increase) with years of seniority in the company. The employer finances this obligation by following an actuarially determined benefits formula and making current payments that will yield the future pension benefit for a retiring employee.

Defined benefit plans generally follow one of three different formulas. The most common approach (54 percent) is to calculate average earnings over the last 3 to 5 years of service for a prospective retiree and offer a pension that is a function of this earnings average and years of seniority. Plans that are considered generous typically target pensions that equal to 50 to 80 percent of final-average earnings. At the low end of the "generosity" scale are plans that target 30 to 50 percent of final-average pay. The second formula (14 percent of companies) for a defined benefits plan uses average career earnings rather than earnings from the last few years: Other things being equal, this usually reduces the benefit. The third formula (28 percent of companies) commits an employer to a fixed dollar amount that does not depend on any earnings data. This figure generally rises with seniority level.

The level of pension a company chooses to offer depends on the answers to several questions. First, what level of retirement compensation does a company want to set, expressed as a function of preretirement earnings? Second, should Social Security payments be a factor when considering the level of income an employee should have during retirements? About two-thirds of all plans have a provision for integration with Social Security benefits.[34] One integration approach reduces normal benefits by a percentage (usually 50 percent) of Social Security benefits.[35] Another feature employs a more liberal benefits formula on earnings that exceed the maximum income taxed by Social Security. Regardless of the formula used, about two-thirds of U.S. companies do not employ the cost-cutting strategy. Once a company has targeted the level of income it wants to provide employees in retirement, it makes sense to design a system that integrates private pension and Social Security to achieve that goal. Any other strategy is not cost-effective.

Third, should other post-retirement income sources (e.g., savings plans that are partially funded by employer contributions) be integrated with the pension

---

[33] U.S. Chamber of Commerce, *Employee Benefits, 1993*, pp. 22, 25.

[34] J. S. Placentini and T. J. Cerino, *EBRI Databook on Employee Benefits*, 1992.

[35] Jerry S. Rosenbloom and G. Victor Hallman, *Employee Benefit Planning* (Englewood Cliffs, NJ: Prentice Hall, 1981).

EXHIBIT 12.6   The High Cost of Job-Hopping (Pensions Based on One Percentage Point for Each year of Service Multiplied by Final Salary)

		Years of Service	Percentage Point Credit		Final Salary	Annual Pension
Employee A	1st job	10	10%	×	$ 35,817 =	$ 3,582
	2st job	10	10	×	64,143 =	6,414
	3rd job	10	10	×	114,870 =	11,487
	4th job	10	10	×	205,714 =	20,571
					Total pension:	$42,054
Employee B	1st job	40	40	×	205,714 =	82,286
					Total pension:	$82,286

Note: Figures assume starting salary of $20,000 and 6% annual inflation rate.
Pay increases match inflation rate.
Source: Federal Reserve Bank of Boston.

payment? Fourth, should seniority factor into the company's payout formula? The larger the role played by seniority, the more important pensions will be in retaining employees. Most companies believe that the maximum pension payout for a particular level of earnings should be achieved only by employees who have spent an entire career with the company (e.g., 30 to 35 years). As Exhibit 12.6 vividly illustrates, this type of strategy hurts job-hoppers.

Defined Contribution Plans

Defined contribution plans require specific contributions by an employer, but the final benefit received by employees is unknown; it depends on the investment success of those charged with administering the pension fund.

There are two popular forms of defined contribution plans. A 401-K plan, so named for the section of the Internal Revenue Code describing the requirements, is a savings-type plan in which employees are allowed to defer income up to $7,000 a year. Employers match employee savings, typically at the level of 50 cents for each dollar deferred. The maximum deferral level may rise from $7,000 depending on changes in the CPI.

The second type of plan is an Employee Stock Ownership Plan. In a basic ESOP, a company makes a tax-deductible contribution of stock shares or cash to a trust. The trust then allocates company stock (or stock bought with cash contributions) to participating-employee accounts. The amount allocated is based on employee earnings. When an ESOP is used as a pension vehicle (as opposed to an incentive program), the employees receive cash at retirement based on the stock value at that time. ESOPs have one major disadvantage that limits their utility for pension accumulations. Many employees are reluctant to "bet" most of their future retirement income on just one investment. If the company's stock

Exhibit 12.7   Relative Advantages of Different Pension Alternatives

Defined Benefit Plan	Defined Contribution Plan
Provides an explicit benefit that is easy to communicate.	Unknown benefit level is difficult to communicate.
Company absorbs risk associated with changes in inflation and interest rates that affect cost.	Employees assume these risks.
More favorable to long-term employees.	More favorable to short-term employees.
Employer costs unknown.	Employer costs known up front.

takes a downturn, the result can be catastrophic for employees approaching retirement age. Despite this disadvantage, ESOPs continue to be popular. One public opinion poll found that about one-half of employees would trade their next pay increase for a share in ownership of their company.[36] Further evidence of ESOP popularity comes from the increase in participation. In 1975 about 250,000 employees were enrolled in ESOPs. That number exceeded 11.3 million by 1991.[37]

Finally, *profit sharing* can also be considered a defined contribution pension plan if the distribution of profits is delayed until retirement. Chapter 10 explains the basics of profit sharing.

Exhibit 12.7 outlines the advantages and disadvantages of these two generic categories of pensions.

Possibly the most important factors noted in Exhibit 12.7 is the differential risk borne by employers on the cost dimension. Defined contribution plans have known costs from year one. The employer agrees to a specific level of payment that changes only through negotiation or through some voluntary action. In contrast, defined contribution plans commit the employer to a specific level of benefit. Errors in actuarial projections can add considerably to costs over the years. Perhaps for this reason, defined contribution plans have been more popular for new adoptions over the past 15 years.

Not surprisingly, both of these deferred compensation plans are subject to stringent tax laws. For deferred compensation to be exempt from current taxation, specific requirements must be met. To qualify (hence labeled a *qualified deferred compensation plan*), an employer cannot freely choose who will participate in the plan. This requirement eliminated the common practice of discriminating in favor of executives and other highly compensated employees. The major advan-

---

[36] Employee Benefit Research Institute, *Fundamentals of Employee Benefit Programs* (Washington, DC: EBRI, 1990).

[37] Placentini and Foley, *EBRI Databook on Employee Benefits, 1992.*

tage of a qualified plan is that the employer receives an income tax deduction for contributions made to the plan even though employees may not yet have received any benefits. The disadvantage arises in recruitment of high-talent executives. A plan will not qualify for tax exemptions if an employer pays high levels of deferred compensation to entice executives to the firm, unless proportionate contributions also are made to lower level employees.

The Appendix to this chapter illustrates one example of the language used in describing pension benefits.

The Employee Retirement Income Security Act (ERISA)

Private pension plans ran into serious criticism in the recession of the early 1970s for a number of reasons. Many people who thought they were covered were the victims of complicated rules, insufficient funding, irresponsible financial management, and employer bankruptcies. Some pension funds, including both employer-managed and union-managed funds, were accused of mismanagement; other pension plans required long vesting periods. ERISA was passed in 1974 to protect the interests of participants in, and beneficiaries of benefit plans.

ERISA *does not require* employers to offer a pension plan. But if a company decides to have one, it is rigidly controlled by ERISA provisions. These provisions were designed to achieve two goals: (1) to protect the interest of 76 million workers who are covered today by private retirement plans and (2) to stimulate the growth of such plans.

The actual success of ERISA in achieving these goals has been mixed at best. In the first two full years of operation (1975–1976), more than 13,000 pension plans were terminated. A major factor in these terminations, along with the recession, was ERISA. Employers complained about the excessive costs and paperwork of living under ERISA. Some disgruntled employers even claimed ERISA was an acronym for Every Ridiculous Idea Since Adam. To examine the merits of these claims, let us take a closer look at the major requirements of ERISA.

General Requirements.   ERISA states that employees are eligible for pension plans beginning at age 21. Employers may require one year of service as a precondition for participation. The service requirement may be extended to two years if the pension plan offers full and immediate vesting.[38]

Vesting and Portability.   These two concepts are sometimes confused but have very different meanings in practice. *Vesting* refers to the length of time an

---

[38] Placentini and Foley, *EBRI Databook on Employee Benefits, 1992.*

employee must work for an employer before he or she receives the employer's contribution into the pension plan. The vesting concept has two components. First, any contributions made by the employee to a pension fund are immediately and irrevocably vested. The vesting right becomes questionable only with respect to the employer's contributions. As mandated by ERISA, and amended by the Tax Reform Act of 1986, the employer's contribution must vest at least as quickly as one of the following two formulas: (1) full vesting after five years or (2) 20 percent after three years and 20 percent each year thereafter (full in seven years).

The vesting schedule an employer uses is often a function of the demographic makeup of the particular work force. An employer who experiences high turnover may wish to use the five-year service schedule. By so doing, any employee with less than five years' service at time of termination receives no vested benefits. Alternatively, the employer may use the second schedule in the hope that earlier benefits accrual will reduce undesired turnover. The strategy adopted, therefore, depends on organizational goals and work force characteristics.

Portability of pension benefits becomes an issue for employees moving to new organizations. Should pension assets accompany the employee?[39] ERISA does not require mandatory portability of private pensions. On a voluntary basis, though, the employer may agree to let an employee's pension benefits transfer to the new employer. For an employer to permit portability, of course, the pension rights must be vested.

Fiduciary Responsibility.   By the year 2000 almost $3 trillion will exist in pension accounts in the United States.[40] Unrestrained investment of these funds by a company representative could lead to substantial abuse.[41] Consequently, ERISA stipulates that the fiduciary entrusted with investment decisions is legally obligated to follow a "prudent-man" rule. Included in the operational definition of a prudent man are certain prohibitions against investments made in self-interest.

Pension Benefit Guaranty Corporation.   Despite the wealth of constraints imposed by ERISA, the potential still exists for an organization to go bankrupt, or in some way fail to meet its vested pension obligations. To protect their workers, employers are required to pay insurance premiums to the Pension Benefit Guaranty Corporation (PBGC) established by ERISA. In turn, the PBGC guarantees payment of vested benefits to employees formerly covered by terminated pension plans.

---

[39] Susan M. Philips and Linda P. Fletcher, "The Future of the Portable Pension Concept," *Industrial and Labor Relations Review* 30 (1977), p. 197.

[40] Placentini and Foley, *EBRI Databook on Employee Benefits, 1992.*

[41] Mark Gertner, "ERISA and the Investment Decision-Making Process: The Past, the Present, and the Future," *Employee Benefits Journal,* June 1985, pp. 28–35.

LIFE INSURANCE

One of the most common employee benefits (offered by about 94 percent of medium to large private sector firms) is some form of life insurance.[42] Typical coverage is a group term insurance policy with a face value of one to two times the employee's salary. Most plan premiums are paid completely by the employer (82 percent of employers).[43] About 45 percent include retiree coverage. The term policy provides protection against loss of life for a specified period, but provides no cash surrender value or investment value. About two-thirds of all policies include accidental death and dismemberment clauses. To discourage turnover, almost all companies cancel this benefit at termination.

Life insurance is one of the benefits heavily affected by the trend to a flexible benefits program. Flexibility is introduced by providing a core of basic life coverage (e.g., $25,000) and then permitting employees to choose more coverage (e.g., in increments of $10,000 to $25,000) as part of their optional package.

MEDICAL AND RELATED PAYMENTS

General Health Care

The American health system costs in excess of $830 billion annually.[44] Health care costs represented 5.9 percent of GNP in 1965, 10.5 percent in 1983, and 14 percent in 1992.[45] By the year 2000, health care spending is expected to account for 17 percent of GNP and 70 percent of business expenditure.[46] More costly technology, increased numbers of elderly, and a system that does not encourage cost savings have all contributed to the rapidly rising costs of medical insurance. In the past 10 years, though, employers have begun to take steps designed to curb these costs. We follow with a discussion of the types of health care systems and these cost-cutting strategies. Exhibit 12.8 explains the three most common health care options.

An employer's contribution to health care costs goes to one of five health care systems: (1) a *community-based system*, such as Blue Cross, (2) a *commercial insurance plan*, (3) *self-insurance*, (4) a *health maintenance organization (HMO)*, or (5) a *preferred provider organization (PPO)*.

---

[42] U.S. Department of Labor, Bureau of Labor Statistics, *Employee Benefits in Medium and Large Firms,* 1989 (Washington, DC: U.S. Government Printing Office, 1990); *Employee Benefits in State and Local Governments,* 1990 (Washington, DC: U.S. Government Printing Office, 1992); *Employee Benefits in Small Private Establishments,* 1990 (Washington, DC: U.S. Government Printing Office, 1991).

[43] Ibid.

[44] Metropolitan Life Insurance Company, "Developments in Medical Care Costs," *Statistical Bulletin,* January–March 1993, p. 29.

[45] Ibid.

[46] Christopher Farrell, "The Scary Math of New Hires," *Business Week,* February 22, 1993, pp. 70–71.

EXHIBIT 12.8   How Health Insurance Options Differ on Key Dimensions

Issue	Traditional Coverage	Health Maintenance Organization (HMO)	Preferred Provider Organization (PPO)
Who Is Eligible?	May live anywhere.	May be required to live in HMO designated service area.	May live anywhere.
Who Provides Health Care?	Patient chooses doctor and health care facility.	Must use doctors and facilities designated by HMO.	May use doctors and facilities associated with PPO. If not, may pay additional copayment/ deductible.
How Much Coverage on Routine, Preventive Level?	Does not cover regular checkups and other preventive services. Diagnostic tests may be covered in part or full.	Covers regular checkups, diagnostic tests, other preventive services with low or no fee per visit.	Same as with HMO if doctor and facility are on approved list. Copayments and deductibles are assessed at much higher rate for others not on list.
Hospital Care.	Covers doctors and hospital bills.	Covers doctors and hospital bills if HMO approved hospital.	Covers doctors and hospitals if PPO approved.

Of these five, plans 1 through 3 (labeled as traditional coverage in Exhibit 12.8) operate in a similar fashion. Two major distinctions exist, however. The first distinction is in the manner payments are made. With Blue Cross, the employer-paid premiums guarantee employees a direct service, including room, board, and any necessary health services covered by the plan. Coverage under a commercial insurance plan guarantees fixed payment for hospital service to the insured, who in turn reimburses the hospital. And, finally, a self-insurance plan implies that the company provides coverage out of its own assets, assuming the risks itself (within state legal guidelines). A Bureau of National Affairs Survey claims that self-funding is on the rise, with 64 percent of the companies surveyed claiming some level of self-funding.[47] The most common strategy is to

---

[47] Personnel Policies Forum, "Health and Dental Benefits," survey no. 149 (Washington, DC: The Bureau of National Affairs, Inc., 1992), p. 4.

have stop-loss coverage, with an insurance policy covering costs in excess of some predetermined level (e.g., $50,000).[48]

The second distinction is in the way costs of medical benefits are determined. Blue Cross operates via the concept of community rating. In effect, insurance rates are based on the medical experience of the entire community. Higher use of medical facilities results in higher premiums. In contrast, insurance companies operate from a narrower experience-rating base, preferring to charge each company separately according to its medical facility usage. Finally, of course, the cost of medical coverage under a self-insurance program is directly related to usage level, with employer payments going directly to medical care providers rather than to secondary sources in the form of premiums.

As a fourth delivery system, health maintenance organizations offer routine medical services at a specific site for a fixed fee. Employees make prepayments in exchange for guaranteed health care services on demand. By emphasizing preventive treatment and early diagnosis, HMOs reduce the need for hospitalization to about one-half the national average.[49] By law, employers with more than 25 employees must offer the option of joining a federally qualified HMO. If the employee opts for HMO coverage, the employer is required to pay the HMO premium or an amount equal to the premium for previous health coverage, whichever is less.

Finally, preferred provider organizations represent a newer form of health care delivery in which there is a direct contractual relationship between and among employers, health care providers, and third-party payers.[50] An employer is able to select providers (e.g., selected doctors) who agree to provide price discounts and submit to strict utilization controls (e.g., strict standards on number of diagnostic tests that can be ordered). In turn, the employer gives employees financial incentives to use the preferred providers. Doctors benefit through increased patient flow, and employers benefit through increased cost savings. And employees benefit through wider choice of doctors than might be available under an HMO.

Health Care: Cost-Control Strategies

Basically, three general strategies help benefits managers control the rapidly escalating costs of health care.[51] First, organizations can motivate employees to change their demand for health care through changes in either the design or the

---

[48] "Self Funding: Many Companies Try it for Health Benefits," *The Wall Street Journal,* June 2, 1987, p. 1.

[49] Janice Ross, "Attacking Soaring Health Benefit Costs," *Pension World* 14, no. 1 (1978), p. 51.

[50] Thomas Billet, "An Employer's Guide to Preferred Provider Organizations," *Compensation Review* 16, no. 4 (1984), pp. 58–62.

[51] Regina Herzlinger and Jeffrey Schwartz, "How Companies Tackle Health Care Costs: Part I," *Harvard Business Review* 63 (July–August 1985), pp. 69–81.

administration of health insurance policies.[52] Included in this category of control strategies are: (1) *deductibles* (the first *x* dollars of health care cost in each year are paid by the employee), (2) *coinsurance rates* (premium payments are shared by company and employee), (3) *maximum benefits* (defining a maximum payout schedule for specific health problems), (4) *coordination of benefits* (ensuring no double payment when coverage exists under the employee's plan and a spouse's plan), (5) auditing of hospital charges for accuracy, (6) requiring preauthorization for selected visits to health care facilities, and (7) mandatory second opinion whenever surgery is recommended.[53] Exhibit 12.9 indicates a rise in utilization of selected cost-management strategies.

The second general cost-control strategy involves changing the structure of health care delivery and participating in business coalitions (for data collection and dissemination). This category includes the use of HMOs and PPOs and the trend to negotiate rates with hospitals and other health care delivery agents.

The last cost strategy is to encourage wellness. No-smoking policies and incentives for quitting smoking are popular. But there is also increased interest in healthier food in cafeterias and vending machines, on-site physical fitness facilities, and early screening to identify possible health problems before they become more serious.[54] There is some evidence that fitness programs also increase

EXHIBIT 12.9   Selected Cost-Control Strategies and Their Utilization over Time

Provision	1984	1986	1988	1990
Preadmission testing	87%	83%	84%	81%
Precertification of length of stay	17	31	61	*
Second surgical opinion	54	83	81	*
Home health care	68	70	77	*
Hospice care	39	52	66	*
Wellness program	15	28	52	50
Annual physical	18	41	36	39
Ambulatory surgical facilities	81	89	89	*

Note: * Information not available.

Source: The Wyatt Company, *Group Benefits Surveys* (Washington, DC: The Wyatt Company, 1988; 1990).

[52] David Rosenbloom, "Oh Brother, Our Medical Costs Went Up Again," Paper presented for March 16, 1988. Health Data Institute, Boston, MA.

[53] Herzlinger and Schwartz, "How Companies Tackle Health Care Costs: Part I"; Regina Herzlinger, "How Companies Tackle Health Care Costs: Part II," *Harvard Business Review* 63.

[54] W. Robert Nay, "Worksite Health-Promotion Programs," *Compensation and Benefits Review* 17, no. 5 (1985), pp. 57–64.

productivity, increase commitment, decrease absenteeism, and decrease turnover.[55]

Short- and Long-Term Disability

A number of benefit options provide some form of protection for disability. For example, workers' compensation covers disabilities that are work related. Even Social Security has provisions for disability income to those who qualify. Beyond these two legally required sources, though, there are two private sources of disability income: employee salary continuation plans and long-term disability plans.

Many companies have some form of salary continuation plan that pays out varying levels of income depending on duration of illness. At one extreme is a typical *sick-leave policy* that continues to pay an employee 100 percent of salary.[56] After "sick day" benefits run out, disability payments begin. The benefit level is typically 50 to 67 percent of salary and may vary with the length of the sickness.[57]

A *long-term disability plan* might begin when the *short-term disability plan* expires, typically after 26 weeks.[58] Long-term disability is usually underwritten by insurance firms and provides 50 to 66 percent of an employee's wages for a period varying between two years and life. As of 1993, about 57 percent of all U.S. businesses provide long-term disability insurance through insured plans, self-administered plans, or trusts.[59]

Dental Insurance

A rarity 20 years ago, dental insurance is now quite prevalent. Dental insurance is a standard inclusion for approximately 84 percent of the major U.S. employers.[60] This translates into more than 100 million workers with some form of dental insurance.

In many respects, dental care coverage follows the model originated in health care plans. The dental equivalent of HMOs (DMOs) and PPOs is a standard delivery system. For example, a DMO enlists a group of dentists who agree to treat company employees in return for a fixed monthly fee per employee.[61]

[55] Loren Falkenberg, "Employee Fitness Programs: Their Impact on the Employee and the Organization," *Academy of Management Review* 12, no. 3 (1987), pp. 511–22.

[56] Employee Benefit Research Institute, *Fundamentals of Employee Benefit Programs.*

[57] Ibid.

[58] Ibid.

[59] *Employee Benefits Survey Data from Benefit Year 1993* (Washington, DC: U.S. Chamber of Commerce Research Center, 1994), pp. 25–26.

[60] Personnel Policies Forum Survey No. 149, "Health and Dental Benefits" (Washington, DC: The Bureau of National Affairs, Inc., 1992), p. 19.

[61] "Dental Insurance Program Gains Favor Among Firms," *The Wall Street Journal,* September 21, 1984, p. 31.

Fortunately for employers, dental insurance costs have not spiraled like health care costs. Dental benefits cost about 10 to 15 percent of the amount employers pay for medical benefits and are rising in cost at about one-half the rate.[62] In part, these relatively modest costs are due to stringent cost-control strategies (e.g., plan maximum payouts are typically $1,000 or less per year), but the excess supply of dentists in the United States has also helped keep costs competitive.[63] Dental costs remain relatively stable at around .7 percent of payroll.[64]

Vision Care

Vision care dates back only to the 1976 contract between the United States Auto Workers and the big three auto makers. Since then, this benefit has spread to other auto-related industries and to parts of the public sector. Most plans are noncontributory and usually cover partial costs of eye examination, lenses, and frames. About 35 percent of medium and large organizations have some form of vision care program.[65]

MISCELLANEOUS BENEFITS

Paid Time Off during Work Hours

Paid rest periods, lunch periods, wash-up time, travel time, clothes-change time, and get-ready time benefits are self-explanatory.

Payment for Time Not Worked

Included within this category are several other self-explanatory benefits:

1. Paid vacations and payments in lieu of vacation.
2. Payments for holidays not worked.
3. Other (payments for National Guard, Army, or other reserve duty; jury duty and voting pay allowances; and time lost due to death in family or other personal reasons).

Judging from employee preferences discussed in the last chapter and from observation of negotiated union contracts, pay for time not worked continues to be a high-demand benefit. Forty years ago it was relatively rare, for example,

---

[62] William McQuiggan, "Evaluating Dental Insurance Packages," *Compensation and Benefits Review*, May–June 1992, pp. 49–52.

[63] Harry Sutton, "Prescription Drug and Dental Programs," *Compensation and Benefits Review* 18, no. 4 (1986), pp. 67–71.

[64] *Employee Benefits Survey Data from Benefit Year 1993* (Washington DC: U.S. Chamber of Commerce Research Center, 1994), p. 27.

[65] Placentini and Foley, *EBRI Databook on Employee Benefits, 1992,* p. 246.

EXHIBIT 12.10   Payment for Time Not Worked

Paid Leave Type	Average Private Sector, 1989	Average State and Local Government, 1990
Rest period	26 minutes/day	29 minutes/day
Holidays	9.2/year	13.6/year
Vacation	9.1 days for 1 year service	12.2 days for 1 year service
	20.4 days for 20 year service	22.1 days for 20 year service
Funeral leave	3.3 days/occurrence	3.7 days/occurrence
Military leave	12 days/year	2 days/year
Jury duty	as needed	as needed
Sick leave	15.4 days/year with full pay after 1 year service	13 days/year with full pay after 1 year service

Source: U.S. Department of Labor Bulletin 2363 (1989); *Employee Benefits in Medium and Large Firms,* 1989; Bureau of Labor Statistics, *Employee Benefits in State and Local Governments,* 1990, Bulletin 2309.

to grant time off for anything but vacations, holidays, and illness. Now many organizations have a policy of ensuring payments for civic responsibilities and obligations. Any pay for such duties (e.g., National Guard and jury duty) is usually nominal, so companies often supplement this pay, frequently to the level of 100 percent of wages lost. There is also increasing coverage for parental leaves. Maternity and, to a lesser extent, paternity leaves are much more common than 30 years ago.

Exhibit 12.10 outlines the average paid leave time for covered employees.

Child Care

As of 1994, approximately 6,000 employers offered child care as a benefit.[66] About 60 percent of all children under six years of age with working mothers are enrolled in organized child care facilities.[67] Over the next 10 years, more and more companies are expected to open day care centers for the preschool age children of employees. In part, these centers are intended as a tool to attract and retain employees. Indeed, Travelers Insurance reports reduced turnover (at a child care cost of $1,200 per child per year), and Mutual Insurance believes that child care is an excellent recruitment tool.[68]

---

[66] Roberta Maynard, "Child-Care Options for Small Firms," *Nation's Business*, February 1994, pp. 43–46.

[67] Placentini and Foley, *EBRI Databook on Employee Benefits, 1992,* p. 353.

[68] Sue Shellenbargen, "Employers Report Gains from Babysitting Aid," *The Wall Street Journal*, July 22, 1991, p. B1.

Legal Insurance

Prepaid legal insurance is still rare, covering about 4 percent of employees in medium to large organizations.[69] Tremendous variety exists in the structure, options, delivery systems, and attorney compensation mechanisms. A majority of plans provide routine legal services (e.g., divorce, real estate matters, wills, traffic violations) but exclude provisions covering felony crimes, largely because of the expense and potential for bad publicity. Employees with legal problems either select legal counsel from a panel of lawyers chosen by the firm (closed-panel mechanism) or freely choose their own lawyers with claims reimbursed by an insurance carrier.

BENEFITS FOR CONTINGENT WORKERS

Approximately one out of every four workers currently employed in the United States can be classified as a member of the contingency work force, including flexible workers, part-time employees, and independent contractors.[70] This group poses a new set of questions for benefits administrators. Should these employees be entitled to benefit coverage? If so, which benefits and how much coverage?

Currently, employers are not required by law to provide any benefits to their contingent workers. However, some companies have found that partial benefit coverage can increase loyalty among contract laborers.[71] Exhibit 12.11 outlines these benefits.

EXHIBIT 12.11   Comparison of Benefit Coverage (Full Time versus Contingent)

	Hours Worked per Week (1990)			
Benefit	*40+ (full time)*	*30–39*	*20–29*	*Less than 20*
Health insurance (medical)	99%	76%	61%	20%
Dental coverage	91	78	53	17
Life insurance	95	66	49	15
Long-term disability	90	52		9
Paid holidays		82		50

Source: Report of a Survey by Hewitt Associates (Washington DC: Bureau of National Affairs, January 1995).

---

[69] Placentini and Foley, *EBRI Databook on Employee Benefits, 1992*, p. 412.

[70] Larry Reynolds, "Washington Confronts Part-Time America," *Management Review*, February 1994, pp. 27–28.

[71] Debbie Galant, "Are Part-Time Workers Getting Their Due?" *Institutional Investor*, July 1993, pp. 45–51.

Summary

Since the 1940s, employee benefits have been the most volatile area in the compensation field. Employee benefits are now a major, and many believe, prohibitive component of doing business. The early 1990s have been dominated by cost-saving efforts to improve the competitive position of American industry. A portion of these savings has come from tighter administrative controls on existing benefits packages. Further savings, as already seen in the auto industry, may come from a reduction in existing benefits packages. The current trend in benefits is flexibility as workers demand a larger voice and more choice in how and when they receive benefits.

Review Questions

1. Name six practices you could implement in health care coverage for a company that could result in cost savings.

2. Why are people concerned about funding Social Security payments if there is currently a surplus (tax exceeds payouts)?

3. Why are defined contribution pension plans gaining in popularity in the United States and defined benefit plans losing popularity?

4. Your company has a serious turnover problem among employees with less than five years' seniority. The CEO wants to use employee benefits to reduce this problem. What might you do in the areas of pension vesting, vacation and holiday allocation, and life insurance coverage to help reduce turnover?

5. Assume you are politically foolhardy and decide to challenge your CEO's decision in question 4 to use benefits as a major tool for reducing turnover. Before she fires you, what arguments might you try to persuade her that there is a better way to achieve her goal? (Hints: Are there other compensation tools that might be more effective in reducing turnover? Might the changes in benefits have unintended consequences on more senior employees? Could you make a cost argument against such a strategy? Is turnover of these employees necessarily bad? (How would you demonstrate that this turnover isn't a problem?)

ILLUSTRATION OF A BENEFITS PROGRAM: PFIZER BENEFITS PROGRAM

Your Benefits at Pfizer

At first glance, the Pfizer Employee Benefits Program—like all such programs—may appear to be an assortment of unrelated plans. Actually, each Pfizer benefit has been developed and improved to take care of you—*and* in many cases your dependents—in certain types of situations when extra financial assistance is needed.

There are four major types of coverage in the Pfizer Employee Benefit Program: survivors' assistance, disability protection, health care, and retirement income—all of which are outlined in this brochure. In addition, you and your family may enjoy many other benefits throughout your active Pfizer career. These include: holidays, vacations, educational assistance, matching gifts, scholarships, military leave and active duty training allowances, and adoption benefits—highlights of which are also shown in this brochure.

All in all, the Pfizer Employee Benefits Program gives you and your family a full range of financial protection and security—above and beyond your regular earnings as an employee. Actually, these benefits represent a substantial *addition* to your earnings and many allow certain tax advantages.

In addition to your Pfizer benefits, Social Security provides income and medical benefits to you and/or your qualified dependents upon disability, death, or retirement. Workers' compensation also provides cash, income, medical, and death benefits to you and certain family members if you qualify as the result of a job-related accident.

As you can see, the various benefits in the Pfizer Program and those provided by law work together to give you and your family well-rounded protection when it's needed most.

Each plan in the Benefit Program has been carefully designed with the welfare of our employees in mind. The plans are continually reviewed to make certain they remain up-to-date and to ensure that they are accomplishing the job they were intended to do. In fact, we feel that the program is one of the best to be found anywhere today.

Survivor Benefits	*Coverage*

Life Insurance
. . . pays benefits to your beneficiary whatever the cause of your death.

Basic—Approximately *two times* your annual compensation—maximum benefit of *$500,000*—until your normal retirement date—reduced amounts thereafter. Part of your Life Insurance continues into retirement—at no cost to you.

Supplemental—Choice of approximately one, two, or three times your annual compensation, up to a maximum benefit of *$500,000*.

Accidental Death and Dismemberment Coverage
. . . pays *additional* benefits to your beneficiary if you die—or to you if you suffer dismemberment as a result of an accident.

Amounts equal to your Basic and Supplemental Life Insurance for:
• loss of life
• loss of any two limbs or entire sight of both eyes (one-half of the coverage for loss of one limb or entire sight of one eye).

Business Travel Accident Insurance
. . . pays *additional* benefits to your beneficiary if you are killed on a covered Company business trip—or to you, if you lose sight or limb.

Six times your annual compensation—*Minimum $50,000/maximum $500,000*—for loss of life, any two limbs or entire sight of both eyes.

One-Half of insurance amount—*Minimum $50,000/maximum $250,000*—for loss of one limb or entire sight of one eye.

Disability Benefits	*Coverage*

Short Term Disability
. . . helps continue part of your pay for temporary absences from work because of illness or injury.

Service	Full Salary	Half Salary
Less than 10 years	6 months	0
10 but less than 15 years	6 months	3 months
15 or more years	6 months	6 months

Long Term Disability Plan
. . . helps continue part of your pay if you become ill or are injured and cannot work.

60% of your insured monthly compensation *up to* a maximum monthly benefit of *$3,600* including Workers' Compensation, Social Security disability benefits and any other Pfizer Group Plan Benefits.

(continued)

Health Care Benefits	*Coverage*
For you and each of your covered dependents: **Comprehensive Medical Plan** . . . provides coverage for a broad range of medical services. Three types of expenses are covered by the Plan—Type A, Type B and Type C.	*TYPE A EXPENSES*—100% of reasonable and customary charges, with no deductible required, for certain cost-effective services such as second surgical opinions, outpatient surgery and outpatient diagnostic x-rays and lab tests. *TYPE B EXPENSES*—100% of reasonable and customary charges for semi-private hospital room and board and special services or intensive care charges *after* the deductibles are met. Most hospital benefits are payable for as long as each hospital confinement lasts—except for confinements for treatment of alcoholism and drug abuse. For those conditions, hospital benefits are payable for up to a lifetime maximum of 365 days. *TYPE C EXPENSES*—80% of reasonable and customary charges for all other covered services and supplies not included as Type A or Type B expenses *after* the deductibles are met.

Health Care Benefits	*Coverage*
	DEDUCTIBLES • Calendar year Plan deductibles of $200 per individual/$500 per family for most Type B and Type C expenses. • Hospital deductible of $100 per confinement—in addition to the calendar year Plan deductible, if not previously satisfied—up to a maximum of three hospital deductibles per person per calendar year. • Services received in a hospital emergency room —$25 deductible per visit for treatment or outpatient surgery within 72 hours of an accident; —$25 per visit deductible *and* calendar year Plan deductible (if not previously satisfied) for all other services performed in a hospital emergency room.

Health Care Benefits	*Coverage*

EMPLOYEE OUT-OF-POCKET MAXIMUM
- An out-of-pocket calendar year maximum of $2,000 per family applies to all covered expenses not reimbursed by the Plan, including the deductibles. Thereafter, the Plan will pay 100% of additional covered charges incurred during the remainder of that calendar year. (Expenses for the treatment of alcohol and drug abuse may not be applied toward the out-of-pocket maximum.)

PLAN MAXIMUMS
- Unlimited lifetime dollar maximum for most covered charges.
- $50,000 per person combined lifetime maximum for outpatient psychiatric visits and outpatient treatment of alcoholism and drug abuse.
- $50,000 per person maximum for hospice care.

Dental Plan

. . . pays benefits for a wide variety of dental procedures—*including orthodontia*—with no deductible at all.

100% of reasonable and customary charges for most forms of preventive and diagnostic care—and
50% of reasonable and customary charges for repair or replacement of natural teeth—up to
$1,000 per person each calendar year—with
$10,000 in lifetime benefits per person—plus
$1,000 in lifetime benefits per person for orthodontia alone.

Retirement Benefits	*Coverage*

Retirement Annuity Plan

. . . is designed to pay an income for life to you and—in the case of your death—to your surviving spouse.

The pension plan has two formulas and the one which produces the *higher* benefit for you is used. One formula provides a benefit based on 1.4% of your Pfizer Career Earnings for service up to 35 years. The other formula provides a benefit based on 1.75% of your Pfizer Career Earnings for service up to 35 years less a portion of your projected Primary Social Security benefit. Career Earnings are determined by multiplying the *average* of your earnings for your highest consecutive five calendar years prior to January 1, 1987 times years of service prior to January 1, 1987 and then adding your actual earnings from 1987 to the date you retire. If you are *not* married when your retirement benefit commences, you will receive a straight life annuity payable only to

(continued)

Retirement Benefits	*Coverage*

you, unless you choose an optional payment method. If you are *married* when payments begin, your benefits will be in the form of a 50% joint and survivor annuity *unless* your spouse signs a waiver and consent form permitting you to choose a payment option other than a joint and survivor annuity. *Normal* retirement is age 65.

Early retirement is any time after age 50 with at least 10 years of service if your age and service equals 65 or more. If you retire early, your pension will be reduced *unless* your age plus service equals 90 or more, and you are at least age 60 when you retire. *Late* retirement is anytime after age 65.

Vesting—i.e., your right to a pension—occurs after 5 years of service.

Savings and Investment Plan
. . . affords you the opportunity to accumulate finds toward retirement through your contributions and Company contributions made on your behalf. Contributions may be made on a before-tax basis, after-tax basis or a combination of both. Company contributions vest at a rate of 20% per year.

Contributions from 2%–15% of your regular earnings, up to the maximum permitted by current laws and regulations, may be made to the Plan. The Company matches these contributions dollar for dollar on the first 2% of your pay that is contributed to the Plan and 50¢ for every dollar on the next 4% of your pay that is contributed to the Plan. You can invest in one, two or all three investment funds. All Company matching contributions are invested in Pfizer common stock. *Vesting* is full and immediate for the value of your own contributions and at 20% for each year in which you participate in the Plan on the value of Company contributions; *up to 100%* after 5 years. If you are married, your spouse will *automatically* be your primary beneficiary *unless* your spouse signs a waiver and consent form permitting you to name someone else as a primary beneficiary.

YOUR TURN:

KRAMER TOOL COATING COMPANY

Background

Kramer Tool Coating company (KTC) is a high technology firm that coats cutting tools by bombarding them with ions of a patented substance. Because of the high cost of the ion chambers needed for this process, KTC has yet to make a profit in its 10 years of existence. Forecasts project, however, that KTC will make money next year, and by 10 years from now (barring drastic changes in cutting tool technology) will boast a return after taxes of $30 million.

KTC is unionized by an independent union comprising workers who used to be employed at a nearby company unionized by the United Auto Workers. When that company went bankrupt, KTC hired 20 of its most skilled individuals. These people are now key members in the independent union. Remembering the bankruptcy, these employees have been reluctant to press for too much, too fast, lest history repeat itself. But it is evident now that the company is past its danger point. The new contract will be the first to include any but the bare minimum of benefits. The old package included the legally required benefits (e.g., workers' compensation, unemployment insurance, Social Security) and a relatively low-cost health care package.

The Situation

The union insists that the next package include a substantial growth in employee benefits. Hard negotiation has determined that the union is willing to forgo substantial wage increase demands in exchange for some gains in the following areas: (1) life insurance, (2) dental insurance, (3) package of short-term (sick days) and long-term disability coverage, and (4) a contributory 401-K pension plan. Life insurance and dental insurance coverage as proposed by the union cost approximately the same amount. Similarly, the disability package and the pension package are about equally expensive. You believe the union will settle for one of the two insurance packages and either the pension or disability coverage. Basically, you are indifferent in terms of costs.

Your Task

The president wants a recommendation about which way to have the labor lawyer negotiate. Consider how current and long-term corporate goals might influence your decision making. Also, do you want any other cost data or projections before making a decision? Are there any benefits that, if adopted, might make another of the requested benefits less necessary? What other information should you collect?

EXHIBIT V.1   The Pay Model

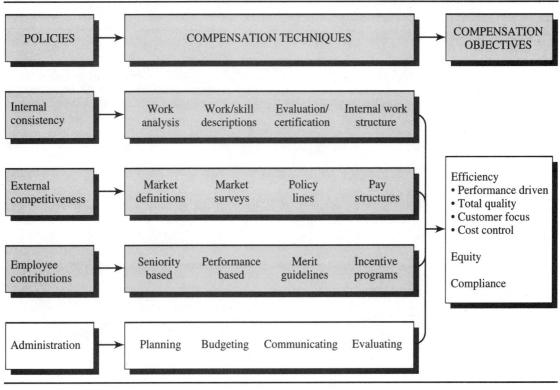

PART V

Compliance

We have now completed the discussion of three strategic policies in the pay model used in this book. The first, which focused on determining the structure of pay, dealt with internal consistency. The second was determining the pay level based on external competitiveness, and the third dealt with determining the pay for employees according to their contributions. Strategic decisions regarding consistency, competitiveness, and contributions are directed at achieving the objectives of the pay system. Specific objectives vary among organizations; helping achieve competitive advantage and treating employees fairly are basic ones.

Before discussing the fourth strategic decision, the nature of administration, we need to consider the significant role that government and legislation play in the management of compensation. Laws and regulations are the most obvious government intervention. Minimum wage legislation, the Equal Pay Act, and Title VII of the Civil Rights Act, among others, regulate pay decisions.

But government is more than a source of laws and regulations. As a major employer, as a consumer of goods and services, and through its fiscal and monetary policies, government affects the demand for labor. It affects the supply of labor by setting licensing standards, appropriating funds for education and training programs that affect skills, and by competing for human resources directly.

This part of the book has two chapters devoted to examining government as a major force in the design and management of pay systems (see Exhibit V.1). Chapter 13 examines government's role in general and also several laws. Pay discrimination is considered in Chapter 14.

 # The Government's Role in Compensation

---

Chapter Outline

The Angry Trout Cafe in Grand Marais, Minnesota, posts a notice on all its tables outlining its tipping policy:

Tipping Policy

Dear customer,

Here at the Angry Trout Cafe we feel the cooks and dishwashers, as well as the servers are an important part of the service you receive and that the entire staff should receive a share of any tip paid for that service. Sharing tips increases team cooperation and provides a more equitable system of employee compensation. However, Minnesota state law prohibits us from having a straight-forward tip-sharing policy. So, we ask you to help us out by defining any amount you choose to pay over the price of your bill as a "discretionary service payment" which is intended to be split in its entirety among all employees. To reduce confusion, we will consider all payments above the amount of the bill to be "discretionary service payments" and any payments intended for only one person should be made when that person is not working at the cafe.

Management

People at the Angry Trout are up front about their desire to circumvent a law they believe harms their "equitable system of employee compensation." While designers of executive pay may not state their intentions so clearly, much of their work is based on creative responses to ever-changing laws and regulations.[1] Actions at the Angry Trout and in executive compensation departments illustrate the continuing process by which any society attempts to address perceived problems through legislation. A problem is defined (executives are overpaid, servers are being taxed on tips they aren't receiving) and corrective legislation is proposed (Corporate Responsibility Act, no tip-sharing policy). If enough support develops, often as a result of compromises and trade-offs, the proposed legislation becomes law. Employers, along with other stakeholders, all attempt to influence the form any legislation will take. Once passed, laws are enforced by agencies through rulings, regulations, inspections, and investigations. Companies respond to legislation by auditing and perhaps altering their practices, and perhaps again lobby for legislative change. Consequently, the regulatory climate—the laws and regulations issued by governmental agencies created to enforce the laws—represents a significant influence on compensation decisions throughout the world.

GOVERNMENT INFLUENCES ON THE IMPLICIT SOCIAL CONTRACT

In Chapter 1, we discussed government's role as a third party to the employment relationship. The exact role government should play in the contemporary workplace depends in part on one's political ideology. Some call for organizations and the government to act in concert to carry out a public policy that protects the interests of employees. Others believe the constant reconfiguring that is inherent in market-based economies is vital to society's well-being; the economy ought to be allowed to adapt and transform, undistorted by government actions. Countries throughout the world address these issues. However, no two countries arrive at precisely the same answers.

As noted in Chapter 1, it is convenient to see the employment relationship as a contractual exchange between the organization and the employer. Such

---

[1] William Gentry and Eric Peress, "Taxes and Fringe Benefits Offered by Employers" (Working paper no. 4764, NBER, 1994).

EXHIBIT 13.1   The Government's Role in the Employment Relationship

Implicit Employment Contract

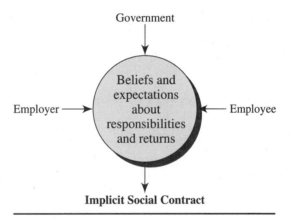

Implicit Social Contract

contracts take many forms, ranging from formal ones, such as those negotiated with unions and professional athletes, to less formal ones, described as expectations and beliefs, often unexpressed and implied. "In simple terms, the implicit contract encompasses the actions employees believe are expected of them and and the responses [e.g., pay, benefits] they expect in return from the employer."[2]

The idea of the implicit employment relationship can be expanded to a social contract that includes a third party, the government, in addition to employees and organizations (Exhibit 13.1). Governments play a crucial role in the employment relationship. Minimum wage, nontaxability of benefits, and other laws all serve to shape the social contract. As you will read in Chapter 18, different countries

---

[2] Denise Rousseau and Martin Greller, "Human Resource Practices: Administrative Contract Maker," *Human Resource Management* 33 (1994), pp. 385–402.

and cultures have different perspectives on the role the government should play in the social contract.

As noted in the Dunlop Commission Report on the Future of Worker–Management Relations:

> The workplace is a centerpiece of the nation's economic performance, concern with productivity, quality, and competitiveness. Our main national asset is a skilled and hard-working workforce. In an ever more global economy, the quality of the workplace affects not only the individual enterprise and its employees, but also national economic growth and productivity performance.[3]

Small wonder that today's governments view themselves as a third party to the employment relationship. Because U.S. workplaces reflect the racial and ethnic diversity of the population and distribute earned income to most of the population, the government has a strong interest in whether that distribution is fair. The quality of the workplace as it affects national economic health informs national debate on minimum wage, health care, the security and portability of pensions, comparable worth, even the quality of public education and the availability of training. So in addition to individuals and employers, government is a key third party to the implicit social contract. Compensation managers need to understand the importance of the implicit social contract as well as government's rightful role in it.

GOVERNMENT INFLUENCES ON PAY

Legislation and public policy set the framework for the employment contract. They can affect pay either directly or indirectly. Laws affect pay directly by specifying certain behaviors and forbidding others. For example, the minimum wage law sets a floor on what an employer must pay, and the Equal Pay Act requires that pay differences among employees doing the same job cannot be based on the sex of the employee. But the government also indirectly affects compensation, as shown in Exhibit 13.2. Governmental actions can affect both the demand and supply of labor; consequently, wages are also affected. Protective legislation often restricts the supply of labor in an occupation. Requiring plumbers to be licensed restricts the number of people who can legally offer plumbing services. Although these licensing requirements are initiated in the name of consumer protection, they also constrain the labor supply, which puts upward pressure on wages for those licensed occupations.

Legislation aimed at protecting specific groups also tends to restrict that group's full participation in the labor supply. Compulsory schooling laws, for example, restrict the supply of 15-year-old employees available to sell hamburgers. In the past, laws intended to protect women from harsh working conditions also limited the hours they could work and the amount of physical labor they

---

[3] Commission on the Future of Worker–Management Relations, *Final Report* (Washington, DC: Department of Labor/Department of Commerce, January 1995).

EXHIBIT 13.2   Indirect Government Influences on Pay

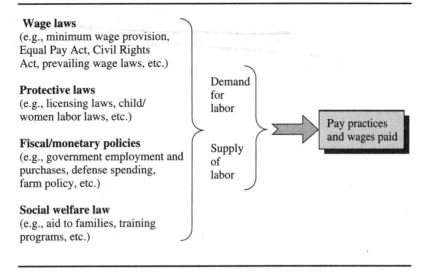

Wage laws
(e.g., minimum wage provision,
Equal Pay Act, Civil Rights
Act, prevailing wage laws, etc.)

Protective laws
(e.g., licensing laws, child/
women labor laws, etc.)

Fiscal/monetary policies
(e.g., government employment and
purchases, defense spending,
farm policy, etc.)

Social welfare law
(e.g., aid to families, training
programs, etc.)

Demand
for
labor

Supply
of
labor

Pay practices
and wages paid

---

could perform. Although the original intent may have been well-meaning, such laws restricted women's access to many good-paying occupations.

Other indirect effects of government on labor supply and hence wages include government-sponsored training and social welfare programs (e.g., aid to families with dependent children). One criticism of the current welfare system is that combined with food stamps and medical care, it provides a better standard of living than working full time at entry-level jobs. Consequently, a financial disincentive to work exists. While there is consensus on the nature of the problem, there is widespread disagreement on solutions.

Government actions also affect the demand for labor in several ways, most directly as a major employer. Employment at all levels of government has grown from around 6 million employees in 1946 to 19.1 million in 1994.[4] In spite of continuing calls for governmental cutbacks, government employment continues to increase, particularly at the state and local level. Yearly growth rates of 5 percent were common in the 1970s and 1980s, and local government employment continues to expand. In many state capitals and county seats the government is the dominant employer; consequently, it is a major force in determining local wages.

In addition to being a major employer, government is a major consumer. Federal expenditures as a percent of the gross national product have risen from 7.3 percent in 1902 to 23.2 percent in 1994.[5] A decision by the government to

---

[4] "Current Labor Statistics: Employment Data," *Monthly Labor Review*, December 1994, p. 84.

[5] *Economic Report of the President*, transmitted to Congress February 1995 (Washington, DC: U.S. Government Printing Office, 1995).

purchase 10 B-757 aircraft from Boeing has a dramatic effect on the demand for labor in Seattle, where Boeing is located.

Government fiscal and monetary policies that affect the economy indirectly affect market forces which, in turn, influence wages. Foreign trade policies, money supply decisions, farm policy—all these governmental actions have indirect effects on wages paid. Restricted farm exports mean that farmers will have less money to spend on supplies and equipment, which means that manufacturers of farm equipment and fertilizer will hire fewer people. Lowered interest rates mean that more people can afford to purchase houses, which means jobs not only for builders and mortgage companies but also for employees of appliance, furniture, and carpet manufacturers. Lower tax rates mean more cash for all taxpayers, which may translate into a boost for all employers and an increased demand for labor. Tax subsidies for hiring disadvantaged youth stimulate demand for such employees. Higher income taxes increase the provision of fringe benefits, which are deductible to the employer and not taxable to employees. So government's effect on wages is wide-ranging and pervasive.

GOVERNMENT AND THE PAY MODEL

Regulatory compliance is one of the objectives of the pay model used in this book. The compensation techniques and the results of those techniques must all comply with the laws.

However, employers frequently try to influence the type of legislation that is passed.[6] They lobby through their governmental relations units or through a consortium of employers, such as Business Roundtable or American Compensation Association. They testify before committees drafting legislation. To influence legislation, compensation managers must establish links with their own firm's law department as well as with professional societies.

Employers also influence court interpretation of legislation through defending their practices during litigation, although this is a costly procedure and not one many employers seek. An example of employer influence on legislation is the Equal Pay Act, in which Congress chose skill, effort, responsibility, and working conditions as factors to define equal work.[7] These factors were chosen largely because Congress became aware of them through lobbying efforts and testimony as criteria commonly used by employers and unions to evaluate jobs. Compensation managers need to put greater emphasis on proactive activities intended to shape the legislation and regulations or to defend sound pay practices in the courts.

Let us now look at some specific compensation legislation.

---

[6] James Ledvinka, *Federal Regulation of Personnel and Human Resource Management* (Boston: Kent Publishing Company, 1982).

[7] Equal Employment Opportunity Commission, *Legislative History of Titles VII and XI of Civil Rights Act of 1964* (Washington, DC: U.S. Government Printing Office, 1968).

FAIR LABOR STANDARDS ACT OF 1938

The Fair Labor Standards Act (FLSA) of 1938 covers all employees (with some exceptions discussed later) of companies engaged in interstate commerce or in production of goods for interstate commerce. FLSA has four major provisions:

1. Minimum wage
2. Hours of work
3. Child labor
4. Equal pay

Minimum Wage

Minimum wage legislation is intended to provide an income floor for workers in society's lowest paid and least productive jobs. When first enacted in 1938, the minimum wage was 25 cents an hour. It has been raised periodically; in 1991, a new minimum of $4.25 took effect. Proposals to increase it to above $5.00 have been considered every year since then. Exhibit 13.3 shows the minimum wage in nominal terms (the actual dollar amount) and in real terms (adjusted to match the consumer price index for November 1994). The graph of real wages translates into purchasing power.

EXHIBIT 13.3

The federal minimum wage in nominal terms and in terms of today's money. Job categories covered by the minimum have varied over the years; some states set higher minimums. Figures are plotted monthly and are adjusted for inflation based on the consumer price index (seasonally adjusted starting in 1972).

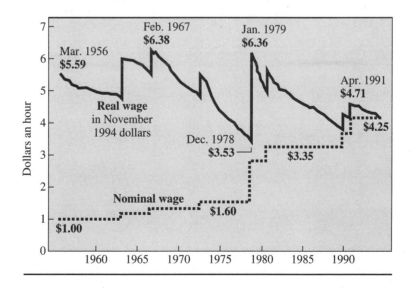

While we all immediately think of teenage employees of fast-food restaurants when we think of a minimum wage earner, in fact only one-third of the roughly four million minimum-wage earners are teenagers.[8] The rest are adults over 25. An additional 5.5 million workers, or nearly 5 percent of the work force, receive wages within 50 cents of the minimum. As legislation forces pay rates at the lowest end of the scale to move up, pay rates above the minimum often increase in order to maintain differentials. This shift in pay structure does not affect all industries equally. For example, the lowest rates paid in the steel, chemical, oil, and pharmaceutical industries are already well above minimum; any legislative change would have little direct impact on employers in these industries. However, retailing and service firms tend to pay at or near minimum wage to many clerks and sales personnel. When legislation results in substantially higher labor costs for these firms, they may consider substituting capital for jobs (e.g., automated inventory control systems, prepacked frozen french fries) or reducing the number of jobs available.

Conventional economic theory says that this job loss falls most heavily on inexperienced and unskilled workers, that is, their perceived value does not equal their actual cost. The high rate of unemployment among teenagers supports this theory. However, a number of recent studies cast doubt on this belief. A decade ago most studies concluded that 1 percent or more of all minimum wage workers lost their jobs for each 10 percent increase in the minimum wage.[9] But more recent studies put the job loss at less than 1 percent, or roughly 40,000 people, if the proposed increase to $5.00 were passed. One study goes even further; it claims no employment effects among fast-food restaurants in New Jersey when that state's minimum wage was increased from $4.25 to $5.05 in 1992. However, others have criticized the New Jersey study for everything from faulty logic to faulty data gathering to faulty statistical analysis.[10] Forty-seven states also have minimum wage laws to cover employees exempt from FLSA.

Minimum wage discussion is also tied up in the social good of the people who are not faring well in the market economy.[11] Some make the case that continuing a low minimum wage permits the continuation of boring, dead-end

---

[8] Louis Uchitelle, "Minimum Wage and Jobs," *The New York Times*, January 12, 1995, pp. D1, D19.

[9] Finis Welch, Donald Deere, and Kevin Murphy, "Estimates of Job Loss with Increasing Minimum Wage," Presentation at 1995 American Economic Association, Washington, DC; David Neumark and William Wascher, "Employment Effects of Minimum and Subminimum Wages: Panel Data on State Minimum Wage Laws," *Industrial and Labor Relations Review* 46, no. 1 (October 1992), pp. 55–81.

[10] David Card and Alan Krueger, "Minimum Wages and Employment: A Case Study of the Fast Food Industry in New Jersey and Pennsylvania," *American Economic Review*, September 1994, pp. 772–93; Lawrence F. Katz and Alan B. Krueger, "The Effect of the Minimum Wage on the Fast-Food Industry," *Industrial and Labor Relations Review* 46, no. 1 (October 1992), pp. 6–21.

[11] David Neumark, "Employment Effects of Minimum and Subminimum Wages: Recent Evidence" (Washington, DC: Employment Policies Institute, February 1993).

jobs that ought to be modernized. Many employers won't bother doing the necessary upgrading and training of employees if they can get by at low pay. Others believe that a higher wage will make it more attractive to people to leave welfare or other government assistance and join the labor market.

So the topic stirs endless debate. What is certain is that people working at or near the minimum wage who continue to work definitely do benefit from mandated minimum wage increases, and other workers in higher level jobs in those same companies may also benefit. Yet as labor costs increase, fewer workers will be hired if the increased costs cannot be passed on to consumers or offset by increased productivity.

Hours of Work

The overtime provision of the FLSA is aimed at sharing available work. It seeks to make hiring more workers a less costly option than scheduling overtime for current employees by requiring payment at one-and-a-half times the standard for working more than 40 hours per week. But the workplace has changed a lot since the law was passed. For current employers, overtime pay is often the least costly option. This is due to (1) an increasingly skilled work force with higher training costs per employee and (2) higher fringe benefits, the bulk of which are fixed per employee. These factors have lowered the point at which it pays employers to schedule longer hours and pay the overtime premium, rather than hire, train, and pay fringes for more employees. Models to examine the break-even points between working overtime and hiring additional workers compare added expense of time-and-a-half wages to the added fringe benefits and training costs required for new hires.

Several amendments to increase the overtime penalty have been proposed over the years. These typically seek to increase the penalty, reduce the standard workweek to less than 40 hours, or repeal some of the exemptions.

Who Is Covered?   Only about 58 percent of all employees are covered by the overtime provision. Determining which jobs are exempt is the most complex part of the act. Some of the exemptions are shown in Exhibit 13.4. Professional, executive, and administrative jobs are exempt. So are many jobs in the transportation industry.

Some exemptions suspend only certain provisions of the act; others suspend all provisions. Some apply to all employees of certain businesses, others to only certain employees. To compound the confusion, exemptions may overlap. Repeated amendments to the act have made the distinction between exempt and nonexempt difficult to determine. One writer observed, "As soon as the distinction between exempt and nonexempt begins to emerge clearly from court cases, the act is amended, setting off a new round of court cases."[12]

---

[12] *Keeping America Competitive* (Washington, DC: Employment Policy Foundation, 1994).

EXHIBIT 13.4   Some Exemptions to the Minimum Wage and Overtime Provisions of the Fair Labor Standards Act

Section 13(a)(1)	Outside salesmen, professional executive, and administrative personnel ("including any employee employed in the capacity of academic administrative personnel or teacher in elementary or secondary schools").
Section 13(a)(3)	Employees of certain seasonal amusements or recreational establishments.
Section 13(a)(5)	Fishing and fish processing at sea employees.
Section 13(a)(6)	Agricultural employees employed by farms utilizing fewer than 500 man-days of agricultural labor, employed by a member of their immediate family, certain local seasonal harvest laborers and seasonal hand harvest laborers 16 years of age or under, and employees principally engaged in the range production of livestock.
Section 13(a)(7)	Employees exempt under Section 14 of the act (certain learners, apprentices, students and handicapped workers).
Section 13(a)(12)	Seamen on foreign vessels.
Section 13(a)(15)	Babysitters employed on a casual basis and persons employed to provide companion services.
Section 7(b)	Certain employees under collectively bargained guaranteed annual wage plans and wholesale or bulk petroleum distribution employees.
Section 7(i)	Certain commissioned salespeople in retail or service establishments.
Section 13(b)(1)	Motor carrier employees.
Section 13(b)(2)	Railroad employees.
Section 13(b)(3)	Airline employees.
Section 13(b)(6)	Seamen.
Section 13(b)(12)	Agricultural employees.
Section 13(b)(15)	Maple sap employees.
Section 13(b)(29)	Employees of amusement or recreational establishments located in a national park or national forest or on land in the National Wildlife Refuge System.

The Wage-Hour Division of the Department of Labor, which is charged with enforcement of the FLSA, provides strict criteria that must be met in order for jobs to be considered professional and exempt from minimum wage and overtime provisions. Professionals must

Do work requiring knowledge generally acquired by prolonged, specialized study, or engage in original and creative activity in a recognized artistic field.
Consistently exercise discretion or judgment.
Do work that is primarily intellectual and nonroutine.
Devote at least 80 percent of their work hours to such activities.

However, contemporary workplace trends that increase employee discretion and omit specific details on duties blur the distinction between exempt and nonexempt. In 1995, a reporter claimed that the *Washington Post* owed him more than $100,000 in overtime accumulated during the six years he covered Washington politics. He said his job merely "required creativity" but did not "depend primarily" on it. But the judge ruled that the job required "invention, imagination, and talent," and thus fell into the category of artistic work and was, therefore, exempt from coverage.[13] Many people accuse reporters of using too much invention and imagination. We will not comment, but Rush Limbaugh probably will.

There are also criteria for exempt status for executives. Executives must

Primarily undertake management duties.

Supervise two or more employees.

Have control (or at least great influence) over hiring, firing, and promotion.

Exercise discretionary powers.

Devote at least 80 percent of their work hours to such activities.

In the 1980s, some fast-food chains were found guilty of giving too many people the title of manager and not paying overtime, even though the work of these "managers" differed only slightly from their coworkers.

What Time Is Covered?   Sometimes counting the hours of work becomes a contest. Exhibit 13.5 details what we mean. Tallying the hours of work is not a piddling matter. In 1993, Iowa Beef Processors was hit with a multimillion dollar bill to cover the overtime wages due to slaughterhouse employees for walking to and from the knife room, waiting to have their knives sharpened, and time spent cleaning equipment. The issue is, When does the workday begin? The Portal-to-Portal Act, passed in 1947 as a result of earlier interpretations and lawsuits surrounding the definition of work time, provides that time spent on activities before beginning the "principal activity" is generally not compensable. In the case of Iowa Beef Processors, the court ruled that the time spent changing into and out of work clothes did not qualify. However, those employees required to wear special protective gear should be compensated for the time it takes to put on the gear as well as for the time spent cleaning tools and protective equipment.

A newer issue is the increased use of "on-call employees" who make themselves available to respond 24 hours a day.[14] Firefighters and other emergency personnel are traditional examples. But with more businesses relying on 24-hour-service from their computer systems, telecommunications and software services personnel must respond quickly to problems outside their regularly scheduled

---

[13] Milo Geyelin, "*Washington Post* Wins Overtime Case by Ex-Reporter," *The Wall Street Journal*, January 5, 1995, p. B1.

[14] *1994–95 Survey of Exempt and Non-Exempt On-Call Practices: Job Site vs. Home-Based* (Dublin, OH: N. E. Fried and Associates, 1994).

Exhibit 13.5   There's No Such Thing as a Free . . .
(Item posted to Internet by D. Shniad)

Gainers Workers Must Pay to Use Bathroom

EDMONTON—Employees at Gainers Inc. are now docked pay for every bathroom break visit made outside of breaks and lunch hour under regulations brought in last week by company owner Burns Meats Ltd.

A notice posted in the meat-packing plant tells employees that abusing washroom visits has lowered productivity. If employees need to use the bathroom outside of breaks, they must report to a supervisor, who records the time of departure and return. The time is tabulated at the end of the week and pay cheques are deducted based on an employee's hourly wage.

"How can they charge you for going to the washroom?" asked one angry employee.

The man said one worker at the plant had a kidney transplant and has to use the washroom often.

"Because of this system, he had to hold it in [between breaks] for a whole week. He went once for three minutes and was charged 43 cents."

Dan McGee of the United Food and Commercial Workers said "the union is deeply concerned about this situation and we're having this situation investigated."

Such washroom rules are rare but there is nothing in the Alberta employment standards code that requires a person to be paid when they don't work, said Kathy Lazowski, a public affairs officer with Alberta Labour. Employees in the province are entitled to a half-hour break after a straight shift of five or six hours. But Ms. Lazowski said a provincial employment standards officers is looking into the dispute.

—Canadian Press

---

workday. Sometimes a flat rate is paid for the added inconvenience of being on call. These payments must be included when computing overtime pay. Gifts or special occasion bonuses do *not* need to be included, because they are at the employer's discretion. When a pay form is promised to employees if certain conditions are met, then those payments must be included as part of an employee's regular rate on which overtime is based. The changing nature of the workplace and of pay systems has led to calls to reform FLSA to allow for more flexible scheduling and easier administration of variable pay plans.

Child Labor

Generally, persons under 18 cannot work in hazardous jobs such as meatpacking and logging; persons under 16 cannot be employed in jobs involving interstate commerce except for nonhazardous work for a parent or guardian. Additional exceptions and limitations also exist. While the intent of the law is straightforward, violations have soared in recent years as the supply of older teenagers dwindles and the service sector of the economy expands. The dramatic increase in violations has caused many states to reexamine child labor legislation.

The fourth major provision of FLSA, equal employment, will be discussed in the next chapter. Equal employment was not covered in the original 1938 FLSA. It was added as an amendment in 1963, called the *Equal Pay Act*, and is today of major importance.

The next group of laws set pay for work done to produce goods and services contracted by the federal government. These are called "prevailing wage" laws.

PREVAILING WAGE LAWS

A government-defined prevailing wage is the minimum wage that must be paid for work done on covered government projects or purchases. The original purpose was to prevent the government from undercutting local workers. For example, if a government project of the magnitude of Hoover Dam were to pay low wages to construction workers, its sheer force of size could drive down the entire wage structure in the area. So the government requires that surveys identify the prevailing wage in an area. That prevailing wage then becomes the mandated minimum wage on the government-financed project.

Contractors object to this requirement because it frequently means that they have to match a wage rate that only a minority of area workers are receiving. Many taxpayers also object because they believe it drives up the cost of government.

A number of laws contain prevailing wage provisions. They vary on the government expenditures they target for coverage. The following are the main prevailing wage laws:

1. Davis-Bacon (1931), which covers mechanics and laborers on public construction projects with expenditures over $2,000.
2. Walsh-Healey Public Contracts Act (1936), which extends the provisions of Davis-Bacon to manufacturers or suppliers of goods for government contracts over $10,000.
3. Service Contract Act (1965), which extends coverage to suppliers of services to the federal government in excess of $2,500 (e.g., cleaning, catering).
4. National Foundation Arts and Humanities Act (1965), which covers professionals, laborers, and mechanics working on projects that receive funding from the Foundation. Only those employees directly engaged in producing or furnishing for the federal contract are covered; other employees of the manufacturer/supplier are not.

Much of the legislation discussed so far was originally passed in the 1930s and 1940s in response to social issues of that time. In the 1960s, the equal rights movements pushed different social problems to the forefront. The Equal Pay

---

EXHIBIT 13.6   Federal Laws: Equal Employment Opportunity

Regulation	Major Provisions
Equal Pay Act	A 1963 amendment to FLSA; equal pay required for male and female workers doing "substantially similar work" in terms of skill, effort, responsibility, and working conditions. Exemptions allowed for seniority, merit pay, and piecework systems.
Title VII of Civil Rights Act	(1) Prohibits discrimination in all employment practices on basis of race, sex, color, religion, origin, or pregnancy. (2) Bennett Amendment links Title VII and the Equal Pay Act by providing that it is not unlawful to differentiate on the basis of sex in determining pay if such differentiation is authorized by the Equal Pay Act.
Age Discrimination Act	Protects employees age 40 and over against age discrimination.
Pregnancy Discrimination Act	Disability and medical benefits plans cannot single out pregnancy for differential treatment. Pregnancy must be covered to same extent that other medical conditions are covered.
Civil Rights Act of 1991	Reestablishes the standards for proving discrimination that had been in general use before 1989 Supreme Court rulings. Allows jury trials and damage awards.

Act and the Civil Rights Act were passed. Because of their substantial impact on human resource management and compensation, they are discussed at length in the next chapter. Additional rights legislation includes the Pregnancy Discrimination Act and the Age Discrimination in Employment Act (Exhibit 13.6).

EQUAL RIGHTS LEGISLATION

Age Discrimination in Employment Act of 1967

The Age Discrimination in Employment Act (ADEA), passed in 1967 and amended in 1978, 1986, and 1990, protects workers age 40 and over from employment discrimination due to age. There are a few exemptions: religious clergy, elected officials, and bona fide executives and policy makers (not middle managers). To date this act has been applied principally to retirement, promotion, and layoff policies, but it covers all personnel decisions. The purpose of the act is to "promote employment of older persons on their ability rather than age; to prohibit arbitrary age discrimination in employment; to help employers and workers find ways of meeting problems arising from the impact of age on employment." The law forbids limiting or classifying employees in any way that would adversely affect their status because of age, reducing any employee's wage rate to comply with the act, or discriminating in compensation or terms of employment because of age.

The 1990 amendment to the act, called the *Older Workers Benefits Protection Act* (OWBPA) extends ADEA coverage to all employee benefits. It was passed as a correction to a 1989 Supreme Court ruling that found legal a state law allowing disability retirements only through age 60. The case involved an employee who became disabled at age 61 and was forced to take early retirement, which provided no medical insurance and whose monthly payments were less than half the amount that disability payments would have been. The Supreme Court found such age-based benefits acceptable, but the public did not, and so a new law was swiftly passed.

OWBPA also contains an "equal benefit or equal cost" principle, which means that benefits for older employees can be less than those for younger employees only if the cost of providing the benefit increases with age. For example, assume that the employer pays $500 for life insurance for each employee. For an employee under age 25, $500 will buy $200,000 worth of insurance. But at age 60, $500 will buy only $50,000 worth of insurance. The employer can provide either the same level of insurance (equal benefit) or pay the same amount per employee for insurance (equal cost).

OWBPA also establishes requirements that must be followed when older employees accept a voluntary retirement package. In cases where an older worker is targeted for layoff, a sweetened benefits package is frequently offered in exchange for a waiver giving up any claim of age discrimination. OWBPA outlines the requirements that must be met before the waiver can be deemed "knowing and voluntary."

Pregnancy Discrimination Act of 1978

This act is actually an amendment to Title VII of the Civil Rights Acts. It requires employers to extend to pregnant women the same disability and medical benefits provided other employees. The Pregnancy Discrimination Act forbids exclusion of pregnancy from the list of disabilities for which the employer compensates absent employees. It does not require an employer to offer a disability plan, nor does it prevent a dollar limit being placed on reimbursement of medical costs. The law merely places disability benefits for pregnant employees on an equal footing with those of nonpregnant employees.

A 1983 court case extends this approach to dependent spouses of employees; a limitation on pregnancy coverage for an employee's spouse is legal only if the same limitation also applies to nonpregnancy-related medical coverage for all dependents. An employer may distinguish between employees and dependents of employees; different levels of coverage to each group is permissible. But different coverage between female dependents and male dependents is not permissible.

WAGE AND PRICE CONTROLS

Governmental wage and price controls limit the size of pay raises and/or price increases. The purpose of these controls is to control inflation at low levels of unemployment.

Wage controls or guidelines can vary in the broadness of application and in the stringency of the standard. The standard for allowable pay increases can range from absolute denial during a freeze to increases equal to some productivity or price change measure. In 1942, for example, wages were frozen at a level that prevailed on September 15 of that year. The government established "going rates" for key occupations and then permitted pay increases up to the minimum of a going rate bracket. Benefits could be instituted only if employers could show that they were customary in an area. The restrictions were deemed necessary because of the demand and supply imbalances created by World War II.

Another freeze was ordered in 1951, but by then many union members had labor contracts that provided automatic wage increases tied to the cost of living as well as annual "productivity" raises. Once stabilization officials decided to permit the continued operation of these contracts, they were forced to sanction similar raises for other groups of employees.

Rather than an across-the-board wage freeze, the Council of Economic Advisers (CEA) in the early 1960s tried a more moderate approach. It tied wage rate and benefit increases to overall productivity increases, reasoning that acceptance of this guide would maintain stability of labor cost per unit of output for the overall economy. But productivity is only one of many factors related to pay, and any national productivity rate is meaningless when applied to a specific employer's productivity.

In 1971 the Nixon administration, facing a 6 percent inflation rate and an unemployment level just over 5 percent, imposed freeze and control measures that rivaled those of World War II. But once the controls were relaxed, inflation rose to 11 percent in 1974.

In the late 1970s, the Council on Wage and Price Stability tried less encompassing voluntary wage guidelines. Employers were provided formulas to determine their own compliance with pay standards. Government purchases favored employers who complied and penalized noncompliance. However, even though flexibility had been a goal of the program, an absolute standard soon developed, along with a bureaucracy to consider exceptions to the standard.

Eventually any freeze or outside control exerted at an arbitrary point in time cannot help but be inequitable to some employers and employees, since the wage-setting process is ongoing. Both unions and managers are united in their concern for the difficulty in maintaining employee equity under wage controls.

How can compensation managers best protect their employees and managers facing government intervention in the wage-setting process? Those companies that seem to suffer the least disruptions are the ones that have sound and flexible compensation systems in place, well-thought-out policies that demonstrably have been followed in the past. Such companies can document what they have done and why they did it, and are far more able to handle government intervention than employers that have no formal pay system and cannot justify their behavior. The same is true with any other area of government interest, be it meeting FLSA pay and recordkeeping requirements, or complying with equal rights legislation. A system based on work- and business-related logic is an employee's and an employer's best protection.

REGULATION OF BENEFITS

We have already mentioned the requirements that benefits packages must be nondiscriminatory on the basis of sex, race, religion, and national origin. Additional governmental effects on benefit options are discussed in Chapter 12. Government has its impact in two ways. The first is by legally requiring that some specific benefits be provided, either at employer expense or as an expense shared between employer and employee. Workers' compensation, Social Security, and unemployment insurance are all legally required. Workers' compensation and unemployment insurance are completely employer-financed, whereas employees and employers jointly contribute to Social Security.

The second way the government influences benefits is through its tax policy. Benefits are, in general, tax free to employees and a tax-deductible expense to employers, providing certain conditions are met. These conditions change frequently, almost with every legislative session, but their general aim is to ensure that a benefits package is structured to be available to all employees rather than to a select few, and to be sure that tax-free cash is not funneled to employees under the guise of benefits, thus escaping the long arm of the Internal Revenue Service. These issues are discussed in the benefits chapters.

Summary

Compliance with laws and regulations can be a constraint and/or an opportunity for a compensation manager. The regulatory environment certainly constrains the decisions that can be made. Once laws are passed and regulations published, employers must comply. But a proactive compensation manager can influence the nature of regulations and their interpretation. Astute professionals must be aware of legislative and judicial currents, to protect both employers' and employees' interests, and to ensure that compensation practices conform to judicial interpretation.

How can a compensation manager best undertake these efforts? First, join professional associations to stay informed on emerging issues and to act in concert to inform and influence public and legislative opinion. Second, constantly review compensation practices and the results of their application. The equitable treatment of all employees is the goal of a good pay system, and that is the same goal of legislation. When interpretations of equitable treatment differ, informed public discussion is required. Such discussion cannot occur without the input of informed compensation managers.

Most of the legislation specifying minimum wages and compensable time was originally passed in the 1930s and 1940s to correct harsh conditions faced by employees, including children. Prevailing wage laws specify a higher minimum for work on government projects, a minimum that is equal to the prevailing rate in an area, which usually translates into a union rate far above the minimum. In the 1960s, legislation addressing equal rights issues had a profound impact on all of U.S. society, including employment relationships. This chapter discussed age discrimination. The many other laws enacted to prevent race and gender discrimination are discussed in the next chapter.

Review Questions

1. What is the nature of government's role in compensation?
 2. Explain why changes in minimum wage can affect higher-paid employees as well.
3. How could a compensation manager examine the effect of minimum wage on a specific employer's labor expense?
4. Your employer's production manager has recommended adding a third shift of workers. What advice can you give?
5. What kinds of proactive activities can an employer undertake to enhance the regulatory environment?
6. Could the pay objective of regulatory compliance ever conflict with other objectives? Could it conflict with the employer's notion of consistency or competitiveness? An employee's notion of equity? If so, how would you deal with such situations?

YOUR TURN:

AMENDING THE MINIMUM WAGE

Over the years, a number of changes have been proposed to the minimum wage provision of the Fair Labor Standards Act. Prepare a brief report outlining the effects of one of the proposed changes listed below. Find out if there is currently any legislative activity regarding this change. You may have to use your library's information service to track current activity.

In your report, answer these questions:

What problem will this change address? Whom will it help? Whom will it hurt? Do you think such a change is a good idea? If you were a legislator, would you vote for such an amendment?

A different student should research each proposed change. Reports should then be presented to the class. Presenters should be prepared to answer questions and defend their votes. After discussion, the entire class will vote on the proposals.

Proposed Changes

a. A youth differential allowing a lower rate for jobs held by unskilled, inexperienced workers.

b. Elimination of the bulk of exemptions.

c. Elimination of the entire minimum wage provision.

d. Index the minimum wage to reflect changes in the CPI. (Chapter 15 contains a discussion of the CPI.)

e. Index the minimum wage to reflect changes in average hourly earnings in private business.

f. Reduce noncompliance by permitting class action lawsuits, increasing penalties, and targeting enforcement efforts.

g. Limit student certification exemptions to high school students.

CHAPTER

Pay Discrimination

Chapter Outline

> The . . . wage curve . . . is not the same for women as for men because of the more transient character of the service of the former, the relative shortness of their activity in industry, the differences in environment required, the extra services that must be provided, overtime limitations, extra help needed for the occasional heavy work, and the general sociological factors not requiring discussion herein. Basically then we have another wage curve . . . for women below and not parallel with the men's curve. [Excerpt from a 1939 pay policy handbook.][1]

Over 30 years have passed since passage of the Equal Pay Act, the first modern statute directed at eliminating discrimination in the job market. This legislation was quickly followed by the Civil Rights Act of 1964. Together, these laws revolutionized the American workplace. Newspaper help-wanted ads specifying "perky gal-Fridays," whites-only local unions, and the pay practice described at the beginning of this chapter are all part of the past. However, women still earn only 76 cents for every dollar earned by men—up a little more than a dime since 1963. African-American and Hispanic women fare worse: 66 cents and 59 cents, respectively.

Many people believed that as women got out of the clerical pool and into professional and managerial occupations and as they accumulated experience and career savvy, the pay gap would close. It hasn't. Today, hourly workers come closest to parity. Female cashiers, for example, make 95 cents to their male counterparts' dollar, but female securities brokers earn only 52 cents for every dollar earned by their male counterparts.[2]

---

[1] The job evaluation manual was introduced as evidence in *Electrical Workers (IUE)* v. *Westinghouse Electric Corp.*, 632 F.2d 1094, 23 FEP Cases 588 (3rd Cir. 1980), cert. denied, 452 U.S. 967, 25 FEP Cases 1835 (1981).

[2] Joan E. Rigdon, "Three Decades After the Equal Pay Act, Women's Wages Remain Far From Parity," *The Wall Street Journal*, June 3, 1993, pp. B1, B6, Alison J. Wellington, "Accounting for the Male/Female Wage Gap Among Whites: 1976 and 1985," *American Sociological Review*, December 1994, pp. 839–48; Audrey Light and Manuelita Ureta, "Early-Career Work Experience and Gender Wage Differentials," *Journal of Labor Economics* 13, no. 1 (1995), pp. 121–54; Emily P. Hoffman, ed., *Essays on the Economics of Discrimination* (Kalamazoo, MI: W. E. Upjohn Institute for Employment Research, 1991).

The law profession illustrates the changes. In 1972, only 4 percent of all U.S. lawyers were women, and 2 percent were African-Americans or of Hispanic origin. In 1982, 15.5 percent were women, and 3.6 percent were African-Americans or Hispanic. By 1993, the percentages were 22.8 percent and 4.9 percent, respectively. So occupational segregation clearly has lessened, particularly for women, and law school enrollments reflect a far greater diversity. However, a recent study concluded that even though women law school graduates start their careers earnings only slightly less per year than do men graduates, 15 years later women graduates are earning only 60 percent as much as men.[3]

We don't mean to pick on lawyers. (Actually, we do, but we won't.) Not all the wage difference is discrimination. But in study after study, in which numerous organization, job, and individual characteristics are controlled, an unexplained pay gap remains. African-American men earn 74 percent and Hispanic men 65 percent of the wages of white men. Many people feel that women and minority group members don't receive pay and benefits commensurate with the work they do, the level of responsibility they hold, or the societal contributions they make.

But what is pay discrimination? How do we recognize it when we see it? How does the law define discrimination? We begin our study of discrimination by distinguishing between access and valuation discrimination.

PAY DISCRIMINATION: WHAT IS IT?

Access discrimination refers to the staffing and allocation decisions made by employers (e.g., recruiting, hiring, promoting, training, and layoffs). Access discrimination denies particular jobs, promotions, or training opportunities to qualified women or minorities. *Valuation discrimination* focuses on the pay women and minorities receive for the jobs they perform. The Equal Pay Act makes it clear that it is discriminatory to pay minorities or women less than males when performing equal work (i.e., working side by side, in the same plant, doing the same work, producing the same results). This definition of pay discrimination hinges on the standard of equal pay for equal work.

But many believe that this definition does not go far enough.[4] They believe that valuation discrimination can also occur when men and women hold entirely different jobs (i.e., when job segregation or access discrimination has forced women or minorities into a limited range of jobs). For example, office and clerical jobs are typically staffed by women, and craft jobs (electricians, welders) are typically staffed by men. Is it illegal to pay employees in one job group less than

---

[3] Robert G. Wood, Mary E. Corcoran, and Paul N. Courant, "Pay Differences among the Highly Paid: The Male-Female Earnings Gap in Lawyers' Salaries," *Journal of Labor Economics* 11, no. 3 (1993), pp. 417–41.

[4] Paula England, *Comparable Worth: Theories and Evidence* (New York: Aldine deGruyter, 1992); H. J. Aaron and C. M. Lougy, *The Comparable Worth Controversy* (Washington, DC: Brookings Institution, 1986).

employees in the other, if the two job groups contain work that is not equal in content or results, but is "in some sense of comparable worth" to the employer?

In this case, the proposed definition of pay discrimination hinges on the standard of equal pay for work of comparable worth. Existing federal laws do not support this standard. However, several states have enacted laws that require a comparable worth standard for state and local government employees. The province of Ontario, Canada, has extended such legislation to the private sector. We shall examine its experience later in this chapter.

So two standards for defining pay discrimination need to be considered: equal pay for equal work, and equal pay for work of comparable worth. For an understanding of the legal foundations of each, let us turn to the legislation and key court cases.

THE EQUAL PAY ACT

The Equal Pay Act (EPA) of 1963 forbids wage discrimination on the basis of gender when

- Employees perform equal work in the same establishment.
- Employees perform jobs requiring equal skill, effort, and responsibility under similar working conditions.

Pay differences between equal jobs can be justified by an *affirmative defense*. Differences in pay between men and women doing equal work are legal if these differences are based on

- Seniority.
- Merit or quality of performance.
- Quality or quantity of production.
- Some factor other than gender.

These terms for comparison and permitted defenses seem deceptively simple. Yet numerous court cases have been required to clarify the act's provisions, particularly its definition of equal.

Definition of Equal

The Supreme Court established guidelines to define equal work in the *Schultz* v. *Wheaton Glass* case in 1970. Wheaton Glass Company maintained two job classifications for selector packers in its production department, male and female. The female job class carried a pay rate 10 percent below that of the male job class. The company claimed that the male job class included additional tasks such as shoveling broken glass, opening warehouse doors, doing heavy lifting, and the like, that justified the pay differential. The plaintiff claimed that the extra tasks were infrequently performed, and not all men did them.[5] Further, these extra tasks performed by some of the men were regularly performed by employees in another classification ("snap-up boys"), and these employees were paid only 2 cents an hour more than the women. Did the additional tasks performed by some members of one job class render the jobs unequal? The court decided not. It ruled the equal work standard required only that jobs be *substantially* equal, not identical. The extra duties performed by the men did not justify paying the men 10 percent more than the women were paid. "Substantially equal work" based on the *Wheaton Glass Company* case has become the standard for assessing whether or not jobs are equal.

Additionally, the courts have generally held that the *actual work performed* is the appropriate information to use when deciding if jobs are substantially equal. This was established in several cases in which it was found that the duties employees actually performed were different from those in the written descriptions of the job.

Definitions of the Four Factors

The Department of Labor provides these definitions of the four factors.[6]

1. Skill: Experience, training, education, and ability as measured by the performance requirements of a particular job.
2. Effort: Mental or physical. The amount of degree of effort (not type of effort) actually expended in the performance of a job.
3. Responsibility: The degree of accountability required in the performance of a job.
4. Working conditions: The physical surroundings and hazards of a job including dimensions such as inside versus outside work, heat, cold, and poor ventilation.

Guidelines to clarify these definitions have evolved through court decisions. For an employer to support a claim of *unequal* work, the following conditions must be met:

1. The effort/skill/responsibility must be substantially greater in one of the jobs compared.
2. The tasks involving the extra effort/skill/responsibility must consume a

---

[5] Plaintiffs are those who bring suit to obtain a remedy for injury to their rights. Defendants are those (usually the employer) who explain practices to answer the suit.

[6] U.S. Department of Labor, *Women Workers Today* (Washington, DC, 1976); U.S. Department of Labor, *The Earnings Gap between Women and Men* (Washington, DC, 1976); U.S. Department of Labor, Interpretive Bulletin, *Equal Pay for Equal Work under the Fair Labor Standards Act* (Washington, DC, August 31, 1971); U.S. Department of Labor, *Brief Highlights of Major Federal Laws and Orders on Sex Discrimination in Employment* (Washington, DC, February 1977).

significant amount of time for *all* employees whose additional wages are in question.

3. The extra effort/skill/responsibility must have a *value commensurate* with the questioned pay differential (as determined by the employer's own evaluation).

The courts have also dealt with equal working conditions.[7] In *Brennan v. Corning Glass Works*, the court ruled that time of day did not constitute dissimilar working conditions. Shift differentials are not illegal, but if they paid, the employer must clearly state that their purpose is to compensate workers for unusual conditions, and they must be separate from the base wage for the job.

Factors Other than Sex

Unequal pay for equal work may be justified through the four affirmative defenses: seniority, merit, performance-based incentive system, or a factor other than sex. Factors other than sex include shift differentials; temporary assignments; bona fide training programs; differences based on ability, training, or experience; and others.[8]

Factors other than sex have been interpreted as a broad exception that may include business reasons advanced by the employer. In *Kouba v. Allstate*,[9] Allstate Insurance Company paid its new sales representatives a minimum salary during their training period. After completing the training, the sales reps received a minimum salary or their earned sales commissions, whichever was higher. The minimum salary paid during training needed to be high enough to attract prospective agents to enter the training program, yet not so high as to lessen the incentive to earn sales commissions after training. Allstate maintained that the minimum salary needed to be calculated individually for each trainee, and the trainee's past salary was a necessary factor used in the calculation. But Allstate's approach resulted in women trainees generally being paid less than male trainees, because women had held lower paying jobs before entering the program. Allstate maintained the pay difference resulted from acceptable business reasons, a factor other than sex.

Lola Kouba didn't buy Allstate's arguments. She argued that acceptable business reasons were limited to "those that measure the value of an employee's job performance to his or her employer." But the court rejected Kouba's argument. It said that Allstate's business reasons for a practice must be evaluated for reasonableness. A practice will not automatically be prohibited simply because wage differences between men and women result.

---

[7] Elizabeth A. Cooper and Gerald V. Barrett, "Equal Pay and Gender: Implications of Court Cases for Personnel Practices," *Academy of Management Review* 9, no. 1 (1984), pp. 84–94.

[8] *Bona fide* is interpreted here as (1) established, either formally or informally, (2) systematically applied in a nondiscriminatory fashion, and (3) communicated to all covered employees. H.R. Rep. No. 309, 88th Cong. 1st Sess. 3 (1963).

[9] *Kouba and EEOC* v. *Allstate Insurance Company*, 691 F.2d 873 (1982).

The court did not say that Allstate's "business" reasons were justified. It did say that Allstate's argument could not be rejected *solely because the practice perpetuated historical differences in pay*. Rather, Allstate needed to justify the business relatedness of the practice.

The case was settled out of court, so no legal clarification of Allstate's rationale was ever provided. Thus, the definition of "factor other than sex" remains somewhat murky. It does seem that pay differences for equal work can be justified for demonstrably business-related reasons. But what is and is not demonstrably business related has not yet been cataloged.

Reverse Discrimination

Several cases deal with the important issue of reverse discrimination against men when pay for women is adjusted. In these cases, men have claimed that they were paid less than women doing similar work, simply because they were men. In one case, the University of Nebraska created a model to calculate salaries based on estimated values for a faculty member's education, field of specialization, years of direct experience, years of related experience, and merit.[10] Based on these qualifications, the university granted raises to 33 women whose salaries were less than the amount computed by the model. However, the university gave no such increases to 92 males whose salaries were also below the amount the model set for them based on their qualifications. The court found this system a violation of the EPA. It held that, in effect, the university was using a new system to determine a salary schedule, based on specific criteria. To refuse to pay employees of one sex the minimum required by these criteria was illegal.

In another case, the male faculty at Northern Illinois University (NIU) sued to have a model the university developed to adjust women faculty salaries applied to them, also.[11] The NIU model was used to allocate a one-time salary adjustment to overcome the results of past discrimination against women, and was not a permanent change in the compensation system. Therefore, the court ruled that it did not need to be applied to men. NIU's approach differed from Nebraska's. NIU made a one-time payment to women to correct past discrimination. Nebraska, on the other hand, developed a new way to calculate salaries and therefore must apply it to all faculty members equally.

---

[10] *Board of Regents of University of Nebraska* v. *Dawes*, 522 F.2d 380, 11 FEP Cases 283 (8th Cir. 1976); 424 U.S. 914, 12 FEP Cases 343 (1976).

[11] *Ende* v. *Board of Regents of Northern Illinois University*, 37 FEP Cases 575 (7th Cir. 1985). Peter Saucier wonders whether affirmative action plans are "a factor other than sex" in "Affirmative Action and the Equal Pay Act," *Employee Relations Law Journal* 11, no. 2 (Winter 1985/86), pp. 453–66. Also see G. Luna, "Understanding Gender-Based Wage Discrimination: Legal Interpretation and Trends of Pay Equity in Higher Education," *Journal of Law & Education* 19, no. 3 (1990), pp. 371–84; Marcia L. Bellas, "Comparable Worth in Academia: The Effects on Faculty Salaries of the Sex Composition and Labor-Market Conditions of Academic Disciplines," *American Sociological Review*, December 1994, pp. 807–21.

More recently, male flight attendants at Northwest Airlines sued to recover back pay comparable to that awarded by Northwest to female attendants who had charged the airline with sex discrimination. The 265 male attendants charged that the airline violated the Civil Rights Act of 1964 by not paying them the back pay when the airline settled with the female attendants. Under a 1992 settlement, the male attendants shared $1 million.

So what does this have to do with compensation management? Viewed collectively, the courts have provided reasonably clear directions. The design of pay systems must incorporate a policy of equal pay for substantially equal work. The determination of substantially equal work must be based on the actual work performed (the job content) and must reflect the skill, effort, and responsibility required, and the working conditions. It is legal to pay men and women who perform substantially equal work differently if the pay system is designed to recognize differences in performance, seniority, quality and quantity of results, or certain factors other than sex, in a nondiscriminatory manner. Further, to minimize vulnerability to reverse discrimination suits, if a new pay system is designed, it must be equally applied to all employees. If, on the other hand, a one-time adjustment is made to correct past problems, it need apply only to the affected group.

But what does this tell us about discrimination on jobs that are *not substantially equal*—dissimilar jobs? Fifty-eight percent of all working women are not in substantially equal jobs as men, so they are not covered by the EPA. For example, suppose that almost all women employees work in one job classification: office/clerical. Further suppose that the employer granted cost of living increases semiannually to all job classes *except* the office/clericals. The office/clerical jobs are not "substantially equal" to the other jobs, so the Equal Pay Act does not apply. Can the office/clerical employees still charge their employer with pay discrimination? Yes, under Title VII of the Civil Rights Act.

TITLE VII OF THE CIVIL RIGHTS ACT OF 1964

Title VII prohibits discrimination on the basis of sex, race, color, religion, or national origin in any employment condition, including hiring, firing, promotion, transfer, compensation, and admission to training programs.[12] Title VII was amended in 1972 and 1978. The 1972 amendments strengthened enforcement and expanded coverage to include employees of government and educational institutions, as well as private employers of more than 15 persons. The pregnancy amendment of 1978, discussed in Chapter 13, made it illegal to discriminate based on pregnancy, childbirth, or related conditions.

Since 1964 the courts have established two theories of discrimination behav-

---

[12] 29 U.S.C. § 206 (d) (1) (1970). Its coverage is broader, also. Employers, employment agencies, labor organizations, and training programs involving 15 or more employees and some 120,000 educational institutions fall under its jurisdictions.

Exhibit 14.1 Discriminatory Behavior

Disparate Treatment	*Disparate Impact*
1. Different standards for different individuals or groups.	1. Same standards have differing consequences.
2. Intent to discriminate may be inferred by behaviors.	2. Discrimination shown by general statistical impact; discriminatory intent need not be present.
3. Employer can justify actions by absence of discriminatory intent and exercise of reasonable business judgment.	3. Employer can justify pay differences through business necessity.

ior under Title VII: (1) disparate treatment and (2) disparate impact. Exhibit 14.1 contrasts the two theories.

Disparate Treatment. Disparate or unequal treatment includes those practices in which an organization treats minorities or women less favorably than others are treated, either openly or covertly. Under this definition, a practice is unlawful if it applies different standards to different employees, for example, based on seniority for women but performance for men (different standards). The mere fact of unequal treatment may be taken as evidence of the employer's intention to discriminate.

Disparate Impact. Personnel practices that have a differential effect on members of protected groups are illegal under the disparate or unequal impact theory of Title VII, unless the differences can be justified as necessary to the safe and efficient operation of the business or are work related. The major case that established this interpretation of Title VII is *Griggs* v. *Duke Power Co.*,[13] in which the Court struck down employment tests and educational requirements that screened out a higher proportion of blacks than whites. Even though the practices were applied equally—both blacks and whites had to pass the tests—they were prohibited because (1) they had the consequence of excluding a protected group (blacks) disproportionately and (2) they were not related to the jobs in question.

Under the disparate impact theory of discrimination, whether or not the employer intended to discriminate is irrelevant. Thus, a personal decision can, on its face, seem neutral, but if the results of it are unequal, the employer must demonstrate that the decision is either work related or a business necessity.

---

[13] *Griggs* v. *Duke Power Co.*, 401 U.S. 414 (1971).

CIVIL RIGHTS ACT OF 1991

The two standards of discrimination—disparate treatment and disparate impact—appeared well established when applied to access discrimination issues. But a 1989 Supreme Court ruling, *Wards Cove Packing* v. *Atonio*, upset the apple cart by ruling that plaintiffs must specify which employment practice had the adverse impact and then link that practice to the resulting imbalance.[14] But as you recall from your introductory human resource management course, trying to isolate the effect of a single personnel practice is like separating the strands of a spider web. Pick up a single strand and find the whole world attached. The Civil Rights Act of 1991 redressed the issue by reestablishing the standards for discrimination that had been in widespread use before 1989. Nevertheless, the two standards remain difficult to apply to pay issues, since pay differences are legal for dissimilar work.

To understand pay discrimination under Title VII, we examine two basic questions.

1. Can pay discrimination exist in different pay rates for dissimilar jobs?
2. What constitutes pay discrimination in dissimilar jobs?

PAY DISCRIMINATION AND DISSIMILAR JOBS

The Supreme Court, in *Gunther* v. *County of Washington*, determined that pay differences for dissimilar jobs may reflect discrimination.[15] In this case, four jail matrons in Washington County, Oregon, claimed that their work was comparable to that performed by male guards. The women matrons also were assigned clerical duties, because guarding the smaller number of female prisoners did not occupy all of the work time.

Both the county's own wage survey and its assessment of job worth had indicated that the matrons should be paid about 95 percent as much as the guards. Instead, their pay was only about 70 percent that of the guards. Lower courts refused to consider the matrons' charge of discrimination on the grounds that their evidence did not meet the equal work requirement of the Equal Pay Act. The Supreme Court overturned the lower courts and stated that a Title VII pay case was not bound by the definitions of equal work or the affirmative defenses of the Equal Pay Act, ruling that "to hold that sex-based wage discrimination violates Title VII only if it also violates the EPA would be denying relief to victims of discrimination who did not hold the same jobs as a higher paid man." The Court also went out of its way to state what it was *not* ruling on:

> We emphasize at the outset the narrowness of the question before us in this case. Respondents' claim is not based on the controversial concept of "compara-

---

[14] *Wards Cove Packing* v. *Atonio*, 57 U.S.L.W. 4583 (1989).
[15] *Gunther* v. *County of Washington*, U.S. Sup. Ct. 451 U.S. 161 (1981).

ble worth,'' under which the plaintiff might claim increased compensation on the basis of a comparison of the intrinsic worth or difficulty of their job with that of other jobs in the same organization or community. Rather, respondents seek to prove, by direct evidence, that their wages were depressed because of intentional sex discrimination, consisting of setting the wage scale level lower than its own survey of outside markets and the worth of the jobs warranted.

(The case was returned to a lower court for additional evidence of discrimination, and was eventually settled out of court.)

Although the *Gunther* case established that charges of pay discrimination on dissimilar (not equal) jobs could be brought under Title VII, it did not consider what might constitute pay discrimination in dissimilar jobs under Title VII. To examine this question, we discuss three possible approaches: (1) where the employer exhibited a pattern of discrimination in many of its personnel practices beyond wage setting, (2) where the employer used market data to justify pay differences, and (3) where the employer conducted a pay equity study using job evaluation to determine jobs of "comparable worth."

Proof of Discrimination: Pattern of Personnel Practices

Under this approach, employees seek to prove that discrimination pervades the entire employment relationship, including the pay system. In *Taylor* v. *Charley Brothers Company,*[16] a wholesale distributor maintained two separate departments based on what products were handled, not on what work was done. For example, warehouse workers who handled frozen food were in department 1; those who handled health and beauty aids were in department 2. Charley Brothers hired only men for the first department; women applicants were not even considered for positions in that department. If female applicants specifically requested department 1, they were told that the work there required greater physical strength, but they were not told that it also paid more. Additional evidence indicated that no males were considered for jobs in department 2, and that both company officials and union officials discouraged female employees from bidding for jobs in department 1. Clearly, the company's hiring and job assignment policies violated Title VII in that women were denied equal access to jobs, but did its pay policies discriminate, too? The Court held that both the EPA and Title VII were violated: Charley Brothers intentionally discriminated in its entire pay system. Women were paid substantially less than men in the all-male department simply because they worked in a department populated only by women, not because the jobs they performed were inherently worth less than jobs performed by men. The Court took as evidence of the company's intent to discriminate the fact that it never had undertaken any type of evaluation of any of the jobs, that it segregated women within the one department, and that officials of

---

[16] *Taylor* v. *Charley Brothers Company*, 25 FEP Cases 602 (W.D. Pa. 1981).

the company made various discriminatory remarks.[17] Sufficient proof of Charley Brothers' intention to discriminate was shown through the pattern of its personnel practices, including pay, regardless of the dissimilarity of the jobs involved.

Most cases are less clear-cut than Charley Brothers. That is why few *pattern-of-practice* cases have been filed in recent years. However, the 1991 Civil Rights Act has reversed the downward trend by allowing for punitive and compensatory damages up to $300,000 per person in addition to back pay in employment class actions. The assumption is that the possibility of larger settlements makes it worthwhile to sift through all the data required to build a pattern-of-practice case. For example, computer consultants logged 2,000 hours reviewing State Farm General Insurance's hiring, promotion, and pay records. Their analysis played a major role in State Farm's 1992 $250 million settlement with 1,000 women who said they had been denied jobs as agents.[18]

Now let us focus on the way in which pay rates for two obviously dissimilar jobs are determined. Examples include the pay rates for nurses versus tree trimmers or nurses versus sanitarians or even professors of nursing versus professors of business administration. If these jobs are dissimilar and if no pattern of discrimination in hiring, promotion, or other personnel decisions exists, then what constitutes pay discrimination?

Proof of Discrimination: Use of Market Data

In the case of *Lemons* v. *City and County of Denver*,[19] nurse Mary Lemons claimed that her job, held predominantly by women, was illegally paid less than the jobs held predominantly by men (tree trimmers, sign painters, tire servicemen, etc.). Lemons claimed that the nursing job required more education and skill. Therefore, to pay the male jobs more than the nurses' jobs simply because the male jobs commanded higher rates in the local labor market was discriminatory. She argued that the market reflected historical underpayment of "women's work." The court disagreed, adding that "market disparities are not among those Title VII seeks to adjust." Thus, the situation identified by *Lemons*—pay differences in dissimilar jobs—did not by itself constitute proof of intent to discriminate.

The courts have continually upheld employers' use of market data to justify pay differences for different jobs. *Spaulding* v. *University of Washington*[20] developed the argument in greatest detail. In this case, the predominantly female faculty of the Department of Nursing claimed that it was illegally paid less than

---

[17] The union was also accused of discrimination against female employees. The courts accepted as evidence discriminatory statements made by union leaders but did not hold them liable for their behaviors, since they had not made the hiring and allocation decisions.

[18] Russell Mitchell and Jonathan Ringel, "The Swat Team of Bias Litigation," *Business Week*, January 23, 1995, pp. 88–89.

[19] *Lemons* v. *City and County of Denver*, 620 F.2d 228 (1980).

[20] *Spaulding* v. *University of Washington*, 35 FEP Cases 217 (9th Cir. 1984).

faculty in other departments. The statisticians for Spaulding presented a model of faculty pay comparisons in "comparable" departments that controlled for the effects of level of education, job tenure, and other factors. They asserted that any pay difference not accounted for in their model was discrimination. But the courts have been dubious of statistics. Such an approach to defining discrimination has been likened to the owner of a missing piece of jewelry concluding that it must be in the kitchen, "because I've looked through every other room in the house." Far better to define discrimination directly, rather than concluding that it is "whatever is left."[21] The *Spaulding* judge observed that the model "unrealistically assumed the equality of all master's degrees, ignored job experience prior to university employment, and ignored detailed analysis of day-to-day responsibilities." Without such data, "we have no meaningful way of determining just how much of the proposed wage differential was due to sex and how much was due to academic discipline."

But the court went beyond criticizing the model. It ruled on the use of competitive market data as a policy. The court held that every employer constrained by market forces may consider market values in setting wages. "Naturally, market prices are inherently job-related." Employers who rely on the market deal with it as a given and do not meaningfully have a "policy" about it in the relevant Title VII sense, according to the court.

Is There a "Market Policy"?   As you recall from Chapter 7, a lot of judgment goes into the wage survey process. Which employers constitute the "relevant market"? Does the relevant market vary by occupation? Do different market definitions yield different wage patterns? Clearly, judgment is involved in answering these questions. Yet the courts have thus far neglected to examine those judgments for possible bias. Perhaps the pattern of judgment does not constitute a "policy" in a Title VII sense.

Spaulding and other court cases have tended to view the market as a given that allows little room for discretion. If that is so, then the employer's role is to "find out precisely what that rate is. If, on the other hand, a *range* of possible wages exists for any given job, then . . . the observed, or measured, market wage will depend on where the wage data is collected, . . . (and) *sampling* becomes critical."[22] Furthermore, "judgment enters into virtually every step of the wage survey process, and each successive judgment may modify the eventual results." It is not at all clear that employers are the "price takers" that the courts have assumed.[23]

---

[21] Orley Ashenfelter and Ronald Oaxaca, "The Economics of Discrimination: Economists Enter the Courtroom," *American Economic Review*, May 1987, pp. 321–25; Victor Fuchs, *Women's Quest for Economic Equality* (Cambridge, MA. Harvard University Press, 1988).

[22] Sara L. Rynes and George T. Milkovich, "Wage Surveys: Dispelling Some Myths about the 'Market Wage,'" *Personnel Psychology*, Spring 1986, pp. 71–90.

[23] Sara L. Rynes, Caroline L. Weber, and George T. Milkovich, "The Effects of Market Survey Rates, Job Evaluation, and Job Gender on Job Pay," *Journal of Applied Psychology* 74, no. 1 (1989), pp. 114–23.

Proof of Discrimination: Jobs of "Comparable Worth"

A third approach to attempting to determine pay discrimination on jobs of dissimilar content hinges on finding a standard by which to compare the value of jobs. The standard must be two things. First, it must permit jobs with dissimilar content to be declared equal or "in some sense comparable."[24] Second, it must permit pay differences for dissimilar jobs that are not comparable. Job evaluation has been proposed as that standard.[25] If an employer's own job evaluation study shows jobs of dissimilar content to be of equal value to the employer, then isn't failure to pay them equally proof of intent to discriminate? The issue has been considered in *AFSCME* v. *State of Washington*.

In 1973, the state of Washington commissioned a study of the concept of comparable worth (discussed later in this chapter) and its projected effect on the state's pay system. The study concluded that by basing wages on the external market, the state was paying women approximately 20 percent less than it was paying men in jobs deemed of comparable value to the state. The state took no action on this finding, alleging it could not afford to do so, so the American Federation of State, County, and Municipal Employees (AFSCME), the employees' union, sued to force implementation of a compensation system based on comparable worth as outlined in the study. The union alleged that since the state was aware of the adverse effect of its present policy, failure to change it constituted discrimination.

But an appeals court ruled that the state was not obligated to correct the disparity. An employer's merely being aware of adverse consequences for a protected group did not constitute discrimination. "The plaintiff must show the employer chose the particular policy because of its effect on members of a protected class."

AFSCME v. *State of Washington* differs from previous cases that used market data in that this is the first case in which the evidence that the jobs were in any sense "equal" was developed by the employer. But even though the state had commissioned the study, it had not agreed to implement the study's results. Therefore, the employer had not, in the court's view, admitted that the jobs were equal or established a pay system that purported to pay on the basis of "comparable worth" rather than markets. Rather than appeal, the parties settled out of court. The state revamped its pay system and agreed to make more than $100 million in "pay equity" adjustments by 1992.

So where does this leave us? Clearly, Title VII prohibits intentional discrimination in compensation if it is based on sex or other proscribed factors, whether or not the employees in question hold the same or different jobs. Discrimination may be proved by direct evidence of an employer's intent (e.g., an overall pattern

---

[24] B. F. Reskin and H. I. Hartmann, eds., *Women's Work, Men's Work: Segregation on the Job* (Washington, DC: National Academy Press, 1986).

[25] *Job Evaluation: A Tool for Pay Equity* (Washington, DC: National Committee on Pay Equity, November 1987); Rynes, Weber, and Milkovich, "Effects of Market Survey Rates, Job Evaluation, and Job Gender on Job Pay."

of behavior that demonstrates disparate treatment). However, "job evaluation studies and comparable worth statistics alone are insufficient to establish the requisite inference of discriminatory motive."[26] The disparate impact standard, in which no proof of discriminatory intent is required, appears to be inappropriate for broad challenges to general compensation policies.

Title VII rulings make it clear that pay discrimination is not limited only to equal jobs; it may also occur in setting different rates for different jobs. It is also clear that the courts are not about to rule the use of external market rates illegal. Further, to prevail in a disparate treatment allegation, plaintiffs need to demonstrate a pattern of discrimination practices that is specific and deliberate— "regularly and purposefully treat(ing) women differently and generally less favorably than men."[27] Simply demonstrating pay differences on jobs that are not equal is insufficient to prove discrimination.

What additional implications for the design and administration of pay systems can be drawn? These court decisions imply that pay differentials between dissimilar jobs will not be prohibited under Title VII if the differences can be shown to be based on the content of the work, its value to the organization's objectives, and the employer's ability to attract and retain employees in competitive external labor markets. The courts appear to recognize that "the value of a particular job to an employer is but one factor influencing the rate of compensation for a job."[28] Absent new legislation, comparable worth is not the law of the land.

ECONOMIC EQUALITY AS A SOCIAL ISSUE

As the statistics given earlier in this chapter show, women and people of color still have not achieved economic parity with white men. So what? Is economic parity a desirable social good? While many believe it is, there is disagreement. The issue is equality of access versus equality of outcomes. Some believe that eliminating gender- and race-related pay differentials on equal jobs and opening access to all jobs constitutes fairness. But many others do not agree. They argue that despite the equal pay standard, women and minorities continue to face severe handicaps in the labor market.[29] To paraphrase Mark Twain, women and minorities are "surrounded by insurmountable opportunities."

---

[26] *American Federation of State, County, and Municipal Employees* v. *State of Washington*, 578 F. Supp. 846 (W.D. Wash. 1983).

[27] *Taylor* v. *Charley Brothers Company.*

[28] *AFSCME* v. *State of Washington.*

[29] Jerald Greenberg and Claire L. McCarty, "Comparable Worth: A Matter of Justice," in *Research in Personnel and Human Resources Management*, vol. 8, ed. K. M. Rowland and G. R. Ferris (Greenwich, CT: JAI Press, 1990); Claudia Goldin, *Understanding the Gender Gap* (New York: Oxford University Press, 1990); Chinhui Juhn, "Decline of Male Labor Market Participation: The Role of Declining Market Opportunities," *Quarterly Journal of Economics* 107 (February 1992), pp. 79–121.

Some say value discrimination remains as a legacy of past discrimination and outright segregation, that is, minorities and women were simply denied access to certain occupations, which artificially created a labor oversupply in another limited range of jobs. According to this view the labor market places a lower value on jobs traditionally held by women and minorities for no other reason than that they were traditionally held by women and minorities. For example, office and clerical jobs are typically staffed by women, and craft jobs (electricians, welders) are typically staffed by men. Is it illegal to pay a secretary less than an electrician, if the two jobs contain work that is not equal in content or results, but is "in some sense of comparable worth or value" to the employer? Under current federal law, it is not. But should it be? A comparable worth standard, or passage of "pay equity" legislation, would make the pay differential illegal. To understand the argument in favor of such a standard, we need to look at a time line of the earnings gap over time: What it is, what causes it, and why it persists.

The Earnings Gap

According to the Bureau of Labor Statistics, white women working full time in 1993 had a median weekly wage equal to 76 percent of the weekly wage earned by white men. The ratio for African-American males was also 74 percent, for African-American females 66 percent, for Hispanic males 66 percent, and for Hispanic females 59 percent. Exhibit 14.2 shows how the wage gap has persisted over time. Although the size of the differences has fluctuated over time, it has been extremely persistent, and always to the advantage of white males. Women of all races are at least narrowing the gap, albeit slowly. However, African-American and Hispanic males seems to be losing ground despite the passage of the Equal Pay Act in 1963, the Civil Rights Acts of 1964 and 1991, and the executive orders that mandated affirmative action in firms doing business with the federal government. What do we know about why that gap exists? Respected economists agree that many complex and subtly interrelated factors are involved (which is why we never sit next to economists at parties).[30]

Some of the more important factors, shown in Exhibit 14.3, include the following:

1. Differences in the occupational attainment and the jobs held by men and women.
2. Differences in personal work-related characteristics and work behaviors.
3. Differences among industries and firms.
4. Differences in union membership.
5. The presence of discrimination.

First let us examine some data, then some conflicting beliefs.

---

[30] See Dave Barry, *Dave Barry Slept Here* (New York: Random House, 1989), p. 25.

EXHIBIT 14.2   Changes in the Wage Gap, 1979–1993: Median Weekly Earnings as Percent of White Male Earnings

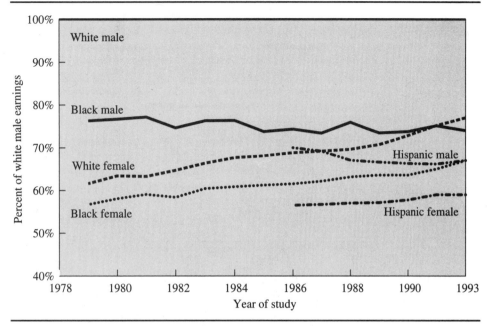

Source: U.S. Department of Labor, Bureau of Labor Statistics, *Employment and Earnings* (Washington, DC, January 1994).

Differences in Occupational Attainment

One of the most important factors that accounts for much of the remaining gap is the difference in the nature of jobs held by men and women. A variety of data illustrate these differences.

The Bureau of Labor Statistics reports that half of all working women in the United States are employed in only 20 percent of the 427 occupations. In addition, among the 427 occupational classes, 80 percent of women work in classes in which at least 70 percent of employees are women. Forty percent of Canadian women work in just 10 job categories. The difference in occupational attainment is the major factor accounting for the earnings gap.[31]

Supporters of comparable worth believe these differences are a reflection of discrimination in society. Discrimination and gender stereotyping in counseling

---

[31] Linda Subich, Gerald Barrett, Dennis Doverspike, and Ralph Alexander, "The Effects of Sex Role-Related Factors on Occupational Choice and Salary," *Pay Equity: Empirical Inquiries* (Washington, DC: National Academy of Science, 1989); Randall K. Filer, "Occupational Segregation, Compensating Differentials and Comparable Worth," *Pay Equity: Empirical Inquiries;* and Elaine Sorensen, "The Crowding Hypothesis and Comparable Worth," *Journal of Human Resources* 25, no. 1, pp. 55–89.

EXHIBIT 14.3   Possible Determinants of Pay Differences

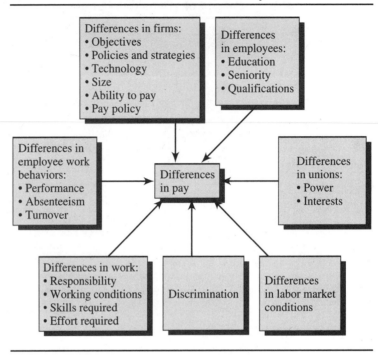

Source: George T. Milkovich, "The Emerging Debate," in *Comparable Worth: Issues and Alternatives*, ed. E. Robert Livernash (Washington, DC: Equal Employment Advisory Council, 1980).

and courses taken in high school, admission to college, and the hiring and promotion practices of employers have all worked, the argument goes, to allocate or crowd women into a limited number of occupations. Because these occupations are typed as women's work, they are devalued. That is, women's jobs pay less because wage discrimination acts on an entire occupation, not only on individual women workers.

On the other hand, the opponents of comparable worth believe that wages are determined primarily by supply and demand; that is, by choices of women and employers. Wages and employment levels are flexible and labor markets adjust, so that the supply available, made up of choices of workers to undertake training required and seek job opportunities, adjusts to equal the demand. If we just get markets competitive and working efficiently, the argument goes, the goal of maximizing profits will eventually lead employees to eliminate discrimination.

According to this view, women make choices about which occupations to train for and when to leave and enter the work force. From this efficient market perspective, women earn less because the jobs they choose have low productivity

EXHIBIT 14.4   Female/Male Earnings Ratio

| | Full-Time Workers Selected Occupations | | | | | |
| | 1979 | | 1986 | | 1993 | |
Occupation	Percent Female	Earnings Ratio	Percent Female	Earnings Ratio	Percent Female	Earnings Ratio
Registered nurses	94.6%	82	92.7%	91	93.3%	101
Bookkeepers, accounting and auditing clerks	88.1	66	93.0	74	90.0	94.4
Nursing aides, orderlies, and attendants	85.1	72	88.3	81	85.9	93.3
Administrative support occupations, misc.	62.9	62	82.4	70	81.9	77.1
Social workers	60.6	83	60.0	73	66.8	86.6
Computer operators	56.6	69	63.8	73	60.1	80.0
Supervisors, food preparation, and service occupations	41.6	72	48.2	67	56.4	67.0
Secondary school teachers	39.7	83	49.1	86	55.1	90.2
Accountants and auditors	34.0	60	44.7	72	51.1	76.6
Computer programmers	28.0	80	39.7	81	30.1	89.8
Janitors and cleaners	15.3	74	21.0	69	23.0	80.2
Supervisors, production occupations	12.9	62	15.1	67	15.5	66.0
Lawyers	10.4	55	15.2	63	29.2	83.7

Source: U.S. Department of Labor, Bureau of Labor Statistics, *Employment and Earnings*, (Washington, DC, January 1994).

and low wages, but those jobs permit women to enter and leave the work force readily; require relatively less training; and are not onerous or dangerous.[32]

Recent data indicate that these occupational patterns are changing. Women are gaining access to a wider array of occupations. Those occupations with the biggest changes tend to be the ones that are growing the fastest. When a strong demand for employees exists, fewer barriers to women's entry exist. Both the wage gap and occupational segregation diminish.[33] Exhibit 14.4 data are from

[32] Elaine Sorensen, "Measuring the Effect of Occupational Sex and Race Composition on Earnings," *Pay Equity: Empirical Inquiries:* "General Accounting Office to Conduct Pay Equity Study of the Federal Workforce" (Washington, DC: National Committee on Pay Equity, March 16, 1989); the entire Spring 1994 issue of *Journal of Human Resources* is devoted to the topic of Women's Work, Wages, and Well-Being; editors are Alice Nakamura and Kathryn Shaw; also see Randall K. Filer, "The Usefulness of Predicted Values for Prior Work Experience in Analyzing Labor Market Outcomes for Women," *Journal of Human Resources* 28 (Summer 1993), pp. 519–37.

[33] Judith Fields and Edward Wolff, "The Decline of Sex Segregation and the Wage Gap, 1970–80," *Journal of Human Resources* 26, no. 4, pp. 608–22.

some selected occupations. For example in 1979, less than 40 percent of secondary school teachers were women; by 1986 it was 49 percent; and by 1993 it was over 55 percent. The earnings ratio among women lawyers had increased from 55 to almost 84 percent. Similar increases occurred for janitors and accountants. However, the earnings ratio for food preparation supervisors has fallen since 1986.

It is a fact that (1) women tend to be employed in female-dominated occupations and that (2) wages in these occupations are relatively lower. It is also a fact that (3) women tend to hold the lower paying jobs in each occupation. So although the percentage of women employed has increased dramatically, new workers are more likely to hold lower paying jobs. Thus, the influx of women into the work force has also tended to hold down women's earnings.

Unfortunately, recent research concludes that a wave of women entering an occupation does not wash away problems. A study of women in science and engineering professions finds that even though they have already cleared the hurdles of misguided high school guidance counselors and/or lack of peer support or role models, women scientists and engineers are almost twice as likely to leave these occupations as males (Exhibit 14.5).[34] Another study of M.B.A.s found that 10 to 15 years after receiving their degree, in addition to a pay gap there is also a gender-based chasm in such subjective measures as career satisfaction, boss appreciation, and feeling of discrimination.[35] Exhibit 14.6 shows the extent of the variance. Fully 46 percent of the women said they had experienced discrimination; only 9 percent of the men said they had. The most common problem women reported was that less qualified men were chosen for promotions over them. Additionally, they felt that discrimination has become more subtle and harder to prove. This study measured perceptions of boss appreciation and discrimination that may or may not correspond to reality; however, it appears that many professional women and minorities believe they operate in less supportive work environments than their white male colleagues.[36]

The Glass Ceiling

Even at the top, women and minorities frequently complain of a "glass ceiling," an invisible barrier that permits them to get close to the top position but keeps them out of the highest jobs. A 1991 report by the Department of Labor (DOL) confirms what other surveys have shown: Few women and even fewer minorities

---

[34] Anne E. Preston, "Why Have All the Women Gone? A Study of Exit of Women from the Science and Engineering Professions," *American Economic Review*, December 1994, pp. 1446–62.

[35] Joy A. Schneer and Frieda Reitman, "The Importance of Gender in Mid-Career: A Longitudinal Study of MBAs," *Journal of Organizational Behavior* 15 (1994), pp. 199–207.

[36] Alison M. Konrad and Kathy Cannings, "Of Mommy Tracks and Glass Ceilings: A Case Study of Men's and Women's Careers in Management," *Relations Industrielles* 49, no. 2 (1994), pp. 303–33.

EXHIBIT 14.5   Percentage of 1982 Scientists and Engineers Who Left the Profession by 1989 by Reason for Departure and Gender

Reason	Males	Females
1. Percentage out of the labor force for family reasons	0.05	3.6
2. Percentage out of the labor force for other reasons	0.4	2.6
3. Percentage nonscience or engineering employment for reasons other than promotion	6.2	10.4
4. Percentage nonscience or engineering employment because of promotion	2.0	1.6
5. Percentage unemployed	2.0	1.9
Total exit rate (percentage not employed in science and engineering), 1989	10.7	20.1

Source: Anne E. Preston, "Why Have All the Women Gone? A Study of Exit of Women from the Science and Engineering Professions," *American Economic Review*, December 1994, pp. 1446–62.

EXHIBIT 14.6   Mid-Career Differences in Income and Impressions (means and frequencies by gender)

Variables		Men	Women
Income 1984	Mean	55.2	50.3
	S.D.	(23.1)	(16.4)
Income 1990	Mean	89.8	79.6
	S.D.	(32.2)	(30.6)
Career satisfaction 1984	Mean	3.87	3.87
	S.D.	(0.77)	(0.73)
Career satisfaction 1990	Mean	3.79	3.51
	S.D.	(0.66)	(0.87)
Boss appreciation	Yes	69%	51%
	To some extent	28	33
	No	3	16
Discrimination	Yes	9	46
	Maybe	9	10
	No	83	44

Source: Joy A. Schneer and Frieda Reitman, "The Importance of Gender in Mid-Career: A Longitudinal Study of MBAs," *Journal of Organizational Behavior* 15 (1994), pp. 199–207.

hold top management jobs in U.S. companies.[37] Among 94 contractors reviewed, women represented only 6.6 percent and minorities only 2.6 percent of executive-level positions (assistant vice president or above). In some of the companies studied, no women or minorities were employed above entry level.

Potential barriers to the movement of women and minorities into top management that were identified in the report include executive recruiting practices that bypass women and minority candidates, a lack of mentoring, and few assignments to high visibility jobs, projects, or training programs. Such barriers can block advancement at different levels of management. The DOL advocates a voluntary glass-ceiling effort that identifies and removes barriers to the movement of more women and minorities into top management, at whatever level of management those barriers exist.

To "encourage" such voluntary efforts, the DOL entered into its first-ever settlement in 1993 resulting from a corporate management review that focused on pay differences in managerial and professional jobs. The Fairfax Hospital in Falls Church, Virginia, paid $604,000 to settle charges alleging that 52 women in management were paid less than men. While the hospital felt it had a sound rationale for differences, the DOL disagreed. Three more settlements were announced in 1994.

A 1989 Supreme Court case addresses promotions to top management. In *Price Waterhouse* v. *Hopkins* (109 S. Ct. 1775), a female plaintiff claimed that although she had generated more billable hours and business than any other partnership candidate, her promotion was denied, at least in part, because she had violated traditional sex role stereotypes. In comments written for the partnership decision, several partners stated that the plaintiff was "macho," "overcompensated for a woman," and "should dress more femininely." The Court agreed that under Title VII, sex, racial, or ethnic stereotypes should not influence promotion decisions. Businesses may be liable unless they can provide evidence that such stereotypes have no influence on high-level promotion decisions. Unfortunately, stereotypes die hard.

A survey of human resource managers identifies these barriers to the top:

- Assigning women and minorities to staff positions that are not viewed as training grounds for top management.
- Discounting women's and minorities' qualifications and performance.
- Providing lower returns to women and minorities (in terms of responsibility, authority, and overall compensation) for their promotions.
- Limiting access of women and minorities to informal networks of higher level managers.
- Using a restricted range of referrals and outside sources when hiring executives.[38]

---

[37] U.S. Department of Labor, *A Report on the Glass Ceiling Initiative* (Washington, DC, 1991).

[38] *Women in Corporate Management: The Results of a Catalyst Survey* (New York: Catalyst, 1990).

Most of these barriers have also been identified by human resource management research. For example, a 1990 review of research on hiring decisions found that in 29 of 34 studies, whites were judged more qualified than minorities who had identical qualifications.[39] Research on performance appraisals also suggests that despite comparable performance, women and minorities do not receive performance ratings equal to those of white men. A common thread running through all this research is that the qualifications and performance of women and minorities are likely to be discounted when the work involved has traditionally been done by white men, when it involves supervision of white men, and when the qualifications for the work are relatively general or subjectively defined. These characteristics—traditionally the domain of white men, supervision of white men, and subjectively defined qualifications—describe many managerial positions, especially those at higher levels.

According to the executive director of the National Committee on Pay Equity, the pay gap and glass ceiling are linked.

> In the career of sales person, a woman sells shoes for an average of $12,400 per year, while a man sells furniture for an average of $20,020 per year. When a supervisory position comes open, at an average salary of $25,000 per year, the woman seems less qualified for the job because it is almost double her current salary, while for the man, the promotion would only provide a $5,000 increase. Furthermore, if the woman were to get an interview for the job, it is unlikely that she would demand double her current pay, but if she agrees to work for less, then she further perpetuates the wage gap, because the male worker is most likely to demand and be granted the $5,000 increase. . . .

Current compensation systems are not self correcting and continue to perpetuate undervaluation of the work performed by minorities and women. This is part of the reason that the wage gap narrows so slowly.[40]

Differences in Personal Work-Related Characteristics

Differences in employee attributes and behaviors help explain the earnings gap. Work-related differences include experience and seniority within a firm, continuous time in the work force, education, and the like. Personal characteristics of

---

[39] T. Cox, Jr., and S. M. Nkomo, "Invisible Men and Women: A Status Report on Race as a Variable in Organization Behavior Research," *Journal of Organizational Behavior* 11 (1990), pp. 419–31; G. N. Powell, "One More Time: Do Female and Male Managers Differ?" *Academy of Management Executive* 4 (1990) pp. 68–75; S. J. Spurr, "Sex Discrimination in the Legal Profession: A Study of Promotion," *Industrial and Labor Relations Review* 43, no. 4 (1990), pp. 406–17; J. H. Greenhaus, S. Parasuraman, and W. M. Wormely, "Effects of Race on Organizational Experiences, Job Performance Evaluations, and Career Outcomes," *Academy of Management Journal* 33 (1990), pp. 64–86; Renae Broderick and Carolyn Milkovich, *Breaking the Glass Ceiling* (Ithaca, NY: Industrial and Labor Relations School, Cornell University, 1991).

[40] Comments of Susan Bianchi-Sand, Executive Director of National Committee on Pay Equity, reported in *Newsnotes*, National Committee on Pay Equity, Fall 1993, p. 4.

questionable work-relatedness include obesity and beauty. Yet empirical studies have found both of these factors related to pay differences.[41] Plain people earn less than average-looking people, who earn less than the good-looking. The "plainness penalty" is 5 to 10 percent.

Experience and Seniority.   Consider experience and seniority differences among full-time workers. On average, men work 6 percent more hours per week than women. By the time men and women have been out of school for 6 years, women on average have worked 1.6 years, or 30 percent less than men. After 16 years out of school, women average half as much labor market experience as men.[42] But these patterns are changing and are likely to continue to change.

Education.   Currently, men and women graduate from college in nearly equal numbers. However, they tend to choose different majors. And college major is the strongest factor affecting income of college graduates.[43] But this pattern is changing, too. In fact, women's improved education, experience, and record of more continuous attachment to the labor market are credited with the lion's share of the narrowing (but persistent) gap in the last decade.[44]

In the study of middle-aged law school grads mentioned earlier in this chapter, the women lawyers did work fewer hours—about 91 percent as long as men.[45] But they were paid substantially (not proportionately) less; they earned only 61 percent of what men earned. Even with differences in work history accounted for, male lawyers continue to enjoy a considerable earnings advantage as well as a higher rate of growth earnings.

Combining Factors.   Although many researchers studied the effects of differences in jobs and occupations and personal characteristics such as experience and education, few studies have looked at their effects on pay differences *over time*. One longitudinal study examined starting and current salaries of men and women hired between 1976 and 1986, using data from within a single Fortune

---

[41] Daniel S. Hamermesh and Jeff E. Biddle, "Beauty and the Labor Market," *The American Economic Review*, December 1994, pp. 1174–94; Susan Averett and Sanders Korenman, "The Economic Reality of 'The Beauty Myth' " (Working paper, National Bureau of Economic Research, 1993).

[42] Fuchs, *Women's Quest for Economic Equality*.

[43] Francine Blau and Marianne Ferber, "Career Plans and Expectations of Young Women and Men," *Journal of Human Resources* 26, no. 4, pp. 581–607; Estelle James, N. Absalam, J. Conaty, and Duc-le To, "College Quality and Future Earnings" (Working paper, Department of Economics, SUNY Stony Brook, Stony Brook, NY, 1989).

[44] June O'Neill and Solomon Polachek, "Why the Gender Gap in Wages Narrowed in the 1980s," *Journal of Labor Economics* 11, no. 1 (1993), pp. 205–28; Francine Blau and Lawrence Kahn, "The Impact of Wage Structure on Trends in U.S. Gender Wage Differentials: 1975–87" (Working paper no. 4748, National Bureau of Economic Research, May 1994).

[45] Wood, Corcoran, and Courant, "Pay Differences Among the Highly Paid."

500 firm.[46] Controlling for education degree, college major, and prior experience, males had a 12 percent higher starting salary than females. Among college graduates, college major was a key determinant of gender differences in starting salaries. When all the variables in the study's model were included, the current salary differential among male college graduates and female college graduates was less than 3 percent. The implication is that women received greater pay increases after they were hired than men did, but differences in starting salary remain important and persistent contributors to gender-related pay differences.

Differences in Industries and Firms

Other factors affecting earnings differences between men and women are the industry and the firms in which they are employed. There is some evidence that within the same occupations, industries that employ higher percentages of women (e.g., retail, insurance) tend to pay a lower average wage than those firms in industries employing higher percentages of men. In other words, office and clerical workers, most likely women, tend to be paid less in retailing than in manufacturing or chemicals.

Differences in the firm's compensation policies and objectives within a specific industry is another factor that accounts for some of the earnings gap. As noted in Chapters 6 and 7, some firms within an industry adopt pay strategies that place them among the leaders in their industry; other firms adopt policies that may offer more employment security coupled with bonuses and gain-sharing schemes. The issue here is whether within an industry some firms are more likely to employ women than other firms and whether that likelihood leads to earnings differences.

Within a firm, differences in policies for different jobs may even exist. For example, many firms tie pay for secretaries to the pay for the manager to which the secretary is assigned. The rationale is that the secretary and the manager function as a team. When the manager gets promoted, the secretary also takes on additional responsibilities and therefore also gets a raise. However, this traditional approach breaks down when layers of management are cut. In 1995, IBM announced pay cuts of up to 36 percent for secretaries who had been assigned to managerial levels that no longer exist. IBM justified the cuts by saying the rates were way above the market. Prior to the reduction, the highest base salary for a senior executive secretary was $70,000 plus overtime.[47]

We also know that the size of a firm is systematically related to differences in wages. Female employment is more heavily concentrated in small firms. Wages of men in large firms are 54 percent higher than wages of men in small firms. That gap was only 37 percent for women in small versus large firms. The study

---

[46] Barry A. Gerhart and George T. Milkovich, "Salaries, Salary Growth, and Promotions of Men and Women in a Large, Private Firm," *Pay Equity: Empirical Inquiries.*

[47] Laurie Hays, "IBM Plans to Slash Secretaries' Salaries in Sweeping Review," *The Wall Street Journal*, May 18, 1995, pp. A3, A7.

of middle-aged lawyers revealed large sex differences in job setting. Men were much more likely than women to be in private practice, and they were twice as likely to practice in large firms (over 50 lawyers). Clearly, these differences are related to pay: the most highly paid legal positions are in private practice law firms, and the larger the law firm, the greater is the average rate of pay. In contrast, men are much *less* likely than the women to be in the relatively low-paying areas of government and legal services. Other studies report that employees in some jobs can get about a 20 percent pay increase simply by switching industries in the same geographic area while performing basically similar jobs.[48]

To the extent that these differences in job setting are the result of an individual's preference or disposition, they are not evidence of discrimination. To the extent that these differences are the result of industry and firm practices that steer women and minorities into certain occupations and industries, or lower-paying parts of a profession, they may reflect discrimination. At the minimum, they require thoughtful exploration.

Recently, a new and interesting approach was used to examine the gender earnings differential. Total pay was divided into base pay and contingent pay that varies with job performance. After controlling for individual characteristics (e.g., education and experience), occupation, and job level, approximately 34 percent of the unexplained pay gap was due to gender differences in performance-based pay.[49] If these differences occur *within* a firm, several possible explanations exist. Perhaps firms are not offering men and women equal opportunities to earn contingent pay; perhaps men and women are treated differently in the evaluations used to determine contingent pay; perhaps men and women differ substantially on performance.

However, if the differences are *across* firms, then perhaps women prefer less pay risk and choose those occupations and firms with less variable pay. While their sample size did not permit the authors to say if the differences were within or across firms, if the pay gap is the result of the way people select their occupations and employers, then we need to understand how pay practices influence those choices.

Differences in Union Membership

Finally, we also know that belonging to a union will affect differences in earnings. Belonging to a union in the public sector seems to raise female wages more than it raises male wages. Little research has been devoted to studying the gender effect of union membership in the private sector.

---

[48] Reuben Gronau, "Sex-Related Wage Differentials and Women's Interrupted Labor Careers—the Chicken or the Egg," *Journal of Labor Economics* 6, no. 31 (1988), pp. 277–301; Barry Gerhart and Nabil El Cheikh, "Earnings and Percentage Female: A Longitudinal Study" (Working paper 89-04, Center for Advanced Human Resource Studies, Cornell University).

[49] Keith W. Chauvin and Ronald A. Ash, "Gender Earning Differentials in Total Pay, Base Pay, and Contingent Pay," *Industrial and Labor Relations Review*, July 1994, pp. 634–49.

Presence of Discrimination

So we know that many factors affect pay; discrimination may possibly be one of them.[50] But we are not in agreement as to what constitutes evidence of discrimination. Although the earnings gap is the most frequently cited example, closer inspection reveals the weaknesses in this statistic.

RESEARCH ON THE EARNINGS GAP: A MIXED BAG

Unfortunately, many studies of the earnings gap have little relevance to understanding discrimination in pay-setting practices. Three examples of these limitations are discussed: the use of unexplained residuals as evidence of pay discrimination, inferring employer-level behavior from aggregate rather than employer-specific data, and problems with proxies.

Unexplained Residual Approach

A standard statistical approach for determining whether discrimination explains part of the gap is to try to relate pay differences to the factors just discussed above (e.g., occupation, type of work, experience, education, and the like). The procedure typically used is to regress some measure of earnings on those factors thought to legitimately influence earnings. If the average wage of men with a given set of values for these factors is significantly different from the average wage of women with equal factors, then the standard statistical approach is to interpret the residual portion of the gap as discrimination. This residual approach brings to mind a comment by popular astronomer Carl Sagan. He observed that although space exploration and research have increased our knowledge of the universe, much remains to be learned. He cautioned, "Just because we can't identify a light doesn't make it a space ship." Many people looking at the earnings gap fall into the same trap. Just because we can't explain all the differences in pay between men and women doesn't make it discrimination.

Must this residual earnings disparity be considered a function of discrimination? Consider studies on the earnings of white men. Studies that attempt to explain differences in white men's earnings, using such factors as jobs held and experience, education, time worked and age, are able to account for about 60 to 70 percent of the differences. How can we logically conclude that the residual unexplained portion is discrimination among white men? Statistical studies are just one type of evidence to consider when deciding whether pay differences are attributable to discrimination.

If they do not tell us what portion of the gap is discrimination, what do these analyses show? They show that the gap is not fully explained by a number of factors: differences in characteristics of men or women employees, differences

---

[50] Donald J. Treiman and H. J. Hartmann, eds., *Women, Work and Wages* (Washington, DC: National Academy Press, 1981).

in jobs they hold, the occupations they are in, the firms in which they are employed, the industry, and so on. But these studies do not eliminate the possibility that the discrepancy is caused by unmeasured variables other than discrimination. Nor can they rule out that wage and earnings differences are the result of voluntary behaviors.

Inferring from Aggregated Data

Many studies of the earnings gap have little relevance to understanding pay discrimination because actual pay decisions are decentralized: made by individual employers, unions, and employees. Most analysis of the earnings gap is conducted at aggregate levels. Studies using aggregate data often do not adequately include factors actually used in wage determination. This is not always because researchers are not aware of these factors; the omissions are due in large part to two problems. First, there is a lack of adequate publicly available data, and second, the proxies used are often too abstract.

Consider a study that treats all employee experiences as equal (measured as age minus years of education minus five years) and all fields of education as equal (measured as years of education completed). Common sense and your own experience tell you that there are differences in the types of experience (whether it is continuous with one employer and the type of training received) and that there are differences in the specialties and quality of education (a four-year degree in social work is not equivalent to a four-year degree in electrical engineering). Anyone knowledgeable in pay determination believes that these differences are important in attracting and retaining the work force necessary for an effective organization. Hence, the differences also affect pay differences. Mr. and Mrs. Jones both have college degrees (his in psychology, hers in computer science), both are in sales (he in shoes and she in computers), and both work for private sector employers (he for J.C. Penney and she for Compaq). They probably earn very different salaries, but most aggregate data would report them to have similar skills and education, and similar jobs.

Problems with Proxies

Years of education often serve as a proxy for all the differences in a person's skills and abilities and quality of the education received. Employee performance may be measured as absenteeism, and differences in firms may be measured as differences in industries, treating each firm within an industry as the same. One study even used the number of children as a proxy for time spent away from the job. We have reached that stage as parents when we better understand a counterpoint, that the number of teenagers one has will increase the time spent on the job and away from home!

Another problem with the proxies used is that mere possession of a qualification or skill does not mean it is work related. Examples of cab drivers, secretaries, and house painters with college degrees are numerous.

Even if legitimate factors fully explain pay differences between men and women, discrimination still could have occurred. First, the factors themselves may be tainted by discrimination. For example, past discrimination against women in the admission to engineering schools may have affected their earnings. Or women may be better qualified on some factors that were omitted in the analysis.

In sum, statistical analysis needs to be treated as part of a pattern of evidence and needs to reflect the wage behaviors of specific firms. If we infer behaviors from unexplained residuals, we can be misled by grossly aggregated data and poor proxies. As one reviewer has written, "It is not the quantity of studies that is lacking; it is the quality."[51]

WAGES FOR "WOMEN'S WORK"

Why are jobs held predominantly by women, almost without exception, paid less than jobs held predominantly by men? Are women's jobs fairly valued by the same standards that are used to value other jobs, or have they been systematically undervalued and/or underpaid?[52] Do job evaluation systems give adequate recognition to job-related contributions in those jobs held primarily by women? The state of Washington conducted a study that concluded that the job of a licensed practical nurse required skill, effort, and responsibility equal to that of a campus police officer. The state paid the licensed practical nurse, on average, $739 a month. The campus police officer was paid, on average, $1,070 a month. These salary differences were not related to productivity-related job content characteristics included in the study.[53]

It is this type of wage difference (e.g., nurses' versus police officers' wages) that is controversial. Some argue that pay differences are the result of consistent undervaluing of work done by women, and it ought to be illegal.[54] If jobs require comparable skill, effort, and responsibility, the pay must be comparable, no matter how dissimilar the job content may be. Pay systems that value jobs based on their current market rates, these critics assert, incorporate and perpetuate the legacy of past access discrimination against women and minorities. Therefore, jobs held predominantly by women and minorities ought to be paid at the market rate for "comparable" or "equivalent" jobs held predominantly by white men.

[51] Donald P. Schwab, "Using Job Evaluation to Obtain Pay Equity," in *Comparable Worth: Issue for the 80's*, vol. 1.

[52] Sharon Toffey Shepela and Ann T. Viviano, "Some Psychological Factors Affecting Job Segregation and Wages," in *Comparable Worth and Wage Discrimination*, ed. H. Remick (Philadelphia: Temple University Press, 1984).

[53] Helen Remick, "Beyond Equal Pay for Equal Work: Comparable Worth in the State of Washington," in *Equal Employment Policy for Women*, ed. Ronnie Steinberg-Ratner (Philadelphia: Temple University Press, 1980), pp. 405–48; Ronnie J. Steinberg, " 'A Want of Harmony': Perspectives on Wage Discrimination and Comparable Worth," in *Comparable Worth and Wage Discrimination*.

[54] Paula England, "Socioeconomic Explanations of Job Segregation," in *Comparable Worth and Wage Discrimination*.

Others respond that pay differences are the result of many factors, not the least of which is the external labor market, for which no acceptable substitute is available.

COMPARABLE WORTH

Comparable worth has been debated off and on since World War II—over 50 years! Proponents continue to lobby for either new legislation or voluntary action on the part of employers that would include the comparable worth standard. Much of this political activity is occurring in state and local governments. By the early 1990s, almost half the states had begun or completed "pay equity adjustments" for state civil service employees.[55] This process is particularly significant because over half of all women in the work force are employed in the public sector.

The Mechanics

Establishing a comparable worth plan typically involves the following four basic steps:

1. *Adopt a single job evaluation plan for all jobs within a unit.* If employees are unionized, separate plans can be prepared for each bargaining unit and take precedence over previous agreements. The key to a comparable worth system is a single job evaluation plan for jobs with dissimilar content.

2. *All jobs with equal job evaluation results should be paid the same.* Although each factor in the job evaluation may not be equal, if the total points are equal, the wage rates must also be equal.

3. *Identify general representation (percentage male and female employees) in each job group.* A job group is all positions with similar duties and responsibilities, requires similar qualifications, is filled by similar recruiting procedures, and is paid under the same pay schedule. Typically, a female-dominated job class is defined as 60 percent or more female incumbents; a male-dominated job class has 70 percent or more male incumbents.

4. *The wage-to-job evaluation point ratio should be based on the wages paid for male-dominated jobs* since they are presumed to be free of pay discrimination.

---

[55] Alice Cook, *Comparable Worth: A Case Book of Experiences in States and Localities, 1986 Supplement* (Honolulu: Industrial Relations Center, University of Hawaii at Manoa); *Survey of State-Government Level Pay Equity Activity, 1988* (Washington, DC: National Committee on Pay Equity, no date); *Pay Equity Implementation Series* (Toronto, Ontario, Canada: The Pay Equity Commission). This is a series of guidelines addressing questions regarding implementation of the province's pay equity legislation.

EXHIBIT 14.7   Job Evaluation Points and Salary

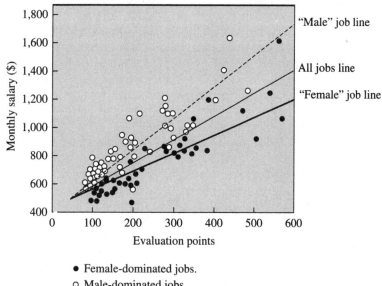

- Female-dominated jobs.
- Male-dominated jobs.

These steps are based on the state of Minnesota's law that mandates comparable worth for all public sector employees (e.g., the state, cities, school districts, libraries).

To understand the mechanics more clearly, consider Exhibit 14.7. The solid dots represent jobs held predominantly by women (i.e., female representation greater than or equal to 60 percent). The circles represent jobs held predominantly by men (i.e., greater than or equal to 70 percent men). The policy line (solid) for the women's jobs is below and less than the policy line for men's jobs (dotted line). A comparable worth policy would use the results of the single job evaluation plan and price all jobs as if they were male-dominated jobs (dotted line). Thus, all jobs with 100 job points would receive $600, all those with 200 points would receive $800, and so on.

Proponents of comparable worth are of two minds when it comes to job evaluation. Some see it as the primary technique for establishing jobs of comparable worth, as illustrated above.[56] Others see it as too subjective to rely on.[57] How

---

[56] Remick, ed., *Comparable Worth and Wage Discrimination* .

[57] Ruth G. Blumrosen, "Wage Discrimination, Job Segregation and Title VII of the Civil Rights Act of 1964," *University of Michigan Journal of Law Reform* 12, no. 397 (1979), pp. 17–23; Richard W. Beatty and James R. Beatty, "Some Problems with Contemporary Job Evaluation Systems," in *Comparable Worth and Wage Discrimination;* Robert Madigan, "Comparable Worth Judgments," *Journal of Applied Psychology* 70, no. 1 (1985), pp. 137–47; Robert Grams and Donald Schwab, "An Investigation of Systematic Gender-Related Error in Job Evaluation,"

dollars are actually attached to job evaluation points is still being debated. Recent applications (step 4) use market rates for male-dominated jobs to convert the job evaluation points to salaries. The point-to-salaries ratio of male-dominated jobs is then applied to female-dominated jobs.

Some question the use of male-dominated jobs rather than all job data to establish the relationship between job evaluation points and pay rates. They argue that using only male-dominated jobs artificially inflates other job rates. The approach presumes that clerical work is subject to identical union and market forces as are police, firefighters, and craft workers. Arbitrators and legislators are struggling with this issue.

Since pay legislation has outlawed lowering any wage to make pay equal, a comparable worth policy may require employers to pay all employees at the highest market line or point-to-dollar ratio that exists for any segment of its employees (steps 3 and 4). This translates into the rate paid for jobs held predominantly by men (Exhibit 14.7, the dotted line). Such an arrangement raises a host of issues:

- Would the unions give up their right to negotiate contracts independent of the pay arrangements in the other segments of the organization; for example, would unions B, C, D, E, etc., have to agree to the same point/dollar relationship as union A, which signed the first agreement?
- If the individual unions negotiated jointly for the same point/pay relationship, would there be any need for more than one union?
- How would an organization entice people into jobs where there were shortages because of distasteful work if there were not premium pay for the same points, or more pay for fewer points?
- If one unit in a firm pays only base salary, will it have to increase its pay level if another unit in the same firm introduces an incentive plan suitable for the business sector in which it competes?
- Must a state pay the same dollars for the same points to employees who work and live in a low-cost rural area as it does to employees in the high-cost large cities?
- Must a high-tech company raise the pay of its accountants (male dominated) to equal the pay of its engineers (also male dominated) for the same points?

Underlying these points is a more basic one, which is whether legally mandating a job evaluation approach is defensible. Many employers do not use job evaluation at all.

Academy of Management Journal 28, no. 2 (June 1985), pp. 279–90; Mark Lengnick-Hall, "The Effects of Group Processes on Bias in Job Evaluation," Paper presented at the Academy of Management Meetings, Washington, DC, 1989.

And of those who do, a partner of Hay Associates observed:

> We, ourselves, do not know of a single case where a large and diverse organization in the private sector concluded that a single job evaluation method, with the same compensable factors and weightings, was appropriate for its factory, office, professional, management, technical, and executive personnel in all profit center divisions and all staff departments.[58]

A mandated job evaluation approach that specifies a hierarchy of jobs seems counter to the direction that most organizations are moving today. A myriad of approaches determine pay ranging from market pricing to skill-based pay to gain-sharing to maturity curves. Nevertheless, politicians continue to introduce legislation that mandates comparable worth. The Fair Pay Act, introduced (but not passed) in 1994, for example, specifies equal pay for equivalent jobs. The work performed in equivalent jobs may be different, but the combination of the jobs' skills, effort, responsibility, and working conditions must be similar. The act also proposes requiring employers to report pay data for each job classification as well as the sex, race, and national origin of employees within each classification. These reports would become public information. The point is to gather more detailed information on pay differences within an occupation in order to compare occupations.

How to determine the *equivalency* referred to in this bill in a bias-free manner is difficult to imagine. We discussed the limitations of job evaluation in earlier chapters. An analysis of Washington State's experience with a comparable worth policy revealed that on job evaluation points for the factors knowledge and skills, mental demands, accountability, and working conditions, the category "mental demands" has a significant negative relationship to pay and the variable "accountability" has zero effect.[59] So only working conditions and knowledge and skills are positively related to pay. Yet the job evaluation points for mental demands and accountability are summed together with the other categories as though they contribute positively to the "worth" of the occupation. People who advocate job evaluation as a vehicle for comparable worth credit the technique with more explanatory power than it possesses.

Ontario's Experience

The province of Ontario, Canada, has accumulated the most extensive experience with comparable worth. The Ontario Pay Equity Act, in effect since 1988, covers both the private and public sectors. Employers are required to compare female-dominated job classes to male-dominated job classes. In jobs of equal value, the

---

[58] Alvin O. Bellak, "Comparable Worth: A Practitioner's View," in *Comparable Worth: Issue for the 80's,* vol. 1.

[59] June O'Neill, Michael Brien, and James Cunningham, "Effects of Comparable Worth Policy: Evidence from Washington State," *American Economic Association Papers and Proceedings,* May 1989, pp. 305–9.

pay in the female class is raised if it is lower than the pay for the male job class. If there is no male job class of the same value, proportional comparisons are made to a male job class of less worth if that class is also paid more than the female class. The law differs from the comparable worth approach described earlier in this chapter in that it requires that job evaluation plans be negotiated with all unions in the facility. Therefore, a single employer may have a number of different plans—one for each bargaining unit plus a different plan for non-unionized employees. The use of multiple plans reduces the number of possible comparisons for women who believe that their jobs are undervalued.

Ontario's law requires comparisons between female-dominated job classes and male-dominated job classes in the same bargaining unit.[60] If the comparison is to a male job class of lower value, the law says that the female job class should be paid equal to the highest wage in that lesser-valued male job class. But what if that highest wage is earned by a management trainee who is only temporarily doing that job? Or what if that wage results from production-related bonuses or incentives? If no comparisons in the same bargaining unit exist, women may compare thoughout the workplace. But if other jobs are valued under a different job evaluation system, it's hard to prove equal value.

The original law left a large percentage of Ontario's working women unaffected because no appropriate comparisons existed. Women who work in female-dominated workplaces such as libraries, day care centers, and nursing homes were not covered because there are no male-dominated job classes at their workplace. A 1992 amendment offers alternative comparisons when no male-dominated job class exists in the same workplace.[61] For an unmatched female job class, an employer examines the relationship or pattern between pay and value for all the male job classes, and uses this relationship or pattern to determine if the female job class is underpaid and if any pay equity adjustment is required. This is the *proportional value* comparison, as opposed to *job-to-job* comparisons. In the public sector only, a third method, *proxy comparison,* is available for predominantly female workplaces where neither job-to-job nor proportional value are applicable. The proxy comparison method borrows job information on similar female jobs in another public sector setting that has male comparators. So, for example, female counselors at a women's shelter might borrow information from female crisis intervention specialists at a nearby hospital if that hospital also had male comparators.

According to a report evaluating compliance with the law, the private sector is closer to compliance than the public sector in terms of developing plans and posting them. However, the size of pay equity adjustments was higher in the public sector. The law requires employers to allocate at least 1 percent of payroll

---

[60] David B. Balkin and Janice L. Miller, "The Influence of Comparable Worth on Human Resource Managers' Pay in Ontario," Working paper, University of Colorado, Boulder, 1995.

[61] *Pay Equity Commission Newsletter*, published periodically by the Pay Equity Office, 150 Eglinton Ave East, Toronto, Ontario M4P 1E8, addresses compliance issues.

each year to equity increases until the pay gaps are eliminated. Not surprisingly, most employers are refusing to allocate more than the mandated 1 percent.

Who Gains? Who Pays?   An issue concerning any comparable worth proposal is whether it will benefit those who were its intended beneficiaries. A report released by Ontario's Pay Equity Commission claims that women in professional and managerial positions have benefitted the most.[62] Lower-paid female-dominant job classes, such as clerical or production workers, that were the targeted beneficiaries were either compared to other low-paying male job classes or not compared at all, because no comparable male job class could be found within the organization. In Washington State between 1983 and 1987, those occupations that received no comparable worth adjustment increased their share of total employment by 5.7 percent. Among those occupations receiving pay adjustments, the larger the adjustment, the larger the decline in employment share (Exhibit 14.8). Economic return on the schooling and work experience of both male and female employees fell.[63]

Employers claim that administrative costs to comply with the legislation have been higher than anticipated—in many cases much higher than the resulting wage adjustments. That's because pay equity can't be done piecemeal. Some employers must adjust their entire pay system. A potential problem in any work site is what happens if clerk X's salary is adjusted to match maintenance worker Y's rate, which also happens to be the rate paid to clerk X's supervisor. Other employers have paid huge consulting fees to find out that their systems are evenhanded. A Toronto consultant cites one company that spent $13,000 analyzing its wages but paid only a few hundred dollars in pay increases.

But lest non-Canadians tut-tut over such a distortion of intent, let us have a moment of sympathy for the University of Minnesota, which settled a discrimination complaint filed by Shyamala Rajender, a former lecturer in its chemistry department. In contrast to the $100,000 that Ms. Rajender received, her lawyers received a cool $2 million.[64]

The issue of administrative cost versus benefit pervades any discussion of legislative mandates:

---

[62] *What Works . . . Experiences with Implementation of the Pay Equity Legislation*, Report prepared for Pay Equity Commission (Toronto: Avesbury Research and Consulting Limited, 1991); *An Evaluation of Pay Equity in Ontario: The First Year*, Report prepared for Pay Equity Commission, (Toronto: SPR Associates, 1991).

[63] O'Neill, Brien, and Cunningham, "Effects of Comparable Worth Policy"; Greg Hundley, "The Effects of Comparable Worth in the Public Sector on Public/Private Occupational Relative Wages," *Journal of Human Resources*, Spring 1993, pp. 318–42; Erica Groshen, "The Structure of the Female/Male Wage Differential," *Journal of Human Resources* 26, no. 3, pp. 457–72.

[64] Ian Maitland, "How the University of Minnesota Was Subverted by Litigation," *Academic Questions*, Winter 1992–93, pp. 85–93; R. E. Azevedo and L. Roth, "Canadian–United States Experience with Comparable Worth: The View from Minnesota," *Labor Law Journal IRRA Spring Meeting* (August 1990), pp. 531–34.

EXHIBIT 14.8   Employment Effects of Comparable Worth*

	1980	1980–83	1983–87
		Absolute Change	
Percentage of Total Employment			
Uncovered	43.7	−2.9	5.7
Low gain	29.1	3.1	−0.6
Medium gain	13.4	1.0	−2.1
High gain	13.8	−1.2	−3.0
		Percentage Change	
Hourly Wage†			
Uncovered	12.29	1.5	−3.0
Low gain	11.19	−5.7	1.6
Medium gain	8.43	−2.1	5.9
High gain	6.66	1.1	11.0

Notes: * Uncovered occupations received no comparable worth adjustment in 1986; low gain occupations received a 2.5 percent adjustment, medium gain, a 2.5–7.5 percent adjustment, and high gain, a greater than 7.5 percent adjustment.

† 1987$.

Source: June O'Neill, Michael Brien, and James Cunningham, "Effects of Comparable Worth Policy: Evidence from Washington State," *American Economic Association Papers and Proceedings*, May 1989, pp. 305–9.

While managers may grumble about compliance with EEO legislation, it is often the case that the human resource practices that firms need to implement in order to protect themselves against potential charges of employment discrimination also improve human resource decisions. Taking employee selection as an example, such legally recommended practices as job analysis and test validation also improve a firm's ability to predict which job candidates will be the best performers after hiring.

Job evaluation, in contrast, makes no such contribution to productive efficiency, and is strictly an administrative convenience that allows firms to rank jobs for pay purposes. Widespread changes would do nothing for the economic performance of the firm. The type of revamping that would ensue . . . . would affect virtually everyone's pay—creating a consultant's dream and an employer's nightmare.[65]

However, it's not clear that low-paid women and people of color, who constitute 53 percent of the work force, care about administrative costs.[66]

---

[65] Anthony F. Buono and Mark Rosen, book review of Paula England, *Comparable Worth*, in *Personnel Psychology*, Winter 1993, pp. 869–73.

[66] Mary Virginia Moore and Yohannan T. Abraham, "Comparable Worth: Is It a Moot Issue? Part II: The Legal and Juridicial Posture," *Public Personnel Management*, Summer 1994, pp. 263–86. This article is part of a series on comparable worth. The first part was published in the Winter 1992 issue of *Public Personnel Management*. The National Committee on Pay Equity is an ac-

Union Developments

Unions support "pay equity" as a concept. Some interpret pay equity to mean comparable worth; others use pay equity as a more all-encompassing, less well-defined term. The amount of union support for comparable worth is directly related to its effects on the union's membership. AFSCME and the Communication Workers of America (CWA) actively support comparable worth and have negotiated comparable worth-based pay increases, lobbied for legislation, filed legal suits, and attempted to educate their members and the public about comparable worth.

The public sector faces little competition for its services and is frequently better able to absorb a wage increase, since public employees are in a better position to pressure lawmakers than are taxpayers. This probably accounts for the relative success of public employees' unions in bargaining comparable worth pay adjustments. But trade-offs between higher wages and fewer jobs make unions in industries facing stiff foreign competition (e.g., International Ladies' Garment Workers' Union and the United Steel Workers) reluctant to aggressively support comparable worth. The beauty of "equity adjustments," from a union's perspective, is that because they are a separate budget item, they do not appear to come at the expense of overall pay increases for all union members. Collective bargaining has produced more comparable worth pay increases than any other approach.

International Developments

Canada has gone further than any nation toward requiring a comparable worth pay standard. Although the province of Ontario extends its law to the private sector, the Canadian Human Rights Act, in effect since 1978, requires that equal pay for work of equal value be paid to federal employees, approximately 10 percent of the country's work force.

The International Labour Organization (ILO) has had a directive since 1951 promoting "equal pay for work of equal value," but this has been generally interpreted to mean equal pay for equal work. The European Community (EC) issued an equal pay directive in 1975, specifying elimination of all discrimination on grounds of sex for the "same work or for work to which equal value is attributed." The 12 member states are free to choose the methods most suitable for complying with the directive. As a result of complaints and subsequent court decisions, both Denmark and the United Kingdom were required to change their laws to incorporate the directive's provisions. In Denmark in 1986, the wage gap in average hourly earnings was 82 percent. In the United Kingdom it was 74 percent.

---

tive lobbying group in support of comparable worth. It publishes a series of newsletters and publications and can be reached at 1126 Sixteenth Street NW, Suite 411, Washington, DC 20036. Telephone (202) 331–7343.

But although passage of laws may not be sufficient, it also may not be necessary. Sweden's Act on Equality between Men and Women at Work, in force since 1980, prohibits sex discrimination but does not specify equal pay for work of equal value. Yet the ratio of women's wages in 1985 was 91 percent. The narrowness of the gap has been attributed in part to the Swedish unions' practice of negotiating the largest increases for the lowest-paid workers, which narrows the wage structure and also the wage gap.[67]

Costs

Opposition to comparable worth legislation is almost a reflex action for many employers. Legislation constrains their ability to act, to redesign pay systems, and to meet changing conditions. In addition, legislation usually translates into increased costs. Nevertheless, some employers that oppose a mandated approach to comparable worth are investigating how it could be implemented and its expected costs.

Private sector data on costs of comparable worth adjustments are not available, for competitive reasons. When adjustments have been made in the public sector, there is a wide variation in the magnitude of costs. Hawaii, for example, appropriated $1 million in 1987 for equity adjustments for white collar workers, even though a task force found only minimal inequities. In 1994, Hawaii conducted another study focusing on blue collar, health care, and nonprofessional hospital workers. In Iowa, $32 million worth of comparable worth adjustments affected 60 percent of the state's employees. In contrast, $20 million of adjustments were shared by about 30 percent of Michigan state employees. However, Michigan concentrated its comparable worth efforts on reclassification of jobs rather than adjusting wage rates based on job evaluation points.[68]

In Minnesota, where coverage extends to all local cities, counties, and school districts, costs statewide have averaged 1.7 percent of payroll for school districts, 4.1 percent for cities, and 3.8 percent for counties. At the state level, adjustments totaling $22.2 million, approximately 3.7 percent of payroll, were negotiated for clerical and health care workers. The case at the end of this chapter is adapted from an arbitration hearing in a Minnesota city. The local police believed their pay raises should be comparable to pay raises police officers in other municipalities were receiving, even though the city's pay equity analysis dictated a wage freeze.

How generalizable are these figures? One writer estimated costs at .7 to 5 percent of payroll but did not report the underlying models used to arrive at

---

[67] "Closing the Wage Gap: An International Perspective" (Washington, DC: National Committee on Pay Equity, October 1988).

[68] Deborah M. Figart, "Evaluating Pay Equity in Michigan: A Strategic Choice Perspective," *Industrial Relations* 34, no. 2 (April 1995) pp. 263–81.

EXHIBIT 14.9   Preliminary Calculations of Comparable Worth's Addition to Wage Bill

Percent Increase = *DF*

where

D = Percent differential between wage for female-dominated occupations and comparable male-dominated occupations

F = Percent of total wages presently paid to members of female-dominated occupations

If $D = 20\%$ $F = 30\%$, comparable worth adds 6 percent to total wage bill.

If $D = 15\%$ $F = 20\%$, comparable worth adds 3 percent to total wage bill.

those estimates.[69] A simple model shown in Exhibit 14.9 allows us to make an initial estimate of the cost of comparable worth adjustments. Perlman and Grune estimate a 50 to 20 percent pay difference in male-female jobs that have the same job evaluation points in most firms.[70] We can use their 20 percent figure as the size of the wage adjustment required and further assume that 25 percent of the firm's entire payroll is earned by people whose wages need to be increased. Based on the formula in Exhibit 14.9, the adjustment is a 5 percent increase in the employer's total wage bill. In organizations in which wage differences are less than 20 percent or a smaller percent of the total wage bill is paid to female-dominated jobs, the percentage would be smaller.

A 5 percent increase in total wage costs may not be too high a price for some employers—those that can pass the costs on in the form of higher prices or increased taxes, or those whose overall labor costs are a very small portion of total costs. Conversely, those employers facing greater competition and with a higher percentage of employees receiving adjustments will find a 5 percent increase in their wage costs intolerable.

Obviously, the model in Exhibit 14.9 oversimplifies the real costs involved. It calculates the cost for only a single period, and it does not include additional costs resulting from benefits tied to pay level (e.g., pensions, overtime pay, social security).

Some advocates of comparable worth try to gain support by using the term *pay equity*—no one wants to be against equity. Others say comparable worth penalizes women who have made the efforts to get the training and experience

---

[69] Cook, *Comparable Worth: A Case Book of Experiences in States and Localities, 1986 Supplement.* See also Richard Arvey and Katherine Holt, "The Cost of Alternative Comparable Worth Strategies," *Compensation and Benefits Review*, September–October 1988, pp. 37–46.

[70] Nancy Perlman and Joy Ann Grune, "Comparable Worth Testimony of the National Committee on Pay Equity," Presented before the U.S. House of Representatives, Subcommittees on Civil Service, Human Resources, and Compensation and Employee Benefits, 1982.

that allowed them to move into higher paying jobs. The concept can evoke strong feelings. But the pay determination process has always had a political aspect. Unionized workers have frequently been able to obtain higher wages than have comparable unorganized workers. So if women can convince employers to adopt comparable worth, why shouldn't they? The issue then becomes whether it should be mandated. Or should it be part of the ongoing collective bargaining process?

The bottom line is that there simply is no intrinsic economic worth to any one job or group of jobs or job structure.[71] Why should a nurse be paid more than a ditch digger? Why should a ditch digger be paid more than a nurse? Within limits, workers are paid what is required—to get people to do work, which is determined through the confluence of many forces: the markets, unions, individual preferences, and so on. Who is to say another system is "fairer"? Fairer to whom?[72]

Summary

Pay discrimination laws require special attention for several reasons. First, these laws regulate the design and administration of pay systems. Second, the definition of pay discrimination, and thus the approaches used to defend pay practices, are in a state of flux. Many of the provisions of these laws simply require sound pay practices that should have been employed in the first place. And sound practices are those with three basic features:

1. They are work related.
2. They are related to the mission of the enterprise.
3. They include an appeals process for employees who disagree with the results.

Achieving compliance with these laws rests in large measure on the shoulders of compensation managers. It is their responsibility to ensure that the pay system is properly designed and managed.

Should comparable worth be legally mandated? Not surprisingly, opinions vary. But how much, if any, comparable worth policy will diminish the earnings differential remains an unanswered question. The earnings differential is attributable to many factors. Discrimination, whether it be access or valuation, is but one factor. Others include market force, industry and employer differences, and union bargaining priorities. Compensation managers need to examine critically traditional pay practices to ensure that they are complying with regulations. Certainly, the focus needs to be on pay dicrimination.

---

[71] June O'Neill, "An Argument against Comparable Worth," in *Comparable Worth: Issue for the 80's,* vol. 1.

[72] Greenberg and McCarty, "Comparable Worth: An Issue of Fairness."

Is all this detail on interpretation of pay discrimination really necessary? Yes. Without understanding the interpretation of pay discrimination legislation, compensation managers risk violating the law, exposing their employers to considerable liability and expense, and lose the confidence and respect of all employees when a few are forced to turn to the courts to gain nondiscriminatory treatment.

Review Questions

1. What is the difference between access discrimination and valuation discrimination?
2. Differentiate between disparate impact and disparate treatment, using pay practices as your examples. (Your illustrative practices may be legal or illegal.)
3. Consider contemporary practices such as skill/competency-based plans, broadbanding, market pricing, and pay-for-performance plans. Discuss how they may affect the pay equity debate.
4. What factors help account for the pay gap?
5. What are the pros and cons of labor market data in settings wages? Can you defend their use?

 6. How would you design a pay system that was based on comparable worth?

p 532

YOUR TURN

WAYZATA POLICE OFFICERS

Background

The following information is based on an actual arbitration case in Wayzata, Minnesota. The parties to the case are the city of Wayzata and the Law Enforcement Union, which represents police officers.

The union requests a 5 percent increase in each of the two years of the contract. It bases its proposal on wage comparisons with police departments in Wayzata's geographic district and with other cities that are demographically comparable, that is, as wealthy as Wayzata. These market comparisons justify the union's salary request.

The city proposes a wage freeze in order to comply with Minnesota's comparable worth legislation, which downgrades the use of market rates. However, the legislation says that any arbitrator award should not exceed the 3.25 percent already granted to the public works employees.

Much of the debate centers around the comparable worth law, which states:

1. Every political subdivision shall establish equitable compensation relationships between female-dominated, male-dominated, and balanced classes of employees.

2. The arbitrator shall consider those compensation relationships, job evaluation studies, any employee objections to those studies, and any other standards appropriate to the arbitration.

3. The relationships shall be equitable if
   a. The compensation for positions that require comparable skill, effort, responsibility, working conditions, and other relevant work-related criteria is comparable.
   b. The compensation for positions that require differing skill, effort, responsibility, working conditions, and other relevant work-related criteria is proportional to the skill, effort, responsibility, working conditions, and other relevant work-related criteria required.

Additional Information

1. Wayzata uses a quantitative job analysis system to support its job evaluation.
2. The dots on Exhibit 1 show the ratios for job evaluation points to wages for a number of jobs in Wayzata's system. The ratio for police officers is extremely high.
3. The lines on Exhibit 1 show a market line generated using regression analysis. Two

EXHIBIT 1   **Wayzata Pay Equity Analysis: Market Line Generated Using Regression Analysis, with Additional Lines Showing 90% of Market and 110% of Market**

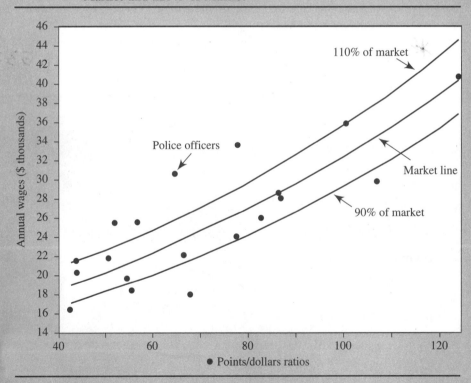

additional lines show 90 percent of the market and 110 percent of the market.

4. The job of patrol officer is male dominated.
5. The CPI increased by 3 percent last year and is projected to increase by a smaller rate next year.

Discussion

Divide the class into thirds. One-third is the union team and presents the union arguments. One-third presents the city's position. The final third of the class makes up the arbitration panel that issues a decision.

Issues for the Union

1. Evaluate the usefulness of job evaluation for the job of police officer. Do not focus on Wayzata's particular system; rather, focus on quantitative job evaluation per se and whether it can really "measure" a wide range of jobs.
2. Justify the high points/dollars ratio for police officers. What do these ratios mean?
3. Justify your market comparisons with other police departments.

Issues for the City

1. How do you respond to criticisms of quantitative job evaluation as applied to the police officers' job?
2. Is the city's financial condition relevant?
3. How should the market data be handled? What are relevant comparisons?

Issues for the Arbitrator

As the arbitrator, you have the legal duty to decide how to weight the usefulness of the job evaluation system against the legislative intent of comparable worth. What conclusions might the legislation lead you to in terms of relevance of market data for determining compensation relationships? What types of data might constitute "other standards" appropriate to interest arbitration? How will your decision about police officers' wages impact the wages of female-dominated professions valued comparably? Should police officers receive awards greater than those for comparable jobs outside law enforcement? Should the financial burden to the city of raising wages for female-dominated classes be a consideration in your decision about police officers' wages? Does the projected rise in price levels as indicated by the CPI make a difference?

Exhibit VI.1 The Pay Model

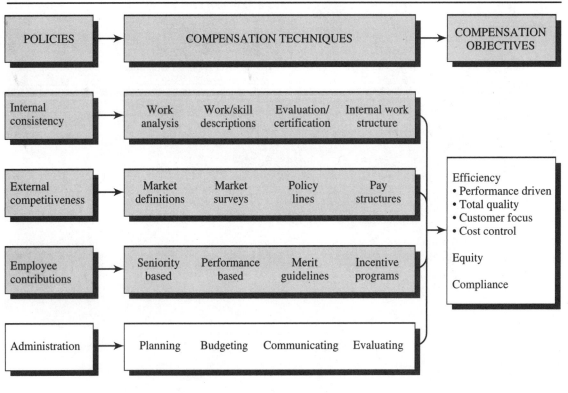

PART VI

Managing the System

Let us return to the pay model shown previously and in Exhibit VI.1. We have covered three basic strategic decisions—consistency, competitiveness, and contribution—along with the specific techniques and decisions required to attain objectives such as achieving competitive advantage, fair treatment of employees, and compliance with regulations. We have also examined in the preceding two chapters the role of government in the design of pay systems and in pay discrimination. Now we take up the fourth, and last, basic strategic decision shown in the pay model, the administration of the system. Many facets of pay administration have already been examined. Yet several important issues remain. These are covered in this final part of the book.

The most important remaining issue concerns managing costs. In fact, one of the key reasons for being systematic about pay decisions is to control costs. Some basic questions that need to be answered include these: What are the labor costs associated with recommended pay decisions? How can the labor costs be contained? How are these costs to be budgeted and managed?

In addition to these questions, other administration issues also need to be considered. The best-designed system in the world will founder if it is ineffectively implemented and managed. Communication is vital. How should the compensation philosophy, strategy, and plan be communicated to employees? How will line managers and employees participate in administering the system? Does the system help achieve the organization's objectives? How can the effectiveness of the pay system be measured or evaluated? We also discuss how to organize the compensation department and consider which activities should be done in-house, which activities should be reengineered and outsourced, and how to use the pay system as a catalyst for change.

The objective of Part VI is to answer these questions and discuss the techniques involved in managing the pay system. Techniques for managing costs, budgeting, and administration are discussed in Chapter 15. Chapter 16 examines compensation systems designed for employee groups working in special circumstances. These include executives, sales personnel, scientists and engineers, contingent workers, and first-level supervisors. As noted throughout the book, unions often play a significant role in the pay determination process, and we treat unions as an extra-special group by giving the topic its own chapter.

No longer can managers of employee compensation overlook international developments. International approaches to employee compensation serve as sources of new, often refreshing ideas, offer insights into competitive practices, and highlight how employees in various countries expect to be paid. Consequently, this book concludes with a chapter devoted to international compensation management.

Budgets and Administration

Chapter Outline

John Russell, former American Compensation Association Board member, was approached by his Missouri community to develop a salary plan for the city. He worked on it diligently and submitted the plan.

Subsequently, he decided to run for the position of alderman on the city council and was elected. His salary program was then brought before the council for a vote. Mr. Russell voted against his own program. He explained his behavior by commenting, "I never realized how tight the budget was!"

Today, managers of compensation should not share Mr. Russell's dilemma. They are business partners. The financial status of the organization, the competitive pressures it faces, and budgeting are integral to managing compensation. The cost implications of decisions such as updating the pay structure, merit increases, or gain-sharing proposals are critical for making sound decisions. Consequently, budgets are an important part of managing compensation: they are also part of managing human resources and the total organization.[1] Creating a compensation budget involves trade-offs among the basic pay policies—how much of the increase in external market rates should be budgeted according to employee contributions to the organization's success compared to automatic across-the-board increases. Trade-offs also occur over short- versus long-term incentives, over pay increases contingent on performance versus seniority, and over direct pay (cash) compared to benefits. Budgeting also involves trade-offs between how much to emphasize compensation compared to other aspects of human resource management. Managers must decide the financial resources to deploy toward compensation compared to staffing (e.g., work force size and job security) compared to training (e.g., work force skills) and so on. The human resource budget implicitly reflects the organization's human resource strategies; it becomes an important part of the human resource plan. Finally, budgeting in the total organization involves allocating financial resources to human resources and/or technology, capital improvements, and the like. So from the perspective of a member of the city council, John Russell ended up making different resource allocation decisions than he might have made from the perspective of the compen-

---

[1] Robert H. Meehan, "Analyzing Compensation Program Costs," in *Compensation Guide,* ed. William Caldwell (Boston, MA: Warren Gorham and Lamont, 1994); Michael Guthman, "Managing Total Labor Costs," *Compensation and Benefits Review,* November–December 1991, pp. 52–60.

sation manager. Today's managers of compensation need to understand and demonstrate how compensation decisions help achieve organization success while treating employees fairly.

The four basic pay policies dealing with consistency, competitiveness, contribution, and administration serve to guide and regulate pay decisions. In turn, the compensation systems (techniques) are designed to be consistent with these policies and to achieve specific pay objectives. Pay systems are intended to serve as mechanisms that assist managers to make better decisions about pay. How the pay systems are used by managers involves the administration of pay.

ADMINISTRATION AND THE PAY MODEL

Consider making pay decisions without a formal system. Under such an arrangement, each manager would have total flexibility to pay whatever seemed to work at the moment. Total decentralization of compensation decision making, carried to a ridiculous extreme, would result in a chaotic array of rates. Employees could be treated inconsistently and unfairly. Managers would use pay to motivate behaviors that achieved their own objectives, not necessarily those of the overall organization. The objectives of individual managers and some employees may be served, but the overall fair treatment of employees and the organization's objectives may be ignored.

This was the situation at the beginning of this century, where the "contract system" set up highly skilled workers as managers as well as workers. The employer agreed to provide the "contractor" with floor space, light, power, and the necessary raw or semifinished materials. The contractor both hired and paid labor. Bethlehem Steel operated under such a "decentralized" contract system. Skilled workers and plant captains had wide discretion; pay inconsistencies for the same work were common. Some contractors demanded kickbacks from employees' pay checks; many hired their relatives and friends. Dissatisfaction and grievances became widespread, resulting in legislation and an increased interest in unions.[2]

Lest we pass the contract system off as ancient history dredged up by overzealous compensation professors, read on. Some contemporary experts at the end of the century are promoting network organizations such as Benetton and Apple Computer, which rely on networks of independent parties to perform the essential functions of their businesses. Networking is linked to the concept of outsourcing. *Outsourcing* means that organizations secure a growing range of services and supplies from independent, external vendors. Ultimately, some see outsourcing driven to its logical extreme as a network of individual contractors or small

---

[2] Sanford M. Jacoby, "Industrial Labor Mobility in Historical Perspective," *Industrial Relations,* Spring 1983, pp. 261–82; T. J. Schlereth, *Victorian America: Transformations in Everyday Life, 1876–1915* (New York: Harper Collins, 1991); E. L. Otey, *Employers' Welfare Work* 123 (Washington, DC: Bureau of Labor Statistics, May 15, 1913).

teams. "All individual workers will be self-employed business units."[3] Look back to the turn of the century, replace the term *contract system* with *outsourcing,* and the contemporary similarities emerge. Will dissatisfaction, unfair treatment, cost sharing, and risk shifting to employees again be the result?

To avoid this result, any management system, including the compensation system, needs to be goal directed. Compensation is managed to achieve the three pay model objectives: efficiency, equity, and compliance. Properly designed pay techniques help managers achieve these objectives. Rather than goal-directed tools, however, pay systems often degenerate into bureaucratic burdens or blindly follow the fads and fashions of the day. Techniques become ends in themselves rather than focusing on objectives. Operating managers may complain that pay techniques are more a hindrance than a help, and these managers are frequently correct. So any discussion of administration must again raise the questions: What does this technique do for us? How does it help us better achieve our objectives? Are employees fairly treated? Although it is possible to design a system that includes internal consistency, external competitiveness, and employee contributions, the system will not achieve its objectives without competent administration.

Although many pay administration issues have been discussed throughout the book, a few remain to be called out explicitly. Therefore, this chapter covers a variety of compensation administration issues, including (1) managing labor costs, (2) variable pay as a cost control, (3) inherent controls, (4) communication, and (5) structuring the compensation function.

MANAGING LABOR COSTS

You already know many of the factors that affect labor costs. As shown in Exhibit 15.1,

$$\text{Labor costs} = \text{Employment} \times \left(\frac{\text{Average cash}}{\text{compensation}} + \frac{\text{Average benefit}}{\text{cost}} \right)$$

Using this model, there are three main factors to control in order to manage labor costs: employment (e.g., number of employees and the hours they work), average cash compensation (e.g., wages, bonuses), and average benefit costs (e.g., health and life insurance, pensions). The cash and benefits factors are this book's focus. However, if our objective is to better manage labor costs, it should be clear that all three factors need attention. Controlling benefit costs were discussed at length in Chapters 11 and 12. Here we concentrate on controlling employment and the average salary.

---

[3] "The New World of Work," and "Sixty-Five Years of Work in America," *Business Week,* October 17, 1994, pp. 76–148; Richard Huber, "How Continental Bank Outsourced its Crowned Jewels," *Harvard Business Review,* January–February 1993, pp. 121–29.

EXHIBIT 15.1 **Managing Labor Costs**

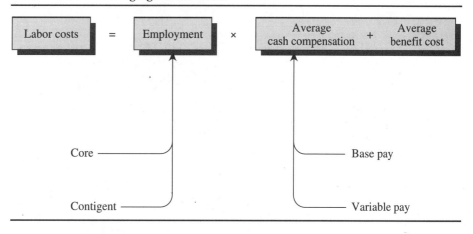

Controlling Employment: Head Count and Hours

Managing the number of employees (head count) and/or the hours worked is the most obvious and perhaps most common approach to managing labor costs. Obviously, paying the same to fewer employees is less expensive. Employers who reduce their work forces get headlines. There is some evidence that announcement of layoffs and plant closings have favorable effects on stock prices because the stock market reacts positively to events designed to improve cash flow and control costs. However, some evidence suggests that the adverse effects of work force reduction, such as loss of trained employees and unrealized productivity, often causes the financial gains of the reductions to be less than anticipated.[4]

To manage labor costs better, many employers attempt to buffer themselves and employees by establishing different relationships with different groups of employees. As Exhibit 15.2 depicts, the two groups are commonly referred to as *core employees,* with whom a strong and long-term relationship is desired, and *contingent workers,* whose employment agreements may cover only short, specific time periods.[5] Rather than expand/contract the core work force, many employers achieve flexibility and control labor costs by expanding/contracting the contingent work force.

---

[4] K. P. DeMeuse, P. A. Vanderheiden, and T. J. Bergmann, "Announced Layoffs: Their Effect on Corporate Financial Performance," *Human Resource Management* 33, no. 4 (1994), pp. 509–30; W. F. Cascio, "Downsizing: What Do We Know? What Have We Learned?" *Academy of Management Executive* 7, no. 1 (1993), pp. 95–104; Max Aquilera-Hellweg, "Getting Beyond Downsizing," *Fortune,* January 10, 1994, pp. 58–63.

[5] G. C. Pierson, "Independent Contractors: Guess Who's Coming to Work," *Legal Report,* Society for Human Resource Management, Summer 1993; "Myths about Contingent Worker Costs," *Work in America Newsletter* 10 (1994), pp. 2–4; Jaclyn Fierman, "The Contingent Workforce," *Fortune,* January 24, 1994, pp. 30–40.

EXHIBIT 15.2   Core and Contingent Employees

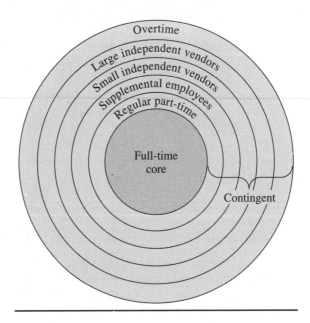

As Exhibit 15.3 shows, most temporary and contingent workers hold jobs in the office and manufacturing plants, but managerial and professional contingent workers are increasing. In Exhibit 15.4 we see a 300 percent increase in the use of temporary workers from 1980 through 1993.

The logic underlying the network organization referred to earlier is to shrink the core and expand the contract or contingent work force. Hence, the fixed portion of labor costs becomes smaller and the variable portion longer. And one can expand/contract the variable portion more easily than the core.

The pay for core employees has been the main focus of this book. What is known about the compensation of contingent employees? Not enough. Contingent workers are not a homogeneous group; their ranks include part-time and full-time employees, temporaries, consultants, "life-of-project" workers, leased employees, and subcontractors. One-fourth of the U.S. work force is estimated to be contingent; this group is growing twice as fast as the overall civilian labor force. The Bureau of Labor Statistics reports that part-time workers earn less per hour and often do not receive employee benefits such as health insurance. However, given the wide mix of employees classified as contingent, we need to be cautious in generalizing. Nevertheless, contingent workers appear to be

EXHIBIT 15.3   Where the Temps Are Working
Based on industry payrolls

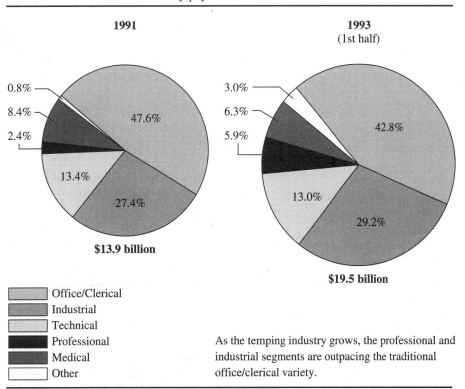

1991

0.8%
8.4%
2.4%
47.6%
13.4%
27.4%

$13.9 billion

1993
(1st half)

3.0%
6.3%
5.9%
42.8%
13.0%
29.2%

$19.5 billion

Office/Clerical
Industrial
Technical
Professional
Medical
Other

As the temping industry grows, the professional and industrial segments are outpacing the traditional office/clerical variety.

EXHIBIT 15.4   The Growing Army of Temps

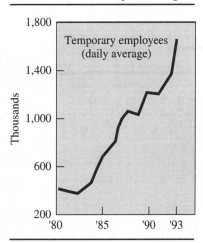

Temporary employees (daily average)

Thousands

1,800
1,400
1,000
600
200

'80   '85   '90   '93

cheaper than core employees, all things considered. And the historical mistreatment of these employees raises a flag of concern for the future.[6]

Rather than defining employment in terms of number of employees, hours of work is often used. For nonexempt employees, hours over 40 per week are more expensive (1.5 × regular wage). Hence, another approach to managing labor costs is to examine overtime hours versus adding to the work force.

Note that the three factors—employment, cash compensation, and benefits costs—are not independent. Overtime hours require higher wages, but avoid the benefits cost of hiring a new employee. Other examples of interdependence are the apparent lower wages (and lack of benefits) for some contingent workers, or a program that sweetens retirement packages to make early retirement attractive. Sweetened retirements drive head count down and usually affect the most expensive head count: older, more experienced employees. Hence, the average wage and health care costs for the remaining (younger) work force will probably be lowered too.[7]

Controlling Average Cash Compensation

Controlling the average cash compensation, as shown in Exhibit 15.1, includes managing average salary level as well as variable compensation payments such as annual bonuses, gain-sharing, or profit sharing.

Average Salary Level.   A wide variety of approaches is used to manage adjustments to average salary level. Here we discuss two basic approaches: (1) *top down,* in which upper management determines pay and allocates it "down" to each subunit and to individual employees for the plan year, and (2) *bottom up,* in which individual employees' pay for the next plan year is forecasted and summed up to create an organization salary budget.

CONTROL SALARY LEVEL: TOP DOWN

Top down, unit level budgeting involves estimating the pay increase budget for an entire organization unit. Once the total budget is determined, it is then allocated to each manager, who plans how to distribute it among subordinates. There are many approaches to unit level budgeting in use. A typical one, controlling the planned pay-level rise, will be considered. A planned pay-level rise is simply the percentage increase in average pay for the unit that is planned to occur.

As shown in Exhibit 15.5, several factors influence the decision about how much to increase the average pay level for the next period: how much the average level was increased this period, ability to pay, competitive market pressures, turnover effects, and cost-of-living.

---

[6] Virginia deRivage, "New Policies for the Part-Time and Contingent Workforce" (Briefing paper, Economic Policy Institute, Washington, DC, 1994).

[7] Nicholas Damico and Barbara Graham, "Early Retirement Incentive Window Plans: New Hurdles," *Benefits Law Journal,* Spring 1992, pp. 89–101.

Exhibit 15.5   What Drives Level Rise?

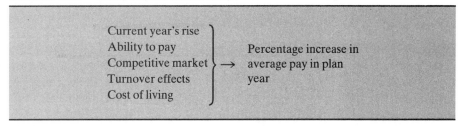

Current Year's Rise

This is the percentage by which the average wage changed in the past year; mathematically:

Percent level rise =

$$100 \times \frac{\text{Average pay at year end} - \text{Average pay at year beginning}}{\text{Average pay at the beginning of the year}}$$

Ability to Pay

The decision regarding how much to increase the average pay level is in part a function of financial circumstances. Financially healthy employers may wish to maintain their competitive positions in the labor market, and some may even share outstanding financial success through bonuses and profit sharing.

Conversely, financially troubled employers may not be able to maintain competitive market positions. The conventional response in these circumstances has been to reduce employment. However, other options are to reduce the rate of increase in average pay by controlling adjustments in base pay and/or variable pay.

Competitive Market

In Chapter 7, we discussed how managers determine an organization's competitive position in relation to its competitors. Recall that a distribution of market rates for benchmark jobs was collected and analyzed into a single average wage for each benchmark. This "average market wage" became the "going market rate" and was compared to the average wage paid by the organization for its benchmark jobs.[8] The market rates adjust differently each year in response to a variety of pressures.

---

[8] Beth Enslow, "Benchmarking Bonanza," *Across the Board*, April 1992, pp. 16–22; Mark Lerner, "Measuring Pay Costs in Your Organization against Pay in Other Organizations," *Personnel*, August 1988, pp. 70–73.

Turnover Effects

Variously referred to as *churn* or *slippage,* the turnover effect recognizes the fact that when people leave (through layoffs, quitting, retiring), they typically are replaced by workers earning a lower wage.[9] Depending on the degree of turnover, the effect can be substantial. Turnover effect can be calculated as annual turnover × planned average increase. For example, an organization whose labor costs equal $1 million a year has a turnover rate of 15 percent and a planned average increase of 6 percent. The turnover effect is 0.9 percent, or $9,000 (0.009 × $1,000,000). So instead of budgeting $60,000 to fund a 6 percent increase, only $51,000 is needed.

The lower average pay will also reduce those benefit costs linked to base pay, such as pensions. So the turnover effect influences both average pay and benefits costs in the total labor cost equation.

Cost of Living

Although there is little research to support it, employees undoubtedly compare their pay increases to changes in their costs of living, and unions consistently argue that increasing living costs justify adjustments in pay.[10]

A Distinction.   It is important to distinguish among three related concepts: the cost of living, changes in prices in the product and service markets, and changes in wages in labor markets. As Exhibit 15.6 shows, changes in *wages* in labor markets are measured through pay surveys. These changes are incorporated into the system through market adjustments in the budget and updating the policy line and range structure. *Price changes for goods and services* in the product and service markets are measured by several government indexes, one of which is the Consumer Price Index. The third concept, *the cost of living*, refers to the expenditure patterns of individuals for goods and services. The cost of living is more difficult to measure because employees' expenditures depend on many things: marital status, number of dependents and ages, personal preferences, and so on. Different employees experience different costs of living, and the only accurate way to measure them is to examine the personal expenditures of each employee.

The three concepts are interrelated. Wages in the labor market are part of the cost of producing goods and services, and changes in wages create pressures on prices. Similarly, changes in the prices of goods and services create needs for increased wages in order to maintain the same lifestyle.

---

[9] Martin G. Wolf, "A Model to Improve Cashflow Payroll Cost Forecasting," *Compensation and Benefits Review,* January–February 1988, pp. 50–57.

[10] Daniel J. B. Mitchell, "Should the Consumer Price Index Determine Wages?" *California Management Review,* Fall 1982, pp. 5–19.

EXHIBIT 15.6   Three Distinct but Related Concepts and Their Measures

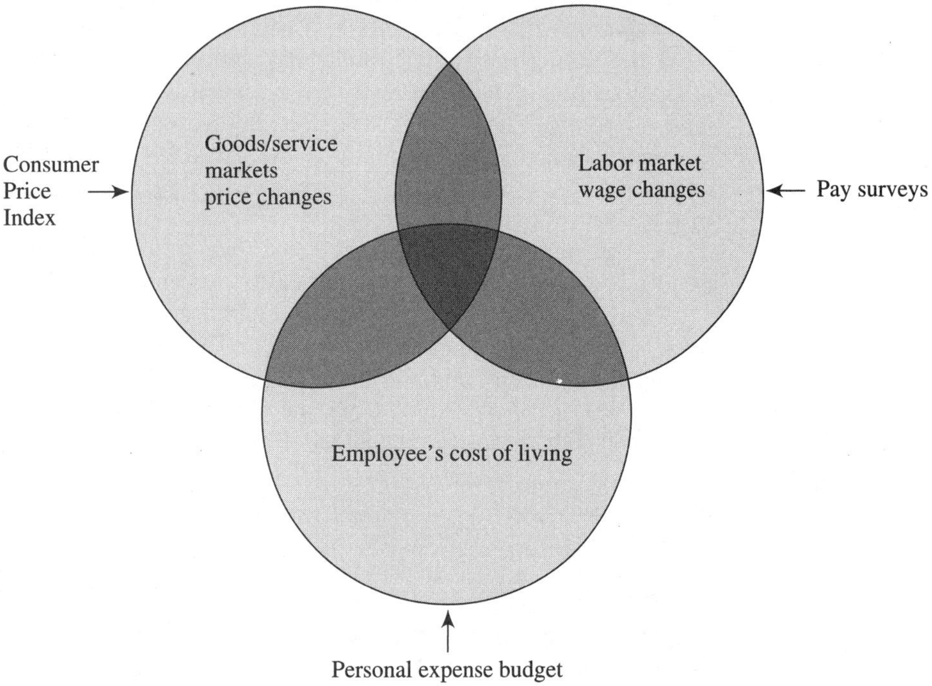

The Consumer Price Index.   Many people refer to the CPI as a "cost of living" index, and many employers choose, as a matter of pay policy or in response to union pressures, to tie wages to it. But in doing so, employers are confounding the concepts of living costs and labor market costs. The CPI does not necessarily reflect an individual employee's cost of living.

The CPI measures changes over time in prices of a hypothetical market basket of goods and services.[11] The present index is based on a 1982–84 study of the actual buying habits of 38,000 individuals. For this study, 265 categories of major expenditures were derived, and weights were assigned based on each category's percentage of total expenditures. For example, the index gives a weighting of 5.02 percent to auto purchases. This means that of the total money spent by all 38,000 people in the 1982–84 study, 5.02 percent of it was spent to buy new cars. This weighting plan measures both the price of cars and the frequency of new car purchases. To determine the new car component for today's

---

[11] For information on the CPI, contact the Bureau of Labor Statistics, Consumer Prices and Indexes: (202) 606–7000.

CPI, today's price of a new car identically equipped to the one purchased in 1982–84 is multiplied by the factor weight of 5.02 percent. The result is called today's *market basket price* of a new car.

The CPI is the subject of public interest because changes in it trigger changes in labor contracts, social security payments, federal and military pensions, and food stamp eligibility, as well as employers' pay budgets. One source estimates that more than one-half of the U.S. population is affected by payout changes tied to the CPI.[12] Tying budgets or payouts to the CPI is called *indexing.* Note that the cost of living is one of the factors shown in Exhibit 15.5 that influences the percentage increase of average salary level. It also may affect cost of benefits faced by employers either through health insurance coverage or pension costs.

There are many variations on the CPI. There is even an index for those readers who plan to lead the "good life." The annual Moet index tracks price changes for a dozen "upper crust" items. In 1994, the biggest increase of all was in the price of a Roll Royce Corniche IV convertible, up 7 percent from 1993 to $269,000. Other items on the Moet index include a Rolex Oyster watch for $13,950, up 5 percent, and a bottle of Dom Perignon, up 4.8 percent to a mere $87. But not to worry; the overall increase last year in the Moet Luxury Index was only 2.3 percent.

The CPI gets no respect these days. One of the main reasons is that the rigid "market basket" bears less and less resemblance to real world purchasing behavior. For example, the index includes the price of Macintosh apples, but if prices for Macintoshes escalate, I switch varieties to golden delicious or crispens. I've even been known to substitute an orange or a banana. Substitutes are not easily handled in the CPI. Another criticism of the index is that it is difficult to include discount prices. Thus, a trip to the car dealer, which the Bureau of Labor Statistics makes, does not really capture the difference between sticker and real prices. And pricing services, especially medical care, is difficult in light of the rapidly changing types and quality of service.

Geographic Differentials.   In addition to the national CPI, separate indexes are calculated monthly for five metropolitan areas and bimonthly for 23 other metropolitan areas and various regions. These local CPIs typically are more variable than the national indexes. They do not, as some mistakenly believe, indicate whether prices are absolutely higher in a particular area. Changes in the CPI indicate only whether prices have increased more or less rapidly in an area since the base period. For example, a CPI of 210 in Chicago and 240 in Atlanta does not necessarily mean that it costs more to live in Atlanta. It does mean that prices have risen faster in Atlanta since the base year than they have in Chicago, since both cities started with bases of 100.

---

[12] "How Reliable Is the Consumer Price Index?" *Business Week,* April 29, 1991, pp. 70–71; "The CPI Overstates Inflation," *Fortune,* February 7, 1994, p. 24.

Locality Pay

Many employers have historically maintained one national pay structure for their managerial–professional work force and separate schedules tied to local pay rates for their blue collar and clerical employees. But variations in living costs as well as external structures in different locations make it difficult to recruit and transfer employees paid on a national schedule. Exhibit 15.7 shows how pay rates and structures vary in different regions of the country. Pay rates in the Far West are substantially above the national averages in 14 of the 15 jobs, and the rank ordering of the jobs is also quite similar. Moving a professional employee to the West from almost anywhere is going to cause two problems. Living costs in general will be higher, and the market rate for that professional is going to be higher. But problems can also occur in structural comparisons. For example, in most regions, an employment interviewer is paid more than an administrative assistant—almost $10,000 more in the Central region. But in the Far West, the administrative assistant has a median wage over $7,000 more than the employment interviewer's.

The FBI's experience with a national pay structure documents the problems the federal government has faced. The general schedule provides guidelines for uniform pay rates across the United States. But in New York, uniform pay rates prescribe starting salaries for FBI agents that are 40 percent less than those for New York City detectives. An FBI agent transferred from Omaha to Boston will be asked to stretch the same pay to cover living costs that are 56 percent higher in Boston than they were in Omaha. The Federal Employee Pay Comparability Act of 1990 (FEPCA) seeks to close any gap between federal employees and employees of local and state government as well as private industry. The act phases in wage adjustments when rates differ from local market rates by more than 5 percent. Private sector employers usually have more flexibility in their pay systems than the federal government. Consequently, they are able to finesse geographic differentials without calling out a specific locality pay policy.

Rolling It All Together

Let us assume that the managers take into account all these factors—current year's rise, ability to pay, market adjustments, turnover effects, changes in the cost of living, and geographic differentials—and decide that the planned rise in average salary for the next period is 6.3 percent. This means that the organization has set a target of 6.3 percent as the increase in average salary that will occur in the next budget period. It does not mean that everyone's increase will be 6.3 percent. It means that at the end of the budget year, the average salary calculated to include all employees will be 6.3 percent higher than it is now.

The next question is, How do we distribute that 6.3 percent budget in a way that accomplishes management's objectives for the pay system and meets the organization's goals?

EXHIBIT 15.7   1993 National and Regional Salary Outlook

A 1993 nationwide survey of 2,200 companies shows the current average pay levels for certain exempt positions in the U.S., by region.

*Median Salary (50th Percentile)	National	Far West	Central	East Central	South	Northeast
General Accountant	$ 25,000	$ 31,200	$ 32,100	$ 30,000	$ 28,779	$ 20,560
Personnel Assistant	26,784	30,000	25,812	26,426	25,225	28,300
Administrative Assistant	27,048	37,200	27,435	27,000	24,890	27,038
Employment Interviewer	28,500	30,000	37,152	29,440	25,396	31,250
Production Planner	31,467	34,600	27,225	30,000	30,680	32,000
Manager Office Services	32,107	31,620	32,400	32,000	34,656	34,075
Programmer/Analyst	35,565	37,200	33,928	33,400	34,886	38,600
Purchasing Agent	37,000	36,665	40,248	36,850	31,000	38,966
Maintenance Supervisor	40,941	41,376	30,000	39,100	45,768	36,876
Personnel Manager	43,232	48,000	40,000	42,000	41,434	44,400
Director of Quality Control	48,940	59,000	39,000	48,060	45,420	52,420
Regional Sales Manager	51,957	53,820	130,000	49,000	48,500	53,857
Controller	60,000	62,520	50,690	56,900	58,000	63,800
Director of Marketing	67,300	75,000	72,700	63,881	61,896	71,000
Legal Counsel	75,000	94,000	68,400	78,000	71,400	78,525

* Salaries refer to median rates. In the survey sample, half of the salaries reported were lower and the other half were higher.

Source: Business & Legal Reports, Inc.

Distributing the Budget to Subunits.   A variety of methods to determine what percentage of the salary budget each manager should receive exists. Some use a uniform percentage, in which each manager gets an equal percentage of the budget based on the salaries of each subunit's employees. Others vary the percentage allocated to each manager based on pay-related problems, such as turnover or performance, which have been identified in that subunit.

Once salary budgets are allocated to each subunit manager, they become a constraint: a limited fund of money that each manager has to allocate to subordinates. Typically, merit increase guidelines are used to help managers make these allocation decisions.

Merit Increase Grids

Merit increase grids as devices to recognize employee performance were discussed in a previous chapter. Here we reconsider them as budget devices. First, they control the reward schedules to help ensure that different managers grant consistent increases to employees with similar performance ratings and in the same position in their ranges. Second, grids help control costs. Examples of grids are included in Chapter 10. Once a grid to deliver a 6.3 percent budget is determined, for example, managers use it to plan each employee's pay increase. The logic and calculations for alternative merit grids are in Chapter 10, Exhibit 10.12.

CONTROL SALARY LEVEL: BOTTOM UP

Bottom-up budgeting requires managers to forecast the pay increases they will recommend during the upcoming plan year. Exhibit 15.8 shows an example of the process involved. Each of the steps within this compensation forecasting cycle is described here.

1. *Instruct managers in compensation policies and techniques.* Train managers in the concepts of a sound pay-for-performance policy and in standard company compensation techniques such as the use of pay increase guidelines and budgeting techniques. Also communicate the salary ranges and market data.
2. *Study pay increase guidelines.* Review with the managers the purpose of increase guidelines and how to use them.
3. *Distribute forecasting instructions and worksheets.* Furnish managers with the forms and instructions necessary to preplan increases.

Exhibit 15.9 is an example of the forecasting worksheets that might be provided. In this exhibit, we see Sarah Ross's performance rating history, past raises, and timing of these raises. Some argue that providing such detailed data and recommendations to operating managers makes the system too mechanical. How would you like your present instructor to look at your overall GPA before

EXHIBIT 15.8   Compensation Forecasting and Budgeting Cycle

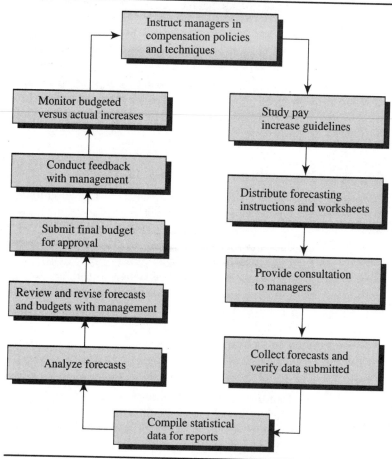

giving you a grade in this course? Pay histories ensure that managers are at least aware of this information and that pay increases for any one period are part of a continuing message to individual employees, not some ad hoc response to short-term changes.

4. *Provide consultation to managers.* Offer advice and salary information services to managers upon request.

5. *Collect forecasts and verify data submitted.* Audit the increases forecasted to ensure that they do not exceed the pay guidelines and are consistent with appropriate ranges.

6. *Compile statistical data for reports.* Prepare statistical data in order to feed back the outcomes of pay forecasts and budgets.

EXHIBIT 15.9   A Pay History Used for Forecasting

Name: Sarah Ross	YEAR END EXPERIENCE: 2	EMPLOYMENT DATE: 08-22-93	YEAR AND SERVICE: 21/04	YEAR FIRST DEGREE: 1993	HIGHEST DEGREE: BS	HIGHEST DISCIPLINE: Acctg.	SOC SEC NO: 458-56-5332
Position: Accountant	CLASSIF LEVEL: 26	EMPL MO LEVEL	DATE ASSIGNED TO POSITION: 08-22-93	DATE ASSIGNED TO CLASS LEVEL OF POSITION: 08-22-93			

Previous Salary Change

DATE	PERFORMANCE RATING	AMOUNT	%	MONTHS INTERVAL	ANNUAL VALUE	FIC	SALARY	UPPER BAND OR RANGE MAX	BAND MIDPOINT	LOWER BAND OR RANGE MIN
02 01 94	2.0						23040			
12 01 94	3.0	1920	8.3	10	10		24960			

Forecast Salary Change

DATE	PERFORMANCE RATING	AMOUNT	%	MONTHS INTERVAL	ANNUAL VALUE	FIC	SALARY	UPPER BAND OR RANGE MAX	BAND MIDPOINT	LOWER BAND OR RANGE MIN
09 01 95		2496	10.0	10	12		27456	30018	28016	25214

7. *Analyze forecasts.* Examine each manager's forecast and recommend changes based on noted inequities among different managers.

8. *Review and revise forecasts and budgets with management.* Consult with managers regarding the analysis and recommended changes.

9. *Submit final budget for approval.* Obtain top-management approval of forecasts.

10. *Conduct feedback with management.* Present statistical summaries of the forecasting data by department and establish unit goals.

11. *Monitor budgeted versus actual increases.* Control the forecasted increases versus the actual increases by tracking and reporting periodic status to management.

The result of the forecasting cycle is a budget for the upcoming plan year for each organization's unit as well as estimated pay treatment for each employee. The budget does not lock in the manager to the exact pay change recommended for each employee. Rather, it represents a plan, and deviations due to unforeseen changes such as performance improvements, unanticipated promotions, and the like are common.

This approach to pay budgeting requires managers to plan the pay treatment for each of their employees. It places the responsibility for pay management on the managers. The compensation manager takes on the role of advisor to operating management's use of the system.[13]

---

[13] Bruce Ellig, "The Compensation Professional in the New Business Environment," *Compensation and Benefits Management,* Autumn 1993, pp. 41–45.

VARIABLE PAY AS A COST CONTROL

Variable pay depends on performance and is *not* "rolled into" (added to) employees' base pay. Thus, the compounding effects of merit pay and across-the-board increases do not occur. Variable pay takes many forms. The essence of variable pay is that it must be reearned each period, in contrast to conventional merit pay increases or across-the-board increases that are added to base pay each year and that increase the base on which the following year's increase is calculated.

Increases added into base pay have compounding effects on costs, and these costs are significant. For example, a $15 a week take-home pay added onto a $40,000 base compounds into $503,116 over 10 years. Here is another chance to use that compounding formula from your accounting class or the compound key on your pocket calculator. If an employee earns $40,000 this year and receives a 5 percent increase every year, after 10 years the new salary is $62,000. The *total cash outflow* to this employee over 10 years is $503,116. In addition, costs for some benefits also increase. By comparison, the organization could keep base pay at $40,000 a year and pay a 26.8 percent bonus every single year for about the same $503,000. That 5 percent increase amounts to only $38 per week before taxes—probably about $15 a week more in take-home pay.

So from a labor cost perspective, conventional increases impact not only the average pay level but also the costs of all benefits contingent on base pay (e.g., pensions). Consequently, the greater the ratio of variable pay to base pay, the more variable (flexible) the organization's labor costs. Reconsider the general labor cost model in Exhibit 15.1; note that the greater the ratio of contingent to core workers and variable to base pay, the greater the variable component of labor costs, and the greater the options available to managers to control these costs.

Although variability in pay and employment may be an advantage for managing labor costs, it may be less appealing from the standpoint of managing equitable treatment of employees. The inherent financial insecurity built into variable plans may adversely affect employees' financial well-being and subsequently affect their behaviors at work and attitudes toward their employers. Managing labor costs is only one objective for managing compensation; other objectives in the pay model include sustaining competitive advantage (productivity, total quality, customer service, and costs) and equitable treatment of employees.

INHERENT CONTROLS

Pay systems have two basic processes that serve to control pay decision making: (1) those inherent in the design of the techniques and (2) the formal budgeting process.

Think back to the several techniques already discussed: job analysis and evaluation, skill/competency-based plans, policy lines, range minimums and maximums, bands, performance evaluation, gain-sharing, and salary increase guidelines. In addition to their primary purposes, these techniques also regulate managers' pay decisions by guiding what managers do. Controls are imbedded in the design of these techniques to ensure that decisions are directed toward the pay system's objectives. A few of these controls are examined below.

Range Maximums and Minimums

These ranges set the maximum and minimum dollars to be paid for specific work. The maximum is an important cost control. Ideally, it represents the highest value the organization places on the output of the work. Under job-based structures, skills and knowledge possessed by employees may be more valuable in another job, but the range maximum represents all that the work produced in a particular job is worth to the organization. For example, the job of airline flight attendant is in a pay range with a maximum that is the highest an airline will pay a flight attendant, no matter how well the attendant performs the job. Pressures to pay above the range maximum occur for a number of reasons—for example, when employees with high seniority reach the maximum or when promotion opportunities are scarce. If employees are paid above the range maximum, these rates are called *red circle rates*. Most employers "freeze" red circle rates until the ranges are shifted upward by market update adjustments so that the rate is back within the range again. If red circle rates become common throughout an organization, then the design of the ranges and the evaluation of the jobs should be reexamined.

Range minimums are just that: the minimum value placed on the work. Often rates below the minimum are used for trainees. Rates below minimum may also occur if outstanding employees receive a number of rapid promotions and rate adjustments have not kept up.

Compa-Ratios

Range midpoints reflect the pay policy line of the employer in relationship to external competition. To assess how managers actually pay employees in relation to the midpoint, an index called a *compa-ratio* is often calculated.

$$\text{Compa-ratio} = \frac{\text{Average rates actually paid}}{\text{Range midpoint}}$$

A compa-ratio of less than 1.00 means that, on average, employees in that range are paid below the midpoint. Translated, this means that managers are paying less than the intended policy. There may be several valid reasons for such a situation. The majority of employees may be new or recent hires; they may be poor performers; or promotion may be so rapid that few employees stay in the job long enough to get into the high end of the range.

A compa-ratio greater than 1.00 means that, on average, the rates exceed the intended policy. The reasons for this are the reverse of those mentioned above: a majority of workers with high seniority, high performance, low turnover, few new hires, or low promotion rates. Compa-ratios may be calculated for individual employees, for each range, for organization units, or for functions.

Other examples of controls designed into the pay techniques include the mutual signoffs on job descriptions required of supervisors and subordinates. Another is slotting new jobs into the pay structure via job evaluation, which helps ensure that jobs are compared on the same factors.

Similarly, an organizationwide performance management system is intended to ensure that all employees are evaluated on similar factors.

Analyzing Costs

Costing out wage proposals is commonly done prior to recommending pay increases. It is also used in preparation for collective bargaining. For example, it is useful to bear in mind the dollar impact of a 1 cent per hour wage change or a 1 percent change in payroll as one goes into bargaining.[14] Knowing these figures, negotiators can quickly compute the impact of a request for a 9 percent wage increase.

Using Computers. If you've been thinking to yourself during these various budgetary calculations that "there's got to be an easier way," you're right. Commercial computer software can analyze almost every aspect of compensation information.

Computers can provide analysis and data that will improve the administration of the pay system. For example, computers can easily compare past estimates to what actually occurred (e.g., the percentage of employees that actually did receive a merit increase and the amount). Spreadsheet programs can simulate alternate wage proposals and compare their potential effects.

But computers have wider applications to compensation administration besides costing, for example, computerized job analysis and job evaluation. Software can also evaluate salary survey data and simulate the cost impact of incentive and gain-sharing options.[15]

COMMUNICATION

Earlier in this book, we stressed that employees must believe that the pay system is fair.[16] Employees' perceptions about the pay system are shaped through the

---

[14] Stephen Holoviak, *Costing Labor Contracts* (New York: Praeger, 1984); Myron Gable and Stephen Holoviak, "Determining the Cost of Supplemental Benefits," *Compensation and Benefits Review,* September–October 1985, pp. 22–23; Robert E. Allen and Timothy J. Keaveny, "Costing Out a Wage and Benefit Package," *Compensation Review,* Second Quarter 1983, pp. 27–39.

[15] *Software for Compensation Professionals* (Scottsdale, AZ: American Compensation Association, 1991).

[16] R. Folger and M. A. Konovsky, "Effects of Procedural and Distributive Justice on Reactions to Pay Raise Decisions," *Academy of Management Journal* 32 (1989), pp. 115–30;

treatment they receive by managers, formal communication programs about their pay and performance, and participation in the design of the system.

Communication or Marketing?

Salaries of the top executives in publicly held corporations are published in prospectuses and often in annual financial reports. Similarly, collective bargaining agreements spell out in detail pay rates for covered employees. And if you know which budget books to examine, you can even find the salaries of most public officials. But these groups constitute only a fraction of all employees. Most employees are not told what their coworkers are being paid. The literature on compensation management usually exhorts employers to communicate pay information; however, there is no standard approach on what to communicate to individuals about their own pay or that of their colleagues.

Some organizations have adopted a marketing approach. Similar to selling products to consumers, the pay system is a product, and employees and managers are the customers. Marketing approaches include consumer attitude surveys about the product, snappy advertising about the pay policies, and elaborate videotapes expounding policies and strengths. The marketing approach aims to directly manage expectations and attitudes about pay. In contrast, the communication approach tends to provide technical details. The marketing approach focuses on the quality and advantages of overall policies and is silent on specifics such as range maximums, increase guides, and the like.

Two reasons are usually given for communicating pay information. The first is that pay delivers a strong message. Considerable resources have been devoted to designing a system that is intended to motivate effective performance and encourage productivity. For the pay system to influence work behaviors and attitudes, managers and employees must understand it.

The second reason is that, according to some research, employees seem to misperceive the pay system.[17] For example, they tend to overestimate the pay of those with lower level jobs and to underestimate the pay of those in higher level jobs. In other words, they tend to think that the pay structure is more compressed than it actually is. If differentials are underestimated, their motivational value is diminished.[18]

Further, there is some evidence to suggest that the goodwill engendered by the act of being open about pay may also affect employees' attitudes toward

---

J. Greenberg, "Reactions to Procedural Injustice in Payment Distributions: Do the Ends Justify the Means?" *Journal of Applied Psychology* 72 (1987), pp. 55–61; R. Folger and J. Greenberg, "Procedural Justice: An Interpretive Analysis of Personnel Systems," in *Human Resources Management,* vol. 3, ed. K. M. Rowland and G. R. Ferris (Greenwich, CT: JAI Press, 1985), pp. 141–83.

[17] Thomas A. Mahoney and William Weitzel, "Secrecy and Managerial Compensation," *Industrial Relations* 17, no. 2 (1978), pp. 245–51.

[18] Milan Moravec, "A 21st Century Communications Tool," *HR Magazine,* July 1993, pp. 77–81.

pay.[19] Interestingly, the research also shows that employees in companies with open pay communication policies are as inaccurate in estimating pay differentials as those in companies in which pay secrecy prevails. However, employees under open pay policies tend to express higher satisfaction with their pay and with the pay system.

Intended and Unintended Consequences.   The first point to be made about pay communication is that if the pay system is not based on work-related or business-related logic, then the wisest course is probably to avoid formal communication until the system is put in order. However, avoiding *formal* communication is not synonymous with avoiding communication. Employees are constantly getting intended and unintended messages through the pay treatment they receive.

The second point is that achieving a fair and equitable pay system requires active involvement and feedback from managers and employees. An open policy helps ensure that employees understand how their pay is determined. The third point is that providing accurate pay information may cause some initial short-term concerns among employees. Over the years, employees probably have rationalized a set of relationships between their pay and the perceived pay and efforts of others. Receiving accurate data may require those perceptions to be adjusted.

Exhibit 15.10 is one major employer's communications policy. Many employers communicate the range for an incumbent's present job and for all the jobs in a typical career path or progression to which employees can logically aspire.

EXHIBIT 15.10   Typical Communications Policy

Program Communications
A.   **To supervisors.** New ranges and guides should be provided to affected supervisors upon approval together with a memo explaining the change and outlining the program review, the changes made, the effective data, the new ranges and guides, and any instructions for communication to employees.
B.   **Supervisors should communicate to affected employees.** Employees should understand that our salary ranges are reviewed periodically and that they are competitive with the market. They should be told the dollar value for their salary range and the A–B–C performance definitions. They should know the supervisor's evaluation of their performance—the reasons for that position in the range. Guides are not discussed.

---

[19] Ed Lawler III, "The New Pay," in *Current Issues in Human Resource Management,* ed. Sara L. Rynes and George T. Milkovich (Plano, TX: Business Publications, 1986), pp. 404–12; John Hannon and George T. Milkovich, "The Relationship Between HR Signals, Reputation, and Performance" (Working paper, CAHRS, 1992).

In addition to ranges, some employers communicate the typical pay increases that can be expected for poor, satisfactory, and top performance. The rationale given is that employees exchange data (not always factual) and/or guess at normal treatment, and the rumor mills are probably incorrect. Providing accurate data may have a positive effect on employee work attitudes and behaviors. One potential danger in divulging increase schedule data is the inability to maintain that schedule in the future for reasons outside the control of the compensation department (e.g., economic or product market conditions). Nevertheless, pay increase data, coupled with performance expectations, should enhance employee motivation, which is a prime objective of the pay system.

Opening the Books.   There are some who advocate sharing all financial information with employees.[20] All of it. For 10 years, employees at Springfield Remanufacturing, a rebuilder of engines, have been given weekly peeks at everything from revenues to labor costs. The employees, who own 31 percent of the company stock, and others argue that this "open book" approach results in high commitment and an understanding of how to maintain competitiveness. Many employers don't share information with such gusto, but they are increasingly disclosing more to their employees. Some are even providing basic business and financial training to help employees better understand the information. Devotees of opening the books and financial training believe these methods will improve attitudes and performance, but there is no research to support them.

At the minimum, perhaps the most important information to be communicated is the work-related and business-related rationale on which pay systems are based. Some employees may not agree with these rationales or the results, but at least it will be clear that pay is determined by something other than the whims or biases of their supervisors.

Participation: Beliefs, Payoffs, and Practices

An often unchallenged premise in this book has been that employee (and manager) participation in the design and administration of pay systems pays off through increased understanding and commitment. As you might expect, research on the effects of employee participation in general shows mixed results.[21] Overall, the evidence suggests that participation does have positive effects, but they are not overwhelming.[22] A recent survey reports employees have no input into the design or implementation in 54 percent of the Fortune 500. Generally, employees

---

[20] "Company Wins Worker Loyalty by Opening the Books," *The Wall Street Journal*, December 20, 1993, p. B2.

[21] John Wagner III, "Participation's Effects on Performance and Satisfaction: A Reconsideration of Research Evidence," *Academy of Management Review* 19, no. 2 (1994), pp. 312–30.

[22] Barry Bluestone, *Negotiating the Future* (New York: Basic Books, 1992).

seem to have input into aspects that are directly related to them (i.e., job descriptions), but not into overall policies, structure, or competitor salary surveys.[23]

Recently the NLRB and the DOL have determined that employee committees formed to advise companies on issues such as pay, benefits and other conditions of work constitute unfair labor practices. Polaroid, a nonunion company, asked a group of employees to help redesign its pay system. The DOL alleged that the employee team was "a super-sophisticated form of employer-dominated labor organization" and should have been democratically elected. In a more important case, Electromation employee teams helped revise a bonus plan that had been discontinued because of wide employee dissatisfaction. The NLRB determined that the teams constituted a company-dominated labor organization because management facilitated and controlled committee discussions. This decision has effectively thrown up a major legal obstacle to formal employee participation (except through certified unions) in the design of pay systems. Recently, the Dunlop Commission has recommended changing the labor laws to overcome this obstacle.[24]

From Administrator to Change Agent

Employee compensation is a powerful signal. Some suggest that restructured pay systems signal major shifts in business strategies or culture. Shifts from conventional across-the-board annual increases to profit sharing or from narrow job descriptions and ranges to broad roles and bands are examples of how management sends signals of major change to employees. Others argue that pay systems should follow rather than lead change. Hence, team-based gain-sharing plans can support the move to high-performance organizations.

Whether pay is a leading catalyst for change or a follower of change, compensation managers need to learn how to implement change. Not only do they need to know the strategic and technical aspects of compensation, they also need to learn how to bargain, resolve disputes, empower employees, and develop teams.

STRUCTURING THE COMPENSATION FUNCTION

Compensation professionals seem to be constantly reevaluating where within the organization the responsibility for the design and administration of pay systems should be located. The organizational arrangements of the compensation function vary widely.

---

[23] Janice Stanger and J. Stephen Heinen, "Alternatives to Employee Task Forces," *Employee Benefits Journal*, June 1994, pp. 18–22.

[24] Tom Kochan and Paul Osterman, *Mutual Gains* (Boston: Harvard Business School, 1994).

Centralization–Decentralization

An important issue related to structuring the function revolves around the degree of decentralization (or centralization) in the overall organization structure. *Decentralized* refers to a management strategy of giving separate organization units the responsibility to design and administer their own systems. This contrasts with a *centralized* strategy, which locates the design and administration responsibility in a single corporate unit. Some firms, such as AT&T and Pacific Gas and Electric, have relatively large corporate staffs whose responsibility it is to formulate pay policies and design the systems. Administration of these policies and systems falls to those working in various units, who often are personnel generalists. Such an arrangement runs the risk of formulating policies and practices that are well tuned to overall corporate needs but less well tuned to each unit's particular needs and circumstances. The use of task forces, with members drawn from the generalists in the affected units, to design new policies and techniques helps diminish this potential problem.

Other more decentralized organizations, such as TRW and GE, have relatively small corporate compensation staffs (three or four professionals). Their primary responsibility is to manage the systems by which executives and the corporate staff are paid. These professionals operate in a purely advisory capacity to other organization subunits. The subunits, in turn, may employ compensation specialists. Or the subunits may choose to employ only personnel generalists rather than compensation specialists, and may turn to outside compensation consultants to purchase the expertise required on specific compensation issues.

Decentralizing certain aspects of pay design and administration has considerable appeal. Pushing these responsibilities (and expenses) close to the units, managers, and employees affected by them may help ensure that decisions are business related. However, decentralization is not without dilemmas. For example, it may be difficult to transfer employees from one business unit to another. Problems of designing pay systems that support a subunit's objectives but run counter to the overall corporate objectives crop up. So, too, does the potential for pay discrimination.

Flexibility within Corporatewide Principles

The answer to these and related problems of decentralization can be found in developing a set of corporatewide principles or guidelines that all must meet. Those principles may differ for each major pay technique. As examples, Exhibits 15.11 and 15.12 are the corporate guides for incentive plans for IBM and TRW business units. IBM's business units worldwide have the flexibility to design incentive plans tailored to each unique business unit's strategies and cultures. The only guidance is to ensure that the principles presented in Exhibit 15.11 (adhere to IBM's basic beliefs, improve financial and business objectives, and so on) are met.

EXHIBIT 15.11   Example of Corporatewide Principles: IBM

Variable Pay Program

Variable pay enhancements to IBM's merit pay system should be developed consistent with the following principles, objectives, and design considerations.

Principles—All variable pay programs must
- Adhere to IBM's basic beliefs.
- Improve IBM's financial/business performance.
- Support human resources strategy and meritocracy.
- Consider local environment/compensation practices.
- Be cost effective/neutral.
- Maintain/enhance IBM reputation.

Objectives
- Contain or reduce costs/enhance affordability.
- Stimulate improved performance.
- Share business success/risk.
- Sharpen focus on business strategy/results.

Keep in mind that the pay system is one of many management systems used in the organization. Consequently, it must be congruent with these other systems. For example, it may be appealing, on paper at least, to decentralize some of the compensation functions. However, if financial data and other management systems are not also decentralized, the pay system may not fit and may even be at odds with other systems.

A final issue related to structuring the responsibility for pay design and administration involves the skills and competencies required in compensation managers. The grandest strategy and structure may seem well designed, well thought out in the abstract, but could be a disaster if people qualified to carry it out are not part of the staff. Our earlier example in which the business subunits were staffed by generalists who were not trained or prepared to design pay systems tailored to the unit's needs illustrates the point. So all three aspects of management—strategy, structure, and staffing—must be considered.[25]

In view of the importance of a well-trained staff, both the American Compensation Association (ACA) and the Society of Human Resource Managers (SHRM) have professional development programs to entice readers into the compensation field.[26]

---

[25] Bruce Ellig, "The Compensation Professional in the New Business Environment," *Compensation and Benefits Management,* Autumn 1993, pp. 41–45.

[26] Schedules and course registration information are available from American Compensation Association, 14040 N. Northsight Blvd., Scottsdale, AZ 85260, and from Society of Human Resource Managers, 606 N. Washington Street, Alexandria, VA, 22314.

EXHIBIT 15.12   Example of Corporatewide Principles: TRW

<table>
<tr><td align="center">Group Incentive Plan Guidelines</td></tr>
</table>

- The design of a group incentive plan must be consistent with the organization's business and human resources strategies, and management and employee values.
- Performance measures must directly influence financial performance. Standards of performance must be at or above target financial levels or at least above the organization's historical levels. Historical performance measurements should be set at a realistic baseline.
- The plan must also address how product quality and customer satisfaction will be enhanced through attainment of the plan's objectives.
- The plan must be designed to be self-funding (i.e., plan-generated compensation is the result of increased profits or decreased costs).
- The plan must provide an equitable return to both the employees and the company. Payouts should be timed to logical milestones within the organization, but as close to the performance event as possible.
- All elements of the plan must be in compliance with applicable national and local laws and regulations.
- The plan should be written for a defined period and contain procedures for responding to changes in the business, work, and economic environment that may affect the plan's performance measures.
- Communication and employee involvement programs must be developed to support the plan. These programs should provide employees with information on how they can influence organization performance. Reports on the organization's progress toward attainment of performance goals should be provided on a timely basis.
- All plans must be approved by the cognizant Group Human Resources director or vice president in conjunction with a review of the plan by Sector Human Resources or Company Compensation for direct reporting groups.

Reengineering and Outsourcing

Reengineering the compensation function involves changing the process of paying people. It means reshaping the compensation function to make it more client or customer focused. Clients probably include employees, managers, owners, and perhaps even real customers of the organization. The basic question asked during reengineering is, "Does each specific activity (technique) directly contribute to our objectives (i.e., to our competitive advantage)?" If some added value isn't apparent, then the technique should be dropped. The next question, directed at those pay activities that do contribute to achieving objectives is, "Should we be doing the specific activity in-house, or can others do it more effectively, that is, should we outsource it?"

Outsourcing is becoming a viable alternative in the compensation (and benefits) field as organizations struggle to cease doing activities that do not directly contribute to objectives. Employee benefits is a major candidate for outsourcing. A commercial for an outsourcing vendor tells the tale:

> Vinnie's Pizza—What a success story! Their pizza and take-out Italian cuisine became so popular that Vinnie had to hire 10 more employees. Vinnie began to spend so much time on pay problems that he changed the name to Vinnie's Pizza and Payroll. Customers asked, what kind of a roll is payroll? Vinnie outsourced payroll and pay administration so he could go back to making dough.

We are experts in pizzas or cars or computers or software. But we are *not* experts in the design and implementation of employee pay schemes. The logic is appealing: Outsource the less essential systems to vendors and consultants who are experts and can do it more efficiently. In a recent survey, about 33 percent of over 1,000 firms reported that they already outsourced major responsibilities for their pay (e.g., market surveys and structure design) and benefits

EXHIBIT 15.13   HR Services Most Frequently Outsourced

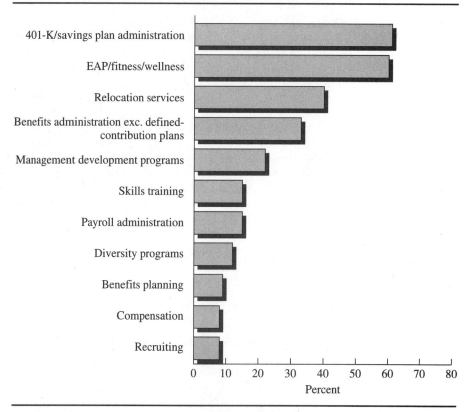

Source: Helen Axel, *HR Executive Review: Outsourcing HR Services* (New York: The Conference Board).

administration. Exhibit 15.13 shows which benefits activities are the most likely to be outsourced.

Cost savings is the apparent major short-term advantage of outsourcing. All those compensation wonks can be laid off or retrained. Major disadvantages of outsourcing include less responsiveness to unique and specific employee–manager problems, less control over decisions that are often critical to all employees (i.e., their pay), and information leaks to rivals and competitors.[27]

CONTROLS AS GUIDELINES: LET MANAGERS BE FREE

One of the major attacks on traditional compensation plans is that they often degenerate into bureaucratic nightmares that interfere with the organization's ability to respond to competitive pressures. Some recommend reducing the controls and guidelines inherent in any pay plan. Hence, banding eliminates or at least reduces the impact of range maximums and minimums. Replacing merit grids with awards and bonuses eliminates the link between the pay increase and the employees' salary position in the range and performance rating. Replacing job evaluation with skill-based plans opens up the freedom to assign employees to a wider variety of work, regardless of their pay and the value of the work they perform.

Such approaches are consistent with the oft-heard plea that managers should be free to manage pay. Or, as some more bluntly claim, pay decisions are too important to be left to compensation professionals. There is a ring of truth to all this. Our experience with many companies is that their pay systems are managed like the worst bureaucratic nightmares in Kafka's *Trial.*

Yet permitting managers to be free to pay employees as they judge best rests on a basic premise: Managers will use pay to achieve the organization's objectives—efficiency, equity, and compliance with regulations—rather than their own objectives. Clearly, some balance between hidebound controls and chaos is required to ensure that pay decisions are directed at the organization goals, yet permit sufficient flexibility for managers and employees to respond to unique situations. Achieving the balance becomes part of the art of managing compensation.

Summary

We have now completed the discussion of the pay administration process. Administration includes control: control of the way managers decide individual employ-

---

[27] B. P. Sunoo and J. Laabs, "Winning Strategies for Outsourcing Contracts," *Personnel Journal,* March 1994, pp. 20–25; "Reengineering the HR Function," *HR Planning Newsletter* 14, no. 2 (1993); M. Hammer and J. Champy, *Reengineering the Corporation* (New York: Harper Business, 1993); Huber, "How Continental Bank Outsourced Its Crowned Jewels."

ees' pay as well as control of overall costs of labor. As we noted, some controls are designed into the fabric of the pay system (inherent controls, range maximums and minimums, etc.). The salary budgeting and forecasting processes impose additional controls. The formal budgeting process focuses on controlling labor costs and generating the financial plan for the pay system. The budget sets the limits within which the rest of the system operates.

Other aspects of administration we examined in this chapter included the fair treatment of employees in communications and participation. The basic point was that pay systems are tools, and like any tools, they need to be evaluated in terms of usefulness in achieving an organization's objectives.

Review Questions

1. How can employers control labor costs?
2. How does the administration of the pay system affect the pay objectives?
3. Why is the structure of the compensation function important?
4. Give some examples of how employers use inherent controls.
5. What activities in administering the pay system are likely candidates to be outsourced? Why?
6. Explain how employee communications and participation influence the effectiveness of the pay system.

Your Turn:

Two Harbors Teachers

Public school teachers typically are paid according to salary schedules that include

1. "Steps" that pay for accumulating experience.
2. "Lanes" that pay for extra college credits.

Steps and lanes operate to boost pay even if the local school board does not grant any across-the-board or cost of living increases.

Critics of such schedules say that they guarantee steadily climbing costs, even in times when a district's finances do not permit increases.

Exhibit 1 shows a simplified salary schedule at Two Harbors, a district that employs 100 teachers and whose enrollment is growing at about 3 percent a year.

A. Calculate the change in salary in year 2 under the following conditions.
   1. Six teachers earning an average salary of $43,444 resign.
   2. Nine teachers are hired at an average of $25,666.
   3. Ninety-four teachers get raises averaging

EXHIBIT 1   Two Harbors Salary Schedule Showing Distribution of 100 Teachers

Year One

Total salaries for 100 teachers —————— $3,110,000
Average salary————————————— 31,100

	B.A. degree	B.A. and credits	M.A. degree	M.A. and credits
Step 5	7 teachers $29,000	18 teachers $33,000	14 teachers $36,000	11 teachers $41,000
Step 4	4 teachers $27,000	6 teachers $30,000	5 teachers $34,000	1 teacher $38,000
Step 3	6 teachers $25,000	4 teachers $28,000	3 teachers $31,000	1 teacher $35,000
Step 2	6 teachers $23,000	2 teachers $26,000	2 teachers $28,000	0 teachers $32,000
Step 1	8 teachers $22,000	1 teacher $24,000	1 teacher $26,000	0 teachers $28,000

Each step represents four years of service; the vertical columns show levels of college credits. In year 2, the faculty moves from an average of 3.86 steps to 3.93 and the proportion of teachers with master's degrees increases from 38 to 39 percent.

$851 as they move up and to the right because of more experience and training.

4. One hundred three teachers are on staff for the year.

5. There are no changes to the salary schedule.

What is the average salary for year 2, and what is the change from the previous year?

B. From year 1 to year 2, the percentage of teachers with master's degrees went from 38 to 39 percent; they also went from an average step ranking of 3.86 to 3.93. How do the results change if the assumptions change? For example,

1. What happens if enrollment declines by 3 percent a year?

2. What happens if the district starts to grow at 6 percent a year?

3. What happens if a nearby college opens an offsite facility that will make it easier for teachers to earn additional credits?

4. What happens if the district increases its entire salary schedule by 5 percent for each of the next two years of its teachers' contract?

C. Take the role of superintendent of the Two Harbors school district. Money is tight, as always. The district is about to launch an expensive technology program to give all classrooms Internet access. A vocal group of parents have taken the lead in demanding the district get "on-line." The teachers are mixed in their support. Some are enthusiastic advocates, others believe it is a waste of resources, a few are personally uncomfortable with the technology. In addition to the equipment, extensive (and expensive) training will be required. Nevertheless, the school board supports the move and wants it to be successful. At the same time, they have stressed the need to hold the line on other expenses in order to support this new foray.

Make the case that the district's ability to pay precludes any adjustments in the salary schedule for the next several years.

D. Take the role of president of the teachers negotiating committee. Make the case that the present salary schedule means that for the majority of teachers, their salaries will not even keep up with inflation. Yet the district is asking them to take on additional tasks without a pay increase. Because training in the new technology will be given within the district and will not receive college credit, it will not change teachers' positions in the schedule.

Make the case that in addition to salary schedule adjustments to help the district remain competitive with comparable school districts, a new way of reimbursing teachers for their new skills is also required.

CHAPTER

Compensation of Special Groups

> The country's in a bind, but I'm cheerful and I'm chipper,
> As I slash employee wages like a fiscal Jack the Ripper,
> And I take away their health care and never mind their hollers,
> And pay myself a bonus of a couple of million dollars.
>
> Mark Russell, Comedian

Managing compensation is so fascinating that even comedians are getting into the act. Mark Russell's satire on executive pay confirms what everyone suspects: that pay, particularly one's own, is determined without apparent justice or reason. This chapter identifies the underlying logic and practices governing compensation of special groups, including executives.

So far we have described compensation programs as if they were fairly uniform across all jobs in an organization. Compensation is determined by analyzing jobs, determining a job's internal worth from a job evaluation, using salary surveys to determine what competitors pay for the job, reconciling discrepancies, and making provisions to recognize individual performance. Not all jobs follow all these stages, though. Indeed, all we have to do is open a newspaper to see that some jobs and some people are singled out for special compensation treatment. Why does Jim Kelly (quarterback, Buffalo Bills) have a contract for more than $20 million over three years? Why does Michael Eisner (CEO, Walt Disney Company) regularly make more than $10 million per year ($202 million in 1993)? Are the value of these jobs and the incumbents in them determined in the same way as compensation is determined for other jobs and employees? The answer is probably no. But why? To answer this question it is useful to work backwards. What jobs get special compensation treatment in a company? Are they basically the same kinds of jobs across companies? If they are the same kinds of jobs, is there any common characteristic(s) that causes companies to devise special compensation packages for these jobs?

When we look at company practices with these questions in mind, a pattern begins to emerge. Special treatment, in the form either of add-on packages not

EXHIBIT 16.1   Conflicts Faced by Special Groups

Special Group	Type of Conflict Faced
Supervisors	Caught between upper management and employees. Must balance need to achieve organization's objectives with importance of helping employees satisfy personal needs. If unsuccessful, either corporate profit or employee morale suffers.
Top management	Stockholders want healthy return on investment. Government wants compliance with laws. Executive must decide between strategies that maximize short-term gains versus directions that focus on the long run.
Board of directors	Face possibility that disgruntled stockholders may sue over corporate strategies that don't "pan out." Help set strategic plans that affect profits.
Professional employees	May be torn between the goals, objectives, and ethical standards of their profession (e.g., should an engineer leak information about a product flaw that may hurt corporate profits?) and the demands of an employer concerned more with the profit motive.
Sales staff	Often go for extended periods in the field with little supervision. Challenge is to stay motivated and continue making sales calls despite little supervision.

received by other employees or of compensation components entirely unique in the organization, tends to focus on a few specific groups. This chapter argues that special groups share two characteristics. First, special groups disproportionately tend to face conflict from the incompatible demands of different stakeholders. And second, the way the job holders resolve this conflict must have important consequences for the success of the company. When both of these conditions are met we tend to find distinctive compensation practices for these special groups. Exhibit 16.1 describes the nature of the conflicts faced by some special groups: supervisors, top management, boards of directors, professional employees, and the sales staff.

As an example of facing conflict that has consequences for the success of the firm, consider how two different organizations compensate their engineers. One is a high technology firm with a strong research and development component. The other organization is a firm in which engineers are not central to its missions. A survey of just such differences in employee composition and organizational strategy found that research and development organizations with heavy concentrations of engineers have devised unique compensation systems that respond to the special needs of their engineers. Organizations with a different focus and with fewer engineers merged this group's compensation with the standard package.[1]

WHO ARE SPECIAL GROUPS?

Supervisors

Remember that supervisors are caught between the demands of upper management in terms of production and the needs of employees in terms of rewards and reinforcements. The major challenge in compensating supervisors centers on equity. Some incentive must be provided to entice nonexempt employees to accept the challenges of being a supervisor. For many years, the strategy was to treat supervisors like lower-level managers. But in so doing, sometimes the existing job evaluation system left these supervisors earning less than some of the employees they supervised. As you might imagine, there was little incentive to take on the extra work. More recently organizations have devised several strategies to attract workers to supervisory jobs. One popular method is to key base salary of supervisors to some amount exceeding the earnings of the most highly paid subordinate in the unit (5 to 30 percent represents the typical differential).[2]

---

[1] J. W. Crim, *Compensating Nonsupervisory Professional Employees* (Ithaca, NY: Research Press, 1978).

[2] E. C. Miller, "Supervisory Overtime, Incentive and Bonus Practices," *Compensation Review*, 10 (1978), pp. 12–25.

EXHIBIT 16.2   Percentage of Firms Paying Supervisors Overtime

	1989	1990	1991	1994
Percentage of firms paying for overtime	34%	36%	38%	40%

Source: Wyatt Data Services (1992, 1994).

EXHIBIT 16.3   Supervisory Variable Pay Plans

Type of Plan	Percent of Supervisors Eligible
Annual bonus	60%
Spot award	72
Lump sum	18
Individual incentive	15
Cash profit sharing	14

Source: Wyatt Data Services Survey of 1,510 companies, as reported in "More Variable Pay for Supervisors," *Compflash* (Saranac Lake, NY: American Management Association, July 1994).

Another method to maintain equitable differentials is simply to pay supervisors for scheduled overtime.[3] Over the past few years, this option has become slightly more popular, as Exhibit 16.2 demonstrates. Companies that do pay overtime are about evenly split between paying straight-time overtime versus time-and-a-half for overtime hours.

Finally, some organizations (about 60 percent) develop special supervisory incentive and bonus plans. Exhibit 16.3 explains these plans.

Corporate Directors

A board of directors generally comprises 10 to 20 individuals who meet on a regular basis to serve a variety of roles in the interest of the corporation and its shareholders. Historically, directors frequently were given the role of rubber-stamping decisions made by top management. Such boards were "stacked" with people affiliated in some way with the organization (e.g., retired corporate officers, suppliers, attorneys). Modern corporate boards have changed considerably. Membership now includes more outside directors (approximately two-thirds)

---

[3] Remember, as exempt employees, the law does not mandate overtime pay for supervisors. This puts them at a disadvantage to subordinates who are paid for overtime.

EXHIBIT 16.4   Major Benefits Offered to Directors in 1994

Benefit	Percent of Companies Offering Benefit	Average Cost per Person
Retirement programs	43%	$13,800
Matching director's gift to college or university	52	3,000
Deferral of cash compensation until retirement	48	2,200
Grants to charity	11	13,000*
Medical insurance	15	2,000
Payment of spouse's travel expenses	32	1,000
Death benefits	21	1,000

Note: * This figure represents 1991 costs. All others are for 1994.
Source: Anne G. Perkins, *Havard Business Review*, January–February 1995, pp. 12–14.

than inside directors (e.g., chief executive officers, corporate officers). Outside members may be unaffiliated business executives, representatives from important segments of society, and major shareholders. The days of rubber-stamped decisions are almost gone. Boards now face increased responsibility for decision making and for the success of the firm. They face the increased risks that disgruntled shareholders might bring suit against them for unprofitable or unpopular corporate decisions. Compensation has not always kept up with this increased responsibility that director's face. Indeed, there is a growing concern that board members are paid too much to perform rubber-stamp duties, but too little to assume today's risks, responsibilities, and pressures.

According to a 1994 survey, the average outside director in an industrial firm earns $57,832 including stock awards averaging $12,323.[4] Exhibit 16.4 shows other forms of compensation that directors receive.

If any trend exists in the compensation of corporate directors, it is toward increased variable compensation. About 51 percent of large firms provide directors with some form of stock compensation.[5] The compensation goal is to make sure that directors make decisions that are in the best interests of the stockholders. This is also true for executives. An obvious way of achieving this goal is to make sure the directors also are stockholders!

---

[4] Anne G. Perkins, *Harvard Business Review*, January–February 1995, pp. 12–14.
[5] Jacqueline M. Graves, "While Directors Get Stock," *Fortune*, October 3, 1994, p. 18.

Exhibit 16.5   Highest Paid Executives, 1982–1993

Year	CEO	Company	Total Pay (millions)
1993	Michael Eisner	Disney	$202.0
1992	Stephen A. Wynn	Mirage Resorts	$ 34.154
1991	Anthony O'Reilly	H. J. Heinz	$ 75.1
1990	Stephen Wolf	UAL	18.3
1989	Craig McCaw	Cellular	53.9
1988	Michael Eisner	Disney	40.1
1987	Charles Lazarus	Toys R Us	60.0
1986	Lee Iacocca	Chrysler	20.5
1985	Victor Posner	DWG	12.7
1984	T. Boone Pickens	Mesa Petroleum	22.8
1983	William Anderson	NCR	13.2
1982	Frederick Smith	Federal Express	51.5

Source: *Business Week*, April 25, 1994, pp. 52–97; *Fortune*, June 14, 1993, pp. 102–11; *The Wall Street Journal Reports*, April 13, 1994.

Chief Executive Officers

How would you like to earn $3.8 million per year? That is the 1993 average compensation (salary plus bonus) for CEOs in major corporations.[6] Exhibit 16.5 shows the total compensation for the *highest paid executive* for each of the past 10 years. Many critics argue that this level of compensation is excessive.[7] Are the critics right? One way to answer the question is to look at the different ways people say that executive compensation is determined and ask, Does this seem reasonable?

Possible Explanations for CEO Compensation   One approach to explain why executives receive such large sums of money involves social comparisons.[8] According to this approach, executive salaries bear a consistent relative relationship to compensation of lower level employees. When salaries of lower level employees rise in response to market forces, top executive salaries also rise to maintain the same relative relationship. In part the data in Exhibit 16.6 support this explanation. Second-level managers earn about two-thirds of the CEO's salary, and those in the third level earn slightly more than one-half of the CEO's salary.

---

[6] *Business Week*, April 25, 1994, p. 55.

[7] Graef S. Crystal, *In Search of Excess* (New York: W. W. Norton, 1991). Based on 200 major companies in seven industries.

[8] Herbert A. Simon, *Administrative Behavior*, 2nd ed. (New York: Macmillan, 1957).

Exhibit 16.6   Ratio of Subordinate Salaries to CEO Salaries across Industries, 1990 versus 1986

Position Relative to CEO	Manufacturing		Banking		Insurance		Construction		Utilities	
	1990	*1986*	*1990*	*1986*	*1990*	*1986*	*1990*	*1986*	*1990*	*1986*
Second level	65	68	66	68	65	67	71	77	65	58
Third level	52	53	55	52	53	54	52	61	52	54

Source: *Top Executive Compensation* (New York: The Conference Board, 1986; 1990).

These ratios have been reasonably stable for more than a decade. The relative relationship breaks down, however, in a comparison of CEO salary to that of lower-level workers. In 1980 the average CEO had a salary that was 42 times that of an ordinary worker. By 1990 that ratio more than doubled to *85 times the wages of ordinary workers.* As a point of reference, the corresponding differential in Japan is less than 20![9] Both these pieces of information suggest that a social comparison explanation is not sufficient to explain why executive wages are as high as they are.

A second approach to understanding executive compensation focuses less on the *difference* in wages between executive and other jobs and more on explaining the *level* of executive wages. The premise in this economic approach is that the worth of a CEO should correspond closely to some measure of company success (e.g., profitability, sales). Intuitively, this explanation makes sense. There is also empirical support.[10] Numerous studies during the past 30 years have demonstrated that executive pay bears some relationship to company success.[11]

One study combined social comparison and economic explanations to try to better understand CEO salaries. Both of these explanations turned out to be significant. Size and profitability affected level of compensation, as did social comparisons. In this study, the social comparison was between CEOs and members of the board of directors. It seems that CEO salaries rose, on average, 51 percent for every $100,000 more that was earned by directors on the board.[12]

---

[9] Margaret Blair, "CEO Pay: Why Such a Contentious Issue?" *The Brookings Review*, Winter 1994, pp. 23–27. This comparison needs to be interpreted with some caution. One counterargument (the Hay Group, *Compflash* [Saranac Lake, NY: American Management Association April 1992, p. 3]) notes that American companies are generally much larger than their foreign counterparts. When compared to like-sized companies in other countries, the U.S. multiple is comparable to the international average.

[10] John A. Byrne, *Business Week*, April 25, 1994, p. 53.

[11] Marc J. Wallace, "Type of Control, Industrial Concentration, and Executive Pay," *Academy of Management Proceedings*, pp. 284–88; W. Lewellan and B. Huntsman, "Managerial Pay and Corporate Performance," *American Economic Review* 60 (1970), pp. 710–20.

[12] Charles O'Reilly, Brian Main, and Graef Crystal, "CEO Compensation as Tournament and Social Comparison: A Tale of Two Theories," *Administrative Science Quarterly* 33 (1988), pp. 257–74.

Recognizing this, some CEOs supposedly lobby to appoint as directors persons who are highly paid in their primary jobs.

A third view of CEO salaries involves the political motivations that are an inevitable part of the corporate world. Sometimes, this argument runs, CEOs make decisions that aren't in the best economic interest of the firm and its shareholders. One variant on this view, labeled *agency theory*, suggests that the normal behavior of CEOs is self-protective: They make decisions to solidify their position and to maximize the rewards they personally receive.[13] As evidence of this self-motivated behavior, consider the following description of how executives ensure their high compensation. This description comes from the experience of a well-known executive compensation consultant, now turned critic, who specialized for years in the design of executive compensation packages.

1. *If the CEO is truly underpaid*: A compensation consultant is hired to survey true competitors of the company. The consultant reports to the board of directors that the CEO is truly underpaid. Salary is increased to a competitive or higher level.

2. *If the CEO is not underpaid and the company is doing well*: A compensation consultant is hired. A list of companies is recommended to the consultant as appropriate for surveying. Companies tend to be selected because they are on the top end in terms of executive compensation. The consultant reports back to the board that its CEO appears to be underpaid. Salary is increased.

3. *If the CEO is not underpaid and the company is doing poorly*: A compensation consultant is hired. The CEO laments to the consultant that wages are so low for top management that there is a fear that good people will start leaving the company and going to competitors. Of course, no one ever asks why the company is underperforming if it has such a good management team. Anyway, the result is that the consultant recommends a wage increase to avoid future turnover.[14]

In each of these scenarios, CEO wages rise. Inevitably, someone points out that such practices lead to outcomes like those experienced in 1990: Profits slid 7 percent but executive compensation rose 7 percent.[15]

One result of the continued rise in CEO compensation has been increasing cries from both shareholders and the general public that executive compensation should be tied to success of the firm. One study found 83 percent agreement with this practice, but only 38 percent believe that firms actually did this.[16] Recent evidence suggests a growing link between pay and performance for executives. The CEO at Merck & Co. took a 11 percent pay cut as the company's profits

---

[13] Kathyrn M. Eisenhardt, "Agency Theory: An Assessment and Review," *Academy of Management Review* 14 (1989), pp. 57–74.

[14] Crystal, *In Search of Excess*.

[15] "The Flap over Executive Pay," *Business Week*, May 6, 1991, pp. 90–96.

[16] Compflash, "At The Top," *Compflash* (Saranac Lake, NY: American Management Association, 1990), p. 1.

dipped 11 percent. Similarly, when Mattel's profits declined 26 percent in 1993, CEO John Amerman took an even larger 41 percent pay cut.[17]

Agency theory argues that executive compensation should be designed to ensure executives have the best interests of stockholders in mind when they make decisions. The outcome has been to use such long-term incentive plans as stock options. Executive decision making is motivated by, and compensated for, improving shareholder wealth.[18] One survey of 500 large industrial firms found that 72 percent had three or more long-term incentive plans.[19] The most common of those plans is some type of *stock option*. In its simplest form, the plan gives an executive the option to purchase shares of the company stock at some future date for an amount equaling the fair market price at the time the option is granted. There is a built-in incentive for an executive to increase the value of the firm. Stock prices rise. Because of the rise in the stock price, the executive profits from the increased value of the stock purchased at the option price.

Although this sounds like an effective tool to motivate executives, there are still many critics.[20] The major complaint is that stock options don't have a downside risk. If stock prices rise the stock options are exercised. If stocks don't improve, the executive suffers no out-of-pocket losses. Some argue that executive compensation should move more toward requiring executives to own stock.[21] With the threat of possible financial loss and the hopes of possible substantial gains, motivation may be higher. Alternatively, firms could require CEOs to meet specific performance objectives before they could exercise their stock options.

The second trend in response to complaints about excessive executive compensation is increasing government regulation. In 1992 the Security and Exchange Commission entered the controversy.[22] Stockholders are now permitted to propose and vote on limits to executive compensation. The 1993 Revenue Reconciliation Act limited employer deductions for executive compensation to $1 million and capped the amount of executive compensation used in computing contributions to and benefits from qualified retirement plans. These and other proposed rule changes signal continued interest in, and closer scrutiny of, all components of executive compensation. The following discussion outlines these different components.

---

[17] John A. Byrne, *Business Week*, April 25, 1994, p. 52.

[18] J. Eaton and H. S. Rosen, "Agency, Delayed Compensation and the Structure of Executive Remuneration," *Journal of Finance* 38, no. 5 (1983), pp. 593–616; G. P. Baker, M. C. Jensen, and K. J. Murphy, "Compensation and Incentives: Practice vs. Theory," *Journal of Finance* 43, no. 3 (1988), pp. 593–616.

[19] Amanda Bennett, "Big Firms Rely More on Options but Fail to End Pay Criticism," *The Wall Street Journal*, March 11, 1992, p. A1.

[20] Ibid.

[21] Ira T. Kay, "Beyond Stock Options: Emerging Practices in Executive Incentive Programs" *Compensation and Benefits Review* 23, no. 6 (1991), pp. 18–29.

[22] Michelle Osborn, "SEC: Executive Pay Is an Issue for Shareholders," *USA Today*, July 13, 1994, p. B1.

Exhibit 16.7   Percentage Breakdown of Executive Compensation Components

Compensation Component	Percentage during 1970s	Percentage during 1980s	Percentage during 1990s
Base salary	60%	40%	38%
Benefits	*	15	10
Perks	*	5	3
Short-term incentive	25	20	23
Long-term incentive	15	34	68

Note: * = Unreported.

Source: Various issues of *The Wall Street Journal*, data from TPF&C, Wyatt Co.; Michael Bishko, "Compensating Your Overseas Executives, Part 1: Strategies for the 1990s," *Compensation and Benefits Review* 22 (May–June 1990); Blair, "CEO Pay: Why Such a Contentious Issue?" *The Brookings Review*, Winter 1994, pp. 23–27.

Components of an Executive Compensation Package   There are five basic elements of most executive compensation packages: (1) base salary, (2) short-term (annual) incentives or bonuses, (3) long-term incentives and capital appreciation plans, (4) employee benefits, and (5) perquisites. Because of the changing nature of tax legislation, each of these elements has received considerable attention in designing executive compensation packages. Exhibit 16.7 traces the trend in the use these components.

One obvious trend is apparent from these data. Companies are placing more and more emphasis on long-term incentives at the expense of base salary. Such a change in emphasis signals the growing importance attached to making decisions that ensure the long-run growth and survival of a company.

Base Salary.   As noted earlier, being competitive is a very important factor in the determination of executive base pay. But this competition is more important within than across industries. As Exhibit 16.8 shows, base salaries vary significantly across industries.

Although formalized job evaluation still plays an occasional role in determining executive base pay, other sources are much more important. Particularly important is the opinion of a compensation committee, usually made up of the company's board of directors (or a subset of the board). Frequently this compensation committee will take over some of the data analysis tasks previously performed by the chief personnel officer, even going so far as to analyze salary survey data and performance records for executives of comparably sized firms.[23]

---

[23] Ernest C. Miller, "How Companies Set the Base Salary and Incentive Bonus Opportunity for Chief Executive and Chief Operating Officers . . . A Compensation Review Symposium," *Compensation Review* 9 (Fourth Quarter 1976), pp. 30–44; Monci Jo Williams, "Why Chief Executives' Pay Keeps Rising," *Fortune*, April 1, 1985, pp. 66–72, 76.

EXHIBIT 16.8   Base Salary of Top Executives

Industry	CEO	Second Highest	Third Highest	Fourth Highest	Fifth Highest
			Organization Level of Executive		
Manufacturing	$463,000	$290,000	$231,000	$207,000	$195,000
Commercial banking	375,000	258,000	218,000	175,000	153,000
Communications	525,000	350,000	306,000	267,000	254,000
Diversified services	375,000	245,000	195,000	175,000	148,000
Energy and natural resources	460,000	312,000	275,000	200,000	180,000
Insurance	350,000	212,000	185,000	155,000	142,000
Utilities	345,000	221,000	173,000	157,000	155,000

Source: E. Arreglado, *Top Executive Compensation* (New York: The Conference Board, 1990).

This signals an increasing trend to closely monitor competitive pay and to improve oversight efforts for CEO compensation.[24]

Bonuses.   Annual bonuses often play a major role in executive compensation and are primarily designed to motivate better performance. Most striking is the rapid rise in popularity of this type of compensation. Less than 10 years ago annual bonuses were favored by about 36 percent of companies. Today 90 percent of executives receive annual bonuses based on performance![25]

Long-Term Incentive and Capital Appreciation Plans.   Exhibit 16.9 further illustrates the increased popularity of one form of long-term incentives, stock option plans. Boards of directors are shifting their focus for executive compensation to long-term achievements, sometimes even at the expense of short-term profits. Exhibit 16.10 identifies the various types of long-term incentives and describes their main features.[26]

Executive Benefits.   Since many benefits are tied to income level (e.g., life insurance, disability insurance, pension plans), executives typically receive higher benefits than most other exempt employees. Beyond the typical benefits outlined in Chapter 12, however, many executives also receive additional life insurance,

---

[24] Based on a William Mercer survey of 506 public firms as reported in the *The Wall Street Journal*, April 23, 1994.

[25] Based on a Buck Consulting, Inc., survey of 256 Fortune 1000 companies. As reported in *Compensation: Human Resource Management* (Chicago, IL: Commerce Clearing House, Inc., 1994).

[26] Other tax reform issues are discussed in Gregory Wiber, "After Tax Reform, Part I: Planning Employee Benefit Programs," *Compensation and Benefits Review* 19, no. 2 (1987), pp. 16–25; Irwin Rubin, "After Tax Reform, Part II," *Compensation and Benefits Review* 20, no. 1 (1988), pp. 26–32.

EXHIBIT 16.9   Trends over Time in the Use of Stock Options for Executives

Industry	1982	1984	1985	1988	1989
Total	**62%**	**66%**	**68%**	**75%**	**75%**
Manufacturing	80	84	82	84	84
Retail trade	63	77	73	—	—
All trade	—	—	—	77	77
Construction (publicly held)	61	62	—	—	—
Insurance: stock	48	43	45	68	76
Commercial banking	44	50	61	74	72
Gas and electric utilities	20	20	24	—	—
All utilities	—	—	—	38	48
Diversified services	—	—	100	70	67
Communication	—	—	—	83	88
Energy	—	—	—	78	81

Source: From various issues of *Top Executive Compensation* (New York: The Conference Board, 1982–1990).

exclusions from deductibles for health-related costs, and supplementary pension income exceeding the maximum limits permissible under ERISA guidelines for qualified (i.e., eligible for tax deductions) pension plans.

Of course, various sections of ERISA and the tax code restrict employer ability to provide benefits for executives that exceed by too great a margin those received by other workers. The assorted clauses require that a particular benefits plan (1) cover a broad cross section of employees (generally 80 percent), (2) provide definitely determinable benefits, and (3) meet specific vesting (see Chapter 12) and nondiscrimination requirements. The nondiscrimination requirement specifies that the average value of benefits for low-paid employees must be at least 75 percent of the average value for highly paid employees.[27]

Executive Perquisites.   Perquisites, or "perks," probably have the same genesis as the expression "rank has its privileges." Indeed, life at the top has its rewards, designed to satisfy several types of executive needs. One type of perk could be classified as internal, providing a little something extra while the executive is inside the company: luxury offices, executive dining rooms, special parking. A second category is company-related but for business conducted externally: company-paid membership in clubs/associations and payment of hotel, resort, airplane, and auto expenses.

---

[27] Dennis Blair and Mark Kimble, "Walking Through the Discrimination Testing Wage for Welfare Plans," *Benefits Quarterly* 3, no. 2 (1987), pp. 18–26. Author's note: At press time, Section 89 of the Tax Code was under serious attack. If repealed, the nondiscrimination laws would change again.

EXHIBIT 16.10 Long-Term Incentives for Executives

Type	Description	Comments
Incentive stock options	Purchase of stock at a stipulated price, conforming with Internal Revenue Code (Section 422A).	No taxes at grant. Company may not deduct as expense.
Nonqualified stock options	Purchase of stock at a stipulated price, not conforming with Internal Revenue Code.	Excess over fair market value taxed as ordinary income. Company may deduct.
Phantom stock plans	Cash or stock award determined by increase in stock price at a fixed future date.	Taxed as ordinary income. Does not require executive financing.
Stock appreciation rights	Cash or stock award determined by increase in stock price during any time chosen (by the executive) in the option period.	Taxed as ordinary income. Does not require executive financing.
Restricted stock plans	Grant of stock at a reduced price with the condition that it may not be sold before a specified date.	Excess over fair market value taxed as ordinary income.
Performance share/ unit plans	Cash or stock award earned through achieving specific goals.	Taxed as ordinary income. Does not require executive financing.

Source: *1990 Executive Compensation Report*, Sibson & Co.

The final category of perquisites should be totally isolated from the first two because of its tax status. This category, called *personal perks*, includes such things as low-cost loans, personal and legal counseling, free home repairs and improvements, personal use of company property, and expenses for vacation homes.[28] Since 1978 various tax and regulatory agency rulings have slowly been requiring companies to place a value on perks so as to tax them as income.[29] If this trend continues, the taxable income of executives with creative perk packages

---

[28] Michael F. Klein, "Executive Perquisites," *Compensation Review* 12 (Fourth Quarter, 1979), pp. 46–50.

[29] R. L. VanKirk and L. S. Schenger, "Executive Compensation: The Trend Is Back to Cash," *Financial Executive*, May 1978, pp. 83–91.

EXHIBIT 16.11   Popular Perks Offered to Executives

Type of Perk	Percentage of Companies Offering Perk
Physical exam	85%
Financial counseling	70
Company car	63
Club memberships	62
First-class air travel	57
Company plane	53
Personal liability insurance	47
Cellular telephone	45
Chauffeur service	35
Airline VIP clubs	30
Reserved parking	29
Home security system	26
Executive dining rooms	20
Home computer	9
Loans	6

Source: Hewitt Associates (1993).

may increase considerably. Exhibit 16.11 illustrates different types of perks and the percentages of companies that offer them.

Professional Employees: Scientists and Engineers

Scientists and engineers are classified as professionals. According to the FLSA, this category includes any person who has received special training of a scientific or intellectual nature and whose job does not entail more than a 20 percent time allocation for supervisory responsibilities.

The compensation of scientists and engineers focuses on rewarding incumbents for their special scientific or intellectual training. Here lies one of the special compensation problems that scientists and engineers pose. Consider the electrical engineer who graduates with all the latest knowledge in the field. For the first few years after graduation this knowledge is a valuable resource on engineering projects in which new applications of the latest theories are a driving force. Gradually, though, this engineer's knowledge starts to become obsolete. Team leaders begin to look to the newer graduates for fresh new ideas. The salaries of scientists and engineers reflect a high correlation between pay increases and knowledge relevance. Early years bring larger than average (relative to employees in other occupations) increases. After 10 years, however, increases drop below average and become down right puny in the 15-to-20-year time frame. Partly because of these salary plateaus, many scientists and engineers make career changes (e.g., move into management) or temporarily leave business and reenter academia to update their technical knowledge. In recent years, some firms have tried to deal with the plateau effect and to accommodate the different career motivations of mature scientists and engineers. The result has been the creation of dual career tracks, as exemplified in Exhibit 16.12.

Notice that dual ladders provide exactly that: two different ways of progressing in an organization, each reflecting different types of contributions to the organization's mission. The *managerial ladder* ascends through increasing responsibility for supervision or direction of people. The *professional ladder* ascends through increasing positions of a professional nature that do not mainly

EXHIBIT 16.12   IBM Dual Ladder

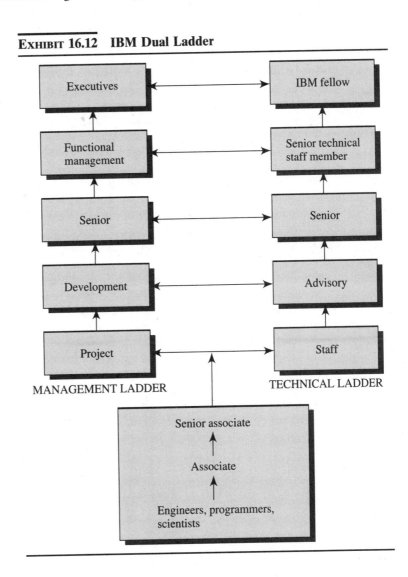

entail the supervision of employees. Scientists and engineers (SEs) have the opportunity at some stage in their careers to consider a management track or continue along the scientific ladder. Dual career ladders offer greater advancement opportunities for SEs. Maximum base pay in the technical track can approximate that of upper management positions.

A second problem in designing the compensation package of scientists and engineers centers on the question of equity. The very nature of scientific knowledge and its dissemination requires relatively close association among SEs across organizations. SEs tend to compare themselves for equity purposes with the graduates who entered the labor market at the same time period. Partially because of this and partially because of the volatile nature of both jobs and salaries in SE occupations, organizations rely very heavily on market data to determine SE base pay.[30] The form of the data involves the construction of maturity curves.

Maturity curves reflect the relationship between SE compensation and years of experience in the labor market. Generally, surveying organizations ask for information intended to measure the half-life of technical obsolescence. In fact, a plot of these data with appropriate smoothing to eliminate aberrations typically shows curves that are steep for the first five to seven years and then rise more gradually as technical obsolescence erodes the value of jobs. Exhibit 16.13 illustrates such a graph with somewhat greater sophistication built into it; that is, different graphs are constructed for different levels of performance. To construct such graphs the surveying organization may also ask for data broken down by broad performance levels. Notice in the illustration that the high performers begin with somewhat higher salaries and the differential continues to broaden over the first few years.

Scientists and engineers also receive compensation beyond base pay. In general, high technology firms place a greater emphasis on the use of performance-based incentives.[31] Common forms of incentives include profit sharing and stock ownership incentives. Other incentives link payment of specific cash amounts to completion of specific projects on or before agreed-upon deadlines. Post hoc bonuses are also paid for such achievements as patents, publications, and attainment of professional licenses.

Finally, organizations have devoted considerable creative energy to development of "perks" to satisfy the unique needs of SEs. Such perks are flexible work schedules, large offices, campus-like environments, and lavish athletic facilities. The strategic importance of SEs to the firm dictates that both mind and body be kept active.

---

[30] Jo C. Kail, "Compensating Scientists and Engineers," in *New Perspectives on Compensation*, ed. David B. Balkin and Luis R. Gomez-Mejia (Englewood Cliffs, NJ: Prentice Hall, 1987), pp. 247–81.

[31] George T. Milkovich, "Compensation Systems in High Technology Companies," in *New Perspectives on Compensation*, ed. Balkin and Gomez-Mejia, pp. 269–77.

Exhibit 16.13   Maturity Curve Showing Years since B. S. Degree Relative to Salary

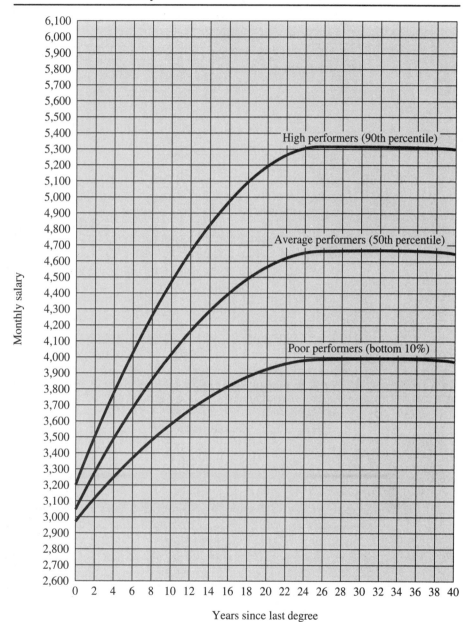

EXHIBIT 16.14   Alternative Sales Pay Plans

Type of Pay Plan	Sales Representative	Sales Managers
Guaranteed base salary plus commission	25%	14%
Guaranteed base salary plus bonus	22	48
Guaranteed base salary plus commission and bonus	21	21
Commission only	15	2
Other arrangements (e.g., base only)	17	15

Source: John Tallitsch and John Moynahan,"Fine Tuning Sales Compensation Programs," *Compensation and Benefits Review*, March–April 1994, pp. 34–37.

Sales Force

The sales staff spans the all important boundary between the organization and consumers of the organization's goods or services. Besides the sales function, or even as part of selling, the sales force must be sensitive to changing consumer tastes and provide rapid feedback to appropriate departments. The role requires individuals with high initiative who can work under low supervision for extended periods of time. The standard compensation system is not designed for this type of job. Indeed, much of the value for sales jobs is determined by factors largely external to the organization and driven by market forces.[32] The challenge is to incorporate these factors in the design of a sales compensation plan. Before discussing these factors, though, Exhibit 16.14 illustrates the different types of sales pay plans.[33]

Designing a Sales Compensation Plan   Four major factors influence the design of sales compensation packages: (1) the special nature of people who enter the sales profession, (2) organizational strategy, (3) competitor practices, and (4) product sold.

The Nature of People Who Enter the Sales Profession.   Popular stereotypes characterize salespeople as heavily motivated by financial reward. One study that supports this stereotype shows salespeople ranking pay significantly higher than five other forms of reward.[34] As a source of satisfaction, pay rated a mean of 83.7 on a scale to 100. Promotional opportunities, sense of accomplishment,

---

[32] John K. Moynahan, *The Sales Compensation Handbook* (New York: Amacom, 1991).

[33] John Tallitsch and John Moynahan, "Fine Tuning Sales Compensation Programs," *Compensation and Benefits Review*, March–April 1994, pp. 34–37.

[34] N. Ford, O. Walker, and G. Churchill, "Differences in the Attractiveness of Alternative Rewards Among Industrial Salespeople: Additional Evidence," *Journal of Business Research* 13, no. 2 (1985), pp. 123–38.

Exhibit 16.15   Average Annual Compensation Change: Midlevel Salesperson

1988	1989	1990	1991	1992
$38,869	$37,073	$39,666	$40,194	$45,278

Source: *Sales & Marketing Management* 145, no. 7 (June 28, 1993) p. 61.

personal growth, recognition, and job security were all less highly regarded. These values almost dictate that the primary focus of sales compensation should be direct financial rewards (base pay + incentives). Exhibit 16.15 shows the level of, and change in, average annual compensation for a midlevel salesperson over the past five years. In general, compensation has not changed much, perhaps reflecting the stagnation in the economy.

Organizational Strategy.   A sales compensation plan should link desired behaviors of salespeople to organizational strategy. Salespeople must know when to stress customer service and when to stress volume sales. When volume is the goal, salespeople should know which products to push the most. Strategic plans signal which behaviors are important. For example, emphasis on customer service to build market share or movement into geographic areas with low potential may limit sales volume. Ordinarily, sales representatives who work under an incentive system will view customer service as an imposition, taking away from money-making sales opportunities. And woe be it to the sales supervisor who assigns a commission-based sales person to a market with low sales potential.

Alternatively, an organization may want to motivate aggressive sales behavior. A straight commission-based incentive plan focuses sales efforts in this direction, to the possible exclusion of supportive tasks (e.g., processing customer returns). These incentive plans include both a statement about the size of the incentive and a discussion of the performance objective necessary to achieve it. Each measure in Exhibit 16.16, of course, corresponds to a different business goal. For example, an organization might use some volume measure such as number of units orders, invoices, or cash received if the business goal is to increase sales growth. Alternatively, if the goal is to improve profit, the appropriate measurement would be gross margin on sales or price per unit. Percentage account erosion would be stressed if improved account retention became a major focus of attention; sales per account might be stressed when account penetration becomes a major organizational goal.

Competitor Practices.   In selecting an appropriate pay level, organizations should recognize that external competitiveness is essential. The very nature of sales means that competitors will cross paths, at least in their quest for potential customers. This provides the opportunity to chat about relative compensation packages, an opportunity that salespeople will frequently take. To ensure that the comparison process is favorable, the organization should identify a compensation-

---

EXHIBIT 16.16   Sales Force Incentive Performance Measures

Performance Measure	Percentage of Companies
Revenue	64%
Customized nonsales performance objectives	40
Profit margin	34
New accounts	30
Units sold	30
Product mix	21
Company/unit performance	19
Expense control	10
Team performance	10
Customer satisfaction	7
Market share	4

Source: Hewitt Associates (1993).

level strategy that explicitly indicates target salaries for different sales groups and performance levels.

Product Sold.   The very nature of the product or service to be sold may influence the design of a compensation system. Consider a very technical product that takes time to understand, present effectively, and sell. Such products are said to have high barriers to entry. Compensation in this situation usually includes a large base pay component, minimizing the risk a sales representative will face and encouraging entry into the necessary training program. At the opposite extreme are products with lower barriers to entry, which are relatively easy to learn to sell. The compensation for these product lines frequently has a higher incentive component, thus paying more for actual sales than for taking the time to learn about them.

Products or services that sell themselves, where sales ability isn't as crucial, inspire different compensation packages than products or services for which the salesperson is more essential to sales. Base compensation tends to be more important with easily sold products. Not surprisingly, incentives become more important when willingness to work hard may make the difference between success and failure. Few jobs fit the ideal specifications for either of the two extremes, represented by straight salary or straight commission plans. A combination plan is intended to capture the best of both these plans. A guaranteed straight salary can be linked to performance of nonsales functions (e.g., customer service), and a commission for sales volume yields the incentive to sell. A plan combining these two features signals the intent of the organization to ensure that both types of activities occur.

We should note that other forms of rewards play a role, albeit a small one, in the total compensation package of salespeople. For example, 44 percent of companies surveyed develop formal recognition programs for high sales performers. Other popular forms of recognition, though, focus on more tangible incentives, offering merchandise and travel for outstanding performance. Of course standard benefits are also provided, with additional features such as company cars and expense accounts thrown in to recognize the distinctive feature of the jobs performed by this special group.

The Contingent Work Force

There is a new force on the labor front. It's called the contingent workforce. In past years these workers might have been called part-timers, temporaries, independent contractors, or even "leased employees." The trend to leaner companies has one main casualty—many workers who were displaced cannot find full-time jobs. Representing about 15 percent of the American workforce, most sources claim this number is only headed upward.[35]

When we look at the compensation programs for this group, it's easy to understand why cost-conscious employers are hiring contingent workers in increasing numbers. According to the 1993 employment cost index, contingent workers average $9 per hour in pay and benefits. This is slightly less than half the amount earned by full-time workers ($18.54).[36]

Contingent workers present one clear compensation challenge: how to integrate them into a workforce where clear salary differences exist, sometimes for the same job. Some experts are particularly concerned about how to integrate teams comprised of full- and part-time workers. Designing incentive pay plans that recognize the distinctive work schedule and contribution differences may sorely test the principles of equity.[37]

Summary

Special groups represent compensation challenges to organizations. Many of the innovations in compensation have started with one of the groups discussed in this chapter and gradually cascaded to other work groups. For example, sales personnel and executives often have been the target of innovative new pay-for-

---

[35] Barbara Solomon, "More Companies Offer Benefits to Part-Time Workers but Growth of Continent Uninsured Bodes Instability," *Compflash* (Saranac Lake, NY: American Management Association, July 1993), pp. 5–7.

[36] "Part-Timers Cost Half the Money, on Average," *Compflash* (Saranac Lake, NY: American Management Association, December 1994), p. 2.

[37] "Part-Time Employees: A Growing Trend," *Benefits*, November 1993, pp. 30–31.

performance plans. Success with these groups leads to further "tests" with other subgroups. Such trials are often the stuff of good human resource practices.

Review Questions

1. Is it possible for occupational groups other than those discussed in this chapter to assume the status of a special group for the purpose of compensation? If your answer is no, explain why not. If your answer is yes, explain why. Use as your example the job of a lawyer in an industry going through deregulation (elimination or revision of some of the rules governing the way firms in the industry do business).

2. For each of the special groups discussed in this chapter, explain how the issue of equity is especially important. Who are the groups against which special group members might compare themselves to determine if compensation is fair?

3. Identify possible explanations for why executives receive such high levels of compensation. Which of the possible explanations in the text seem least likely? Why?

4. Why are external market wages so important in the determination of wages for professionals (scientists and engineers) and sales personnel.

5. If the trend toward increased use of contingency workers extends into the next millenium, what types of equity problems do you foresee? If the numbers grow substantial, what are the implications? To help you answer this question you might want to compare the experiences under the two-tier wage systems discussed in Chapter 17. How are contingent workers hired after a two-tier system is implemented? As numbers increase, so too does power. Might this influence design of a compensation system?

YOUR TURN:

COMPENSATION OF SPECIAL GROUPS

Madeira Research, Inc., is a government contractor providing design and testing for all-terrain combat vehicles and functional weaponry. Fifty-five percent of all MRI costs are traceable to wages and benefits.

Of the 312 employees, 118 are scientists/engineers. Salary surveys for competitors in the region (basically a 200-mile radius) show the following information (randomly chosen from a larger survey printout).

Employee #	Company	Highest Relevant Degree Received	Number Years since Degree Received	Salary ($ per Year)
1	A	B.S.	3	39,000
2	B	M.S.	6	58,800
3	B	M.S.	3	50,400
4	A	Ph.D.	7	95,900
5	C	B.S.	6	48,000
6	A	Ph.D.	9	105,300
7	A	M.S.	4	53,200
8	C	Ph.D.	3	77,100
9	C	B.S.	7	51,000
10	D	Ph.D.	6	91,200
11	D	M.S.	9	67,200
12	D	M.S.	7	61,600
13	C	Ph.D.	4	81,800
14	B	B.S.	9	57,000
15	A	B.S.	4	42,000

Discussion Questions

1. From the information provided can you identify any pattern to the market rates for scientists/engineers? What is the pattern and how strong is it?

2. Assuming you want to lead the market by 10 percent, how much should you pay the following two scientists from your company?

	Degree	Yrs. since Degree Received	Last Performance Rating	Salary
#1	M.S.	5	Very Good	_____
#2	Ph.D.	8	Excellent (top rating)	_____

CHAPTER

Union Role in Wage and Salary Administration

Chapter Outline

Many experts believe that unions are currently facing their most critical challenge of the last 50 years.[1] Between 1954 and 1987, union membership fell 50 per-

---

[1] Aaron Bernstein, "Why Lane Kirkland Looks Like a Lame Duck," *Business Week*, February 13, 1995, p. 44; Thomas A. Kochan, Harry C. Katz, and Robert B. McKersie, *The Transformation of American Industrial Relations* (New York: Basic Books, 1986), pp. 221–23.

cent.[2] During roughly that same period, the union success rate in certification elections (winning rights to represent previously nonunion workers) fell from 60 percent to approximately 45 percent.[3]

One popular explanation for this decline is that management is taking an increasingly hard stance against unions in general and union demands in particular. Much of this management opposition to unions is spurred by increasing pressure from both domestic and international companies. Management increasingly resists wage increases that would give nonunion competitors, both domestic and foreign, a competitive price advantage. The end result of these competitive pressures is a declining union-nonunion wage differential. In fact, one study shows that a 10 percent rise in import share (a popular measure of international competition) has the effect of lowering the union wage differential by approximately 2 percent.[4]

Such competitive pressures during the 1980s and early 1990s have triggered lower than normal wage increases in unionized firms and even some wage concessions. Accompanying these wage trends is an increasing pessimism about the continued viability of unions in American industry. One survey of union employees covering changing attitudes during the 1983–1984 period reported a decline from 53 percent to 41 percent in positive answers to the question: "Are unions necessary for equitable labor relations?"[5] More recent surveys report similar attitudes toward unions (Exhibit 17.1).

EXHIBIT 17.1   Attitudes in the Labor Management Area

Question	Percentage of Response	
	Yes	Other
Are workers better off with a union?		
Overall response	49%	51%
Union respondents	83	17
Management respondents	46	54
Do you view unions favorably?	44	56
Do you view management favorably?	64	36
Do you favor right to work laws?	70	30
(bans mandatory union membership)		

Source: Media General Associated Press Poll (1989).

[2] Kirkland Ropp, "State of the Unions," *Personnel Administrator* 32, no. 7 (1987), pp. 36–41.

[3] Richard B. Freeman, *On the Divergence of Unionism among Developed Countries* (Working paper no. 2817, National Bureau of Economic Research, 1989).

[4] David A. Macpherson and James B. Steward, "The Effect of International Competition on Union and Non-Union Wages," *Industrial and Labor Relations Review* 43, no. 4. (1990), pp. 434–46.

[5] R. Wayne Mondy and Shane Preameaux, "The Labor Management Power Relationship Revisited," *Personnel Administrator*, May 1985, pp. 51–54.

Despite these pessimistic statistics, though, it would be a mistake to conclude that the impact of unions on wage and salary administration is minor. Even in a nonunion firm, external union activity influences the actions taken by wage and salary administrators. This chapter outlines the general factors affecting wages in unionized firms and then illustrates the specific impact of unions in wage determination. Four specific areas of union impact are discussed: (1) on general wage and benefit levels, (2) on the structure of wages, (3) on nonunion firms (known as *spillover*), and (4) on wage and salary policies and practices in unionized firms. The final discussion focuses on union response to the changing economic environment of the 1980s and the alternative compensation systems that have evolved in response to these changes.

GENERAL FACTORS AFFECTING WAGES IN UNIONIZED FIRMS

Some interesting economic realities have made compensation decision making a crucial factor in organizational success for the 1990s. First, it is increasingly apparent that international competition has a significant impact on the profitability of U.S. enterprises. Our ability to compete, in both domestic and foreign markets, continues to decline.[6] As our product prices become noncompetitive in the international market, the result, as any executive in the auto industry during the past decade can attest, can be catastrophic.

The United States is also experiencing significant changes in the composition of industries. Fewer manufacturing and more service jobs are being created. Most of these new jobs come from small firms. In fact, between 1980 and 1986, 63 percent of all new positions were generated in small firms.[7] Both these small firms fighting to survive and larger firms striving to combat foreign competition seek ways to control labor costs. To understand the direction these efforts take in unionized settings, it would help first to understand the factors affecting wage determination in unionized organizations. These factors include (1) productivity, (2) changes in the cost of living, (3) ability of an employer to pay, and (4) comparability among wage rates (equity).[8] Not surprisingly, each of these issues has received considerable attention lately, and the outcome of this attention may well be dramatic changes in compensation of unionized employees.

Productivity

Although the United States has the highest per worker productivity of any country in the world, yearly increases in productivity have lagged far behind most other industrial countries over the past decade. Although this decline is undoubtedly due to a host of factors, including slow modernization rates in key

---

[6] Paula Voos, ed., *Contemporary Collective Bargaining in the Private Sector* (Madison, WI: Industrial Relations Research Association, 1993).

[7] Ibid.

[8] Daniel Quinn Mills, *Labor Management Relations* (New York: McGraw-Hill, 1989).

manufacturing sectors, a portion of the blame for lower productivity continues to be directed at unions. The sources of these complaints are twofold. First, union contracts establish staffing practices or other work rules that artificially reduce output. Examples of such practices include minimum crew size requirements and provisions limiting subcontracting. Second, union-initiated strikes obviously restrict output during the term of the strike.

Alternatively, some experts suggest that in the presence of unions, output enhances. This argument suggests that unions negotiate higher wages and vent grievances against management. Advocates say that by improving satisfaction and lowering turnover, unions have a positive impact on net productivity.[9]

No matter the outcome of these debates, management is acting as if unions cause lower productivity. The result has been an increasingly tougher stand in negotiations and more agreements that tie wage increases to productivity increases. Further, unions increasingly agree to productivity bargaining positions that permit greater employee involvement and focus on total quality management. A host of compensation changes has resulted, including incentive systems, profit sharing plans, and merit-based pay plans. Later in this chapter we will discuss the nature of these changes and the role of unions in this process.

Cost of Living

Cost of living adjustments are designed to increase wages automatically during the life of the contract as a function of changes in the consumer price index. During the inflation-ridden 1970s, unions made a strong drive for these escalator clauses. Indeed, by 1978, COLA clauses had made broad inroads on the labor management scene, despite evidence that such contract clauses failed to keep workers "whole" with respect to inflation.[10] More recently, though, unions have exhibited less interest in bargaining for COLA clauses. This shift is probably traceable to deceleration of the consumer price index during the mid- and late-1980s. Historically, unions have clamored for COLAs during periods of high inflation and deemphasized them when inflation rates were more tolerable. Now that the inflation rate has moderated in the past several years, fewer unions consider COLA clauses a vital element of a total package. The number of workers covered by COLA clauses in negotiated contracts declined from 59 percent in 1980 to 49 percent in 1985.[11] Since 1987 the extent of COLA coverage has leveled off. Today, approximately 32 percent of the 5.7 million workers covered by major agreements have COLA clauses in their contracts.[12]

---

[9] Richard Freeman, "Individual Mobility and Union Voice in the Labor Market," *American Economic Review*, May 1976, pp. 361–68.

[10] Victor J. Sheifer, "Collective Bargaining and the CPI: Escalation v. Catch-Up," *Proceedings of the 31st Annual Meeting, Industrial Relations Research Association Series*, 1978, pp. 257–63.

[11] Richard Henderson, "Contract Concessions: Is the Past Prologue?" *Compensation and Benefits Review* 18, no. 5 (1986), pp. 17–30.

[12] Arthur Sloane and Fred Whitney, *Labor Relations* (Englewood Cliffs, NJ: Prentice Hall, 1994); Voos, *Contemporary Collective Bargaining in the Private Sector.*

Despite the decreased current interest in them, escalator clauses deserve discussion, if only in anticipation of future bouts with inflation and renewed interest in this contractual safeguard. All COLAs have two common elements: some measure of change in living costs and a formula to adjust wages as a function of these changes in living costs. The most common measure of change in living costs is the consumer price index prepared by the Bureau of Labor Statistics. Recall from Chapter 15 that the CPI provides an estimate of the change in cost of a market basket of goods (as many as 4,000 individual items may be priced every month to determine changes in the cost patterns). The cost of this market basket is compared against a base-period cost to determine change.

The second element of an escalator clause is the formula for adjusting wages as the CPI changes. The most common formula provides for a 1 cent increase in wages for each 0.3 to 0.4 percent rise in the CPI.[13]

Ability to Pay and Wage Comparability within Industries

The third factor affecting wage levels in unionized organizations is an employer's ability to pay. In profitable years, unions reason that part of the profits should accrue to the work force responsible for much of the organization's success. This argument plays a role in the eventual determination of bargained wage levels. What follows then is well-known by the U.S. consumer. Product prices are raised and labor cost increases are cited as a major reason. In the past, this pattern usually did not cause problems. Consumers continued to purchase what remained a competitively priced product compared to the same product offered by other firms in the industry.

In large part, this continued competitiveness can be explained by introducing the fourth factor affecting wage levels: comparability among wage rates. As one group of workers representing one firm received wage increases, product competitors agreed to similar demands from their work force. The result was labor cost and product price increases that rose relatively uniformly through the industry. As long as unions were able to control wage increases within an industry (usually by organizing the whole industry), no employer suffered a disproportionate wage increase or the resulting noncompetitive product price! Employers were content to go along with this situation as long as they received a reasonable return on investment and their market share remained unaffected. What they failed to realize, and what must be considered in future wage negotiations, is the rapid internationalization of product markets: Increased imports during the 1980s and 1990s and the rapid internationalization of product markets caused major retrenchments for such diverse industries as shoes, apparel, steel, autos, consumer electronics, and capital goods.[14] Spurred by the need to compete with international producers, several of these industries (e.g., auto and steel) negoti-

---

[13] Sheifer, "Collective Bargaining and the CPI: Escalation v. Catch-Up."

[14] John A. Fossum, *Labor Relations: Development, Structure, Process* (Burr Ridge, IL: Richard D. Irwin, 1989).

ated major wage and work rule concessions.[15] The auto industry is a classic example. Japanese autoworkers receive compensation worth approximately one-half that of their U.S. counterparts. As long as Japan assumed a small role in the auto market, U.S. auto manufacturers were concerned primarily about wages relative to domestic manufacturers. As Japan increased its market share due to competitive price/quality differentials, however, the comparable wage differential loomed larger and larger. This differential played a large role in United Auto Workers (UAW) concessions to both Ford and General Motors in 1982.

Is the auto industry unique, or are wage concessions a new, and potentially permanent, feature of the industrial relations scence? One view argues that current wage concessions represent "much ado about nothing."[16] As evidence, this faction points out that during the depression (1929–1933), average hourly earnings fell 22 percent. In contrast, the height of the "wage concession" period was marked by a 22 percent rise in average hourly earnings (1981–1986).[17] A second view argues that wage concessions are real and have been a fixture of the industrial relations scene at different times during the entire 20th century.[18] For example, in 1908 the glass bottle blowers accepted a 20 percent wage cut in the hope of fighting automation. During the 1930s, concessions were a regular feature in the construction, printing, and shoe industries. Concessions were also made in the apparel and textile industries during the 1950s. Continuing into the 1980s, major contract concessions occurred in eight industries: air transport, food stores, shoe manufacturing, primary metals, metal cans, transportation equipment, textiles, and trucking.[19] Exhibit 7.2 illustrates the pattern of wage changes over the last decade.

Notice that the magnitude of union wage settlements declined markedly in the early 1980s. Concessions generally were concentrated in small firms, in high wage paying firms, and in firms will relatively low levels of unionization.[20]

It would be a mistake to assume that concessions come only in the form of straight-forward wage reductions. Other concession strategies exist. Because of their increasing prominence, we discuss three further variations of concessions.

One further type of concession comes in the form of *lump-sum awards*. Although not traditionally cast as a concession, lump-sum awards do fit this category. Workers receive a lump sum of money at a specified time. The dollar amount is not factored into their base salary. For example, in September 1988

---

[15] Ibid.

[16] John Dunlop, "Have the 1980s Changed U.S. Industrial Relations?" *Monthly Labor Review* 5 (1988), pp. 29–34.

[17] Ibid.

[18] Richard Freeman and James Medoff, *What Do Unions Do?* (New York: Basic Books, 1984).

[19] Robert Gay, "Union Contract Concessions and Their Implications for Union Wage Determination" (Working paper no. 38, Division of Research and Statistics, Board of Governors of the Federal Reserve System, 1984).

[20] Linda Bell, "Union Wage Concessions in the 1980s: The Importance of Firm Specific Factors," *Industrial and Labor Relations Review* 48, no. 2 (1995), pp. 258–75.

EXHIBIT 17.2 Types of First-Year Wage Adjustments in Major Agreements

	Percentage of Workers				
Wage Adjustment	*1980*	*1983*	*1988*	*1989*	*1990*
Wages decreased	–0–%	15%	2%	< 1%	< 1%
No change	< 1	22	20	20	4
Increase less than 4%	4	14	50	44	60
Increase more than 4%	95	48	28	37	35

Source: Bureau of Labor Statistics, Department of Labor, *Current Wage Developments*, various issues.

Revlon and the UAW began working under a contract that awarded workers a lump sum equal to 100 hours of pay rather than a 5 percent increase in base salary. Lump-sum awards save companies money in two ways. Consider a worker with an initial salary of $10,000 dollars. A 5 percent increase would raise base wages to $10,500. Employee benefits tied to base wages (e.g., life insurance is typically provided as some percentage of base wages) would rise correspondingly. During the next year of the contract, any percent increase is applied to the new base of $10,500. Contrast this with a lump-sum award equal to 5 percent. Employees still receive $500, but it is given as a separate check, not added to base wages. The award does not affect benefit costs, and any future percentage raises are applied to a base of $10,000, not $10,500. The difference may be small for one worker during one year, but over many workers and across many years, the savings can be substantial. In 1991, fully 37 percent of all contracts provided for lump-sum payouts.[21]

An additional form of concession consists of a *back-loaded wage clause.* Approximately 27 percent of all workers covered by contracts negotiated in 1989 had back-loaded clauses included.[22] These contracts specify low increases during the early years of the contract and larger increases at the back end. Given the time value of money (a fixed dollar amount is worth more now than later), backloading reduces the overall cost of the wage packages for employers.

A final type of concession centers on reductions in benefit costs. According to a study by a Washington consulting firm, employee health insurance premiums represent a cost drain equal to about one-fourth of net earnings for many American corporations.[23] Not surprisingly, this has led many employers to try shifting the costs of health insurance premiums more to employees. An analysis of union contracts by the Bureau of National Affairs found premium cost sharing in 19 percent of contracts in 1986 and 28 percent of contracts in 1989.[24] For example,

---

[21] Commerce Clearing House, *Labor Law Reports*, no. 280, February 7, 1992.

[22] Department of Labor, "Current Wage Developments," March 1990, p. 5.

[23] "Labor Leaders Agree on a Health Care Position," *Los Angeles Times*, February 20, 1991, p. D5.

[24] Bureau of National Affairs, *Basic Patterns in Union Contracts* (Washington, DC: Bureau of National Affairs, 1989).

the International Brotherhood of Electrical Workers was asked to increase both its annual deductibles for medical care and its deductible for prescription drugs in its 1991 contract negotiation with GTE Florida. The deductible rose from $260 to $265 for single health care coverage and from $780 to $795 for family coverage. The deductible for prescription drugs doubled to $8.[25]

Examples of other types of concessions are numerous. For example, the General Motors Stamping plant workers in Fairfield, Ohio, agreed to a 50 percent cut in paid vacations during the last contract negotiation in exchange for greater job security and other forms of management trade-offs.[26] However, we can expect wage concessions to level off or drop during the 1990s. Many union leaders and workers believe the words of mine worker president Trumka who calls concession: "A form of suicide by degrees."[27]

THE IMPACT OF UNIONS IN WAGE DETERMINATION

Union Impact on Wage and Benefit Levels

The first compensation issue concerns whether the presence of a union in an organization raises the level of wages and benefits of workers above what they would be if the company were not unionized. The commonly held belief among workers is that unions do have a wage impact. More than 80 percent of the respondents to a quality-of-employment survey believed that unions improved the wages of workers.[28] Efforts to determine whether this perception is accurate have been a focus of research for at least 40 years.

Unfortunately, comparing the union versus nonunion wage and benefit differential is no easy chore. Several measurement problems are difficult to overcome. The ideal situation for estimating union impact would compare numerous organizations that were identical except for the presence or absence of a union.[29] Any wage differences among these organizations could then be attributed to unionization. Unfortunately, few such situations exist. One alternative strategy adopted has been to identify organizations within the same industry that differ in level of unionization. For example, consider company A, which is unionized, and company B, which is not. It is difficult to argue with assurance that wage differences between the two firms are attributable to the presence or absence of a union. First, the fact that the union has not organized the entire industry weakens its power base (e.g., strike efforts to shut down the entire industry could be thwarted by nonunion firms). Consequently, any union impact in this example

[25] "Current Wage Developments," *Monthly Labor Review*, July 1991, p. 138.

[26] Ibid.

[27] As reported in Sloane and Witney, *Labor Relations*.

[28] Thomas A. Kochan, "How American Workers View Labor Unions," *Monthly Labor Review*, April 1979, pp. 23–31.

[29] Allan M. Carter and F. Ray Marshall, *Labor Economics* (Burr Ridge, IL: Richard D. Irwin, 1982).

might underestimate the role of unions in an industry in which percentage of unionization is higher. A second problem in measuring union impact is apparent from this example. What if company B grants concessions to employees as a strategy to avoid unionization? These concessions, indirectly attributable to the presence of a union (the union in company A), would lead to underestimation of union impact on wages.

A second strategy for estimating union impact on wages is to compare two different industries that vary dramatically in the level of unionization.[30] This strategy suffers because nonunionized industries (e.g., agriculture, service) are markedly different from unionized industries in the types of labor employed and their general availability. Such differences have a major impact on wages independent of the level of unionization and make any statements about union impact difficult to substantiate.

One source of continuing data on unionized and nonunionized firms is the Bureau of Labor Statistics. Between 1969 and 1985, union wage premiums more than doubled from 17.6 to 35.6 percent.[31] Between 1979 and 1988, union versus nonunion pay differential increased in 6 industries and decreased in 9 (of 15 selected industries).[32] Historically, differentials have experienced multiple-year upswings followed by multiple-year downswings. The 1950s were characterized by a widening of the union wage impact, followed by constriction in the 1960s, an enlargement from 1969 to 1983, and another constriction from 1983 to the present.[33] Since 1983, the nonunion sector has been securing larger wage increases than the unionized sector, partially due to unions' acceptance of lump-sum payments in lieu of increases in base wage.[34]

Perhaps the best conclusion about union versus nonunion wage differences comes from a summary analysis of 114 different studies.[35] Two important points emerge:

1. Unions do make a difference in wages. Union workers earn somewhere between 8.9 percent and 12.4 percent more than their nonunion counterparts.

2. The size of the wage gap varies from year to year. During periods of higher unemployment, the impact of unions is large. When economies are strong, the union-nonunion gap is small. Part of the explanation for this time-based phenomenon is related to union resistance to wage cuts during recessions and the relatively slow responses of unions to wage increases during inflationary periods (because of rigidities or lags introduced by the presence of multiyear labor contracts).

---

[30] Michael L. Wachter and William H. Carter, "Norm Shifts in Union Wages: Will 1989 Be a Replay of 1969?" in *Brookings Papers on Economic Activity*, ed. William C. Brainard and George L. Perry (Washington, DC: The Brookings Institution, 1989), pp. 233–76.

[32] Kay E. Anderson, Philip M. Doyle, and Albert E. Schwenk, "Measuring Union-Nonunion Earnings Differences," *Monthly Labor Review* 113 (1990), pp. 26–38.

[33] Wachter and Carter, "Norm Shifts in Union Wages: Will 1989 Be a Replay of 1969?"

[34] Anderson, Doyle, and Schwenk, "Measuring Union-Nonunion Earnings Differences."

[35] Stephen B. Jarrell and T. D. Stanley, "A Meta Analysis of the Union-Non Union Wage Gap," *Industrial and Labor Relations Review* 44, no. 1 (1990), pp. 54–67.

In addition, research indicates that the presence of a union adds about 20 to 30 percent to employee benefits.[36] Unions also have an impact on the difference between wages for selected groups. Wage differentials between workers who are different in terms of race, age, service, skill level, and education appear to be lower under collective bargaining.[37]

Similar studies of union–nonunion wage differentials exist for employees in the public sector.[38] In a summary of 13 public sector union studies, Lewin concluded that the average wage effect of public sector unions is approximately 5 percent. As Lewin notes, this wage differential is smaller than typically assumed and certainly smaller than is estimated for the private sector. Of course, this 5 percent average masks some large variations in wage increases for different occupational groups in the public sector. The largest gains for public sector employees are reported for fire fighters, with some studies reporting as much as an 18 percent wage differential attributable to the presence of a union. At the other extreme, however, teachers' unions (primarily affiliates of the National Education Association and the American Federation of Teachers) have not fared as well, with reported impacts generally in the range of 1 to 4 percent.[39]

The Structure of Wage Packages

The second compensation issue involves the structure of wage packages. One dimension of this issue concerns the division between direct wages and employee benefits. There is evidence that union employees have employee benefit packages that are about 20 to 30 percent higher than nonunion employees have. Whether because of reduced management control, strong union-worker preference for benefits, or other reasons, unionized employees also have a higher percentage of their total wage bill allocated to employee benefits.[40] Typically, this shows up in the form of higher pension expenditures or higher insurance benefits.[41] One

---

[36] Freeman and Medoff, *What Do Unions Do?*

[37] R. Freeman and J. Medoff, "The Impact of Collective Bargaining: Illusion or Reality?" in J. Steiber, R. McKersie, and D. Q. Mills, *U.S. Industrial Relations 1950–1980: A Critical Assessment* (Madison, WI: IRRA, 1981).

[38] David Lewin, "Public Sector Labor Relations: A Review Essay," in *Public Sector Labor Relations: Analysis and Readings,* ed. David Lewin, Peter Feuille, and Thomas Kochan (Glen Ridge, NJ: Thomas Horton and Daughters, 1977), pp. 116–44.

[39] For a discussion of the reasons for this smaller public sector union impact see Lewin, *Public Sector Labor Relations: Analysis and Readings.*

[40] Bevars Mabry, "The Economics of Fringe Benefits," *Industrial Relations* 12 (1973), pp. 95–106.

[41] Robert Rice, "Skill, Earnings and the Growth of Wage Supplements," *American Economic Review* 56 (1966), pp. 583–93; George Kalamotousakis, "Statistical Analysis of the Determinants of Employee Benefits by Type," *American Economist,* Fall 1972, pp. 139–47; William Bailey and Albert Schwenk, "Employer Expenditures for Private Retirement and Insurance Plans," *Monthly Labor Review* 95 (1972), pp. 15–19.

particularly well-controlled study found unionization associated with 24 percent higher levels of pension expenditures and 46 percent higher insurance expenditures.[42]

A second dimension of the wage structure issue is a relatively new phenomenon. Along with the concession bargaining movement have come two-tier pay plans. Basically a phenomenon of the union sector, two-tier wage structures differentiate pay based upon hiring date. A contract is negotiated that specifies that employees hired after a given target date will receive lower wages than their higher seniority peers working on the same or similar jobs. From management's perspective, wage tiers represent a viable alternative compensation strategy. Tiers can be used as a cost control strategy to allow expansion or investment or as a cost-cutting device to allow economic survival.[43] Two-tier pay plans initially spread because unions viewed them as less painful than wage freezes and staff cuts among existing employees. The trade-off was to bargain away equivalent wage treatment for future employees! Remember, this is a radical departure from the most basic precepts of unionization. Unions evolved and continue to endure, in part, based on the belief that all members are equal and should receive equal pay for equal work. Two-tier plans are obviously at odds with this principle. Lower-tier employees, those hired after the contract is ratified, receive wages 50 to 80 percent lower than employees in the higher tier.[44] The contract may specify that the wage differential may be permanent, or the lower tier may be scheduled ultimately to catch up with the upper tier. Eventually, the inequity from receiving different pay for the same level of inputs may cause employee dissatisfaction.[45] Consider the Roman emperor who implemented a two-tier system for his army in 217 A.D.[46] He was assassinated by his disgruntled troops shortly thereafter. Although such expressions of dissatisfaction are unlikely today, Exhibit 17.3 indicates a number of problems related to two-tier programs.

The future of two-tier structures is uncertain. Some predict that they will continue to increase in popularity; others indicate a decline in contracts with two-tier structures.[47] This latter view is best supported by the Bureau of National Affairs annual surveys of employer bargaining objectives. Between 1988 and 1989, there was a 14 percent decline (from 95 to 81 percent) in firms expecting

---

[42] Loren Solnick, "Unionism and Fringe Benefits Expenditures," *Industrial Relations* 17, no. 1 (1978), pp. 102–7.

[43] James E. Martin and Thomas D. Heetderks, *Two-Tier Compensation Structures: Their Impact on Unions, Employer, and Employees* (Kalamazoo, MI: W. E. Upjohn Institute for Employment Research, 1990).

[44] Mollie Bowers and Roger Roderick, "Two-Tier Pay Systems: The Good, the Bad and the Debatable," *Personnel Administrator* 32, no. 6 (1987), pp. 101–12.

[45] James Martin and Melanie Peterson, "Two-Tier Wage Structures: Implications for Equity Theory," *Academy of Management Journal* 30, no. 2 (1987), pp. 297–315.

[46] "Two-Tier Wage Systems Falter as Companies Sense Workers' Resentment," *The Wall Street Journal*, June 16, 1987, p. 1.

[47] Martin and Heetderks, *Two-Tier Compensation Structures: Their Impact on Unions, Employer, and Employees.*

EXHIBIT 17.3   Experiences with Two-Tier Systems (in Percentages)

Have two tiers	28
Do not have two tiers	72
Reasons for Not Adopting Two-Tier System	
1. Labor unrest	14
2. Morale problems	10
3. Productivity declines	2.3
4. Insufficient benefit from system	26
5. Other	27
Concessions Granted by Management to Obtain Two-Tier System	
1. None	72
2. Increased employee security	7
3. Restricted subcontracting	2
4. Bonus	4
5. Reframe from shifting operations overseas	0
6. Increased salary to incumbents	10
7. Other	10

Note: Based on a sample of 434 companies in 1986.

Source: Towers, Perrin, Forster, and Crosby, "Survey of Company Experiences with Two-Tier Wage Systems" (Washington, DC: Towers, Perrin, Forster, and Crosby, 1986).

to continue two-tier structures and a decrease from 18 to 12 percent of firms contemplating implementation of two-tier structures.[48] Hughes aircraft, under attack for sloppy work by the Navy, abolished its two-tier wage system. Your friendly U.S. Postal Service also agreed to eliminate its two-tier plan. By 1992 such plans existed in only 5 percent of newly bargained labor contracts.[49]

Union Impact: The Spillover Effect

Although union wage settlements have declined in recent years, the impact of unions in general would be understated if we did not account for what is termed the *spillover effect*. Specifically, employers seek to avoid unionization by offering workers the wages, benefits, and working conditions won in rival unionized firms. The nonunion management continues to enjoy the freedom from union

---

[48] Bureau of National Affairs, "Agreements with Two-Tier Wage Plans Continue to Decline to 1987, Study Says," *Labor Relations Week*, March 2, 1988, pp. 201–2; Bureau of National Affairs, "Employer Bargaining Objectives, 1989," *Collective Bargaining Negotiations and Contracts* 1131 (October 6, 1988), pp. 951–58.

[49] Sloane and Whitney, *Labor Relations*.

"interference" in decision making, and the workers receive the spillover of rewards already obtained by their unionized counterparts. Several studies document the existence and importance of this phenomenon, providing further evidence of the continuing role played by unions in wage determination.[50]

Role of Unions in Wage and Salary Policies and Practices

Perhaps of greatest interest to current and future compensation administrators is the role unions play in administering wages. The role of unions in administration of compensation is outlined primarily in the contract. The following illustrations of this role are taken from major collective bargaining agreements in effect between 1977 and 1992.[51]

   1. *Basis for pay.* The vast majority of contracts specify that one or more jobs are to be compensated on an hourly basis and that overtime pay will be paid beyond a certain number of hours. Notice the specificity of the language in the following contract clause, and the growing trend to lessen excessive overtime.

   a. Overtime will be paid at one and a half (1½) times the rate for any hours worked over eight (8) hours per day or forty (40) hours per week whichever is greater or normal scheduled shift hours provided that the employee has worked all scheduled days or has a legitimate excuse. The Company may require proof.

   b. There shall be no pyramiding of overtime.

   c. (1) All employees will be expected to work reasonable overtime. Reasonable overtime shall be defined as working up to ten (10) overtime hours in a work week. Any overtime work in excess of reasonable overtime hours in a work week shall be voluntary.

   (2) Where known by the Employer, notice of necessary overtime on a normal work day shall be given by mid-shift and for necessary overtime on a sixth or seventh day, by the end of the shift on the fourth day. Employees may be excused from overtime work in cases of emergency or where legitimate reason is given at the time overtime is assigned.

   (3) Overtime work on the sixth and seventh days in a work week will be given to the senior qualified employees, by line, who have

   [50] Loren Solnick, "The Effect of Blue Collar Unions on White Collar Wages and Fringe Benefits," *Industrial and Labor Relations Review* 38, no. 2 (1985), pp. 23–35; Lawrence Kahn, "The Effect of Unions on the Earnings of Nonunion Workers," *Industrial and Labor Relations Review* 31, no. 1 (1978), pp. 205–16.

   [51] U.S. Department of Labor, *Major Collective Bargaining Agreements: Wage Administration Provisions Bulletin 1425–17* (Washington, DC: Bureau of Labor Statistics, 1978); General Motors–UAW, "Agreement between General Motors Corporation and the UAW" (September 1984); Bureau of National Affairs, "Wage Patterns and Wage Data," in *Collective Bargaining Negotiations and Contracts*, 18.10-18.993 (Washington, DC: Bureau of National Affairs, 1984).

worked on the same type product lines during the prior five (5) days. Relief operators shall be assigned by the Company.

(4) No employee will be required to work more than twelve (12) hours in a given work day but may volunteer to do so if they choose.

(5) No employee may be required to work more than seven (7) consecutive days without a day off. However, an employee may waive the day off and then be scheduled another seven (7) consecutive days without a day off.[52]

Further, many contracts specify that a premium be paid above the worker's base wage for working nonstandard shifts:

> The . . . rates are based on day work and the following differentials are paid in addition thereto for the various shift classifications:
>
> An individual scheduled to work days, afternoons, and nights on rotating shifts Monday through Friday, inclusive, shall receive a differential of twenty-eight cents ($.28) per hour for all hours worked.
>
> An employee scheduled to work a straight night shift, including or excluding Sundays and holidays, shall receive a differential of thirty-two cents ($.32) per hour for all hours worked.[53]

Alternatively, agreements may specify a fixed daily, weekly, biweekly, or monthly rate. In addition, agreements often indicate a specific day of the week as payday and sometimes require payment on or before a certain hour. The following contract clause illustrates this requirement.

> The company will continue to pay wages earned on a weekly basis. The first shift will be paid on/or before 7:30 A.M. Friday; the second shift will be paid on/or before 3:30 P.M. Friday; and the third shift will be paid on/or before 11:30 P.M. Thursday.[54]

Much less frequently, contracts specify some form of incentive system as the basis for pay. The vast majority of clauses specifying incentive pay occur in manufacturing (as opposed to nonmanufacturing) industries. Many of these clauses provide for union-management discussion of incentives:

> It is agreed that all matters pertaining to piece work, incentive pay, and bonus are subject to discussion between the company and the union. . . .
>
> All work being performed on incentive basis shall have the allowance established prior to the start of the job; and this allowance and description of the job shall be furnished to the men performing the work at the beginning of the shift or job, except in cases where the allowance for the work to be performed is to be divided between individuals or groups, in which case the allowance shall be given to the individual or group prior to the end of the shift. If the allowance

---

[52] Agreement between Dunkirk Ice Cream, Co. and Teamsters Local 264, 1993–1997.

[53] Collective Agreement between U.S. Vanadium Corp.–Niagara Falls, NY, and Oil, Chemical and Atomic Workers International Union Local 8-250, November 2, 1989–November 2, 1992.

[54] General Motors–UAW, "Agreement between General Motors Corporation and the UAW"; Bureau of National Affairs, "Wage Patterns and Wage Data," 1987.

and the description are not furnished as required above, the job shall be considered day work.

Incentive allowance rates will not be reduced after work has been started upon the particular job or after the completion of the particular job covered by the allowance, except when some reduction is made in the quantity of work originally specified or where the method of performing the work has been revised.[55]

2. *Occupation-wage differentials.* Most contracts recognize that different occupations should receive different wage rates. Within occupations, though, a single wage rate prevails.[56] The following contract clause illustrates differentials.

Crane Operator	$14.85
Bricklayer	14.83
Garage Mechanic	14.60
Lab Technician	14.31
Truck Driver	14.31
Janitor	13.05[57]

Although rare, some contracts do not recognize occupational/skill differentials. These contracts specify a single standard rate for all jobs covered by the agreements. Usually such contracts cover a narrow range of skilled groups.

3. *Experience/merit differentials.* Single rates are usually specified for workers within a particular job classification. Single-rate agreements do not differentiate wages on the basis of either seniority or merit. Workers with varying years of experience and output receive the same single rate. Alternatively, agreements may specify wage ranges. The following example is fairly typical.[58]

Labor-Grade	Minimum							Maximum
19	$9.66	$9.91	$10.15	$10.39	$10.92	$11.40	$11.92	$12.40
18	8.99	9.22	9.46	9.67	10.16	10.60	11.05	11.54
17	8.34	8.55	8.77	8.98	9.41	9.84	10.26	10.67

The vast majority of contracts requiring wage ranges specify seniority as the basis for movement through the range. *Automatic progression* is an appropriate

---

[55] Ibid.

[56] Collective Agreement between U.S. Vanadium Corp.–Niagara Falls, NY, and Oil, Chemical and Atomic Workers International Union Local 8-250.

[57] Buffalo Color Corporation and United Steel Workers of America, 12330, June 13, 1991–present.

[58] AVX Corporation and IBEW, expired December 1993.

name for this type of movement through the wage range, with the contract frequently specifying the time interval between movements. This type of progression is most appropriate when the necessary job skills are within the grasp of most employees. Denial of a raise is a significant exception and frequently is accompanied by the right of the union to submit any wage denial to the grievance procedure.

At the other extreme of management intervention, some agreements permit management to shorten the time between automatic progressions for workers with outstanding performance records. For example,

> Nothing in this provision shall prevent the employer from granting individual increases more frequently than each 16 weeks if, in its judgment, they are merited.[59]

A second strategy for moving employees through wage ranges is based exclusively on merit. Employees who are evaluated more highly receive larger or more rapid increments than do average or poor performers. Within these contracts, it is common to specify that disputed merit appraisals may be submitted to grievance. If the right to grievance is not explicitly *excluded*, the union has the implicit right to it.

The third method for movement through a range combines automatic and merit progression in some manner. A frequent strategy is to grant automatic increases to the midpoint of the range and permit subsequent increases only when merited on the basis of performance appraisal.

4. *Other differentials.* A number of remaining contractual provisions deal with differentials for reasons not yet covered. The first example deals with differentials for new and probationary employees. About one-half of major agreements refer to differentials for these employees. The most common rate designation is below or at the minimum of the rate range. For example,

> New employees hired on or after the effective date of this Agreement, who do not hold a seniority date in any General Motors plant and are not covered by the provisions of Paragraph (98b) below, shall be hired at a rate equal to eighty five (85) percent of the maximum base rate of the job classification. Such employees shall receive an automatic increase to: (1) ninety (90) percent of the job classification at the expiration of one hundred and eighty (180) days, (2) ninety-five (95) percent of the maximum base rate of the job classification at the expiration of three hundred and sixty-five (365) days, (3) the maximum base rate of the job classification at the expiration of five hundred and forty-five (545) days.[60]

The second example of contractual differentials deals with different pay to unionized employees who are employed by a firm in different geographic areas. Very few contracts provide for different wages under these circumstances, despite

---

[59] Goodyear and Oil, Chemical, and Atomic Workers.
[60] Alside Supply Center and UAW District 65.

the problems that can arise in paying uniform wages across regions with markedly different costs of living.

The final category in which differentials are mentioned in contracts deals with part-time and temporary employees. Few contracts specify special rates for these employees. Those that do, however, are about equally split between giving part-time/temporary employees wages above full-time workers (because they have been excluded from the employee benefits program) and below full-time workers.

5. *Vacations and holidays.* Vacation and holiday entitlements are among clauses frequently found in labor contracts. They, too, use very specific language, as the following example illustrates:

The length of service increments shown below are based on the employee's length of service as of June 20 of the vacation year.

		Days Off
0 to 6 months		None
6 months to 2 years	2% of annual earnings	5
2 to 4 years	3% of annual earnings	7½
4 to 7 years	4% of annual earnings	10
7 to 10 years	5% of annual earnings	12½
10 to 14 years	6% of annual earnings	15
14 to 18 years	7% of annual earnings	17½
18 to 22 years	8% of annual earnings	20
22 to 25 years	9% of annual earnings	22½
25 years & over	10% of annual earnings	25

All of the above percentages will be mulitplied by 1.1 to arrive at the vacation pay due on June 20 of each contract year. The 1.1 multiplier applies to this section only.

18.02   Vacation pay will be distributed to the employees on June 20, or the last working day before June 20 each contract year.

A) Employees who desire vacation pay at the time they take it must notify the Company in writing at the time they submit their vacation preference as described in 18.06a. Any vacation pay remaining will be paid to the employee on the next pay day immediately following May 1st.

B) An employee returning from layoff will not be able to take vacation time during the first 30 work days following recall.[61]

6. *Wage adjustment provisions.* Frequently in multiyear contracts, some provision is made for wage adjustment during the term of the contract. These adjustments might be specified in three major ways: (1) deferred wage increases, (2) reopener clauses, and (3) cost of living adjustments or escalator clauses. A deferred wage increase is negotiated at the time of initial contract negotiations

---

[61] PeerLess-Winsmith, Inc., and International Union of Electronics, Electrical, Technical, Salaried Machine and Furniture Workers, AFL–CIO, 1991–1994.

**EXHIBIT 17.4   Popularity of Different Wage Clauses
(Frequency Expressed as Percentage of Contracts)**

	1948	1957	1966	1975	1983	1989	1992
Deferred increases	n.a.	33%	72%	88%	94%	77%	89%
Wage reopeners	40%	36	13	8	7	9	5
COLA clauses	n.a.	18	15	36	48	35	34

n.a. = Not tabulated until trend emerged.

Source: Bureau of National Affairs, *Basic Patterns in Union Contracts* (Washington, DC: Bureau of National Affairs, 1992).

with the timing and amount specified in the contract. A reopener clause specifies that wages, and sometimes such nonwage items as pension/benefits, will be renegotiated at a specified time or under certain conditions. Finally, a COLA clause, as noted earlier, involves periodic adjustment based typically on changes in the consumer price index:

> The amount of the cost-of-living allowance payable on each Effective Date of Adjustment will be determined by comparing the three month average CPI-W for the adjustment period to the base. $.01 per hour for each full .4 of a point change that the three month average CPI-W for the adjustment period exceeds the base will be added to any cost-of-living allowance payable effective December 5, 1988. The cost-of-living allowance will be paid as a separate rate per hour for all hours for which employees receive pay from the company.[62]

An analysis of trends in wage negotiations by the Bureau of National Affairs confirms that unions have lost some power in securing these types of wage increases. As Exhibit 17.4 suggests, deferred increases, wage reopeners, and cost of living adjustments have all lost popularity in recent years.

Geographically, as Exhibit 17.5 indicates, deferred increases predominate in New England, and cost of living clauses and lump-sum payments are most common among contracts covering multiple regions. Wage reopeners are most frequent in the Southeast and Southwest.

UNIONS AND ALTERNATIVE REWARD SYSTEMS

It is unlikely that the internationalization of business and the increased cost pressures that organizations face signal the death of traditional long-term labor contracts. Rather, union response is likely to center on ensuring that industries buffeted by deregulation and intense competition are able to control labor costs.

---

[62] Collective Agreement between Goodyear Tire & Rubber Company–Niagara Falls, NY, and Oil, Chemical, and Atomic Workers Local 8-277, December 10, 1988–December 9, 1991.

EXHIBIT 17.5   **Wage Clauses by Geographic Area**
              (Frequency Expressed as a Percentage of Contracts in
              Each Region)

	Deferred Increases	Active Cost of Living Escalators	Lump-Sum Payments	Reopeners
All regions	89%	25%	23%	5%
Middle Atlantic	95	18	22	2
Midwest	100	21	18	4
New England	100	27	15	—
North Central	89	27	25	3
Rocky Mountain	90	20	30	10
Southeast	83	15	23	15
Southwest	85	15	15	15
West Coast	89	22	11	—
Multiregion	77	48	39	8

Source: Bureau of National Affairs, *Basic Patterns in Union Contracts* (Washington, DC: Bureau of National Affairs, 1992).

This signals continued moderation in annual wage increase demands, increased willingness to consider work rule changes, renewed interest in cooperative labor-management relations, and further experimentation with profit sharing and other wage proposals that increase cost competitiveness. This section covers the likely union response to these alternative compensation systems.

Lump-Sum Awards

As discussed earlier, lump-sum awards are one-time cash payments to employees that are not added to an employee's base wages. These awards are typically given in lieu of traditional merit increases, which are more costly to the employer. This higher cost results because merit increases are added to base wages and because several employee benefits (e.g., life insurance and vacation pay) are figured as a percentage of base wages. Lump-sum payments may become a reality of union contracts. Cost and competitive pressures continue for companies, and these payments represent a compromise that neither party accepts, but endures.

Employee Stock Ownership Plans

An alternative strategy for organizations hurt by intense competition is to obtain wage concessions in exchange for giving employees part ownership in the company. For example, in both the 1988 and previous contract the teamsters negotiated a provision permitting local trucking companies and teamster employees to set up ESOP plans.[63] The National Master Freight Agreement specifies that employees will receive 49 percent ownership in a trucking company in exchange for wage concessions of no more than 15 percent over five years. So far, these plans have not been very effective in keeping marginal firms from eventually declaring bankruptcy. Approximately 20 such contracts have been negotiated, but only three still exist. Most of the remaining firms went out of business.[64]

ESOPs have been more successful in the airline industry in which soaring fuel costs and fare wars have severely damaged several companies. Three firms (Western, Republic, and PSA) turned around heavy loss years and became profitable after negotiating ESOPs.[65] These plans specify that employees get 12 to 32 percent of the airline's stock in exchange for 10 to 20 percent wage concession. In 1987, ESOP meant $33 million in payment to Republic employees.[66] Although unions typically agree to stock ownership plans only to keep organizations afloat, occasionally such programs result in considerable rewards for union employees.

Pay-for-Knowledge Plans

Pay-for-knowledge plans do just that: pay employees more for learning a variety of different jobs or skills. For example, Chrysler's agreement with the UAW specifies that journeymen will receive extra pay per hour for learning new trades. By coupling this new wage system with drastic cuts in the number of job classifications, organizations have greater flexibility in moving employees quickly into high demand areas. Unions also may favor pay-for-knowledge plans because they make each individual worker more valuable and less expendable to the firm. In turn, this also lessens the probability that work can be subcontracted out to nonunion organizations.

Gain-Sharing Plans

In the 1970s and early 1980s, gain-sharing plans were viewed as very effective ways to align workers and management in efforts to streamline operations and cut costs. Any cost savings resulting from employees working smarter were split according to some formula between the organization and the workers. The result has been some impressive gains for unionized companies with such group-based incentive plans. Across a large sample of unionized companies, performance

---

[63] Bureau of National Affairs, *Changing Pay Practices: New Developments in Employee Compensation* (Washington, DC: Bureau of National Affairs, 1988).

[64] Ibid.

[65] Given that all three of these airlines were acquired by other airlines between 1986 and 1987, it is not entirely clear whether ESOPs can be acclaimed as the sole reason for increased profitability over time.

[66] Joan C. Szabo, "Giving Workers a Company Stake," *Nations Business*, vol. 82, June 1994, pp. 54–55.

increased almost 20 percent more than when gain- or profit sharing plans were implemented.[67]

In the past few years, though, several companies have become disenchanted by gain-sharing plans. Parker Pen, Gould Battery, and Ingersol-Rand all recently terminated gain-sharing plans.[68] One of the main problems centers on early productivity improvement plateaus. Payouts are sometimes tied to continued increases in savings. When savings level off, the "gains" shared with workers drop correspondingly.[69] Not surprisingly, unions are not enthusiastic about making changes that continue to benefit the organization but that result in wage gains for employees only in the short term.

Rather than opposing gain-sharing, though, the most common union strategy is to delay taking a stand until real costs and benefits are more apparent.[70] Politically, this may be the wisest choice for a union leader. As the data in Exhibit 17.6 indicate, there are numerous possible costs and benefits to union membership

EXHIBIT 17.6   Union Perceptions of Advantages/Disadvantages of Gain-Sharing

Percentage in Agreement	
Advantages	*Disadvantages*
1. Increased recognition (95%)	1. Management may try to substitute for wage increases (94%)
2. Better job security (94%)	2. Management can't be trusted (88%)
3. More involvement in job activities (94%)	3. Peer pressure to perform may increase (77%)
4. More money (94%)	4. Don't trust/understand bonus calculations (76%)
5. More feeling of contributing to firm (86%)	5. Union influence is undermined (66%)
6. Increased influence of union (70%)	6. Increased productivity may reduce need for jobs (64%)

Source: T. Ross and R. Ross, "Gainsharing and Unions: Current Trends," in *Gainsharing: Plans for Improving Performance*, ed. B. Graham-Moore and T. Ross (Washington, DC: Bureau of National Affairs, 1990).

[67] W. N. Cooke, "Employee Participation Programs, Group Based Incentives, and Company Performance," *Industrial and Labor Relations Review* 47, no. 4 (1994), pp. 594–610.

[68] John Zalusky, "Labor's Collective Bargaining Experience with Gainsharing and Profit-Sharing," Paper presented at the IRRA 39th Annual Meeting, December 1986, pp. 175–82.

[69] *Changing Pay Practices: New Developments in Employee Compensation*, 1988.

[70] T. Ross and R. Ross, "Gainsharing and Unions: Current Trends," in *Gainsharing: Plans for Improving Performance*, ed. B. Graham-Moore and T. Ross (Washington, DC: Bureau of National Affairs, 1990), pp. 200–13.

for agreeing to a gain-sharing plan. Until the plan is actually implemented, though, it is unclear what the impact will be in any particular firm.

Profit Sharing Plans

Unions have debated the advantages of profit sharing plans for at least 80 years.[71] In 1948, Walter Reuther, then president of the CIO (which became the AFL–CIO in 1955), championed the cause of profit sharing in the auto industry. The goal of unions is to secure sound, stable income levels for the membership. When this is achieved, subsequent introduction of a profit sharing plan allows union members to share the wealth with more profitable firms while still maintaining employment levels in marginal organizations. We should note, though, that not all unions favor profit sharing plans. As indicated by recent grumblings of employees at General Motors, inequality in profits between firms in the same industry can lead to wage differentials for workers performing the same work. Payouts to Ford employees on the profit sharing plan totaled $9,400 between 1984 and 1988. During the same period, General Motors employees received less than $1,500.[72] Ford employees continue to receive higher payouts than their GM counterparts. Most General Motors employees would argue that the difference in payout cannot be traced to the fact that Ford employees work harder or smarter. In fact, the difference in profitability, the UAW argues, is due to management decision making. Therefore, the argument runs, workers should not be penalized for factors beyond their control.

Summary

The United States no longer can view itself as the dominant economic power in the world. Other countries continue to make inroads in product areas traditionally the sole domain of U.S. companies. The impact of this increased competition has been most pronounced in the compensation area. Labor costs must be cut to improve the U.S. competitive stance. Alternative compensation systems to achieve this end are regularly being devised. Unions face a difficult situation. How should they respond to these attacks on traditional compensation systems? Many unions believe that crisis demands changing attitudes from both management and unions. Labor and management identify compensation packages that both parties can abide. Sometimes these packages include cuts in traditional forms of wages in exchange for compensation tied more closely to the success of the firm. We expect the remainder of the 1990s to be dominated by more innovation in compensation design and increased exploration between unions and management for ways to improve the competitive stance of U.S. business.

---

[71] Zalusky, "Labor's Collective Bargaining Experience with Gainsharing and Profit-Sharing"; William Shaw, "Can Labor Be Capitalized?" *American Federationist*, June 1910, p. 517.

[72] *Changing Pay Practices: New Developments in Employee Compensation*, 1988.

Review Questions

1. Assume, as local union president, that you have just received valid information that the bankruptcy of the company employing your workers is imminent. What types of wage concessions might your union be able to make? Which of these are likely to have the least negative impact on your union workers' wages in the short term (one year)? Which represent the greatest cost savings potential for the company in the short term? Which is most likely to create internal dissension between different factions of the union?

2. Assume that you are a researcher working for the AFL–CIO. Your boss just gave you the assignment of designing a study to show the wage impact of unions in the restaurant industry. What problems must you surmount in figuring out what is, and what is not, a wage difference that is due to the union?

3. Why do union employees dislike profit sharing plans? Would you expect this feeling to be stronger for unionized than nonunionized workers? Why or why not?

4. Suppose an employee has a $30,000 base wage. Assume that she receives a 5 percent performance award at the end of each year for five years. What are the five-year cost savings for distributing this award as an annual lump-sum bonus rather than as an annual merit increase?

5. Under what economic circumstances do unions favor COLA clauses? Why do fewer contracts specify COLA clauses today than 10 years ago?

Your Turn:
General Technology

The Company

General Technology (GT) is an international producer of burglar alarm systems. To crack the international market, GT must comply with quality standards as set by the International Organization for Standardization (ISO). Compliance requires that all products and processes pass a series of 17 strict criteria, the so-called ISO 9000 audit.

The Union

The Technology Workers of America (TWA) organized GT's Buffalo division in 1979. In the last contract, both parties agreed to have a three-person panel listen to all disputes between union and management concerning the proper classification of jobs.

Your Role

You are the neutral third party hired to hear the dispute described below. The union representative has voted in the union's favor, and management has sided with management's position. You will break the tie. How do you vote and why? Some experts would argue that enough evidence is presented here for you to make a decision. See if you can figure out what the logic was that led to this conclusion. Further, list what other information you would like to have and how that might influence your decision.

The Grievance

A job titled Technical Review Analyst I with responsibility for ISO 9000 audits is slotted as a tier 3 job.[1] Union believes that this job should be evaluated as a tier 4 job. Management contends that both this job and its counterpart in tier 4 (Senior Technical Review Analyst) should be graded in tier 3.

Summary of Important Points in the Union Case

The union asserts, and management agrees, that the only difference historically between auditors classified as Technical Review Analysts I (tier 3) and those classified as Senior Technical Review Analysts (tier 4) was the presence or absence of one task. That task was the performance of systems tests. Only tier 4 personnel performed this work, and this yielded the higher tier classification. With the introduction of ISO 9000 audits, the systems test component of the tier 4 job was eventually phased out and both tier 3 and tier 4 auditors were asked to perform the ISO 9000 audit. The union and management agree that the systems test work previously performed by tier 4 employees was easier (and less valuable to the company) than the new ISO 9000 work now being performed. However, the union maintains that this added responsibility from the ISO 9000 audit, which involves about 150 hours of training, is sufficiently complex to warrant tier 4 classification. As partial support, the union provided a list of attendees to one ISO 9000 training session and noted that many of the attendees from other companies are managers and engineers, asserting this as evidence of the complexity involved in the audit material and the importance attached to this job by other firms.

The union also presented evidence to support the assertion that tier 3 personnel performing ISO 9000 audits are doing work of substantially the same value as the old grade 310 work.[2] This grade, as agreed by both the union and the company, is equivalent to the new tier 4.

Summary of Important Points in Management Case

Management's case includes four major points. First, management argues that a Technical Review Analyst performing ISO 9000 audits has a job that is similar in complexity, responsibility, and types of duties to jobs previously classified as grade 308 and 309. Jobs in these old grades are now slotted into tier 3, per the contract.

Second, management presented evidence that many of the duties performed in the ISO 9000 audits were performed in a series of prior audits, variously labeled Eastcore MPA, QSA 1981, and QPS 1982. This long and varied history of similar duties, management contends, is evidence that ISO 9000 does not involve higher level or substantially different (and hence no more valuable) duties than have been performed historically.

Third, management presented both notes and a memorandum from W. P. Salkrist (the company job evaluation expert) in support of his argument that the audit job with ISO 9000 responsibilities should be classified as a tier 4 job. Prior to introduction of the ISO 9000 audit, neither the union nor management had found any reason to complain about the existing prior job evaluations of the tier 3 and tier 4 review analysts.

Fourth, management provided evidence that these jobs at other facilities, *with other local contract provisions and conditions*, were all classified into tier 3.[3]

---

[1] Tier 1 is the low end and tier 5 is the highest for all skilled craft jobs. Different evaluation systems are used for management and for clerical employees.

[2] The former job evaluation system broke jobs down into many more grades. As of the last contract, jobs are now classified into one of five tiers or grades.

---

[3] Union strongly contests the introduction of this information. In the past, management has vehemently argued that conditions at other facilities should not be introduced because local contracts were negotiated, with different trade-offs being made by the different parties. Union believes that this same logic should now apply if a consistent set of rules is to evolve.

CHAPTER

International Pay Systems

Change is part of modern market-based economies and consequently part of the employment relationships embedded in them. It is yesterday's news that the terms and conditions under which people work are changing. Over 70 percent of the Fortune 500 multinationals report that they have restructured over the past five years. Forty percent responded that they were either in the midst of restructuring or that it was ongoing and continuous.[1] This means downsizing, layoffs, redefined work roles, more variable pay, greater risk, and general uncertainty.

Change in the employment relationship is not isolated in the United States. It is happening globally. Major Japanese employers are restructuring. Nissan and Toyota have modified their lifetime employment promises to long-term security within a group of companies, not necessarily the parent company.[2] Japanese employers report they are increasingly using ability and performance-based pay with less emphasis on seniority.[3] European companies are searching for ways to control the rate of labor cost increases and beginning to experiment with variable pay and performance-based appraisal.[4] And talk about jolting change—consider Russia and Central Europe, where employees in these post-communist economies face the challenge of revising pay systems that were dictated by central government authorities without business or market-related logic.[5] Indeed, a friend operating in Russia recently suggested that "the most effective pay delivery system is a brown bag under the table."

So employment relationships are changing, and pay systems around the world are changing, too. A framework can help understand and manage this change. Without such a framework, the changes appear chaotic. With the framework, they may appear only ambiguous, ill-conceived, or inappropriate. However, they may also become more understandable and manageable.

---

[1] H. Axel, *HR Executive Review: Downsizing* (New York: The Conference Board, 1993).

[2] Shintaro Hori, "Fixing Japan's White-Collar Economy: A Personal View," *Harvard Business Review*, November–December 1993, pp. 157–72; Yoshio Sasajima, "Changes in Labour Supply and Their Impacts on Human Resource Management: The Case of Japan," *International Journal of Human Resource Management*, February 1993, pp. 29–44.

[3] Sachiko Imada, "The Labour Market that Could Best Serve the Demand for Human Resources" Hiroshi Sato, "Personnel Management in Japanese Corporations," Takashi Araki, "Flexibility in Japanese Employment Relations and the Role of the Judiciary," Presentations at Japan Institute of Labour, Tokyo American Club, February 8, 1994, Tokyo; also Tadashi Amaya, "Recent Trends in Human Resource Development," *Japan Industrial Relations Series,* no. 17 (Tokyo: Japan Institute of Labour, 1994).

[4] David Soskice, "Wage Determination: The Changing Role of Institutions in Advanced Industrialized Countries," *Oxford Review of Economic Policy* 6, no. 4, pp. 36–61; David Soskice, "The German Wage Bargaining System," in *IRRA 46th Annual Proceedings*, ed. Paula Voos (October 1994), pp. 349–58; Anuska Ferligoj, Janez Prasnikar, and Vesna Jordan, "Competitive Strategies and Human Resource Management in SMEs" (Working paper, University of Ljubljana, 1994.)

[5] "Pay Setting Headache in Eastern Europe," *IDS European Report* 389 (May 1994), pp. 21–22; Lowell Turner, "From 'Old Red Socks' to Modern Human Resource Managers?" (Working paper 94-28, Center for Advanced Human Resource Studies, Cornell University, 1994); Jacob C. Manakkalathil and Piotr Chelminski, "The Central European Three: Opportunities and Challenges," *SAM Advanced Management Journal*, Summer 1993, pp. 28–34.

SOCIAL CONTRACTS

As we noted in Chapters 1 and 13, looking at compensation as part of the social contract offers a useful framework for understanding and managing employee pay. Exhibit 18.1 depicts the employment relationship with the actions employees believe are expected of them and the responses (e.g., pay, benefits, opportunities) they expect in return. This concept can expand to include the role of government. The implicit employment and social contracts are the keystones of modern societies' economic and social well-being. As you read this chapter, it should be clear that different countries and cultures hold differing beliefs about the role and responsibilities of governments, employers, unions, and employees.

A recent study contrasting U.S. and German pay systems illustrates the point. It concluded that "in the U.S. you work hard to advance to keep a good job, to keep from falling into a shallow social safety net . . . . whereas the

EXHIBIT 18.1   Implicit Employment and Social Contracts

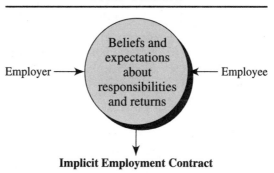

Implicit Employment Contract

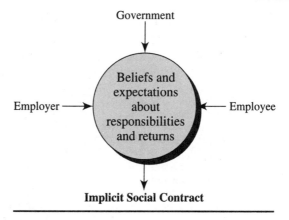

Implicit Social Contract

German pay system and social benefits system is close to a guaranteed annual income."[6] A typical German employee's marginal tax rate (percent tax on each additional dollar or mark earned) is 30 percent higher than in the United States. As a result, the return for working extra hours or working harder to receive a gain-sharing bonus is smaller in Germany. But in exchange for their higher taxes, German employees receive more generous social benefits, such as welfare and unemployment payments, national health care, plus subsidized college and apprenticeship programs.

So understanding how to manage employee compensation in Germany requires an understanding of the social contract, that is, understanding the role played by government, employees, and employers. Efforts to change employee compensation systems—for example, to make them more responsive to customers, encourage innovative and quality service, or control costs—must be managed within the context of the relevant social contract.

A note of caution as you read this chapter. National and regional generalizations are often as misleading as personal stereotypes. To claim that all organizations in Germany or Japan or the United States operate in some similar way ignores variations and differences. Considerable variety among company practices within any country exists. The basic premise of this section is that social, cultural, and economic conditions within each nation or region, taken as a whole, form distinct social and employment relationships. Understanding these relationships is useful for managing employee compensation. But do not assume uniformity within a country.

GLOBAL COMPARISONS

Three related factors define the differences in various employment relationships: (1) managerial autonomy based on culture and laws, (2) patterns of ownership within financial markets, and (3) structures to accommodate trade union and employee involvement.[7]

Managerial autonomy refers to the degree of freedom or discretion to make choices. Most U.S.-based organizations have relatively greater freedom (i.e., it is less costly) to change employee pay practices than in Europe. 3M, a global

---

[6] Linda Bell and Richard Freeman, "Why Do Americans and Germans Work Different Hours?" (Working paper 4808, National Bureau of Economic Research, 1994).

[7] Chris Brewster, "Developing a 'European' Model of Human Resource Management," *International Journal of Human Resource Management*, December 1993, pp. 765–854; Thomas Kochan, "The Future of Employer-Employee Relations," Working paper 94-23 (Center for Advanced Human Resource Studies, Cornell University, 1994); Miriam Rothman, Dennis R. Briscoe, and Raoul C. D. Nacamulli, eds. *Industrial Relations Around the World* (Berlin: Walter deGruyter, 1993); Klaus Schwab and Claude Smadja, "Power and Policy: The New Economic World Order," *Harvard Business Review*, November–December 1994, pp. 40–45; Alice Lam, "The Utilization of Human Resources: A Comparative Study of British and Japanese Engineers in Electronics Industries," *Human Resource Management Journal* 4, no. 3, pp. 22–40.

company based in St. Paul, Minnesota, is currently encouraging all its units to pursue performance-based pay in order to sustain growth. 3M units in the United States are trying out a variety of gain-sharing and bonus plans. At 3M Singapore, the notion of performance-based bonuses is old hat. Bonuses equivalent to two months' salary are paid every six months. On the other hand, 3M Europe, headquartered in Brussels, was told by the Belgian government that its proposed performance-based pay plan may be illegal. In an effort to control inflation and promote egalitarian values, Belgium passed a law that made all forms of new pay beyond that set by the nationally negotiated labor agreements illegal. Generally, European Union (EU) countries constrict actions at the national level via wage agreements negotiated by industrywide or nationwide employers and union associations.[8]

Recently, Japanese employment relationships have also been changing. Traditionally, Japan's employment relationship has been supported by "three pillars":

1. Lifetime security within the company.
2. Seniority-based pay and promotion systems.
3. Enterprise unions (decentralized unions that represent blue-collar workers within a single company). This structure contrasts with industrywide unions such as United Auto Workers in the United States or I.G. Metall, the largest trade union in Germany.[9]

Increasingly, Japanese companies are using performance-based approaches for pay and promotion (though seniority still is important, as you will read later in this chapter), MBO-style performance appraisal is commonly used to assess managerial performance, and employment security is defined as *long time* rather than lifetime.[10] The Japanese government regulates layoffs.[11]

On the whole, businesses have greatest freedom of action in the United States, less in Japan, and are the most constrained in Europe, particularly in Germany. In both Europe and Japan, government has a greater involvement in

[8] *Social Europe: The Social Dimension of the Internal Market* (Brussels: Directorate-General for Employment, Social Affairs, and Education, 1988); Sanford M. Jacoby, ed., *The Workers of Nations* (New York: Oxford University Press, 1995); Soskice, "German Wage Bargaining System."

[9] Yoko Sano, "Changes and Continued Stability in Japanese HRM Systems: Choice in the Share Economy," *International Journal of Human Resource Management*, February 1993, pp. 11–27; Motohiro Morishima, "The Japanese Human Resource Management System: A Learning Bureaucracy," in *Human Resource Management in the Pacific Rim: Institutions, Practices and Values,* ed. J. Devereaux Jennings and Larry Moore (New York: Walter deGruyter, in press).

[10] "The Appreciation of 'Lifetime Employment System and Job Mobility' in Toyota" (Toyota White Paper, Tokyo, 1993); "Business Restructuring and Effective Use of Human Resources," *Productivity in Japan* 7, no. 3 (Alexandria, VA: Japan Productivity Center for Socio-Economic Development).

[11] Johannes Schregle, "Dismissal Protection in Japan," *International Labour Review* 132, no. 4 (1993), pp. 507–20.

EXHIBIT 18.2   Pay and Social Costs Adjusted to Reflect Purchasing Power
(Comparative Compensation Costs in U.S. Dollars*)

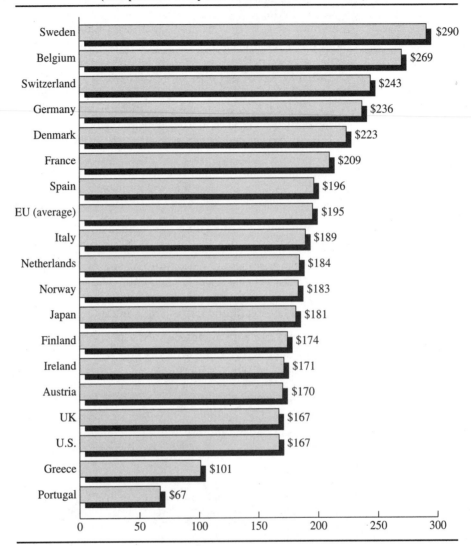

Sweden	$290
Belgium	$269
Switzerland	$243
Germany	$236
Denmark	$223
France	$209
Spain	$196
EU (average)	$195
Italy	$189
Netherlands	$184
Norway	$183
Japan	$181
Finland	$174
Ireland	$171
Austria	$170
UK	$167
U.S.	$167
Greece	$101
Portugal	$67

* Using OECD average 1993 exchange rates adjusted for GDP purchasing parities relative to those in the United States.
Source: Sedgwick Noble Lowndes (1994).

social policy and welfare programs. And the costs of these social welfare programs are considerable.[12] As Exhibit 18.2 shows, U.S. employers' *total employment costs*, including pay and social programs, are lower than in Japan and most of Europe. Employer costs for pay and social programs are 8 percent higher in

[12] "Taxes and Benefits Take A Big Bite Out of U.S. Pay," *Compflash* (Saranac Lake, NY: American Management Association, 1994), p. 4.

Japan, 25 percent higher in France, 41 percent higher in Germany, and 61 percent higher in Belgium.

Ownership and financial markets also affect the employment relationship and social contract. Patterns of ownership differ greatly. In the United States, corporate ownership and access to capital is far less concentrated than in most other countries. In Korea, for example, six conglomerates control a significant portion of the Korean economy, and the six are closely linked with specific families (e.g., Hyundai and Samsung). In Germany, most major companies are closely allied and owned largely by a small number of influential banks and the Bundesbank, its national bank.[13] These patterns of ownership make certain types of pay systems almost nonsensical. For example, linking performance bonuses to increased shareholder value or offering stock options to employees makes little sense for German, Korean, or Japanese firms.[14] Japanese, Korean, and European governments take a greater interventionist role in their economies.

Trade unions and employee involvement clearly differ among nations, and these differences influence employee compensation. Europe is highly unionized: 85 percent of Sweden's work force belong to unions, the UK figure is about 40 percent, and France about 12 percent. In addition, laws in France, Belgium, and Germany require the establishment of worker councils. The exact rules vary among nations, but compared to the United States, worker councils and unions significantly affect any proposed changes in pay.[15]

The EU is commited to maintaining the role of the *social partners,* as it calls employers and trade unions. The EU is trying to provide common labor standards in all its member countries. The purpose of standards is to avoid "social dumping," or the relocation of a business in a country with lower standards and labor costs. At present, hourly labor costs vary substantially among the countries, although sometimes the low labor costs are accompanied by low productivity. Exhibit 18.3, for example, shows 1991 hourly labor costs, adjusted for purchasing power, that range from 6 ECUs (the EU currency) in Portugal to 19.56 ECUs in Germany, and social protection benefits that range from 1,617 ECUs in Portugal to 5,797 ECUs in Luxembourg. However, each nation's history of labor law, cultural values, and political ideologies complicates attempts to develop systemwide regulations.[16]

Exhibit 18.4 summarizes some of the different approaches to pay and benefits

---

[13] Kirsten S. Wever and Christoper S. Allen, "Is Germany a Model for Managers?" *Harvard Business Review*, September–October 1992, pp. 36–43; "21st Century Capitalism," *Business Week*, special 1994 issue.

[14] Michael Byungnam Lee, Vida Scarpello, and B. Wayne Rockmore, "Strategic Compensation in South Korea's Publicly Traded Firms," Presentation at 10th World Congress of the International Industrial Relations Association, June 1995, Washington DC; Michael Byungnam Lee, "Business Strategy, Participative Human Resource Management and Organizational Performance: The Case of South Korea" (Working paper, Georgia State University, 1994).

[15] "The German Industrial Relations System: Lessons for the United States?" *National Planning Association* 15, no. 3 (December 1993), entire issue.

[16] Barbara A. Lee, "The Effect of the European Community's Social Dimension on Human Resource Management in U.S. Multinationals: Perspectives from the United Kingdom and

EXHIBIT 18.3   Productivity, Hourly Labor Costs, Social Protection Benefits, and Unemployment Rates in the European Community

	GDP per Person,* 1991 (PPS)	Hourly Labor Costs, 1991 (PPS)	Social Protection Benefits per Person, 1991 (PPS)	Unemployment Rates (%), 1992
Belgium	16,193	18.94	4,191	8.1%
Denmark	16,576	18.01	4,609	9.5
Germany	18,345	19.56	4,952	4.5
Greece	7,397	9.23	1,669	7.7 (1991)
Spain	11,964	13.31	2,433	18.0
France	17,250	14.33 (1988)	4,803	10.0
Ireland	10,815	13.33	2,240	17.8
Italy	15,890	14.33 (1988)	3,991	10.3
Luxembourg	19,636	13.43 (1988)	5,797	1.9
Netherlands	15,551	15.42 (1988)	5,101	6.7
Portugal	9,064	6.00	1,617	4.8
United Kingdom	14,732	13.88	3,653	10.8
EC Average	15,432	—	3,930	9.5

Data are expressed in ECUs (the EC currency), adjusted for purchasing power parities (PPS).

Note: * Gross domestic product at market prices per person.

Source: Eurostat, *Basic Statistics of the Community* (Luxembourg: Office for Official Publications of the European Communities, 1993).

regulations. The United Kingdom specifies the fewest requirements with no minimum wage, no maximum hours, and no formal methods for employee participation. France, Belgium, and the Netherlands have the most generous minimum annual vacations.

Perhaps most striking for managing pay is that many European countries have nationally negotiated wage agreements that set the floor for wages of all unionized employees in the country. Such national-level decision making reduces the ability of organization-level managers to attempt to tailor or craft their pay system to fit their organization's unique business strategy. Hence the basic business strategy-based model

Business Strategy	→	HR Strategy	→	Compensation Strategy	→	Employee	→	Competitive Advantage

needs to be modified to include the direct impact of various laws and regulations.

France," *Human Resource Management Review* 4, no. 4 (1994), pp. 333–61; Neil Millward, Mark Steens, David Smart, and W. R. Hawes, *Workplace Industrial Relations in Transition* (Brookfield, VT: Dartmouth Publishing Company, 1992); John T. Addison and W. Stanley Siebert, "Recent Developments in Social Policy in the New European Union," *Industrial and Labor Relations Review*, October 1994, pp. 5–27; Christopher L. Erickson and Sarosh Kuruvilla, "Labor Costs and the Social Dumping Debate in the European Union," *Industrial and Labor Relations Review*, October 1994, pp. 28–47.

EXHIBIT 18.4 Employment Practices and Policies among EC Countries

Country	Minimum Pay	Maximum Hours (including overtime)	Minimum Annual Vacation	Employee Participation
Belgium	Yes	8 per day; 40 per week	4 weeks	Works councils
Denmark	No, but must conform to one of two compulsory wage systems	Depends on collective agreement	2.5 days per month	Employee representatives on board of directors where there are more than 30 employees
France	Yes	10 per day 39 per week (includes 5 Saturdays)	2.5 days per month	Employee and union representatives
Germany	No, but if a collective agreement exists, this provision must be included	8 per day 48 per week	18 days	Works councils
Greece	Yes	48 per week	4 weeks (after 1 year's employment)	Works councils
Ireland	No	No generally applicable statutory maximum	3 weeks	No formal requirements
Italy	Collective agreement	48 per week 8 per day	Collective agreement	National collective bargaining agreements; requires consultation
Luxembourg	Yes	40 per week 8 per day	25 working days (5 days' holiday equals 1 week)	Employee representatives; joint works councils; employee directors
The Netherlands	Yes	48 per week 8.5 per day 5.5 days per week	4 weeks	Works council in undertakings with 35 or more employees
Portugal	Yes	Office workers: 42 hours per week Others: 48 per week; 8 per day.	Not less than 21 days nor more than 30 days	Workers' commissions and registered trade unions
Spain	Yes	40 per week 9 per day	2.5 days per month	Employee delegates and committees; employee directors
United Kingdom	No	No	No requirements	No formal requirements

Source: Adapted from *Personnel*, October 1989, p. 22 and updated, and from Dworkin and Lee, 1992.

In summary, employee compensation is part of the overall employment relationship that in turn operates within the social context. European and Japanese social contracts are distinctive. The relationships among laws, organizations, employees, and unions are also distinctive to each country.

These interrelationships bring to mind the old children's game of rock crushes scissors, scissors cuts paper, and paper covers rock. Rock, scissors, and paper interact with each other in the same way that culture, employment relationships, and economic forces interact.[17] Culture and laws sustain and support the employment relationships, which in turn influence and shape how organizations and employees economically compete. Economic competitiveness recalibrates and forces changes in the culture and laws. Thus, the forces are inevitably intertwined.

COMPENSATION: TRANSLATION PLEASE?

Compensation does not mean the same thing in every culture. In the United States, we equate compensation with wages and benefits given in exchange for effort or work. The notion of compensation in Sweden, Norway, and Germany includes the idea of exchange but not necessarily wages and benefits. Rather, compensation implies an exchange of time and effort, as in, I will work for three hours in your garden if you will care for the kids tonight or repair my car. The German phrase *zahlung leitsen*, meaning "make payment for," is perhaps Germany's closest phrase implying compensation. *Zahlung leitsen* indicates achievement. The meaning is derived from German shoemakers who skillfully crafted shoes that fit the wearer's foot. They "fit the standard" or "measured up." Hence, the notion that achievement that measures up deserves recompense.

The translation of compensation into the Japanese word *hosho* implies protection or guarantee. The notion of trust in a guarantee is a cornerstone of the traditional Japanese workplace. A Japanese employer, like a parent in a family, makes a commitment to care for family members. The relationship is not really an exchange; it certainly is not a reward for performance. Rather, it is more like the expectation that parents will provide food, clothing, and shelter for their children. In return, children are expected to be members of the family and support it. Compensation in this traditional Japanese sense is an understood and expected obligation.

So what difference do these definitions make? They demonstrate how the notion of compensation must be broader than a purely monetary exchange. And the financial relationship must be aligned with various expectations about the employment relationship.

---

[17] Theodore C. Bestor, "Visible Hands: Auctions and Institutional Integration in the Tsukiji Wholesale Fish Market" (Working paper no. 63, Columbia University Center on Japanese Economy and Business, 1992).

INTERNATIONAL WAGE COMPARISONS

In Chapter 7 we discussed the numerous difficulties in measuring a market wage rate. Many large companies face difficulties of even greater magnitude when they try to compare their labor costs with those of foreign competitors. Comparisons among societies as different as the United States and Japan, for example, can be very misleading. Even if wages appear the same, expenses for health care, living costs, and typical company-provided perquisites such as dormitories and commuting allowances all complicate the picture. Comparisons between a specific U.S. firm and a specific Japanese firm may be even more misleading. Accurate data are difficult to obtain. Statistics may not be publicly available or may not completely specify what is or is not included. A number of different comparisons may all be valid, but all may paint different pictures. Exhibit 18.5, for example, shows three different wage comparisons between Caterpillar, Inc., in the United

EXHIBIT 18.5   Comparing Labor Costs

Caterpillar compared its hourly U.S. labor costs with those of its own joint venture in Japan, under the theory that the Japanese venture has costs similar to those of Komatsu:

Caterpillar	Shin Caterpillar Mitsubishi
$22.26/hour cash compensation plus $10/hour in benefits	About $20.25/hour plus $5/hour in benefits

The UAW examined cash compensation at Cat and Komatsu, but didn't include the added cost of benefits:

Caterpillar	Komatsu
$20.91/hour	$19.66/hour

Add in recent wage increases and changes in exchange rates, and there's little difference in annual cash compensation:

Caterpillar	Komatsu
$39,350	$39,700

Source: Robert L. Rose and Masayoshi Kanabayashi, "Comparing U.S.–Japan Labor-Cost Data Can Be Murky," *The Wall Street Journal*, June 4, 1992, p. B4.

States and Komatsu, Ltd., a Japanese competitor. These comparisons were offered by various parties during a 1992 strike by the UAW against Caterpillar in Peoria, Illinois.

Mexico provides a closer-to-home example. A Bureau of Labor Statistics comparison of hourly compensation costs in 29 countries (Exhibit 18.6) shows wages in Mexico at only 11 percent of those in the United States. However, another source, Hewitt Associates, puts the "effective labor cost" in Mexico at about $6.00 per hour compared to $16.70 in the United States, for a ratio of 36

EXHIBIT 18.6   **Indexes of Hourly Compensation Costs for Production Workers in Manufacturing**
[Index, United States = 100]

Country or Area	1975	1980	1985	1988	1989	1990	1991	1992	1993
United States	100	100	100	100	100	100	100	100	100
Canada	94	88	84	97	104	107	110	106	97
Mexico	23	22	12	9	10	11	12	14	16
Australia	88	86	63	82	87	88	87	81	73
Hong Kong	12	15	13	17	19	21	23	24	26
Israel	35	38	31	55	54	57	56	56	—
Japan	47	56	49	91	88	86	94	101	114
Korea	5	10	9	16	22	25	29	30	32
New Zealand	50	54	34	59	54	56	54	49	48
Singapore	13	15	19	19	22	25	28	31	32
Sri Lanka	4	2	2	2	2	2	3	—	—
Taiwan	6	10	12	20	25	26	28	32	31
Austria	71	90	58	104	99	119	116	126	120
Belgium	101	133	69	114	108	129	127	137	127
Denmark	99	110	62	109	101	120	117	124	114
Finland	72	83	63	113	118	141	136	123	99
France	71	91	58	93	88	102	98	104	97
Germany*	100	125	74	131	124	149	147	157	152
Greece	27	38	28	38	38	45	44	46	—
Ireland	48	60	46	72	67	79	78	83	—
Italy	73	83	59	101	101	119	119	121	95
Luxembourg	100	121	59	99	95	110	107	—	—
Netherlands	103	122	67	114	105	123	118	127	120
Norway	106	117	80	133	128	144	139	142	120
Portugal	25	21	12	20	21	25	27	32	27
Spain	40	60	36	61	62	76	78	83	69
Sweden	113	127	74	121	122	140	142	152	107
Switzerland	96	112	74	129	117	140	139	144	135
United Kingdom	53	77	48	76	74	85	88	89	76

Notes: * Former West Germany; dash indicates data are not available.

percent.[18] The difference between the two estimates stems largely from supplemental pay required by either Mexican law or custom. Hewitt reports that it is standard practice in Mexico to pay one month's pay as a Christmas bonus plus 80 percent of base for vacation bonuses plus punctuality bonuses. In addition, Mexican law dictates workers be paid 365 days per year.[19] Arthur Andersen, another consulting firm, reports that due to shortages of trained Mexican managers, they often earn 20 to 30 percent more than their U.S. counterparts. Unfortunately, all these calculations were made before the December 1994 devaluation of the Mexican peso, a move which seriously disrupted the economy. The point of including all this information is to show that some data are useful only for gross comparisons and understanding trends over time. But anyone designing a pay system in one of these countries must obtain current local data and understand local culture and customs.

Just in case you are looking at these data to decide where to begin your own career, perhaps one more comparison might be of interest: paid vacation days per year (Exhibit 18.7).[20] European workers average 25 paid vacation days (in Dusseldorf and Madrid, as many as 30). Brazilian law mandates 22 vacation days for managers *and* a vacation bonus of as much as one-third of a month's base salary. By contrast, workers in Seoul, Los Angeles, Houston, and Chicago enjoy only an average of 11 vacation days per year.

EXHIBIT 18.7   Vacation Allowances (Days)

Country	Legal Minimum	Typical Practice	Holidays	Total Annual
Brazil	22	22	11	33
Canada	10	20	11	33
France	25	25–30	16	46
Germany	15	30	16	46
Hong Kong	7	20–30	17	47
Japan	19	20	16	36
Mexico	14	15–20	19	39
Sweden	30	30	14	44
United Kingdom	0	25–30	9	39
United States	0	20	10	30

Source: William M. Mercer, consultants.

---

[18] Mary Greiner, Christopher Kask, and Christopher Sparks, "Comparative Manufacturing Productivity and Unit Labor Costs," *Monthly Labor Review*, February 1995, pp. 26–41; Melvin M. Brodsky, "Labor Market Flexibility: A Changing International Perspective," *Monthly Labor Review*, November 1994, pp. 53–60.

[19] "Mexican Labor's Hidden Costs," *Fortune*, October 17, 1994, p. 32.

[20] *International Benefit Guidelines* (New York: William M. Mercer, 1994).

Exhibit 18.8   The Hamburger Standard

	Big Mac Prices		Actual $ Exchange Rate 5/4/94	Implied PPP† of the Dollar	Local Currency Under(−)/Over(+) Valuation** (%)
	In Local Currency*	In Dollars			
United States‡	**$2.30**	**$2.30**	—	—	—
Argentina	Peso3.60	3.60	1.00	$ 1.57	+57%
Australia	A$2.45	1.72	1.42	1.07	−25
Austria	Sch34.00	2.84	12.0	14.8	+23
Belgium	BFr109	3.10	35.2	47.39	+35
Brazil	Cr1,500	1.58	949	652	−31
Britain	£1.81	2.65	1.46‡‡	1.27‡‡	+15
Canada	C$2.86	2.06	1.39	1.24	−10
Chile	Peso948	2.28	414	412	−1
China	Yuan9.00	1.03	8.70	3.91	−55
Czech Rep	CKr50	1.71	29.7	21.7	−27
Denmark	DKr25.75	3.85	6.69	11.2	+67
France	FFr18.5	3.17	5.83	8.04	+38
Germany	DM4.60	2.69	1.71	2.00	+17
Greece	Dr620	2.47	251	270	+8
Holland	Fl5.45	2.85	1.91	2.37	+24
Hong Kong	HK$9.20	1.19	7.73	4.00	−48
Hungary	Forint169	1.66	103	73.48	−29
Italy	Lire4,550	2.77	1,641	1,978	+21
Japan	¥391	3.77	104	170	+64
Malaysia	M$3.77	1.40	2.69	1.64	−39
Mexico	Peso8.10	2.41	3.36	3.52	+5
Poland	Zloty31,000	1.40	22,433	13,478	−40
Portugal	Esc440	2.53	174	191	+10
Russia	Rouble2,900	1.66	1,775	1,261	−29
Singapore	$2.98	1.90	1.57	1.30	−17
S. Korea	Won2,300	2.84	810	1,000	+24
Spain	Ptas345	2.50	138	150	+9
Sweden	Skr25.5	3.20	7.97	11.1	+39
Switzerland	SFr5.70	3.96	1.44	2.48	+72
Taiwan	NT$62	2.35	26.4	26.96	+2
Thailand	Baht48	1.90	25.3	20.87	−17

Notes: * Price vary locally. † Purchasing-power parity: local price divided by price in United States. ** Against dollar. ‡ Average of New York, Chicago, San Francisco and Atlanta. ‡‡ Dollars per pound.

Source: McDonald's.

Standard of Living: Basket of Goods versus Big Mac

If comparing labor costs is difficult, comparing living costs and standards is even more complex. The Bank of Switzerland uses a uniform basket of goods based on European consumer habits, which includes the prices for 137 items from clothing to transportation to personal care.[21] A woman shopping for a summer dress, jacket, skirt, shoes, and tights will find Tokyo the most expensive place to shop ($2,300), whereas Nairobi ($50) and Bombay ($120) are best buys. Tokyo is equally expensive for a man. If he wants a blazer, shirt, jeans, socks, and shoes, he will need to come up with $1,800 to pay for a medium-priced outfit.

If your tastes don't run to blazers and jackets, the *Economist* takes a Big Mac approach. Rather than pricing a complex basket of goods and services, the magazine uses the price of a Big Mac in different locations.[22] According to Exhibit 18.8, the average price of a Big Mac in the United States is $2.30 (average of 4 cities), in China 9.00 yuan ($1.03 U.S.), in Canada $2.86 ($2.06 U.S.), and in Russia 2,900 rubles (about $1.66 U.S.).

Why is this standard of living data important for managing compensation? These comparisons permit adjustments for international employees who transfer among countries to maintain *purchasing power parity*. Purchasing power parity comes up again in this chapter when we discuss expatriate pay.

Purchasing Power

There are several ways to calculate purchasing power.[23] A common approach is to divide hourly wages by the cost of a standard basket of goods and services. Another approach is to calculate the working time required to buy an item such as a 1-kilogram loaf of bread: 7 minutes in London, 15 minutes in Tokyo, 27 minutes in Montreal, and 12 minutes in Chicago. Or to buy a Big Mac: 14 minutes in Chicago, 36 minutes in London, and 90 minutes in Mexico City. The Big Mac (plus fries) attains luxury status in Nairobi, Caracas, and Lagos; an employed person must toil three hours (Nairobi), four hours (Caracas) or almost two days (Lagos) to afford it. (Hold the fries.)

COMPARING SYSTEMS

We have made the point that pay systems differ around the globe, and those differences relate to the nature of the social contracts in various cultures. In this section we compare several compensation systems. Examples from Japanese and European companies are contrasted with the U.S. examples that have been discussed throughout the book. The caution about stereotyping raised earlier

---

[21] Daniel Kalt and Manfred Gutmann, eds., *Prices and Earnings Around the Globe* (Zurich: Union Bank of Switzerland, 1994).

[22] "Big Mac Currencies," *Economist*, April 9, 1994, p. 88.

[23] Kalt and Gutmann, eds., *Prices and Earnings Around the Globe*.

applies here as well. Even in nations described by some as homogeneous, pay systems differ from business to business. For example, two well-known Japanese companies, Toyota and Toshiba, have designed different pay systems. Toyota places greater emphasis on external market rates, uses far fewer levels in its structure, and places greater emphasis on individual-based merit and performance pay than does Toshiba. So as we discuss "typical" systems, remember that differences and experimentation exist everywhere.

The Pay Model: Strategic Choices

The pay model used throughout the book guides our discussion of pay systems in different countries. Our experience suggests that all organizations face similar strategic issues, but that the relative importance among them differs greatly. You will recognize the basic choices, which seem universal:

- Objectives of pay systems.
- External competitiveness.
- Internal consistency.
- Employee contributions.
- Administration.

But if the choices are universal, the decisions are not. Some of these differences are best explained by the governmental laws and regulations that reflect national cultures and politics. For example, German and Japanese tax laws make stock options unattractive. Not surprisingly, the use of stock options is practically nil in both countries.

Relative Importance Differs

In many Central European countries and a good number of EU nations (e.g., Belgium, France, and Germany) nationally negotiated wage agreements set a floor on pay levels.[24] The effect is to decrease the emphasis on market pricing and the need for competitive market data. Some organizations in these countries use *adders,* or steps above the floor, to compensate for increased experience or skill. Trimo, a package fabrication company in the Central European country of Slovenia, adds three steps to each floor rate. Trimo hopes to establish a lead position in its market and attract and hold on to more highly educated and skilled workers. However, Trimo's structure is the exception. More often, when national-level negotiations establish the "going rate," it is no longer used to help

---

[24] "The German Industrial Relations System: Lessons for the United States?" *National Planning Association* 15, no. 3 (December 1993), entire issue; Soskice, "German Wage Bargaining System."

achieve competitive advantage. In contrast to U.S.-based companies, organizations in the EU place relatively less importance on market surveys and competitive positions.

In addition to nationally negotiated agreements, regulation in some countries is so strict that it is difficult to manage any part of employee compensation to help achieve competitive advantage. In effect, decisions about pay are taken out of the hands of the organization and placed in the hands of regulators and nationwide associations. Sweden and Belgium are such countries. Sweden is so constrained by laws and national agreements that all Swedish organizations have very similar pay systems. However, global competitive forces are pressuring organizations in all countries to seek to control labor costs and attempt to use performance-based pay plans. This in turn is putting pressure on regulators and negotiators to modify their social contracts.

In sum, while the strategic choices in the pay model are universal, their relative importance differs considerably around the globe. Competitive global pressures are forcing changes in many national regulations regarding pay decisions.

JAPANESE PAY SYSTEMS

Traditional Japanese pay systems tend to emphasize the person rather than the job; seniority and skills possessed rather than job-work performed; promotions based upon supervisory evaluation of trainability, skill/ability levels, and performance rather than on performance alone; internal consistency and equity over competitors' market rates; and lifetime job security rather than security based on the performance of the organization and the individual.

Components of Pay in Japan

It is convenient to describe Japanese pay systems in terms of three basic components: base pay, bonuses, and allowances/benefits.[25]

Base Pay. Base pay accounts for 60 to 80 percent of an employees' monthly pay, depending on the rank in the organization. Base pay is not based on job evaluation or market pricing (as predominates in North America) nor is it attached to specific job titles. Rather, it is based on a combination of employee characteristics: career category, years of service, and skill/performance level.

---

[25] Tadashi Amaya, "Recent Trends in HR Development" and Tadashi Amaya, Seminar for Foreign Business in Japan and Labour Issues, Presentations at Tokyo Club, 1994; Hideo Inohara, "Personnel Appraisal in Japanese Companies," bulletin no. 128, Sophia University Business Series (Tokyo: Sophia University, 1990); Takao Kato and Mark Rockel, "Experiences, Credentials, and Compensation in the Japanese and U.S. Managerial Labor Markets: Evidence from New Micro Data," *Journal of the Japanese and International Economies* 6 (1992), pp. 30–51.

Career.   Five career categories prevail in Japan: (1) general administration, (2) engineer/scientific, (3) secretary/office, (4) technician/blue collar job, and (5) contingent. Workers in the first two categories are called white-collar workers.

Years of Service.   Seniority is a major factor in determining base pay. Management creates a matrix of pay and years of service for each career category. Exhibit 18.9 shows a matrix for general administration work. Age is often used rather than years of service because they are equivalent in the Japanese system of lifetime employment. Companies meet periodically to compare their matrixes, which accounts for the similarity among companies. In general, salary increases with age until 50 years old and then is reduced. Employees can expect annual increases no matter what their performance level until age 50, though the amount of increase varies according to individual skills and performance.

Skills and Performance.   Each skill is defined by its class (usually 7–13) and rank (1–9) within the class. Exhibit 18.10 illustrates a skill salary chart for the General Administration career category. Classes 1 and 2 typically include associate (entry) and senior associate work; 2, 3, and 4 supervisor and managerial; 5, 6, and 7 managerial, general director, and so on. Employees advance in rank as a result of their supervisor's evaluation of their

- Effort (e.g., enthusiasm, participation, responsiveness).
- Skills required for the work (e.g., analytical, decision making, leadership, planning, process improvement, teamwork).
- Performance (increasingly, MBO-style ratings).

Mitsui's appraisal form in Exhibit 18.11 is typical of most appraisals.

EXHIBIT 18.9   Salary and Age Chart for General Administration Work

*Age	†Salary	Age	Salary	Age	Salary	Age	Salary
		31	$1,900	41	$2,900	51	$3,800
22	$1,000	32	2,000	42	3,000	52	3,700
23	1,100	33	2,100	43	3,100	53	3,600
24	1,200	34	2,200	44	3,200	54	3,500
25	1,300	35	2,300	45	3,300	55	3,400
26	1,400	36	2,400	46	3,400	56	3,300
27	1,500	37	2,500	47	3,500	57	3,200
28	1,600	38	2,600	48	3,600	58	3,100
29	1,700	39	2,700	49	3,700	59	3,000
30	1,800	40	2,800	50	3,800	60	2,900

Notes: * Age 22 is typical entry age with college degree. † Monthly salary.

EXHIBIT 18.10   Skill Chart for General Administration Work

	Associate	Senior Associate	Supervisor		Manager	General Director	
	Class 1	*Class 2*	*Class 3*	*Class 4*	*Class 5*	*Class 6*	*Class 7*
Rank 1	$ 600	$1,600	$2,600	$3,100	$3,600	$4,500	$5,500
Rank 2	700	1,700	2,650	3,150	3,750	4,700	6,000
Rank 3	800	1,800	2,700	3,200	3,800	4,900	
Rank 4	900	1,900	2,750	3,250	3,900	5,100	
Rank 5	1,000	2,000	2,800	3,300	4,000		
Rank 6	1,100	2,100	2,850	3,350	4,100		
Rank 7	1,200	2,200	2,900	3,400			
Rank 8	1,300	2,300	2,950	3,450			
Rank 9	1,400	2,400	3,000	3,500			

To illustrate how the system works, let us consider a graduate fresh from college who enters at class 1, rank 1. After one year, this new *salaryman* and all those hired at the same time are evaluated by their supervisors on their effort, abilities, and performance. Early in the career (the first three years), effort is more important; in later years abilities and performance receive more emphasis. The number of ranks an employee moves each year (and therefore the increase in base pay) depends on this supervisory rating (e.g., A = 3 ranks; B = 2 ranks; C = 1 rank; D = 0 ranks).

Theoretically, a person with an A rating could move up three ranks in class each year and shift to the next class in three years. However, most companies require both minimum and maximum years of service within each class. So even if you receive four straight A ratings, you would still remain in class 1 for the minimum of six years. Class 2 may also have a six year minimum time, and so on. Conversely, if you received four straight D grades, you would still get promoted to the next skill class after spending the maximum of 10 years in class 1. These minimum and maximum times in class effectively change this skill system into one based on both seniority and skill.

The logic underlying this approach is revealing. On the one hand, setting a minimum time in each class helps ensure that the employee knows the work and returns value to the company. On the other hand, the system also slows the progress of high-potential performers. And even the weakest performers eventually advance. Indeed, some report that weak performers eventually can get to the top of the pay structure though they do not get the accompanying job titles or responsibility.

The system reflects the traditional Japanese saying, "A nail that is standing too high will be pounded down." An individual employee will not want to stand out. Employees work to advance the performance of the group or team rather than themselves.

Exhibit 18.11   Mitsui Annual Appraisal of Performance (Summary)

Name: Job grade:

Age: Years in the grade:

School:

Appraisal	Rating				
	A	B	C	D	E

Last year's appraisal:
  First-half appraisal
  Second-half appraisal
	___
	___
		___
		___
			___
			___
				___
				___
					___
					___

Attendance					

Performance:
  Quantity
  Quality
	___
	___
		___
		___
			___
			___
				___
				___
					___
					___

Ability:
  Planning/judgment
  Improvement
  Negotiation
  Leadership
	___
	___
	___
	___
		___
		___
		___
		___
			___
			___
			___
			___
				___
				___
				___
				___
					___
					___
					___
					___

Work attitude:
  Positiveness
  Cooperation
  Responsibility
	___
	___
	___
		___
		___
		___
			___
			___
			___
				___
				___
				___
					___
					___
					___

General appraisal
  First appraisal
  Second appraisal
  Adjustment
  General appraisal
  All-company adjustment
  Final decision
	___
	___
	___
	___
	___
	___
		___
		___
		___
		___
		___
		___
			___
			___
			___
			___
			___
			___
				___
				___
				___
				___
				___
				___
					___
					___
					___
					___
					___
					___

Key: Outstanding (A); Superior (B); Standard (C); Inferior (D); Very inferior (E).

We can use Exhibits 18.9 and 18.10 to calculate base salary using a Japanese system. Sato-san joined a Japanese company after his graduation from Keio University. After 11 years in general administration work, he is at skill class 2, rank 7. His recent A appraisal means he could move three ranks, which would promote him to class 3, rank 1. However, classes 1 and 2 require six years minimum in each, so he must wait another year before receiving the promotion to skill class 3 (six years in class one and six years in class 2). So his base pay is calculated as

> Salary for years of seniority (10) or age 33 (Exhibit 18.9, $2,100) +
> Salary for class 2 and skill rank 9 (Exhibit 18.10, $2,400)
> = $2,100 + $2,400
> = $4,500 per month or $54,000/year

The increase this year was $100 per month for the additional age (or year of service) plus $200 per month for the increase from rank 7 to rank 9 in class 2. The $300 per month total increase equals 7 percent.

Under the traditional Japanese system, increases in annual base pay are relatively small (7 percent for Sato-san's superior performance, compared to 10 to 12 percent for star performers in many U.S. merit systems), though they compound over time just as conventional merit and across-the-board increases in the United States. However, since the Japanese system is so seniority based, labor costs increase as the average age of the work force increases. In fact, one of the major problems facing Japanese employers is the increasing labor costs caused by the cumulative effects of annual increases combined with lifetime employment security.[26]

Bonus.   Bonuses account for between 20 and 40% of annual salary, depending on the level in the organization. Generally, the higher up you are, the larger the percent of annual salary received as bonus. Many writers assume that the Japanese bonus is similar to U.S. profit sharing bonus in that it is based on some measure of performance.[27] But some caution in interpretation is required. For blue-collar and unionized employees, management calls the bonus a *gratuity*.[28] Unions avoid this term, however; they describe bonuses as an *expectable* additional payment to be made regularly, twice a year (July and December), even in bad financial times. Each bonus for workers is the equivalent of about two months' salary. While there is some fluctuation based on the firm's performance,

[26] Brenton R. Schlender, "Japan's White Collar Blues," *Fortune*, March 21, 1994, pp. 67–69; Yoko Sano, "Changes and Continued Stability in Japanese HRM"; Morishima, "The Japanese Human Resource Management System: A Learning Bureaucracy."

[27] Martin Weitzman, *The Share Economy* (Cambridge, MA: Harvard University Press, 1984).

[28] Ryohei Magota, "The Bonus System in Japan," *Labor Issues Quarterly*, Summer 1994, pp. 6–8; Sano, "Changes and Continued Stability in Japanese HRM."

the differences over time are small.[29] According to the Japan Institute of Labour, for most employees (managers excepted), bonuses are in reality variable pay that helps control the employers' cash flow and labor costs, but are not intended to act as a motivator or to support improved corporate performance.

Japanese labor laws encourage the use of bonuses to achieve cost savings by omitting bonuses from calculations of many other benefits costs.[30] For example:

- Calculations for pension plan contributions (2.25 percent of each employees' salary) exclude bonuses.
- Health insurance premiums are 4.1 percent of salary, but only .5% of bonus.
- Overtime pay calculations (at least 25 percent of base pay) exclude bonuses.
- Calculations for severance pay and earlier retirement allowances exclude bonuses.

So the cost savings offered by emphasizing bonuses rather than base pay can add up. Sano has observed, "In the rest of the world a bonus is defined as a reward or dividend of profits to employees. In Japan, however, the bonus is assumed to be a part of regular earnings, except for top management. In the recent past, the actual amount of bonus never decreases, even in hard times."[31]

She further emphasizes the traditional importance of the timing of the bonuses. In Japan both the summer festival and new year are traditional gift giving times; in addition, consumers tend to make major purchases during these periods. Employees use their bonuses to cover these expenses. Thus, "The bonus system is deeply rooted in [Japanese life] and an indispensable source of income."[32]

Even though bonuses for blue-collar employees are not strongly linked to performance, bonuses for white-collar employees are increasingly performance based. While they continue to retain elements of the traditional guaranteed payment, Japanese banks, automobile companies, and other large companies are beginning to base bonuses on corporate, unit, and individual performance, much like many U.S. companies. At the highest executive level, it is even becoming common for bonuses to be cut if the firm's performance slips. Indeed, poor corporate earnings is such a loss of face that some executives resign. Contrast this with many U.S. executives who continue to get pay increases while they drive their companies' performance down.[33]

Allowances.   The third characteristic of Japanese pay systems, the allowance, comes in a variety of forms: family allowances, commuting allowances, housing

---

[29] "Corporate Benefits as a Competitive Tool in Japan," *Japan Economic Institute Report* (Washington DC: Japan Economic Institute), 1990.

[30] Sano, "Changes and Continued Stability in Japanese HRM."

[31] Ibid.

[32] Magota, "The Bonus System in Japan."

[33] Graef S. Crystal, *In Search of Excess* (New York: W. W. Norton, 1991).

and geographic differential allowances, and so on.[34] Company housing, which often includes rent or mortgage subsidies as well as dormitories for single employees, is a substantial cost. Life-passage payments are made when an employee marries or experiences a death in the immediate family. Commuting allowance is also important. A recent survey reported that employees who took public transportation received about 9,000 yen (approximately $90 per month) for commuting. Family allowances include extra pay that varies with number of dependents. Toyota provides about 17,500 to 18,000 yen ($175 to $180) a month for the first dependent and about 4,500 to 5,500 yen ($45 to $55) for additional dependents.[35] Some employers even provide matchmaking allowances for interested employees.

Experience suggests that many of these allowances would be considered discriminatory in the United States. For example, housing allowances for unmarried women have traditionally been lower than men's because the women were expected to live with their parents. Many Japanese employers still expect women to retire upon marriage or motherhood. These practices and expectations appear to be changing, albeit slowly.

The history of some of these allowances reveals very pragmatic roots. But like many practices in the United States, the allowances remain long after the need. An example is the contemporary family allowance that originated as a "rice allowance" during the late 1940s and early 1950s. At that time, Japanese workers needed extra money to feed their families because of the country's hyperinflation.[36]

Legally Mandated Benefits

Legally mandated benefits in Japan include Social Security, unemployment, and workers' compensation. Although these three are similar to the United States, Japanese employers also pay premiums for mandated health insurance, preschool child support, and employment of the handicapped. The references include more detail on Japanese benefits.[37]

Changing and Building on Traditional Approaches

Japan's traditional seniority-based approach, based not on specific jobs or performance but rather on the length of service with a company, is changing. The traditional approach resulted in very similar treatment of all employees of the same age with similar education. However, contemporary pay systems are more complex. Aging work forces mean increased labor costs. Controlling labor costs

---

[34] Sangyo Rodo Chosasho, "Prevalence of Preferences," *Industry and Labor Research Center*, Chingin-Jijo, March 5, 1993.

[35] "Corporate Benefits as a Competitive Tool in Japan."

[36] Ibid.

[37] William M. Mercer, *International Benefit Guidelines.*

under a seniority-based system requires rapid expansion so that younger, lower-wage employees can also be hired in order to keep average labor costs down. The slowed expansion that Japan has been experiencing in the last few years, coupled with seniority-based pay, means that Japanese labor costs have climbed faster than their international competitors'. Faced with these pressures, many Japanese companies are trying to maintain *long-time* (rather than lifetime) employment while they also look for other ways to reward younger and more flexible employees. As a result, considerable variation in pay systems is beginning to emerge among Japanese companies.[38]

EXHIBIT 18.12   Strategic Similarities and Differences: An Illustrated Comparison

	Japan	*U.S.*
Objectives	Long-term focus High commitment Egalitarian—internal fairness Flexible work force Control cash flow with bonuses	Short/intermediate focus High commitment Performance—market—meritocratic Flexible work force Cost control; varies with performance
Internal consistency	Person based: age, ability, performance determines base pay Many levels Small pay differences	Work based: jobs, skills, accountabilities Fewer levels Larger pay differences
External competitiveness	Monitor age-pay charts Consistent with competitors	Market determines base pay Compete on variable and performance-based pay
Employee contribution	Bonuses vary with performance only at higher levels in organization Performance appraisal influences promotions and small portion of pay increases	Increases based on individual, unit, and corporate performance Increased percentage of total pay
Advantages	Supports low to normal/high commitment Greater predictability Flexibility—person based Performance over long term	Supports performance–competitor focus Costs vary with performance Encourages "wild ducks" (innovators) Focus on short-term payoffs (speed to market)
Disadvantages	High cost of aging work force Discourages unique contributors Discourages women and younger employees	Skeptical workers, less security Fosters "What's in it for me?" No reward for investing in long-term projects

---

[38] Sano, "Changes and Continued Stability in Japanese HRM."

Strategic Comparisons

Japanese and U.S. organizations appear to have different strategic approaches to pay. Exhibit 18.12 uses the basic strategic choices outlined in the pay model—objectives, internal consistency, competitiveness, contribution, and administration—as a basis for comparisons. Japanese organizations set pay objectives that focus on the long term (age and security), support high commitment (seniority–ability based), are more egalitarian (smaller pay differences), signal the importance of company and individual performance (company bonuses, individual promotions), and encourage flexible workers (person-based pay). U.S. companies, in contrast, focus on the short term (less job security); emphasize cost control (variable pay based on performance); reward performance improvement (individual, unit, and corporate), meritocracy, and innovation (individual rewards); and encourage flexibility (broadbanding and skill based).

These objectives are achieved by emphasizing different policies. U.S. firms are increasingly setting base pay according to market pricing (competitive position), the work (job and person), and employee contributions (performance-based pay). In Japan, person-based factors (seniority–ability and performance) are increasingly used to set base pay. Market comparisons are monitored in Japan, but internal consistency remains far more important.

Each approach has advantages and disadvantages. Clearly, the Japanese approach is consistent with low turnover/high commitment, greater acceptance of change, and the need to be flexible. U.S. firms face higher turnover (which is not always a disadvantage) and greater skepticism about change (i.e., what's in it for me?). U.S. firms clearly encourage innovation and wild ducks; they also recognize the enormous talent and contributions to be tapped from work force diversity. Japanese pay systems face challenges from the high costs associated with an aging white-collar work force, its limited use of women's capabilities, and emerging efforts to reward innovative individuals. The U.S. challenges include the impact of increased uncertainty and risk among employees, its short-term focus, and employees skepticism about change.

GLOBAL SNAPSHOTS

Discussing how companies approach pay plans in other countries in the same detail as we did the Japanese system requires another textbook. (Groan!) So Exhibit 18.13 offers some highlighted comparisons (sigh of relief . . .) based on the major strategic decisions in the pay model.

Internal Consistency.   Person-based systems are used to determine base pay in Japan and Korea and in high technology firms in Egypt and Mexico.[39] Most

[39] Gordon Betcherman, Kathryn McMullen, Norm Leckie, and Christina Caron, eds., *The Canadian Workplace in Transition* (Kingston, Ontario; IRC Press, 1994); "Focus on International

EXHIBIT 18.13 Global Comparisons

	China (PRC)	Egypt	Germany	India	Japan
Internal Consistency	• Hierarchical levels • Small differentials • Job based and negotiated with government agencies	• Relatively hierarchical • Skill/knowledge based, especially technical • Small differentials	• Relatively hierarchical • Primarily job based • Modest differentials between levels	• Job based and *caste based*; jobs at the bottom levels determined by the caste system • Higher level jobs are job based	• Person based; seniority–ability factors • Hierarchical with small differentials • Differences compound with tenure
External Competitiveness	• Lack of data and markets • Emphasis on preferential access to scarce goods and services • Government agencies control wages; shift to noncash and off-the-books forms	• Lack salary surveys • Government guarantees jobs with low pay to college graduates	• National rates negotiated by employer and union association • Government and Bundesbank major players in negotiations • Increasing interest in surveys and market data	• Oversupply of highly qualified labor, forcing wages down; many highly educated workers leave the country	• Comparisons within industry • Relative labor costs and work force productivity important factors • Private comparisons among Japanese firms • Consultant surveys among multinationals

Employee Contribution	• Growing interest in incentives based on individual and facility performance	• High interest in performance based; up to 40% of pay based on company results • High inflation and high taxes decrease impact of performance increases	• Increases based on seniority, inflation, and across-the-board guarantees • Increasing interest in performance bonuses, up to 20% in some cases • Performance small percentage of total pay	• Low-caste workers have little incentive to do better; excellence by the individual threatens the caste system and is not rewarded • Payment Bonus Act of 1965 requires profit sharing with a minimum of 8.33%	• Increased interest in individual merit and group-based pay • Traditional bonuses (twice yearly) used as variable cost • Performance based pay small percentage of total pay • Emerging use of performance appraisal
Benefits	• Major strategic tool; company provides services such as housing, showers, medical, scarce commodities, transportation, and day care	• Moderate mandatory benefits of vacation pay, medical, and retirement	• National health care and national pensions • High mandated; costly layoff severance allowance • Discretionary; cars	• Mandatory retirement and pension benefits • Typical package includes housing, traveling, and geographic allowances	• Mandated: national health care, and retirement; layoff allowances • Discretionary: commuting, housing, family, sports facilities, vacations retreats
Nature of Administration	• Centralized • Emphasize government connections • Focus on benefits/ services	• Government taxes and regulations limit the use of pay as a strategic tool • Centralized with low participation • Search for nontaxable "payments"	• Government policies and regulations major factor • Centralized • Less use of pay as strategic source of competitive advantage	• Government laws major factor; regardless of profit level or performance level, employee's pay cannot go down • Layoffs are illegal	• Increasingly using pay as strategic device • Tax regulations major influence; retaining allowances; only base pay included in pension, medical, retirement calculations

(continued)

Eхнівіт 18.13 *(concluded)*

	Korea	Mexico	Russia	Slovenia	United Kingdom
Internal Consistency	• Person based, seniority, ability, and competencies • Hierarchical with small differentials	• Relatively hierarchical levels • Primarily job based with skill based in high tech • Modest differentials	• Hierarchical • Appearance of job based • Small differentials	• Modest to low hierarchies • Small differentials • Job and skill based	• Relatively hierarchical levels • Primarily job based • Modest differences among levels
External Competitiveness	• Mobility among companies relatively common • Surveys of wages and labor costs • Competitive position important for attracting and retaining workers	• Competitive forces influencing pay of higher-skilled workers • Surveys based upon work conduct • Overall labor cost relatively low; yet, 10 to 25 percent premium for scarce talent	• Lacks markets and data; setting pay is guessing game • Personal negotiations based on expertise	• National negotiated rates with unions, employers, and the government • Rates paid above negotiated rate to attract needed talent	• Reduced reliance on national rates negotiated by employers and union associations; more on industry specific data • White-collar based on "London rates" • Increasing use of surveys and competitive market data
Employee Contribution	• Increasing use of performance-based pay • Companywide bonuses at least once a year	• Increases based on seniority, inflation, and across-the-board guarantees • Growing interest in performance based • Performance about 5 percent of total pay	• Transition from old, out-of-date piece rates and across-the-board government mandated increases • Facility level incentives	• Increasing use of profit sharing, gain-sharing, and performance appraisals	• Increase based on seniority, inflation, and across-the-board guarantees • Growing use of performance based (75 percent use individual based and 50 percent use unit or firm based) • Performance still small percentage of total pay

656

Benefits	• Mandatory national health care and retirement • Generally sparse benefits; few companies pay overtime or holidays	• Moderate mandatory medical, retirement, low cash allowances • Christmas bonus (15 days' pay) and vacation bonus (25 percent of pay) • Mandated profit sharing; 10 percent of pretax profits	• Major strategic tool; offer scarce goods and services, medical care, improved housing, access to quality products	• High mandated coverage: medical care, pensions, and vacations/holidays	• Slight trend away from company cars, though it is still a major symbol of status • National health care and pensions • Paid leaves (25 days) plus national holidays • Lunch and parking allowance
Nature of Administration	• Government policies and regulations not enforced stringently	• Government regulations major factor • Acquired rights; if a benefit or bonus is paid for two years, employee has a right to it • Centralized • Low costs and increased use of incentives as strategic aspects	• High inflation and uncertainty • Preferential access to scarce goods and service (nontaxed) • Individual negotiations	• Government policies major factor • Increased use of performance based as a strategic tool	• Government policies and regulations a major influence • Centralized and open • Early efforts at using pay strategically have not had impact on administration • Increasing effort to use employee reviews

companies in the EU and the United States use some form of job basis for setting base pay, though some careers (engineering and computer related) are based on person factors (type of degree, years since degree, maturity-curve performance). And knowledge and competency approaches are receiving increasing attention.

External Competitiveness.   North America and the United Kingdom remain relatively unique in the importance they place on labor and product-market competitors to set base pay. Japanese and Korean companies emphasize internal more than external factors.[40] As already noted, employers and union associations negotiate national rates of pay in many countries in Europe and Asia. These rates act as the going rates for entire industries. By establishing national rates for different types of work, pay is no longer a variable to be managed.

Employee Contributions.   An increased interest in performance-based pay seems to be a global trend. The percentage of total pay that is based on performance varies greatly due to tax rates, culture, and ideology. For example, the Communist Party objected to wage differences by saying they do no good and lead to social inequality. China rationalized communism with a Confucian quote: "Do not worry about scarcity only about unevenness." The United Kingdom and United States seem to place greatest emphasis on performance-based approaches.

Benefits.   Taxes and government regulation are major influences on the management of pay around the globe. In Mexico, an *acquired rights* law requires that if a benefit, service, or bonus is paid two years in a row, it becomes an employee's right.[41] So consultants caution employers new to Mexico to go slow with benefits and other services. Both India and Mexico mandate profit sharing; 10 percent

---

Benefits," *Employee Benefit Plan Review,* November 1994, pp. 32–37; Gilian Flynn, "HR in Mexico: What You Should Know," *Personnel Journal,* August 1994, pp. 34–44; Richard D. Kantor and Michael Richerson, "The Egyptian Compensation Environment: Where Change is the Only Constant," *Benefits and Compensation International,* March 1993, pp. 18–22; Arturo J. Fisher and Douglas J. Carey, "Mexico in the Dawn of NAFTA: The Human Resources Environment," *Journal of International Compensation and Benefits,* July–August 1994, pp. 9–15.

[40] Michael Byungnam Lee, "South Korea," in Raoul C. Nacamulli, Miriam Rothman, and Dennis R. Brisco, eds., *Industrial Relations Around the World* (New York: Walter DeGruyter, 1993), pp. 245–69; Korea Labor Institute, *Korea's Labor Unions* (Seoul, Korea: Korea Labor Institute, 1989); Korea Labor Institute, *Quarterly Labor Review* (Seoul, Korea: Korea Labor Institute, 1991); Michael Byungnam Lee, "Bonuses, Unions, and Labor Productivity in South Korea," *Journal of Labor Research,* in press; *Benefit Policies for Third Country Nationals, U.S. Expatriates, and Key Local Nationals* (New York: Kwasha Lipton, 1994); William Brown and Janet Walsh, "Pay Determination in Britain in the 1980s: The Anatomy of Decentralization," *Oxford Review of Economic Policy* 7, no. 1, pp. 44–59; Tony Buxton, Paul Chapman, and Paul Temple, *Britain's Economic Performance* (London: Routledge, 1994); Byong-moo Yang, "Trends, Problems and Directions for Improvement for Korean Industrial Relations," Presentation at forum on Labour-Management Cooperation, October 1994, Tokyo, Japan.

[41] Flynn, "HR in Mexico."

of pretax profits must be distributed to employees. In addition, most developed and emerging economies have some form of national health care supplied by employer- and employee-paid premiums.[42]

In centralized command-control economies that are experimenting with market-based approaches such as China, managing employee compensation presents unique challenges.[43] Government agencies still control base-pay determination, but noncash payments are highly valued by employees. A survey reported that after higher pay, Chinese employees say they want scarce goods and services such as housing; medical care; access to hard-currency goods like fresh fruit, meat, and fish; transportation; and allowances for meals, clothing, and laundry. Similar conditions existed in the United States in earlier periods. Ford Motor Company provided cafeterias, dentists, social workers, home economists, and English tutors to its work force in the 1920s and 1930s, since so many of the workers were immigrants who were unfamiliar with American customs.

Just a brief review of the differences in Exhibit 18.13 should convince you that international compensation involves more than exporting U.S.-style systems.

EXPATRIATE PAY

When multinational organizations decide to open facilities in an international location, one of the many decisions they face is the type of personnel to hire. International subsidiaries choose among a mix of expatriates (expats, someone whose citizenship is that of the employer's base country; for example, a Japanese citizen working for Sony in Toronto), third country nationals (TCNs, someone whose citizenship is neither the employer's base country nor the location of the subsidiary; for example, a German citizen working for Sony in Toronto), and local country nationals (LCNs, citizens of the country in which the subsidiary is located; for example, Canadian citizens working for Sony in Toronto). One obvious choice is to staff the subsidary with individuals whose citizenship corresponds to the country of origin for the subsidiary: LCNs. Hiring LCNs has advantages. The company saves relocation expenses and avoids concerns about employees adapting to the local culture. Employment of LCNs satisfies nationalistic demands for hiring locals. Only rarely do organizations decide that hiring LCNs is inappropriate.

Expats or TCNs may be brought in for a number of reasons. The foreign assignment may represent an opportunity for selected employees to develop an international perspective; the position may be sufficiently confidential that

[42] William M. Mercer, *International Benefit Guidelines;* "Focus on International Benefits," *Employee Benefit Plan Review;* "Corporate Benefits as a Competitive Tool in Japan."

[43] Paula DeLisle and Sherman Chin, "Remunerating Employees in China—The Complicated Task Faced by Foreign Firms," *Benefits and Compensation International*, September 1994, pp. 16–20; Irene Hau-siu Chow, "Chinese Workers' Attitudes towards Compensation Practices in the People's Republic of China," *Employee Relations* 14, no. 3 (1992), pp. 41–55.

information is only entrusted to a proven domestic veteran; the particular talent demanded for a position may not be readily available in the local labor pool. Exhibit 18.14 catalogues a number of reasons for asking employees to take work assignments in another country. Designing expatriate pay systems that help achieve such varied objectives is a challenge.

Only about 1 percent of the international work force comprised of U.S. and European multinational companies is expatriates. About 4.2 percent of the international work force for Japanese manufacturing companies are expatriates (i.e., Japanese nationals working in other countries). Sony manufacturing facilities in Italy employ mostly Italians, although a regional operations manager is a Japanese expatriate; Sony manufacturing facilities in Mexico employ mostly Mexicans. However, the plant manager and controller are Japanese expatriates. The greater use of expatriates by Japanese companies maintains greater control of the subsidiaries. However, there is some evidence that managerial job satisfaction and even profitability of the subsidiaries suffer as a result.[44]

Varying Objectives

Expatriates are a relatively small, yet critical and costly group of international employees; and the number of expatriates per large U.S. multinational company has declined over the past decade. In 1993, there were about 60 expatriates per U.S. multinational company, compared to about 120 per U.S. company in 1983.[45] There are two explanations for this decline. One is that the objectives for overseas assignments are shifting. Earlier, transferring technologies and the need for specific skills in scarce supply in local economies were the primary reasons for hiring expatriates. More recently, developing a global perspective among key employees has become more important. This shift is consistent with the increasing educational levels globally and the growing international importance of sales for U.S. firms. Indeed, our experience is that two very different groups of employees are receiving global assignments. One group is higher-level managers and executives who must make strategic decisions about global opportunities and competition. The other group is recent college graduates who receive relatively short overseas assignments as part of their career development.

Costs. It is a challenge to design a pay system for employees who are being assigned overseas to meet a variety of corporate objectives. In addition, expatriate assignments are expensive. For example, a company that sends a U.S. employee (base salary of $80,000) with a spouse and two children to London for three years can expect to spend $800,000 to $1,000,000. Obviously, the high cost of

---

[44] Vlado Pucik, "The Challenges of Globalization: The Strategic Role of Local Managers in Japanese-Owned U.S. Subsidiaries" (Working paper, Cornell University, 1993).

[45] *International Total Remuneration,* certification course T9 (Scottsdale, AZ: American Compensation Association, 1995); Cal Reynolds, "International Compensation," in *Compensation Guide,* ed. William A. Caldwell (Boston: Warren, Gorham and Lamont, 1994).

Exhibit 18.14 Why Expatriates Are Selected

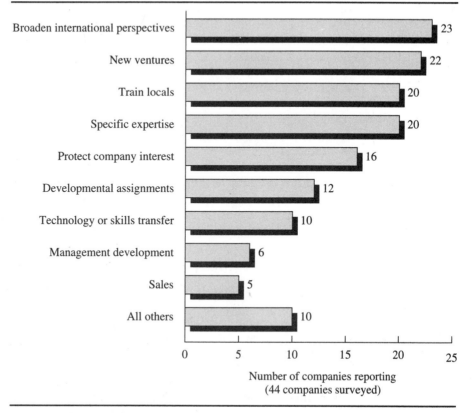

Number of companies reporting
(44 companies surveyed)

Source: Organization Resources Counselors Inc.

expatriate assignments needs to be offset by the value of the contributions the employee makes.[46]

Fairness.   Fairness is in the eye of the beholder. In expatriate compensation, fairness is measured against the compensation expatriates would have received had they stayed in their home country and by comparisons to the pay received by local nationals (i.e., Tanzanians manufacturing toothpaste in Tanzania for Colgate-Palmolive). The expatriate pay must be sufficient to encourage the employee to take the assignment yet not so attractive that local nationals will feel unfairly treated or that the expatriate will refuse any future reassignments. Expatriate compensation systems are forever trying to be like Goldilocks' porridge: not too high, not too low, but just right. However, the relevant standard

---

[46] "What It Costs to House Expatriates Worldwide" (New York: Runzheimer International, 1994).

for judging fairness may not be home-country treatment. It may be the pay of other expats, that is, the expat community, or it may be local nationals. And how do local nationals feel about the allowances and pay levels of their expat coworkers? Very little research tells us how expats and those around them judge the fairness of expat pay.[47]

Employee Preferences.   Beyond work objectives, costs, and fairness, an additional consideration is employees' preferences for international assignments. For many European and Asian companies, their home markets are a relatively small part of the total product market. So working in another country at some point in a career is part of understanding your market. Yet for many U.S. employees, leaving the United States means leaving the action. They may worry that expatriate experience sidetracks rather than enhances a career. Employees undoubtedly differ in their preferences for overseas jobs, and preferences can vary over time. Having children in high school, elderly parents to care for, divorce, and other life factors exert a strong influence on whether an offer to work overseas is a positive or negative opportunity. Research does inform us of the following:

- 68 percent of expatriates do not know what their jobs will be when they return home.
- 54 percent return to lower-level jobs. Only 11% are promoted.
- Only 5 percent believe their company values overseas experience.
- 77 percent have less disposable income when they return home.
- More than half of returning expatriates leave their company within one year.

Unfortunately, while research does highlight the problem, it does not offer much guidance for designers of expat pay systems.[48] Consequently, we are at the mercy of conjecture and beliefs.

Elements of Expatriate Compensation

A shopping list of items, such as those in Exhibit 18.15, that can make up expatriate compensation includes everything from household furnishing allow-

---

[47] Angelo DeNisi and T. P. Sommers, "In Search of Adam's Other: Re-Examination of Referents Used in the Evaluation of Pay," *Human Relations* 43 (1990), pp. 497–511.

[48] *Expatriate Dual Career Survey Report* (New York: Windham International and National Foreign Trade Council, 1992); Garry M. Wederspahn, "Costing Failures in Expatriate Human Resources Management," *Human Resource Planning* 15, no. 3, pp. 27–35; Steve Jones, "Lessons from the Relocation Experience of Early Transferees," *International Compensation and Benefits*, May/June 1993, pp. 60–64; Michael S. Schell and Ilene L. Dolins, "Dual-Career Couples and International Assignments," *International Compensation and Benefits*, November–December 1992, pp. 25–29; Carolyn Gould, "Can Companies Cut Costs by Using the Balance-Sheet Approach?" *International Compensation and Benefits*, July–August 1993, pp. 36–41; David E. Molnar, "Repatriating Executives and Keeping Their Careers on Track," *International Compensation and Benefits*, November–December 1994, pp. 31–35; Ken I. Kim, Hun-Joon Park, and Nori Suzuki, "Reward Allocations in the United States, Japan, and Korea: A Comparison of Individualistic and Collectivistic Cultures," *Academy of Management Journal* 33, no. 1 (1990), pp. 188–98.

EXHIBIT 18.15 Common Allowances in Expatriate Pay Packages

Financial Allowances
   Reimbursement for tax return preparation
   Tax equalization
   Housing differential
   Children's education allowance
   Temporary living allowance
   Goods and services differential
   Transportation differential
   Foreign service premium
   Household furnishing allowance
   Currency protection
   Mobility premium
   Home-leave allowance
   Stopover allowance
   Subsidized health and fitness facilities
   Hardship premium
   Completion bonus
   Assignment extension bonus
   Extended work week payment

Social Adjustment Assistance
   Emergency leave
   Home leave
   Language training (manager)
   Company car/driver
   Assistance with locating new home
   Access to high-quality, Western health care
   Club membership
   General personal services (e.g., translation)
   Personal security (manager and family)
   General culture-transition training (manager)
   Social events
   Career development and repatriation planning
   Training for local culture customs (manager)
   Orientation to community (manager and family)
   Counseling services
   Rest and relaxation leave
   Domestic staff (excluding child care)
   Use of company-owned vacation facilities

Family Support
   Language training (family)
   Assistance locating schools for children
   General culture-transition training (family)
   Training for local culture's customs (family)
   Child care providers
   Spousal employment in firm
   Assistance locating spousal employment outside firm

ances to language and culture training, spousal employment assistance, and rest and relaxation leaves for longer-term assignments. Usually such lists are organized into four major components: salary, taxes, housing, and general-services allowances and premiums.

Salary.   The base salary plus incentives (merit, eligibility for profit sharing, bonus plans, etc.) for expatriate jobs is usually determined via job evaluation or competency-based plans. 3M, for example, applies a recently designed international job evaluation plan for its international assignments. Common factors describe different 3M jobs around the world. With this system, the work of a regional HR manager in Brussels can be compared to the work of an HR manager in Austin, Texas, or Singapore. Most companies attempt to apply the procedures they use to value domestic operations to expatriate jobs.

Beyond salaries and incentives, the intent of the other components is to help keep expatriate employees financially whole and minimize the disruptions of the move. This basically means maintaining a standard of living about equal to their peers in their home or base country. This is a broad standard, one that has often resulted in very costly packages from the company's perspective, but often "good deals" for the expatriate.

Taxes.   Income earned in foreign countries has two potential sources of income tax liability.[49] With few exceptions (Saudi Arabia is one), foreign tax liabilities are incurred on income earned in foreign countries. For example, money earned in Japan is subject to Japanese income tax, whether earned by a Japanese or a Korean citizen. The other potential liability is the tax owed in the employees' home country. The United States has the dubious distinction of being the only developed country that taxes its citizens for income earned in another country, even though that income is taxed by the country in which it was earned. So money beyond $70,000 earned in Japan by an American citizen is subject to both Japanese income tax and U.S. income tax. Employers handle this through *tax equalization*.[50] The employer takes the responsibility of paying whatever income taxes are due to either the host country and/or the home country. Taxes are deducted from employees' earnings up to the same amount of taxes they would pay had they remained in their home country.

This allowance can be a substantial amount. For example, the marginal tax rates in Belgium, the Netherlands, and Sweden can run between 70 to 90 percent. So if the expatriate is sent to a lower-tax country (lower than the U.S.), the company keeps the difference. If the expatriate's assignment is in a higher-tax country, the company makes up the difference. The logic here is that if the

---

[49] Monica M. Sabo, "Tax-Effective Compensation Planning for International Assignments," *International Compensation and Benefits*, January–February 1995, pp. 24–28; Charles J. Boyland, "A Short Guide to U.S. Expatriate Taxes," *Journal of International Compensation and Benefits*, July–August 1992, pp. 45–50.

[50] Reynolds, "International Compensation."

employee kept the windfall from being assigned to a low-tax country, then getting this person to accept assignments elsewhere would become difficult. Additionally, the unearned windfall has the potential to create a sense of unfairness among other employees (local nationals and other expatriates). Tax equalization takes income tax considerations out of the equation when an employee is deciding whether to accept an expatriate position.

Housing.   Most international companies pay allowances for housing or provide company-owned housing for expatriates. "Expatriate colonies" often grow up in sections of major cities where international companies tend to locate their expatriates. The difficulty comes in determining what is appropriate housing, and in some cases, finding affordable versions of it. Depending on the type of package used, an employee may be given some or all of the choice in the matter. Our experience is that this allowance is a very important part of the expatriate's compensation package, especially for American employees. Americans often face challenges adapting to relatively less spacious conditions compared to expatriates from other countries. Japanese citizens working for Toshiba in the U.S. are often delighted with the available housing when coming to the United States, since it tends to be more spacious than what is available in Tokyo. Perhaps Americans take their wide open spaces for granted. Providing expatriates with appropriate housing seems to have a major impact on the success of the assignment.

Service Allowances and Premiums.[51]   A friend in Moscow cautions that when we take the famed Moscow subway, we must be sure to pay the fare at the beginning of the ride. The reason is that inflation is so high that if we wait to pay until the end of the ride, the fare will be more than we can afford! Cost of living allowances, club memberships, transportation assistance, child care and education, spousal employment, local culture training, and personal security are some of the many service allowances and premiums expatriates receive.

The logic supporting these allowances is that foreign assignments require the expatriate to (1) work with less direct supervision than a domestic counterpart, (2) often live and work in strange and sometimes uncongenial surroundings, and (3) represent the employer in the host country. The size of the premium is a function of both the expected hardship and hazards in the host country and the type of job. So an assignment in London will probably yield less service and premium allowances than one in Tehran, where Death to Americans Day is still a national holiday.[52] Balance against this the objectives for the expatriate assignment and the type of job. A more senior career expatriate assigned for three to five years to manage a joint venture in Tehran will receive very different service and premium allowances than a newly graduated software engineer on an 18-month product design and support assignment in London.

---

[51] *Benefit Policies for Third Country Nationals, U.S. Expatriates, and Key Local Nationals.*
[52] *Guide to Major Holidays Around the Globe* (Zurich: Union Bank of Switzerland, 1992).

Some research tells us that the components of expatriate compensation packages do affect expenses, commitment to the employer, job satisfaction, and willingness to accept other assignments.[53] A recent study reported that expatriates' beliefs about how sufficient the allowances were plus their perceptions of the employers' support for their situation influences their commitment and intentions. Thus, managing the implicit psychological contract via good communications is an important part of expatriate compensation.

The Balance Sheet Approach

Most North American, European, and Japanese global firms use the balance sheet approach to pay expatriates.[54] As you can tell from the name, this approach borrows from accounting, where credits and debits must balance. It is based on the premise that employees on overseas assignments should have the same spending power as employees in the home country. Therefore, the home country is the standard for all payments. The approach has three objectives:

1. Ensure mobility of expatriate talent to global assignments as cost effectively as feasible.
2. Ensure that expatriates neither gain nor lose financially.
3. Minimize adjustments required of expatriates and their dependents.

Of these, the last two, minimizing financial effects and adjustments, seem to receive the major emphasis. Until recently, efforts to link expatriate pay to improving performance and cost effectiveness received less attention.

Exhibit 18.16 depicts the balance sheet approach. Home country salary is the first column. The salary (based on job evaluation, market surveys, merit and incentives) is divided into the components discussed earlier (taxes, housing, service allowances and premiums) plus a "reserve" to cover savings or other financial obligations (e.g., alimony) or discretionary payments. These components are used because each varies as salary and number of dependents change. As salary increases, taxes and reserves may increase, but the percentage of salary going for housing and goods and services may decline. As number of dependents increase, percent salary going for reserve may decrease, and housing and goods and services increase.

Note that the proportion set for each of the components are *norms* (i.e., assumed to be "normal" for the typical expatriate) set to reflect consumption patterns in the home country. They are not actual expenditures. These norms are based on surveys conducted by consulting firms. Using these norms is supposed to

---

[53] Richard A. Guzzo, Katherine A. Noonan, and Efrat Elron, "Expatriate Managers and the Psychological Contract," *Journal of Applied Psychology* 7, no. 4 (1994), pp. 617–26; Rosalie Tung, "Selection and Training Procedures of U.S., European, and Japanese Multinationals," *California Management Review* 25 (1982), pp. 57–71.

[54] Reynolds, "International Compensation."

Exhibit 18.16   Balance Sheet Approach

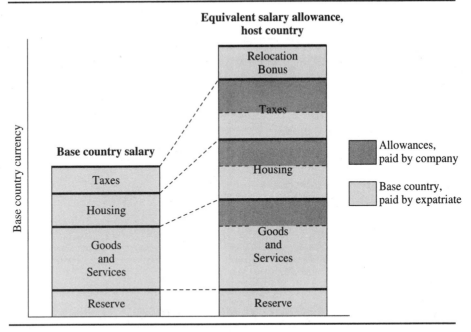

avoid negotiating with each individual. But any experienced expatriate will tell you no one is "typical"; this approach permits a lot of flexibility.

So now two basic building blocks for expatriate salaries are in place: the home country's salary for the job the expatriate will be doing plus the norms of home-country expenditures (four categories) for someone earning that salary. If any building block is wrong, the rest of the system is also wrong.

The next building block is the equivalent costs experienced by the typical expatriate in the host country where the assignment is located. For example, if a profile for a manager earning $80,000 shows typical housing costs of $2,000 a month in the United States, the expatriate will be expected to pay $2,000 a month for housing in the host country. If similar housing costs $3,000, the company pays the difference. In the illustration, taxes, housing, and goods and services components are all greater in the host country than in the home country. The expatriate bears the same level of costs (white area of column two) as at home. The employer is responsible for the additional costs (shaded area). (Changing exchange rates among currencies are considered in these allowance calculations.)

Despite the inherent difficulties in comparing apples and oranges (and other goods and services), most major companies use some index of cost of living abroad provided by consulting firms, the State Department, or the United Nations. For example, Runzheimer International supplies comparative cost of living data for

EXHIBIT 18.17   What It Costs to House Expatriates Worldwide

This chart shows typical annual housing costs of relocated employee families based on a U.S. expatriate family of four, having a moderate base salary. The housing costs listed coincide with typical housing costs for both homes or apartments rented by the expatriate families. Homes that expatriates rent vary in size from three to four bedrooms, depending on location. In addition to rental costs, the annual expenses include utilities, insurance, maintenance, and taxes.

Location	Total Annual Housing Cost
Tokyo	$ 118,200
Hong Kong	84,645
Paris	71,359
London	51,634
Caracas	46,258
Frankfurt	46,083
Mexico City	44,806
Rio de Janeiro	38,195
Chicago	28,894

Source: Runzheimer International.

different cities around the globe.[55] A $75,000 cost for a typical family of four in Chicago translates into about $41,000 in Warsaw, $73,000 in Rome, $151,000 in Seoul, and $210,000 in Tokyo. Exhibit 18.17 shows recent Runzheimer comparisons for housing costs.

Relocation Incentive.   The balance sheet approach is really designed to equalize the purchasing power of expatriates in similar jobs across the globe with what they would have in their home country. However, equalizing pay may not motivate an employee to move to another country, particularly if the new location has less personal appeal. Therefore, many employers also offer some form of financial incentive or bonus to encourage the move. Column 2 of Exhibit 18.16 shows relocation bonuses or lump sum payments that some companies use at each transfer or move. These bonuses typically equal around three months of base pay. Four out of five U.S. multinational corporations pay relocation bonuses to induce people to take expatriate assignments.[56]

However, if gaining international experience is really one of the future competencies required by organizations, then the need for such premiums ought to be less, since the overseas experience should increase the likelihood of future promotions. However, research reveals that U.S. expatriates feel their U.S. organizations still do not appreciate or value their international expertise.[57] So the

---

[55] Runzheimer International, "What It Costs to House Expatriates Worldwide."

[56] Ibid.; also *Expatriate Dual Career Survey Report* (New York: Windham International and National Foreign Trade Council, 1992).

[57] Tung, "Selection and Training Procedures of U.S., European, and Japanese Multinationals."

rhetoric of the value of global competencies has yet to match the reality; hence the need for relocation incentives.

Alternatives to Balance Sheet Approach.   The balance sheet approach was refined in the 1960s and 1970s when most expatriates were technical employees of U.S. oil companies. But the business environment and the reasons for expatriate assignments have changed since then. Consequently, many employers are exploring changes to their traditional balance sheet approach. The wider variety of objectives for international assignments, costs, administrative complexities, and the reluctance of expatriates to change to a location with fewer allowances have pushed organizations to try alternatives. A few of these alternatives are described below.[58]

Negotiation simply means the employer and employee find a mutually agreeable package. This approach is most common in smaller firms with very few expatriates. The arrangements tend to be relatively costly (or generous, de pending on your point of view), create comparability problems when other people are asked to locate overseas ("but Mike and Sarah got . . ."), and need to be renegotiated with each transfer ("You are going to take away my chauffeur and three domestic servants here in the Philippines just to send me to London? Guess again!").

Another alternative, *localization*, ties salary to the host (local) country salary scales and provides some cost of living allowances for taxes, housing, and dependents. The allowances tend to be similar to those under the balance sheet, but the salary can vary. The down side is that individual salaries vary with the location (average rate for an engineer in Geneva is $55,000 compared to $41,300 in Rome and $32,000 in Bristol) rather than with the job or performance.

While the balance sheet approach ties salary to the home country, the *modified balance sheet* ties salary to a region (Asia-Pacific, Europe, North America, Central America, and South America). The logic is that if an employee of a global business who relocates from San Diego, California, to Portland, Maine, receives only a moving allowance, why should all the extras be paid for international moves of far less distance (i.e., from Germany to Spain)? In Europe, many companies no longer view those European managers who work outside their home country as expats. Instead, they are Europeans running their European businesses.

Another common modification is to decrease allowances over time. The logic is that the longer the employee is in the host country, the standard of living should become closer to that of a local employee. For example, if Americans eat a $10 pizza twice a week in the United States, should they eat a $30 pizza

---

[58] Jack W. Eads and Douglas J. Carey, "Expatriate Compensation: Managing the Bottom Line," *International Compensation and Benefits*, May–June 1994, pp. 27–33; Mary E. Myhr, "Linking Expatriate Pay to Assignment Objectives," *International Compensation and Benefits*, March–April 1994, pp. 37–43; S. E. Wimbush, "Expatriate Compensation and the High Price of Old Assumptions," *International Compensation and Benefits*, March–April 1994, pp. 51–56.

EXHIBIT 18.18   Total Remuneration—Chief Executive Officer

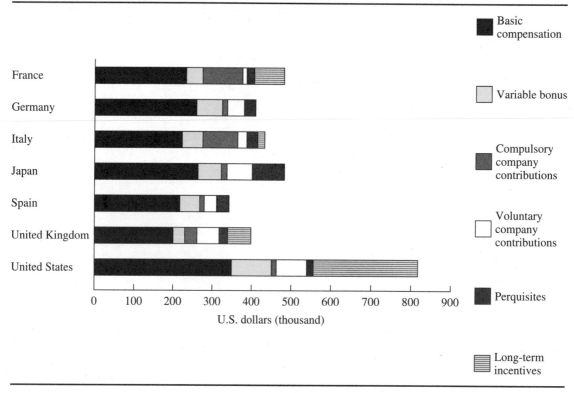

Source: Towers Perrin Inc.

twice a week in Tokyo, at the employer's expense? More typically, after a couple of months, the expatriate will probably learn where the nationals find cheaper pizza or will develop a taste for the local cuisine; in any event, the yearnings for Chicago-style deep dish with pepperoni ought to diminish. So while these modified plans minimize the impact of changes in standards of living at the first stage (one to three years) of the assignment, after three to five years some of the allowance becomes equal to allowances paid to local national employees. The major exception seems to be taxes and housing. The main purpose of the modified balance sheet seems to be to reduce costs; it pays little attention to performance, ensuring fairness, or satisfying preferences of expats.

The *lump-sum/cafeteria approach* offers expats more choices. This approach sets salaries according to the home-country system and simply offers employees lumps of money to offset differences in standards of living. So, for example, a company will still calculate differences in cost of living. But instead of breaking them into housing, transportation, goods and services, and so on, the employee simply receives a total allowance. Perhaps one employee will trade less spacious housing for private schooling and tutors for the children; another employee will make different choices. The logic is to avoid paying for items the employee does not value. These approaches may offer employees flexibility to minimize their taxes. We know of one expatriate, for example, who purchased a villa and a winery in Italy with his allowance. He has been reassigned to Chicago, but still owns and operates his winery. This arrangement was probably not an objective of the expatriate pay system, yet he made trade-offs in his living arrangements to retain most of his lump sum.

Expatriate Systems → Objectives? *Quel Dommage!*

Talk to experts in international compensation, and you soon get into complexities of taxes, exchange rates, housing differences, and the like. What you do not hear is how the pay system affects competitive advantage, customer satisfaction, quality, or other performance concerns. They do emphasize maintaining employee purchasing power and minimizing disruptions and inequities. But the lack of attention to improving performance or ensuring that the expatriate assignment is consistent with organization objectives remains.

BORDERLESS WORLD → BORDERLESS PAY?

Many multinational corporations are attempting to create a cadre of global managers, managers who operate anywhere in the world in a borderless manner.[59] To support this flexibility, some are also designing borderless or at least regionalized pay systems. One testing ground for this approach is the EU. One of the difficulties with borderless pay is that base pay levels and the other components depend so much on cultural attitudes about executive pay. Exhibit 18.18 compares the components of total remuneration among CEOs in different countries.[60] Note that the major differences are the overall levels among countries (with the U.S. sticking out like a sore thumb) and the use of long-term incentives (stock options). Several EU countries, notably Germany and Spain, as well as Japan, do not use long-term incentives, primarily because they are taxed so heavily. Nevertheless, perhaps the strongest pressure to harmonize managerial pay systems is that managers in global companies are no longer expatriates from their home countries but true global managers running global businesses.

Focusing on expatriate compensation may blind companies to the issue of adequate rewards for employees who are seeking global career opportunities. Ignoring such employees causes them to focus only on the local operations and pay less attention to the broader goals of the global firm. It is naive to expect

---

[59] Vlado Pucik, Noel Tichy, and Carole K. Barnett, eds., *Globalizing Management* (New York: Wiley, 1992).

[60] Takao Kato, "Chief Executive Compensation and Corporate Groups in Japan: New Evidence from Micro Data," *International Journal of Industrial Organization*, in press; Laura Mazur, "Europay," *Across the Board*, January 1995, pp. 40–43.

commitment to a long-term global strategy in which local executives have little input and receive limited benefits. Paradoxically, attempts to localize top management in subsidiaries may reinforce the gap in focus between local and global management.

A successful global organization must learn from its experiences in each locality in order to become truly global rather than "multilocal." Consequently, a pay system that helps the organization achieve this objective is required. At least a partial disassociation of pay from job descriptions may help foster behavior consistent with the notion of a borderless organization.

While HR systems in Japanese, U.S., and European multinationals may be strikingly dissimilar, they share a challenge of rewarding potentially promising employees with adequate opportunities that lead to more responsibility and opportunities for career growth. The successful managerial mix of locals, third country nationals, and home-office employees is a goal that has so far eluded most of the multinationals. Those who do manage to mobilize global human resources will gain a substantial competitive edge. However, global utilization of managerial skills will probably not be achieved without a properly structured global reward system.[61]

Summary

Studying employee compensation only in your neighborhood, city, or country is like a horse with blinders. Removing the blinders by adopting a global perspective will deepen your understanding of local or national issues. Anyone interested in compensation needs to adapt a global perspective. The internationalization of businesses, financial markets, trade agreements, and even labor markets is affecting every workplace and every employment relationship. And employee compensation, so central to the workplace, is embedded in the political–socioeconomic arrangements found in each nation—the social contract. Examining employee compensation in the framework of the implicit social contracts offers insights into various approaches to pay.

Any attempt to manage employee compensation to help achieve organization success and competitive advantage while sustaining fair treatment for employees needs to take place within the changing social contracts that are occurring globally.

The basic premise of this book has been that compensation systems have a profound impact on individual behavior, organization success, and social well-being. We believe this holds true within all national boundaries and among nations as well.

---

[61] Pucik, Tichy, and Barnett, eds., *Globalizing Management.*

YOUR TURN:

INTERNATIONAL COMPENSATION

Your Assignment

1. Recommend a new compensation policy that will attract and retain U.S. engineers to the Madrid office.
2. Analyze and assess the present policy on expatriates, specifically the mix of U.S. expatriates and local country nationals (LCNs).

The following information is provided for use in this case:

1. A memo outlining Medico's present expatriate pay policy.
2. Some definitions of pay elements in the expatriate policy.
3. Letter from a consultant describing approaches to expatriate pay.
4. A memo from a former Medico expatriate outlining reasons for quitting.

Use this information to answer the questions at the end of the case.

Background

Medico Instruments is a manufacturer of specialty medical instruments. The CEO has asked you to look at their expatriate pay system. The company is headquartered in Provo, Utah, with branch offices all over the world. Many of these offices are staffed by some United States citizens, called expatriates, who work in these foreign locations, usually on a temporary basis. The rest of the office is staffed by local country nationals (LCNs), who are citizens of the country in which the office is located.

By an examination of internal Medico memos and discussions with their HR department, you learned that last week, one of the U.S. expatriates, an instruments engineer, quit in Madrid. This made three voluntary quits in six months for the Madrid office. All three expatriates cited low pay among the reasons for their departure.

Medico InterOffice Memorandum

Here is the summary you requested of the features we presently offer to employees working in our overseas offices. Most of the policy was updated two years ago. We follow a "balance sheet" approach with the following additional elements:

- A pre-move visit to the foreign location for the employee and his/her spouse.
- Pre-move cultural and language training for employees and their families.
- Provision of a company-paid car in the foreign location for the duration of the employee's stay.

- Shipping and/or storage costs for the employee's belongings.
- Emergency travel arrangements in case of death or illness of a family member back in the United States.

The following is compensation information you requested about our expatriate engineers in Madrid. Please note that when this plan was implemented, the dollar was worth 140 pesetas (PTA).

	Pesetas	U.S. Dollars
Base salary	$10,920,000	$ 78,000
Profit sharing	280,000	2,000
Foreign service premium	700,000	5,000
Tax equalization	574,000	4,100
Housing allowance	980,000	7,000
Subtotal	*13,454,000*	*96,100*
Benefits	3,640,000	26,000
Total	$17,094,000	$122,100

From: The Gray Group
To: Medico Instruments

Here is the information you requested on the different types of expatriate plans.

Balance Sheet Approach

This is by far the most common method used to pay expatriates. It attempts to enable the expatriate to maintain a standard of living roughly equivalent to the standard of living prior to taking the assignment. Expenses are broken down into four major categories: Income taxes, housing, goods and services, and reserve (or as discretionary accounts, e.g., savings, investments, etc.). Each component is measured in home country currency and varies with income level and family size. Costs of comparable income taxes, housing, and goods and services are then measured in the host country, and the expatriate is "equalized" to the base country for each component.

Here is an example based upon the information you sent me regarding the Madrid location.

	U.S. Expenditures	Madrid Equivalent	Allowance in U.S. Dollars
Taxes	$17,000	$ 20,000	$ 3,000
Housing	13,000	21,000	8,000
Goods and services	34,000	40,000	6,000
Discretionary account	24,000	24,000	—
Total	$88,000	$105,000	$17,000

Notice that total U.S. expenditures were $88,000, about equivalent to the employee's salary (excluding benefits). The company pays the expatriate the amounts in Allowance (the third column) plus usual salary (column 1). Therefore, the expatriate will be paid $105,000. However, the purchasing power of the expatriate will be about the same as it was back in the United States at a salary of $88,000. The intent is that financially, the expat will neither gain nor lose.

The balance sheet has been criticized as too complex and too expensive: the expat ends up spending the extra allowance. An alternative is simply lump the allowance into base and incentives.

Lump-Sum Approach

In this method, the company provides the expatriate with an amount of money (a lump sum), in addition to base pay and any incentive pay, that the expatriate can spend in any way. This method is similar to the balance sheet approach in that many of the calculations to determine the lump are the same. However, the major difference is that all of the money can be spent on one thing without drastically affecting the compensation. For example, under a lump-sum approach, choosing to live in a small apartment would free up funds for other items. But under the balance sheet approach, the smaller apartment would mean a smaller allowance. So there is little incentive to not spend the entire allowance.

The major drawback to lump sum is that variations in currency exchange rates may severely cut buying power; it depends upon which goods the lump-sum calculation is based.

Cafeteria Style

This method is very similar to the lump-sum approach, except that the employer offers a number of options the employee can choose from. Usually a list is created, and expatriates are given a limit on the number of options they can choose. This method only works if it does not force expatriates to choose between two highly desirable options such as a life insurance policy and home leave.

Please note that all methods are designed to keep the expats purchasing power the same on assignment as in their home country. The expat allowances are not based on performance or what competitors do, but rather on the estimates of a particular location's living costs. However, competitors' practices can be surveyed to gauge your practices.

Medico InterOffice Memorandum

To: C. Me
From: Seedy Rom, Project Engineer
Re: Expatriate Pay

I was an expatriate on assignment in Madrid only four months ago. However, I could not stand to live there any longer, so I requested a transfer back to stateside. I have a wife and two small children, and I could no longer expect them to face the poor living standards and working conditions in Madrid.

As my records should show, my performance ratings have been consistently superior and my supervisors reported that I was due for a promotion in 3 months. My decision to leave is based on my pay.

I recognize that my pay package appears very large compared to the one I had in the States. Yet, it was very expensive to support my family and myself here in Madrid. I wanted to be able to provide my family everything they had in the States. I should be able to do that. My family should not suffer just because I accepted an assignment in Madrid.

I was also made to feel very uncomfortable at work. Most of the other workers there were Spanish. While they didn't really know the amount I was making, I always felt they had a good idea. They made considerably less than I did, even though they were doing the same job I was. I felt they resented me, primarily because of the differences in compensation. This made it difficult to work with them.

Finally, it was not very clear what my role would be when I returned to the States. I may not have my old job waiting for me when I return.

Just for your information, here are some comparative prices. Note the size of the allowance required to offset the differences in costs.

Tuition at an English speaking private school comparable to home country education

Madrid	$1,400,000 pesetas per year	$10,000 per year
United States		7,000 per year

Required allowance: $3,000

3 bedroom, 2 bath duplex with community pool and tennis facilities

Madrid	$23,800,000 pesetas	$170,000
United States		160,000

Required allowance: $10,000

2,000 sq ft single dwelling home with full yard

Madrid	$42,000,000 pesetas	$300,000
Provo		260,000

Required allowance: $40,000

These data make my point about Medico's low expatriate allowances. My current salary is $80,000 (including my $2,000 profit sharing bonus). My housing allowance is only $7,000 and the foreign service premium is only $5,000. Just my children's school and my housing exceeds this $12,000 allowance by $1,000. A comparison:

	Actual Cost	Medico Allowance
Children's schooling	$ 3,000	$ 5,000 (total FS premium)
Housing in duplex	10,000	7,000
	$13,000	$12,000

A thousand dollar shortfall just on these two items! I had to pay for the opportunity to work in Spain!

Some Definitions

Foreign Service Premium   Financial incentive to induce an employee to take an assignment overseas. In this period of globalization, many companies have abandoned this premium, theorizing that employees should be pleased to have the chance to work abroad.

Hardship Premium   Financial incentive to induce an employee to take an assignment in difficult or dangerous living conditions. Usually between 10 and 25 percent of base salary, it is sometimes referred to as hazard pay.

Housing Allowance   Set sum of money used for accommodations, or in very lengthy assignments (3 years+), buy a place to live.

Tax Protection   The company agrees to pay taxes for any amount over what the employee paid in the home country. If the tax amount is less than the employee paid at home, employee usually gets to keep the windfall.

Tax Equalization   The company deducts what the employee used to pay in taxes from base salary and agrees to pay all taxes and fees while the employee is on assignment abroad.

Questions

Prepare a memo that includes the following:

1. Your preliminary evaluation and analysis of expatriate pay at Medico. Critical problems to address in Medico's expat pay plan include: Should Medico provide some hardship premium for all assignments? Should Medico match its competitors' policies? What is the primary objective of the Medico expat plan: Motivate volunteers for foreign assignments? Make foreign assignments a "great deal"? Encourage a small contingent of employees to become permanent foreign workers?

2. Your recommendations. For example, would you recommend increasing the emphasis on base pay, short-term, or long-term incentives? What is your rationale?

3. What additional information do you recommend Medico collects before making its final decision? How would you use this information? Please be specific.

Glossary of Terms

Ability Refers to an individual's capability to engage in a specific behavior.

Ability to Pay The ability of a firm to meet employee wage demands while remaining profitable; a frequent issue in contract negotiations with unions. A firm's ability to pay is constrained by its ability to compete in its product market.

Access Discrimination Focuses on the staffing and allocation decisions made by employers. It denies particular jobs, promotions, or training opportunities to qualified women or minorities. This type of discrimination is illegal under Title VII of the Civil Rights Act of 1964.

Across-the-Board Increases A general adjustment that provides equal increases to all employees.

Adjective Checklist An individual (or job) rating technique. In its simplest form, it is a set of adjectives or descriptive statements. If the employee (job) possesses a trait listed, the item is checked. A rating score from the checklist equals the number of statements checked.

Age Discrimination in Employment Act (ADEA) of 1967 (Amended 1978, 1986, and 1990) Makes nonfederal employees age 40 and over a protected class relative to their treatment in pay, benefits, and other personnel actions. The 1990 amendment is called the *Older Workers Benefit Protection Act.*

Agency Theory A theory of motivation that depicts exchange relationships in terms of two parties: agents and principals. According to this theory, both sides of the exchange will seek the most favorable exchange possible and will act opportunistically if given a chance. As applied to executive compensation, agency theory would place part of the executive's pay at risk, to motivate the executive (agent) to act in the best interests of the shareholders (principals), rather than in the executive's own self-interests.

All-Salaried Work Force Both exempt employees (exempt from provisions of the Fair Labor Standards Act), who traditionally are paid a salary rather than an hourly rate, and nonexempt employees receive a prescribed amount of money each pay period that does not primarily depend on the number of hours worked.

Alternation Ranking A job evaluation method that involves ordering the job description alternately at each extreme. All the jobs are considered. Agreement is reached on which is the most valuable, then the least valuable. Evaluators alternate between the next most valued and next least valued and so on until the jobs have been ordered.

American Compensation Association (ACA) A non-profit organization for training compensation professionals.

Appeals Procedures Mechanism created to handle pay disagreements. They provide a forum for employees and managers to voice their complaints and receive a hearing.

Balance Sheet   A method for compensating expatriates based upon the belief that the employee not suffer financially for accepting a foreign-based assignment. The expatriate's pay is adjusted so that the amounts of the financial responsibilities the expatriate had prior to the assignment are kept at about the same level while on assignment—the company pays for the difference.

Base Pay   *See* Base Wage.

Base Wage   The basic cash compensation that an employer pays for the work performed. Tends to reflect the value of the work itself and ignore differences in individual contributions.

Basic Pay Policies   Include decisions on the relative importance of (1) internal consistency, (2) external competitiveness, (3) employee contributions, and (4) the administration of the pay system. These policies form the foundation for the design and administration of pay systems and serve as guidelines for managing pay to accomplish the system's objectives.

Bedeaux Plan   Individual incentive plan that provides a variation on straight piecework and standard hour plans. Instead of timing an entire task, a Bedeaux plan requires determination of the time required to complete each simple action of a task. Workers receive a wage incentive for completing a task in less than a standard time.

Behaviorally Anchored Rating Scales (BARS)   Variants on standard rating scales in which the various scale levels are anchored with behavioral descriptions directly applicable to jobs being evaluated.

Benchmark Conversion   Matching survey jobs by applying the employer's plan to the external jobs and then comparing the worth of the external job with its internal "match."

Benchmark (or Key) Jobs   A prototypical job, or group of jobs, used as reference points for making pay comparisons within or without the organization. Benchmark jobs have well-known and stable contents; their current pay rates are generally acceptable, and the pay differentials among them are relatively stable. A group of benchmark jobs, taken together, contains the entire range of compensable factors and is accepted in the external labor market for setting wages.

Benefit Ceiling   A maximum payout for specific benefit claims (e.g., limiting liability for extended hospital stays to $150,000).

Benefit Cutbacks   Similar to wage concessions, negotiations by some employers with employees to eliminate or reduce employer contributions to selected benefits options.

Best Pay Practices   Compensation practices that allow employers to gain preferential access to superior human resource talent and competencies (i.e., valued assets), which in turn influence the strategies the organization adopts.

BLS   *See* Bureau of Labor Statistics.

Bonus   A lump-sum payment to an employee in recognition of goal achievement.

Bottom Up Approach to Pay Budgeting   Under this approach individual employees' pay rates for the next plan year are forecasted and summed to create an organization's total budget.

Broadbanding   Collapsing a number of salary grades into a smaller number of broad grades with wide ranges.

Budget   A plan within which managers operate and a standard against which managers' actual expenditures are evaluated.

Bureau of Labor Statistics   A major source of publicly available pay data. It also publishes the Consumer Price Index.

Cafeteria (Flexible) Benefit Plan   A benefit plan in which employees have a choice as to the benefits they receive within some dollar limit. Usually a common core benefit package is required (e.g., specific minimum levels of health, disability, retirement, and death benefit) plus elective programs from which the employee may select a set dollar amount. Additional coverage may be available through employee contributions.

Capital Appreciation Plans   *See* Long-Term Incentives.

Career Paths   Refers to the progression of jobs within an organization.

Central Tendency   A midpoint in a group of measures.

Central Tendency Error   A rating error that occurs when a rater consistently rates a group of employees at or close to the midpoint of a scale irrespective of true score performance of ratees. Avoiding extremes (both high and low) in ratings across employees.

Churn *See* Turnover Effect.

Civil Rights Act Title VII of the Civil Rights Act of 1964 prohibits discrimination in terms and conditions of employment (including benefits) that is based on race, color, religion, sex, or national origin.

Civil Rights Act of 1991 Reestablishes the standards for proving discrimination that had been in general use before the 1989 Supreme Court rulings. Allows jury trials and damage awards.

Claims Processing Begins when employee asserts that a specific event (e.g., disablement, hospitalization, unemployment) has occurred and demands that the employer fulfill a promise for payment. As such, a claims processor must first determine whether the act has, in fact, occurred.

Classification Job evaluation method that involves slotting job descriptions into a series of classes or grades that cover the range of jobs and that serve as a standard against which the job descriptions are compared.

Clone Error Giving better ratings to individuals who are like the rater in behavior or personality.

Coinsurance Employees share in the cost of a benefit provided to them.

Commission Payment tied directly to achievement of performance standards. Commissions are directly tied to a profit index (sales, production level) and employee costs; thus, they rise and fall in line with revenues.

Comparable Worth A doctrine that maintains that women performing jobs judged to be equal on some measure of inherent worth should be paid the same as men, excepting allowable differences, such as seniority, merit, and production-based pay plans, and other non-sex-related factors. Objective is to eliminate use of market in setting wages for jobs held by women.

Compa-Ratio An index that helps assess how managers actually pay employees in relation to the midpoint of the pay range established for jobs. It estimates how well actual practices correspond to intended policy. Calculated as the following ratio:

$$\text{Compa-Ratio} = \frac{\text{Average rates actually paid}}{\text{Range midpoint}}$$

Comparators Used in Ontario, Canada's, pay equity legislation. Refers to jobs deemed appropriate for wage comparisons between male- and female-dominated job classifications.

Compensable Factors Job attributes that provide the basis for evaluating the relative worth of jobs inside an organization. A compensable factor must be work related, business related, and acceptable to the parties involved.

Compensating Differentials Economic theory that attributes the variety of pay rates in the external labor market to differences in attractive as well as negative characteristics in jobs. Pay differences must overcome negative characteristics to attract employees.

Compensation All forms of financial returns and tangible services and benefits employees receive as part of an employment relationship.

Compensation Budgeting A part of the organization's planning process; helps to ensure that future financial expenditures are coordinated and controlled. It involves forecasting the total expenditures required by the pay system during the next period as well as the amount of the pay increases. Bottom up and top down are the two typical approaches to the process.

Compensation Differentials Differentials in pay among jobs across and within organizations, and among individuals in the same job in an organization.

Compensation Objectives The desired results of the pay system. The basic pay objectives include efficiency, equity, and compliance with laws and regulations. Objectives shape the design of the pay system and serve as the standard against which the success of the pay system is evaluated.

Compensation at Risk *See* Earnings at Risk.

Compensation System Controls Basic processes that serve to control pay decision making. They include (1) controls inherent in the design of the pay techniques (e.g., increase guidelines, range maximums and minimums), and (2) budgetary controls.

Competency Basic units of knowledge and abilities employees must acquire or demonstrate in a competency-based plan in order to successfully perform the work, satisfy customers, and achieve business objectives.

Competency Based Links pay to the depth and scope of competencies that are relevant to doing the work. Typically used in managerial and professional work where what is accomplished may be difficult to identify.

Competency Analysis A systematic process to identify and collect information about the competencies required for the person and the organization to be successful.

Competitive Objective The midpoints for each pay range. The pay policy line that connects the midpoints becomes a control device: compensation must be managed to conform to these midpoints if the organization is to maintain the pay policy it has specified.

Competitive Position The comparison of the compensation offered by one employer relative to that paid by its competitors.

Compression Very narrow pay differentials among jobs at different organization levels as a result of wages for jobs filled from the outside (frequently these are entry-level jobs) increasing faster than the internal pay structure.

Congruency The degree of consistency or "fit" between the compensation system and other organizational components such as the strategy, product-market stage, culture and values, employee needs, union status.

Consolidated Omnibus Budget Reconciliation Act (COBRA) Employees who resign or are laid off through no fault of their own are eligible to continue receiving health coverage under employer's plan at a cost borne by the employee.

Consumer Price Index (CPI) Published by the Bureau of Labor Statistics, U.S. Department of Labor, it measures the changes in prices of a fixed market basket of goods and services purchased by a hypothetical average family.

Content Theories Motivation theories that focus on *what* motivates people rather than on *how* people are motivated. Maslow's need hierarchy theory and Herzberg's two-factor theory fall in this category.

Contingency Work Force A growing work force that includes flexible workers, temporaries, part-time employees, and independent contractors. The pay and benefits of contingent workers tend to be about half the pay and benefits of noncontingent workers.

Contingent Employees Workers whose employment is of a limited duration (part-time or temporary).

Contributory Benefit Financing Plans Costs shared between employer and employee.

Contributory Financing Refers to an employee benefit that is partially paid for by the employee.

Conventional Job Analysis Methods Methods (e.g., functional job analysis) that typically involve an analyst using a questionnaire in conjunction with structured interviews of job incumbents and supervisors. The methods place considerable reliance on analysts' ability to understand the work performed and to accurately describe it.

Cooperative Wage Study (CWS) A study undertaken by 12 steel companies and the United Steel Workers to design an industrywide point plan (the Steel Plan) for clerical and technical personnel.

Coordination of Benefits. Efforts to ensure that employer coverage of an employee does not "double pay" because of identical protection offered by the government (private pension and social security coordination) or a spouse's employer.

Core Employees Workers with whom a long-term full-time work relationship is anticipated.

Cost Containment Attempts made by organizations to contain benefits costs, such as imposing deductibles and coinsurance on health benefits or replacing defined benefit pension plans with defined contribution plans.

Cost of Living Actual individual expenditures on goods and services. The only way to measure it accurately is to examine the expense budget of each employee.

Cost of Living Adjustments (COLAs) Across-the-board wage and salary increases or supplemental payments based on changes in some index of prices, usually the Consumer Price Index (CPI). If included in a union contract, COLAs are designed to increase wages automatically during the life of the contract as a function of changes in the Consumer Price Index (CPI).

Cost of Living Increase *See* Cost of Living Adjustments.

Cost Savings Plans Group incentive plans that focus on cost savings rather than on profit increases as the standard of group incentive (e.g., Scanlon, Rucker, Improshare).

CPI *See* Consumer Price Index

Culture The informal rules, rituals, and value systems of an organization that influence the way employees behave.

Davis-Bacon Act of 1931 Requires most federal contractors to pay wage rates prevailing in the area.

Deductibles Employer cost-saving tool by which the employee pays first *x* number of dollars when a benefit is used (e.g., hospitalization). The employer pays subsequent costs up to some predetermined maximum.

Deferred Compensation Program Provide income to an employee at some future time as a compensation for work performed now. Types of deferred compensation programs include stock option plans and pension plans.

Defined Benefits Plan A benefits option or package in which the employer agrees to give the specified benefit without regard to cost maximum. Opposite of defined contribution plan.

Defined Contribution Plan A benefits option or package in which the employer negotiates a dollar maximum payout. Any change in benefits costs over time reduces the amount of coverage unless new dollar limits are negotiated.

Differentials Pay differences among levels within the organization, such as the difference in pay between adjacent levels in a career path, between supervisors and subordinates, between union and nonunion employees, and between executives and regular employees.

Direct Compensation Pay received directly in the form of cash (e.g., wages, bonuses, incentives).

Disparate (Unequal) Impact Standard Outlaws the application of pay practices that may appear to be neutral but have a negative effect on females or minorities, unless those practices can be shown to be business related.

Disparate (Unequal) Treatment Standard Outlaws the application of different standards to different classes of employees unless they can be shown to be business related.

Dispersion Distribution of rates around a measure of central tendency.

Distributive Justice Fairness in the amount of reward distributed to employees.

DOLs Original Department of Labor methodology of job analysis. It categorized data to be collected as (1) actual work performed and (2) work traits or characteristics. Actual work performed is further refined into three categories: worker functions (what the worker does), work fields (the methods and techniques employed), and products and services (output).

Double-Track System A framework for professional employees in an organization whereby at least two general tracks of ascending compensation steps are available: (1) a managerial track to be ascended through increasing responsibility for supervision of people and (2) a professional track to be ascended through increasing contributions of a professional nature.

Drive Theory A motivational theory that assumes that all behavior is induced by drives (i.e., energizers such as thirst, hunger, sex), and that present behavior is based in large part on the consequences or rewards of past behavior.

Dual Career Ladders Two different ways to progress in an organization, each reflecting different types of contribution to the organization's mission. The managerial ladder ascends through increasing responsibility for supervision or direction of people. The professional track ascends through increasing contributions of a professional nature that do not mainly entail the supervision of employees.

Dual Coverage In families in which both spouses work, dual coverage refers to coverage of specific claims from each spouse's employment benefit package. Employers cut costs by specifying payment limitations under such conditions.

Earnings-at-Risk Plans *See* Risk Sharing.

Efficiency Pay Objective Involves (1) improving productivity and (2) controlling labor costs.

Efficiency Wage Theory A theory to explain why firms are rational in offering higher than necessary wages.

Employee Benefits That part of the total compensation package, other than pay for time worked, provided to employees in whole or in part by employer payments (e.g., life insurance, pension, workers' compensation, vacation).

Employee Contributions Refers to comparisons among individuals doing the same job for the same organization.

Employee Equity *See* Employee Contributions.

Employee-Pay-All Financing Refers to an employee benefit that is fully paid for by the employee.

Employee Retirement Income Security Act of 1974 (ERISA) An act regulating private employer pension and welfare programs. The act has provisions that cover eligibility for participation, reporting, and disclosure requirements, establish fiduciary standards for the financial management of retirement funds, set up tax incentives for funding pension plans, and establish the Pension Benefit Guaranty Corporation to insure pension plans against financial failures.

Employee Services and Benefits Programs that include a wide array of alternative pay forms ranging-from payments for time not worked (vacations, jury duty) through services (drug counseling, financial planning, cafeteria support) to protection (medical care, life insurance, and pensions).

Employer of Choice The view that a firm's external wage competitiveness is just one facet of its overall human resource policy, and competitiveness is more properly judged on overall policies. So challenging work, high calibre colleagues, or an organization's prestige must be factored into an overall consideration of attractiveness.

Entitlement Employee belief that returns and/or rewards are due regardless of individual or company performance.

Entry Jobs Jobs that are filled from the external labor market and whose pay tends to reflect external economic factors rather than an organization's culture and traditions.

Equal Employment Opportunity Commission (EEOC) A commission of the federal government charged with enforcing the provisions of the Civil Rights Act of 1964 and the EPA of 1963 as it pertains to sex discrimination in pay.

Equalization Component As a part of an expatriate compensation package, equalization is one form of equity designed to "keep the worker whole" (i.e., maintain real income or purchasing power of base pay). This equalization typically comes in the form of tax equalization, housing allowances, and other allowances and premiums.

Equal Pay Act (EPA) of 1963 An amendment to the Fair Labor Standards Act of 1938 prohibiting pay differentials on jobs which are substantially equal in terms of skills, efforts, responsibility, and working conditions, except when they are the result of bona fide seniority, merit, or production-based systems, or any other job-related factor other than sex.

Equity Absolute or relative justice or "fairness" in an exchange such as the employment contract. Absolute fairness is evaluated against a universally accepted criterion of equity, while relative fairness is assessed against a criterion that may vary according to the individuals involved in the exchange, the nature of what is exchanged, and the context of the exchange.

Equity Pay Objective Fair pay treatment for all the participants in the employment relationship. Focuses attention on pay systems that recognize employee contributions as well as employee needs.

Equity Theory A theory proposing that in an exchange relationship (such as employment) the equality of outcome/input ratios between a person and a comparison other (a standard or relevant person/group) will determine fairness or equity. If the ratios diverge from each other, the person will experience reactions of unfairness and inequity.

ESOP (Employee Stock Ownership Plan) A plan in which a company borrows money from a financial institution using its stock as a collateral for the loan. Principal and interest loan repayment are tax deductible. With each loan repayment, the lending institution releases a certain amount of stock being held as security. The stock is then placed into an Employee Stock Ownership Trust (ESOT) for distribution at no cost to all employees. The employees receive the stock upon retirement or separation from the company. TRASOPs and PAYSOPs are variants of ESOPs.

Essay An open-ended performance appraisal format. The descriptors used could range from comparisons with other employees through adjectives, behaviors, and goal accomplishment.

Exchange Value The price of labor (the wage) determined in a competitive market; in other words, labor's worth (the price) is whatever the buyer and seller agree upon.

Executive Prerequisites (Perks) Special benefits made available to top executives (and sometimes other managerial employees). May be taxable income to the receiver. Company-related perks may include luxury office, special parking, and company-paid membership in clubs/associations, hotels, resorts. Personal perks include such things as low-cost loans, personal and legal counseling, free home repairs and improvements, and so on. Since 1978, various tax and agency rulings have slowly been requiring companies to place a value on perks, thus increasing the taxable income of executives.

Exempt Jobs Jobs not subject to provisions of the Fair Labor Standards Act with respect to minimum wage and overtime. Exempt employees include most executives, administrators, professionals, and outside sales representatives.

Expatriate Colony   Sections of large cities where expatriates tend to locate and form a ghetto-like community that takes on some of the cultural flavor of the expatriates' home countries. An example of an expatriate colony would be the Roppongi section of Tokyo, where many Americans live while working in Japan.

Expatriates   Employees assigned outside their base country for any period of time in excess of one year.

Expectancies   Beliefs (or subjective probability climates) individuals have that particular actions on their part will lead to certain outcomes or goals.

Expectancy (VIE) Theory   A motivation theory that proposes that individuals will select an alternative based on how this choice relates to outcomes such as rewards. The choice made is based on the strength or value of the outcome and on the perceived probability that this choice will lead to the desired outcome.

Experience Rating   Insurance premiums vary directly with the number of claims filed. Experience rating is applied to Unemployment Insurance and Workers' Compensation, and may be applied to commercial health insurance premiums.

External Competitiveness   Refers to the pay relationships among organizations and focuses attention on the competitive positions reflected in these relationships.

External Equity   Fairness in relation to the amount paid in the relevant external market.

Extrinsic Rewards   Rewards that a person receives from sources other than the job itself. They include compensation, supervision, promotions, vacations, friendships, and all other important outcomes apart from the job itself.

Face Validity   The determination of the relevance of a measuring device on "appearance" only.

Factor Comparison   A job evaluation method in which jobs are assessed on the basis of two criteria: (1) a set of compensable factors and (2) wages for a selected set of jobs.

Factor Scales   Reflect different degrees within each compensable factor. Most commonly five to seven degrees are defined. Each degree may also be anchored by the typical skills, tasks and behaviors, or key job titles.

Factor Weights   Indicate the importance of each compensable factor in a job evaluation system. Weights can be derived either through a committee judgment or statistical analysis.

Fair Labor Standards Act of 1938 (FLSA)   A federal law governing minimum wage, overtime pay, equal pay for men and women in the same types of jobs, child labor, and recordkeeping requirements.

Family and Medical Leave Act of 1993   Entitles eligible employees to receive unpaid leave up to 12 weeks per year for specified family or medical reasons, such as caring for ill family members or adopting a child.

Fat Grades   The wide range of flexibility permitted in broadband pay structures in defining job responsibilities. Fat grades support redesigned, downsized, or seamless organizations that have eliminated layers of managerial jobs. Employees may move laterally across a band in order to gain depth of experience.

Federal Employee Pay Comparability Act of 1990 (FEPCA)   Seeks to close any pay gap between federal employees and employees of local and state government as well as private industry. The act phases in wedge adjustments when rates differ from local market rates by more than 5 percent.

Federal Insurance Contribution Act (FICA)   The source of social security contribution withholding requirements. The FICA deduction is paid by both employer and employee.

First Impression Error   Developing a negative (positive) opinion of an employee early in the review period and allowing that to negatively (positively) color all subsequent perceptions of performance.

Flat Rates   A single rate, rather than a range of rates, for all individuals performing each job. Ignores seniority and performance differences.

Flexible Benefits   *See* Cafeteria (Flexible) Benefit Plan.

Flexible Benefits Plan   Benefits package in which employees are given a core of critical benefits (necessary for minimum security) and permitted to expend the remainder of their benefits allotment on options that they find most attractive.

Flexible Compensation   The allocation of employee compensation in a variety of forms tailored to organization pay objectives and/or the needs of individual employees.

Forms of Compensation   Pay may be received directly in the form of cash (e.g., wages, bonuses, incentives) or indirectly through series and benefits (e.g., pensions, health insurance, vacations). This definition excludes other forms of rewards or returns that employees may receive, such as promotion, recognition for outstanding work behavior, and the like.

Forms of Pay *See* Forms of Compensation.

Functional Job Analysis (FJA) A conventional approach to job analysis that is followed by the U.S. Department of Labor. Five categories of data are collected: what the worker does; the methodologies and techniques employed; the machines, tools, and equipment used; the products and services that result; and the traits required of the worker. FJA constitutes a modification of DOLs methodology and is widely used in the public sector.

Gain-Sharing or Group Incentive Plans Incentive plans that are based on some measure of group performance rather than individual performance. Taking data on a past year as a base, group incentive plans may focus on cost savings (e.g., the Scanlon, Rucker, and Improshare plans) or on profit increases (profit sharing plans) as the standard to distribute a portion of the accrued funds among relevant employees.

Gantt Plan Individual incentive plan that provides for variable incentives as a function of a standard expressed as time period per unit of production. Under this plan, a standard time for a task is purposely set at a level requiring high effort to complete.

General Schedule (GS) A job evaluation plan used by the U.S. Office of Personnel Management for white collar employees. It has 18 "grades" (classes). Most jobs are in 15 grades; the top three are combined into a "supergrade" that covers senior executives.

Generic Job Analysis Generalized, less detailed data collection at a level used to write a broad job description that covers a large number of related tasks. The result is that two people doing the same broadly defined job could be doing entirely different, yet related, tasks.

Geographic Differentials *See* Locality Pay.

Glass Ceiling A subtle barrier that keeps women and minorities out of the very highest executive positions.

Global Approach Substitutes a particular skill and experience level for job descriptions in determining external market rates. Includes rates for all individuals who possess that skill.

Group Incentive Plans *See* Gain-Sharing or Group Incentive Plans.

Halo Error An appraiser gives favorable ratings to all job duties based on impressive performance in just one job function. For example, a rater who hates tardiness rates a prompt subordinate high across all performance dimensions exclusively because of this one characteristic.

Halsey 50–50 Method Individual incentive method that provides for variable incentives as a function of a standard expressed as time period per unit of production. This plan derives its name from the shared split between worker and employer of any savings in direct costs.

Hay System A point factor system that evaluates jobs with respect to know-how, problem solving, and accountability. It is used primarily for exempt (managerial/professional) jobs.

Health Maintenance Act Requires employers to offer alternative health coverage options (e.g., Health Maintenance Organizations) to employees.

Health Maintenance Organization (HMO) A non-traditional health care delivery system. HMOs offer comprehensive benefits and outpatient services, as well as hospital coverages, for a fixed monthly prepaid fee.

Hierarchies (or Job Structures) Jobs ordered according to their relative content and/or value.

High-Commitment Practices Prescribes high base pay, sharing successes only (not risks), guaranteed employment security, promotions from within, training and skill development, employee ownership, and long-term perspective. High-commitment practices are believed to attract and retain a high-committed workforce that will become the source of competitive advantage.

Hit Rate The ability of a job evaluation plan to replicate a predetermined, agreed-upon job structure.

Horn Error The opposite of a halo error; downgrading an employee across all performance dimensions exclusively because of poor performance on one dimension.

Human Capital Theory An economic theory proposing that the investment one is willing to make to enter an occupation is related to the returns one expects to earn over time in the form of compensation.

Hybrid Policy   Pay plan that includes base pay set at or below competitive market rates *plus* performance-based bonuses that vary with the unit's profitability.

Integrated Manufacturing Strategies   Organization strategies designed to gain competitive advantage such as just-in-time manufacturing, statistical quality control, and advanced technologies.

Implicit Contract   The unwritten implied agreements, or patterns of reciprocal obligations and returns, between employers and employees. This includes reciprocal understandings about the nature of risks involved in wages, benefits, and employability.

Implicit Social Contract   The beliefs and expectations held by a person of the inputs they are expected to make to society, and the outputs they are expected to get in return.

Improshare (IMproved PROductivity through SHARing)   A gain-sharing plan in which a standard is developed to identify the expected hours required to produce an acceptable level of output. Any savings arising from production of agreed-upon output in fewer than expected hours are shared by the firm and the worker.

Incentive   Inducement offered in advance to influence future performance (e.g., sales commissions).

Incentive Stock Options (ISOs)   A form of deferred compensation designed to influence long-term performance. Gives an executive the right to pay today's market price for a block of shares in the company at a future time. No tax is due until the shares are sold.

Increase Guidelines   Inherent compensation system controls. They specify amount and timing of pay increases on an organizationwide basis.

Indirect Compensation   Pay received through services and benefits (e.g., pensions, health insurance, vacations).

Individual-Based Systems   They focus on employee rather than job characteristics. Pay is based on the highest work-related skills employees possess rather than on the specific job performed.

Individual Incentive Plans   Incentive compensation that is tied directly to objective measures of individual production (e.g., sales commissions).

Institutional Theory   Theory that organizations base their practices to a large extent on what other organizations are doing.

Instrumentality   The perceived contingency that an outcome (performing well) has another outcome (a reward such as pay).

Internal Consistency   Refers to the pay relationships among jobs or skill levels within a single organization and focuses attention on employee and management acceptance of those relationships. It involves establishing equal pay for jobs of equal worth and acceptable pay differentials for jobs of unequal worth.

Internal Equity   *See* Internal Consistency.

Internal Labor Markets   The rules or procedures that regulate the allocation of employees among different jobs within a single organization.

Internal Pricing   Pricing jobs in relationship to what other jobs within the organization are paid.

Interrater Reliability   The extent of agreement among raters rating the same individual, group, or phenomena.

Inventories   Questionnaires in which tasks, behaviors, and abilities are tested. The core of all quantitative job analysis.

Job Analysis   The systematic process of collecting and making certain judgments about all of the important information related to the nature of a specific job. It provides the knowledge needed to define jobs and conduct job evaluation.

Job-Based Systems   Focus on jobs as the basic unit of analysis to determine the pay structure; hence, job analysis is required.

Job Classes or Grades   Each represents a grouping of jobs that are considered substantially similar for pay purposes.

Job Cluster   A series of jobs grouped for job evaluation and wage and salary administration purposes on the basis of common skills, occupational qualifications, technology, licensing, working conditions, union jurisdiction, workplace, career paths, and organizational tradition.

Job Competition Theory   Economic theory that postulates a "quoted" wage for a job irrespective of an individual's qualifications. Because the most qualified applicants will be hired first, later hires will be more costly because they will require more training or will be less productive.

Job Content   Information that describes a job. May include responsibility assumed and/or the tasks performed.

Job Description   A summary of the most important features of the job as it is performed. It identifies the job and describes the general nature of the work, specific task responsibilities, outcomes, and employee characteristics required to perform the job.

Job Evaluation   A systematic procedure designed to aid in establishing pay differentials among jobs within a single employer. It includes classification, comparison of the relative worth of jobs, blending internal and external market forces, measurement, negotiation, and judgment.

Job Evaluation Committee   Usually having a membership representing all important constituencies within the organization. It may be charged with the responsibility of (1) selecting a job evaluation system, (2) carrying out or at least supervising the process of job evaluation, and (3) evaluating the success with which the job evaluation has been conducted. Its role may vary among organizations.

Job Evaluation Manual   Contains information on the job evaluation plan and is used as a "yardstick" to evaluate jobs. It includes a description of the job evaluation method used, descriptions of all jobs, if relevant, a description of compensable factors, numerical degree scales, and weights. May also contain a description of available review or appeals procedure.

Job Family   Jobs involving work of the same nature but requiring different skill and responsibility levels (e.g., computing and account-recording is a job family; bookkeeper, accounting clerk, tellers are jobs within that family).

Job Grade   *See* Pay Grade.

Job Hierarchy   A grouping of jobs based on their job-related similarities and differences and on their value to the organization's objectives.

Job Pricing   The process of assigning pay to jobs, based on thorough job analysis and job evaluation.

Job Structure   Relationships among jobs inside an organization, based on work content and the job's relative contribution to achieving organization's objectives.

Job-to-Job Comparison   Method of pay equity adjustment prescribed by Ontario, Canada's, pay equity legislation. Looks at working conditions, knowledge, and skills needed to perform the job regardless of gender. The relative worth of the job is compared to that of others in determining pay. Removes use of market data for setting pay.

Just Wage Doctrine   A theory of job value that posited a "just" or equitable wage for any occupation based on that occupation's place in the larger social hierarchy. According to this doctrine, pay structures should be designed and justified on the basis of societal norms, custom, and tradition, not on the basis of economic and market forces.

Key Jobs   *See* Benchmark (or Key) Jobs.

Knowledge Analysis   The systematic collection of information about the knowledge or skills required to perform work in an organization.

Knowledge Blocks   The different type of knowledge or competencies required to perform work.

Knowledge Systems   Linking pay to additional knowledge related to the same job (depth) (e.g., scientists and teachers) or to a number of different jobs (breadth) (e.g., technician).

Labor Demand   In economic models, the demand for labor is a curve that indicates how the desired level of employment varies with changes in the price of labor when other factors are held constant. The shape of the labor demand curve is downward sloping. Thus, an increase in the wage rate will reduce the demand for labor in both the short and long run.

Labor Supply   In economic models, the supply of labor is a curve or schedule representing the average pay required to attract different numbers of employees. The shape of the labor supply curve varies depending on the assumptions. In perfectly competitive markets, an individual firm faces a horizontal (elastic) supply of labor curve.

Lag Pay Level Policy   Setting a wage structure to match market rates at the beginning of plan year only. The rest of the plan year, internal rates will lag behind market rates. Its objective is to offset labor costs, but it may hinder a firm's ability to attract and retain quality employees.

Lead Pay Level Policy   Setting a wage structure to lead the market throughout the plan year. Its aim is to maximize a firm's ability to attract and retain quality employees and to minimize employee dissatisfaction with pay.

Least Squares Line   In regression analysis, the line fitted to a scatterplot of coordinates that minimizes the squared deviations of coordinates around the line. This line is known as the *best fit line.*

Legally Required Benefits   Benefits that are required by statutory law: workers' compensation, social security, and unemployment compensation are required in the United States. Required benefits vary among countries. Companies operating in foreign countries must comply with host country compensation and benefits mandates.

Leniency Error   Consistently rating someone higher than is deserved.

Leveling   Weighting market survey data according to the closeness of the job matches.

Level of Aggregation   Refers to the size of the work unit for which performance is measured (e.g., individual work group, department, plan, or organization) and to which rewards are distributed.

Level Rise   The percentage increase in the average wage rate paid.

Percent level rise =

$$100 \times \frac{\text{Avg. pay year end} - \text{Avg. pay year beginning}}{\text{Avg. pay at the beginning of the year}}$$

Lifetime Employment   Most prevalent in Japanese companies, this refers to the notion of an employee staying with the same company for their entire career, despite possible poor performance on the part of either the employee or the company.

Linear Regression   A statistical technique that allows an analyst to build a model of a relationship between variables that are assumed to be linearly related.

Line of Sight   Refers to an employee's ability to see how individual performance affects incentive payout. Employees on a straight piecework pay system have a clear line of sight—their pay is a direct function of the number of units they produce; employees covered by profit sharing have a fuzzier line of sight—their payouts are a function of many forces, only one of which is individual performance.

Local Country Nationals (LCNs)   Citizens of a country in which a U.S. foreign subsidiary is located. LCNs' compensation is tied either to local wage rates or to the rates of U.S. expatriates performing the same job. Each practice has different equity implications.

Locality Pay   Adjusting pay rates for employees in a specific geographic area to account for local conditions such as labor shortages, housing cost differentials, and so on.

Long-Term Disability (LTD) Plan   An insurance plan that provides payments to replace income lost through an inability to work that is not covered by other legally required disability income plans.

Long-Term Incentives   Inducements offered in advance to influence longer rate (multiyear) results. Usually offered to top managers and professionals to focus on long-term organization objectives.

Low-High Approach   Using the lowest- and highest-paid benchmark job in the external market to anchor an entire skill-based structure.

Lump-Sum Award   Payment of entire increase (typically merit based) at one time. Amount is not factored into base pay so any benefits tied to base pay also don't increase.

Lump-Sum Bonus   *See* Lump-Sum Award.

Managed Care   Refers to steps taken to contain health care and Workers' Compensation costs, such as switching to preferred provider organizations for health care delivery, utilization-review procedures and medical bill audits.

Management by Objectives (MBO)   An employee planning, development, and appraisal procedure in which a supervisor and a subordinate, or group of subordinates, jointly identify and establish common performance goals. Employee performance on the absolute standards is evaluated at the end of the specified period.

Marginal Product of Labor   The additional output associated with the employment of one additional human resources unit, with other factors held constant.

Marginal Productivity Theory (MPT)   By contrast with Marxist "surplus value" theory, MPT focuses on labor demand rather than supply and argues that employers will pay a wage to a unit of labor that equals that unit's use (not exchange) value. That is, work is compensated in proportion to its contribution to the organization's production objectives.

Marginal Revenue of Labor The additional revenue generated when the firm employs one additional unit of human resources, with other factors held constant.

Market Pay Lines Summarize the distribution of market rates for the benchmark jobs under consideration. Several methods to construct the lines can be used: a single line connecting the distributions' midpoints (means or medians), or the 25th, 50th, and 75th percentiles. Often the lines are fitted to the data through a statistical procedure, such as regression analysis.

Market Pricing Setting pay structures almost exclusively through matching pay for a very large percentage of jobs with rates paid in the external market.

Maturity Curves A plot of the empirical relationship between current pay and years since a professional has last received a degree (YSLD), thus allowing organizations to determine a competitive wage level for specific professional employees with varying levels of experience.

Merit Pay A reward that recognizes outstanding past performance. It can be given in the form of lump-sum payments or as increments to the base pay. Merit programs are commonly designed to pay different amounts (often at different times) depending on the level of performance.

Merit Pay Increase Guidelines Tie pay increases to performance. They may take one of two forms: The simplest version specifies pay increases permissible for different levels of performance. More complex guidelines tie pay not only to performance but also to position in the pay range.

Merrick Plan Individual incentive plan that provides for variable incentives as a function of units of production per time period. It works like the Taylor plan, but three piecework rates are set: (1) high—for production exceeding 100 percent of standard; (2) medium—for production between 83 percent and 100 percent of standard; and (3) low—for production less than 83 percent of standard.

Middle and Top Management Employees above the supervisory level who have technical and administrative training and whose major duties entail the direction of people and the organization. They can be classified as special groups to the extent the organization devises special compensation programs to attract and retain these relatively scarce human resources. By this definition, not all managers above the supervisory level qualify for consideration as a special group.

Minimum Wage A minimum wage level for most Americans established by Congress as part of the FLSA of 1938.

Motivation An individual's willingness to engage in some behavior. Primarily concerned with (1) what energizes human behavior, (2) what directs or channels such behavior, and (3) how this behavior is maintained or sustained.

Multiskill Systems Link pay to the number of *different jobs* (breadth) an employee is certified to do, regardless of the specific job he or she is doing.

Mutual Commitment Compensation A pay strategy that combines high wages with an emphasis on quality, innovation, and customer service. Based on the belief that high wages are essential to reinforce cooperation and participation and will provide a better living standard for all employees.

National Electrical Manufacturing Association (NEMA) A point factor job evaluation system that evolved into the National Position Evaluation Plan sponsored by NMTA associates.

National Metal Trades Association Plan (NMTA) A point factor job evaluation plan for production, maintenance, and service personnel.

National Position Evaluation Plan A point factor job evaluation system that evolved from the former plan. Today, the plan is sponsored by 11 management/manufacturing associations and is offered under the umbrella group, NMTA associates.

Need Theories Motivation theories that focus on internally generated needs that induce behaviors designed to reduce these needs.

Noncontributory Financing An employee benefit that is fully paid for by the employer.

Nonexempt Employees Employees who are subject to the provisions of the Fair Labor Standards Act.

Nonqualified Deferred Compensation Plans A plan does not qualify for tax exemption if an employer who pays high levels of deferred compensation to executives does not make proportionate contributions to lower level employees.

Nonqualified Stock Options Gives an executive the right to purchase stock at a stipulated price; the excess over fair market value is taxed as ordinary income.

Objective Performance-Based Pay Systems Focus on objective performance standards (e.g., counting output) derived from organizational objectives and a thorough analysis of the job (e.g., incentive and gain-sharing plans).

Occupational Diseases Diseases that arise out of the course of employment, not including "ordinary diseases of life," for which Workers' Compensation claims can be filed.

Occupational Safety and Health Act (OSHA) of 1970 Designed to improve working conditions in industry, thereby reducing worker accidents and job-related illnesses.

On-Call Employees Employees who must respond to work-related assignments/problems 24 hours a day. Firefighters, SPCA humane officers, and other emergency personnel are traditional examples. Increasingly, this group includes technical workers such as software service personnel.

Organizational Culture The composite of shared values, symbols, and cognitive schemes that ties people together in the organization.

Organizational Values Shared norms and beliefs regarding what is socially, organizationally, and individually right, worthy, or desirable. The composite of values contributes to form a common organizational culture.

Outlier An extreme value that may distort some measures of central tendency.

Outsourcing The practice of hiring outside vendors to perform functions that do not directly contribute to business objectives and in which the organization does not have comparative advantage.

Paired Comparison A ranking job evaluation method that involves comparing all possible pairs of jobs under study.

Pay Bands Combining separate job classifications into a smaller number of divisions, called *bands*. Created to increase flexibility.

Pay Discrimination It is usually defined to include (1) access discrimination that occurs when qualified women and minorities are denied access to particular jobs, promotions, or training opportunities and (2) valuation discrimination that takes place when minorities or women are paid less than white males for performing substantially equal work. Both types of discrimination are illegal under Title VII of the Civil Rights Act of 1964. Others argue that valuation discrimination can also occur when men and women hold entirely different jobs (in content or results) that are of comparable worth to the employer. Existing federal laws do not support the "equal pay for work of comparable worth" standard.

Pay Equity *See* Comparable Worth.

Pay-for-Knowledge System A compensation practice whereby employees are paid for the number of different jobs they can adequately perform or the amount of knowledge they possess.

Pay-for-Performance Plans Pay that varies with some measure of individual or organizational performance, such as merit pay, lump-sum bonus plans, skill-based pay, incentive plans, variable pay plans, risk sharing, and success sharing.

Pay Grade One of the classes, levels, or groups into which jobs of the same or similar values are grouped for compensation purposes. All jobs in a pay grade have the same pay range—maximum, minimum, and midpoint.

Pay Increase Guidelines The mechanism through which performance levels are translated into pay increases and, therefore, dictate the size and time of the pay reward for good performance.

Pay Level An average of the array of rates paid by an employer.

Pay Level Policies Decisions concerning a firm's level of pay vis-à-vis product and labor market competitors. There are three classes of pay level policies: to lead, to match, or to follow competition.

Pay Mix Relative emphasis among compensation compotents such as base pay, merit, incentives, and benefits.

Pay Objectives *See* Compensation Objectives.

Pay Plan Design A process to identify pay levels, components, and timing that best match individual needs and organizational requirements.

Pay Policy Line Represents the organization's pay-level policy relative to what competitors pay for similar jobs.

Pay Ranges   The range of pay rates from minimum to maximum set for a pay grade or class. They put limits on the rates an employer will pay for a particular job.

Pay Satisfaction   A function of the discrepancy between employee perceptions of how much pay they *should* receive and how much pay they *do* receive. If these perceptions are equal, an employee is said to experience pay satisfaction.

PAYSOPs (Payroll-Based Tax Credit Employee Stock Ownership Plans)   A form of TRASOP in which the tax credit allotted to plan sponsors who permit and match voluntary employee contributions is payroll based, not investment based.

Pay Structures   The array of pay rates for different jobs within a single organization; they focus attention on differential compensation paid for work of unequal worth.

Pay Techniques   Mechanisms or technologies of compensation management, such as job analysis, job descriptions, market surveys, job evaluation, and the like, that tie the four basic pay policies to the pay objectives.

Pay with Competition Policy   This policy tries to ensure that a firm's labor costs are approximately equal to those of its competitors. It seeks to avoid placing an employer at a disadvantage in pricing products or in maintaining a qualified work force.

Pension Benefit Guaranty Corporation   To protect individuals from bankrupt companies (and pension plans!), employers are required to pay insurance premiums to this agency. In turn, the PBGC guarantees payment of vested benefits to employees formerly covered by terminated pension plans.

Pension Plan   A form of deferred compensation. All pension plans usually have four common characteristics: (1) they involve deferred payments to a former employee (or surviving spouse) for past services rendered; they all specify (2) a normal retirement age at which time benefits begin to accrue to the employee, (3) a formula employed to calculate benefits, and (4) integration with social security benefits.

Percentage Pay Range Overlap   *See* Range Overlap.

Performance-Based Pay   *See* Pay-for-Performance Plans.

Performance Dimension Training   Training performance appraisers about the performance dimensions on which to evaluate employee performance.

Performance Evaluation (or Performance Appraisal)   A process to determine correspondence between worker behavior/task outcomes and employer expectations (performance standards).

Performance Ranking   The simplest, fastest, easiest to understand, and least expensive performance appraisal technique. Orders employees from highest to lowest in performance.

Performance Share/Unit Plans   Cash or stock awards earned through achieving specific goals.

Performance Standard   An explicit statement of what work output is expected from employees in exchange for compensation.

Performance Standard Training   Training that gives performance appraisers a frame of reference for making ratee appraisals.

Perquisite   Also known as a "perk"; the extras bestowed on top management, such as private dining rooms, company cars, first class airfare.

Phantom Stock Plan   Stock plan in which an increase in stock price at a fixed future date determines the cash or stock award. These are called phantom plans because the organization in question is not publicly traded. Stock price, therefore, is an illusion. The "phantom price" is derived from standard financial accounting procedures.

Planned Compa-Ratio Budgeting   A form of top-down budgeting in which a planned compa-ratio rather than a planned level rise is established to control pay costs.

Planned Level Rise   The percentage increase in average pay that is planned to occur after considering such factors as anticipated rates of change in market data, changes in cost of living, the employer's ability to pay, and the efforts of turnover and promotions. This index may be used in top-down budgeting to control compensation costs.

Planned Level Rise Budgeting   A form of top-down budgeting under which a planned level rise rather than a planned compa-ratio is established as the target to control pay costs.

Point (Factor) Method   A job evaluation method that employs (1) compensable factors, (2) factor degrees numerically scaled, and (3) weights reflecting the relative importance of each factor. Once scaled degrees and weights are established for each factor, each job is measured against each compensable factor and a total score is calculated for each job. The total points assigned to a job determine the job's relative value and hence its location in the pay structure.

Policy Capturing Approach to Factor Selection *See* Statistical Approach to Factor Selection.

Policy Line A pay line that reflects the organization's policy with respect to the external labor market.

Portability Transferability of pension benefits for employees moving to a new organization; ERISA does not require mandatory portability of private pensions. On a voluntary basis, the employer may agree to let an employee's pension benefit transfer to an individual retirement account (IRA), or, in a reciprocating arrangement, to the new employer.

Portal-to-Portal Act of 1947 Defines compensable working time to include only the "principal activity" unless the custom is otherwise.

Position Analysis Questionnaire (PAQ) A structured job analysis technique that classifies job information into seven basic factors: information input, mental processes, work output, relationships with other persons, job context, other job characteristics, and general dimensions. The PAQ analyzes jobs in terms of worker-oriented data.

Position Description Questionnaire (PDQ) A quantitative job analysis technique.

Preferred Provider Organization (PPO) Health care delivery system in which there is a direct contractual relationship between and among employers, health care providers, and third-party payers. An employer is able to select providers (e.g., selected doctors) who agree to provide price discounts and submit to strict utilization controls.

Pregnancy Discrimination Act of 1978 An amendment to Title VII of the Civil Rights Act. It requires employers to extend to pregnant employees or spouses the same disability and medical benefits provided other employees or spouses of employees.

Prevailing Wage Laws A government-defined prevailing wage is the minimum wage that must be paid for work done on covered government projects or purchases. In practice, these prevailing rates have been union rates paid in various geographic areas. The main prevailing wage laws are (1) Davis-Bacon (1931), (2) Walsh-Healey Public Contracts Act (1936), and (3) McNamara-O'Hara Service Contract Act (1965).

Procedural Equity Concerned with the process used to make and implement decisions about pay. It suggests that the way pay decisions are made and implemented may be as important to employees as the results of the decisions.

Procedural Justice Fairness in the procedures used to determine the amount of reward employees will receive.

Process Theories Motivation theories that focus on *how* people are motivated rather than on *what* motivates people (e.g., drive, expectancy, and equity theories).

Product Market The market (or market segments) in which a firm competes to sell products or services.

Professional Employee An employee who has specialized training of a scientific or intellectual nature and whose major duties do not entail the supervision of people.

Profit Sharing Plan Focus on profitability as the standard for group incentive. These plans typically involve one of three distributions: (1) cash or current distribution plans provide full payment to participants soon after profits have been determined (quarterly or annually); (2) deferred plans have a portion of current profits credited to employee accounts, with cash payments made at time of retirement, disability, severance, or death; and (3) combination plans incorporate aspects of both current and deferred options.

Progression through the Pay Ranges Three strategies to move employees through the pay ranges: (1) automatic or seniority-based progression, which is most appropriate when the necessary job skills are within the grasp of most employees; (2) merit progression, which is more appropriate when jobs allow variations in performance; and (3) a combination of automatic and merit progression. For example, employers may grant automatic increases up to the midpoint of the range and permit subsequent increases only when merited on the basis of performance appraisal.

Proportional Value Method of pay equity adjustment prescribed by Ontario, Canada's, pay equity legislation. Can be used to make equity adjustments for female workers when no male-dominated job class exists in the same workplace. An employer examines the relationship or pattern between pay and value for all the male job classes to determine if a pay equity adjustment is required.

Proxy Comparison   Method of pay equity adjustment used only in the public sector in Ontario, Canada. Predominately female workplaces (e.g., libraries, day care centers) borrow job information on similar female jobs in other public sector settings that have male comparators.

Psychological Contract   Perceptions and beliefs on the part of individuals regarding the terms and conditions of the employment relationship. Psychological contracts differ from implied contracts insofar as they describe individual perceptions of mutual obligation not necessarily observable and verifiable by others.

Purchasing Power   The ability to buy goods and services in a certain currency, determined by exchange rates and availability of goods. Companies must determine purchasing power when allocating allowances to expatriates.

Qualified Deferred Compensation Plan   To qualify for tax exemption, a deferred compensation program must provide contributions or benefits for employees other than executives that are proportionate in compensation terms to contributions provided to executives.

Quantitative Job Analysis (QJA)   Job analysis method that relies on scaled questionnaires and inventories that produce job-related data that are documentable, can be statistically analyzed, and may be more objective than other analysis.

Range Maximums   The maximum values to be paid for a job grade, representing the top value the organization places on the output of the work.

Range Midpoint   The salary midway between the minimum and maximum rates of a salary range. The midpoint rate for each range is usually set to correspond to the pay policy line and represents the rate paid for satisfactory performance on the job.

Range Minimums   The minimum values to be paid for a job grade, representing the minimum value the organization places on the work. Often rates below the minimum are used for trainees.

Range Overlap   The degree of overlap between adjoining grade ranges is determined by the differences in midpoints among ranges and the range spread. A high degree of overlap and narrow midpoint differentials indicate small differences in the value of jobs in the adjoining grades and permit promotions without much change in the rates paid. By contrast, a small degree of overlap and wide midpoint differentials allow the manager to reinforce a promotion with a large salary increase. Usually calculated as

$$\frac{\text{Percentage}}{\text{overlap}} = \\ 100 \times \frac{\begin{array}{l}\text{Maximum rate for} \\ \text{lower pay grade}\end{array} - \begin{array}{l}\text{Minimum rate for} \\ \text{higher pay grade}\end{array}}{\begin{array}{l}\text{Maximum rate for} \\ \text{lower pay grade}\end{array} - \begin{array}{l}\text{Minimum rate for} \\ \text{lower pay grade}\end{array}}$$

Ranges   *See* Pay Ranges.

Range Width or Spread   The range maximum and minimum are usually based on what other employers are doing and some judgment about how the range spread fits the organization, including the amount of individual discretion in the work. Usually calculated as

$$\frac{\text{Range maximum} - \text{Range minimum}}{\text{Range minimum}}$$

Ranking   A simple job evaluation method that involves ordering the job descriptions from highest to lowest in value.

Ranking Format   A type of performance appraisal format that requires the rater to compare employees against each other to determine the relative ordering of the group on some performance measure.

Rater Error Training   Training performance appraisers to identify and suppress psychometric errors such as leniency, severity, central tendency, and halo errors when evaluating employee performance.

Rating Errors   Errors in judgment that occur in a systematic manner when an individual observes and evaluates a person, group, or phenomenon. The most frequently described rating errors include halo, leniency, severity, and central tendency errors.

Rating Formats   A type of performance appraisal format that requires raters to evaluate employees on absolute measurement scales that indicate varying levels of performance.

Recency Error   The opposite of first impression error. Performance (either good or bad) at the end of the review period plays too large a role in determining an employee's rating for the entire period.

Red Circle Rates   Pay rates that are above the maximum rate for a job or pay range for a grade.

Reengineering   Changes in the way work is designed to include external customer focus. Usually includes organizational de-layering and job restructuring.

Regression   A statistical technique for relating present pay differentials to some criterion, that is, pay rates in the external market, rates for jobs held predominantly by men, or factor weights that duplicate present rates for all jobs in the organization.

Reinforcement Theories   Theories such as expectancy and operant conditioning theory grant a prominent role to rewards (e.g., compensation) in motivating behavior. They argue that pay motivates behavior to the extent merit increases and other work-related rewards are allocated on the basis of performance.

Relative Value of Jobs   Refers to their relative contribution to organizational goals, to their external market rates, or to some other agreed-upon rates.

Relevant Markets   Those employers with whom an organization competes for skills and products/services. Three factors commonly used to determine the relevant markets are: the occupation or skills required, the geography (willingness to relocate and/or commute), and the other employers involved (particularly those who compete in the product market).

Reliability   The consistency of the results obtained. That is, the extent to which any measuring procedure yields the same results on repeated trials. Reliable job information does not mean that it is accurate (valid), comprehensive, or free from bias.

Reopener Clause   A provision in an employment contract that specifies that wages, and sometimes such nonwage items as pension/benefits, will be renegotiated under certain conditions (changes in cost of living, organization, profitability, and so on).

Reservation Wage   A theoretical minimum standard below which a job seeker will not accept an offer, no matter how attractive the other job attributes.

Resource Dependency   The theory that internal pay structures are based on the differential control jobs exert over critical resources.

Responsibility-Oriented   Job descriptions that focus on outcomes. Recognizes broad accountability for the accomplishment of results that help the organization attain its objectives.

Restricted Stock Plan   Grants stock at a reduced price with condition that it not be sold before a specified date.

Revenue Act of 1978   Primarily simplified pension plans, added tax incentives for individual retirement accounts (IRAs), and adjusted requirements for ESOPs. The act also provided that cafeteria benefit plans need not be included in gross income and reaffirmed the legality of deferring compensation and taxes due on it for an employee.

Revenue Reconciliation Act of 1993   Limits employer deductions for executive compensation to $1 million and caps the amount of executive compensation used to compute contributions to and benefits from qualified retirement plans.

Reward System   The composite of all organizational mechanisms and strategies used to formally acknowledge employee behaviors and performance. It includes all forms of compensation, promotions, and assignments; nonmonetary awards and recognitions; training opportunities; job design and analysis; organizational design and working conditions; the supervisor; social networks; performance standards and reward criteria; performance evaluation; and the like.

Risk Sharing   An incentive plan in which employee base wages are set below a specified level (e.g., 80 percent of the market wage) and incentive earnings are used to raise wages above the base. In good years an employee's incentive pay will more than make up for the 20 percent shortfall, giving the employee a pay premium. Because employees assume some of the risk, risk sharing plans pay more generously than success sharing plans in good years.

Rowan Plan   Individual incentive plan that provides for variable incentives as a function of a standard expressed as time period per unit of production. It is similar to the Halsey plan, but in this plan a worker's bonus increases as the time required to complete the task decreases.

Rucker Plan   A group cost savings plan in which cost reductions due to employee efforts are shared with the employees. It involves a somewhat more complex formula than a Scanlon plan for determining employee incentive bonuses.

Salary   Pay given to employees who are exempt from regulations of the Fair Labor Standards Act, and hence do not receive overtime pay (e.g., managers and professionals). "Exempts" pay is calculated at an annual or monthly rate rather than hourly.

Salary Continuation Plans   Benefit options that provide some form of protection for disability. Some are legally required, such as Workers' Compensation provisions for work-related disability and Social Security disability income provisions for those who qualify.

Salary Sales Compensation Plan   Under this plan, the sales force is paid a fixed income not dependent on sales volume.

Sales Compensation   Any form of compensation paid to sales representatives. Sales compensation formulas usually attempt to establish direct incentives for sales outcomes.

Scaling   Determining the intervals on a measurement instrument.

Scanlon Plan   A group cost savings plan designed to lower labor costs without lowering the level of a firm's activity. Incentives are derived as the ratio between labor costs and sales values of production (SVOP).

Self-Insurance   An organization funding its own insurance claims, for either health or life insurance or Workers' Compensation.

Seniority Increases   These tie pay increases to a progression pattern based on seniority. To the extent performance improves with time on the job, this method has the rudiments of paying for performance.

Severity Error   The opposite of leniency error. Rating someone consistently lower than is deserved.

Shirking Behavior   The propensity of employees to allow the marginal revenue product of their labor to be less than its marginal cost; to be lax. One measure of shirking is the number of disciplinary layoffs.

Short-Term Disability   *See* Workers' Compensation.

Short-Term Incentives   Inducements offered in advance to influence future short-range (annual) results. Usually very specific performance standards are established.

Short-Term Income Protection   *See* Unemployment Insurance.

Sick Leave   Paid time when not working due to illness or injury.

Signaling   The notion that an employer's pay policy communicates to both prospective and current employees what kinds of behaviors are sought. Applicants may signal their likely performance to potential employees through their personal credentials such as experience or educational degrees.

Simplified Employee Pension (SEP)   A retirement income arrangement intended to markedly reduce the paperwork for regular pension plans.

Single Rate Pay System   A compensation policy under which all employees in a given job are paid at the same rate instead of being placed in a pay grade. Generally applies to situations in which there is little room for variation in job performance, such as an assembly line.

Skill Analysis   A systematic process to identify and collect information about skills required to perform work in an organization.

Skill Based   Links pay to the depth and/or breadth of the skills, abilities, and knowledge a person acquires/demonstrates that are relevant to the work. Typically applies to operators, technicians, and office workers where the work is relatively specific and defined. The criterion chosen can influence employee behaviors by describing what is required to get higher pay.

Skill-Based/Global Approach to Wage Survey   This approach does not emphasize comparison of pay for specific jobs. Instead, it recognizes that employers usually tailor jobs to the organization or individual employee. Therefore, the rates paid to every individual employee in an entire skill group or function are included in the salary survey and become the reference point to design pay levels and structures.

Skill-Based Pay System   *See* Pay-for-Knowledge System.

Skill Blocks   Basic units of knowledge employees must master to perform the work, satisfy customers, and achieve business objectives.

Skill Requirement   Includes experience, training, and ability as measured by the performance requirements of a particular job.

Slippage   *See* Turnover Effect.

Social Contract   Reciprocal understandings involving a critical third party to the employment exchange (e.g., the government). Public policies such as minimum wages, tax laws, social security, and union–management regulations play a significant role in the employment exchange.

Social Information Processing Theory (SIP)   Counters need theory by focusing on external factors that motivate performance. According to SIP theorists, workers pay attention to environmental cues (e.g., inputs/outputs of coworkers) and process this information in a way that may alter personal work goals, expectations, and perceptions of equity. In turn, this influences job attitudes, behavior, and performance.

Social Security   The Social Security Act of 1935 established what has become the federal old-age, survivors, disability, and health insurance system. The beneficiaries are workers that participate in the social security program, their spouses, dependent parents, and dependent children. Benefits vary according to (1) earnings of the worker, (2) length of time in the program, (3) age when benefits start, (4) age and number of recipients other than the worker, and (5) state of health of recipients other than the worker.

Special Groups   Employee groups for whom compensation practices diverge from typical company procedures (e.g., supervisors, middle and upper management, nonsupervisory professionals, sales, and personnel in foreign subsidiaries).

Spillover Effect   This phenomenon refers to the fact that improvements obtained in unionized firms "spill over" to nonunion firms seeking ways to lessen workers' incentives for organizing a union.

Spillover Error   Continuing to downgrade an employee for performance errors in prior rating periods.

Spot Award   One-time award given to individual employees for exceptional performance; also called a Spot Bonus.

Standard Hour Plan   Individual incentive plan in which rate determination is based on time period per unit of production, and wages vary directly as a constant function of product level. In this context, the incentive rate in standard hour plans is set based on completion of a task in some expected time period.

Standard Rating Scales   Characterized by (1) one or more performance standards being developed and defined for the appraiser and (2) each performance standard having a measurement scale indicating varying levels of performance on that dimension. Appraisers rate the appraisee by checking the point on the scale that best represents the appraisee's performance level. Rating scales vary in the extent to which anchors along the scale are defined.

Statistical Approach to Factor Selection   A method that uses a variety of statistical procedures to derive factors from data collected through quantitative job analysis from a sample of jobs that represent the range of the work employees (or an employee group) per-

form in the company. It is often labeled as *policy capturing* to contrast it with the committee judgment approach.

Stock Appreciation Rights (SARs)   SARs permit an executive all the potential capital gain of a stock incentive option (ISO) without requiring the purchase of stock and, thus, reduce an executive's cash commitment. Payment is provided on demand for the difference between the stock option price and current market price.

Stock Purchase Plan (Nonqualified)   A plan that is, in effect, a management stock purchase plan. It allows senior management or other key personnel to buy stock in the business. This plan has certain restrictions: (1) the stockholder must be employed for a certain period of time, (2) the business has the right to buy back the stock, and (3) stockholders cannot sell the stock for a defined period.

Stock Purchase Plan (Qualified)   A program under which employees buy shares in the company's stock, with the company contributing a specific amount for each unit of employee contribution. Also, stock may be offered at a fixed price (usually below market) and paid for in full by the employees.

Straight Piecework System   Individual incentive plan in which rate determination is based on units of production per time period; wages vary directly as a constant function of production level.

Straight Ranking Procedure   A type of performance appraisal format that requires the rater to compare or rank each employee relative to each other employee.

Strategic Issues   Critical considerations in compensation design such as congruency between the pay system and the strategy, the organization's culture and values, employee needs, and the nature of the union relationships.

Strategy   The fundamental direction of the organization. It guides the deployment of all resources, including compensation.

Subjective Performance-Based Pay Systems   Focus on subjective performance standards (e.g., achievement of agreed-upon objectives) derived from organizational objectives and a thorough analysis of the job.

Substantive Equity   In contrast with procedural equity, refers to the equity of the outcomes (results such as pay level, structure, and employee differentials) of the pay system.

Success Sharing   An incentive plan (e.g., profit sharing or gain-sharing) in which an employee's base wage is constant (e.g., set as 100 percent of market wage) and variable pay adds on during successful years. Because base pay is not reduced in bad years, employees bear little risk; their total pay will likely be less than it would be under a risk sharing plan in good years.

Supplemental Unemployment Benefits (SUB) Plan   Employer-funded plan that supplements state unemployment insurance payments to workers during temporary periods of layoffs. Largely concentrated in the automobile, steel, and related industries.

Surplus Value   The difference between labor's use and exchange value. According to Marx, under capitalism wages are based on labor's exchange value—which is lower than its use value—and, thus, provide only a subsistence wage.

SVOP (Sales Value of Production)   This concept includes sales revenue and the value of goods in inventory.

Task Oriented   Job descriptions that describe individual jobs in detail based on a prescribed set of duties.

Tax Equalization Allowances   A method whereby an expatriate pays neither more nor less tax than the assumed home-country tax on base remuneration. The employer usually deducts the assumed home-country tax from monthly salary and reimburses the employee for all taxes paid in the country of assignment and any actual home-country tax on company remuneration only.

Taylor Plan   Individual incentive plan that provides for variable incentives as a function of units of production per time period. It provides two piecework rates that are established for production above (or below) standard, and these rates are higher (or lower) than the regular wage incentive level.

Team Incentive   Group incentive restricted to team members with payout usually based on improvements in productivity, customer satisfaction, financial performance, or quality of goods and services directly attributable to the team.

Third Country Nationals (TCNs)   Employees of a U.S. foreign subsidiary who maintain citizenship in a country other than the United States or the host country. TCNs' compensation is tied to comparative wages in the local country, the United States, or the country of citizenship. Each approach has different equity implications.

Thrift Savings Plans   The typical thrift plan is designed to help American workers in meeting savings goals. The most common plan involves a 50 percent employer match on employee contributions up to a maximum of 6 percent of pay.

Title VII of the Civil Rights Act of 1964   A major piece of legislation prohibiting pay discrimination. It is much broader in intent than the EPA, forbidding discrimination on the basis of race, color, religion, sex, pregnancy, or national origin.

Top-Down Approach to Pay Budgeting   Also known as unit-level budgeting. Under this approach, a total pay budget for the organization (or unit) is determined and allocated "down" to individual employees during the plan year. There are many approaches to unit-level budgeting. They differ in the type of financial index used as a control measure. Controlling to planned level rise and controlling to a planned compa-ratio are two typical approaches.

Topping Out   When employees in a skill-based compensation plan attain the top pay rate in a job category by accumulating and/or becoming certified for the top-paid skill block(s).

Total Compensation   The complete pay package for employees including all forms of money, benefits, services, and in-kind payments.

Total Reward System   Includes financial compensation, benefits, opportunities for social interaction, security, status and recognition, work variety, appropriate work load, importance of work, authority/control/autonomy, advancement opportunities, feedback, hazard-free working conditions, and opportunities for personal and professional development. An effective compensation system will utilize many of these rewards.

Tournament Theory   The notion that larger differences in pay are more motivating than smaller differences. Like prize awards in a golf tournament, pay increases should get successively greater as one moves up the job hierarchy. Differences between the top job and second highest job should be the largest.

TRASOP (Tax Reduction Act Employee Stock Ownership Plan)   A form of Employee Stock Ownership Plan (ESOP) that meets specific requirements of the Tax Reform Act of 1975, as amended.

Turnover Effect   The downward pressure on average wage that results from the replacement of high-wage-earning employees with workers earning a lower wage.

Two-Tier Pay Plans   Wage structures that differentiate pay for the same jobs based on hiring date. A contract is negotiated that specifies that employees hired after a stated day will receive lower wages than their higher seniority peers working on the same or similar jobs.

Unemployment Benefits   *See* Unemployment Insurance.

Unemployment Compensation   *See* Unemployment Insurance.

Unemployment Insurance (UI)   State-administered programs that provide financial security for workers during periods of joblessness. These plans are wholly financed by employers except in Alabama, Alaska, and New Jersey, where there are provisions for relatively small employee contributions.

Unequal Impact   *See* Disparate (Unequal) Impact Standard.

Unequal Treatment   *See* Disparate (Unequal) Treatment Standard.

U.S. Expatriates (USEs)   American citizens working for a U.S. subsidiary in a foreign country. Main compensation concerns are to "keep the expatriates whole" relative to U.S.–based counterparts and to provide expatriates with an incentive wage for accepting the assignment in a foreign country.

Universal Job Factors   Factors that could theoretically be used to evaluate all jobs in all organizations.

Use Value   The value or price ascribed to the use or consumption of labor in the production of goods or services.

Valence   The amount of positive or negative value placed on specific outcomes by an individual.

Validity   The accuracy of the results obtained. That is, the extent to which any measuring device measures what it purports to measure.

Valuation Discrimination   Focuses on the pay women and minorities receive for the work they per-form. Discrimination occurs when members of these groups are paid less than white males for performing substantially equal work. This definition of pay discrimination is based on the standard of "equal pay for equal work." Many believe that this definition is limited. In their view, valuation discrimination can also occur when men and women hold entirely different jobs (in content or results) that are of comparable worth to the employer. Existing federal laws do not support the "equal pay for work of comparable worth" standard.

Variable Pay   Tying pay to productivity or some measure that can vary with the firm's profitability.

Vesting   A benefit plan provision that guarantees that participants will, after meeting certain requirements, retain a right to the benefits they have accrued, or some portion of them, even if employment under their plan terminates before retirement.

VIE Theory   *See* Expectancy (VIE) Theory.

Wage   Pay given the employees who are covered by overtime and reporting provisions of the Fair Labor Standards Act. "Nonexempts" usually have their pay calculated at an hourly rate rather than a monthly or annual rate.

Wage Adjustment Provisions   Clauses in a multilayer union contract that specify the types of wage adjustments that have to be implemented during the life of the contract. These adjustments might be specified in three major ways: (1) deferred wage increases—negotiated at the time of contract negotiation with the time and amount specified in the contract, (2) cost-of-living adjustments (COLAs) or escalator clauses, and (3) reopener clauses.

Wage and Price Controls   Government regulations that aim at maintaining low inflation and low levels of unemployment. They frequently focus on "cost push" inflation, limiting the size of the pay raises and the rate of increases in the prices charged for goods and services. Used for limited time periods only.

Wage Survey   The systematic process of collecting information and making judgments about the compensation paid by other employers. Wage survey data are useful to design pay levels and structures.

Walsh-Healey Public Contracts Act of 1936 A federal law requiring certain employers holding federal contracts for the manufacture or provision of materials, supplies, and equipment to pay industry-prevailing wage rates.

Work or Task Data Involve the elemental units of work (tasks), with emphasis on the purpose of each task, collected for job analysis. Work data describe the job in terms of actual tasks performed and their output.

Worker or Behavioral Data Include the behaviors required by the job. Used in job analysis.

Workers' Compensation An insurance program, paid for by the employer, designed to protect employees from expenses incurred for a work-related injury or disease. Each state has its own workers' compensation law.

YSLD Years since a professional has last received a degree.

Zones Ranges of pay used as controls or guidelines within pay bands that can keep the system more structurally intact. Maximums, midpoints, and minimums provide guides to appropriate pay for certain levels of work. Without zones employees may float to the maximum pay, which for many jobs in the band is higher than market value.

Name Index

Subject Index